Oracle Internals

Tips, Tricks, and Techniques for DBAs

Oracle Internals

Tips, Tricks, and Techniques for DBAs

Edited by

Donald K. Burleson

CRC Press is an imprint of the
Taylor & Francis Group, an **informa** business
AN AUERBACH BOOK

Oracle Internals
Tips, Tricks, and Techniques for DBAs

OTHER AUERBACH PUBLICATIONS

ABCs of IP Addressing
Gilbert Held
ISBN: 0-8493-1144-6

Application Servers for E-Business
Lisa M. Lindgren
ISBN: 0-8493-0827-5

Architectures for e-Business
Sanjiv Purba, Editor
ISBN: 0-8493-1161-6

A Technical Guide to IPSec Virtual Private Networks
James S. Tiller
ISBN: 0-8493-0876-3

Building an Information Security Awareness Program
Mark B. Desman
ISBN: 0-8493-0116-5

Computer Telephony Integration
William Yarberry, Jr.
ISBN: 0-8493-9995-5

Cyber Crime Field Handbook
Bruce Middleton
ISBN: 0-8493-1192-6

Enterprise Systems Architectures
Mark Goodyear, Editor
ISBN: 0-8493-9836-3

Enterprise Systems Integration, 2nd Edition
Judith Myerson
ISBN: 0-8493-1149-7

Information Security Architecture
Jan Killmeyer Tudor
ISBN: 0-8493-9988-2

Information Security Management Handbook, 4th Edition, Volume 2
Harold F. Tipton and Micki Krause, Editors
ISBN: 0-8493-0800-3

Information Security Management Handbook, 4th Edition, Volume 3
Harold F. Tipton and Micki Krause, Editors
ISBN: 0-8493-1127-6

Information Security Policies, Procedures, and Standards: Guidelines for Effective Information Security
Thomas Peltier
ISBN: 0-8493-1137-3

Information Security Risk Analysis
Thomas Peltier
ISBN: 0-8493-0880-1

Information Technology Control and Audit
Frederick Gallegos, Sandra Allen-Senft, and Daniel P. Manson
ISBN: 0-8493-9994-7

Integrating ERP, CRM, Supply Chain Management, and Smart Materials
Dimitris N. Chorafas
ISBN: 0-8493-1076-8

New Directions in Internet Management
Sanjiv Purba, Editor
ISBN: 0-8493-1160-8

New Directions in Project Management
Paul C. Tinnirello, Editor
ISBN: 0-8493-1190-X

Oracle Internals: Tips, Tricks, and Techniques for DBAs
Donald K. Burleson, Editor
ISBN: 0-8493-1139-X

Practical Guide to Security Engineering and Information Assurance
Debra Herrmann
ISBN: 0-8493-1163-2

TCP/IP Professional Reference Guide
Gilbert Held
ISBN: 0-8493-0824-0

Roadmap to the e-Factory
Alex N. Beavers, Jr.
ISBN: 0-8493-0099-1

Securing E-Business Applications and Communications
Jonathan S. Held
John R. Bowers
ISBN: 0-8493-0963-8

Oracle Internals

Tips, Tricks, and Techniques for DBAs

Edited by

Donald K. Burleson

CRC Press is an imprint of the
Taylor & Francis Group, an **informa** business
AN AUERBACH BOOK

CRC Press
Taylor & Francis Group
6000 Broken Sound Parkway NW, Suite 300
Boca Raton, FL 33487-2742

First issued in hardback 2017

CRC Press is an imprint of Taylor & Francis Group, an Informa business

Chapter 44, "Oracle 8i Buffer Cache: New Features," copyright ©2000 by John Beresniewicz and Savant Corporation. Printed with permission.

Chapter 47, "Eliminating Space Reorganizations in Oracle 8i," copyright ©2000, Robin Schumacher. Printed with permission.

Library of Congress Cataloging-in-Publication Data

Oracle internals: tips, tricks, and techniques for DBAs/ edited by Donald K. Burleson
p. cm.
Includes bibliographical references and index.
ISBN 0-8493-1139-X
1. Oracle (Computer file) 2. Relational databases. I. Burleson, Donald K.

QA76.9.D3 0729 2001
005.75'6—dc21 2001032077

This book contains information obtained from authentic and highly regarded sources. Reprinted material is quoted with permission, and sources are indicated. A wide variety of references are listed. Reasonable efforts have been made to publish reliable data and information, but the author and the publisher cannot assume responsibility for the validity of all materials or for the consequences of their use.

Neither this book nor any part may be reproduced or transmitted in any form or by any means, electronic or mechanical, including photocopying, microfilming, and recording, or by any information storage or retrieval system, without prior permission in writing from the publisher.

All rights reserved. Authorization to photocopy items for internal or personal use, or the personal or internal use of specific clients, may be granted by CRC Press LLC, provided that $1.50 per page photocopied is paid directly to Copyright Clearance Center, 222 Rosewood Drive, Danvers, MA 01923 USA. The fee code for users of the Transactional Reporting Service is ISBN 0-8493-1139-X/02/$0.00+$1.50. The fee is subject to change without notice. For organizations that have been granted a photocopy license by the CCC, a separate system of payment has been arranged.

The consent of CRC Press LLC does not extend to copying for general distribution, for promotion, for creating new works, or for resale. Specific permission must be obtained in writing from CRC Press LLC for such copying.

Direct all inquiries to CRC Press LLC, 2000 N.W. Corporate Blvd., Boca Raton, Florida 33431.

Trademark Notice: Product or corporate names may be trademarks or registered trademarks, and are used only for identification and explanation, without intent to infringe.

Visit the Auerbach Publications Web site at www.auerbach-publications.com

© 2002 by CRC Press LLC
Auerbach is an imprint of CRC Press LLC

No claim to original U.S. Government works

Library of Congress Card Number 2001032077

ISBN 13: 978-1-138-41655-0 (hbk)
ISBN 13: 978-0-8493-1139-0 (pbk)

Contributors

MICHAEL R. AULT, *Consultant, DMR Consulting Group, Alpharetta, Georgia*

SIKHA BAGUI, *Lecturer, Department of Computer Science, University of West Florida, Pensacola, Florida*

CHARLES BANYAY, *Manager, Deloitte Consulting, Toronto, Ontario, Canada*

JOHN BERESNIEWICZ, *Technical Product Manager, Precise Software Solutions, Montgomery Village, Maryland*

BRADLEY D. BROWN, *Chairman and Chief Architect, The Ultimate Software Consultants, Lakewood, Colorado*

WILLIAM G. BROWN, *Senior Consultant, Symmetry Corp., San Rafael, California*

DONALD K. BURLESON, *Editor, Kittrell, North Carolina*

TONY CALALANO, *Consultant, The Ultimate Software Consultants, Chicago, Illinois*

TREVOR CLARKE, *Management Consultant, Deloitte Consulting, Toronto, Ontario, Canada*

HERVÉ DESCHAMPS, *Technical Manager, Oracle Corporation, Miami, Florida*

RICHARD EARP, *Associate Professor, Department of Computer Science, University of West Florida, Pensacola, Florida*

JEFFERY FELDMAN, *Manager, Deloitte Consulting, Toronto, Ontario, Canada*

HOWARD FOSDICK, *Independent Database Administrator, Chicago, Illinois*

FREDERICK GALLEGOS, *CISA, CDE, CGFM, MSBA, Audit Advisor and Faculty Member, Computer Information Systems Department, California State Polytechnic University, Pomona, California*

JONATHAN GENNICK, *Oracle Database Administrator, Writer, and Editor, O'Reilly & Associates, Cambridge, Massachusetts*

RICK GREENWALD, *Author, Evanston, Illinois*

ROMAN KAB, *President, Optimum Computing Resources, Cary, North Carolina*

PAUL KORZENIOWSKI, *Freelance Writer, Sudbury, Massachusetts*

RICHARD LEE, *Senior Consultant, Operations Reengineering, Deloitte & Touche Consulting Group, Toronto, Ontario, Canada*

JONATHAN LEWIS, *Independent Oracle Consultant, Surrey, England*

CHARLES MANSFIELD, *Independent Oracle Contractor, Hillsborough, North Carolina*

PAUL MUNDELL, *Consultant, West Hollywood, California*

JOHN ADOLPH PALINSKI, *Oracle Developer, Midwestern Public Utility, Omaha, Nebraska*

RAJ PANDE, *Database Administrator, Merrill Lynch, Dayton, New Jersey*

DMITRY PETROV, *Oracle Database Administrator, St. Petersburg, Russia*

ELLEN ROBINSON, *Founder, CEO, and President, Dot to Dot Communications, Denver, Colorado*

BRUCE D. RODGERS, *Domestic Sales Vice President, SEEK Systems, Inc., Seattle, Washington*

J.B. SASTRY, *Technical Manager, Systems Performance Group, Oracle Consulting Services, Denver, Colorado*

ROBIN SCHUMACHER, *Vice President, Product Management, Embarcadero Technologies, Inc., New Albany, Indiana*

GARY E. SHARPE, *President and Chief Executive Officer, Terascape Software, Needham, Massachusetts*

SERG SHESTAKOV, *Oracle Database Administrator, St. Petersburg, Russia*

ANUNAYA SHRIVASTAVA, *Financial and Manufacturing Applications, Computech Answers, Detroit, Michigan*

DAVID C. SISK, *Database Administrator and Internal Technology Consultant, Rhone-Poulenc, Research Triangle Park, North Carolina*

MICHAEL J.D. SUTTON, *Adm.A., CMC, ISP, MIT, Business Process and Document Management Services Group Director, Rockland, Ottawa, Ontario, Canada*

BIJU THOMAS, *Oracle Database Administrator, Renaissance Worldwide, Inc., Fort Worth, Texas*

MARK B. WALLACE, *Independent Consultant, Los Angeles, California*

GUANG SHENG WAN, *Oracle Database Administration Consultant, Pittsburgh, Pennsylvania*

Alex Watts, *Principal Consultant, Kraftware Systems, Kent, England*

Joseph C. Yin, *Senior Programmer Analyst, ITA Corporate Engineering, Qualcomm Incorporated, San Diego, California*

Contents

Introduction

Since the inception of *Oracle Internals* we have been very fortunate to have some of the world's leading Oracle gurus contribute highly technical material to our publication.

Today's Oracle professionals are now challenged more than ever before to keep pace with the Oracle technology. Oracle has evolved from a simple relational database into one of the most complex E-commerce platforms ever devised. It is not enough for today's Oracle professional to just understand the Oracle database. Rather, the Oracle professional must also understand the components of Web server technology, XML, Oracle security, Oracle and Java, and a host of other areas that are very important so that Oracle administrators can do their jobs properly.

The rapid rate of technology change mandates that periodicals such as *Oracle Internals* exist so that practicing Oracle professionals can keep pace with the information needed to survive. This driving need for technical tips was the main reason for the creation and ongoing success of *Oracle Internals.* The typical Oracle professional no longer has the luxury of being able to keep up with the technology and read all of the new manuals to understand the new features within each new release of Oracle. Instead, he or she relies on *Oracle Internals* to provide comprehensive and in-depth tips and techniques for using the new technology.

Oracle Internals has been very favorably received by the Oracle community, in part because of the wonderful content of the articles, and in part because of the need arising within the Oracle community for highly detailed technical information on complex technical topics.

Just as the Oracle professional is challenged to keep pace with technology, *Oracle Internals* is challenged with finding top-notch technical articles that can be used to assist Oracle professionals in maximizing the utilization of their knowledge to incorporate of all of Oracle's new features.

This book is the culmination of the best articles from *Oracle Internals* over the past two years. It is our hope that you will find these in-depth studies of Oracle to be both informative and useful.

I

ORACLE APPLICATIONS DEVELOPMENT TECHNIQUES

The first area we present is one regarding Oracle applications tips and techniques. As is known, Oracle supports a host of different front ends, all the way from Visual Basic, to PowerBuilder, Web HTML, and Oracle's native development tools. There is a great deal of demand from the marketplace for people who have expertise in the development of Oracle applications and can provide tips for the rapid and successful development of custom applications. This section also discusses the Oracle Applications product platforms and how Oracle managers can use Oracle Apps to fully implement the various Oracle Applications modules. The area of Oracle applications is one of the broadest within the Oracle field.

Rather than concentrating on a specific product, *Oracle Internals* provides solicited information regarding Oracle Forms, Oracle Developer, and other applications tools that directly impact the performance and configuration of the Oracle database.

The chapters in this section derive from a wealth of sources — from Hervé Deschamps, a senior Oracle corporate technical manager, to John Palinski, a noted author and expert on Oracle developer tools.

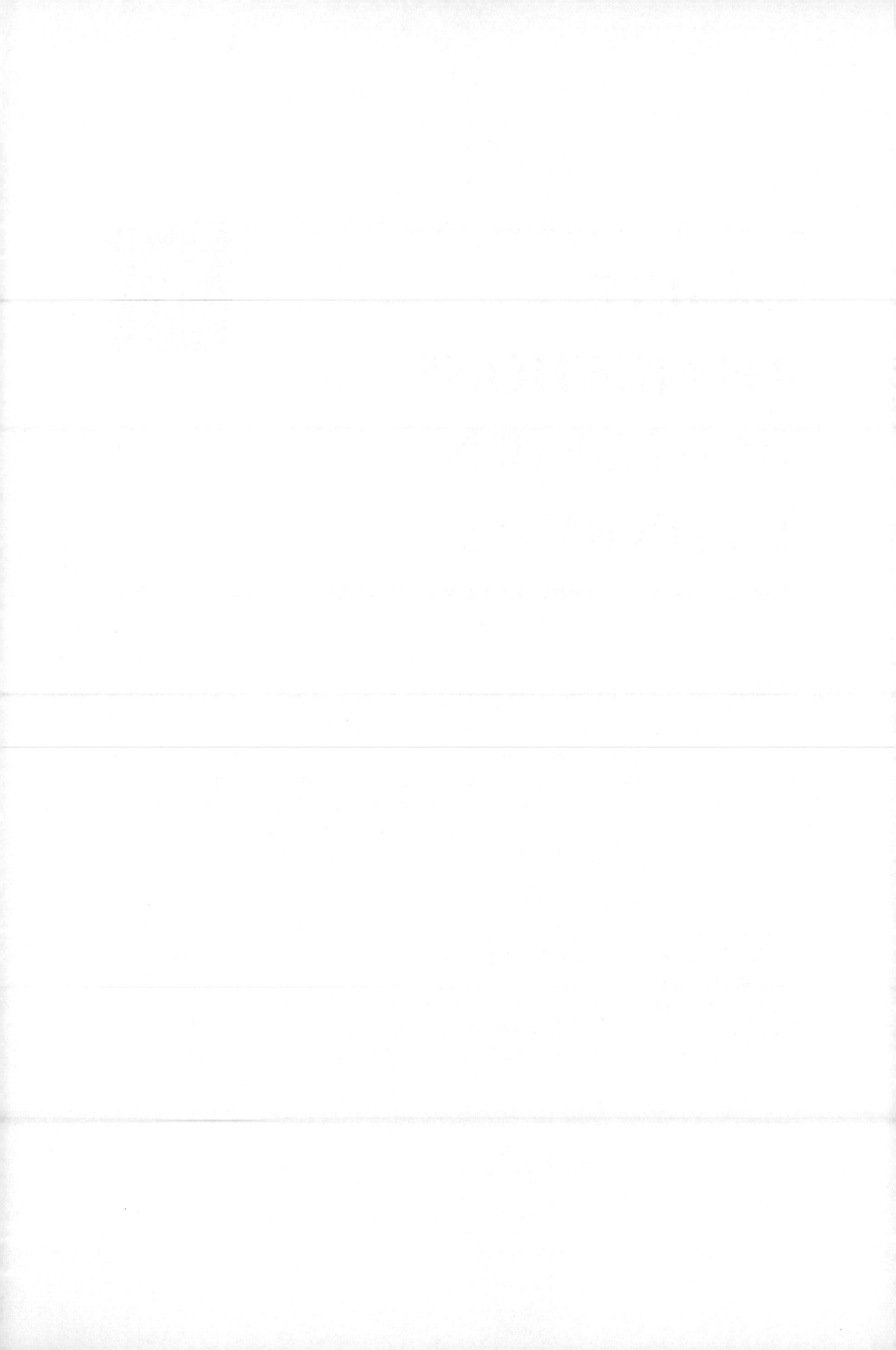

Chapter 1

A Practical Example of Data Conversion

Charles Banyay

Conversion — the word is enough to dim the enthusiasm of most systems developers. The word instills fear in some, trepidation and loathing in others. Regardless of the nature of the project with which she or he is involved, if there is any conversion effort involved, the reaction is the same. Exclude it from project scope! Let someone else do it! Although some might suspect that there may be some religious connotation here, and rightly so, the topic of this article is not converting from one religion to another. Nor is the topic software conversion, although this would be closer to the mark. This article deals with the various forms of the conversion of data.

Even if the project promises to be primarily development or implementation, which is usually the dream of most developers, and even if it involves some of the latest state-of-the-art technology, the word "conversion" immediately throws a pall over all the luster and glitter and dims the hopes of an interesting endeavor. Most systems implementations involve some form of conversion. When the software changes, the data model or the data itself often changes with it.

For some reason, conversions have come to be associated with the mundane, boring, and tiresome aspects of systems implementation. Most developers would consider conversion efforts as boring, tiresome, and devoid of interesting challenges, when compared to the implementation of state-of-the-art technology.

This is a misconception in many instances. Conversion efforts can be as challenging as any state-of-the-art technology. They can exercise the most creative abilities of technology professionals. An entire book chapter probably could be devoted to discussing the possible reasons behind the general lack of enthusiasm for the conversion effort. This chapter, however, will focus on examining the following:

0-8493-1139-X/02/$0.00+$1.50
©2002 by CRC Press LLC

- Different types of conversion efforts that one encounters during systems implementation projects
- The Taxonomy of the conversion effort
- Common pitfalls that can have rather detrimental effects on the overall effort if one is not aware of them and does not take the necessary precautions beforehand

Classifying Data Conversions

There are a number of different ways to classify a data conversion. One of the most common ways is to classify it by what is involved in the conversion effort. This could be one or more of the following:

- Converting from one hardware platform to another (e.g., a host system upgrade [on PCs this is done on a matter-of-fact basis almost daily])
- Converting from one operating system to another (e.g., UNIX to NT)
- Converting from one file access method to another (e.g., converting from an indexed or flat file structure into a DBMS)
- Converting from one coding structure or format to another (e.g., from EBCDIC to ASCII)
- Converting application software such as upgrading versions of an application or replacing one application with another (e.g., replacing an outmoded payroll application with a state-of-the-art pay benefits system)

One of the most common pitfalls of conversions is to combine into one conversion effort a change of too many variables, for example, changing hardware, operating system(s), file access method(s), and application software all at once. Sometimes this cannot be avoided. Ideally, however, as few as possible of the variables should be changed at once. With only one variable changing, error detection and correction is the simplest. Any problem can be attributed to the change of the single variable and thus can be rectified by analyzing the single variable. With combinations and permutations, the effort increases exponentially.

Unfortunately, as often happens in life, the ideal state is the exception. In general, it is a rare conversion that does not have some combination of the above variables changing at once. The taxonomy of each, however, can be explored individually, as can most of the pitfalls. Some combinations will have unique pitfalls simply due to the combination of changes in variables.

Change in Hardware

In general, the simplest conversion is upgrading hardware, assuming that all of the other variables remain constant, that is, operating systems, file access method, coding structure and format, and application software. This can best be illustrated in the PC world. PCs have been continuously upgraded with relative ease from one configuration to another for the past 10 years. As long as the operating system does not change, the upgrade in hardware usually involves nothing more than copying the files from one hard disk to another. This migration of files is usually accomplished with the assistance of some standard utilities. Using utilities rather than custom-developed software lowers the amount of effort involved in ensuring that the files have migrated successfully. Most utilities provide fairly good audit trails for this purpose. Even files on the same floppies can be used in a 286, 386, 486, or Pentium machine. Data on floppies do not require any conversion.

In environments other than personal computers, the same simplicity of conversion generally holds true. Upgrading from one main frame configuration to another is relatively easy. Changing configurations of a minicomputer, such as from one AS/400 to a more powerful configuration of the same or from one HP/3000 to a more powerful HP/3000, does not usually require significant effort. These kinds of conversions generally are imperceptible to the users and are done without much involvement from the user community. There usually is no requirement for any user testing or programmer testing. This cannot be said for the more complex conversions such as changes in the operating system.

Migrating from One Operating System to Another

Changes to the operating system are generally more complicated from a conversion perspective than changes to hardware. The complexity, however, is usually more pronounced at the application software rather than the data level. There is considerable insulation by the operating system of the application software and associated data from the hardware. In general, there is little to insulate the application software from the operating system. Object-oriented approaches are slowly changing this fact, but for now it is safe to say that a change in operating system requires a more complex conversion effort than a change in hardware.

For individuals who primarily have limited their involvement with technology to the WINTEL world, conversion complexity due to changes in operating system may come as a surprise. In the WINTEL world, one generally can change from DOS to Windows 3.x to Windows 95 (or higher) with few or limited problems. In fact, most users do this on a regular basis. This may imply that changes in an operating system are as simple as changes in hardware. This is a misconception. The people at Microsoft® and to a limited extent at Intel have spent innumerable hours to ensure that there exists a degree of compatibility between these operating systems that does not exist in any other environment.

Even in the WINTEL world this compatibility is breaking down. As the move to NT accelerates, this is becoming evident. Users moving to NT have discovered that many of their favorite software programs are not functioning as they would like them to, or the programs are not functioning at all.

Although some form of conversion effort is usually involved when operating systems are changed, the changes in operating system more definitely impact the application software than the data. The impact on any of the data is usually from indirect sources, such as from a change in one of the other variables such as data format or file access method. Different operating systems may support only different data coding structures or different file access methods.

Changes in File Access Method

It is not often that one changes a file access method while leaving the operating system and the application system the same. The general reasons for doing this would be suspect unless the current file access method was being abandoned by whomever was providing support. Another valid reason for changing the file access method may be if a packaged application system vendor released a new version of its application. This new version may offer a new data architecture such as an RDBMS. There may be valid reasons, such as better-reporting capability using third-party tools, for upgrading to this new version with the RDBMS. For whatever reason, a change in file access method usually requires some form of change in data architecture.

A simple illustration of this change in the underlying data architecture would be in converting a flat file sequential access method to an indexed file access method. Some form of indexing would have to be designed into the file structure resulting in a change in the underlying data architecture. A more complex example would be in changing from a sequential access method to a database management system.

This change, at a minimum, would involve some degree of data normalization and a break-up of the single segment or record structure of the file. The resultant change in data architecture would be quite substantive. This type of conversion generally is not simple and requires a comprehensive conversion utility. In the case where it is a packaged application being upgraded, the vendor would probably provide the conversion utility. In the case where a custom-developed application is being converted, the conversion utility would probably have to be custom-developed as well.

In either case, the tasks are straightforward. All of the data must be converted. Every record must have a corresponding entry or entries in some table or tables. Each field in the source file needs to be transferred to the target database. Field conversion is not required. There is only a limited degree of selection involved. The conversion utility is run against the source data to create the target data store. Often, there are a number of intermediate steps. Different tables or segments of the database may be created in different steps. The resultant data is verified at each step. Taking a step-by-step approach, one can minimize the number and extent of the reruns of the conversion. This is another example of minimizing the number of variables that can change at once.

There are a number of approaches to ensuring that the resultant data store has the required integrity. These approaches are identical to the ones used to ensure the integrity of data that is converted due to a change in the application software.

The extent of the effort depends on the degree of reliability that is required. The effort has an obvious cost. The lack of data integrity also has a cost. A financial system requires a high degree of data integrity. It can be argued that the data controlling the operation of a nuclear power station requires an even higher degree of integrity.

Migrating from One Application System to Another

Changing or upgrading applications always requires converting data from the old to the new application. These conversions are generally the most complex and require the most effort.

One of the first steps in the conversion process is to decide which is the driving application. What is most important in the conversion process? Is it being exhaustive in converting the data in the old application or ensuring that the new application has the required fields that it needs to operate effectively? This may not be intuitively obvious. This is not to imply that the decision as to which data to convert is at the whim of the person designing the conversion programs.

There is always a base amount of data that must be converted. Many old applications, however, accumulate various codes and indicators over the years that either lose meaning over time or are particular to that application and are not required in a new application. This situation is more particular to operational applications such as payroll, materials management, etc. When converting data in an operational application, the emphasis is on converting the minimum amount of current data for the new application to fulfill its role and be able to operate. The data requirements of the new application drive the conversion design.

Recordkeeping applications, on the other hand, such as document management systems and pension administration systems need to retain almost all of the information within the current database. These applications generally hold a tremendous amount of history that needs to be retained. Recordkeeping applications as a rule require that the emphasis be on being exhaustive in converting all of the information within the current database. The data requirements of the old application drive the conversion design.

Generally speaking, converting operational applications is considerably easier than converting recordkeeping applications. Populating fields necessary for the operation of a particular piece of software can be done in various ways. New information required for the effective operation of the new application, which is not available from the old application, can be collected from other repositories. This is generally the most time-consuming and complex way of meeting the data requirements of the new application. On the one extreme of the conversion continuum is the possibility of disregarding the old application completely and satisfying the data requirements of the new application by collecting the data from original sources. This approach is particularly useful when the data integrity of the old application is very suspect.

New information can also be provided as defaults based on other data, which are available from the old application. For example, in classifying employees for payroll purposes, give each employee the same classification based on the department where they work. In some instances new information can be fudged if the new data is not critical to the output required. For example, if source medium for an invoice is a required field in a new accounts payable application and it is not a current business requirement to keep source medium, then it could be assumed that all invoices are on paper and the information fudged with that indicator.

Being exhaustive and ensuring that all of the data in an old application is converted to a new application is, as a rule, more complex than meeting the data requirements of a new application. The complexity is not just in the conversion. The old application must be analyzed much more thoroughly to ensure that all of the data is understood and put into proper context. The converted data must be screened much more thoroughly to ensure that everything has been converted appropriately and is in the proper context within the new application. In addition, there are still the data requirements of the new application to consider.

Converting historical information often requires shoehorning existing data into fields that were not designed for that data. Very often, field conversions are required. For various reasons there may be an array of information in the old application for which there is only one field in the new application. Pension administration systems are notorious for this. For example, it is not uncommon to have numerous pension enrollment dates depending on the prior plans of which an individual was a member. The new application, especially if it is not sophisticated, may provide only one pension enrollment date.

Acquisitions, mergers, and changes in union agreements and government legislation can wreak havoc with historical recordkeeping systems. These then result in a conversion nightmare when one of these applications needs to be converted to a new application system. A very common experience is that the conversion routines often approach the complexity of artificial intelligence applications. These are the conversions that tax the abilities of even the most experienced developers. These conversions are also the ones that are potentially the most interesting and challenging to complete.

Once the driving application is determined, the next decision, which is basic to any conversion, is whether an automated conversion is the most effective way of transferring the data to the new application. In certain instances, an automated conversion may not be possible. For example, if the source data architecture or the data format is not known and cannot be determined, and there is no export utility provided by the application, then it would be very difficult to develop an automated conversion utility. In certain instances, it is simply not cost-effective to develop an automated conversion utility. If the volume of source data is relatively low and the complexity of the data requires conversion routines approaching the complexity of artificial intelligence routines, then a manual conversion effort may be more cost-effective.

The next conversion decision that must be made is how to get the data into the new application. For some reason, many application system designers never think of the initial population of their application with the relevant data. It is as if this is supposed to occur by magic. There are four basic ways of populating the new application. In order of relative complexity, these are:

1. Using a bulk load facility if one is provided by the target application
2. Generating input transactions into the new application if the application is transaction based and the format of the transactions is known
3. Real-time data entry through keystroke emulation
4. Creating the target database so that it is external to the application

Bulk load facilities are often provided by packaged application system vendors. If a bulk load facility is not provided, then the vendor often provides the necessary APIs so that a bulk load facility can be developed. Bulk load facilities are the most effective tools with which to populate a new application. The bulk load facility generally provides the necessary native edit and validation routines required by the application, while providing the necessary audit capabilities with which to determine the degree of success of the conversion.

If a bulk load facility is not provided and cannot be developed from vendor-provided APIs, then the next best thing is to generate the transactions that ordinarily would be used to enter data into the system. In this way, the data is cleansed by the application-provided routines, and one is ensured that the resultant data has the required integrity from the application perspective and is appropriately converted. This approach generally requires multiple conversion routines, possibly one per transaction type, and multiple iterations of the conversion as the transactions are loaded.

If neither of the previous methods for converting the data is available, then one can explore using keystroke emulation as a method of entering the data. There are numerous keystroke emulation or screen scraping utilities available that can assist in this endeavor. The trick here is to generate flat files from the source application and then to assemble screens of information that ordinarily are used by the application for data entry. The application is in essence fooled into behaving as if a client was communicating with it for data entry.

There are some technical limitations or challenges with this approach. With large volumes of information, multiple clients with multiple client sessions may have to be established. This is dependent on the efficiency of the client application. The slower the client application and the higher the volume of data, the greater the number of clients who need to operate simultaneously. The more client sessions, the higher the risk of malfunction. Auditing this type of conversion effort is usually quite challenging. The audit process needs to be very thorough to ensure that all of the data is converted. As with the previous approaches to conversion, by using this process one is still assured that the data that does make it to the new application has been validated and edited by the application-provided routines.

As a last resort, if it is determined that none of the above alternatives are feasible or available, then one can attempt to use the following approach. The tool of last resort is to convert the data from the source application by constructing the target database from outside the application. In the past, when applications and application data architectures were relatively simple (i.e., a flat file structure), this approach was used quite frequently. The trick here is that the conversion designer must have an intimate knowledge of the application design and underlying data architecture and the context of the data. With a simple application and a simple data architecture, this is not a daunting requirement. With today's complex application packages, however, this approach is almost not supportable. For example, creating the application database for an SAP implementation outside the application would be out of the question.

Once the decision is made as to which approach to use for the conversion, the actual conversion routines need to be written and tested just like any piece of application code. There usually is no user testing required at this point. When the routines are ready and thoroughly tested, the time comes for the actual conversion. This is the trickiest part of the entire effort. It is rare to have the luxury of ample time between running the conversion and certifying the resultant database for live operation. The planning of the actual conversion, checking the resultant database, and certifying the data must be planned with military precision.

Checking the data is usually done using multiple independent audit trails, at least providing the count of data records converted and some hash totals on certain fields. The amount of effort expended is usually commensurate with the cost and impact of an error. The users of the data must be involved and have the final sign-off. Whatever audit trails are used, the results and associated statistics must be kept in archives for at least the first few years of operation of the new application. A copy of the source database used for the conversion should also be archived, together with some application code that can access the data for reporting purposes. If questions with regard to the conversion process arise at a later date, then one has something to go back to for verification.

After a successful conversion, the final step involves decommissioning the old application. This sounds much simpler than it actually is. It is not unusual — in fact, it is often absolutely mandatory — that the old and the new applications be run in parallel for some specified time period. Weaning users from the old application can sometimes be a major challenge. That, however, is not a subject for a chapter on conversions, but is more in the realm of change management.

Conclusion

As the preceding discussion illustrates, conversions are not as boring and lacking in challenges as most professionals assume. Neither are conversions as frightening as they are made out to be. Most systems implementations involve some form of data conversion. When the software changes, the data model or the data itself often changes with it. Conversion software design and development can challenge the most creative juices of the most skilled developers. Conversions can be interesting and fun. Keep this in mind the next time you hear the word "conversion."

Chapter 2

Using Wizards in an Oracle Developer 6i Form

John Adolph Palinski

Wizards are a series of pages that step a user through tasks. Wizards are a recently developed tool employed in a variety of software products. They are used throughout the Oracle development products. A Database block wizard, a Layout wizard, and a LOV wizard exist in Oracle's Form Builder. Oracle's Report Builder has a Report wizard, a Chart wizard, and a Web wizard. Oracle is not the only software developer to employ wizards. Microsoft Access employs a Database wizard to prompt the user to enter criterion for the database. Oracle has provided us with a class that enables the developer to employ wizards in a form. This chapter explains how to use this class.

Wizard Illustration

To illustrate the use of a wizard in a form, this chapter explains how to create a simple wizard that can be used to populate an employee database. The wizard will have five pages that accomplish the following:

1. The first page welcomes the user to the New Employee Entry wizard.
2. The second page allows the user to enter company-related employee information such as payroll number, employment date, and classification.
3. The third page allows the user to enter personnel information such as address and social security number.
4. The fourth page allows the user to enter any tool purchase information. Employees often buy their initial set of tools when they are hired.
5. The fifth and final page is a congratulations page notifying the user that the process is complete. The records will be saved after the page is closed.

0-8493-1139-X/02/$0.00+$1.50
©2002 by CRC Press LLC

Next, Previous, Cancel, and Finish buttons will be placed on the appropriate pages. They will allow the user to navigate within the wizard and terminate the wizard when desired.

Wizard Class

The wizard class contains a number of components that will enable you to develop the wizard. These components are placed inside the form. These components are:

- *A PL/SQL library named Wizard.pll:* it can be located in the \orant\tools\devdem60\demo\forms directory.
- *A form object library:* this library is the Stndrd20.olb file and is also located in the \orant\tools\devdem60\demo\forms directory.

The Wizard.pll library contains a package called Wizard. It contains three procedures and three package variables. The following are the procedures and their descriptions:

- *Wizard_begin:* this procedure launches the wizard.
- *Wizard_finish:* this procedure closes (or hides) the wizard.
- *Wizard_show:* this procedure displays the desired page.
- *Page_name:* this is a varchar2 package variable that contains the name of the currently displayed page.
- *Page_number:* this is a number package variable that contains the sequence number of the currently displayed page.
- *Page_count:* this is a number package variable that contains the maximum number of sequential pages the wizard can display.

The second class component is the form components that reside in the Stndrd20.olb object library. The object library contains an object group under the Components tab. The desired object group is called "Wizard." This group contains the following form items:

- *A database block called Wiz_bar:* this block will contain four navigation buttons called Cancel, Finish, Next, and Back. It also contains a display item called Page_text.
- *A stacked canvas called Wiz_bar:* Exhibit 2.1 displays this canvas; it contains the navigation buttons on the Wiz_bar database block.
- *A form window called Window1:* this is the default window for the form.
- *A form window called Wiz_Window:* this is the window that will display the wizard.
- *A visual attribute called Wiz_standard:* the attribute sets the Foreground Color property black, the Background Color property white, the Fill Pattern property transparent, the Font Name property MS Sans Serif, and the Font Size property 8.

Exhibit 2.1 Wiz_bar Stacked Canvas
(A "Finish" exists beneath the Next button)

PAGE_TEXT	<Back	Next >	Cancel

Creating the Example Wizard

For the most part, creating a wizard is the same as creating any other form. You need to create database blocks and place the items on a canvas. The difference is that a normal form generally has one content canvas and occasionally other stacked canvases are displayed. The wizard will be displaying multiple stacked canvases in a sequence, allowing the user to move back and forth between the canvases. The following are the steps needed to create the five-page wizard discussed in the "Wizard Illustration" section of this chapter.

1. Create a new form module.
2. Attach the Wizard.pll library to the form module.
3. Locate the Stndrd20.olb object library and attach the library to Forms Developer.
4. Click on the Component tab of the object library and drag the Wizard object group from the object library to Object Group node of your form.

At this point, you have the pre-built components within your form. You can now create the canvases. You will need to create a canvas for each of the pages. In this illustration, five pages are needed. One for the Welcome, one for the Employee-At-Work data, one for the Employee-At-Home data, one for the Employee-Tool-Purchases, and one as a Congratulations.

1. Create the canvases for each of the pages in the wizard. It is extremely important that all of the canvases are stacked canvases.
2. Select all of the canvases and open a multiple item property palette. Set common height, width, canvas type, and background colors (and any other settings you desire).

You are now ready to create the database blocks. The information resides in two related tables: Employee and Emp_tools. The Employee table contains unique information about each employee. This table contains items that will appear on both the second and third pages of the wizard. Although the items appear on two pages, you only need one database block. You will put the database block's items on different canvases. The Emp_tools table is a detail table that contains instances of employee tool purchases

1. Create the database blocks (one for the Employee table and one for the Emp_tools table). Do not use the Layout Wizard to place the database block items on the respective canvases. Because one of the blocks contains items on two canvases, it is easier to group select the items for each canvas and change the Canvas property using a multiple item property palette.
2. Place each of the data items on the proper canvas.
3. Open and format each canvas. Reposition the items and add images or other desired boilerplate.

Exhibits 2.2 through 2.6 illustrate the formatted canvases

Each of the wizard canvases must be sized the same. They must have the same Height, Width, Viewport Height, and Viewport Width properties. This is necessary to prevent the Wizard_begin procedure from having to resize the Wizard window.

Exhibit 2.2 Initial Wizard Page

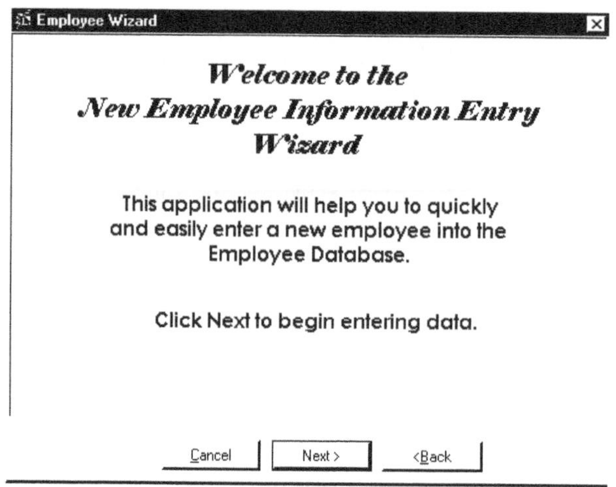

Exhibit 2.3 Second Wizard Page

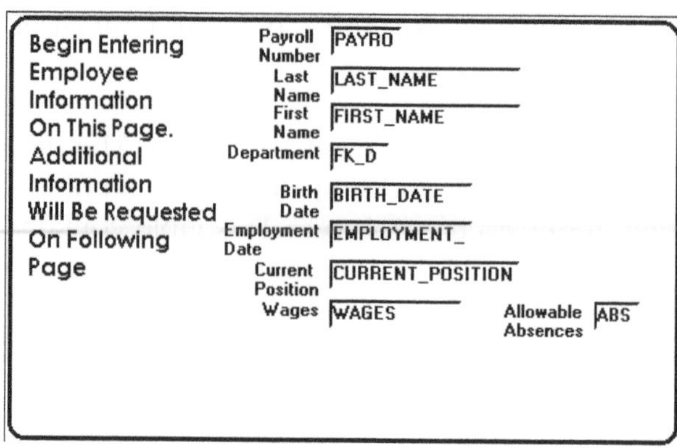

Exhibit 2.4 Third Wizard Page

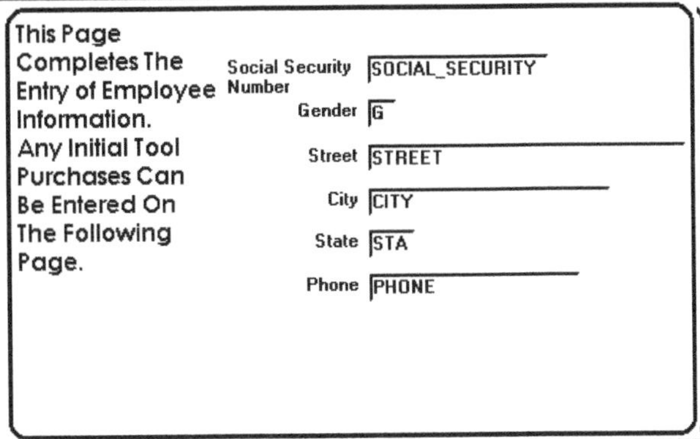

Exhibit 2.5 Fourth Wizard Page

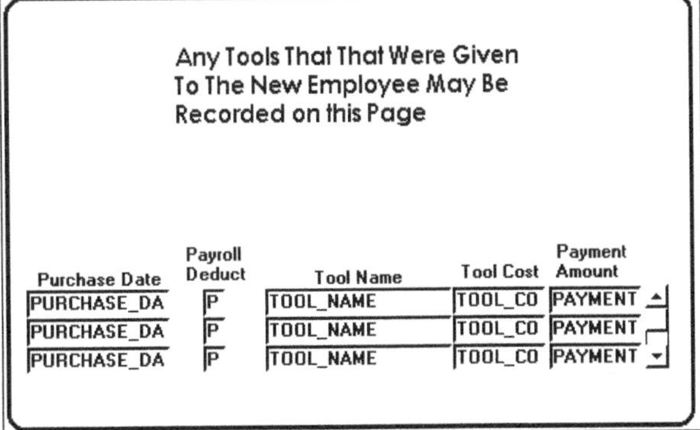

Exhibit 2.6 The Final Wizard Page

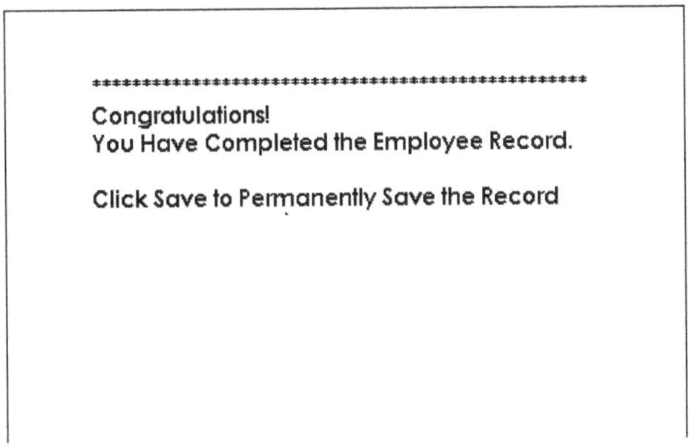

****

Congratulations!
You Have Completed the Employee Record.

Click Save to Permanently Save the Record

On the last canvas (Exhibit 2.6), place a small text item. This item can be placed on any of the blocks, but must be a non-database item. This item will be called Holder and will be placed on the Employee block. The purpose of the item is to receive the focus when the wizard navigates to the Congratulations page. You cannot navigate to this page without the item.

1. Create a non-database item called Holder on the Employee block. Be sure that it is placed on the final wizard canvas. The Height and Width properties should be set to 1 to reduce visibility.
2. Set each canvas's Height, Width, Viewport Height, and Viewport Width properties.

The wizard will use the Wiz_bar stacked canvas illustrated in Exhibit 2.1. This canvas has Back, Next, Cancel, and Finish buttons. The Next button overlays the Finish button. Wizard private package procedures will enable, disable, and change the visibility of the Next button. If you would like to see the Finish button at all times, it can be moved from the beneath the Next button.

The Wizard_begin procedure will display the first wizard screen and the Wiz_bar canvas. It will display the Wiz_bar canvas beneath the page. Note that the Page_text item on the canvas is intended to display the total number of pages in the wizard and the number of the current page.

1. Format the Wiz_bar canvas. It should have the same Width property as the wizard pages. Other properties such as Background or Height can be set to preference.
2. Set the Height property of the window that displays the wizard pages. The value should be the sum of the page height and the Wiz_bar tool canvas.

The user should only navigate to the next screen by pressing the proper button. In the next step, you should set the Next Navigable item properties so that navigation between pages does not occur by item tabbing.

Set the Next Navigable item property for the last tabbed item on each page. The value should be the first item that is to receive the focus on the page.

The next series of steps is to make the navigation buttons on the Wiz_bar canvas work. This requires a When-Button-Pressed trigger for each button. The buttons will use the Wizard library procedures to perform the needed functionality. Exhibit 2.7 illustrates the PL/SQL for the Cancel button. This code block first clears the wizard of any data, without committing it. The Wizard_finish package procedure hides (i.e., closes) the Wizard window. However, the developer must navigate to an appropriate item or the current page will redisplay. The Exit_form subprogram performs this function. If you want to return to a different canvas within the form, use the Go_item or Go_block built-ins.

Create a When-Button-Pressed trigger for the Cancel button using the code block in Exhibit 2.7.

Exhibit 2.7 PL/SQL Code for the Cancel Button When-Button-Pressed Trigger

```
-- This removes the Wizard Window.
   clear_form (no_commit);
   Wizard.Wizard_Finish;
   exit_form;
-- If you would like to display a base canvas rather than leaving
-- the form, use a go_item or go_block subprogram rather than
-- the exit_form

End Listing
```

Exhibit 2.8 illustrates the PL/SQL code block used in the Back button's trigger. This trigger navigates to the previous wizard page. It uses the Wizard.Page_number package variable to compute the previous page number. It also has provisions to prevent the user from navigating to the Welcome page. The user will hear a bell alarm and will see a message if this navigation is attempted.

You should notice that the actual navigation between pages is with the Go_item built-in. The Wizard procedures do not perform navigation. Navigation within the wizard is done in the tradition Forms manner.

Create a When-Button-Pressed trigger for the Back button using the code block in Exhibit 2.8.

Exhibit 2.8 PL/SQL Code for the Back Button When-Button-Pressed Trigger

```
declare
-- Computes the number of the previous wizard page
    next_page number default Wizard.Page_Number-1;
begin
-- Navigate to the appropriate page
    if next_page = 1 then
-- The following two lines prevent the user from navigating to the Welcome Page.
      bell;
      message ('You are on the first Employee Entry page');
    else
      if next_page = 2 then
           go_item('EMPLOYEE.PAYROLL_NUMBER');
         elsif next_page = 3 then
           go_item('EMPLOYEE.SOCIAL_SECURITY_NUMBER');
         elsif next_page = 4 then
           go_item('EMP_TOOLS.PURCHASE_DATE');
      end if;
      -- Set the page number to previous page and display it
      Wizard.Wizard_Show(next_page);
      -- The name of the new canvas is in package variable
      -- Wizard.PageName
    end if;
end;
```

Exhibit 2.9 PL/SQL Code Block for the Next Button's When-Button-Pressed Trigger

```
declare
   next_page number default Wizard.Page_Number+1;
begin
--Navigate to the appropriate page
   if next_page = 2 then
      go_item('EMPLOYEE.PAYROLL_NUMBER');
      -- Set the page number to previous page and display it
      Wizard.Wizard_Show(next_page);
      -- The name of the new canvas is in package variable
      -- Wizard.PageName
   elsif next_page = 3 then
      go_item('EMPLOYEE.SOCIAL_SECURITY_NUMBER');
      Wizard.Wizard_Show(next_page);
   elsif next_page = 4 then
      go_item('EMP_TOOLS.PURCHASE_DATE');
      Wizard.Wizard_Show(next_page);
   elsif next_page = 5 then
      go_item('employee.holder');
      Wizard.Wizard_Show(next_page);
   else
      bell;
      message('You are on the last page of the Wizard');
   end if;
end;
```

Exhibit 2.9 illustrates the PL/SQL code block used to navigate to the next wizard page. This code is placed into a When-Button-Pressed trigger for the Next button. It is similar in nature to Exhibit 2.8. It prevents the user from navigating past the last page by using a bell and wizard. Notice that it uses the Employee.holder non-database item as the navigation point of the last page.

Create a When-Button-Pressed trigger for the Next button using the code block.

The PL/SQL code block for the Finish button is:

```
commit;
   Wizard.Wizard_Finish;
   exit_form;
```

It is a very simple code block that commits the data entered in the form, hides the wizard, and closes the application. Similar to the Cancel button, the Exit_form built-in can be replaced by the Go_item or Go_block built-in if navigation to a base canvas is desired.

Create a When-Button-Pressed trigger for the Finish button using the code block in Exhibit 2.7.

At this point, we are ready for the script that will launch the wizard. Wizards can be launched from a hierarchical item using a When-Tree-Node-Selected trigger, from a button or many other Form components. I have chosen for this example to make the wizard its own application or form module. A When-New-Form Instance trigger launches the wizard. This trigger is fired when the form is launched.

The Wizard.Wizard_begin function initializes all of the wizard variables and sets up the wizard:

```
--start the Wizard
declare
   a boolean;
begin
   a := wizard.wizard_begin('page1,page2,page3,page4,page5',
   --Canvas pages separated by commas
   'Employee Wizard', FALSE);
end;
```

It also displays the first page. The function has three parameters. These are:

1. *A list of wizard pages*: This list is a text expression or string listing the canvas names of the wizard pages in the order that they will be displayed. Commas should separate the canvas names and the entire list should be enclosed by single quotation marks.
2. *A text expression that will be used as the title for the wizard*: The expression should be enclosed by single quotes.
3. *A boolean that determines whether the Page_text item will be used*: The Page_text item displays the Number of the current wizard page and the maximum number of pages. A value of True displays the information; a value of False causes the information to be hidden.

Create a When-New-Form-Instance trigger using the PL/SQL code.

At this point, the wizard is ready. However, you may want to add a Form level Key-Others trigger and a Key-Next-Item. This will prevent the user from being able to use any of the function keys and still allow the user to tab between items. Because the example wizard is a new employee entry form, the user should not be executing queries or performing other default functions. The sample form has a Key-other trigger with a single line of code (null;). This will disable the normal function keys. The Key-Next-Item trigger has one built-in, next_item. This will allow the user to tab.

Exhibit 2.10 illustrates one of the completed wizard pages. It displays both the page and the button bar. Wizards such as this example can be a simple and effective tool for walking users through complex sets of entry data.

Exhibit 2.10 Finished Wizard Page

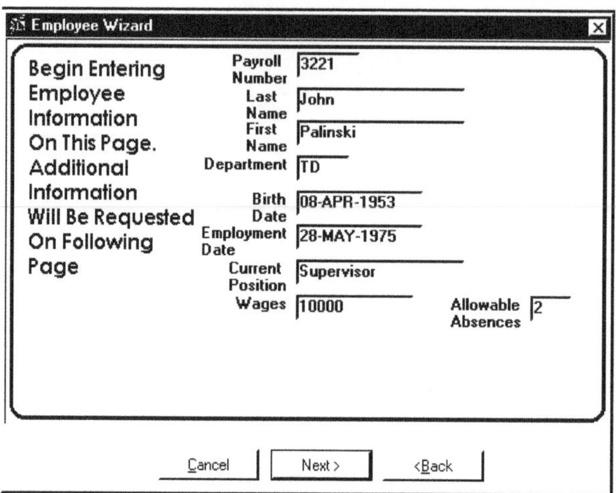

Chapter 3

Using Oracle's Developer 6i to Create a Record Directory

John Adolph Palinski

A favorite Oracle Developer 2000/6i form that I place in every system that I develop is called a Record Directory. This application has been the base from which I design/develop each of my systems. This application continues to be a favorite of the users I support, and I believe you will find it a favorite of your user base. This chapter discusses the theory behind this application and explains how to develop it for your Oracle Developer client/server or Web-based systems.

Why I Designed a Record Directory

I have developed a large number of systems in my career as a developer. Each of these systems consisted of several applications that allowed the user to record, update, or view detail attributes about an entity. Examples of entities are projects, work orders, customers, orders, parts, transformers, and baseball cards.

At the heart of each system that I develop is the Record Directory. It is a user favorite because it allows the user to simply and quickly identify the desired entity instance and drill-down (navigate) to more detailed views (Oracle forms) of the instance. Because I use this application in every system that I develop, there is an extremely low learning curve for newly implemented systems.

Despite the usefulness of the Record Directory, I have not found a single purchased system I am familiar with (Indus, Peoplesoft) that uses the design. These purchased systems cause users to struggle in identifying entity instances. When my company purchases Oracle-based software, my user base generally requests that a Record Directory and other applications be developed for these systems.

0-8493-1139-X/02/$0.00+$1.50
©2002 by CRC Press LLC

Why do I use a Record Directory rather than a standard Oracle form as a search tool? The first form that I designed in the mid-1980s was an Oracle form that displayed one record. It had one text item (work order) that could be used to enter an argument as search criteria. My company used approximately 9000 work orders per year. I quickly noticed that users had difficulty identifying the specific work order. Users could not remember the numbers, or they remembered a number, but it was sometimes several digits off. I quickly realized that users needed a special type of application to easily identify records. The ideal search application should have the following qualities:

- *Multiple search items:* This allows the user to retrieve records based on multiple arguments.
- *Multiple record display area:* This allows the user to identify the exact record from a set of records that share common traits.
- *Tools or buttons:* This allows the user to navigate to subsidiary screens that display detailed information about the selected instance.

Oracle forms have outstanding search capabilities and have some of the above features. They allow the user to use any text item on the form as a search field. A developer can also place tools on the form for navigation to detailed forms. However, there are several problems with a typical Oracle form. These problems are:

- *Search criteria disappear when records are retrieved.* If additional searches are needed, the user must remember the original search values, place the form into the Enter Query mode, and re-enter the search values — a tedious and time-consuming process.
- *A non-tabular form only shows one record.* If the query returns multiple records, the user often does not realize that additional records are available by scrolling or that he or she must scroll through the records to find the needed record.

The Record Directory application eliminates these problems. Whether on the Web or client/server, your users will get enhanced productivity using this application.

The Record Directory

A Record Directory application generally consists of two data blocks. The top block is a form-style non-base table block consisting of text items used as search criteria. A non-base table block is needed to keep the search criteria on the form. A regular block flushes values from text items before the data block is placed into the Enter Query mode.

Exhibit 3.1 A Typical Record Directory

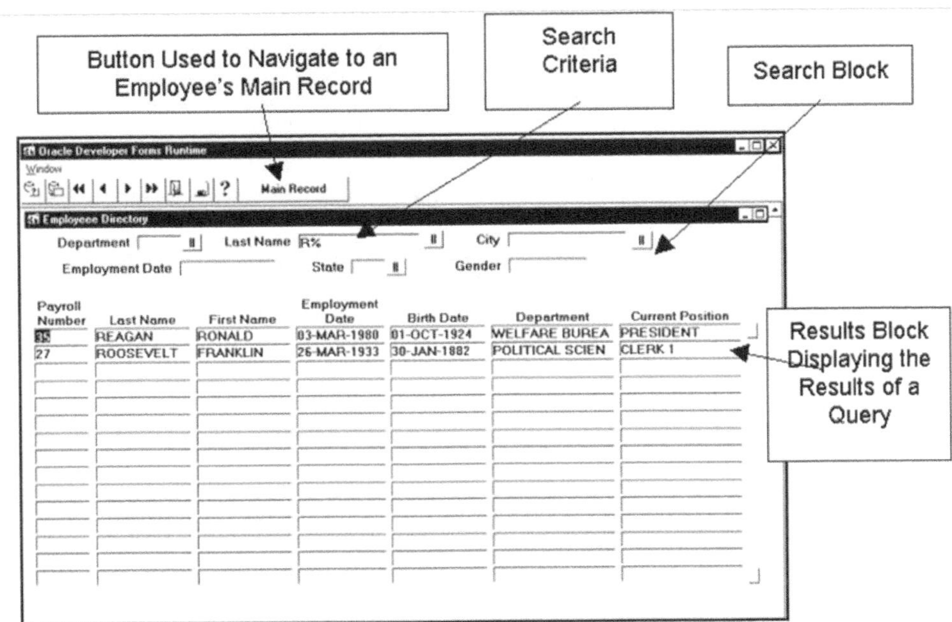

The second data block is a multi-record tabular data block used to display the results of the query. It is a database table block that contains items for each of the search text items and the items that are displayed from the database. Because the Search block always retains the search values, it is not necessary to display this item on the Results block because all retrieved values must match the search value. This frees form real estate and allows the developer to place other items on the displayed row.

The form also has a toolbar that contains tools for each of the applications the user may be interested in navigating. Queries are initiated by pressing the F7 and F8 function keys or selecting the Query tool. It is not necessary (and undesirable) to place the form into the Query mode to enter search values. The "Copy From" property on the Results block items will copy values from the Search block. This eliminates the need for the Query mode.

Exhibit 3.1 illustrates a directory for an employee database.

Creating the Record Directory

The first step in creating this type of application is to create the database block that displays the results of the database query.

Note: This chapter assumes that the reader has some Form Builder skill. Only tasks relevant to the Record Directory are mentioned. It is assumed that the reader knows how to create stacked canvases within a form.

1. Create a new form module.
2. Create a new database block using the Data Block Wizard. The block will display the results of the query. The block can be based on a view, table, or stored procedure. This block is called the Results block for the remainder of this chapter. ***Note:*** This database block must contain all columns that display result values and columns that are used as search arguments.
3. Launch the Layout Wizard for the database block created in Step 2. Perform the following:
   a. Select only the database block items that are displayed.
   b. This block should be tabular (i.e., Record Orientation block property set to vertical).
   c. The block should also display multiple records (i.e., Number of Records Displayed block property set to 10 or above).
4. Launch the Layout Editor and format the Results block and the form canvas to suit.

This application is designed to allow the user to move to other forms. When the user returns to the Record Directory from the called subsidiary screens, it is often difficult to determine which record is the currently selected record. For this reason, it is important to signify the currently selected record. Use a Visual Attribute with a Foreground property setting of Red.

5. Create a Visual Attribute. The Foreground Color property is set to "Red."
6. Set the Results Block Current Visual Attribute property to the visual attribute created in Step 5.

I do not generally allow users to update records displayed on the Results block. This allows me to avoid having to place edits into this form. Users update records on the detail screen. Step 7 prevents users from adding, updating, and deleting any record on this block.

7. Open the property palette for the Results data block. Set the following properties:
   a. Insert Allowed No
   b. Update Allowed No
   c. Delete Allowed No
8. Multi-select all of the items on the Results block. Open a multi-item property palette for the items. Set the following properties:
   a. Required No
   b. Case Insensitive Query Yes
   c. Query Length 100
9. Create a *non-basetable* block. The best way is to select the Data Blocks object on the Object Navigator and press the Create tool. When the Alert is launched, select the "Build a New Data Block Manually" option. For the purposes of this chapter, this block is called Search.

10. Open the Search block's property palette. Set the Database Data Block property to "No."
11. Expand the Results block Items object. Multi-select all of the items that will be used as search arguments. Copy these items.
12. Select the Search block Items object. Paste the items selected in Step 11.

The items pasted into the Search block will be overlaying the copied items from the Results block. You will need to change some of the Search block items properties.

13. Select all of the items on the Search block. Open a multi-item property palette.
14. Change the following item properties:

a. Required	No
b. Database Item	No
c. X Position	0
d. Y Position	0
e. Visible	Yes
f. Canvas	Name of the current canvas

The Search block's items will now be visible and located on the top-left corner of the form.

15. Open the Layout Editor and drag the Search block's items to the proper location.
16. Format the Search block's items to suit.

The following step is needed to synchronize the items on the two blocks. It is important that the values from Search block items are copied to the corresponding items on the Results block.

17. Select and open a property palette for an item on the Results block that has a corresponding item on the Search block.
18. Change the Copy Value From property on the Results block item to the name of the corresponding item on the Search block. Be sure to use both the block and item names (i.e., search.fk_department).
19. Repeat Steps 17 and 18 until all Results block items corresponding to Search block items are completed.

The design of the application requires that the form not be placed in the Enter-Query mode. It requires the Results block to execute a query whenever the Enter-Query and Execute-Query function keys are pressed. The following steps will enable this functionality.

20. Create a form level, Key-Entqry trigger. Use the following PL/SQL code:

```
Go_block ('results');
Execute_query;
```

21. Create a form level, Key-Exeqry trigger. Use the same code as in Step 20.

At this point, the basic functionality of the directory application is ready for use. You may do additional formatting, place a pop-up menu, or add a tool bar or LOVs as needed.

To operate the application, enter values in the Search fields and press the Enter-Query or Execute-Query function keys.

Navigating to Other Applications

The Directory application is designed to help the user easily locate the desired entity instance (record(s)). After identification, the user can navigate or drill-down to other windows that contain more detailed information about the entity instance.

An effective way to accomplish this navigation is to place a button or tool on the form for each of the navigable windows. (*Note:* A tool is simply an iconified button.) The buttons can be placed on the form or on a tool bar. The biggest issue is whether the called window will be a stacked canvas (that has it own window) within the directory application or another form application.

If the application is Web-enabled, I recommend that you create stacked canvases enclosed by a window within your initial form. This will cause the download time of the initial Web form to be longer, but will also increase the performance when navigating to the new window. Because it is a stacked canvas that has been downloaded, the user will not have to download the form from the Web. The user will only need to send a database call to Oracle and receive the data. Because it is quite common for a user to view the detail windows for numerous records, this is a good technique to use.

Performance is better in a client/server environment. Form executable files (.fmx) do not have to be interpreted into HTML as is done for Web forms. This means the client/server form will be displayed quicker than a Web form. You may find it easier to develop detail screens as separate applications. If so, you may want each of your called windows to be a separate form module.

To navigate from the directory to a detail window for the selected record, several things must be done, including:

1. The primary key of the selected record must be identified and placed into a global variable.
2. The proper detail window must be opened.
3. The primary key value of the selected record must be passed to the called window so that it can be used as a search argument.
4. A query is then executed on the database block within the called window.

The following PL/SQL script (Exhibit 3.2) can be used to call the detail window if it is another application. When the user presses the button for the form, the primary key value of the selected record is passed to a global variable. The new form is then called using the Call_form procedure.

Exhibit 3.2 When-Button-Pressed Trigger That Launches Another Form Module

```
:global.primary_key := :results.primary_key
Call_form ('form_name');

End Listing
```

Note: Values that may vary in practice are in italics.

I use either the Call_form or Open_form procedures because they do not close the Directory. When the user closes the detail window, the original directory should reappear with the same records displayed. Either procedure will perform this function. Use of the New_form procedure will close the Directory. The difference between the Call_form and Open_form procedures is that Call_form uses the same Oracle sesssion and Open_form establishes a new one.

The next task is to pass the primary key value to the detail window and execute a query populating the data block. This is done with a When-New-Form-Instance trigger. The trigger uses the global variable to populate the data block's Where property. This ensures that the proper record will be displayed. A query is then executed on the data block. Exhibit 3.3 illustrates this trigger.

Exhibit 3.3 When-New-Form-Instance Trigger That Populates the Called Form

```
Set_block_property ('block_name', default_where,
   'primary_key = :global.primary_key');
Go_block ('block_name');
Execute_query;

End Listing
```

If you are calling a stacked canvas within the Directory form, only one trigger is needed, and it is somewhat simpler to implement. Exhibit 3.4 illustrates a typical trigger. To call a stacked canvas, the Go_item or Go_block built-ins are used. The act of navigating to the block will cause the stacked canvas to be displayed.

Exhibit 3.4 When-Button-Pressed Trigger That Calls a Stacked Canvas

```
Set_block_property ('block_name', default_where,
   'primary_key = :results. Primary_key');
Go_block ('block_name');
Execute_query;

End listing
```

To close the stacked canvas and return to the directory, perform the following:

1. Place a button on the called canvas.
2. Create a When-Button-Pressed trigger for the button. Use the following built-in procedure:

```
Go_block ('search');
```

Conclusion

You will find that a Directory is an extremely useful tool, whether to identify records or to modify the database. Users will learn to operate the directory far quicker than they would a normal form. Better yet, the design of this application can be used with other types of development languages. I have built the same basic type of application using Visual Basic, C++, and even other archaic languages no one remembers. In all cases, the users quickly took to the concept and continually requested the application.

Chapter 4

Using Hierarchical Tree Items in Oracle's Developer 6i

John Adolph Palinski

A hierarchical tree is a form item that displays data in the form of a tree. Each node or branch of the tree has the ability to expand or collapse. This item is similar to Developer 6i's Object Navigator or Windows Explorer, and is very useful when the user has a great deal of related data to search through to find or drill-down to the proper lower level data. Examples of the type of data that can be displayed in this manner are department and employees or a machine and its associated parts lists. The hierarchical tree item allows the user to initially display a list of the various machines. After a machine is identified, the tree branch can be expanded, displaying the part list for the item. It is even possible to navigate from the hierarchical tree to another form containing detailed information about the selected record.

Populating the Hierarchical Tree Item

Hierarchical tree items are contained in non-database table blocks and they are the only item in the block. The tree item has a property called Data Query. This property contains a five-expression Select statement that will be used to retrieve the data into the tree item. To repeat, the Select clause can only contain five expressions. Each of the expressions has a specific purpose. The expression functionality follows:

- *Expression 1.* This expression contains a value that expresses the state of the record. State indicates whether the record is shown (expanded), not shown (collapsed), or shown at the same level as the parent record. A value of "1" will cause the record to be shown. A value of "–1" will cause the record to be hidden with the parent record marked as having

0-8493-1139-X/02/$0.00+$1.50
©2002 by CRC Press LLC

children record. A value of "0" will cause the record to be displayed at the same level as the parent. This expression is referenced as tree property **Ftree.node_state.**

- *Expression 2.* This expression contains a value that ranks the record in the hierarchy. For example, if the record is a grandparent, it would have a value of 1; if it were the parent, it would have a value of 2; and finally, the child record would have a value of 3. This expression is referenced as tree property **Ftree.node_depth.**
- *Expression 3.* This expression contains the value that will be displayed in the tree when the record is displayed. The value can be literal text if the node is a description of the next level of records or the name of a table column if it represents the actual table values. This expression is referenced as tree property **Ftree.node_label.**
- *Expression 4.* This expression identifies the icon that can be shown next to the node. This feature is comparable to the icons used in Object Navigator to represent various objects (i.e., canvas, data blocks, items). The referenced icons must be located in the current working directory or the directory listed in the UI_ICON string value in the registry. A value of null can be used if no icon is desired. This expression is referenced as tree property **Ftree.node_icon.**
- *Expression 5.* This expression contains a value that is used to identify the record used on the current node. It is generally the primary key of the record that supplied the value and can be used when navigating to another form. This expression is referenced as tree property **Ftree.node_value.**

The most difficult part of using the hierarchical tree item is developing the Select statement that will put the proper rank on each record and sort the records. Records are displayed in the tree as they are retrieved or sorted from the database.

The easiest type of hierarchical tree query is one for recursive data. This means the data comes from one table and each record is related to another record in the same table. Examples of this type of data are university courses that are a prerequisite for another course. Each record in the table has a Prerequisite column that contains a Course ID value. The field is a foreign key to the Course ID column on the same table.

A second example is an employee record that contains the employee number of the employee's immediate supervisor. Oracle provides a sample table called EMP with employee records that have such a recursive relationship. Using the Start With and Connect By Clauses, the records can be easily ordered and analyzed, as Exhibit 4.1 illustrates. As you can see, the Start With/Connect By clauses prepare the data for display in a hierarchical item in the proper order. The clauses analyze and sort the data properly.

However, in the real world, very little data is recursive. Most data comes from different tables. This requires the developer to perform special work. The data can be assembled and ranked properly using the Union All set operator. The records retrieved by each Select statement are given their own

Exhibit 4.1 Using the Start With and Connect By Clauses to Order and Rank Rows Records By Level

```
SQL> column employee_name format a40
SQL> select level, empno, mgr,
  2  lpad(' ', level * 2)||ename employee_name
  3  from emp
  4  start with mgr is null
  5  connect by prior empno = mgr;<Records are ordered by level

    LEVEL      EMPNO       MGR        EMPLOYEE_NAME
    ---        ---         --         --------
    1          7839                   KING
    2          7566        7839       JONES
    3          7788        7566       SCOTT
    4          7876        7788       ADAMS
    3          7902        7566       FORD
    4          7369        7902       SMITH
    2          7698        7839       BLAKE
    3          7499        7698       ALLEN
    3          7521        7698       WARD
    3          7654        7698       MARTIN
    3          7844        7698       TURNER
    3          7900        7698       JAMES
    2          7782        7839       CLARK
    3          7934        7782       MILLER

14 rows selected.

SQL>

End listing
```

level. The problem occurs when the ordering occurs. Ordering is not done by rank.

For example, the data has the following characteristics:

1. The highest rank has a textual description called Departments.
2. The next level is the various department names (i.e., Census Dept., Interior Des.).
3. The lowest level is the employees.

To rank the data properly, the textual description has a rank of 1, the department names have a rank of 2, and employees have a rank of 3. Exhibit 4.2 illustrates the Select statement and its output.

The statement in Exhibit 4.2 can be used in the hierarchical tree item because it has all the proper components. However, it will not produce the desired results because the data is not sorted properly. Employees will be listed after all department names and not after the name of their own department.

Records are displayed in the hierarchical tree exactly as retrieved by the select statement. The employee for each department should follow the proper department name. The developer needs to find a way to properly sort the

Exhibit 4.2 Select Statement Ranking and Sorting Departments and Employees

```
SQL> select -1 state, 1 lvl, 'DEPARTMENTS' displ_val, null icn, null val
from dual
union all
select -1 state, 2, department_name, null, department
from department
union all
select -1 state, 3, last_name||', '||first_name, null,
   to_char(payroll_number)
from employee;

STATE   LVL   DISPL_VAL                I VAL
---     --    -----                    ---
-1      1     DEPARTMENTS
-1      2     CENSUS DEPT              CEN
-1      2     INTERIOR DESIGN          INT
-1      2     POLITICAL SCIEN          POL
-1      2     TREASURY DEPAR           TRF
-1      2     WELFARE BUREAU           WEL
-1      3     BUSH, GEORGE             36
-1      3     CARTER, JIMMY            34
-1      3     CLINTON, WILLIAM         37
-1      3     COOLIDGE, CALVIN         25
-1      3     EISENHOWER, DWIGHT       29
-1      3     FORD, GERALD             33
-1      3     HOOVER, HERBERT          26
-1      3     JOHNSON, ANDREW          21
-1      3     JOHNSON, LYNDON          31
-1      3     KENNEDY, JOHN            30
-1      3     NIXON, RICHARD           32
-1      3     REAGAN, RONALD           35
-1      3     ROOSEVELT, FRANKLIN      27
-1      3     TAFT, WILLIAM            23
-1      3     TRUMAN, HAROLD           28
-1      3     WILSON, WOODROW          24

22 rows selected.
```

records. Level will not work as a sort criterion. The ordering task is further complicated in that only five expressions can be included in the Select statement used within the property.

This dilemma is solved in the following manner:

1. Add a sixth expression to the query.
2. The value in the sixth record will be used to determine the proper sorting. With regard to the example, the sixth expression in the first Select statement should have a value of A because these records relate to the highest node. This will cause that record to be sorted to the top of the list. The sixth expression in the second clause should be the value of Department from the Department table. The value used in the third clause should be a concatenation of the Fk_department, last_name, and first_name columns in the Employee table. This will cause the employee records to be sorted within the proper department records.
3. Create a view of the Select statement created in Step 2.

4. Use the view in the Data Query property item. Use the first five expressions in the Select clause and the sixth expression in the Order By clause.

Exhibit 4.3 illustrates the Select statement/view with the sixth expression, the Select statement used in the Data Query property, and the results of the query.

The Select statement shown in Exhibit 4.3 produces the correct results. This technique should allow you to easily assemble and sort data from many tables when a recursive relationship does not exist.

Creating the Hierarchical Item on the Form

Creating the SQL to populate the Hierarchical item is the most difficult part of the procedure to create the item. The following steps can be followed to complete the task:

1. Create a non-database table block. The tree must be the only item on the block, and the block's Number of Records Displayed property should be set to 1.
2. Open the Layout Editor.
3. Click the Hierarchical tool (displayed on the right).
4. Draw or size the Hierarchical item by clicking and dragging.
5. Set the properties of the item, especially the Data Query property.
6. Create a trigger to populate the tree item. A common trigger is a Pre-form trigger. The following is a sample trigger that can be used:

```
Ftree.populate_tree('block_name.tree_item_name');
```

The form can now be executed and the tree populated. FTREE is the name of a built-in package that contains several procedures that can be used with trees. They are listed later in the chapter.

Hierarchical Tree Item Specific Properties

Hierarchical tree items contain several properties that are peculiar to the item. These properties, along with a description, are contained in Exhibit 4.4.

Populating Other Blocks or Forms Based upon the Selected Node

It is possible to populate forms or other blocks based on the selected node. For example, a form containing a tree item can also contain a database block called Employee. Such a block could be based on the Employee table from the third Select statement in Exhibit 4.3. This statement uses

Exhibit 4.3 Select Statement and View to Properly Order Employee Data

a) View with sixth expression in line 13

```
SQL> create or replace view
  2  department_employees as
  3  select 1 state, 1 lvl 'DEPARTMENTS'
  4  displ_val, null icn, null val, 'A'
  5  sort_value
  6  from dual
  7  union all
  8  select 1 state, 2, department_name, null
  9  department, department
 10  from department
 11  union all
 12  select 1 state, 3, last_name ||', '||first_name, null,
        to_char(payroll_number),
 13  fk_department||last_name||first_name
 14  from employee;

View created.
```

b) Data query property statement

```
SQL> select state, lvl, displ_val, icn, val
  2  from department_employees
  3  order by sort_value
  4  ;

STATE   LVL     DISPL_VAL               I VAL
-----   -----   ---------------------   ---------------
1       1       DEPARTMENTS
1       2       CENSUS DEPT             CEN
1       2       INTERIOR DESIGN         INT
1       3       BUSH, GEORGE            36
1       3       COOLIDGE, CALVIN        25
1       3       EISENHOWER, DWIGHT      29
1       3       FORD, GERALD            33
1       3       TRUMAN, HAROLD          28
1       2       POLITICAL SCIEN         POL
1       3       CLINTON, WILLIAM        37
1       3       JOHNSON, ANDREW         21
1       3       JOHNSON, LYNDON         31
1       3       KENNEDY, JOHN           30
1       3       NIXON, RICHARD          32
1       3       ROOSEVELT, FRANKLIN     27
1       3       WILSON, WOODROW         24
1       2       TRESURY DEPAR           TRF
1       2       WELFARE BUREAU          WEL
1       3       CARTER, JIMMY           34
1       3       HOOVER, HERBERT         26
1       3       REAGAN, RONALD          35
1       3       TAFT, WILLIAM           23
```

`payroll_number` as the data value or fifth expression. Thus, the data value for this node can be used as the primary key for identifying a record and populating a new Employee block.

A block-level "When-tree-node-selected" trigger is used to populate the Employee block. Each time a node is selected, the trigger will fire. The trigger

Exhibit 4.4 Hierarchical Tree Specific Properties

Property Name	*Description*
Allow Empty Branches	This property determines whether nodes that contain children will display the collapsed/expanded symbol. The default value of "Yes" will show the symbol on nodes that do not contain children. A value of "No" will suppress them.
Multi-selection	This property determines whether the user can select multiple items while holding down the Shift button. A value of "No" will disable this function. A value of "Yes" will allow multi-selection.
Show Lines	This property determines whether a line links the Tree nodes. Set the value to "Yes" to display the lines, and to "No" to suppress the lines.
Show Symbols	This property determines whether the nodes can be expanded and collapsed. A value of "No" will disable the functionality and a value of "Yes" will enable it. When the "No" value is selected, the tree will be fully expanded.
Record Group	This property contains the name of the Record Group to be used to supply data to the tree. This property should not be filled in if the Data Query property is populated.
Data Query	This property contains a select statement that is used to supply data to the tree. This property should not be filled in if the Record Group property is populated.

is placed on the same block as the tree item. Exhibit 4.5 is a sample trigger. This trigger uses the Ftree.get_tree_node_property function to return selected values from the tree item.

Each time the trigger is fired, it first determines whether the selected node was for an Employee record. If it was not, a message is displayed informing

Exhibit 4.5 Sample When-Tree-Node-Selected Trigger

```
declare
   ranknumber := 0;
begin
   rank:=
   ftree.get_tree_node_property('tree_control.tree4',
      :system.trigger_node, ftree.node_depth);
   if rank = 3 then
      go_block ('employee');
      set_block_property ('employee',
   default_where,

   'payroll_number='||ftree.get_tree_node_property('tree_control.tree4',
      :system.trigger_node, ftree.node_value));
      execute_query;
   else
      message ('Please select an employee node');
   end if;
end;

End listing
```

the user that an incorrect node was selected. If a valid node is selected, the executable within the If statement is launched and the Employee block is populated based on the value supplied from the Ftree.get_tree_node_property function.

The tree values or parameter in the Ftree.get_tree_node_property function are:

1. Tree_control.tree4: the block and Tree item names
2. System.trigger_node: system value containing the value of the currently selected node
3. Ftree.node_depth: the rank or depth property

Built-In Triggers

Exhibit 4.6 contains the Ftree package built-ins that can be used with hierarchical trees.

Exhibit 4.6 Built-In Triggers for Tree Items

Name	*Description*
Get_tree_property	Retrieves a specific tree property for a target node
Set_tree_property	Sets a specific tree property for a target node
Get_tree_selection	Returns the values for selected nodes
Set_tree_selection	Selects or highlights the target node
Get_tree_node_property	Retrieves a property for a target node
Set_tree_node_property	Sets a property for a target node
Get_tree_node_parent	Determines the ID of the parent of the target node
Find_tree_node	Locates the next node that has a data value that matches the target value
Populate_tree	Launches the query and places the results into the tree
Add_tree_data	Adds a new set of data under the identified node
Add_tree_node	Adds a new node to the tree under the identified node
Populate_group_from_tree	Places the data within the tree into an existing record group
Delete_tree_node	Removes a node from the tree

Exercises

1. Create a hierarchical tree item for departments and their employees. Be sure that the first level displays the word "Departments."
2. Create a second block on the form created in 1. This block will contain information about the selected employee. Create a trigger that populates this block when an employee is selected on the tree.

3. Modify the hierarchical tree to show Employee Tool and Eyeglass Purchases. The hierarchy should contain the labels "Tools" and "Eyeglasses."

Chapter 5

Populating Oracle Form Hierarchies Incrementally at Runtime

John Adolph Palinski

Chapter 4 described how to use hierarchical items in an Oracle Form. This chapter builds on what we have seen in that chapter. Hierarchical items are an Item type that was added with Developer 6.0. The item allows the records returned form of a Select statement to be added to the item. The items are displayed in a hierarchy similar to Forms Object Navigator or Windows Explorer. It is an excellent tool for quickly locating the desired record and drilling down into more detail.

Much of the data in databases is contained in grandfather, father, and child relations. For example, a company may have a number of departments. Each department has employees, and each employee can have eyeglass and tool purchases. This relationship can be seen in Exhibit 5.1.

A Hierarchical item is an excellent tool to explore the records for a particular instance (i.e., department, employee). Using a hierarchy for the database depicted in Exhibit 5.1, at the highest level, the hierarchy will show a list of departments. Expanding a particular Department node will display the department's employees. Expanding the Employee node will cause the tool and eyeglass purchases to be displayed. This type of procedure is called "drilling down" and can be employed with almost every database.

A Problem with Hierarchical Items

Chapter 4 described how to create and populate a Hierarchical item and associate a corresponding data block with the selected node or record.

0-8493-1139-X/02/$0.00+$1.50
©2002 by CRC Press LLC

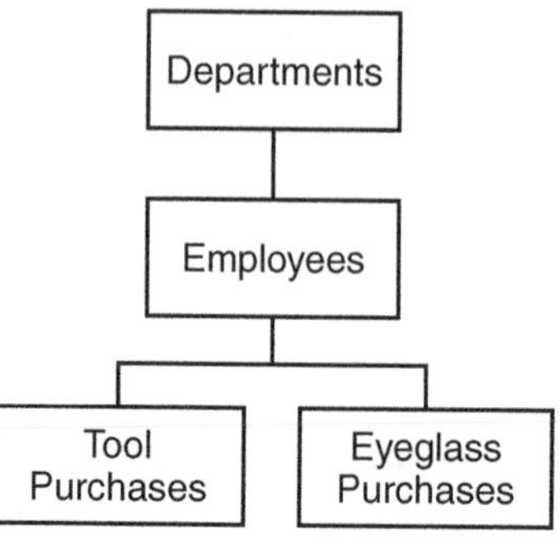

Exhibit 5.1 Table Relationship Drawing

However, the chapter did not mention one serious problem with the Hierarchical item. This problem is the amount of data that can be potentially displayed in the item. A Hierarchical item is similar to an LOV. It accepts the results of a Select statement. If the initial Select statement retrieves a large amount of records, Forms must load all of these records into memory. This can take a lot of time, wasting your system's resources as well as the user's time. The technique discussed in Chapter 4 focused on how to load the hierarchy at one time.

If your Hierarchical item can contain a large number of records, a better way is to initially load as little data into the Hierarchical item as is necessary. As the user begins to drill down, add the additional data to the Hierarchical item at that time. This will minimize the data contained in memory and the time needed to initially display the form. In Chapter 4, I explained how to load all of the possible data into the Hierarchical item when the form is displayed using a Pre-form trigger. In this chapter, I attempt to show how to minimize the initial load and populate the Hierarchical item incrementally. This will make the item a much more practical tool for your real-world databases.

Designing the Hierarchy

The first step is to design the hierarchy and the Select statement that will populate the hierarchy. In the previous chapter, I described how to create the hierarchy using a script containing several Select statements combined with Union set operators. This new approach requires this Select statement to be broken down into numerous individual Select statements or Record groups. Each individual level in the hierarchy requires its own statement. The Pre-form trigger launches the Grandfather-level Select statement. The other Select statements are launched when specific nodes are selected or activated.

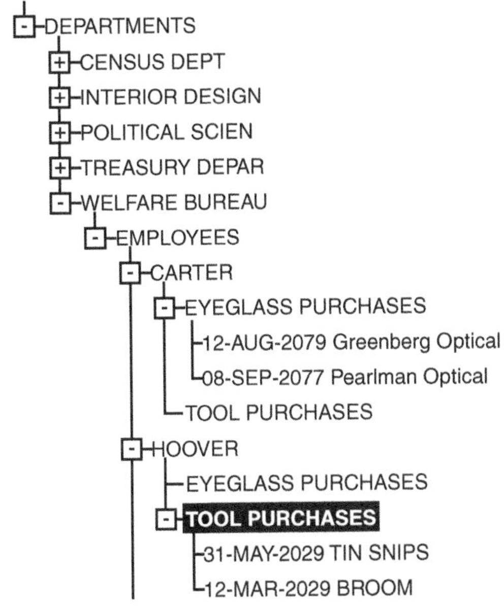

Exhibit 5.2 Department Hierarchy

To illustrate, assume you design the hierarchy displayed in Exhibit 5-2. This hierarchy has the following characteristics:

- The top node is the text value "Departments."
- Below the "Departments" node will be a node for each department displaying the name of the department.
- Expanding the department node will cause a node containing the text value "Employees" to appear.
- The Pre-form trigger will populate each of the above three nodes.
- Double-clicking the "Employees" node will activate the node and cause the department's employees to be displayed under the node. If the department does not have employees, the node will be collapsed.
- Each of the child nodes under the "Employees" node will contain the name of an employee.
- Below each of the "Employee" nodes will be two child nodes at the same level. The first will contain the text value "Eyeglass Purchases" and the second will be "Tool Purchases."
- Double-clicking the "Eyeglass Purchases" node will activate the node and cause the employee's eyeglass purchases to be displayed. If the employee does not have eyeglass purchases, the node will be collapsed.
- Double-clicking the "Tool Purchases" node will activate the node and cause the employee's tool purchases to be displayed. If the employee does not have tool purchases, the node will be collapsed.

Exhibit 5.3 View Used in the Pre-Form Trigger to Add the Departments

```
create or replace view dept_list as
select 1 state, 1 depth, 'DEPARTMENTS' displ_value, null icn, null pk,
   'A'sort_value
from dual
union
select -1 state, 2, department_name, null, department, department
from department
union
select -1 state, 3, 'EMPLOYEES', null, department, department||'A'
from department;
```

Views, Select Statements, and Record Groups

Chapter 4 suggested that a View be created for the Select statements used in the hierarchy. This technique allows the developer to sort the records properly. Following this technique means four Views need to be created. A View is needed to retrieve the records for each of the events affecting the item (i.e., launching the form, double-clicking the "Employees" node, double-clicking the "Eyeglass Purchases" node, and double-clicking the "Tool Purchases" node).

Exhibit 5.3 contains the View for the first Select statement that initially populates the Hierarchical item via the Pre-Form trigger. This View loads the text value node "Departments," the department name node, and the "Employees" text value node into the item.

The next View (see Exhibit 5.4) will be used in the When-Node-Activated trigger to populate the employees of the selected department. You might notice two things:

1. This View is using the same depth values as used in the View in Exhibit 5.3. Forms will not put these nodes at the same level as the nodes created by the View in Exhibit 5.3. It will put the employee nodes one level lower than the selected node and the two expression nodes two levels lower.
2. Each of the records has the department number as the last field. This is necessary in order to select only the records from the View that match the selected department node.

Exhibit 5.4 View Used in the When-Node-Activated Trigger to Populate Employees

```
create or replace view employee_list as
select 1 state, 1 depth, last_name displ_value, null icn,
   payroll_number pk, last_name||first_name sort_value, fk_department
from employee
union
select -1, 2, 'EYEGLASS PURCHASES', null,
   payroll_number, last_name||first_name||'Y', fk_department
from employee
union
select -1, 2, 'TOOL PURCHASES', null,
   payroll_number, last_name||first_name||'Z', fk_department
from employee;
```

Exhibit 5.5 View Used in the When-Node-Activated Trigger to Populate an Employee's Eyeglass Purchases Hierarchy

```
create or replace view eyeglass_list as
select 1 state, 1 depth, to_char(purchase_date,'DD-MON-YYYY')||'
     '||optician displ_value,null icn, fk_payroll_number pk,
     to_char(purchase_date,'YYYY-MON-DD') sort_value
from glasses;
```

These same two features also appear in the Views in Exhibits 5.5 and 5.6. The View in Exhibit 5.5 will be used in the When-Node-Activated trigger to populate the hierarchy with the eyeglass purchases for the selected employee, and the View in Exhibit 5.6 will be used in the When-Node-Activated trigger to populate the hierarchy with the tool purchases for the selected employee.

Exhibit 5.6 View Used in the When-Node-Activated Trigger to Populate an Employee's Tool Purchases Hierarchy

```
create or replace view tool_purchase_list as
select 1 state, 1 depth, to_char(purchase_date,'DD-MON-YYYY')||'
     '||tool_name displ_value,null icn, fk_payroll_number pk,
     to_char(purchase_date,'YYYY-MON-DD') sort_value
from emp_tools;
```

Record Groups

After creating the Views, the form can be created. A Hierarchical item can be created along with a separate non-database block. Two different built-in subprograms are available to populate the Hierarchical item. These are:

- **ftree.populate_tree.** This built-in will be used to initially populate the tree. It will reside in the Pre-Form trigger.
- **ftree.Add_Tree_Data.** This built-in will be used to populate individual branches. It will reside in the When-Node-Activated trigger.

Each of the built-in subprograms can use a Select statement or a Record group, based on the Views to retrieve the needed records. The Ftree.populate_tree trigger can use the Data Query property or the Record Group property of the Hierarchical item. The Add_Tree_Data built-in has a parameter for a text string that contains the Select statement or a text string using the name of a Record group contained within the form. **It is best to use a Record group.**

The reason it is better to use a Record group is because the Select statements used within the form require a Where clause and a bind variable as an argument. For example, the statement retrieving records from the Tool_purchase_list View will only want to retrieve records for the employee selected on the hierarchy. It is much easier to reference a bind variable contained on the form from a Record group than as a text literal in a parameter list.

Exhibit 5.7 Record Group Select Statements

```
                              /* Record Group (DEPT) Statement That
                              Initially Populates the Hierarchy Using the
                              Pre-form Trigger*/
select state, depth, displ_value, ICN, pk
from dept_list
order by SORT_value

                              /*Record Group (EMPS) Statement That
                              Populates the Employees Using the When-node
                              activated Trigger*/
select state, depth, displ_value, icn, pk
from employee_list
where fk_department = :holder.val_char
order by sort_value

                              /*Record Group (GLASSES) Statement That
                              Populates the Eyeglass Purchases Using the
                              When-node-activated Trigger*/
select state, depth, displ_value, icn, pk
from eyeglass_list
where pk = to_number(:holder.val_char)
order by sort_value desc

                              /*Record Group (TOOLS) Statement That
                              Populates the Tool Purchases Using the
                              When-node-activated Trigger*/
select state, depth, displ_value, icn, pk
from tool_purchase_list
where pk = to_number(:holder.val_char)
order by sort_value desc
```

Exhibit 5.7 illustrates the Select statements that comprise the four Record groups used in the example form. Notice that the latter three statements contain the bind variable `:holder.val_char.` This argument determines the records that will be selected by the latter three Record groups. It is a character type of item that is located on a non-database block on the form.

Triggers

After creating the Record groups, populate the Hierarchical item's Record Group property with "DEPT," the name of the initial Record group. A Pre-Form trigger can then be created with the following statement:

```
ftree.populate_tree('block2.tree4');
```

The parameter within the built-in is the name of the Hierarchical item and the Database block it resides on.

The next step is to create the When-Node-Activated trigger that adds children records to the activated node. This type of trigger is fired when a node item is double-clicked. A When-Node-Selected trigger or a When-Node-Expanded trigger could also be used. I prefer to use the When-Node-Selected, which fires when a node is clicked once, to execute a script that populates a corresponding data block. I also prefer to have the user double-click a node to add children records rather than expanding the node. Any of these triggers can be successfully used, depending on your design style.

Regardless of the type of trigger, the PL/SQL within the trigger is the same. The script (see Appendix 5.1) must perform the following functions:

- Identify the node that was activated. This determines the Record group to be used.
- Populate the bind variable with the primary key for the selected node (i.e., department id, payroll_number)
- Ensure that the children for a node are only added *once.*
- Make sure the children nodes appear in an expanded rather than collapsed manner.

At this point, you should be able to execute your form and the Hierarchical item will operate similar to the one shown in Exhibit 5.2. A When-node-selected trigger could be added to the form. This trigger is ideal for populating data blocks that correspond to the selected node.

Limiting the Display of the Initial Set of Nodes

In the previous example, the Select statement used in the Record group for the Pre-Form trigger did not contain a Where clause. This will cause all of the grandparent records to appear in the Hierarchy. In some instances, you may not want all of these records to appear. If this layer consists of a large amount of data and you would like to limit the initial set of records, I would recommend the following:

1. Delete the Pre-Form trigger.
2. Create another Record group similar to the "DEPT" Record group. Add a Where clause containing a bind variable to this Record group. You may also consider using the Like operand in the Where clause with a concatenated '%' with the bind variable (i.e, `:holder.init_val || '%'`).
3. Place the Form item used as a bind variable on the form.
4. Change the Pre-Form trigger to a Key-Execute-Query trigger using the script contained in Exhibit 5.8.

Exhibit 5.8 Key-Execute Trigger Used to Initially Populate the Hierarchical Item

```
if :holder.var_char is null then Ftree.populate_tree ('block2.tree4');
                                 /* This subprogram uses the Record group
                                 without the bind variable. */
   else
                                 /* Since the Form Item has a value, the
                                 Record group with the bind variable should
                                 be used. The following command changes the
                                 Record group of the hierarchical item.*/
   set_tree_property ('block2.tree4, record_group, 'DEPT1');
     ftree.populate_tree('block2.tree4);
```

This last technique will change the way your Form operates. The Hierarchical item will only be populated when the Key-execute-query (F8) button is pressed. If the user wants to limit the search, a value can be placed in the `:holder.init_val` Form item. This will limit the number of records that will be loaded. If the user leaves this item blank, the Hierarchical item will display all of the records.

Using this technique along with the ones discussed in Chapter 4 will allow you to develop exceptional applications that allow your users to easily move around the data in their database.

Appendix 5.1. REQUEST and REQUEST_LINES

```
REQUEST
declare html_results varchar2(4000);-- max is 2000 for v7
   begin
   html_results := utl_http.request('http://www.tusc.com');
   -- process html_results
end;

REQUEST_LINES
declare pieces utl_http.html_pieces;
   begin
           pieces := utl_http.request_lines('http://www.tusc.com');
           for i in 1 .. pieces.count loop
   -- process each piece
   -- refer to each piece as pieces(i)
   end loop;
end
```

Appendix 5.2 When-Node-Activated Trigger Used to Populate the Hierarchical Item Incrementally

```
DECLARE
htree item;                  /*Holds the id of the hierarchy*/
current_nodeftree.node;      /*Holds the id of the activated node*/
executed_num number;         /*Holds the value indicating success or failure after
                             a Record group is populated*/
node_val varchar2(100);      /*Holds the value of the activated node*/
BEGIN                        /*Step 1: Populate a variable with the hierarchy id*
   /htree := find_item('block2.tree4');
                             /*Step 2: Populate a variable with the id of the
                             activated node*/
   current_node := :system.trigger_node;
                             /*Step 3: Populate a variable with the value for the
                             record displayed on the activated node. Records with
                             a value have never had child records added. Records
                             with a value of ' ' have had records added*/
   node_val := ftree.get_tree_node_property(htree,current_node,ftree.node_value);
                             /*Step 4: Determine whether the current node has had
                             child records added. If node_val = ' ', then records
                             have been added and the trigger will perform on more
                             work. If a different value exists, child records may
                             be available for the. The tasks in the if-then
                             structure should be executed*/
```

Appendix 5.2 When-Node-Activated Trigger Used to Populate the Hierarchical Item Incrementally (continued)

```
  if node_val != ' ' then
                              /*Step 5: Place the value of the activated node
                              record into a form item. This value will be used in
                              the form record group's Where clause to extract the
                              proper records*/
    :holder.val_char := Ftree.Get_Tree_Node_Property(htree, current_node,
      Ftree.node_value);
                              /*Step 6: Place the label of the activated node into
                              a form item. This value is used to determine which
                              Record group to use for extracting records*/
    :holder.label := Ftree.Get_Tree_Node_Property(htree, current_node,
      Ftree.node_label);
                              /*Step 7: Populate the appropriate Record group and
                              add the records to the hierarchy. The first if-then
                              construct is used if the activated node is an
                              "Employee" node. The second construct is used if the
                              activated node is an "Eyeglass Purchases" node. The
                              last construct is used if the activated node is a
                              "Tool Purchases" node.*/
                              /*Beginning of the first if-then construct*/
    if :holder.label = 'EMPLOYEES' then
                              /*Step 7a: Populate the Record group.*/
      executed_num := populate_group('emps');
                              /*Step 7b: Add the contents of the Record group as
                              children to the activated node*/
      Ftree.Add_Tree_Data(htree, current_node, Ftree.parent_OFFSET,
          ftree.last_child, Ftree.record_group, 'emps');
                              /*Beginning of the second if-then construct*/
      elsif :holder.label='EYEGLASS PURCHASES' then executed_num :=
          populate_group('glasses'); Ftree.Add_Tree_Data(htree, current_node,
          Ftree.parent_OFFSET, ftree.last_child, Ftree.record_group, 'glasses');
                             /*Beginning of the third if-then construct*/
      elsif :holder.label = 'TOOL PURCHASES' then executed_num :=
          populate_group('tools'); Ftree.Add_Tree_Data(htree, current_node,
          Ftree.parent_OFFSET, ftree.last_child, Ftree.record_group, 'tools');
    end if;
                              /*Step 8:If child records are added to the
                              hierarchy, this construct will change the activated
                              node value to ' '. This prevents the node from being
                              populated again. The construct also expands the newly
                              populated node which causes the records to be
                              displayed */
  if :holder.label in ('EMPLOYEES', 'EYEGLASS PURCHASES', 'TOOL PURCHASES')then
                              /*Step 8a: Changes the activated node value to ' '.*/
  Ftree.Set_Tree_Node_Property(htree, current_node, Ftree.NODE_value, ' ');
                              /*Step 8b:Expands the activated node displaying the
                              newly added child nodes */
  Ftree.Set_Tree_Node_Property(htree, current_node, Ftree.NODE_state,
    ftree.expanded_node);
  end if;
 end if;
end;
```

Chapter 6

Oracle Designer 2.1.2.API: Enforcing Column Naming Standards

Hervé Deschamps

The bigger the project, the more important the naming standards. This chapter focuses on column naming standards. We present a simple technique and a utility to enforce it. Of course, this technique can be extended to tables, foreign key, indexes, modules, entities, attributes, etc. The utility in this chapter was tested by the author on a number of versions of Oracle's CASE tool, from Designer 2000 1.3.2 to Oracle Designer 2.1.2.

Part of the task of enforcing naming standards can be reduced to a simple search and replace function, just as in a word processor. For example, we can look for all instances of the character string MODIFIED and replace them with MDFD. Or replace IDENTIFICATION with ID, PURCHASE with PURCH, and CUSTOMER with CUST. A column named CUSTOMER_IDENTIFICATION would then become CUST_ID. Unfortunately, there is no search and replace utility in Oracle Designer 2.1.2. This task can be done manually at the risk of inconsistencies and typing mistakes. In practice, it is seldom performed because it is extremely tedious; thus, volunteers are scarce because it requires maintenance when the data model changes and because it is too time-consuming for tight project timescales. We will show how we can put a script together that will do this for us. This script issues a few calls to the Oracle Designer API. It can be run several times throughout the duration of the project.

This technique is not all there is to enforcing standards in Oracle Designer, but it can save considerable time. Please feel free to paste the code in SQL*Plus as you go along.

First, we need a simple table with two columns and one primary key constraint:

0-8493-1139-X/02/$0.00+$1.50
©2002 by CRC Press LLC

```
create table case_abbrev
( full_word varchar2(50),
abbrev_word varchar2(50))
/
alter table case_abbrev
add constraint cabb_pk primary
key
(full_word)
using index
/
```

It is on purpose that we did not create a primary key or unique key on the abbreviation. This is because several long words like IDENTIFIER and IDENTIFICATION are often abbreviated the same way: ID.

Exhibit 6.1 lists some typical values that we can insert in this table.

Exhibit 6.1 Typical Values to be Inserted

full_word	*abbrev_word*
CUSTOMER	CUST
ORDER	ORD
MODIFIED	MDFD
CREATED	CRTD
PURCHASE	PURCH
DRAWING	DRW
IDENTIFICATION	ID
NUMBER	NO
INDICATOR	IND
CUSTOMER	CUST

```
insert into case_abbrev values ('CUSTOMER','CUST')
/
insert into case_abbrev values ('ORDER','ORD')
/
insert into case_abbrev values ('MODIFIED','MDFD')
/
insert into case_abbrev values ('CREATED','CRTD')
/
insert into case_abbrev values ('PURCHASE','PURCH')
/
insert into case_abbrev values ('DRAWING','DRW')
/
insert into case_abbrev values ('IDENTIFICATION','ID')
/
insert into case_abbrev values ('NUMBER','NBR')
/
insert into case_abbrev values ('INDICATOR','IND')
/
```

Once we have this, we can already do a bit of impact analysis: "Dear Sql*Plus, show me all the search and replace that my utility would do if I ran it" (see Appendix 6.1).

Now that the scene is set, you can just run the script in the next table. But before you do, bear in mind that changing column names may have an impact on:

- Views
- Module
- Check constraints
- Triggers
- Database procedures, functions, and packages

It is a good idea to enforce standards from the beginning of design and in a continuous way (see Appendix 6.2). Waking up at the end of design or build will be very costly to the project.

If you have taken a close look at the code, you may have noticed that this utility can very easily be enhanced to perform a lot more than a simple search/replace. The only place that you have to change for this is function abbrv_name. You can, for example, make sure that the name of all DATE columns like DATE_ORDER_TAKEN end in _DT: ORD_TAKEN_DT.

If you really have analyzed the code, you may think that this utility could have a problem with columns containing several words to be replaced (e.g., PURCHASE_ORDER_NUMBER). You may doubt my seriousness no more, I have thought about it too. This is why I select the column again after each update:

```
ciocolumn.sel(cur_guilty_column.col_id ,col);
```

A number of times I encountered the error that follows when running this script:

```
RME-00011: Operation 'upd' on COLUMN has failed
CDA-01003: <no message text found>
Activity aborted with API errors
```

The first time I was confronted with that error was because I had accidentally typed the character <TAB> in one of my abbreviated column names in table case_abbrev. The second time, I abbreviated DESCRIPTION as DESC, which is a reserved Oracle word that must not be used as a column name. In both cases, I simply updated the table case_abbrev and moved on. If you get the same error, you will need to locate the offending value. The quickest way to do this is to un-comment the two debug lines of code in the middle of the script and run it again.

Appendix 6.1 Impact Analysis

```
prompt
prompt

rem     *****************************************************
rem     *
prompt  * This utility reports the columns that violate the
prompt  * naming conventions in Designer 2000.
prompt  * It uses table case_abbrev that contains all the words
prompt  * that must be abbreviated, and the standard abbreviation.
rem     *
rem     *****************************************************
prompt
prompt
prompt

set arraysize 1
set pagesize 1000
set linesize 150
col table_name format a30
col column_name format a30
col incorrect_word format a20
col correct_to format a10

spool guilty_col
break on table_name on column_name

-- Report on "Guilty" Columns
select tab.name table_name,
col.name column_name,
abv.full_word incorrect_word,
abv.abbrev_word correct_to
from ci_columns col,
ci_application_systems app,
case_abbrev abv,
ci_table_definitions tab
where col.table_reference = tab.id and
tab.application_system_owned_by = app.id and
app.name = upper('&&app_name') and
app.version = &&app_version and
col.name like '%'||full_word||'%'
order by tab.name, col.name, abv.full_word
/

spool out
```

Appendix 6.2 Enforcing Standards

```
set serveroutput on
set verify off
rem *******************************************************
rem *
rem * This utility enforces column naming conventions using
rem * Designer 2000.
rem * It uses table case_abbrev that contains all the words
rem * that must be abbreviated, and the standard abbreviation.
rem * It also uses function abbrv_name to reformat the
rem * "guilty" column.
rem *
rem *******************************************************

declare
  col ciocolumn.data;
  act_status varchar2(1);      -- Activity status
  act_warnings varchar2(1);    -- Activity warning flag

  v_app_id number(38);
  cursor get_application_id (p_app_name  varchar2,
       p_app_version  number) is
    select id
    from ci_application_systems
    where name = p_app_name and
      version = p_app_version;
  unknown_application_system exception;
  pragma exception_init(unknown_application_system, -20103);

  cursor guilty_columns (p_app_id number) is
    select tab.name tab_name,
      col.id col_id,
      col.name col_name,
      full_word full_word,
      abbrev_word abbrev_word
    from ci_columns col,
      case_abbrev,
      ci_table_definitions tab
    where col.table_reference = tab.id and
      tab.application_system_owned_by = p_app_id and
      col.name like '%'||full_word||'%';
  cur_guilty_column guilty_columns%rowtype;


  function abbrv_name(
       p_original_name in varchar2,
       p_key_word in varchar2,
       p_abbrev_word in varchar2)
    return varchar2 is
  begin
    return (replace(p_original_name,p_key_word,p_abbrev_word));
  end;
```

(continues)

Appendix 6.2 Enforcing Standards (continued)

```
  procedure instantiate_messages is
    m_facility varchar2(3);
    m_code number;
    arg1 varchar2(240);
    arg2 varchar2(64);
    arg3 varchar2(64);
    arg4 varchar2(64);
    arg5 varchar2(20);
    arg6 varchar2(20);
    arg7 varchar2(20);
    arg8 varchar2(20);

begin
    -- Report all violations regardless of the activity status
    for viol in (select * from ci_violations) loop
      dbms_output.put_line( cdapi.instantiate_message(
      viol.facility,viol.code,
      viol.p0,viol.p1,viol.p2,
      viol.p3,viol.p4,viol.p5,
      viol.p6,viol.p7 ) );
    end loop;
    -- Pop messages off the stack and format them into
    -- a single text string
    while cdapi.stacksize > 0 loop
      rmmes.pop( m_facility,m_code,arg1,arg2,arg3,arg4,arg5,
      arg6,arg7,arg8);
      dbms_output.put_line(cdapi.instantiate_message
      ( m_facility,m_code,arg1,arg2,arg3,arg4,arg5,arg6,arg7,arg8));
    end loop;
  end;

begin

  -- Get Application ID
  open get_application_id(upper('&&app_name'),&&app_version);
  fetch get_application_id into v_app_id;
  if get_application_id%notfound then
    raise_application_error(-20103,
      'Sorry, the application that you have entered is unknown.');
  end if;
  close get_application_id;


  -- Initialize API if not already done
  if cdapi.initialized = false then
    -- Initialize the API globals
    cdapi.initialize(upper('&&app_name'), &&app_version);
  end if;

  -- Set DBMS Output Buffer to Max Size
  dbms_output.enable(1000000);

  for cur_guilty_column in guilty_columns(v_app_id) loop
    cdapi.open_activity;

    -- Get the guilty column's record.
    ciocolumn.sel(cur_guilty_column.col_id ,col);
```

Appendix 6.2 Enforcing Standards (continued)

```
      -- Correct the column name.
      -- Uncomment 2 lines below for debugging.
      -- dbms_output.put_line(col.v.name ||' <-
         ('||cur_guilty_column.full_word||
      --
',' ||cur_guilty_column.abbrev_word||').');
      col.v.name := abbrv_name(col.v.name,
         cur_guilty_column.full_word,
         cur_guilty_column.abbrev_word);
      col.i.name := TRUE;

      -- Update the column
      ciocolumn.upd(cur_guilty_column.col_id, col);

      -- Validate the update
      cdapi.validate_activity(act_status,act_warnings);

      -- Get feedback
      instantiate_messages;
      cdapi.close_activity(act_status);

      -- If the activity did not close successfully, roll back
      -- all changes made during the activity
      if act_status != 'Y' then
         cdapi.abort_activity;
         dbms_output.put_line('Activity aborted with constraint
            violations');
      else
         dbms_output.put_line(cur_guilty_column.tab_name||'.'||
            cur_guilty_column.col_name);
      end if;
   end loop;
exception
   when unknown_application_system then
      dbms_output.put_line('Sorry, the application that you have '||
         'entered is unknown.');
      cdapi.abort_activity;
   when others then
      -- If any messages have been posted on the stack, then print them
      -- now and then roll back all changes made during the activity
      if cdapi.stacksize > 0 then
         -- Print all messages on the API stack
         while cdapi.stacksize > 0 loop
         dbms_output.put_line(cdapi.pop_instantiated_message);
         end loop;
         if cdapi.activity is not null then
         cdapi.abort_activity;
         dbms_output.put_line('Activity aborted with API errors');
         else
         dbms_output.put_line('API Session aborted with API errors');
         end if;

      -- Otherwise, this must have been an ORACLE SQL or internal error so
      -- roll back all changes made during the activity and re-raise the
      -- exception
      else
```

(continues)

Appendix 6.2 Enforcing Standards (continued)

```
         if cdapi.activity is not null then
         cdapi.abort_activity;
         dbms_output.put_line('Activity aborted with ORACLE internal
           errors');
         else
         dbms_output.put_line('API Session aborted with ORACLE internal
           errors');
         end if;
         raise;
      end if;
END;
/
```

ORACLE WEB DEVELOPMENT

One of the most interesting new areas of Oracle development is the idea of using Oracle as a back end to systems that are delivered on the Internet. To embrace E-commerce systems, Oracle has completely reconfigured its product line to allow for the simple development of Oracle Web applications, and provides easy-to-use end-user tools such as Oracle WebDB and Oracle Portals for the purpose of developing fast, robust applications that access Oracle over the Internet.

This section includes some of the best work from Bradley D. Brown of TUSC Software, and Hervé Deschamps of Oracle technical support. It is very important for today's Oracle professional to understand the suite of Oracle Web development tools, as well as to have an in-depth understanding of the internal communications between HTTP and XML.

The Internet is becoming the *de facto* standard for Oracle front ends, whether the application is on the Internet or on a local area network. The HTTP format is quickly becoming the standard method for Oracle developers to create and deliver systems that interact within the Oracle database. Hence, this section is indispensable for all Oracle professionals who need to understand the intricacies and nuances of Oracle Web development.

Chapter 7

Building a .com from the Ground Up

Bradley D. Brown
Ellen Robinson

Building a .com or E-business from the ground up sounds daunting, doesn't it? Actually, there are two aspects to the process that you must consider: business and technical. You've got to get through the business aspects before you can begin the technical.

To begin the process, you first need a concept. If you're reading this article, you may already have a concept in mind. In fact, many people establish an idea by seeing a gap in an existing business or service. Many entrepreneurs search the world for a gap they can fill. The idea phase should encompass not only the concept but the objectives and strategies as well. Are you selling a product or other people's products? What kind of volume do you project? How much time will you invest in maintaining and supporting your .com? These are just a few of the questions you must address in the concept phase. You also want to set the key goals of the planning process.

The most effective approach to move from concept to venture is what we refer to as building the "no-brainer" plan. In other words, customers, investors, and employees who learn about the concept will agree that your concept is a "no-brainer" — there is a clear, unmet, and large customer need and a clear path to transform the idea into a viable business. It must be obvious as to how you will accomplish making your idea a reality. It is best if your concept is easy to explain.

Do you remember the letter that Mark Twain wrote in which he implied that if he had more time, he would have written a shorter letter? Isn't that the truth? It takes a lot of time to make the complex sound simple. Take the time to turn your concept into something you can easily explain.

0-8493-1139-X/02/$0.00+$1.50
©2002 by CRC Press LLC

Building the Customer/Business Cases

The first step in building a compelling "no-brainer" case for your idea is to start with the customer and to build the *customer* case. To do so effectively you need to spend time validating why a customer would want your services (defining the value proposition). In other words, the customer is going to love this because — why? Be sure to include cost and timesaving. The customer really needs to love your product, relative to its costs. Is this a new product or service venture? If it is, you need to focus on using technology to drive real business process innovation in the industry, not just another way to do the same things. On the other hand, are any behavior changes involved with using the product or service? Keep in mind that required behavioral changes are difficult to justify.

After building the customer case, it's time to ensure that there is a real business or profit opportunity by understanding and building the *business* case. Your work here should be focused on understanding the size of the market, potential competitors, and the general profit potential of the business. You will need to take a stab at defining your revenue model (e.g., subscription, licensing, advertising, commerce, etc.), pricing your service, understanding the costs of your business, and determining in what share of the market you can make "good" money. If you determine that you need a market share greater than 15 to 20 percent — beware. In fact, if you need as little as 5 percent of the entire market, even that level of market penetration is extremely difficult to achieve. Most sophisticated investors are looking for markets bigger than $10 billion (this is the low bar); so if you plan to take on venture capital, be prepared. Another critical area for you to address while building the business case is your plans for building the management team. Unless you're exceptionally well-connected, you can't do this alone! Now is the time to consider your strengths and weaknesses and how they will affect the success of starting a new venture. What is the likelihood of attracting other talented individuals to this venture? What will be your approach to do so?

Developing the Business Plan

Once you have built a "no-brainer" customer and business case for your idea, you can develop your business plan. Your business plan is a very important component of your success. It represents your "roadmap" toward a successful venture. We won't get into the details of the business plan, as there are numerous resources available to assist this. Just keep in mind that this is the presentation you'll be taking to potential investors to finance your .com. If you are a nonbusiness person, you may even want to consider a business advisor or consultant to work with on your business plan.

You may want to sit down before you read this next section. It can take up to eight months — sometimes longer (working on it nearly full-time) — to gather enough information to write a complete business plan. If you already have all the information you need from your own experience and you can just sit down and write (without researching every detail), the time spent will probably be much shorter. It's unlikely that you can really build a compelling, investor-ready plan without time spent on research, personal interviews, etc. Unless you've raised some "friends and family" money in this stage (and if you have, you probably won't be paying yourself with it), you've got to live without income during this phase. It's difficult, if not impossible, to effectively accomplish this work while retaining other full-time employment. If you are not fully immersed, it will not be a comprehensive plan. Depending on your situation, this may be too high-risk for you.

Marketing will be covered in your business plan, but we'd like to address a few key areas. Make sure your marketing analysis is comprehensive and thorough. You have to know the market you are about to enter. Set specific goals and develop strategies on how to reach those goals. Determine how you will advertise and promote your .com. Success or failure of any business often hinges on marketing. The investors will all ask how you plan to penetrate the market you're going after. Remember that to create a consumer-based brand name in the .com space today, it will cost far in excess of $20 million.

The business plan must include a well-thought-out timeline for launching and growing the venture. This timeline will include your plans and milestones to develop the product. For example, month one would include storyboarding the entire application. Month two would be used to determine functionality within the release of your prototype (document management, profiling, etc.). You would determine the components that can be purchased versus built. During month two you might select a team for design, development, graphics, etc. You would develop a detailed product schedule for your first release of the "real" thing. You would also develop a high-level project schedule for future releases.

Months three through six might flow something like this. In month three you would focus on negotiating with hardware and software vendors and also complete and approve the design of your .com. Month four would encompass development completion, including unit testing and complete system testing of the prototype. You would release your prototype in month five and your "real" version in month six.

Don't forget about methodology. Cover your storyboard design with transactive content and the five Cs of design: Cool, Content, Context, Contact, and Control. Review your technical architecture, including the open architecture (CORBA, UNIX, TCP/IP). Explain why your choice is scalable, reliable, and recoverable — and why these are important. Show how it is a proven technology and how it is portable across platforms. Also demonstrate that it has high availability, which is where an Oracle solution really comes into play.

Review the software you will use for your .com (for example, Oracle8i RDBMS, Oracle Application Server, Java and PL/SQL, XML, and SQL*Net, SSL, and the Apache Web Listener). Be prepared to address questions on why you have chosen this particular software. Expound on Oracle8i and include information on Oracle iFS, Java VM in the Database, Seamless interactions (Java-SQL-PL/SQL), SQLJ — Embedded SQL in Java, enhanced JDBC Drivers, Web monitoring, partitioning, and unlimited database size.

Show the N-Tier Architecture of your .com. This basic drawing will bring together the technical architecture in an easy-to-understand way for your potential investors.

Examine the browser you will use and what it encompasses. As an example, HTML and Java-Script cookies are used to store encrypted user ID, limited plug-ins (i.e., Adobe Acrobat Reader), limited Java, and XML later. Explain why your choice is bandwidth friendly and why this is important. For example, our site will have a dial-up focus, small graphics, and low color requirement.

Hardware/Software

Next you need to discuss hardware — what you will use initially (e.g., Intel Multiprocessor Pentium) and the long-term solution (e.g., Sun Solaris 2.6+). Demonstrate how you will scale up your hardware and how quickly and easily it can be done.

Review where your site will be hosted and why. For example, if you host your site at an ASP, it's close to the backbone (so it's fast), and you have 24x7 system support, mission-critical redundancy, and backup and recovery capabilities.

Address whether you will buy or build your .com solutions. I suggest building only if there is nothing available to buy or no reasonably priced solution. With the numerous products available on the market today, you should be able to buy most, if not all, of the software for your site. Your job will be to put it all together.

Be prepared to discuss who your Project Team is composed of and everyone's role; for example, technical architect, design team, graphic artist, developer, content provider (users), testing team (users), project management, and database administrator.

Present your team development tools, such as Oracle Application Server and the Java, PL/SQL, Perl or LiveHTML Cartridge, Oracle Designer for CASE/Modeling, Macromedia Dreamweaver for HTML Development, Tool for Oracle Application Developers (TOAD) or another PL/SQL editor, WebAlchemy for converting HTML to PL/SQL, WebTrends for site analysis, and Oracle Reports as your reporting tool. How does Oracle Developer Forms fit into your architecture?

Security

Review the site security and what it entails (for example, SSL, application authentication, domain and IP restriction, basic and digest authentication, and database user authentication). Be prepared to discuss the firewall security as well.

Domain Name Registration

By the way, early on in this business planning process, even when your idea is written on a cocktail napkin, it's a good idea to select a domain name, determining if it's available, and register it. If you have ideas about the name, you will, in fact, want to register it before too much time passes.

Registering your own dot.com, or domain name, is pretty simple and usually costs about half of what your Internet service provider (ISP) would charge to do the work for you.

The first step in registering a domain name is to find out if it is available. There are several ways to investigate. You can simply type in the address you want and see if your browser finds it (e.g., www.tusc.com). Keep in mind that there may be several names registered and taken, but not necessarily used. Many companies have registered as many combinations of their domain name as possible because they don't want anyone else to lay claim to their Web addresses.

The best option is to go to Network Solutions, Inc. (NSI). NSI has been the only provider of domain name services in the .com, .net, and .org top-level domains since 1993. However, new registers are currently being tested, with more on the way. Log onto NSI's free online search area at www.networksolutions.com and enter the Web address you want to use, pick an extension (i.e., .com, .net or .org), and then hit the Search button. If the address is available in .com, you should also pick the other two extensions to protect your Internet identity.

Once you find your .com name, there is additional information you need before you can submit your request to register. You must contact your ISP for two Internet Protocol (IP) addresses. IP addresses are the numbers computers use to identify your domain name. If you don't have a domain name server to register, then NSI can provide you with a domain server until you have one of your own.

Once you have your IP addresses, you can register online by going to www.internic.net. and using their Domain Name Template Generator. InterNIC (Internet Network Information Center) is a group maintained by the National Science Foundation, Network Solutions, Inc. (NSI), and AT&T. It is in charge of handling all the requests for domain names. You can also find a link to www.networksolutions.com on this page to do your search for a domain name.

Just complete the form in the Domain Name Template Generator and follow the directions on how to submit, etc. You're billed for the rights to the domain name for two years and then pay an annual fee. It's that easy!

Money

Now let's talk money! Once you have the business plan information in place, you can start thinking about financing, a critical phase of building your .com. You must have the financial backing for your .com or it will never make it off the ground. We're not talking about a few thousand dollars or even a few hundred thousand dollars. The financial backing you're looking for runs into the millions — yes, millions of dollars.

Where are you going to get millions of dollars? How do you find the right people to talk to? How do you determine who to talk to and what to talk about? There are several components you must have in place before you can even begin the financing stage. You can't even talk to potential investors or venture capital people without an executive summary from your business plan, a presentation, and a financial plan, etc. If you are looking to raise money to prove your concept (prove your initial customer case), this is called seed or early stage money. If you have a proven concept and are looking for additional funds to launch your business, this is called first round financing. Later rounds of financing are used to grow the business. Venture capital firms often prefer to provide financing for a particular stage of the business (e.g., early stage or later stage only), so you will need to align your search with the type of funds you are looking for. If the investment you're looking for is less than $1 million, "angel investors" tend to look for investments of this size.

There are many books and resources that will define the various "stages" of a venture (e.g., seed, early stage, xyz stage, late stage, and pre-IPO stage). In general, you are probably at the seed stage (or most probably friends and family pre-seed stage) if you are starting from an idea on a cocktail napkin or have a basic prototype and need money to:

- Do the research
- Fly around to talk with customers
- Hire some consultants to help in various areas
- Further develop customer/business cases

You might need $100,000 (more if you need to spend money on technology) just to see if there is even a business here.

If you've done all the work above, you'll probably need money to "prove the concept," which means actually getting the product or service developed and building a small team of business and technical people to get real customers. Today, people are typically raising $1,000,000 to $1,500,000 to move through the "prove the concept" phase. This, of course, depends on how much money it really takes (the driver for something more than this amount of money would be expensive technology; the business costs are fairly well-defined). And, one can only raise this amount of money if there really appears to be a large market opportunity. This is where the greatest risk is involved for investors; but if it is successful, this is where the greatest amount of financial value (and personal reward) is created.

There is a lot of jargon and characterization of investor types for the various stages. This stage is where the term "angel" comes in. Angels are unlikely to invest the entire $1,000,000+ amount, but a group of "angels" might. An "angel" can be a successful entrepreneur who has made a substantial amount of money and wants to get directly involved with new companies, versus one who gives money to a venture capital fund and remains a passive investor. It is really any high-net-worth individual who is a sophisticated investor, recognizing all the risks at this stage.

The other type of investor would be a seed or early stage venture capitalist. This would mean that the venture capital fund has specifically set a strategy around taking this type of risk, working with companies in this stage, and with their partners. By the way, this would be called the venture capital's "sweet spot" (the stage, and then other descriptors around the type of companies in which that venture capital invests). Given the amount of risk at this stage (if you can't prove the concept, you lose the entire investment) and the amount of support the entrepreneur requires (patient investors, investors with experience in the space with contacts, knowledge, ideas, etc.), this is not a good time to take more money from friends and family.

Finding investors to talk to should start (and hopefully finish) within the entrepreneur's own "six degrees of separation." In other words, contacts are key. It is extremely rare to have much success by simply shipping a business plan around without direct exposure to the investor(s) receiving it (unless the entrepreneur has a notable reputation). There are just too many opportunities being presented at the present time. If an entrepreneur is "light here" with contacts, convince a service professional (lawyer, accountant, business consultant, etc.) to support you and ask to use that person's contacts. This usually means calling on your behalf or sending a plan directly to the targeted investors. This really is tough if the entrepreneur is a real techie without any business contacts. There are people who will take a percentage and do fundraising. This certainly is an option if someone needs it, but probably difficult to find someone you can trust and who works well with you.

When you meet with investors, you need to have the most comprehensive plan possible. You can capture the key elements in an executive summary and a presentation, but you should be prepared with the finished plan to "close" the investment deal. The business plan will provide additional information and your overall thinking. For example, relative to the product development cycle, are product roll-out needs addressed? A project kick-off plan must be in place. Will you have more than one project phase or version? Will you have new versions every quarter? Every six months?

Investor Buy-In

Once an investor has "bought in to your concept," it is time to have that person buy into the company. The central discussion regarding an investor's investment will be around what is called a "pre-money valuation" of the company. A pre-money valuation of your venture is defined as what the value of your venture is immediately prior to accepting a round of financing. Believe it or not, with a solid customer and business case, a good business plan, and a few key members of the management team at least identified, your venture already has a value, and this valuation will be heavily negotiated during the financing process. The valuation ultimately determines the percentage of the company an investor receives in return for the money invested, which ultimately determines the investor's return on that investment some time in the future (usually when the venture is sold or does an IPO). It's important to understand what drives valuations and then determine where this venture fits within these parameters. The valuation process is as much art as science, and you would be well-advised to get some good support here. Nevertheless, there are probably very good ranges one can expect if a venture breaks into the professional investment range at all. Basically, investors at each stage are looking for a return commensurate with their risk. This is *after* the investor determines that if the venture successfully penetrates the market (this is where the risk is calculated), there is really a market large enough to be worthwhile. The investor at this stage probably needs to see a potential for the venture to be "worth" hundreds of millions of dollars over the next three to five years.

For example, an investor willing to invest $1 million in an early stage might desire a future return of $10 million (10 times the initial investment). If the $1 million is the only sum of money ever needed, and if the venture "harvested" $100 million, the investor would have assumed 10 percent of the company to achieve its goals. Usually, the venture will need additional investors in later stages, so what drives the investor's goals (the initial portion of the company you give away) will also include a calculation for future "dilution." For example, if after the $1 million is spent and another round of $10 million is needed, those investors may require 30 percent of the company beyond the dilution of the initial investors (as well as the founder and employees.) In the simple example of the initial investor having 10 percent, this stake would be diluted to 7 percent, and now the venture would have to harvest $142 million to return at 10 times the original investment. All these types of projections are what goes on in the initial valuation (and all subsequent valuations), and this is what ends up leading to seed companies "giving away" anywhere from 30 to 60 percent of their companies in the first round of financing.

Other Concerns

In addition to negotiating pre-money valuations, there are several other terms the entrepreneur must be aware of and negotiate in any financing, i.e., board participation, employee stock option pools, etc. There are several other areas to take into consideration under the business aspect umbrella. When can or should you go public? When should you think about a CEO to take the business to the next level? Where do you fit into your organization — CEO? CIO? Idea dreamer?

If you are a pure techie with hopes of successfully emerging from the seed stage with a viable business, you will need a CEO with a business and probably a sales and marketing background. Basically, at any stage, there needs to be a combination of business and technical expertise to handle the scale of the business at that size. If you are a techie, you will play as key a role as the business members, but *no one* does it on his or her own. Whether you become VP of Development, CTO, or CIO probably depends primarily on your business acumen and leadership skills. But you will always be the "evangelist." You have to be able to convince people to "sign-up" with your idea and work *very* hard to contribute to the success of the venture.

Your financing is in place; your business plan is on track; now you can delve into the technical side of building your .com. Some of the initial legwork was already done in the business planning stage: selecting applications, determining goals, resource costing, and choosing the right tools.

Although you came up with a basic design concept to present to your investors, you need to get down to the nuts and bolts of designing your site. Truly great Web applications are designed to be practical. That means they are well-planned, easy to use, easy to maintain, intuitive, open (support most browsers without plug-ins), relevant, and addictive. Make sure you employ Netiquette in your design, which includes avoiding too much information on your home page and sending users just what they need. Keep in mind features you can use and limitations you have with regard to software and hardware.

Prototyping and testing are important components of the design phase and were included in your methodology for that reason. Your prototype lays the groundwork for later versions. Testing will uncover the positive and negative aspects of your site before you "go live."

Once your design is finished, you can move onto installation and configuration. Make sure your architecture components are in place, configure your hardware, and install and configure your software — Oracle Application Server. Security and logging should be taken care of, as well as establishing virtual hosts. Keep in mind optional software such as Oracle Designer and Developer.

Next, we move into the development phase. The tools you will need are HTML and JavaScript for client-side development, and PL/SQL and Perl for server-side development (both CGI and cartridges). Most projects will usually include a combination of the two. File system operations must be developed either against the Web server or against the data server. Address cookies and ports/security issues. Database authentication needs to be done and a locking method chosen. Now is a good time to develop a library of routines including a generic error routine. If you write your documentation in Word, create bookmarks for context-sensitive positions and save as HTML; you can use this for your online documentation. Use the Listener logs to track usage, do research, and perform market analysis.

Your next step is testing, debugging, and tuning. Keep in mind that your site requires more testing than standard business applications and must encompass back-end (server) code testing, browser (client) variations, network issues, and security and hacker issues. Things to consider during your testing are browsers supported, network and modem speeds, and reliance upon Java, JavaScript, and cookies because client (PC) configurations may have these "turned off."

When tuning for throughput, make sure you address the following areas:

- Balance processing between client and server.
- Offload FTP, mail, and database services to other servers.
- Generate static HTML for standard reports using UTL_FILE, DBMS_JOBS.
- Regularly check to make sure the site is up.
- Tune cartridge instance parameter accordingly.
- Use net.medic to analyze your network.

Do not forget application tuning of SQL queries, PL/SQL and PL/SQL packages, CGI, Perl, and other dynamic programs. And last, but not least, tune the graphics; that is, reduce the color count, use thumbnails when possible, etc.

Implementation

Now you are ready to implement your site. Remember, you only have one chance to make a first impression. Jazz up your site. Check your use of animated images, sound, etc. Keep in mind that it is easy to refine your application once it has been implemented, but it is considerably less costly (about 1000 times less expensive, in fact) to make the modifications to a design document. Address all the aspects of security, from protection, from physical tampering/environmental disasters, to network firewall, to proxy server. Develop a written security policy.

Once up and running, your Web Listener log files, along with data you store about your .com users or customers, can also provide you with some useful marketing analysis information. You should be able to pull the following information from your site:

- Demographics: sex, race, age, education, home value, family size, income
- Psychographics: self-concept, attitude, interests, opinions, beliefs, preferences, personality traits
- Clickographics: attention span, focus, appetite, impulsiveness, judgment, analytical skills
- Communigraphics: communication skills, cooperation, participation

The use of this information will result in predictive marketing, which will then increase page hits and sales, decrease sales costs, etc.

It is important to determine the steps you will use to implement application changes. You should also define a policy on change control. This is something you will use again and again in the future, so it is best to take care of it now. There is no need to keep recreating the wheel; in addition, you will ensure uniformity for future changes.

The last item under the support and maintenance umbrella is determining the methods of contacting your help desk. Will customers e-mail, phone, or fax in their problems — or will they have all three options? Determine the turn-around time for each method and establish policies.

Planning for the Future

Your final step in this process is planning for the future. What will the future bring? Faster networks and cheaper and cheaper memory, to name a few.

However, technology is changing so fast that it is difficult to predict what lies down the road 10, 25, or 50 years from now. What you really need to focus on is Web site development. Where are you today? Where do you want to go? What do you need to be aware of?

Three key areas you should to take into consideration for your future planning decisions include:

1. The future of the .com is transactive content as defined by *Forrester Reports*.
2. Web sites will need to incorporate interpersonal skills.
3. Thin-client computing is around to stay.

Building a .com from the ground up is very similar to opening up a retail store. The business plan must be developed, marketing analysis performed, financing obtained, employees hired, etc. The major difference is the end result — an actual storefront versus a virtual storefront. One last thought before you begin this process.

> Do not go where the path may lead, go instead where there is no path and leave a trail.
>
> —Ralph Waldo Emerson

Chapter 8

Rapid Web Deployment with WebDB

Serg Shestakov
Dmitry Petrov

Web-enabling an Oracle database can be a complicated task for developers not familiar with Oracle Application Server or Oracle Developer Server. What if a customer wants dynamic Web application and cannot wait? Is there any software on the market for really rapid development of secure, scalable, and reliable Web applications? WebDB is just that tool. There are two very important advantages to WebDB. First, the client side is browser-only. We use a browser to develop, deploy, and administer Web applications. Second, all the application logic, interfaces, and development tools are stored directly in the Oracle database; thus, WebDB automatically inherits Oracle's security, scalability, and reliability features.

This chapter shows the fast track for developing dynamic Web applications with WebDB. We take a look at WebDB features, including managing database objects, users, roles and access rights, and building interface components. Then we discuss step-by-step procedures for developing simple Web interfaces to Oracle data. We also show case studies for a table-based form, Query by Example form, master-detail form, and dynamic page. In the end, we consider how to create a menu integrating all our case studies. To achieve this goal, we discuss how to manage WebDB users, how to build database objects, and how to interface components.

Running WebDB

Now let us outline the environment that will be used for our study. On the server side running Oracle 8.1.5 database under Sun SPARC Solaris 2.7, we

0-8493-1139-X/02/$0.00+$1.50
©2002 by CRC Press LLC

have installed WebDB 2.1. To simplify administration, we have created a new operating system user and added it into the dba group. Installation itself is a pretty straightforward process. The installer connects under SYS to target Oracle database and compiles the PL/SQL Web Toolkit. Then it adds a WebDB Listener component to specified $ORACLE_HOME. Note that WebDB Listener should be installed into its own $ORACLE_HOME, different from those running target Oracle database — that is why we recommend running WebDB under a dedicated operating system user. WebDB supports any Oracle database, starting with version 7.3.4. The client can use any standard browser. Oracle recommends using Netscape 4.0.8 and above, or Microsoft IE 4.0.1 with Service pack 1 and above.

Before developing applications, we must start WebDB Listener. During installation, we specified port number 7777 and hostname myhost, and now we refer to these parameters to start a listener. The corresponding command is listed below. To run this command, we log on as the WebDB Listener owner. Note that we specify background execution:

```
wdbstart myhost 7777 &
```

To run WebDB listener automatically at server startup on a UNIX platform, we can append this line to the database starting script (e.g., S83dbstart) placed under the /etc/rc2.d directory. The wdbstart is itself a start script that sets environment variables and runs WebDB daemon, the wdblsnr process.

How to Manage Users

When we installed the WebDB toolkit, we specified Oracle database user WebDB to hold the WebDB repository and Database Access Descriptor (DAD) called WebDB_DAD. The latter is a virtual directory name. Before we can use our DAD, we should configure it. For this purpose, we invoke an administration page located at http://myhost:7777/_admin/gateway.htm. The browser opens the DAD configuration form where we define the connect string and default homepage for our WebDB_DAD. Note that the connection string should correspond to valid entry in server-side tnsnames.ora. We can also specify a default username and password for public access. Actually, all changes are stored in the configuration file wdbsvr.app located at $ORACLE_HOME/listener/cfg. To make sure the changes will take effect, we can stop the WebDB Listener (wdblsnr myhost 7777 stop) and run it again (wdblsnr myhost 7777 start).

Now when the listener process is up and running, we can try connecting to it from the client browser. The location prefix for application URLs has the following format: http://<hostname>:<port>/ <DAD>. In our case, we specify the following connection prefix: http://myhost:7777/ WebDB_DAD. Because we did not specify a default logon, when we try to connect to this

Exhibit 8.1 Oracle WebDB Main Menu

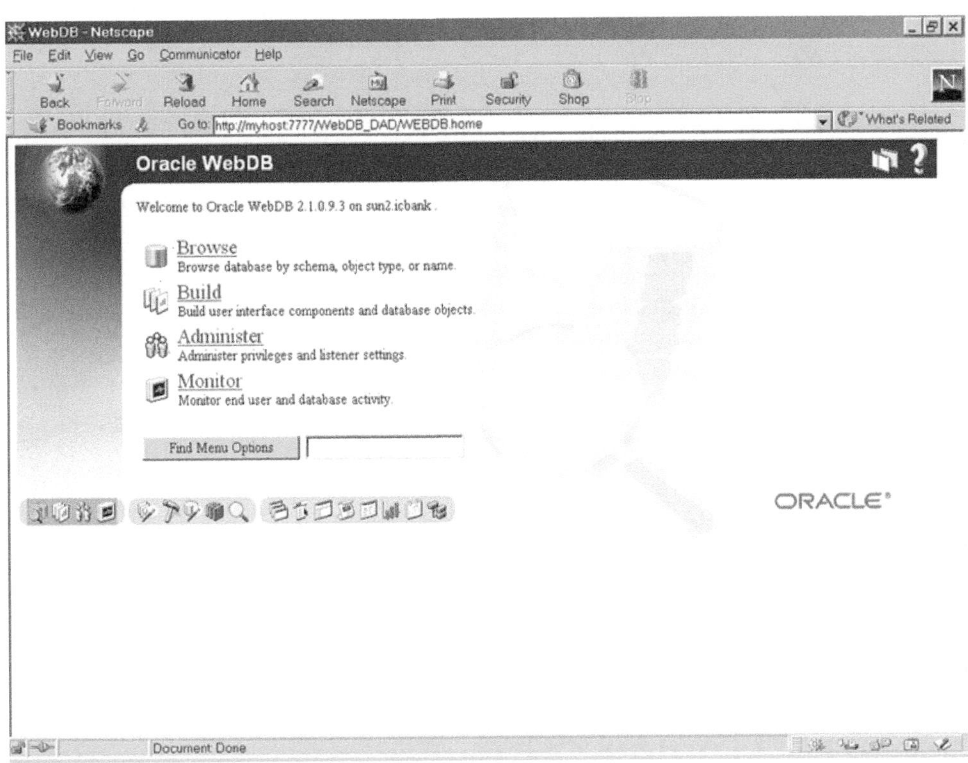

location, we will be prompted for username and password. WebDB users correspond to Oracle database users having access to WebDB repository. By this time, we have created the only user — our `WebDB`. Upon successful logon, we will see the main menu (see Exhibit 8.1) with four options: browsing the database, building interfaces as well as building the sites themselves with Web DB, administering privileges and WebDB listeners, and monitoring users and database (Monitoring is a ready-to-run application written entirely with WebDB). The Monitoring application simplifies many routine DBA tasks and turns WebDB into a useful tool for remote administration. The toolbar placed at the bottom of the page consists of three sections: the first section duplicates the main menu; the second section links to basic tools; and the third section duplicates the menu for managing user interface components.

Because the WebDB user has a DBA role granted, for security reasons we do not recommend using it for applications development. For this purpose, we will create another user; follow the "Administer" menu item and in the administration form click the "User Manager" item. We must fill the "Create a New User" form (see Exhibit 8.2) indicating usual Oracle user data; that is, username, password, default, and temporary tablespaces. Also, do not forget to check both checkboxes — "WebDB Developer" and "Component Building Scheme." For our new user, `WEB_DEVELOPER`, the former checkbox will enable access to the WebDB toolkit, and the latter will help share components

Exhibit 8.2 Adding the WEB_DEVELOPER

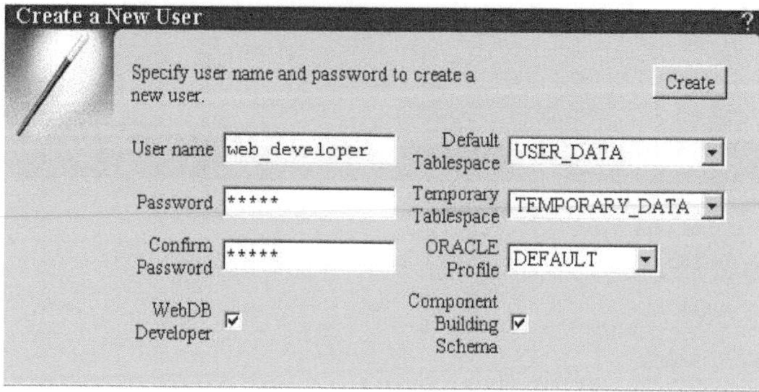

with other developers. Then we apply changes and follow the "Roles" tab to add the RESOURCE role.

If we want to share database objects and interface components with other developers, we should go to the "Build Privileges" tab and enable sharing with other users. For example, we can share components with predefined user SCOTT. When we install WebDB, it creates useful sample objects and components for user SCOTT, and for simplified development, we can reuse its interface components.

How to Build Database Objects

Of course, we can create database objects manually by running commands from the SQL*Plus console. For most common tasks, we do not need SQL*Plus; WebDB has a graphical interface for building tables, indexes, triggers, views, sequences, synonyms, and packages. For our example applications, we will need tables. There are two ways to get to the "Build Database Objects" form. We can go back to the main menu of Oracle WebDB, follow the "Build" option and choose the "Database Objects" item; or we can use a shortcut: click the corresponding icon on the toolbar. In general, we do not recommend using the built-in context search (Find Menu Options button). Next, we run the "Create Table" wizard. In the wizard's first page, we specify the table owner (`WEB_DEVELOPER`) from the pop-up menu, enter table name (`DEPT`), and proceed to the next page where we define table structure — column names, types, etc. (see Exhibit 8.3).

For the `DEPT_ID` column, we specify that it should be a primary key not having null values. Then we proceed to the next page where we define table storage parameters; that is, default tablespace, sizes of initial and next allocated extents (`1m` each), and minimum and maximum numbers of extents (2 and 128, respectively). Finally, wizard is ready to create the table; we just need to click the OK button.

To insert data into our `DEPT` table, we can use the Browse option from the main menu. In this query wizard, we need to specify user schema (`WEB_DEVELOPER`); we can type it manually or choose from the dictionary

Exhibit 8.3 Defining Structure for the DEPT Table

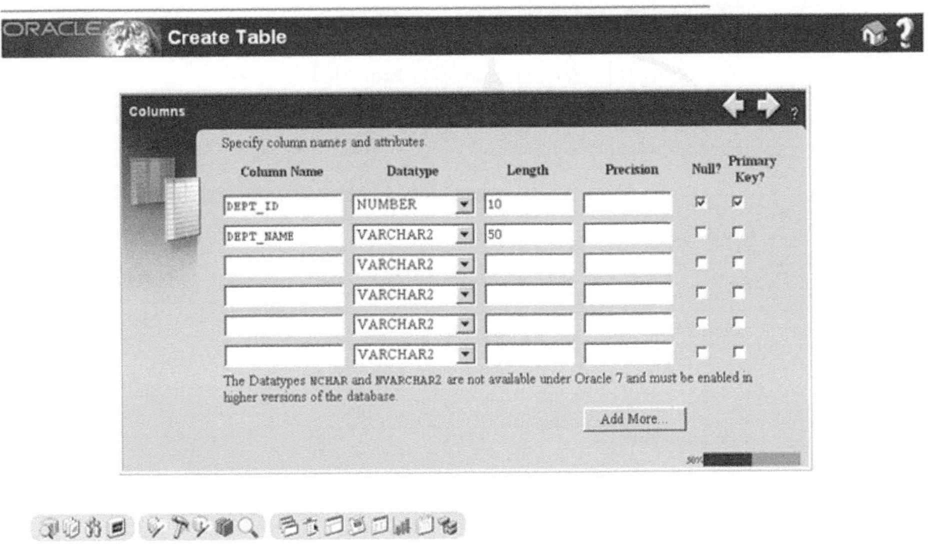

by clicking on an icon near the field. Also, we pick up the database object type (Table) from the pop-up menu and enter search topic (D%). We click the Browse button and query returns all tables beginning with "D." Now we click on our table displayed in query results and this will start the "Query and Update Table" form. There we enter two attributes: new department ID (`DEPT ID`) and name (`DEPT NAME` A) (see Exhibit 8.4) and click the Insert New Rows button. WebDB will show the results saved.

In a similar manner, we insert several rows and click the Query button; Exhibit 8.5 shows the resulting `DEPT` table. Note that we can apply different filters while querying; this is very useful for large tables. Using the Query & Update button, we can edit and delete rows.

To speed up access, we will create an index for the `DEPT_NAME` column called `I_DEPT_NAME.` We can run the Create Index wizard from the Build Database Objects menu. On the first page, we specify the owner, index name, and uniqueness; on the second page, we choose Table from the pop-up list. Next, we indicate table column(s) to index and proceed to the next page where we define the storage parameters just as we did for the table. Finally, we click the OK button to create the index and check its definition. Exhibit 8.6 shows all the index parameters. To try the master-detail example, we need another table called `EMP.` Exhibit 8.7 illustrates its structure defined as we did for the `DEPT` table.

Note that if we want to create a foreign key referencing the `DEPT` table, we need to run the corresponding command manually from the SQL*Plus console. Now we fill the `EMP` table using "Query and Update Table" page just as we did for the `DEPT` table. Exhibit 8.8 shows the `EMP` table opened with the Query & Update button.

Exhibit 8.4 Inserting Rows into the DEPT Table

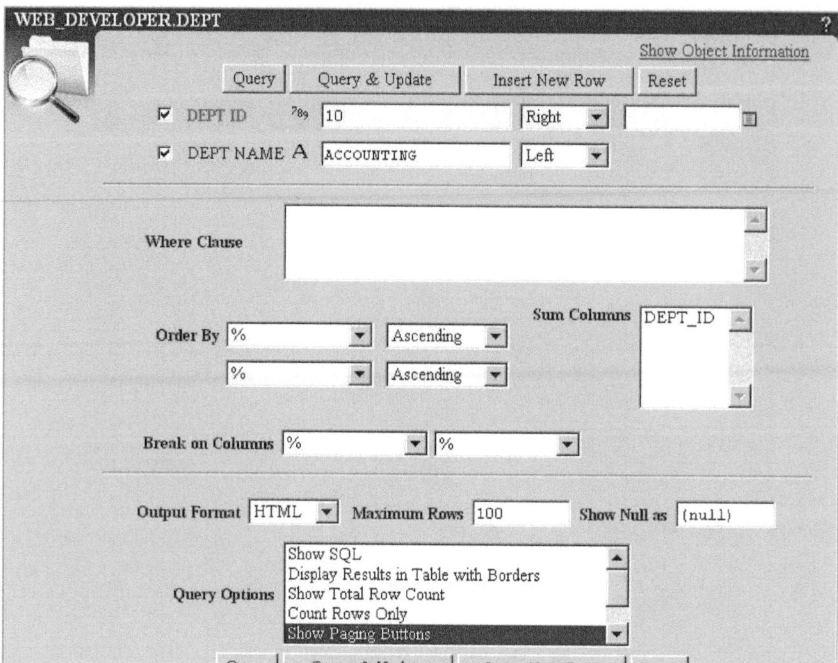

How To Build Interfaces

By this time, we have defined database objects and stored initial user information there. To design an interface with WebDB, we follow the "Build" link from the main menu and choose the "User Interface Components" option. This option helps to create many useful components, including forms, parameterized reports, link-based menus, different HTML-based charts, frame-based screens, etc.

Now we will build a form. Choose the "Forms" components from the menu to get to the "Form Building" page. There are several form types supported by WebDB: forms based on tables/views, forms based on stored procedures, Query by Example forms, and master-detail forms. We will show how to create and run table-based, QBE-based, and master-detail forms.

Exhibit 8.5 The Resulting DEPT Table

DEPT ID	DEPT NAME
10	ACCOUNTING
20	RESEARCH
30	SALES
40	OPERATIONS

Row(s) 1 - 4

Exhibit 8.6 The Resulting `I_DEPT_NAME` Index

Wednesday November 01, 2000 15:37

Index: I_DEPT_NAME

These tables show index information from the ORACLE data dictionary views ALL_INDEXES and ALL_IND_COLUMNS

OWNER	WEB_DEVELOPER
INDEX NAME	I_DEPT_NAME
TABLE OWNER	WEB_DEVELOPER
TABLE NAME	DEPT
TABLE TYPE	TABLE
UNIQUENESS	NONUNIQUE
TABLESPACE NAME	USER_DATA
INI TRANS	2
MAX TRANS	255
INITIAL EXTENT	524288
NEXT EXTENT	524288
MIN EXTENTS	1
MAX EXTENTS	2147483645
PCT INCREASE	0
FREELISTS	1
FREELIST GROUPS	1
PCT FREE	10
STATUS	VALID

Table-based Forms

Now we will design a form based on `DEPT` table. We choose the "Forms on Tables/Views" option from the "Create a New Form" combo box and click the Create button. This opens the first page of the "Create Forms" wizard where we choose the schema owner (`WEB_DEVELOPER`) from the pop-up list

Exhibit 8.7 The `EMP` Table Structure

Columns

Specify column names and attributes.

Column Name	Datatype	Length	Precision	Null?	Primary Key?
EMP_ID	NUMBER	10		☑	☑
EMP_NAME	VARCHAR2	50		☐	☐
DEPT_ID	NUMBER	10		☐	☐
	VARCHAR2			☐	☐
	VARCHAR2			☐	☐
	VARCHAR2			☐	☐

The Datatypes NCHAR and NVARCHAR2 are not available under Oracle 7 and must be enabled in higher versions of the database.

Add More...

50%

Exhibit 8.8 Editing the EMP Table Contents

Action	EMP ID	EMP NAME	DEPT ID
Update	7369	SMITH	20
Update	7499	ALLEN	30
Update	7521	WARD	30
Update	7566	JONES	20
Update	7654	MARTIN	30
Update	7698	BLAKE	30
Update	7782	CLARK	10

Row(s) 1 - 7

Back: Database Tables, Database Objects

and name our form. We will call it DEPT_FORM. The next page offers us the choice between two layouts: structured (this is default layout) and unstructured, and the developer writes it in HTML. To simplify development, we choose structured layout.

Then we proceed to the next page ("Formatting and Validation") where we can change the default setting for our form — background image and font, colors to use, etc. With the next wizard page we can specify what operations we want to apply and define button names and locations — we specify all the operations (Insert, Update, Delete, Query and Reset). The next page, "Text Options," is used to enter title, header, footer, and help information. This time we just change the form title to "Table DEPT". The next page, called "Advanced PL/SQL code," is for configuring PL/SQL blocks. Code can be executed before and after displaying the page or processing the form, before displaying the footer, and after displaying the header. It resembles triggers for Oracle Forms, and it is a useful feature for customizing the page. For example, to display current date next to the form title, we can add the following string, calling the print function from Oracle Web's htp package to "before displaying the page" section:

```
htp.print(SYSDATE);
```

Then we proceed to the next page and apply changes. Now we will show how to run and edit the form: we choose the "Form" icon from the toolbar, proceed to the "Find Existing Form" section, choose owner (WEB_DEVELOPER), and click the Find button. In search results, we click on the form name and enter the "Manage Component" page. We can also get there from a list of recently edited forms (third section of the "Form Building" page). Exhibit 8.9 shows the "Manage Component" page.

This page has a menu with six options to run, edit, define parameters, restrict access privileges, monitor, or manage the form. From this page we learn that WebDB automatically supports version control. Pay attention to the information shown in the "Run Link" section. It contains two working URLs for running this form. The first URL (in our case, it is WEB_DEVELOPER.-DEPT_ FORM.show)

Exhibit 8.9 Managing the `DEPT_FORM`

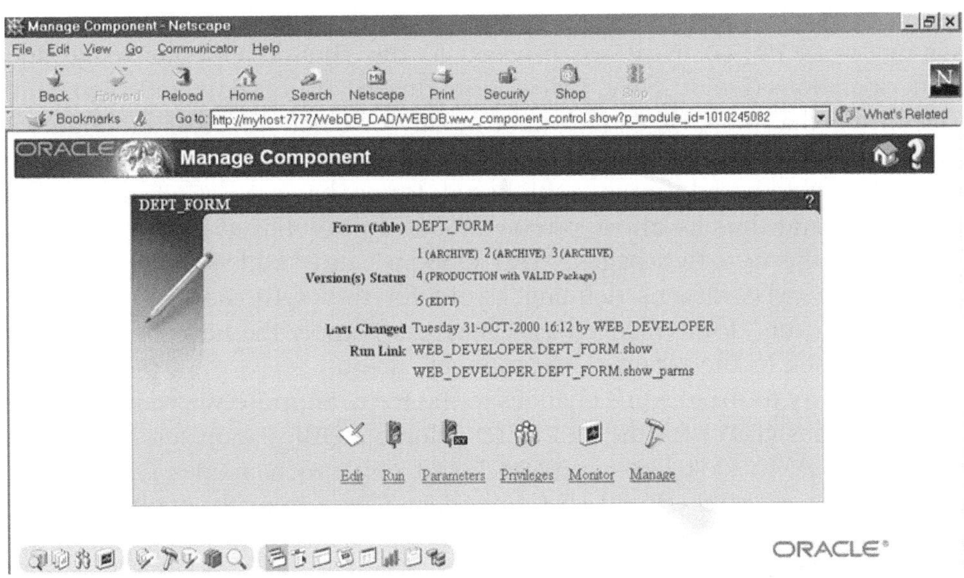

is for running the form with default parameters; and the second URL (`WEB_DEVELOPER.-DEPT_FORM.show_parms`) is for running the form with interactive prompting for parameters, where `show` and `show_parms` are standard WebDB procedures written in PL/SQL. Remember the connection prefix previously discussed: the production URL is composed of prefix and form URL, like this:

```
http://myhost:7777/WebDB_DAD/WEB_ DEVELOPER.DEPT_FORM.show
```

The "Run" option actually calls the above-listed URL. Because we use structured layout, we have one field per line. If it is not applicable, we can design our own lay-out in HTML.

To change the settings we choose with "Create Forms" wizard, return to the "Manage Component" main menu, and follow the "Edit" option. For example, to add a comment, we choose the "Text Options" tab and enter the desired text in the "Help Text" section. At runtime, we can access this message by clicking the question mark link in the upper-right corner. To grant user SCOTT access to this form, we return to the "Manage Component" menu and click the "Privileges" link. We can enter the grantee name manually or choose him/her from the dictionary.

QBE-Based Forms

The next form type we consider is QBE based. We can run the QBE form wizard like we did in designing the previous form: choose "Query by Example (QBE) Forms" from the first section of the "Form Building" page. In the first step, we choose the owner (`WEB_DEVELOPER`) and enter the form name

(DEPT_QBE). On the next page, the "Table/View Columns" we use to mark columns, define format (QBE form can present data in three formats: HTML, Excel, or ASCII), and order rows. We specify 20 rows, ASCII format, and sorting by DEPT_ID. Next we proceed to the "Button Options" page and mark operations (Query, Save, Batch, Reset, Insert), its location, and alignment. This means that the QBE form cannot modify or delete records, although we can define and save queries.

Unlike table-based forms, QBE-based forms have a lot of predefined parameters and thus its show_parms mode can be utilized by the end user. That's why the next two pages, "Text Options" and "Add Advanced PL/SQL code," have two columns defining layout for the "QBE Results" form and "QBE Parameters" form, respectively. Finally, we apply the new form and this brings us back to the "Manage Component" menu.

Now we try to make some changes to the form. Suppose we want to create a list of values (LOV) for the DEPT_ID column, "QBE Parameters" page. We want our LOV to look like a pop-up list of department names replacing its numbers. We click the "Build UI Components" icon from the toolbar, follow the "Shared Components" link, and choose the "List of Values" option. In the first section of the "Manage List of Values" page, we specify the dynamic type of LOV and click the Create button. The Create wizard consists of only one page. We specify the owner (WEB_DEVELOPER), name the LOV (DEPT_LOV), and choose the format (pop-up). WebDB supports all standard Oracle Forms LOV formats: checkboxes, combo boxes, pop-ups, radio groups, and multiple selects. Next, we manually enter the SQL query. The first column is a display value, and the second column defines the actual value passed to the LOV component. We can build a query addressing columns belonging to different tables or views. Exhibit 8.10 shows the resulting page. Note we can share this component with other developers using the Privileges list.

Now it is time to save our LOV component and try to deploy it. We click the "Add LOV" button and follow the "Edit" link from the "Manage Components" menu. There, we click on the "Column Formatting" tab. For the DEPT_ID field, we invoke a list of available LOVs and choose the WEB_DEVELOPER.DEPT_LOV.

To open the "QBE Parameters" page, we follow the "Parameters" link from the "Manage Component" menu. With the "QBE Parameters" page (see Exhibit 8.11), we overwrite the default settings changing sorting order to DEPT_NAME and output format type to HTML. We see that our LOV works fine; Department ID is displayed as a pop-up. To run a QBE form, we click the Query button. The results are presented as an HTML table.

Master-Detail Forms

Now we design a master-detail form for DEPT and EMP tables. We build it in a similar manner, starting "Master-Detail Forms" wizard from the first section of "Form Building" page. The steps are similar to those for table-based and QBE-based forms but there are several peculiarities: we name it DEPT_EMP_MD,

Exhibit 8.10 Creating a List of Values

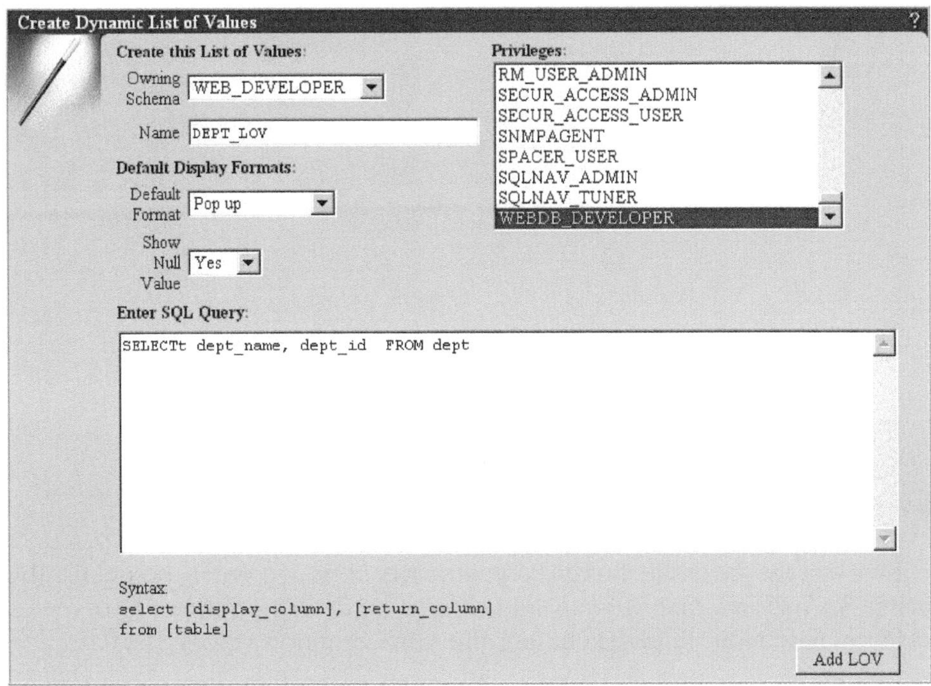

choose DEPT and EMP tables from the WEB_DEVELOPER schema, and specify join condition using the DEPT_ID column. Once we have created the form, we can run it. The best way to run a master-detail form is to call its `show_parms` method and click the Query button. This leads to the master table (see Exhibit 8.12).

Exhibit 8.11 Configuring the QBE Form

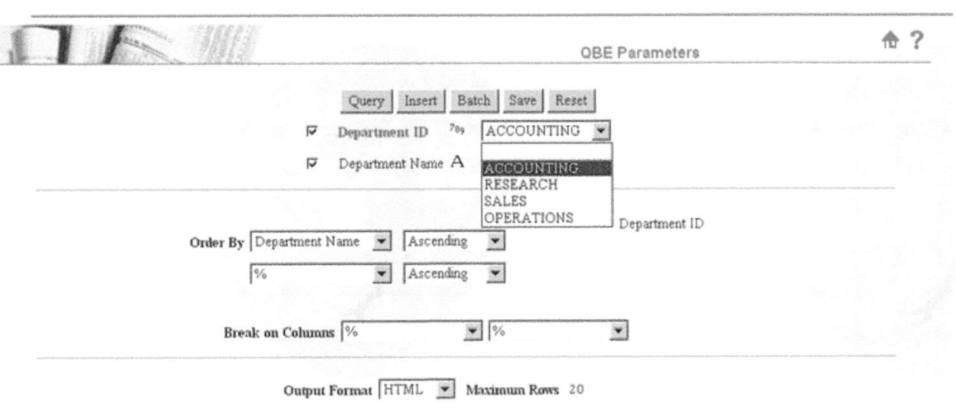

Exhibit 8.12 Browsing the Master Table

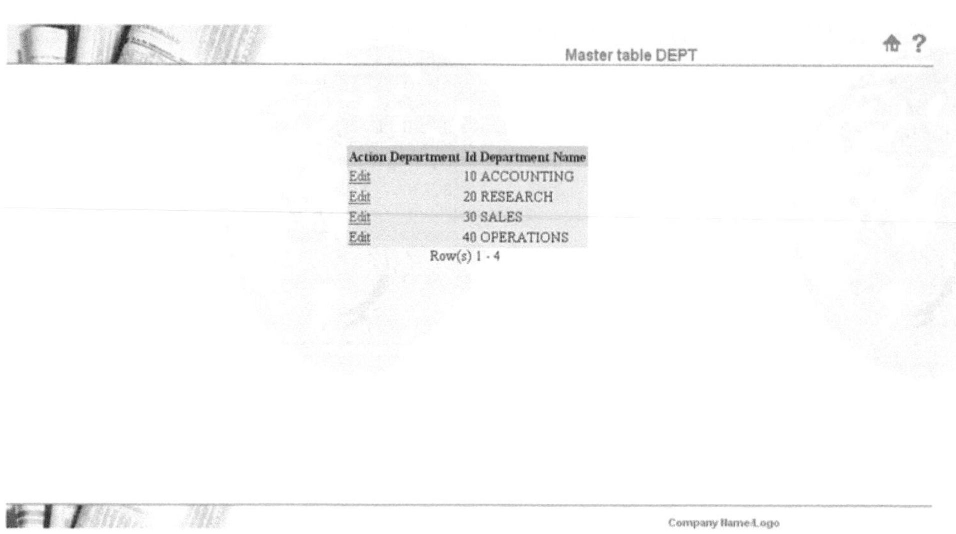

Action	Department Id	Department Name
Edit	10	ACCOUNTING
Edit	20	RESEARCH
Edit	30	SALES
Edit	40	OPERATIONS

Row(s) 1 - 4

If we follow the "Edit" link for some master row, we enter the detail table. Exhibit 8.13 shows that we can add, delete, and edit its rows. Also we can modify master table fields excluding the join condition (`DEPT_ID`).

Dynamic Pages

This is a very useful and powerful feature for a person familiar with Oracle PL/SQL. With Dynamic Pages, we can embed Oracle PL/SQL code within the HTML page. It requires manual programming, of course. Predefined WebDB

Exhibit 8.13 Editing the `EMP` Table

Detail table EMP

Save Form | Delete

Department Id 20

Department Name RESEARCH

Employee Id	Employee Name	Department Id	Delete
7876	ADAMS	20	☐
7902	FORD	20	☑
7566	JONES	20	☐
7788	SCOTT	20	☐
7369	SMITH	20	☐
			Insert
			☐
			☐
			☐
			☐

Row(s) 1 - 5

Company Name/Logo

interface components have limited functionality. Using dynamic pages, a developer can avoid using default WebDB interfaces and try to create his or her own. Try to design a simple report as a Dynamic Page. To get to the "Manage Component" menu for Dynamic Pages, we can click the icon on the toolbar called "Dynamic Pages, HTML with SQL." This option can also be reached if we choose the "Dynamic Pages" item from the "User Interface Components Menu." Then we click the Create button; this will open a "Create Dynamic Page" wizard.

The first two steps are important. First we choose the schema (`WEB_DEVELOPER`) and enter the dynamic page name (`DYN_PAGE`). Then we enter the HTML code. The example below declares HTML document and defines its title and header.

```
<HTML>
<HEAD> <TITLE>Example</TITLE> </HEAD>

<BODY>
<H1>Example of A Dynamic Page</H1>
```

Suppose we want to print a list of department and employee names ordered by department name. We can do it easily with single Oracle SQL command. Each section of the PL/SQL code in Dynamic Page must be wrapped with the `<ORACLE>` tag. The following section of code illustrates this:

```
<ORACLE>
SELECT d.dept_name, e.emp_name
   FROM emp e, dept d
   WHERE d.dept_id=e.dept_id
   ORDER BY d.dept_name
</ORACLE>
```

We can also use standard Oracle Web packages, htp and htf, familiar to many developers. Now we can close the dynamic HTML page with:

```
</BODY>
</HTML>
```

Next, we run our dynamic page following the "Run" option of the "Manage Component" menu. The results are displayed as pure HTML code (see Exhibit 8.14). Note that there is another way to solve similar tasks: that is, WebDB Reports. This interface component has an interactive interface for configuring the layout of the SQL query. The Reports component lacks Dynamic Pages flexibility because we are bound to only one Select statement.

Menus

Now we show how the menu can help us put together our three forms and the dynamic page. To build a menu, we can click the "Menus" icon at the toolbar or follow the "Menus" link from the "User Interface Components" page. There, we run the Create wizard. First we choose the owner and enter the component name as we did before. Next we enter the main page called

Exhibit 8.14 Running the Dynamic Page

Example of A Dynamic Page

ACCOUNTING	CLARK
ACCOUNTING	KING
ACCOUNTING	MILLER
RESEARCH	SMITH
RESEARCH	ADAMS
RESEARCH	FORD
RESEARCH	SCOTT
RESEARCH	JONES
SALES	ALLEN
SALES	BLAKE
SALES	MARTIN
SALES	JAMES
SALES	TURNER
SALES	WARD

"Menu Options." We define Role Security. It works like Oracle Forms security: each menu item can be assigned to some role; if this role was not granted to user, the user cannot access the menu item. We choose WEB_DEVELOPER role to own the entire menu. Next we title the main menu as Examples (field Name). Now we click the green plus icon by the Examples and choose the "Add Submenu" option. Then we go to the new submenu and change its title to "Forms." Likewise, we change its default Role Security from PUBLIC to WEB_DEVELOPER. To include all our forms in the menu, we click the green plus (+) icon by the Forms and choose "Add Item" option three times. For each item we define Name, Role Security, and Link. In a similar manner, we click the green plus (+) icon by the Examples and choose "Add Item" option to link our Dynamic Page. Exhibit 8.15 illustrates this process for a master-detail form.

Exhibit 8.15 Building a Menu

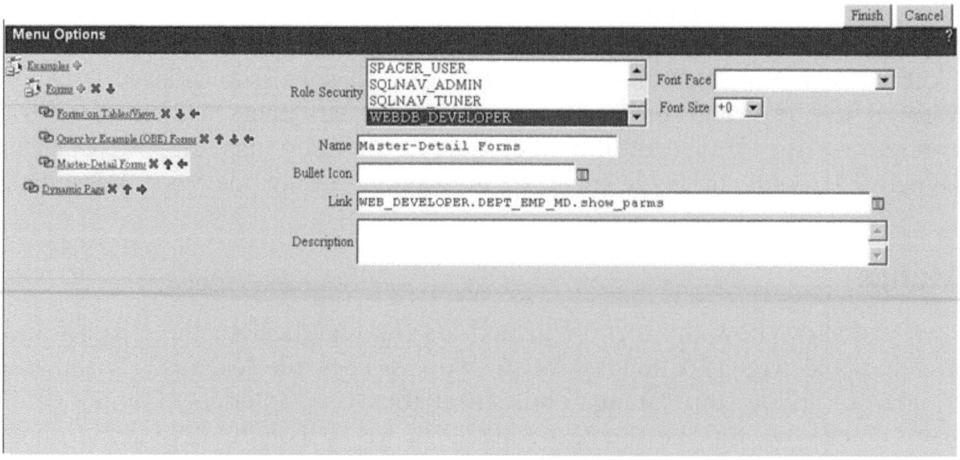

Finish Cancel
Menu Options
Examples
Forms
Forms on Tables/Views
Query by Example (QBE) Forms
Master-Detail Forms
Dynamic Pages
Role Security SPACER_USER SQLNAV_ADMIN SQLNAV_TUNER WEBDB_DEVELOPER
Font Face
Font Size +0
Name Master-Detail Forms
Bullet Icon
Link WEB_DEVELOPER.DEPT_EMP_MD.show_parms
Description

Note that each Link value we define in a format `<Owner>.<Component name>.<procedure>` and we call the `show` method for the table-based view and dynamic page and the `show_pars` method for the QBE-based and master-detail forms. We can run our menu from its "Manage Component" menu or manually.

Conclusion

In this chapter we discussed how to start working with WebDB quickly. It is a perfect and easy-to-deploy tool that does not require advanced Oracle skills. Even the end user can develop a dynamic Web site with WebDB. The client side is 100 percent browser-enabled. Now we know how to start WebDB Listener and what the WebDB Toolkit is. We showed how to administer users, how to create and browse database objects, how to design, run, and administer basic interface components — forms, dynamic pages, and menus. A strong advantage of WebDB is that its logic is stored entirely within Oracle Database; thus, WebDB has built-in security, reliability, and scalability.

Chapter 9

Introduction to iAS for the OAS Administrator

Bradley D. Brown

This is a whole new product; this is not OAS with a minor facelift. This really is a new product. OAS was based on the Spyglass listener, whereas iAS is based on the Apache listener. OAS could integrate with other listeners such as Apache, Netscape, and Microsoft listeners, but iAS works exclusively with Apache.

Is Apache a Good Choice?

Apache owns the HTTP server in both numbers and ongoing market share (more than 60 percent). In fact, there were more than 12.2 million servers running the Apache server as of August 2000 (see Exhibit 9.1). Apache installations continue to grow at a staggering pace (see Exhibit 9.2). iAS uses Apache version 1.3.

Why is Apache so big? This is a lengthy discussion in-and-of itself, but it is safe to point out a few of the major advantages of Apache.

- It screams.
- It is free (no cost).
- It is open source.
- Everybody uses it.
- It has a huge developer base
- It is extensible.

How Does Apache Rate?

If you're interested in a comparison of Web servers, you can find a great comparison at http://webcompare.internet.com/cgi-bin/quickcompare.pl. Exhibit 9.3 shows how Apache rates according to Server Watch.

0-8493-1139-X/02/$0.00+$1.50
©2002 by CRC Press LLC

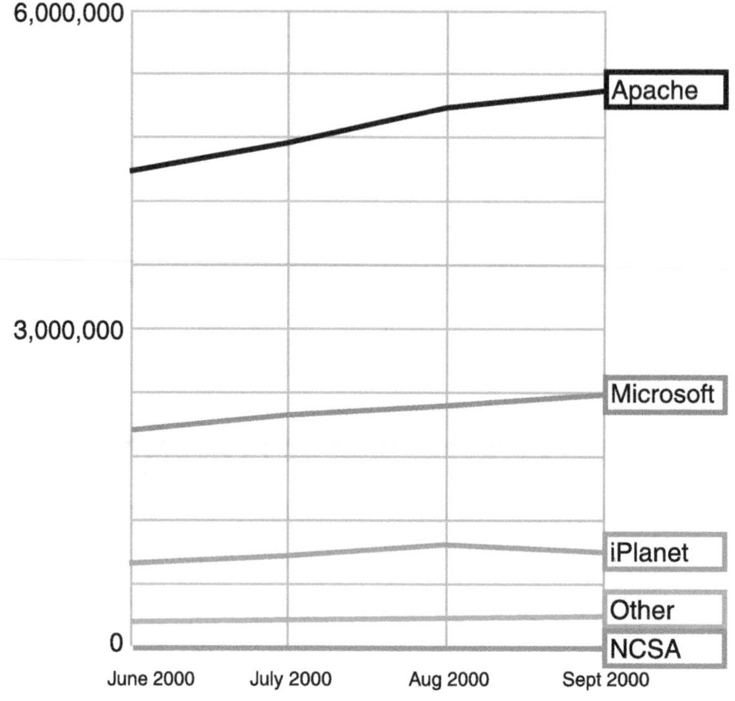

Exhibit 9.1 Servers Installed

No More Cartridges

OAS used persistent modules called cartridges to support development using languages such as PL/SQL, Perl, and Java. iAS uses third-party modules, abbreviated as mods. iAS mods include mod_plsql (migrate for PL/SQL cartridge), mod_perl (migration for Perl cartridge), mod_jserv (migration for JWeb cartridge), and mod_php (migration for LiveHTML cartridge). There is no current migration path for the CWeb cartridge.

Developer Server migrates as Forms and Reports Server. Servlets are the migration path for Java servlets in OAS. EJB and JServer are the migration paths for the JCO, ECO, and EJB cartridges. You can find considerable documentation about available third-party modules at www.apache.org. These are written using the Apache Module API (in fact, it would be pretty easy to write your own mod_plsql because you just have to call the database using the native Oracle drivers and, at the end, read from the PL/SQL table array and display the information to standard output).

Because the PL/SQL cartridge was the primary cartridge used for OAS development, this chapter focuses primarily on the migration to mod_plsql. However, it is important to note that although the PL/SQL migration is generally effortless, the Java (JWeb) to JServ migration is not.

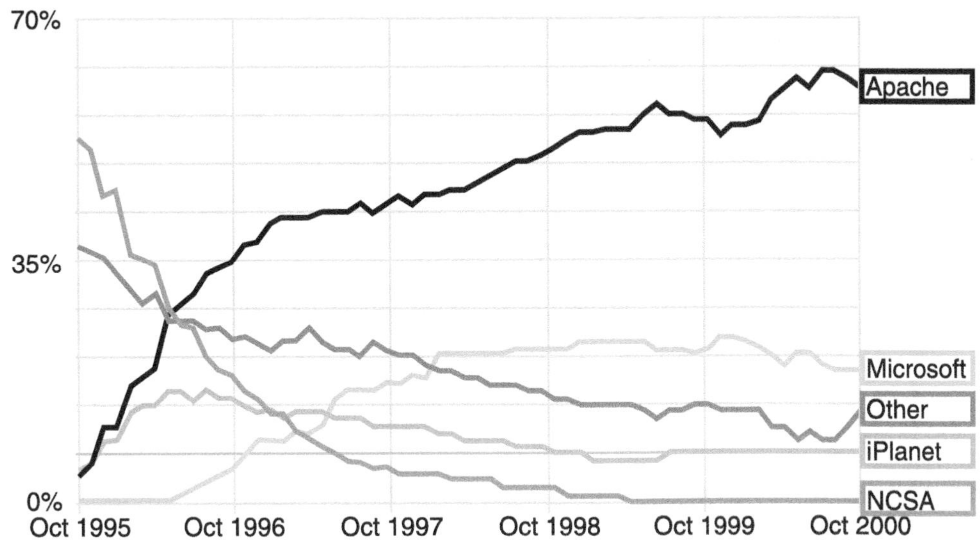

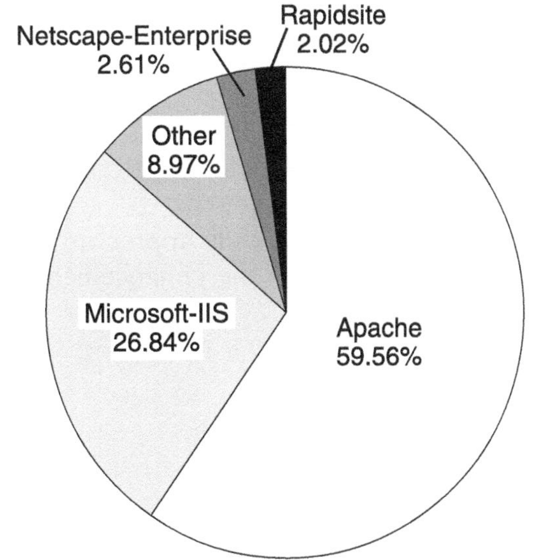

Exhibit 9.2 Market Share

Reliability

Performance

Ease of Use

Tech Support

Exhibit 9.3 How Apache Rates

Does This Affect OAS Applications?

Fortunately, although this is a major architectural change, it does not affect your existing OAS applications in any major consequence. In fact, the effects to your applications are very minor. The primary differences are within the following areas:

- The ability to run PL/SQL from an O/S file no longer exists.
- The way that file uploads and downloads are handled has changed (stored in user schema and numerous enhancements).
- There have been path changes for running PL/SQL program units.
- Flexible parameter passing now requires a pipe in the URL.
- Positional parameter passing is no longer available.

The really good news is that your code is **not** generally affected. The PL/SQL Web Toolkit (from htp to htf to owa_util) is still exactly the same as it was in OAS. So, the good news is that your application code will generally not require modification. The only code that will require modifications are code segments that used any of the above OAS features. From my experience, for most Web applications, this means little to no changes will be required.

Enhancements

If you developed using OAS, you will really appreciate many of the enhancements that were added to iAS. Some of the enhancements (beyond significant performance improvements) include:

- Deauthentication
- New CGI parameters
- PL/SQL Server pages

Deauthentication

When using OAS, you could use database authentication to allow a user to log into the database to run a query, but you could not log the user off. To accomplish this, the user had to exit the browser. Not any more! iAS provides the ability to log off of Oracle using *logmeoff* in the following format:

```
http://myhost/pls/myDAD/logmeoff
```

New CGI Parameters

There are many new CGI parameters that you will find of great value when developing your applications. The example data shown is from executing the following URL:

```
http://tusc_bdb/pls/examples/brad?in_dept_no=10
```

The new parameters of most impact include:

- REMOTE_USER (examples): this will contain the Oracle username that the user connects with
- DAD_NAME (examples): the name of the DAD that the user connected with
- QUERY_STRING (in_dept_no=10): finally, you can access the parameters that were passed to your procedure

PL/SQL Server Pages (PSPs)

iAS also supports PL/SQL Server Pages. WebDB has had PSPs for a long time — they just had a different name. In WebDB, PSPs were called Dynamic Pages, but they were stored in the database as the uncompiled HTML with embedded PL/SQL.

I am personally not a big Server Page (xSP) fan. The primary reason that I am not a fan of xSPs is because of the performance implications they typically suffer from (with the exception of Cold Fusion Server Pages and now PSPs, too). If you are not familiar with server pages, they are simply HTML pages with embedded tags for dynamic processing. The dynamic processing code is a particular programming language. PSPs use PL/SQL as the programming language. Microsoft IIS uses Active Server Pages (ASPs), which uses Visual Basic as the programming language. No surprise here, but Java Server Pages use Java.

The reason that xSPs typically have performance issues is because the code cannot be stored in a compiled format (it is embedded into the PL/SQL code); therefore, they are slower than compiled options. However, HTML programmers usually love xSPs because they can edit the code with their favorite HTML editor. Oracle has provided the best of both worlds with PSPs. Why is that? Because they simply convert the PSP into a mod_plsql routine. In other words, they convert the PSP into a stored procedure. The PSPs are loaded into the database using the *loadpsp* command, which has the following format:

```
loadpsp [-replace] -user login [<page1> <page2> ...]
```

For example:

```
loadpsp -replace -user examples/examples mypsp.psp
```

Upon completion of loading your PSP, you will receive a message similar to the following:

```
"mypsp.psp": procedure "mypsp" created.
```

At this point, you can now call your procedure (e.g., mypsp) through mod_plsql. The really important thing to note is that there is absolutely no performance issue because the PSP is stored in a compiled format in the database. This is mighty powerful! It is also important to note just how you format your PL/SQL code (as the server language) within the PSP file. Here is an example of mypsp.psp; you will notice that the PL/SQL code is wrapped within the `<%` and `%>` tags:

```
<% declare cursor emp_cur is select * fromscott.emp; begin %>
<html>
<head>
<title>My First PSP</title>
</head>
<body>
<h1>Employee List</h1>
<table border=1>
<tr><th>Name</th><th>Salary</th></tr>
<% for emp_rec in emp_cur loop %>
<tr><td>
<% htp.print(emp_rec.ename); %>
</td><td>
<% htp.print(emp_rec.sal); %>
</td></tr>
<% end loop; %>
</table>
</body>
</html>
<% end; %>
```

After loading this file into the database, the following stored procedure is created:

```
PROCEDURE mypsp AS
   BEGIN NULL;
   declare cursor emp_cur is select * from
   scott.emp;begin
htp.prn('
<html>
<head>
<title>My First PSP</title>
</head>
<body>
<h1>Employee List</h1>
<table border=1>
<tr><th>Name</th><th>Salary</th></tr>
');
   for emp_rec in emp_cur loop
htp.prn('
<tr><td>
');
   htp.print(emp_rec.ename);
htp.prn('
</td><td>
');
   htp.print(emp_rec.sal);
htp.prn('
</td></tr>
');
   end loop;
htp.prn('
```

```
</table>
</body>
</html>
');
   end;
htp.prn('
');
   END;
```

iAS Installation

The installation of iAS was easy, as long as I had enough memory and disk space. I tried to install iAS on a couple of machines that OAS previously ran just fine on, but they were undersized for memory and disk space for iAS. I made numerous attempts to get iAS running on these machines, but I never could get it running. So, I bought a new 750-MHz laptop with a 30GB hard drive and 512MB of memory. iAS installed just fine on my new laptop. In fact, it was effortless.

iAS and the database require a lot of memory and disk space. However, after installing iAS (the full-blown version, which includes Developer Server), Oracle Portal, Developer, Designer, and Discoverer on my laptop, I still had about 23GB left. OAS never performed well (i.e., flat out didn't work) if you didn't have a network card installed or without the loopback adapter installed to fake TCP/IP out. iAS runs just fine without a network card and responds to the loopback IP of 127.0.0.1.

iAS Configuration

After installing iAS, you will need to configure a DAD. The initial installation provides a home page for the site that lists "mod_plsql," as can be seen in Exhibit 9.4. As you probably noticed, there is not an administration or node manager port like you had in OAS. The documentation mentions that the iAS administration is browser based, which might lead you to believe that Oracle created such functionality for the administration of the Apache server. This is not true. The add-ons, such as mod_plsql, have a browser-based administration component, but the general Apache administration is performed by editing operating system configuration files (primarily the httpd.conf file), as discussed below. Rather than replace the default index.html file, you will likely want to rename it for future administration of iAS.

The URL to access the PL/SQL DAD configuration is: http://myhost/pls/simpledad/admin_/gateway.htm. The resulting page will look similar to Exhibit 9.5.

To create a new DAD, first click on "Gateway Database Access Descriptor Settings," which will display a page similar to the page shown in Exhibit 9.6. As you can see, I have already created a number of DADs. Next, to create a new DAD, click on "Add Default (blank configuration)" under the "Add

Exhibit 9.4 iAS Initial Main Page

Exhibit 9.5 mod_plsql Configuration

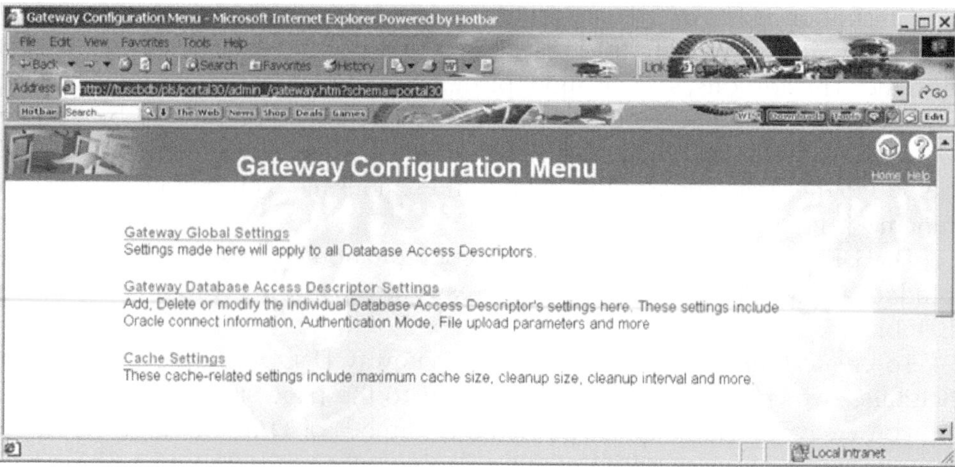

Exhibit 9.6 DAD Configuration

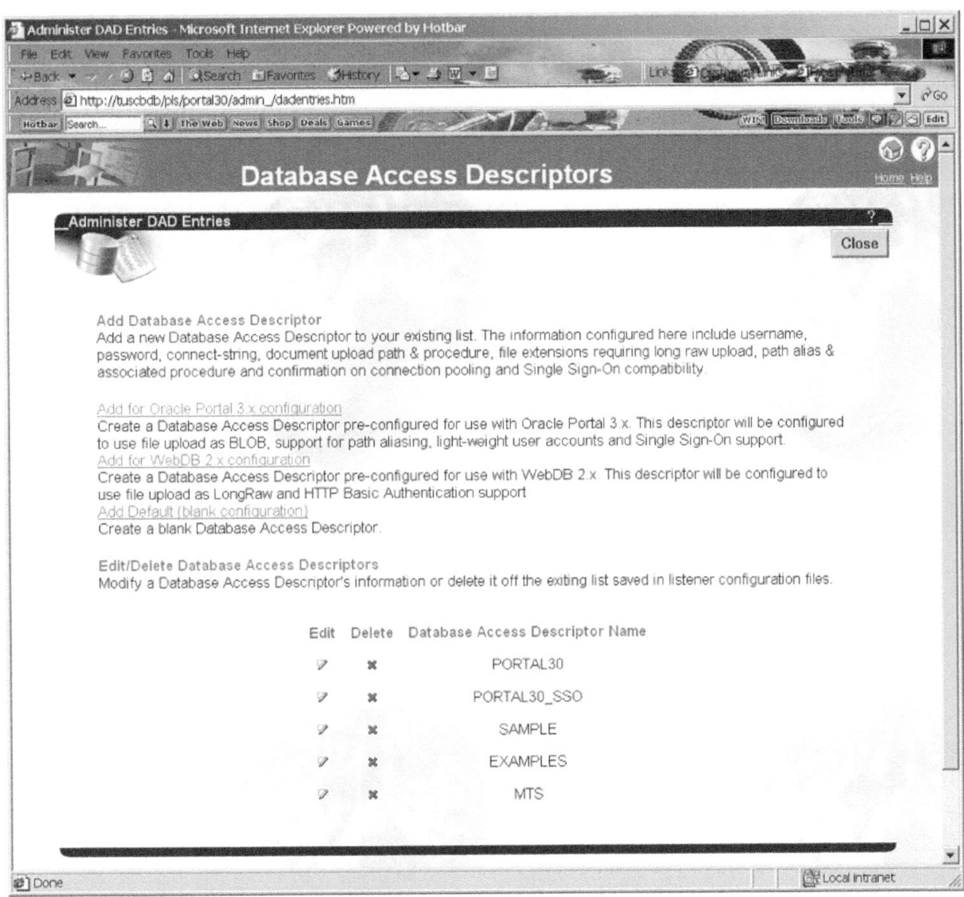

Database Access Descriptor" subheading, which will display a page similar to Exhibit 9.7.

The primary fields that need to be filled in include:

- *Database Access Descriptor Name:* DAD name, which will be used as part of your URL
- *Schema Name:* schema that OAS will connect to (that contains your application code or access to it)
- *Oracle User Name and Oracle Password:* if left blank, database authentication will be used
- *Oracle Connect String*

The rest of the fields can be left as they are, but let me take a minute to explain each now:

Exhibit 9.7 Create a DAD

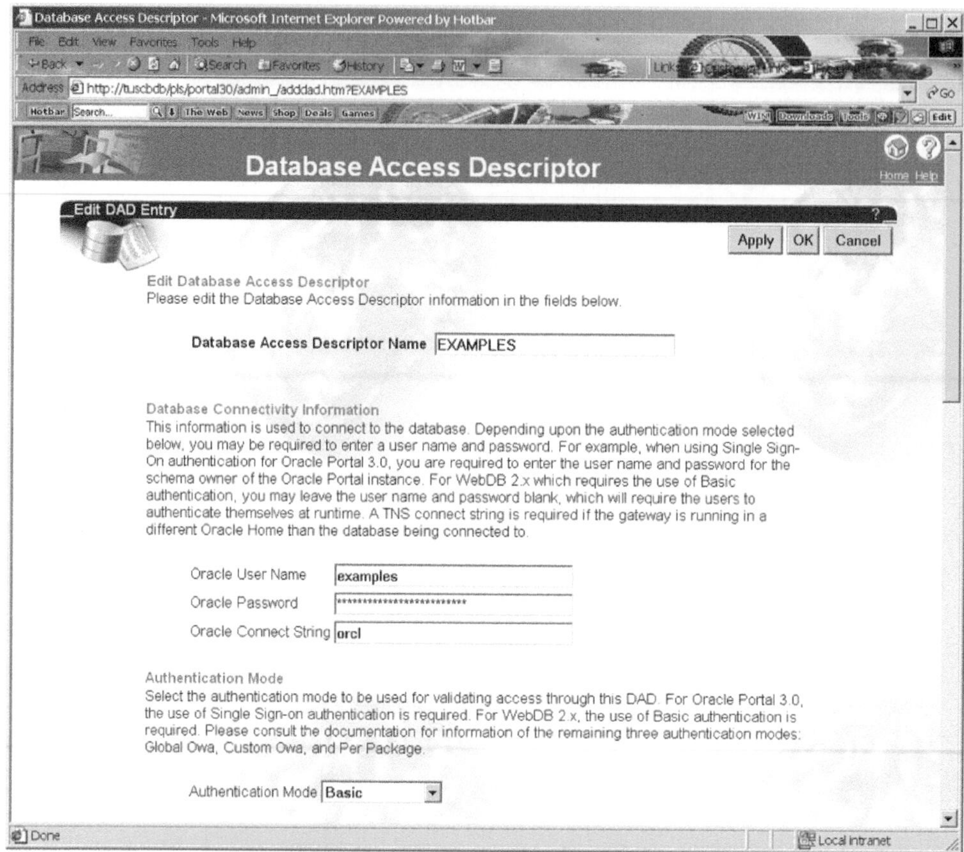

1. When using Single Sign-On authentication for Oracle Portal 3.0, you are required to specify the user name and password for the schema in which Oracle Portal is installed.
2. If you are using iAS along with WebDB 2.x, which requires a Basic Authentication Mode, you can leave the User Name and Password blank. This will require users to authenticate themselves at runtime (i.e., database authentication)
3. Authentication modes are defined as follows:
   a. *Basic:* authentication is performed using basic HTTP authentication. Most applications will use Basic authentication.
   b. *Global OWA:* authorization is performed in the OWA package schema, just like in OAS.
   c. *Custom OWA:* authorization is performed using packages and procedures in the user's schema, or if not found, in the OWA package schema — again, just like OAS.
   d. *PerPackage:* authentication is performed by packages and procedures in the user's schema — again, OAS-like.

e. *Single Sign-On:* authentication is performed using the Oracle Single Sign-On feature of the Login Server. You can use this mode only if your application is set up to work with the Login Server.

4. Session Cookie ID: the session cookie name only for Oracle Portal 3.X installations that participate in a distributed environment; however, you might be able to have some fun with this.
5. Session State Flag: it is important to note that the "Session State" flag is what was previously titled "Client Sessions" in OAS.
6. Shared Connections: choose whether, after processing one URL request, the database connection should be kept open to process future requests. In most configurations, choose Yes for maximum performance. The mod_plsql cleanup thread cleans up database sessions that have not been used for 15 minutes.
7. Connection Pool Parameters: specify the size of the connection pool. This is the maximum number of database connections kept open at one time for this DAD. If a request for another connection comes in after the maximum number is reached, one of the connections is closed to serve this request. You will need to adjust this number, depending on your server, its capacity, and the number of connected users. As a rule of thumb, set this number between 5 and 20 for a medium-sized installation (approximately 200 users). Note that this field is ignored when the UNIX Oracle HTTP server (powered by Apache) is used with mod_plsql. In a UNIX configuration, each server process keeps one database connection pooled for each DAD. Thus, the maximum number of Oracle HTTP server (powered by Apache) processes currently alive is the maximum size of the connection pool for each DAD. If the number of processes grows, the pool size grows and the gateway creates new connections. When a process dies, connections are closed. The maximum number of server processes can be configured through Oracle HTTP Server (powered by Apache) configuration files. When NT Oracle HTTP server (powered by Apache) is used with mod_plsql, configuration files govern the maximum number of threads that will simultaneously be serving requests. The "Maximum Number of Open Connections" field governs the maximum number of connections that can be kept open. Therefore, to ensure correct behavior on NT, specify a value that is equal to the maximum number of threads specified in the Apache server configuration file. If this number is smaller, some requests may be rejected if threads are idle to serve, but maximum connection limit has already been reached.
8. Default (Home) Page: the name of the PL/SQL procedure that will be invoked when none is specified as part of the URL itself. For example, if you specify a default home page of myapp.start_here and an end user enters this URL in a browser: http://myapp.myserver.com/pls/myapp/ will automatically update the URL to http://myapp.myserver.com/pls/myapp/myapp. start_here.

9. Document Access Information: this is the old OWA_CONTENT stuff, repackaged and using specific schema and tables to start the information into.
10. Path Aliasing: for the Alias, enter the keyword that will be used by mod_plsql to send some browser requests to a specific stored procedure. For example, if you enter URL as a Path Alias and AliasProcHandler as the Path Alias Procedure, any URL that starts with the keyword URL will be sent to the AliasProcHandler procedure for processing. The default for this field is URL. For the procedure field, specify the name of the stored procedure that will be called for a path alias request. The default value for this field is <schema>.wwpth_api_alias.process_download.

Calling Your DAD

Now that you have created your DAD, you would probably like to call it from the browser. I had an existing application that was running in OAS within my database. I did not reinstall the PL/SQL Web Toolkit; I used the packages from OAS and everything worked just fine. I simply created my DAD (examples) as described above and then called it using the following syntax:

```
http://myhost/pls/examples/assist.main_menu
```

In OAS, my URL looked like this:

```
http://myhost/examples/assist.main_menu
```

You will notice that iAS has a second component to reach the DAD — specifically, "/pls." You can modify this (in the plsql.conf configuration file), but you do need a two-part component to the virtual path, which wasn't required in OAS.

Need a One-Part Virtual Path?

You might be saying something like, "That means I'll have to change my application code!" It has been my experience that the application code typically uses relative pathing, so it is not affected by this change. However, it has also been my experience that static pages often refer to an absolute path to reach your DADs. Therefore, it may be a requirement for you to remap the virtual path to work for a one-part path. To accomplish this requires modifications to the httpd.conf configuration file. This file can be found in the apache/apache/conf directory. Although the online documentation is pretty good, I would highly recommend buying an Apache administration book, such as *Professional Apache* by Peter Wainwright.

Step 1: You need to turn on the URL rewriting capabilities of Apache. To do so, you must uncomment the following line that you'll find in the *httpd.conf* file:

```
LoadModule rewrite_module
modules/ApacheModuleRewrite.dll
```

Step 2: After the following line,

```
AddModule mod_ssl.c
```

Add the following statement:

```
AddModule mod_rewrite.c
```

You must write your logic that will rewrite URLs. This is done with a basic grep and edlin type substitution. I placed the code after the following line in the configuration file:

```
DefaultType text/plain
```

Then I placed the following statements:

```
RewriteEngine on
RewriteRule ^/plsql/(.*)$ /pls/plsql/$1 [R]
RewriteRule ^/examples/(.*)$ /pls/examples/$1 [R]
RewriteRule ^/mts/(.*)$ /pls/mts/$1 [R]
```

If you read the above syntax, I'm searching for the virtual path that begins with /plsql/, /examples/ or /mts/, and I'm replacing that syntax with /pls/plsql/, /pls/examples, or /pls/mts/.

Now when I execute the following URL:

```
http://myhost/examples/assist.main_menu
```

Apache then replaces that URL with:

```
http://myhost/pls/examples/assist.main_menu
```

and my URL that I was using in OAS now works in iAS!

Directory Mappings

Another important component to an HTTP server is the virtual directory mappings that you have likely defined from the virtual root to the specific virtual directories.

Setting the Virtual Root

The virtual root for the HTTP server is established by setting the *DocumentRoot* command in the *httpd.conf* file as follows:

```
DocumentRoot "c:\oracle\iAS\Apache\Apache\htdocs"
```

Virtual Directories

Virtual directories are established in the Alias section of the *httpd.conf* file:

```
Alias /websites/ "c:\websites\websites/"
```

Virtual Hosts

Virtual hosts can be defined in Apache. Virtual hosts are defined using the NameVirtualHost and VirtualHost directives as follows:

```
NameVirtualHost 192.168.3.220
<VirtualHost 192.168.3.220>
  ServerName rentcondo
  ServerAdmin brownb@tusc.com
DocumentRoot"c:\Websites\Websites\CondoSite"
</VirtualHost>
<VirtualHost 192.168.3.220>
  ServerName tuscbdb
  ServerAdmin brownb@tusc.com
DocumentRoot"c:\oracle\portal\Apache\Apache\htdocs"
</VirtualHost>
<VirtualHost 192.168.3.220>
  ServerName mts
  ServerAdmin brownb@tusc.com
  DocumentRoot "c:\websites\mts"
</VirtualHost>
```

The above specification will direct all references to "rentcondo," "tuscbdb," and "mts" to the document root specified above. Note that if the above specification does not appear to go to the directory you expect, your directory name may be specified incorrectly (i.e., there should be no trailing slash on the DocumentRoot).

Also note that the UseCanonicalName directive **must** be set to Off for this to work. The default is On, so be sure to change this as follows:

```
UseCanonicalName Off
```

A useful tip that I came across was to use "Include conf/virtualhost.conf" rather than including all of your virtual host specifications directly into your *httpd.conf* file. This makes it easy to have another program write a part of the config file (without affecting the entire *httpd.conf* file). There are also methods to set the virtual host name without changing the *httpd.conf* file using the RewriteRule command — these methods are discussed in the online Apache documentation.

Restricting Access: IP and Domain

Apache supports far more complex methods of authentication than did Spyglass. The IP- and domain-based restrictions are roughly the same as Spyglass. For example, for IP-based restriction, you might specify:

```
order deny, allow
deny from all
allow from 127.0.0.1
```

The above says to first base the restrictions on deny, then allow. In other words, deny from everybody, but then allow 127.0.0.1 to access a specific directory. Note that restrictions are permitted down to a directory level in Apache.

If you wish to grant access to class C of an IP, in Spyglass, you would indicate +192.168.2.*; whereas in Apache, you do not put the asterisk. For example:

```
allow from 192.168.2
```

Domain-based restriction is similar to IP-based restriction with Apache. For example:

```
allow from .tusc.com
```

The above means to allow all clients coming from the tusc.com domain. Note that there is not an asterisk, but there is a period.

HTTP Header Authentication

Where Apache really differentiates itself from Spyglass is that Apache can even restrict based on HTTP header information. For example:

```
SetEnvIf Referer
^http://www.tusc.com/secure/links.html origin_ok
<Directory /logged_in_users_only/>
order deny,allow
deny from all
allow from env=origin_ok
</Directory>
```

The above example will allow users to access the "/logged_in_users_only/" directory if the user originated from the *...links.html* HTML file. The SetEnvIf command checks to see if an environmental variable equals a specific string and, if so, sets the environmental variable (in this case, `origin_ok`) to true.

Note that we allow the user to access this directory if the environmental variable `origin_ok` is true. Imagine the power you can create with this functionality.

Basic and Digest Authentication

File-based user authentication is supported in Apache. First, you must create (and maintain) a password file at the operating system level. To create the file, use the "htpasswd" program for Basic authentication and use the "htdigest" program for Digest authentication. For example:

```
htpasswd -c password.file brownb
```

The above command will create an authentication file named password.file and will prompt for a username/password for the first username (brownb). "htpasswd" will automatically store the password in the IMD5 format (encrypted password); you can optionally store passwords in an unencrypted format (would not recommend this). As mentioned, authentication methods can be combined in Apache. To allow users to enter a username and password or if the user is coming from the IP address 192.168.2.202, you might use the following syntax for the /website/Protected directory:

```
<Location "/website/Protected/">
  AuthName "Registered"
  AuthType Basic
  AuthUserFile "c:\websites\password.file"
  require valid-user
  order deny,allow
  deny from all
  allow from 192.168.2.202
  Satisfy any
</Location>
```

Note that the "Location" directive uses virtual directory names, whereas the "Directory" directive uses physical directory names. They both perform the same function (restricting access), but simply allow two methods of pointing to the directory.

Realm Authentication

Apache also allows you to restrict access to groups as follows:

```
<Location "/website/Protected/AdminOnly/">
  AuthName "Registered Administrators"
  AuthType Basic
  AuthUserFile "c:\websites\password.file"
  AuthGroupFile "c:\websites\groups.file"
  require group admin
</Location>
```

Note that you must assign users to groups. These groups (in this example) are stored in the *groups.file* file. You can create the *groups.file* file with a text editor (i.e., vi or Notepad). The format of the data in the file is:

```
groupname: username1 username2
```

For example, to put the user brownb in the admin group would look like this:

```
admin: brownb
```

.htaccess

Any of the above directory directives can be placed in the *httpd.conf* file or they can be placed in an operating system file named *.htaccess.* I would not recommend using *.htaccess* files, as this makes it more difficult to administer the server if you need to scan through directories to view security information. It is much easier to administer if everything is in one file (i.e., *httpd.conf*). Therefore, to disable searching for the *.htaccess* file, you can specify:

```
<Directory />
AllowOverride None
</Directory>
```

This directive will turn off the searching for the *.htaccess* file globally. This is also good for security and performance.

Directory Indexing

For the directories in your site, you can allow indexing (or not) at a directory level. Directory indexing simply shows a list of filenames in the directory if the directory does not contain an initial file (i.e., *index.html*). With Spyglass, you could only index an entire site (or not). You should only index directories that need to be indexed (for security reasons). In the directory directives, you can just specify the following:

```
Options Indexes
```

MIME Types

MIME types can be found in *conf/mime.types* file.

GUI httpd.conf Editors

After reading the above directives for configuring Apache, you are probably really missing that nice GUI editor that OAS provided for administration. Well, it is gone. Apache does not have a GUI browser-based administration tool. However, the Apache organization recommends a number of GUI tools at gui.apache.org. The tool that would appear to be the most highly recommended is Comanche (www.comanche.org). After downloading this tool, you will be able to edit a majority of the *httpd.conf* file with a GUI editor. Unfortunately (surprisingly actually), it is a client/server tool — not a browser-based tool. Exhibit 9.8 shows the Comanche tool. Two things are worth noting about Comanche:

1. To select an object, you cannot click on the graphic for the object (such as the folder icon), you **must** click on the text. This is a bit counter-intuitive, but you will get used to it.
2. To configure an object, you must right-click on the object's text and then select "Configure."

If you have been editing the *httpd.conf* file "the long way," you will probably like Comanche. If you are still using line mode in SQLDBA, you probably will not like this tool.

Exhibit 9.8 Comanche

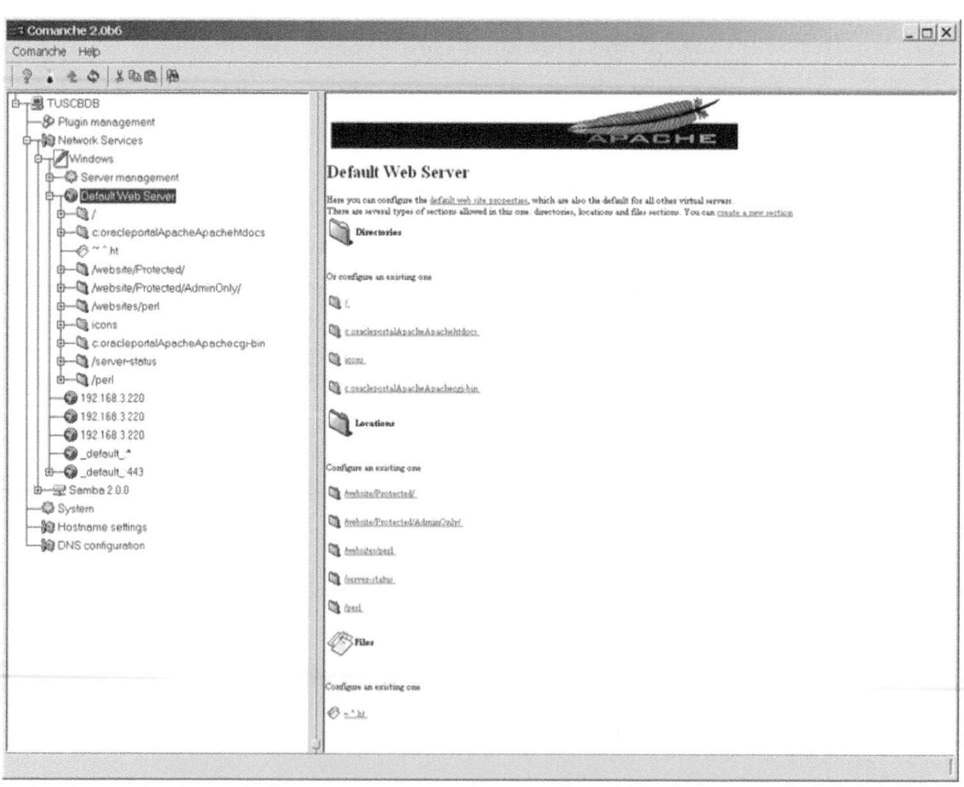

Operating Systems

It is worth mentioning that iAS (i.e., Apache) runs better, faster, and more efficiently on UNIX than it does on NT. This has to do with the use of threads (NT) rather than separate processes or forks (UNIX).

Summary

It would appear that Oracle is migrating internally to iAS pretty quickly. Check out http://www.netcraft. com/survey/developers/oracle.html for a complete list of the HTTP servers that Oracle is running. I was amazed to see that some internal sites (like govt.oracle. com) are still running OWAS 2.1 and other groups (like www-ess2.us.oracle.com) are running NCSA. If you are curious about other vendors, check out http://www.netcraft.com/survey/developers/ — it is interesting to note that Microsoft even uses Apache, as do most of the vendors listed.

As you can tell, this is much more than a name change and a simple version upgrade of OAS. iAS is a robust, powerful product that every company will want to use, especially every Oracle shop. Best of luck with your iAS development.

Acknowledgment

A special thanks to www.netcraft.com for providing graphics and statistics.

Chapter 10

Viewing Performance Data with OAS

Serg Shestakov

Using dynamic HTML is a fast and convenient way to display most vital database performance indicators from the remote location. Any database administrator (DBA) can easily write and deploy custom HTML reports with Oracle Application Server (OAS). This chapter provides an introduction to the OAS dynamic HTML mechanism, shows how to create a secure database scheme for viewing performance data, gives tips for configuring OAS, and explains how to write and run a simple PL/SQL application.

How OAS Works

Cartridge server is a powerful engine inside the OAS. Each OAS application consists of one or more cartridges. Some cartridges implement application logic, and some only provide access to logic.

An HTTP listener is responsible for accepting HTTP requests. The listener either handles the request — if the user wants static HTML/CGI script — or forwards the request to the dispatcher. The dispatcher, in turn, redirects the request to the cartridge instance of the appropriate type.

One of the most popular OAS cartridges is the PL/SQL cartridge. It is responsible for executing logic stored in a database scheme. The PL/SQL cartridge is identified by its virtual name presented in URL. Upon receiving the request, the PL/SQL cartridge connects to the Oracle database using the Database Access Descriptor (DAD), runs the requested stored procedure, and returns HTML output to the user. OAS generates HTML output using packages included into the PL/SQL Web Development Toolkit. With TNS service, the PL/SQL cartridge can connect to the remote Oracle database. This chapter explains how

0-8493-1139-X/02/$0.00+$1.50
©2002 by CRC Press LLC

to configure the PL/SQL cartridge, link it to the listener and database, develop an application for the PL/SQL cartridge, and run the application on the Web.

Configuring OAS

Let's assume that a UNIX server named oashost already has the OAS 4.0 software installed under the Oracle user; the port number for administration purposes is 8888, and the OAS node is called website40. First, you logon to the server as an OAS software owner and start the node manager:

```
owsctl start -n website40 -nodemgr
```

Using the Web browser, you connect to the node manager (http://oashost:8888) and follow the OAS Manager link. This calls the navigational tree, where you open the Oracle Application Server section, proceed to the DB Access Descriptor form, and click the Add button (green plus icon) to create a new DAD. The following values should be specified in the appeared window: DAD's name (oasdad), Oracle database username (oasuser) and its password, database host name, SID and TNS service name. Don't forget to click the checkboxes below to create the user, and do not store the database password with the DAD for better security.

Finally, OAS Manager will prompt for SYS password to create the user and the DAD. The oasuser scheme will be primarily used to keep the Web logic, although it can be used for storing some custom tables with performance statistics. In this case, it is reasonable to change the default tablespace. This can be done by clicking the Advanced button at the bottom of the current DAD's editing window.

Dynamic HTML needs protection, and OAS provides several authentication mechanisms. To simplify user management, it is reasonable to use native Oracle database accounts. Under the Oracle Application Server section, you proceed to the Security form and click the Basic_Oracle section. There you define a group of users (oasgroup) and a realm the group belongs to (oasrealm). You link the realm to the DAD and the database role — namely, the oasdad and the oasrole. When you request any dynamic HTML page using this DAD, you will be prompted for the Oracle database username and password.

An HTTP listener is the next OAS component to configure. You proceed to the HTTP Listeners form and click the Add icon. This will bring up the Add Listener form where you will be asked for a node (you can pick it up from the list), listener name (oaslis), and TCP/IP port number (5500). You can leave other fields with the default values and click the Submit button. Finally, you proceed to the HTTP Listeners form and run the new listener with the Start button.

Once the listener is up and running, you need to configure a cartridge to run the PL/SQL logic and generate HTML pages on-the-fly. Using the navigational tree, you go to the Applications form and click the Add icon. There you select the application type from the pull-down menu (PL/SQL) and click the Apply button. This brings up the next wizard's window, where you specify the application name, its display name for navigational tree (OASAPP), version (1.0), and click "Apply." Note that the application starts automatically with the first user request.

Now it is time to create a new cartridge for the application. You proceed to the OASAPP component of the navigational tree, expand it, and go to the Cartridges form. There you click the "+" icon to add a new cartridge and proceed in manual mode. In the "Add PL/SQL Cartridge" window, one needs to type in the cartridge name, display the name and virtual path (oasplsql), and select the DAD (oasdad) from the pull-down menu. Once the changes have been applied, it is time to turn on the protection mechanism. Refresh the navigational tree and subsequently click "OASAPP," "Cartridges," "Configuration," and "Virtual Path" to bring up the Virtual Paths form. There, enter the application's virtual path (/OASAPP/oasplsql/) and map it to the physical path of the PL/SQL cartridge (%ORAWEB_HOME%/bin). In the Protection section, turn on the Basic_Oracle authentication mechanism for the /OASAPP/oasplsql/ virtual path using the OASREALM. Don't forget the trailing slash ("/"); it will tell the OAS to protect all sub-paths of the virtual path.

As a result, you have the properly configured Oracle Application Server. In general, OAS is designed to work in a distributed environment. In the simplest case, the PL/SQL cartridge can connect using TNS service to the remote Oracle database and run stored procedures generating HTML on-the-fly.

Writing a Sample Application

A sample application for viewing performance data will consist of the PL/SQL procedures. Because the application will access certain system dictionary views, it is necessary to grant the appropriate SELECT privileges to the OAS user. You will need the DBA account to perform this operation. Note that here you address views directly using the V_$ prefix, although public synonyms for the views have the V$ prefix:

```
grant select on SYS.V_$DATABASE to oasuser;
grant select on SYS.V_$ROLLSTAT to oasuser;
grant select on SYS.V_$LIBRARYCACHE to oasuser;
grant select on SYS.V_$ROWCACHE to oasuser;
```

The DAD is linked to some Oracle database role. This role is used by the Basic_Oracle authentication mechanism, and this role must be created and granted to the oasuser:

```
create role oasrole;
grant oasrole to oasuser;
```

Let's logon to the Oracle database as oasuser and start writing the main procedure; call it Perf_Viewer. To make clear the common logic of OAS applications, we will keep the procedure logic as simple as possible. The

Perf_Viewer will run without parameters, detect and print in HTML format the current Oracle database name, calculate some hit ratios, and display its values colored according to the known thresholds.

The main procedure starts with its declaration. Here you see four variables: DB_name, rbs_ratio, lib_ratio, and dict_ratio. The variable DB_name will be used to store the Oracle database name as specified in the V$DATABASE system dictionary view. The variable rbs_ratio holds the rollback segments waits/gets ratio, the lib_ratio indicates the library cache reloads/pins ratio, and the dict_ratio indicates the data dictionary cache misses/gets ratio.

```
create or replace procedure Perf_Viewer is

  DB_name varchar(9);
  rbs_ratio number(5,2);
  lib_ratio number(5,2);
  dict_ratio number(5,2);

begin
```

The next section of code selects the database name into the DB_name variable and prints the HTML header. The header contains a title with the database name. This title will be displayed at the top of the browser's window. To generate HTML output, we use the htp package. It is a part of the PL/SQL Web Developer Toolkit and was installed earlier under the oasuser.

```
select name into DB_name from V$DATABASE;
htp.headOpen;
htp.title('Performance data for the database ' || DB_name);
htp.headClose;
```

The htp.headOpen and htp.headClose produce tags for opening and closing the HTML header — the <head> and the </head>, respectively. The htp.title tags receive the string parameter as a document title. A typical HTML header generated by the above-listed section of code may appear as:

```
<head>
<title>Performance data for the database TEST</title>
</head>
```

Here's one trick for using the PL/SQL Web Developer Toolkit: developers familiar with the HTML tags may find it convenient to use the htp.print (or the htp.p for short) procedure whenever possible. This means more power and flexibility as compared with the numerous predefined procedures and gives a quick start because it requires less learning. For example, PL/SQL generating the same HTML output can be recoded as:

```
htp.p('<head>');
htp.p('<title>Performance data for the database '
  || DB_name || '</title>');
htp.p('</head>');
```

Now we need to get back to the Perf_Viewer procedure. The listing below shows the PL/SQL code for opening a body of the HTML document (the <body> tag) and displaying an average-sized header identical to the document's title. Note that the document body is centered by using the <div> tag with its align attribute set to "center."

```
htp.bodyOpen;
htp.p('<div align="center">');
htp.p('<h3>Performance data for the database ' || DB_name || '</h3>');
```

Before printing the performance report, calculate the indicators. You can find the algorithms in any Oracle Server Tuning guide. You'll need several indicators to illustrate how to create a simple HTML table. The first indicator is a rollback segments waits/gets ratio, and it is calculated by querying the V$ROLLSTAT system dictionary view. If its value is less than 99 percent, you may need additional rollback segments.

```
select round( 100-sum(waits)*100/ sum(gets), 2)
  into rbs_ratio from V$ROLLSTAT;
```

The next two indicators are related to SGA tuning — a library cache reloads/pins ratio and a dictionary cache misses/gets ratio. We will fetch them from the V$LIBRARYCACHE and V$ROWCACHE, respectively. The library cache area may not be sufficient and should be increased if its hit ratio is less than 99 percent, and your data dictionary cache performance is considered satisfactory if its hit ratio exceeds 90 percent.

```
select round( 100-sum(reloads)*100/ sum(pins), 2)
  into lib_ratio from V$LIBRARYCACHE;

select round( 100-sum(getmisses)*100/ sum(gets), 2)
  into dict_ratio from V$ROWCACHE;
```

With all three ratios in place, you can now build a simple HTML table for highlighting some performance bottlenecks. The table will consist of two columns displaying the ratio name and its value. The table begins with the <table> tag. You can customize the table by setting its attributes; for example, this adds borders and sets table width to 70 percent:

```
htp.p('<table border=2 width=70%>');
```

The table row can be highlighted using the bgcolor attribute of the <tr> tag. The code below prints the light yellow table header. The "Value" column is centered by setting the align attribute of the <td> tag.

```
htp.p('<tr bgcolor="#FFCCCC"><td>Ratio</td>');
htp.p('<td align="center">Value</td></tr>');
```

Now the hit ratios are known and the table rows can be printed. HTML is a powerful presentational language — let us use its strength. For example, it is useful to highlight the problematic performance indicators in the report. When a performance indicator is displayed, it is compared with a given threshold. If the indicator is within the allowable limits, the row color is set to white; otherwise, print the hit ratio in red. This sequence of actions applies to each hit ratio and thus this code block can be declared as an additional procedure; call it Print_Row. The Print_Row procedure will take three parameters: hit ratio name, its value, and the threshold. You will need a string variable to keep the current color:

```
create or replace procedure Print_Row
   (message in varchar2, ratio in number,
   threshold in number) is

   current_color varchar2(9);

begin
```

In the beginning of the procedure, we set the current color to white, compare the ratio value with the given threshold, and change the current color to red if necessary.

```
current_color:='FFFFFF';
if ratio<threshold then
   current_color:='FF0000';
end if;
```

The final section of the procedure prints the table row using the current color. Note that the Print_Row should be compiled first because the main procedure depends on it. When developing complex applications, it is reasonable to wrap dependent procedures into packages.

```
htp.p('<tr bgcolor="' || current_color ||
   '"><td>' || message || '</td><td align="center">' ||
   to_char(ratio,'990.99') || '</td></tr>');

end;
/
```

If there is a need to include another performance indicator to the Web report, you just calculate its value and call the Print_Row. With this procedure, the application becomes compact and easy to manage. Now return to the main procedure and we will see how to print all three performance indicators calling the Print_Row:

```
Print_Row('Rollback Segments Ratio', rbs_ratio, 99);
Print_Row('Library Cache Ratio', lib_ratio, 99);
Print_Row('Data Dictionary Cache Ratio', dict_ratio, 90);
```

When finishing a Web document, do not forget to close all opened HTML sections. The opening and closing tags are used in a stack-like order: last opened, first closed. In our case, the table is closed first, the `<div>` tag is closed next, and in the end, the body and the document itself are closed.

```
    htp.p('</table></div>');
    htp.p('</body></html>');

end;
/
```

Running the Sample Application

Both procedures, the Print_Row and the Perf_Viewer, should be compiled under the oasuser scheme. If the compilation succeeds, it is time to run the application on the Web. You had better restart the OAS site manually to make sure all the configuration changes will take effect. You logon to the oashost under the oracle user and run the following commands:

```
owsctl stop -s website40
owsctl start -s website40
```

Now go to your client machine and connect the browser to the application's URL. OAS listener will pass the address to the dispatcher. The latter will detect by the virtual path what type of cartridge is requested (the PL/SQL cartridge) as well as the cartridge name (OASAPP).

```
http://oashost:5500/OASAPP/oasplsql/Perf_Viewer
```

The request will be passed to any available instance of the PL/SQL cartridge or a new one will be created. The user will be prompted for the login name (oasuser) and the password. An authorized users will see the Web report with highlighted performance bottlenecks.

Conclusion

This chapter focused on how to build a simple OAS application for viewing performance data. Dynamic HTML is a perfect tool for reporting database performance. Pages generated by the PL/SQL cartridge can be viewed from anywhere with minimal effort. All you need is a notebook and dial-up access to the OAS host. With OAS, you can easily move your favorite performance tuning scripts to the Web and feel even more comfortable. Locate bottlenecks with the click of a mouse! Scripts will require minor modifications because they are already written in PL/SQL — just develop a Web wrapper for them. Write in native PL/SQL — there is no need to learn Java. As compared with command-line consoles such as SQL*Plus, Web reports are much easier to run and view. Web tools for remote administration save time and boost productivity.

Many other useful features for remote administration of Web applications have been omitted from this discussion, including organizing the hypertext cross-links, drilling-down the Oracle data, etc.

Chapter 11

Top DBA Scripts for Web Developers

Bradley D. Brown
Tony Calalano

Database administrators and Web developers: why can't they be friends? Developing effective Web applications requires the pooled talents of both. However, more often than not, an adversarial relationship exists between these two roles.

There are several DBA topics that every Web developer should know to work toward the same goal of developing effective Web applications. The Web developer and DBA should be pooling talents. There needs to be a common ground between the two groups. If developers had a better knowledge of DBA topics, they could be proactive and solve some potential problems without bothering the DBA.

A Web Developer's Perspective on V$ Views

What Are the V$ Views?

V$ views are dynamic views that contain information about the current state of the database. The data in the views is real-time and updated by the database. This information is not stored in the physical file system, but rather in the virtual file system, commonly referred to as the System Global Area (or SGA). The "V" in V$ means *virtual.* Information that can be extracted from the database includes the state of the database, performance, and backup. DBAs and the Oracle database kernel typically access this information. However, developers will find that there is "gold" in the V$ views for them too. The following valuable queries can be executed by Web developers to return valuable information from the database. These queries can be placed into a

0-8493-1139-X/02/$0.00+$1.50
©2002 by CRC Press LLC

procedure in the database and then be executed from a Web interface (browser).

Open Cursors

The following query can be used to determine all cursors that are currently open. The query will display what queries each user is executing:

```
SELECT    oc.user_name, st.sql_text
FROM      v$open_cursor oc, v$sqltext st
WHERE     oc.address = st.address
AND       oc.hash_value = st.hash_value
ORDER BY  oc.user_name, st.pieces;
```

Review the number of open cursors when, for example, a user complains that the database is slow. Instead of calling the DBA immediately, run this query to see what users are doing. Are they doing inserts, deletes, or updates to the database? What will be returned by this query is every cursor (implicit or explicit) that users are currently executing. Each open cursor takes up memory in the SGA. Keep in mind that implicit cursors are not closed automatically. What if the code uses `DBMS_SQL`, but someone forgets to close the cursor?

SQL Area

The following query can be used to determine what SQL statements are currently being executed. Because the query is ordered by `disk_reads`, the poorest performing queries will be sorted to the top:

```
SELECT    parsing_user_id, executions, loads, sorts, command_type,
            disk_reads, sql_text
FROM      v$sqlarea
ORDER BY  disk_reads
```

Session I/O

The following query can be used to monitor the I/O activity for a particular session:

```
SELECT    a.sid, a.username, b.block_gets, b.consistent_gets,
          b.physical_reads, b.block_changes, b.consistent_changes
FROM      v$session a, v$sess_io b
WHERE     a.sid = b.sid
ORDER BY  a.sid, a.username
```

Users Logged On

The following query can be used to determine the number of users currently logged onto a system. If the user is logged on more than once, that user will be sorted to the top. If a "group" DAD is used, rather than using Database Authentication, it may happen that the DAD account is logged in numerous times. Running this query will determine how many procedures are being concurrently executed, information that can help the Webmaster tune the PL/SQL cartridge minimum instance parameter:

```
SELECT    username, count(*)
FROM      v$session
WHERE     username NOT IN ('SYS','SYSTEM')
GROUP BY  username
ORDER BY  count(*)
```

Why is it important to know who is logged on? There are a number of reasons: it can be helpful to see how many current users are logged on versus the number of users expected to be logged on at any point in time; to make sure everyone is logged off before performing maintenance; or to limit the maximum number of connections for a specific database user. SESSIONS_PER_USER is a parameter that the DBA can set to limit the number of concurrent sessions a particular user can have.

SQL Statements per Session

The following query can be used to determine the SQL statements being executed by a particular user. This query is typically executed when a particular user complains about the performance of the system. It is useful when using Database Authentication; however, without Database Authentication, the query will show the same user name for all Web users' queries.

```
SELECT    a.sid, a.username, b.sql_text
FROM      v$session a, v$sqltext b
WHERE     a.sql_address = b.address
AND       a.sql_hash_value = b.hash_value
ORDER BY  a.username, a.sid, b.piece
```

Objects Accessed per Session

The following query can be used to determine all objects that are currently being accessed by a user.

```
SELECT    a.sid, a.username, b.owner, b.object, b.ob_typ
FROM      v$session a, v$access b
WHERE     a.sid = b.sid
```

Understanding and Using the Oracle Data Dictionary

What information is in the data dictionary?

One of the most important parts of an Oracle database is its data dictionary. The data dictionary is a read-only set of tables that provides information about its associated database. The tables are owned by SYS.

Exhibit 11.1 A Set of Views

Prefix	*Scope*
USER_	User's view of the objects owned by a particular user
ALL_	Expanded user's view, including all objects the user can access
DBA_	Database administrator's view, containing objects that all users can access

What are the differences between the ALL_, USER_, and DBA_ tables? The views of the data dictionary serve as a reference for all database users. Access to the data dictionary views is done via the SQL language. Certain views are accessible to all Oracle users, while others are intended for DBAs only. The data dictionary consists of sets of views. In many cases, a set consists of three views containing similar information, distinguished from each other by prefixes (see Exhibit 11.1).

Extracting and Searching Source from the Data Dictionary

The actual source code of a stored procedure, package, or function is stored in the data dictionary. To determine what code contains a certain segment of text, the following query can be used to return the name of the procedure or function that contains the text:

```
SELECT    DISTINCT name
FROM      all_source
WHERE     text LIKE '%vehicle_model%';
```

Once the procedure or function is returned, the following query can be used to extract the actual source code:

```
SELECT    text
FROM      all_source
WHERE     name = 'GET_PRICES'
AND       type = 'FUNCTION'
ORDER BY  line;
```

Determining Dependencies of Objects

Some types of schema objects can reference other objects as part of their definition. For example, a view is defined by a query that references tables or other views. A procedure's body can include SQL statements that reference other objects in the database. An object that references another object as part of its definition is called a dependent object, while the object being referenced is a referenced object (see Exhibit 11.2).

The following query can be executed to produce a report of objects in the database and its dependent objects:

Exhibit 11.2 Dependent Objects and References Objects

Dependent Objects	*Referenced Objects*
View	Table
Procedure	View
Function	Sequence
Package Specification	Synonym
Package Body	Procedure
Database Trigger	Function
	Package Specification

```
SELECT    DECODE(referenced_type,
   'NON-EXISTENT', '.....',
   referenced_type)|| ' ' ||
   referenced_owner || '.' ||
   referenced_name r_name,
   ' is referenced by: ' || type
   || ' ' || owner || '.' || name name,
   ' Referenced Link: ' ||
   DECODE(referenced_link_name, null, 'none',
   referenced_link_name) r_link
FROM      sys.dba_dependencies
WHERE     owner NOT IN ('SYS', 'SYSTEM')
ORDER BY  1,2;
```

All schema objects in the database have a status: invalid or valid. If a procedure, function, or view is invalid, Oracle attempts to recompile the object the next time it is accessed. If the object fails the recompilation, an error message is returned.

It is a good practice to periodically check the status of all objects in the schema. This can be easily accomplished with the following query:

```
SELECT    owner,object_name,object_type
FROM      all_objects
WHERE     status = 'INVALID'
```

As Web developers make changes to database objects, objects may become invalid. This occurs when an object that a procedure references has changed or the actual object has a compilation error. It is a good practice to compile all objects in a schema when all changes have been completed. The developer can compile each individual object or use the `DBMS_UTILITY.COMPILE_ALL` procedure. This procedure can be used to compile all procedures, functions, and packages in the specified schema. Perform the query again to determine that all objects are valid.

What Indexes Are Available on a Table?

Developers need to construct queries that perform well. Knowing what indexes are available on a particular table is a must. The following query against the data dictionary can be used to get this valuable information:

```
SELECT     index_name, column_name, column_ position
FROM       all_ind_columns
WHERE      table_name = 'ACCOUNT'
ORDER BY   index_name,column_position
```

UTL HTTP

One can actually develop a PL/SQL script that will collect information from all databases, going through a particular DAD, running a particular script, and returning the information as text, letter variables in a table, or whatever. The information can then be used to build a database full of the just-pulled data. Another possibility is to create a bunch of disparate systems to be hit. If all systems are on the Web, set up a key list names entry to go to each independent database and collect specified information and create a data warehouse of data dictionary information.

Standards

It is important to establish standards for the development team. Standards provide and ensure a consistent look and feel to a Web site that the company may wish to portray. Actually, it is good practice to establish standards for all procedures and terms on a regular basis. The PL/SQL code standards released to Web developers become key due to the sheer amount of PL/SQL code that will be developed in Web applications. Creating standards will help shorten development time because expectations are established, and there is no need to start from the ground up each time.

Examples could include standardizing the authentication model that is required for all procedures. A DBA may also want to implement certain table structures that are essential for Web applications. Or, there is a table that Oracle calls OWA Browsers that gives a browser specific parameters that can be set. For example, a table says that the Netscape version 3.0 browser actually does support tables, and this type of information can be looked up in a table. Another example would be to have a users' table, instead of having a database user that creates a session table to keep track of all of the state information as well.

Other common items that should be standardized include:

- Table names
- Column names
- SIDS
- Authentication model

The more standards in place, the easier it is to interpret the requirements and expectations when developing effective Web applications.

`OWA_Chart` Procedure

A unique feature that we often use is the `OWA_Chart` procedure provided by the government at govt.us.oracle.com. This package allows the creation of bar graphs for information pulled from the database. Table space information could be graphed, then actually allow a link. Or, start with any one of the graphs and drill down from there to receive more detailed information. Utilizing the `OWA_Chart` package also allows creation of graphs with various hierarchies; for example, dependencies that allow drilling down for additional information. One report could spawn another.

Log Analyzer

The log analyzer allows review of the Web application server's activity and then provides reports. For example, the log analyzer can display different statistics, such as total bytes transferred, the most frequently accessed URLs, and more. The raw information for these reports is stored by the logger.

Although there are many tools for measuring performance, such as Web Trends or ILUX, loading the log analyzer data directly into the database may be able to service all needs. The information that is logged can provide customized reports. For example, I've created a number of graphs and reports from this information. The reports and graphs show the days of the week that the site was hit, along with the number of hits per day, per hour of the day, etc.

Tuning Code

An important way to develop better applications is to teach Web developers how to tune code; this way, they are aware of the thought processes involved that could potentially solve initial design problems. A recommended solution is to get everyone involved in an "explain plan session," which teaches the intricacies of the explain plan — similar to the `V$SQLAREA` view. This way, Web developers can go out and sort through the information and try to analyze which of their queries are performing poorly from a hit standpoint like a top ten. Teaching Web developers how to tune code is a great way to be proactive and potentially save coding time down the road.

Debugging the Hits in a Web Environment

As mentioned, if Database Authentication is not being used (which is the case for most Oracle Web sites), consider another method of tracking "users." There is a package called `DBMS_APPLICATION_INFO` that contains a procedure, `SET_MODULE`, which allows setting of two parameters: `MODULE` and `ACTION`.

Fill these parameters (creatively) to monitor system performance per user, even without Database Authentication.

For example, when authenticating users with a custom authentication mechanism (in every procedure or using OWA_INIT.authorize), set MODULE to the current procedure name and set ACTION to the name of the authenticated user. If this isn't enough information, then set these parameters to concatenated information.

At any rate, if this information is set in each procedure that is run (and possibly for each SQL statement run in the procedures), it will enable monitoring which specific Web user is running which procedure. This can be accomplished because V$SESSION, V$SQLAREA, and other views now (as of version 7.3) contain the MODULE and ACTION columns. Therefore, for any of the above V$ queries, MODULE and ACTION columns can be queried. For example, if we look at the query from the V$SESSION view above that pulls the SQL statements per session and include our new columns, the query would look like this:

```
SELECT    a.sid, a.username, a.module, a.action, b.sql_text
FROM      v$session a, v$sqltext b
WHERE     a.sql_address = b.address
AND       a.sql_hash_value = b.hash_value
ORDER BY  a.username, a.sid, b.piece
```

This query will now tell us not only the statement that is running, but also the user who is running the query and the procedure in which the statement can be found. This is useful information for tuning purposes. Rest assured that in the future most all packaged query analysis tools will query and report information from these new columns.

There is a packaged procedure called OWA_UTIL.WHO_CALLED_ME that will identify the procedure that called the generic procedure. When using the OWA_INIT.authorize procedure for authentication, set the user name for the session at this level and then use DBMS_APPLICATION_INFO.SET_ACTION in each procedure. This procedure allows setting the ACTION (or procedure in our case) for the current MODULE.

Summary

DBAs and Web developers can get along. In fact, they can be the best of friends. By providing access to these queries to developers, DBAs can actually do themselves a favor. By analyzing this information, developers can save DBAs some time and energy. There are many more queries that can be run to help determine and improve the performance of applications. Take the time to understand the value of the V$ views; they will soon become the best tools.

Chapter 12

Web-Based Testing and Capacity Planning

Trevor Clarke

Everyday, more and more companies are entering the E-marketplace by offering their products and services through the Internet. This shift has led to fundamental changes in the product-development life cycle. The challenges facing CIOs and IT managers have increased accordingly as they are expected to deliver complex applications and application environments in less time than traditional client/server applications in order to meet the more sophisticated demands of their customers and to remain competitive. Consequently, a much more rigorous testing process, completed in a shorter timeframe, is required.

Coupled with this new medium of transacting business is a much larger marketplace, which makes it increasingly difficult for IT managers to predict loads and appropriately provision infrastructure. Failure to sufficiently provision the infrastructure will result in performance degradations and, ultimately, the loss of customers. This chapter addresses two key challenges facing CIOs and IT managers, including Web-based testing and capacity planning in a rapidly changing Internet environment.

The Added Complexities

Web-based systems introduce many additional and different complexities over traditional client/server systems and the earlier mainframe environments. As businesses go online, there are many unknowns that could adversely affect the success of their E-business venture. The following list identifies some of the major complexities and unknowns that your testing organization will have to consider to ensure a quality service:

0-8493-1139-X/02/$0.00+$1.50
©2002 by CRC Press LLC

- ***Speed.*** The increased competition faced by companies doing business on the Internet has resulted in shorter development life cycles. To meet customer expectations, companies have to respond quickly to market demands and continuously improve their site to keep existing customers and attract new customers. Testing must also be completed in much shorter timeframes than experienced with client/server solutions.
- ***Scenario development.*** A key challenge with Web-based systems is the development and testing of all possible scenarios of user interaction with the system. For transaction-based systems, rigorous testing needs to occur to ensure the integrity of transactions as users may willingly or unwillingly be disconnected from the system. Also, transaction integrity needs to be ensured during peak activity when performance degradations and system time-outs are more likely. Finally, the testing organization also needs to consider that users may freely navigate forward or backward within a Web site and may cause unwanted duplication of transactions.
- ***Performance testing.*** Ensuring the performance of your Web-based system is another key challenge as some components are not under direct control of your enterprise. The system or the network could cause performance issues in a Web-based environment. Keynote, The Internet Performance Authority, indicates that Internet performance problems are generally not server problems.[1] They demonstrated that most performance problems occur out in the Internet infrastructure between the users and Web servers at network access points (NAPs), routers, or in a Domain Name Server (DNS). Assuring performance could equate to your company's ability to attract and keep customers loyal to your Web site.
- ***Capacity planning.*** Effectively planning the capacity of your systems and networks becomes difficult as your business becomes global when online. Ineffective planning could lead to excessive performance issues that result in loss of customers.
- ***Security.*** Additional security risks are associated with Web-based systems as they operate in a relatively "open" environment and could provide access to your company's confidential systems and data by unauthorized users. Simple bugs in the Web server could enable users to corrupt or steal data from the system or even render your systems unavailable.
- ***Multiple technologies.*** A complete testing cycle would include all possible software configurations that users leverage to access with your site (primarily Netscape™ or Microsoft Explorer™). Configurations may include various browser versions and service packs.

The Testing Cycle

Utilizing typical client/server testing approaches will not address the many added complexities resulting from a Web-based system. Additionally, the more aggressive time schedules involved in Web site development projects result in a need for your organization to develop a different and effective approach.

Defining Testing Scope

Determining the testing scope is critical to the success of a Web-based testing project. Due to the short timeframe associated with Web site testing, it can become difficult to test all components of the application and network. When possible, testing the complete Web-based environment is ideal. However, when time and budget constraints are incorporated, your organization may need to determine critical requirements and potential high-risk areas and focus testing efforts on these areas.

Critical requirements and high-risk areas can be determined by analyzing the requirements to determine the functionality that is most important to the success of the Web site, the areas within the Web site that will draw most customer focus (both positive and negative), and areas of the Web site that pose security threats.

Testing scope can include the complete system environment, including network performance testing. Alternatively, testing scope can be isolated to a particular module of the Web site or system environment (e.g., Web server, application server, database, etc.). Although not every component of the Web-based application or infrastructure can be tested before production, it is recommended that testing continue post-production for components not initially tested.

Test Planning

Based on the testing scope, the testing organization needs to plan the testing phase, including the types and timing of tests to be performed in both the pre- and post-release stages. The following testing types would be executed in a complete testing cycle:

- ***Unit testing.*** Unit testing is the process of testing individual application objects or functions in an isolated environment before testing the integration with other tested units. Unit testing is the most efficient and effective phase in terms of defect detection.
- ***Integration testing.*** The purpose of integration testing is to verify proper integrated functioning of the modules (objects, functions) that make up a subsystem. The focus of integration testing is on crossfunctional tests rather than on unit tests within one module.
- ***End-to-end testing.*** End-to-end testing is a comprehensive test of the integration of subsystems and interfaces that make up the Web site. Typically, end-to-end testing models all scenarios of user or business activity possible on your Web site. Included within this testing phase is the verification of all links to other Web sites, whether internal or

external (referred to as link testing). Link testing is a key activity that should be completed on a recurring basis as Web sites tend to change URLs or are discontinued

- ***Security testing.*** Although implemented security measures are considered part of the end-to-end solution, this testing type is kept separate due to its importance. Security testing involves two key processes. The first is the assurance that unauthorized users are blocked from accessing data and systems not intended for the user population. The second involves the testing of the data encryption techniques employed by your organization.
- ***Regression testing.*** Regression testing ensures that code changes made during application testing or post-production have not introduced any additional defects into previously tested code.
- ***Usability testing.*** Usability testing ensures that the presentation, flow, and general ergonomics of your Web site are accepted by the intended user community. This testing phase is critical as it enables your organization to measure the effectiveness of the content and design of your Web site, which ultimately leads to the ability to attract and keep customers.
- ***Stress testing.*** Stress testing observes the capabilities of production hardware and software to continue to function properly under a predetermined set and volume of test scenarios. The purpose of stress testing is to ensure that the system can maintain throughput and efficient operation under different load conditions. Stress testing enables your organization to determine what conditions are likely to cause system (hardware or software) failures. This testing phase needs to consider the possible hardware platforms, operating systems, and browsers used by customers. Results from stress testing are also a key component used for capacity planning (capacity planning is discussed later in this chapter).
- ***Performance testing.*** Performance testing observes the response times of your systems (i.e., Web server, database, etc.) and capabilities of your network to efficiently transmit data under varied load conditions. Performance testing should enable your organization to determine and resolve bottlenecks within the application and infrastructure. Performance testing should also consider the possible hardware platforms, operating systems, and browsers used by customers.

If testing scope has been limited to a certain aspect of the system and network environment, only a limited set of tests will be completed in the pre-production phase. Based on the priorities set in the scoping phase, the test manager needs to determine the set of test types and resources required in the pre-production testing phase and those that will be completed in the post-production phase. The minimum testing that needs to occur for code changes is unit and integration testing for the modules affected by the code change.

The requirement for much quicker development and testing cycles has led to the creation of sophisticated software quality tools that automate many of the test types described above. Key competitors in this marketplace include Segue Software, Mercury Interactive, RadView Software, and RSW Software. The following paragraphs describe the solutions offered by each company.

Segue Software: Segue Software's Silk™ family of E-business testing products automates several threads of the testing process, including functional (unit) and regression testing (SilkTest™), load and performance testing (SilkPerformer™), and scenario testing (SilkRealizer™). Segue also provides professional services to help install and configure the Silk products to test your company's products.

Additional value-added products in the Silk line include SilkMonitor™ (24 × 7 monitoring and reporting of Web, application, and database servers), SilkObserver™ (end-to-end transaction management and monitoring of CORBA applications, SilkMeter™ (access control and usage metering), and SilkRadar™ (automated defect tracking).

For more information, visit Segue Software's Web site at www.segue.com.

Mercury Interactive: Mercury Interactive provides the Astra™ suite of Web-based testing products. Specific modules include Astra LoadTest™, to test scalability and performance, and Astra Quick Test™, for functional and regression testing. Additional value-added tools include Astra Site Manager™ to manage the Web site and identify problems and user "hotspots."

For more information, visit Mercury Interactive's Web site at www.mercuryinteractive.com.

Radview Software: Radview's WebLoad™ product line provides tools for verifying application scalability and integrity. Scalability and integrity refer to load and functional testing. Additional products include WebLoad Resource Manager™ to facilitate and coordinate testing and resources in the development life cycle.

For more information, visit Radview Software's Web site at www.radview.com.

RSW Software: RSW's e-Test™ suite of products provides solutions to test the functionality, scalability, and availability of Web-based applications. e-Load™ is used for load and scalability testing while e-Tester™ is used for functional and regression testing. Additional value-added modules include e-Monitor, which provides 7 × 24 monitoring of deployed applications.

For more information, visit RSW Software's Web site at www.rswoftware.com.

To significantly decrease the time required to perform testing, it is recommended to assess your organizations testing requirements and choose an automated software quality tool to expedite repetitive testing tasks. Additionally, these test tools will enable your organization to perform stress testing, which is key to ensuring sufficient network and server resource levels for the production environment.

Capacity Planning

Effective performance testing is difficult without an accurate depiction of future loads. Many companies simply over-engineer hardware and networks at high costs to minimize potential performance issues leading to service degradations or deal with performance issues on a reactive basis. Reacting to performance issues in today's highly competitive marketplace could ultimately lead to the loss of customers during system downtime or periods of poor performance. Planning capacity is a critical step required to ensure the future performance of your Web-based environment. The key components involved are network, server (e.g., memory, CPU, I/O), and storage capacity.

Establishing performance benchmarks and subsequently estimating future growth is critical to planning the capacity of the network and servers. Although benchmarks are published by the Standard Performance Evaluation Corporation for Web servers (www.specbench.org), their uses are limited and do not accurately represent a real-world integrated Web environment. Alternatively, benchmarks can be determined through stress testing and mapping of performance (e.g., response times) to specific network or hardware configurations under varying loads. Modeling tools and techniques can also be used to determine performance characteristics under varying loads.

Once initial benchmarks are established, future production loads can be estimated using historical growth statistics or growth estimated by various Internet analyst groups (e.g., IDC, GartnerGroup, and Forrester Research). Subsequently, the growth forecasts can be put to test to determine the resource and scalability requirements of the network and hardware in the future. Note that peak loads of three to four times average loads should be tested during the stress test phase. An additional stress testing consideration is to model higher-volume loads for cyclical periods. For example, online retailers may have much higher loads during the Christmas period than during the remainder of the year. Ensuring performance, especially during these peak periods, will have an impact on Web site success. For this reason, overprovisioning hardware or network components to a certain level is justified.

Although effective capacity planning should enable your systems to handle future growth, monitoring of your networks and server resources should continue to ensure that capacity is within acceptable limits.

Conclusions

Web-based applications have resulted in many challenges for the testing community. The ability of an organization to effectively prioritize the components requiring testing and to rapidly execute the tests is a requirement in a competitive E-marketplace. Leveraging the tools designed specifically for Web-based testing will enhance the organization's ability to get a quality product to market faster. Finally, proactive capacity planning rather than reactive performance issue resolution will result in greater customer satisfaction and ultimately in greater revenue.

Note

1. "Top 10 Discoveries About the Internet," Keynote Systems, Inc., 1998.

Chapter 13

HTTP Listeners

Bradley D. Brown

The Hypertext Transfer Protocol (HTTP) listener is a process that communicates using HTTP and cycles as it waits for requests coming across TCP/IP on a specific port (or on multiple ports). The HTTP listener, generically called the Web listener, translates virtual directories into physical directory locations. HTTP listeners traditionally support two types of virtual directories, defined as "normal" and "cgi" directories. The main difference between the two is how the files are handled. When users request a file from a normal directory, the file is sent directly to the browser (e.g., an HTML file). A file requested from a cgi directory is assumed to be a program that needs to be executed, which will, in turn, dynamically generate HTML or HTTP data. A Web server is a server that contains one or more Web listeners. If you are looking for a *standard* Web server, I have found more than 150 on the market. You can find a good list of Web servers (and other information, such as marketshare statistics, who is using each Web server, etc.) at www.netcraft.com. The most popular Web servers are free. Oracle's Application Server, however, is much more than a standard Web server. Because most Web servers are free, I can only assume that Oracle never intended to be in the Web server business. The Spyglass listener that is Oracle licensed is packaged with the Web listener. Oracle's Web solution (OAS) provides the base functionality of a standard Web server and much more.

Using the Oracle Listener

As previously mentioned, Oracle's listener is actually a Spyglass listener. If you install OAS and set up listeners through the node manager port, you will actually be configuring the underlying Spyglass listeners. From an integration and support standpoint, I feel it is easiest to use one vendor's product — keep it simple silly (KISS). In other words, use the Oracle listener. If you are

0-8493-1139-X/02/$0.00+$1.50
©2002 by CRC Press LLC

already running one of the following listeners: Microsoft IIS, Netscape Fast-Track, Netscape Enterprise, or Apache — you can register the listener with OAS or you can elect to use the Oracle/Spyglass listener.

A number of tests were conducted to determine if one listener outperformed another in terms of reliability. The findings basically indicated that a listener is a listener. Most listeners will crash when you reach about 1000 characters in a GET operation.

Configuring IIS, Netscape FastTrack, Netscape Enterprise, or the Apache Listener with OAS

To test whether Microsoft's IIS listener could be easily registered with OAS, I performed the following steps:

1. Installed Microsoft's Option Pack 4 (note this is not Service Pack 4, but Option Pack 4) for NT (if I were running a Microsoft NT Server on my PC, rather than the copy of NT Workstation, IIS would already have been installed). This installation proides an IIS listener running on port 80.
2. Rebooted my PC and waited for all of the services to come up.
3. Navigated to the OAS node manager (i.e., port 8888) through the browser.
4. From the node manager, ran OAS Utilities. Drilled into Register External Listeners and selected Microsoft. When you do this, OAS then scans the standard ports (80, 443, and 8080) to determine if there is an IIS listener on one of those ports. If not, it will prompt you for the port to scan. Otherwise, OAS will show you a list of server names and ports that are running IIS.
5. Selected the server (click the checkbox) and port to register. The final step was also pretty simple. I just selected Register Checked Listeners. At that point, you should get a "success" message.
6. Although I did not find this anywhere in the documentation, I rebooted the server once again.
7. After the reboot, go back to the node manager and start OAS.
8. To verify that everything works properly, just execute a cartridge URL like a PL/SQL procedure from the IIS port.
9. The external listener should now work well.

Undoing the Registration of IIS, Netscape FastTrack, Netscape Enterprise, or the Apache Listener from OAS

If you change your mind and decide you would rather not use one of these listeners as your externally registered listener, it is simple to undo the registration. Perform the following steps:

1. Start up the node manager (i.e., port 8888) through the browser.
2. Run OAS Utilities and drill into Unregister External Listeners.
3. Similar to the registration process, you will then see the name(s) of the server(s) and ports that are external and registered. Select the server (click the checkbox) and port that you wish to unregister. Select Unregister Checked Listeners.
4. You should then receive a success message.
5. Once again, although I did not see this step in any documentation, I rebooted the server.
6. After the server started backup, I went back to the node manager, started OAS, and away we went.

Comparing IIS Speed with Oracle (Spyglass)

Previously, I stated that a listener is a listener in terms of reliability. Well, what about performance? To test a listener's performance in terms of URL execution speed, I ran a PL/SQL routine that takes about 1/100th of a second to execute if executed by itself. The PL/SQL routine is called get_emps. Then, I wrote a second routine (get_emps_100_times) using UTL_HTTP to call the get_emps URL 100 times. From the browser, I executed the get_emps_100_times routine 11 times in a row using each of the listeners (Oracle and IIS).

When using the Oracle listener, the first time OAS ran get_emps_100_times, it took 8.52 seconds. The first time you execute a PL/SQL procedure, it will take a little longer because the Oracle DB must physically read the data from the disk. Thereafter, the data is cached in the SGA. The average time for subsequent executions was 4.57 seconds.

Then I removed the Oracle listener and installed Microsoft's IIS listener. The first time I executed get_emps_100_times, the routine took 12.96 seconds. Thereafter, on average, the routine took 5.83 seconds for the next ten executions.

Using this performance benchmark, you can see that it takes longer to run OAS components (in this case, the PL/SQL cartridge) using the IIS than it does through the Oracle listener.

Turning File Caching Off

If you have used OAS version 3 on NT, especially while in the development phase of your project, you were probably extremely frustrated by locked static HTML files. If you are not familiar with this problem, you are fortunate. In version 3, all static HTML files were cached and locked once the server called the HTML page. If you had any hopes of editing the file, you needed to stop the listener, edit the file, and restart the listener.

If you liked this feature, you can still enable it in OAS version 4. However, in version 4, fortunately, you have the option of turning the file caching off. Turning this feature off will cause the file to be read from the disk every

Exhibit 13.1 Recommended TCP/IP Parameter Settings for a Web Server

Parameter	*Recommended Value*
tcp_conn_req_max_q	1,024
tcp_close_wait_interval	3,000
tcp_rexmit_interval_min	1,500
tcp_xmit_hiwat	65,536
tcp_xmit_lowat	24,576
tcp_recv_hiwat	65,536

time — in other words, it is not cached (or locked); therefore, you can edit the file anytime you wish.

Tuning Your TCP/IP Parameters

Sun regularly updates the Solaris operating system components, such as the Transmission Control Protocol/Internet Protocol (TCP/IP) subsystem, that are heavily used by OAS. Whatever your operating system, make sure you have installed the latest patches. Exhibit 13.1 contains Oracle's recommended TCP/IP parameter settings for a Web server.

Guarding Your Base Domain Name

By now, most companies have registered the company domain name. For example, our base domain is tusc.com. Typically, your e-mail address is the same name as this base domain name (e.g., Bradley_Brown@tusc.com). If you are using Microsoft Exchange Server on an NT box, be careful. Your base domain name, in this example tusc.com, is registered to a specific IP, and if a user types **tusc.com** in his browser, the browser will attempt to perform an HTTP operation on port 80 to that specific box (i.e., your mail server). When you install Microsoft NT Server, it automatically installs IIS on that server. Therefore, if a user simply types **tusc.com,** which resolves to the IP address of the Exchange Server, the user may see the default IIS home page. This would certainly confuse users. I have seen smaller ISPs that are not aware of this problem. Because ISPs typically virtually host a number of sites, the page that displays may be a totally different company's Web site.

Starting and Stopping OAS

In Oracle Application Server (OAS) version 4, the WRB is still around, but Oracle simplified the command to start and stop the entire site. Prior to version 4, you could not stop the WRB through a browser; you always had to perform this function through the command line. However, version 4 enables you to start and stop the WRB and all of the listeners (with the exception of the node manager) through the node manager. In prior versions, I usually wrote a script to stop and start the entire Web server.

Setting the Rescan Interval

The default value for the rescan interval parameter is 0, meaning that directories are checked for file changes each time a file is accessed. Ideally, you would set this value to a high number on a production site because changes to static files would rarely be made — or at least scheduled.

Analyzing Why the Listener Does Not Notice that File Permissions Have Changed

The listener caches the modification date and time of the directory and all the files within. If a URL is unavailable because of permission problems, and you fix that problem, the listener will continue to say that the URL is unavailable because the directory modification date and time have not changed; it does not check the file itself. Renaming the file and then changing it back again will force the listener to see the change — the modification date and time will be set accordingly.

Troubleshooting Why You Cannot Access the Node Manager

After installing OAS, you might find that you cannot access the node manager port. During the installation, OAS prompts you for the name of the server. The value displayed is typically the name of the machine, including the full domain name. Try accessing the node manager by specifying the entire name of the machine, including the domain name. If that does not work, look in the file %oraweb_admin/site_name/http.../node/svnode.cfg — you will typically see two entries in the file that indicate how to specify the name of the machine from the browser. In version 3.x, only one entry was added, which was the full domain name of the machine.

Copying a Listener from Another Server

The easiest way to copy the configuration information from one server to another is to copy the listener.cfg file. Before copying the file, create a listener with the virtual name you wish to use and shut down the listener. Then, back up the listener.cfg file that OAS creates and copy the listener.cfg file from the other server to the new server.

Configuring the Listener to Run on Port 80 on a UNIX Machine

On UNIX, all ports less than 1024 are restricted ports. Therefore, port 80 is a restricted port. There is a script located at $ORACLE_HOME/orainst/oasroot.sh that will modify permissions on the oraweb process such that it can run on the protected port of 80.

Summary

So, is a listener a listener? That all depends on what you are looking for. Almost any listener can provide base functionality, and tests indicate that most listeners are fairly reliable. However, if speed, flexibility, and additional features are important to you, the list of options narrows considerably. Oracle's Spyglass listener is one of the best I have found, but you will need to make that call yourself, based on your business requirements.

Notes

Brown, B.D., *Oracle 8i Web Development* (Berkley CA: Osborne/McGraw-Hill, 1999).

Chapter 14

Introduction to UTL_HTTP

Bradley D. Brown

New built-in packages magically appear in each new "dot" release of the Oracle database. The power behind these packages often amazes me. For example, several versions ago, DBMS_JOBS, a cron-like (UNIX background process scheduler) package; DBMS_PIPES, a message-queuing package; and UTL_FILE, a text file reader–writer, were added to the built-in database packages. Each of these brought a new level of powerful features to users' programming fingertips.

The UTL_HTTP package was added in version 7.3.3. Maybe it is just because my world tends to revolve around the Internet architecture and applications, but I was instantly compelled to review the documentation for this new built-in package, see how it worked, and experiment. Wow! Was I ever excited about the power and potential behind this new package.

What is UTL_HTTP?

UTL_HTTP is a package that allows HTTP requests to be made directly from the database. Now that is power! UTL stands for utility. HTTP stands for HyperText Transfer Protocol, the protocol that transfers Web pages or HTML (HyperText Markup Language). By coupling UTL_HTTP with the DBMS_JOBS package, reoccurring requests from the database server out to the Web can be easily scheduled. The results of running UTL_HTTP contain the HTML from the requested HTML page (or URL). UTL_FILE has two options for calling the package. Method one (REQUEST) returns its results as one varchar2 string (maximum of 4000 characters — actually version 7 of the Oracle engine supports a maximum of 2000 characters; but, for simplicity, we will refer to the maximum for version 8, or 4000 characters). Method two (REQUEST_LINES) returns its results as a series of varchar2 strings in a PL/SQL table (essentially an array).

0-8493-1139-X/02/$0.00+$1.50
©2002 by CRC Press LLC

UTL_HTTP really provides the capability to be able to make an HTTP request out to the Web from the database engine! Why do this? To help give an idea of the potential behind this package, here are examples of how this package can be used for practical business purposes.

First, let's say someone needs to track a company's current stock price — current meaning updated information every 15 minutes. Historically, this was accomplished by getting a market feed from a vendor that provided such a service, which was usually expensive. Today, this information is available on a number of Web sites, including NYSE, NASDAQ, and Yahoo! Therefore, by making an HTTP request and receiving the resulting HTML back, the stock price can be extracted from the page and inserted into the database. This can be accomplished with UTL_HTTP by making a request against the Yahoo! Web server, receiving the stock price (in HTML), parsing it out, and storing that information in the Oracle database.

A similar example might be to query competitors' Web sites for their price lists. Use this information for internal research or customers' comparison shopping purposes — right from the company site. Or, pull price lists from vendors so the purchasing department will always get the best price. Any one of these requests could be easily accomplished with UTL_HTTP.

UTL_HTTP can build Cyber robot-like software that searches a Web site and stores key information in Oracle tables. An indexing application could contain indexes of keywords and the URLs to the pages that contain the keywords or it could contain a map of the site index, dynamically built.

Another example might start with wanting to generate a static page from dynamic information. What if a public relations department wants to publish a new page weekly and this information is to be displayed on the home page? Allowing them to edit the HTML as described above would not be efficient; they could easily modify the page's look and feel, which is probably not the desired result, especially since there is likely to be much more information on the home page than in these news stories. The other option would be to store the dated news stories in the database and write a PL/SQL procedure that pulls these news stories into the home page dynamically. Because this information only changes weekly, it is not practical for the page to be dynamically generated for every request. However, by using UTL_HTTP along with UTL_FILE and DBMS_JOBS, the issue can be addressed. UTL_HTTP would be used to call the dynamic page generating routine; UTL_FILE would be used to write the resulting HTML set to a static HTML file; and DBMS_JOBS would be used to schedule this procedure to run weekly.

A final example might go something like this: a need arises to create "semi-static" HTML files for a site. Perhaps these files have been created and maintained with a tool such as Macromedia's Dreamweaver or Notepad, and some of the developers might be experienced content creators using a tool or editing HTML, but they may not be experienced PL/SQL developers. In this case, it is preferable that they be able to maintain this content using a tool rather than editing PL/SQL code. But let's extend the functionality of the HTML just a touch and say that, based on the user's profile information, the background image needs to be varied. In other words, users should be able to customize their experience on the site — sometimes referred to as providing user controls or customerization. HTTP servers service static HTML pages, so they cannot dynamically change the background image based on the user. Oracle's Web server can use the PL/SQL cartridge to dynamically generate HTML pages, but this requires PL/SQL programming knowledge. There is a free tool (available on Oracle's government Web site — govt.us.oracle.com) called WebAlchemy that will reverse-engineer HTML code into PL/SQL code. However, if every page were run through WebAlchemy, it would then require PL/SQL knowledge to modify them from there: each page would be totally dynamic and therefore more difficult to maintain. Rather, store and main-tain the HTML in an HTML file and use that file as a template. Using `UTL_HTTP`, collect the HTML, then use PL/SQL commands to replace the background image for the page accordingly. This example will be demonstrated below.

UTL_HTTP Specifics

`UTL_HTTP` contains two functions; specifically, `REQUEST` and `REQUEST_LINES`. `REQUEST` is a function that returns a string variable (4000 character maximum). `REQUEST` will return a string that contains up to the first 4000 bytes of the HTML result returned from the HTTP request to a specific URL. In other words, if more than 4000 characters are in the resulting HTML received, characters 4001 and beyond will be truncated.

According to the package specification: Package `UTL_HTTP` contains function `REQUEST` for making HTTP callouts from PL/SQL programs. Function `UTL_HTTP.REQUEST` may not be called directly from an SQL statement (because its return type is not supported in a query); however, it may be called from the body of another function that is called directly from an SQL statement (and that returns a type that is legal for a function called from SQL; that is, CHAR). The input parameters to the `REQUEST` function are URL and PROXY. URL is a varchar2 string that will contain the URL to be called. PROXY contains the IP address or domain name for the proxy server; the default is NULL (meaning there is no proxy server).

The `REQUEST_PIECES` function also calls a URL and can accept a PROXY server value. However, `REQUEST_PIECES` returns a PL/SQL table (array structure) of varchar2 strings containing the entire site's HTML output (or at least up to 32,767 times 4000 characters of the page).

According to the `UTL_HTTP` specification, the function `REQUEST_LINES` takes a URL as its argument and returns a PL/SQL-table of strings, which are the successive pieces of the HTML response obtained from the HTTP request to that URL.

`REQUEST_LINES` accepts three parameters: `URL`, `MAX_PIECES`, and `PROXY`. `URL` and `PROXY` are described above. `MAX_PIECES` represents the maximum number of "pieces" to return. The default value is 32,767.

The UTL_HTTP package also contains a data-type of HTML_PIECES, which is a varchar2 PL/SQL table. This datatype should be used in conjunction with the REQUEST_LINES function.

REQUEST and REQUEST_LINES are typically just called with a URL (unless you have a proxy server) as follows:

```
REQUEST
declare html_results
varchar2(4000); -- max is 2000 for v7
begin
  html_results := utl_http.request
  ('http://www.tusc.com');
  .... -- process html_results
end;

REQUEST_LINES
declare pieces
utl_http.html_pieces;
  begin
    pieces := utl_http.request_
    lines('http://www.tusc.com');
    for i in 1 .. pieces.count
loop
  ... -- process each piece
  ... -- refer to each piece as pieces(i)
  end loop;
end;
```

Some things worth noting include:

1. Although it seems repetitious, http:// (the protocol) is specified in the URL.
2. Note the use of the PL/SQL-table method COUNT to discover the number of pieces returned, which may be zero or more.
3. When using REQUEST_LINES, MAX_PIECES is optional. It is the maximum number of pieces (each 4000 characters in length except for the last, which may be shorter) that REQUEST should return. If provided, that argument should be a positive integer.

Exceptions

If initialization of the http-callout subsystem fails (for environmental reasons such as lack of available memory), then exception UTL_HTTP.INIT_ FAILED is raised:

```
init_failed exception;
```

When the HTTP call fails (for example, because of failure of the HTTP daemon or because the argument to REQUEST cannot be interpreted as a URL because it is NULL or has non-HTTP syntax), then exception UTL_HTTP.REQUEST_FAILED is raised:

```
request_failed exception;
```

Note that these two exceptions, unless explicitly caught by an exception handler, will be reported by this generic message:

```
ORA-06510: PL/SQL: unhandled
user-defined exception
```

This error could be misleading, in that it reports the error as a "user-defined" exception although each is defined in this system package. The full error message looks like this:

```
OWS-05101: Execution failed due to Oracle error 6510
ORA-06510: PL/SQL: unhandled user defined exception
ORA-06512: at 'SYS.UTL_HTTP', line 108
ORA-06512: at 'WWW_USER.USE_ TEMPLATE', line 43ORA-06512: at line 1
```

If any other exception is raised during the processing of the http request (e.g., an out-of- memory error), then function `REQUEST` re-raises that exception.

When no response is received from a request to the given URL after about 30 to 60 seconds (because no site corresponding to that URL is contacted), the result may either be a formatted HTML error message like the one found here (with a proxy server) or the dreaded 6510 error (without a proxy server). For example:

```
Fatal Error 500
Can't Access Document:
http://www.sitedoesntexist.com
Reason: Can't locate remote host:
www.sitedoesntexist.com.

CERN-HTTPD3.0A
```

If the requested URL does not exist on a valid server, an error message will appear:

```
The requested URL was not found.
```

Do not expect `UTL_HTTP.REQUEST` to succeed in contacting a URL unless it can be contacted using a browser on the same machine (and with the same privileges, environment variables, and so forth). If `UTL_HTTP.REQUEST` fails to contact an HTTP site, please try contacting that same URL with a browser to verify network availability from the machine.

Request or Request_Lines?

As demonstrated, there are two methods to call `UTL_HTTP`: specifically `REQUEST` and `REQUEST_LINES`. So why use `REQUEST` rather than `REQUEST_LINES`? In my opinion, as good programming practice, always use `REQUEST_LINES`; `REQUEST` has a maximum of 4000 characters it can process.

Excess characters in the string are simply truncated, which is likely to cause a problem in the application. There is no guarantee that the page won't exceed that size so I recommend using REQUEST_LINES.

Extracting Information from Other Sites

In the first example, we said we wanted to track a company's current stock price. For this example, suppose the company is Oracle, whose symbol is ORCL. We can capture this information (in a non-table or no-frills format) from quote.yahoo.com using the following URL:

```
http://quote.yahoo.com/q?s=orcl&o=t
```

The resulting HTML contains the page displaying the results for the current stock price for the symbol ORCL. In this HTML, it contains the following line in it:

```
<a href='/q?s=ORCL&d=t'>ORCL</a>
Nov 25 <b>34 5/8</b> <font
color='#ff0020'>-3/8</font>
<font color='#ff0020'>-
1.07%</font> 4,019,400 <small>
```

To find this specific information, we could use the *instr* command to find something like >ORCL</a> as the start of our pricing information and <small> as the end of our pricing (and volume) information as follows:

```
Start_pos := instr (html(x),
>ORCL</a>Ô);
End_pos := instr (html(x),
<small>, start_pos+1);
```

We could extract the key information as follows:

```
Key_information := substr
(html(x), start_pos, end_pos -
start_pos);
```

The string variable key_information would now contain the date of the information (Nov. 25), the current stock price (34 5 /8), the change from yesterday's close (–3/8), the percentage up or down for the day (–1.07 percent), and the shares traded. By parsing out this line, we can easily insert these pieces of data into an Oracle table. If we used DBMS_JOBS to schedule this procedure to run every 15 minutes, we could easily capture the company's stock price every 15 minutes.

Using a Template

A previous example discussed our desire to use a static HTML file as our template and modify something in the HTML based on something like a user's profile, which might contain a background image of choice. The procedure in Appendix 14.1 accepts a URL as its input parameter and then uses REQUEST_LINES to read the static HTML file. Next, it splits the first 4000-character string into two pieces — we're assuming the BODY command is going to be within the first 2000 characters. The reason we split this into two lines is because we are going to add characters to the BODY section and if we attempted to add characters to a 4000-byte string, we would exceed the maximum length and get an error. Once we've split the line into two variables, we find the BODY tag and modify it accordingly. Then, we send the completed HTML data to the user's browser.

Semidynamic Pages

Our final example demonstrated generating a static page from dynamic information when a public relations department wanted to publish a weekly news page as part of the company home page. Because this information only changes weekly, we didn't want the page to be dynamic for every request. To accomplish this, use REQUEST_LINES as demonstrated. However, instead of using htp.prn to send this page to the user's browser, we use UTL_FILE to open a file and then write this information to a static HTML file. By also using DBMS_JOBS, we can schedule a regeneration of the home page every week.

What About Cookies?

If the page being called sends a cookie to the browser or is looking for a cookie, it will not receive one from UTL_HTTP. If the called application can function without a cookie value, UTL_HTTP will receive its results as expected. However, if the called application requires the cookie to continue, the application will fail; at this point, UTL_HTTP will simply receive the HTML that the called Web server generates.

Notable Oracle Web Application Server Issue

As a final point, I'd like to mention that we were using UTL_HTTP for a Web application running on version 8.0.4 of the Oracle RDBMS. Our application embedded UTL_HTTP into its Web-based procedures. The function we were calling was much like the USE_TEMPLATE procedure above. The application worked just fine; however, we migrated the application to a version 7.3.3 database and we instantly had problems with this procedure. I immediately suspected an issue with UTL_HTTP, so I went into SQL*Plus and ran the procedure through the database. It worked! After considerable time and effort, we realized that there was a bug that prevented us from calling UTL_HTTP from a Web-based procedure but not from the database directly — or via SQL*Plus.

Appendix 14.1 Use_template Procedure

```
PROCEDURE use_template
(in_url    varchar2)
AS
profile_rec tusc_util.profile_cur%rowtype := tusc_util.get_profile_info;
html_pieces  UTL_HTTP.html_pieces;
html         varchar2(4000);
html2        varchar2(4000);
upper_html   varchar2(4000);
head_pos     number(4);
ss_pos       number(4);
ls_pos       number(4);
ls2_pos      number(4);
body_html    varchar2(4000);
protocol     varchar2(100);
BEGIN
   /*
   Author:    Bradley Brown
   Date:      10/1/98
   Description:   This procedure uses any URL (html file) and replaces the
                  BODY command w/ Our own BODY command with the background
                  image of this user.
   History:  BDB - 10/1/98 Ñ Created procedure
   */
   html_pieces: = UTL_HTTP.request_pieces(in_url);
   html:        = substr(html_pieces(1),1,2000);
   upper_html:  = upper(html);
   html2:       = substr(html_pieces(1),2001);
   head_pos:    = instr(upper_html, '<HEAD>');
   ss_pos:      = instr(in_url, '//');
   ls_pos:      = ss_pos + 2;
   <<search_last_slash>>
   ls2_pos:     = instr(in_url, '/', ls_pos+1);
   if ls2_pos > 0 then
     ls_pos:    = ls2_pos;
     goto search_last_slash;
   end if;
   html:         = substr(html, 1, head_pos-1) || '<HEAD><BASE HREF=' ||
              substr(in_url, 1, ls_pos) ||
              '>' || substr(html, head_pos+6);
   upper_html   = upper(html);
   ss_pos:      = instr(upper_html, '<BODY');
   ls_pos:      = instr(upper_html, '>', ss_pos);
   body_html:   = htf.bodyOpen(profile_rec.custom_background_image,
   cattributes => 'bgcolor="#FFFFFF"');
   html:        = substr(html, 1, ss_pos-1) || body_html || substr(html,ls_pos+1);
   htp.prn(html || html2);
   for x in 2 .. html_pieces.count loop
   htp.prn(html_pieces(x));
   end loop;
END;
```

The UTL_HTTP package holds incredible promise for developers of all sorts. It provides a link from the individual database to the entire world (wide Web).

Chapter 15

Portal 3.0: Moving Folders Across Content Areas with Its API

Hervé Deschamps

Portal has a very friendly user interface that lets you copy and move folders. This is illustrated in Exhibit 15.1. However, that interface only lets you move and copy within the same content area. This is very frustrating for users because they have a genuine need to re-use content from one area of their Web site into another or to reorganize its structure. As of Portal 3.0.8 and earlier, users are forced to recreate the source content in the destination content area or duplicate the source content area and trim the excess. Not an ideal workaround, especially if they need to merge two content areas.

This chapter shows you, step by step, how we created a portlet that enables users to copy a folder and its sub-folders anywhere, including across content areas. We also show you a very similar portlet that lets users move a folder and its sub-folders anywhere. These portlets make use of the undocumented part of the Portal API. They are really not very complex once you know what calls to make and what tables to look at.

Step 1: Creating an Application in Portal

The first step is to create a place in Portal from which we can call our Copy and Move utility. There are several ways to do this in Portal. We chose to create an application with two forms. The first form is used to call the Copy utility. The second form is used for the Move utility. Each form captures values for two parameters required by our utilities: the source folder and the destination folder. Both forms also make use of a list-of-value (LOV) module in

0-8493-1139-X/02/$0.00+$1.50
©2002 by CRC Press LLC

Exhibit 15.1 The Portal Interface to Copy Folders

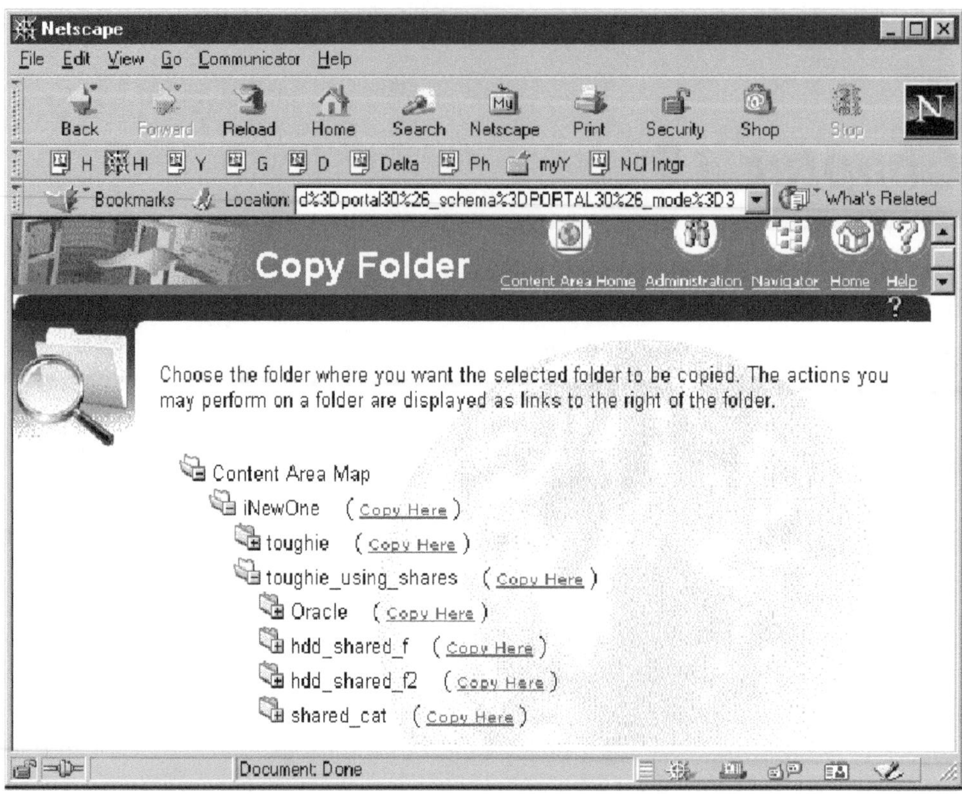

order to facilitate folder selection for the user. All components are illustrated in Exhibit 15.2.

The LOV component is defined as a pop-up format and uses the following hierarchical query:

```
select LPAD(title,length(title)+(level-1)*6,‘.’),name||‘::’||
   to_char(id)||‘::’||to_char(siteid)||‘::’||language
from wwv_corners
where siteid >10          -- only user defined folders
start with parentid = 0
connect by parentid = prior id and
             siteid   = prior siteid and
             language = prior languag
```

The table `wwv_corners` is owned by the Portal30 schema in the database unless the person who installed Portal on your server used a different schema. `Wwv_corners` contains all folder information for all folders defined in Portal, including the internal folders that come with the product. Folders constitute a hierarchy; a folder may contain other folders that in turn may contain others, etc.

There are a few tricks to the table `wwv_corners`. It also contains content area information. A content area is really a top-level folder. All content area folders have their ID set to 1 and the parent folder ID set to 0. Yes, ID is NOT the primary key. Incidentally, you will find that there is no folder record with ID equal to 0; thus, you could not have a foreign key from `parentid`

Exhibit 15.2 The Components of the Copy and Move Utilities

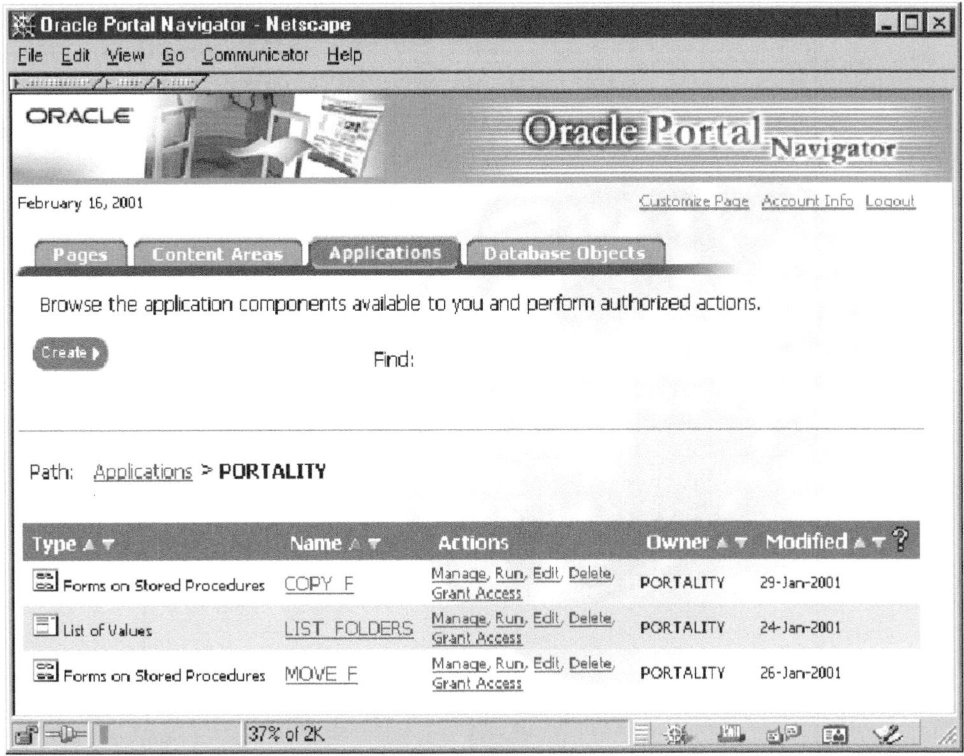

to `id`. Each content area corresponds to one and only one site referred to by the column `siteid`. Site information can be found in table `wwsbr_sites$`.

The Select statement used by a Portal List-of-Values is always formatted in the same way. Only two columns are taken into account. The first column provides the values displayed as a picking list to the users. The second value is the one returned to the module calling the list of value. In our case, you will notice that the first column presents a hierarchy of folder titles. The hierarchy is constructed with the "start with" and the "connect by" clauses of the Select statement. The second column is a concatenation of four columns in the `wwv_corners` table: `name` (Folder Name), `id` (Corner ID), `siteid` (ID of the content area to which the folder belongs), and `language`. (`id`, `siteid`, `language`) compose the primary key of the `wwv_corners` table. They truly identify a given Portal folder in a unique way, across content area and at any level of the folder hierarchy.

The resulting list of value is illustrated in Exhibit 15.3.

Step 2: Creating the Package Called by the Interface

The two forms COPY_F and MOVE_F are based on the two procedures documented in Appendix 15.1: `copy_f` and `move_f`. We used the Portal wizard to create a standard tabular form based on the procedure you pick.

Exhibit 15.3 Hierarchical List of Value

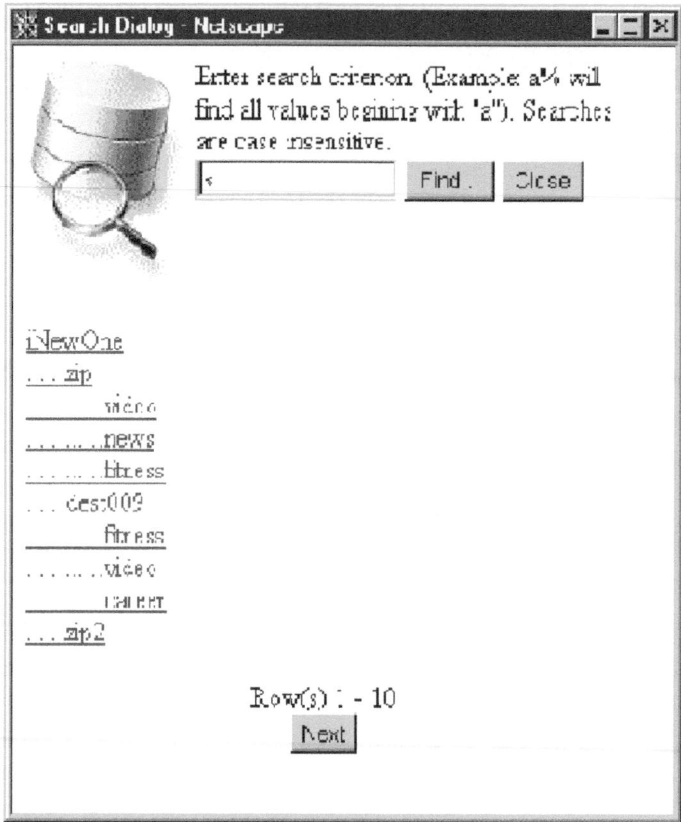

The wizard creates a field for each parameter of the procedures chosen. You can then give each field a user-friendly prompt and associate them with the list-of-value module defined above.

Code for the Procedure Called by the Portal Form Components

The procedures on which the parameter forms are based are only stubs owned by the Portal schema that call the real package that performs the actual work.

Once the three modules are defined within the application, it is important to publish the forms "Copy_f" and "Move_f" as Portlets so that you can use them within a page. This can be done by first checking that the application is exposed as a provider: click on link "Grant Access" for the application, and check the box "Expose as Provider." Then, for forms "Copy_f" and "Move_f," click on their link "Grant Access" and check the box "Publish to Portal."

Step 3: Coding the Copy

Now we are in pure PL/SQL territory. This chapter section is not intended to teach PL/SQL to the reader. PL/SQL is a prerequisite for any Portal API-based utility programming. What we will reveal here is a number of undocumented calls that you can make to the Portal API. This API is also used by the Portal product itself; using it is a very safe way to create and manipulate content. What is not at all safe is to try to issue direct inserts and updates to the Portal database tables.

For the sake of brevity, the code presented in Appendix 15.2 has been simplified. We removed auditing, debugging, validation, presentation, and exception processing because it does take about half of the total number of lines and does not provide readers with any information that they do not have already. We also removed most comments because this chapter explains the code much better than do the comments. The complete code is available from the author.

Core Code Necessary to Copy a Folder Across Content Areas

Step 1 explained how we encoded a folder unique ID composed of four parts: folder name, id, siteid, and language. The separator used between each part is ::. Thus, in Appendix 15.2, the parameters `p_f_source` and `p_f_dest` would receive values such as `Admin::5210::34::us`, which designates the Admin folder whose internal ID is `5210`, belongs to Content Area `34`, and whose language is `English US`. You can obtain a list of the 47 languages available in a Portal 3.0.6 standard install from http://www.iherve.com.

So, in Appendix 15.2, we used a great number of lines (15 to 58) to do a simple thing: split up two parameters into eight variables. The `snip_between` function that we use is one of several reusable components that we have grouped in a `util` package. `Snip_between` is using `substr` and `instr` to crop text between the nth occurence of a certain tag and the nth occurence of another tag. You can also obtain this code from the author who will soon start working on a split function such as Perl's.

Once we have parsed the values for `l_f_source_name`, `l_f_source_id`, `l_f_source_siteid`, `l_f_source_language`, `l_f_dest_name`, `l_f_dest_id`, `l_f_dest_siteid`, and `l_f_dest_language`, we validate them and throw exceptions if necessary. We chose not to show this mundane code to keep the readers focused on the meat of this chapter.

Lines 61 to 65 in Appendix 15.2 are a little puzzling and deserve a detailed explanation. They are a workaround feature of the Portal 3.0.6. API. It turns out that the API `wwv_cornerdb.copy` procedure requires the name of the folder copy to be different from the name of the original folder in only one case: when you choose the root folder level (ID=1) of a content area for the destination. This is the error that Portal will report if that rule is violated:

```
ERROR at line 1:
ORA-20102:
ORA-06512: at "PORTAL30.WWSBR_STDERR", line 437
ORA-06512: at "PORTAL30.WWV_CORNERDB", line 724
ORA-06512: at line 4
```

The workaround is simple: give a temporary name to the copy folder, run the API copy (lines 67 to 77), and update the name afterward (lines 80 to 84).

The API function `wwv_cornerdb.copy` has other parameters that we do not use. You can extend the functionality presented here by making use of `p_newtitle` to create a new title for the copy folder. `p_copylayout` can be used to prevent the copy of the source folder layout. Setting `p_copychildcorners` to 0 prevents the copy for the sub-folders of the source folder. You can also set `p_copyitems` to 0 so that only folders are copied — not the items they contain. Finally, the access rights are taken care of by `p_copyaccess`.

So with minimal programming we have put together a `copy_f` procedure that can copy a folder at any level of the hierarchy, including the root level, anywhere within that same hierarchy, even across content areas. However, this procedure has limitations. When copying across content areas, `copy_f` does not copy categories, custom folder types, or custom item types and their attributes. The only way to make this work is to create these categories, folder type, item type, and attributes as shared objects. You can also enhance `copy_f` and `move_f` to do this for you.

Step 4: Coding the Move

The `move_f` procedure is very similar to the `copy_f` procedure explained in Step 3. It basically copies the source to the destination and then deletes the source (see Appendix 15.3). Only the delete part is a little bit more complex and dangerous.

Core Code Necessary to Move a Folder Across Content Areas

Lines 17 to 22 in Appendix 15.3 are the same workaround as explained in Step 3. Lines 24 to 34 run the Portal API standard copy routine and lines 35 to 41 conclude the workaround started in lines 17 to 22.

Once the content is moved, lines 43 to 52 take care of the deletion of the source folder. If the source folder was the root folder of a given content area, then we choose not to delete the entire content area because that would also remove categories, navigation bars, perspectives, styles, and custom types. Instead, we only delete all the folders within that content area. This is done in lines 44 to 45 by calling our generic procedure `f_content_delete`, as detailed in Appendix 15.4.

Generic Procedure to Delete the Content of a Given Folder, But Not the Folder Itself

The cursor defined in lines 4 to 9 in Appendix 15.4 retrieves all folders within a given folder. The next cursor in lines 10 to 15 retrieves all items in that same folder. Lines 18 to 24 make use of the first cursor to delete each folder's sub-folders and their own sub-folders. Lines 26 to 34 do the same thing with items unless the folder is a root level 1, in which case it will contain no items.

Step 5: Running the Portlets

So now that you have the elements necessary to copy and move folders across content areas, all that is left to do is present these utilities as portlets in a user-friendly page and maybe even make that page a generic utility page and the default page of an administrative user. Or, you could just run these two utilities from the Application Tab in Portal if you want them to remain a super-user module only.

Appendix 15.1 `copy_f` and `move_f`

```
create or replace package body portality_i as
   procedure copy_f        (p_f_sourcein varchar2,
            p_f_destin varchar2
            ) is
   begin
     portality_db.copy_f(p_f_source,p_f_dest);
   end; -- procedure copy_f

   procedure move_f        (p_f_sourcein varchar2,
            p_f_destin varchar2
            ) is
   begin
     portality_db.move_f(p_f_source,p_f_dest);
   end; -- procedure move_f
end; -- package body portality_i
/
```

Appendix 15.2 Simplified Code

```
   procedure copy_f        (p_f_source    in varchar2,
                            p_f_dest      in varchar2
                            ) is
      l_f_source_name       varchar2(1000);
      l_f_dest_name         varchar2(1000);
      l_f_source_language   varchar2(1000);
      l_f_dest_language     varchar2(1000);
      l_newname             varchar2(1000);
      l_f_source_id         number;
      l_f_source_siteid     number;
      l_f_dest_id           number;
      l_f_dest_siteid       number;

   begin
      -- Decompose the parameters
      l_f_source_name := util.snip_between
         ( p_source => p_f_source,
           p_begin  => null,
           p_end    => '::');
      l_f_source_id := util.tonumber
```

(continues)

Appendix 15.2 Simplified Code (continued)

```
      ( util.snip_between (p_source        => p_f_source,
                           p_begin         => '::',
                           p_end           => '::',
                           p_begin_occur  => 1,
                           p_end_occur    => 2));
   l_f_source_siteid := util.tonumber
      (util.snip_between  (p_source        => p_f_source,
                           p_begin         => '::',
                           p_end           => '::',
                           p_begin_occur  => 2,
                           p_end_occur    => 3)
);
   l_f_source_language := util.snip_between
     (p_source => p_f_source,
      p_begin  => '::',
      p_end    => null,
      p_begin_occur => 3);
   l_f_dest_name := util.snip_between
     (p_source => p_f_dest,
      p_begin  => null,
      p_end    => '::');
   l_f_dest_id := util.tonumber
     (util.snip_between ( p_source        => p_f_dest,
                          p_begin         => '::',
                          p_end           => '::',
                          p_begin_occur   => 1,
                          p_end_occur     => 2));
   l_f_dest_siteid := util.tonumber
     (util.snip_between ( p_source        => p_f_dest,
                          p_begin         => '::',
                          p_end           => '::',
                          p_begin_occur   => 2,
                          p_end_occur     => 3));
   l_f_dest_language := util.snip_between
                        ( p_source        => p_f_dest,
                          p_begin         => '::',
                          p_end           => null,
                          p_begin_occur   => 3);

   -- Call Copy. l_newname calculation is a workaround a Portal feature.
   if l_f_dest_id = 1 then
     l_newname := 'temporary_Name';
   else
     l_newname := l_f_source_name;
   end if;
   l_result := wwv_cornerdb.copy (
                          p_id                => l_f_source_id,
                          p_newparentid       => l_f_dest_id,
                          p_newname           => l_newname,
                          p_copylayout        => 0,
                          p_copychildcorners => 1,
                          p_copyitems         => 1,
                          p_copyaccess        => 1,
                          p_level             => 1,
                          p_siteid            => l_f_dest_siteid,
                          p_copysiteid        => l_f_source_siteid);

   if l_f_dest_id = 1 then
     update  wwv_corners
     set     name = l_f_source_name
```

Appendix 15.2 Simplified Code (continued)

```
        where    id = l_result and
                 siteid = l_f_dest_siteid and
                 language = l_f_source_language;
      end if;
   end; -- procedure copy_f
```

Appendix 15.3 Deleting the Source

```
procedure move_f (p_f_source in varchar2,
                  p_f_dest   in varchar2
                  ) is
   l_f_source_name         varchar2(1000);
   l_f_dest_name           varchar2(1000);
   l_f_source_language     varchar2(1000);
   l_f_dest_language       varchar2(1000);
   l_newname               varchar2(1000);
   l_f_source_id           number;
   l_f_source_siteid       number;
   l_f_dest_id             number;
   l_f_dest_siteid         number;
begin
   -- Decompose the parameters
   <same code as in copy_f>

   -- Call Copy. l_newname calculation is a workaround a Portal feature.
   if l_f_dest_id = 1 then
      l_newname := 'temporary_Name';
   else
      l_newname := l_f_source_name;
   end if;

   l_result := wwv_cornerdb.copy (
                          p_id                => l_f_source_id,
                          p_newparentid       => l_f_dest_id,
                          p_newname           => l_newname,
                          p_copylayout        => 0,
                          p_copychildcorners  => 1,
                          p_copyitems         => 1,
                          p_copyaccess        => 1,
                          p_level             => 1,
                          p_siteid            => l_f_dest_siteid,
                          p_copysiteid        => l_f_source_siteid);
   if l_f_dest_id = 1 then
     update wwv_corners
     set    name = l_f_source_name
     where  id = l_result and
            siteid = l_f_dest_siteid and
            language = l_f_source_language;
   end if;

   if l_f_source_id = 1 then -- if the source folder is a root folder then
     f_content_delete     ( p_siteid     => l_f_source_siteid,
                            p_language   => l_f_source_language);
   else  -- if not root
     wwv_cornerdb.remove (
                            p_id         => l_f_source_id,
                            p_language   => 'us',
```

(continues)

Appendix 15.3 Deleting the Source

```
                              p_siteid     => l_f_source_siteid
                              );
   end if;
end; -- procedure move_f
```

Appendix 15.4 f_content_delete

```
procedure f_content_delete (p_siteid   in number,    -- mandatory
                            p_f_id     in number     default 1,
                            p_language in varchar2   default 'us') is
   cursor sub_f is
      select  id
      from    wwv_corners
      where   parentid = p_f_id and
              siteid = p_siteid and
              language = p_language;
   cursor items is
      select  id
      from    wwv_things
      where   cornerid = p_f_id and
              siteid = p_siteid and
              language = p_language;
begin
   -- for each sub-folders
   for cur_sub_f in sub_f loop
      -- remove the folder
      wwv_cornerdb.remove (
         p_id         => cur_sub_f.id,
         p_language   => p_language,
         p_siteid     => p_siteid);
   end loop; -- each sub folders

   if p_f_id != 1 then   -- Root folders do not contain items
      -- for each item in sub-folder
      for cur_item in items loop
         wwv_thingdb.removeitem(
            p_thingid  => cur_item.id,
            p_siteid   => p_siteid,
            p_language => p_language);
      end loop; -- for cur_item in items
   end if;
end; -- procedure f_content_delete
```

Chapter 16

Not WebDB 3.0, Not iPortal, But Oracle Portal

Bradley D. Brown

This is an entirely new product; this is not WebDB with a minor facelift; this really is a new product. The old stuff (functionality) still exists under the covers, but it is just the development tool now...it used to be "the product." Although Oracle did not like to position it as a developer wizard, they did like to say that WebDB was a content management tool. It is now truly a content management tool.

In other words, Oracle finally figured out the niche for WebDB. In fact, Oracle was simply ahead of its time. When I wrote *Oracle8i Web Development,* the WebDB product manager did not like how I positioned the product. At that time, there was a lot of talk of V3, but nobody had seen it. The product manager was right; I did not position the product correctly — at least not V3 of WebDB...or Oracle Portal. It really is an entirely new product.

Thus this was not simply a marketing name change; the name truly changed. As the product went through the beta cycles, it went through several names. At first, the name was simply going to be the next version of WebDB — that is, WebDB 3.0. The next name that I heard was iPortal, which was formally announced. Then, in the last hour, the name became Oracle Portal.

Coincidentally, some time ago, we (TUSC) registered the oracleportal.com domain name. We has hoped to put up a site that consolidated all of the Oracle information available out there — a portal for Oracle developers. It was a good idea!

What is Oracle Portal?

What exactly is Oracle Portal supposed to be? It is an easy-to-use, browser-based software for developing and deploying enterprise portals. Oracle claims

0-8493-1139-X/02/$0.00+$1.50
©2002 by CRC Press LLC

that the product allows "end users" to easily organize and publish information to better serve customers, drive revenue, and improve employee efficiency. "End users" is likely a stretch if the users are going to develop components that query your database. However, end users can maintain content. Oracle also points out that it is the perfect solution for fast-paced environments that demand efficient and organized ways to access enterprise information through self-service features. You have to love self-service applications!

Oracle lists three primary bullets for what Oracle Portal (WebDB) provides:

- Integrated Web publishing services for self-service content publishing and dynamic data publishing
- An intuitive portal framework for organizing, structuring, and customizing corporate information
- A centralized environment for portal deployment, management, monitoring, and maintenance

What the Heck Is a Portal?

Have you heard the word "portal" enough now? Although there is a lot of hype about portals, I am not sure that everyone knows just what a portal is. So, first take a look at the word "portal" as defined in Webster's:

> **por·tal** (pôrtl, pr-) *n.* 1. A doorway, an entrance, or a gate, especially one that is large and imposing. 2. An entrance or a means of entrance: *the local library, a portal of knowledge.*

Wow, "*Especially...large and imposing!*" That sure reminds me of a company I used to work for. Now take a look at an industry definition according to *whatis.com*:

> **Portal** is a new term, generally synonymous with gateway, for a World Wide Web site that is or proposes to be a major starting site for users when they get connected to the Web or that users tend to visit as an anchor site. There are general portals and specialized or niche portals. Some major general portals include Yahoo, Excite, Netscape, Lycos, CNET, Microsoft Network, and America Online's AOL.com. Examples of niche portals include Garden.com (for gardeners), Fool.com (for investors), and SearchNT.com (for Windows NT administrators).

A number of large access providers offer portals to the Web for their own users. Most portals have adopted the Yahoo style of content categories with a text-intensive, faster-loading page that visitors will find easy to use and to return to. Companies with portal sites have attracted much stock market investor interest because portals are viewed as able to command large audiences and numbers of advertising viewers.

Typical services offered by portal sites include a directory of Web sites, a facility to search for other sites, news, weather information, e-mail, stock quotes, phone and map information, and sometimes a community forum. Excite is among the first portals to offer users the ability to create a site that is personalized for individual interests.

The above definition does an excellent job of defining just what a portal is, doesn't it? As you can imagine, this is exactly what you can hope to build for your company. You could look at this as your main menu for your entire company's applications.

Installation

As of this writing, the production version of Oracle Portal has not yet been released. As with most beta versions, you must have the latest and greatest database version installed for the beta to work. So be sure to install Oracle Portal in its own DB instance. You must be running version 8.1.6 of the Oracle RDBMS. This is the version of the database that is shipped with the beta version. Believe me, I attempted to install with other versions and it did not work. As far as the installation goes, this was the biggest *trick* of all — follow the directions.

Portals and Portlets

Now that you understand the term "portal," I have another new term to share with you. This is Oracle's very own term. The term is "portlets." This is actually a cool new concept. So what are portlets?

A portlet is information that is placed within a region on a page. All portlets come from a data source registered with Oracle Portal, called a portlet provider. Oracle Portal itself is a portlet provider because certain aspects of the product have been made available so that you can include them on your own pages. The Main tab on the WebDB home page, for example, contains five portlets, all from WebDB (see Exhibit 16.1).

New Look and Feel

The product has an entirely new look and feel. One of the really cool features is how a user has control over his or her own page look and feel, just like in my.yahoo.com. For example, Exhibit 16.2 displays how the home page looks for one user.

Edit Your Profile

Each user can control not only the look and feel of his or her page, but can edit his or her own profile, right online. This is a feature that I typically tell

Exhibit 16.1 Main Tab on WebDB Home Page

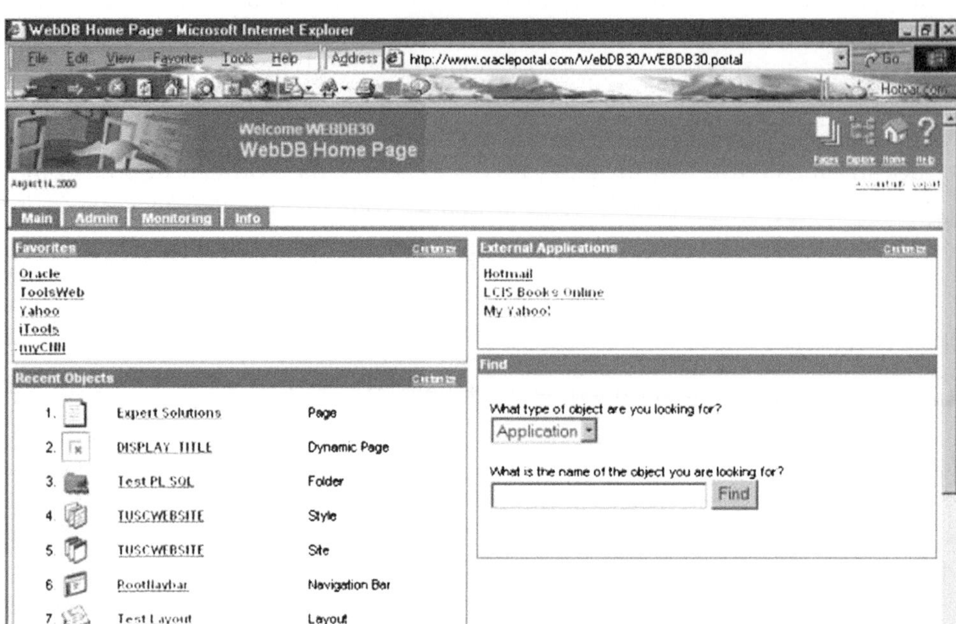

people to build into their applications (this is "Collect" in my "7 Cs"), but Oracle Portal does this for you (see Exhibit 16.3).

Control Your Own Look

As mentioned, the user can edit his or her own home page look and feel by clicking on "Customize Page." In my "7 Cs," I call this "Control." The user can move portlets, delete them, and add new ones (see Exhibit 16.4). In Exhibit 16.4, you can see that some portlets are part of the default look (those with checks next to them) and some were added by the user (those that can be deleted).

The user can click on "Add Portlet" (see Exhibit 16.5) to add new portlets to his or her page. You can see that in Exhibit 16.4, we added the "Excite Stocks" portlet to our page. The user will see the screen in Exhibit 16.6 when adding portlets. Of course, this is a control that you can provide to the user or not; it is your call.

Create an Account Online

The functionality that WebDB provides by default allows administrators to add users. It is important to point out that prior versions of WebDB used database

Exhibit 16.2 How the Home Page Looks for One User

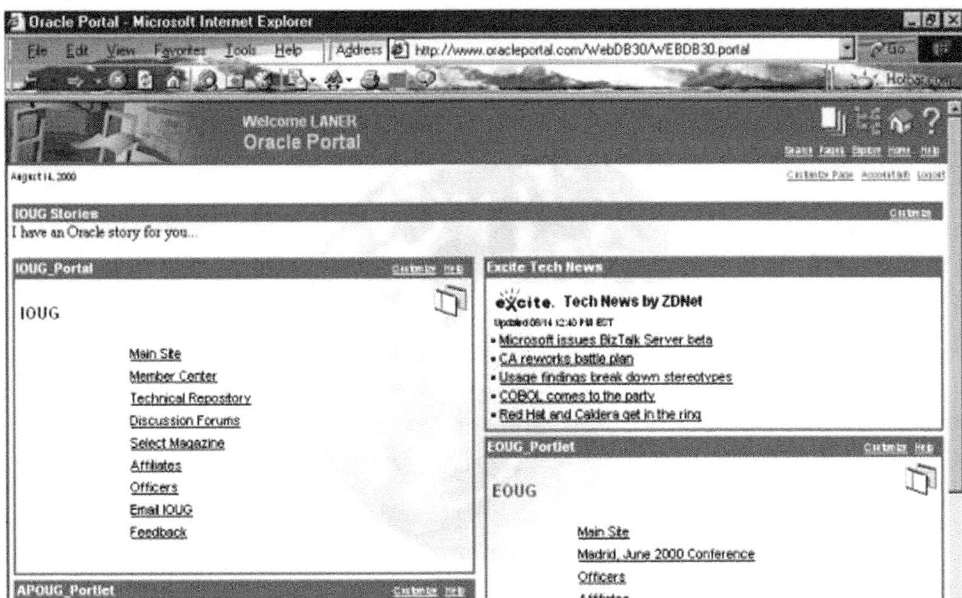

schema accounts and database authentication for user control. This was an issue for most DBAs. However, Oracle Portal stores usernames and security information in a set of Oracle tables. This not only makes the DBAs happy, but it will also make you, as a developer, happy.

However, we recently developed a portal application. This application required that users be able to create a portal account (just like you can on MyYahoo). After creating an account, the application must e-mail the login information to the user. Therefore, we created our own "create your own account" functionality. The procedures to support this functionality can be found at www.tusc.com in the documents section. Just search for "Oracle Portal" to find these procedures.

Exhibit 16.7 demonstrates the "create a user page" that is part of this functionality. As mentioned, this information is then stored into the Oracle Portal supporting tables.

Publish as Portlet

As you can see in Exhibit 16.8, the development functionality is the same functionality as before (form, report, chart, calendar, etc.), but now every object that you create can be published as a portlet.

Exhibit 16.3 Editing a Profile Online

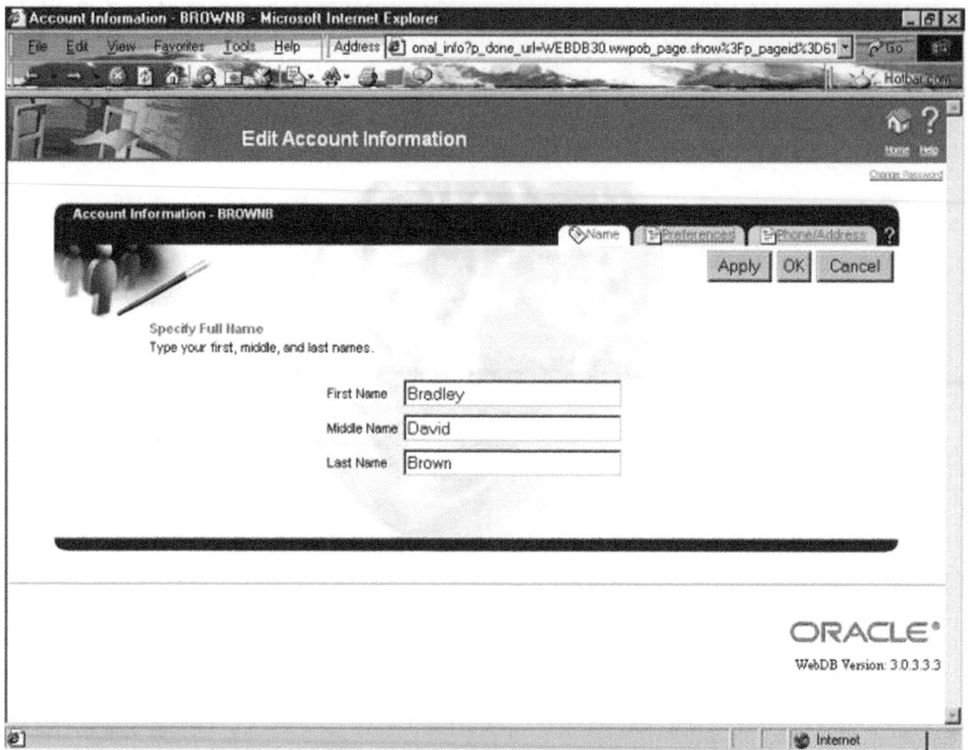

Finding Objects

Some components of the user interface are far less developer-friendly than in the previous version. In fact, I always seem to have difficulty finding the objects that I have created. However, to find your objects, simply click on the "Explore" icon (see Exhibit 16.5).

After clicking on "Explore," click on "Applications" and choose the application that you want to explore (you can choose shared components for those components shared by all applications), and then click the specific component you wish to view, edit, etc. Exhibit 16.9 provides a list of shared components.

Build a Portlet

When I first received the beta version along with the Portlet Developers Kit, I started dreaming up portlets that I could build; I developed a list of about 20. After further research, I discovered that many of the portlets I thought of are going to be in the production release — which is great. For example, I planned to develop a portlet to pull content from other pages using utl_http, but this is slated to be in the production release. However, you can develop your own portlets to integrate into Oracle Portal; so dream away.

Exhibit 16.4 Moving, Deleting, and Adding Portlets

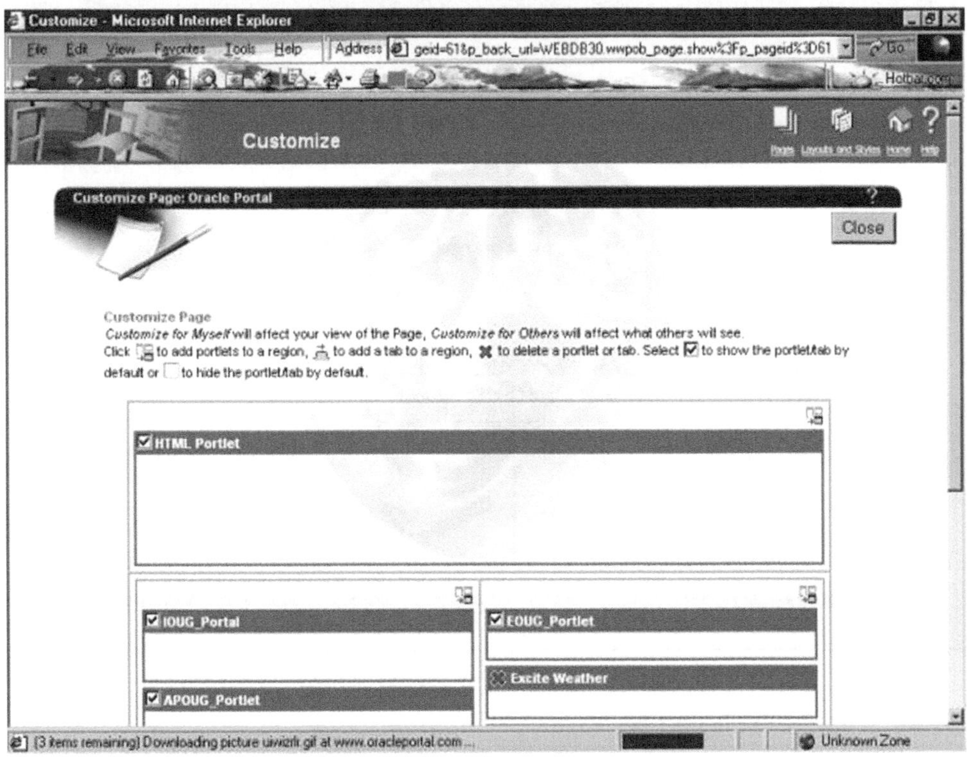

Exhibit 16.5 Icons Used

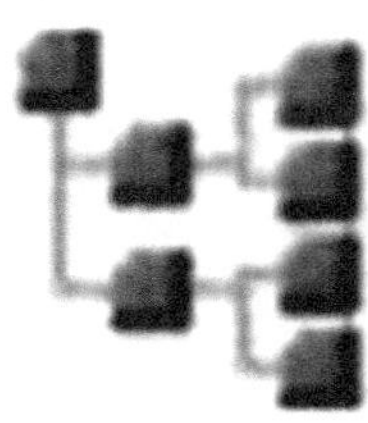

Exhibit 16.6 Screen for Adding Portlets

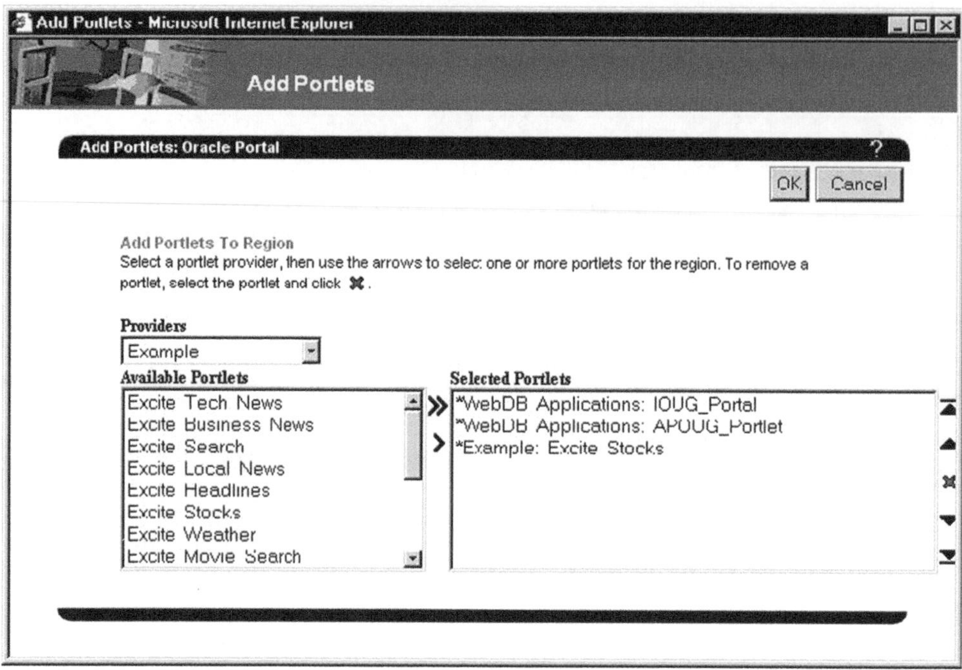

Exhibit 16.7 Creating a User Page

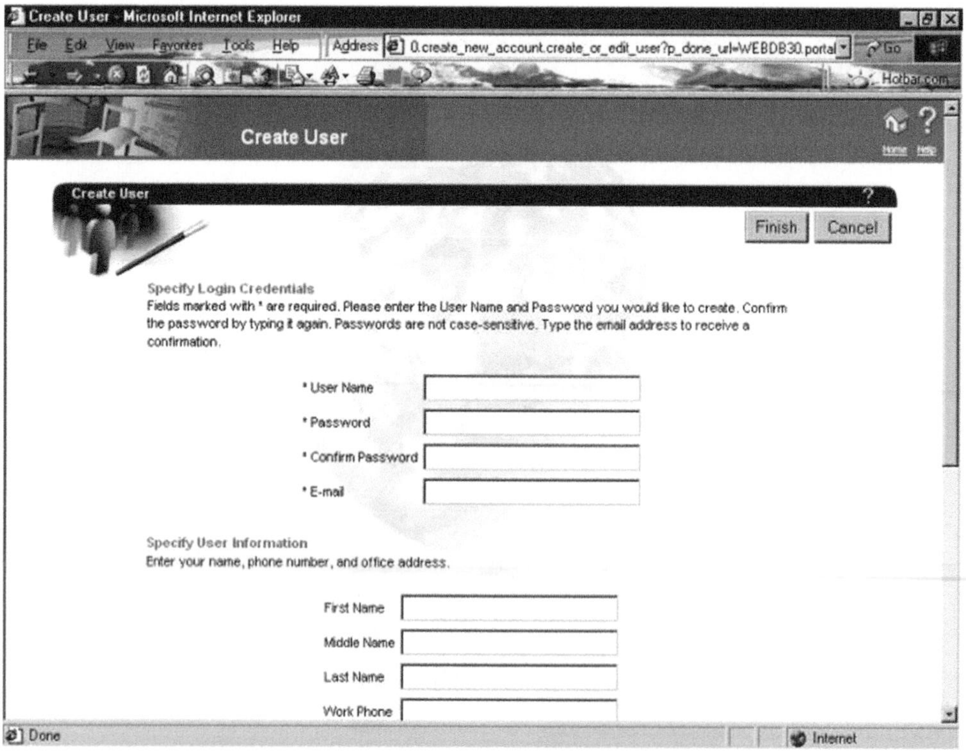

Exhibit 16.8 Development Functionality

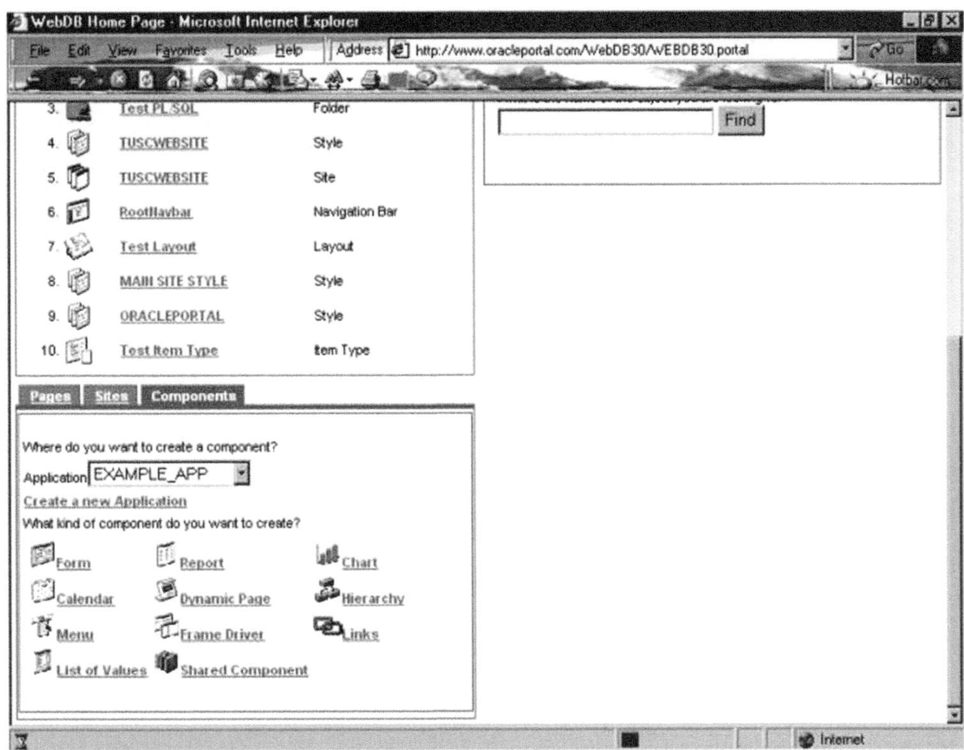

Build a Default Page for Everyone

With Oracle Portal, you can easily create your own default look-and-feel that every user will see when he or she visits your site (prior to logging in). Exhibit 16.10 displays a page I created and set as the default page.

Bugs?

There are many bugs in the beta version; so beware! Additionally, there is limited documentation provided with the product. For example, one bug I discovered was that when I copied an object, the portlet name remained unchanged. This made it very confusing when I started placing portlets on a page. I was, however, able to modify the underlying data in the Oracle Portal tables to fix the problem. At any rate, Oracle has promised significant changes (and bug fixes) between the beta and production versions — so hang on!

Version Control

This version is also missing some of the advanced authorization and rollout features that you might expect in a portal product. For example, items get

Exhibit 16.9 Shared Components

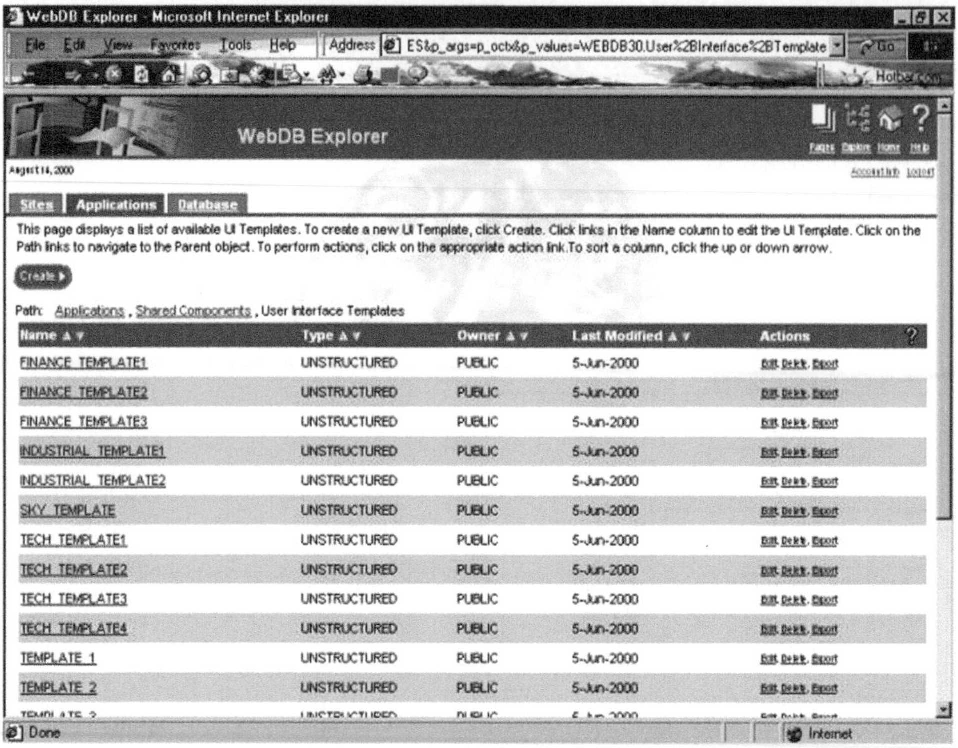
WebDB Explorer - Microsoft Internet Explorer
File Edit View Favorites Tools Help
Address ES&p_args=p_octx&p_values=WEBDB30.User%2BInterface%2BTemplate
WebDB Explorer
Sites Applications Database
This page displays a list of available UI Templates. To create a new UI Template, click Create. Click links in the Name column to edit the UI Template. Click on the Path links to navigate to the Parent object. To perform actions, click on the appropriate action link. To sort a column, click the up or down arrow.
Create
Path: Applications, Shared Components, User Interface Templates
Name Type Owner Last Modified Actions
FINANCE_TEMPLATE1 UNSTRUCTURED PUBLIC 5-Jun-2000 Edit, Delete, Export
FINANCE_TEMPLATE2 UNSTRUCTURED PUBLIC 5-Jun-2000 Edit, Delete, Export
FINANCE_TEMPLATE3 UNSTRUCTURED PUBLIC 5-Jun-2000 Edit, Delete, Export
INDUSTRIAL_TEMPLATE1 UNSTRUCTURED PUBLIC 5-Jun-2000 Edit, Delete, Export
INDUSTRIAL_TEMPLATE2 UNSTRUCTURED PUBLIC 5-Jun-2000 Edit, Delete, Export
SKY_TEMPLATE UNSTRUCTURED PUBLIC 5-Jun-2000 Edit, Delete, Export
TECH_TEMPLATE1 UNSTRUCTURED PUBLIC 5-Jun-2000 Edit, Delete, Export
TECH_TEMPLATE2 UNSTRUCTURED PUBLIC 5-Jun-2000 Edit, Delete, Export
TECH_TEMPLATE3 UNSTRUCTURED PUBLIC 5-Jun-2000 Edit, Delete, Export
TECH_TEMPLATE4 UNSTRUCTURED PUBLIC 5-Jun-2000 Edit, Delete, Export
TEMPLATE_1 UNSTRUCTURED PUBLIC 5-Jun-2000 Edit, Delete, Export
TEMPLATE_2 UNSTRUCTURED PUBLIC 5-Jun-2000 Edit, Delete, Export
Done
Internet

published directly into production without release management. This is a bit scary for most companies.

After the Install

After you install Oracle Portal, be aware that a DBA account is created in your database. The username is webdb30 and the password is the same. Be sure to change the password right away. Additionally, a matching Oracle Portal account (stored in the Oracle Portal tables) is created. Be sure to update this account's password.

Publishing a Portlet

After clicking on the object to create (see Exhibit 16.11), you will notice that the wizards look very familiar if you are acquainted with WebDB 2.1. In fact, although some functionality has been added to each of the objects, you will find the wizard very familiar and comfortable. However, when you are finished, you will see a new option (see Exhibit 16.12): specifically, "Run as Portlet."

If you run the object "not as a portlet," it is bigger; but it also contains the headers and other formatting options (see Exhibit 16.13). Exhibit 16.14 displays the object as a portlet. If you attempt to publish this object as a

Exhibit 16.10 Default Page

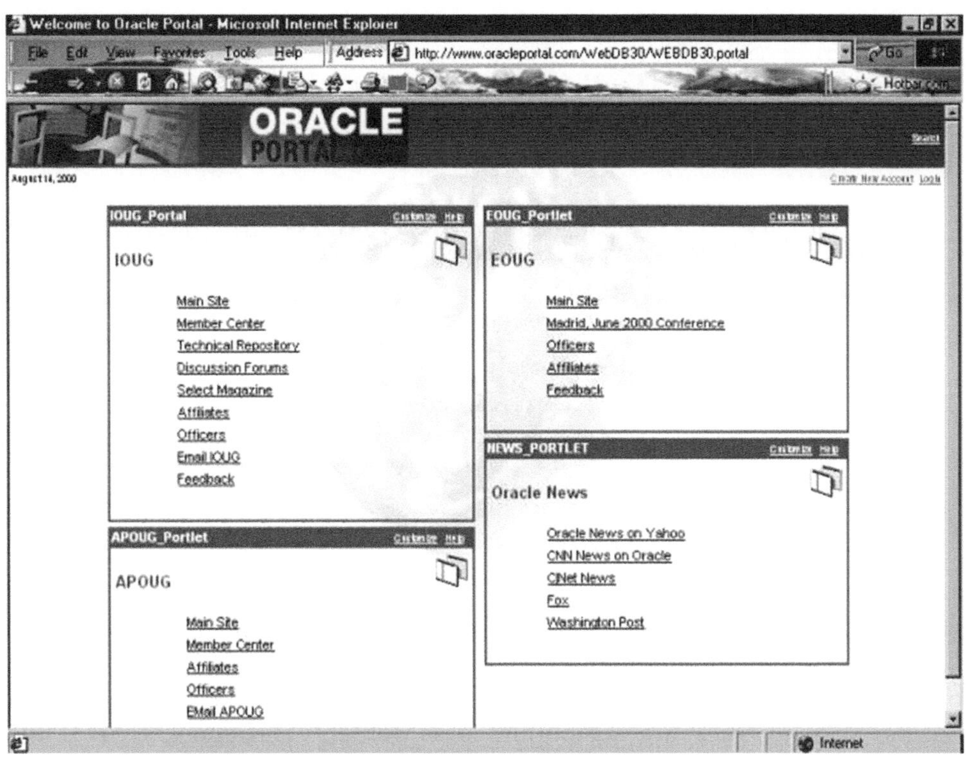

Exhibit 16.11 Creating an Object

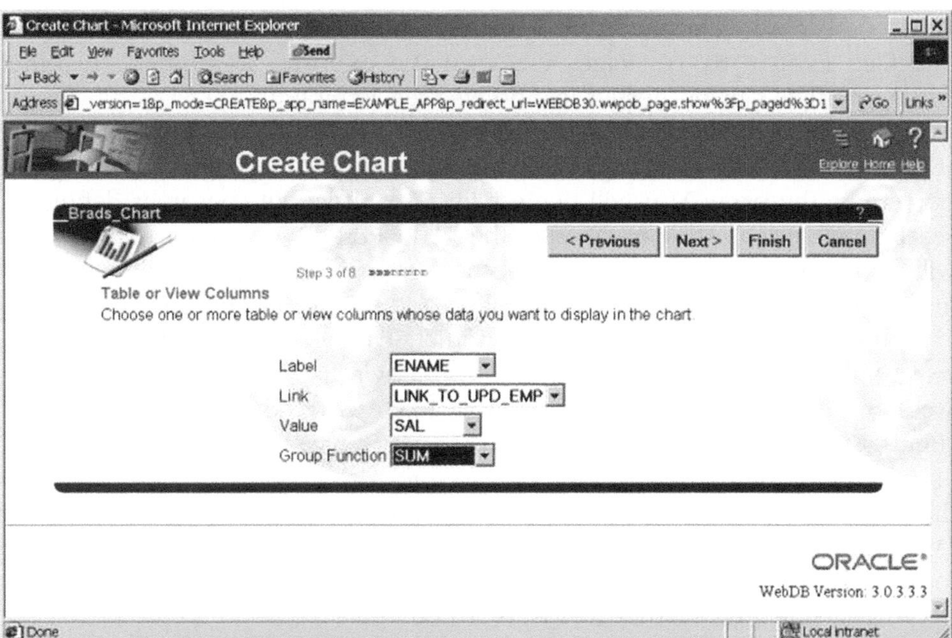

Exhibit 16.12 "Run as Portlet" Option

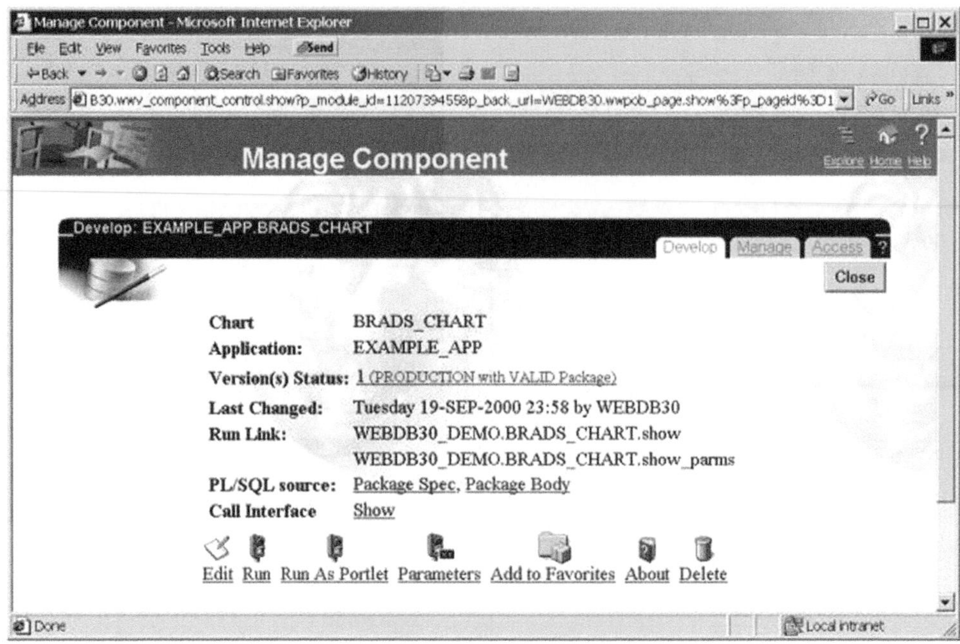

portlet, you cannot; that is, until you "Publish to Portal." The default functionality is that objects are not published as portlets. This checkbox is found under the "Access" tab (see Exhibit 16.15).

Placing a Portlet

Portlets are placed on pages. You can edit an existing page or create a new one (see Exhibit 16.16). Pages can even be exposed as portlets. In other words, portlets can be nested in portlets (see Exhibit 16.17).

Pages also have a default layout and style that you can define (Exhibit 16.18). After defining the layout and style for the page, you can place portlets on the page. You will begin with a blank layout (per your definition; see Exhibit 16.19). As you can see, the "Add Portlet" icon (see Exhibit 16.5) will allow you to add a portlet to a section on the page. Simply click this icon in the section of the page that you wish to add the portlet (Exhibit 16.20).

You can select the provider of the portlet. To include Oracle Portal objects, select "WebDB Applications" from the drop-down list box (can you tell this is WebDB 3.0?). You wll notice in Exhibit 16.20 that the chart created earlier (Brads_Chart) is available as a portlet object, which we selected. In Exhibit 16.21, I selected a portlet for each section on the page. Also note that I was customizing this page for "Others," but also have the option of customizing the page for "MySelf." As one might expect, if you change it for "MySelf," it only affects the look of the page that you see. Exhibit 16.22 displays the final result.

What a powerful feature this is; is it not?

Exhibit 16.13 Running the Object "Not as a Portlet"

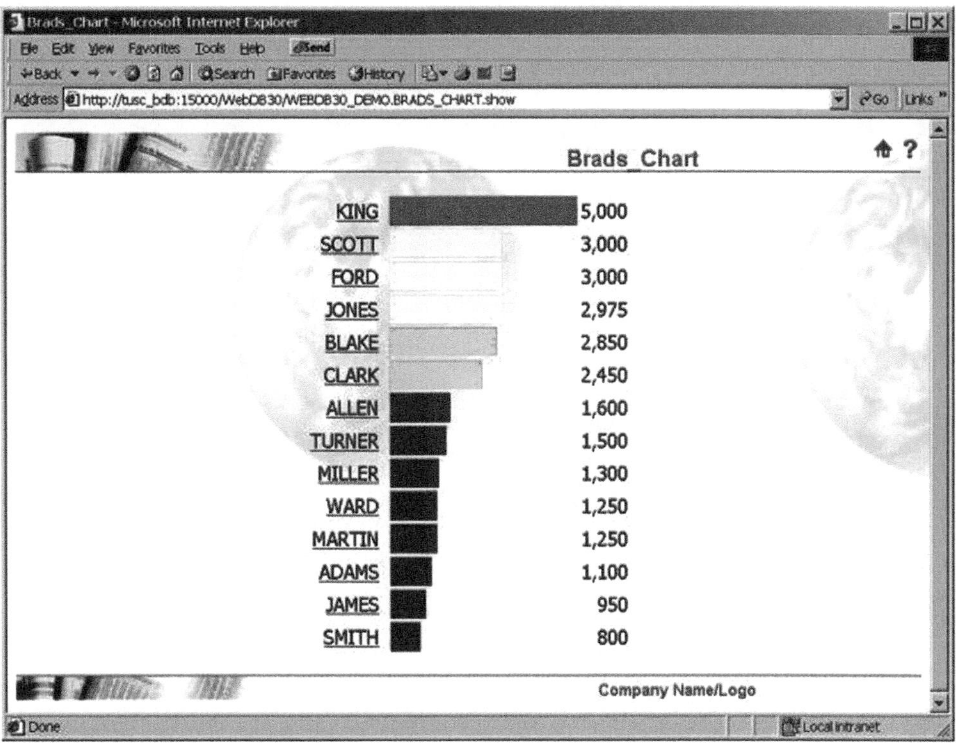

Exhibit 16.14 The Object as a Portlet

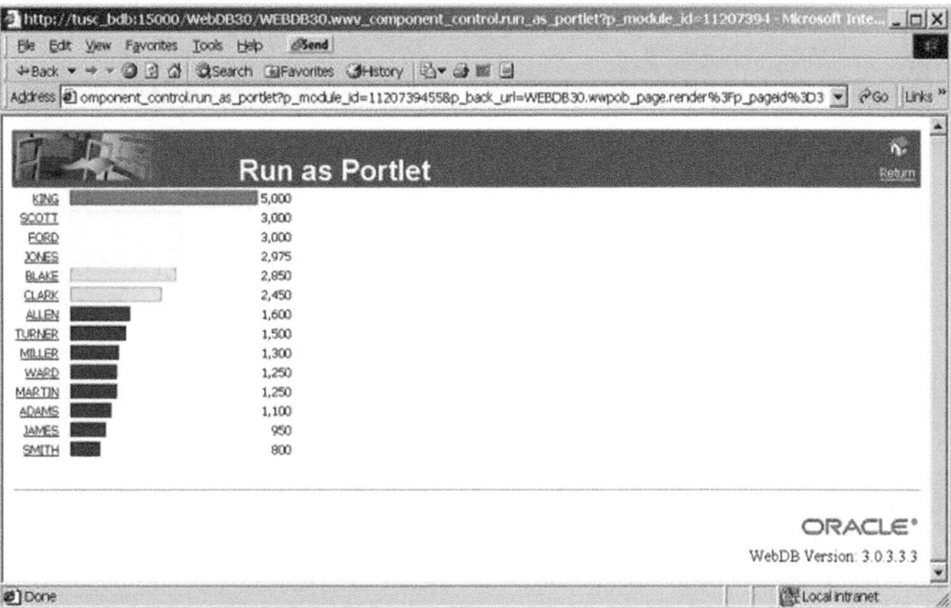

Exhibit 16.15 Checkbox under the "Access" Tab

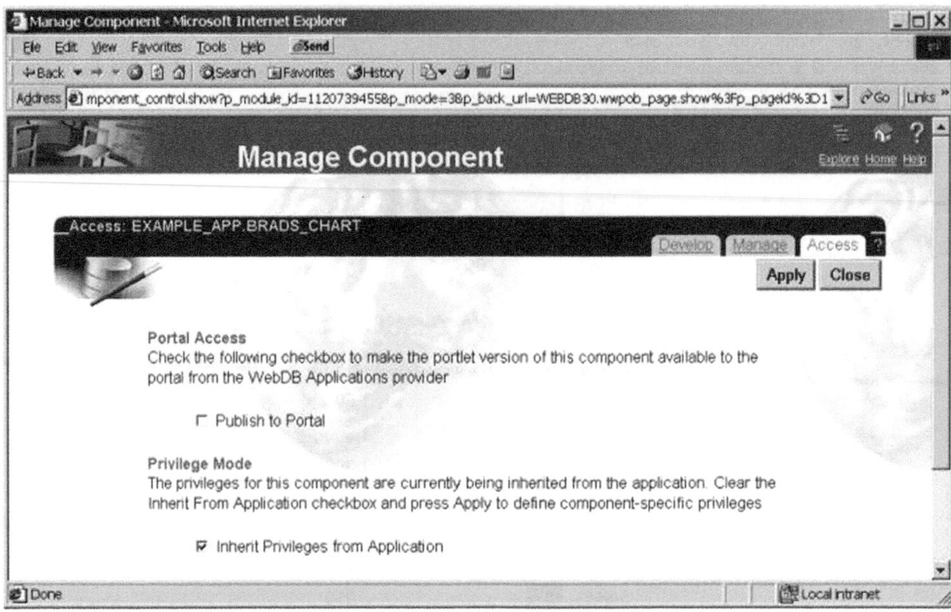

Exhibit 16.16 Editing an Existing Page or Creating a New One

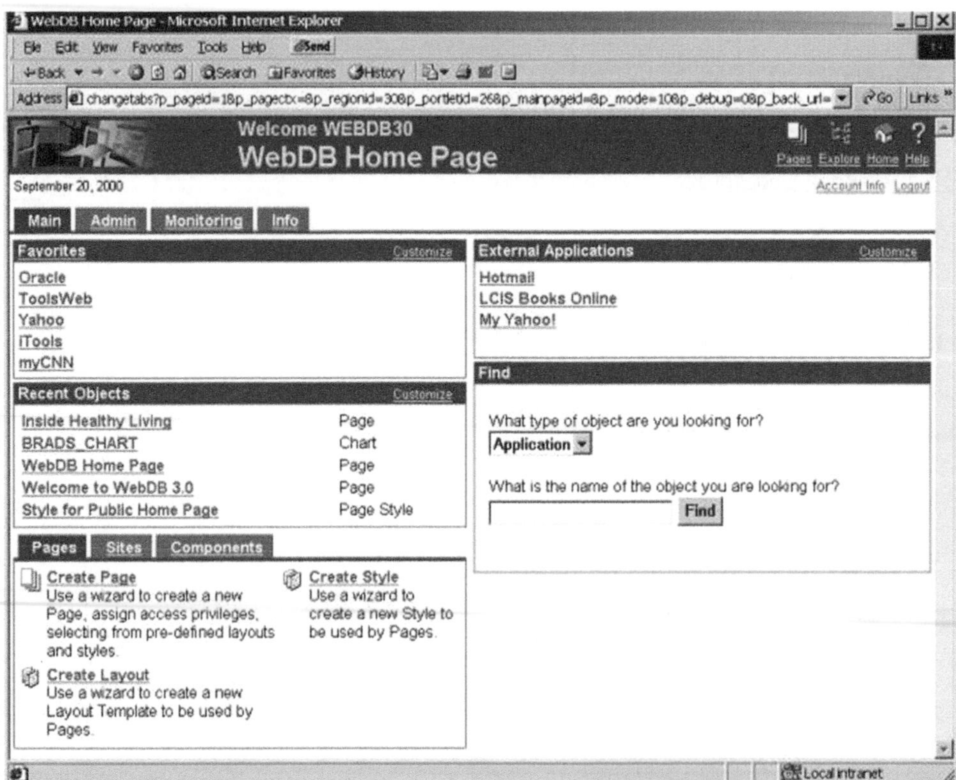

Exhibit 16.17 Portlets Nested in Portlets

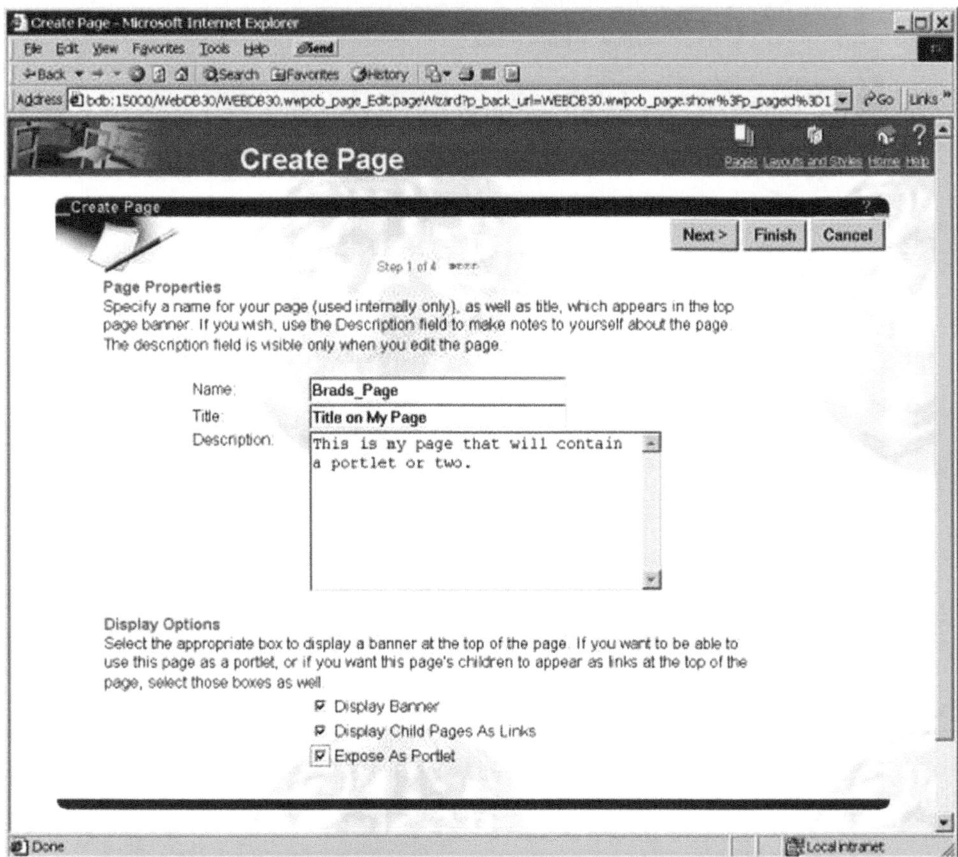

Summary

As you can tell, this is much more than a name change and a simple version upgrade of WebDB. Oracle Portal is a robust, powerful product that every company will want to use. Best of luck with your Oracle Portal development.

Exhibit 16.18 Defining the Default Layout and Style

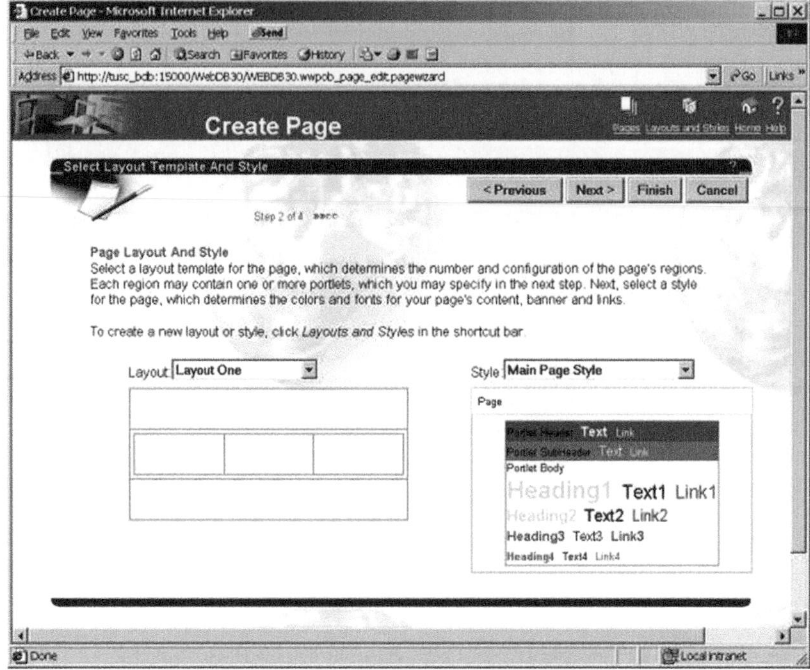

Exhibit 16.19 Blank Layout

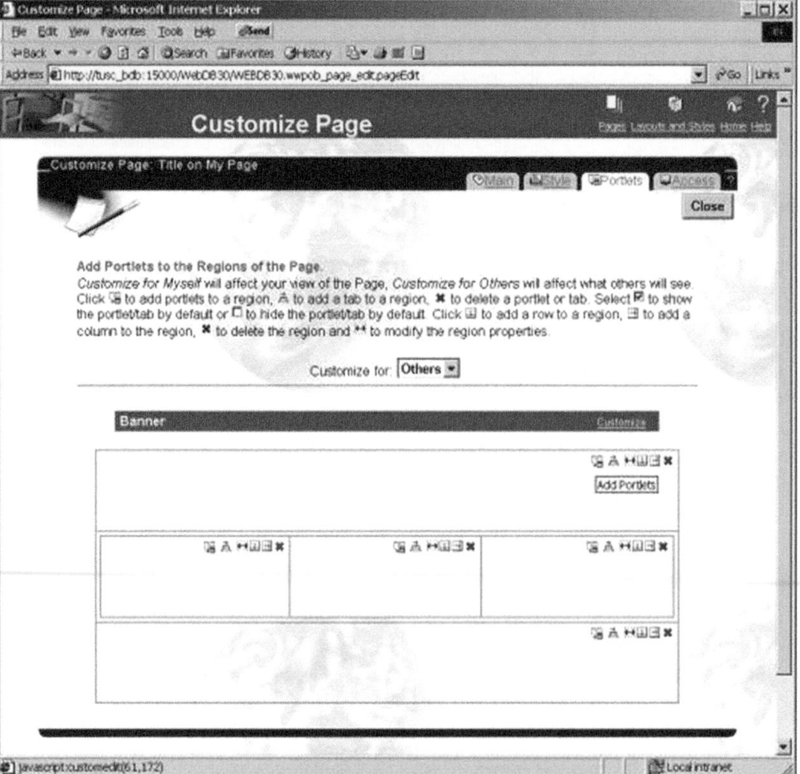

Exhibit 16.20 Adding a Portlet

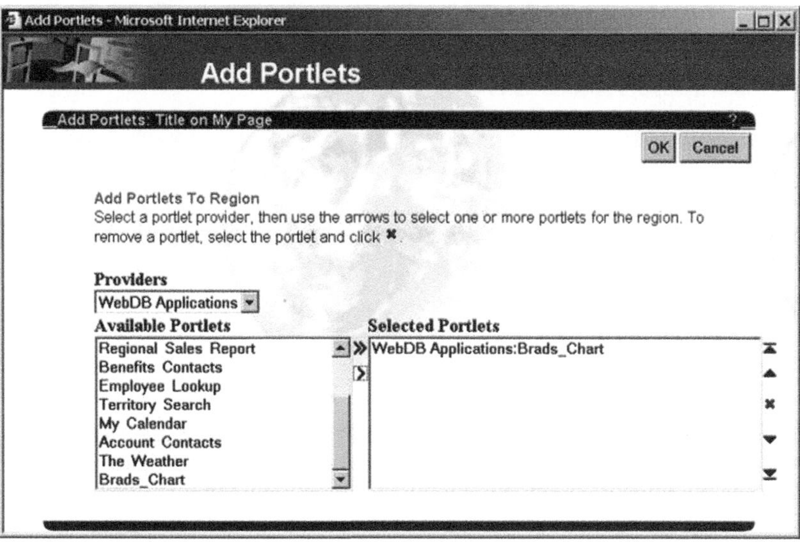

Exhibit 16.21 One Portlet Selected for Each Section

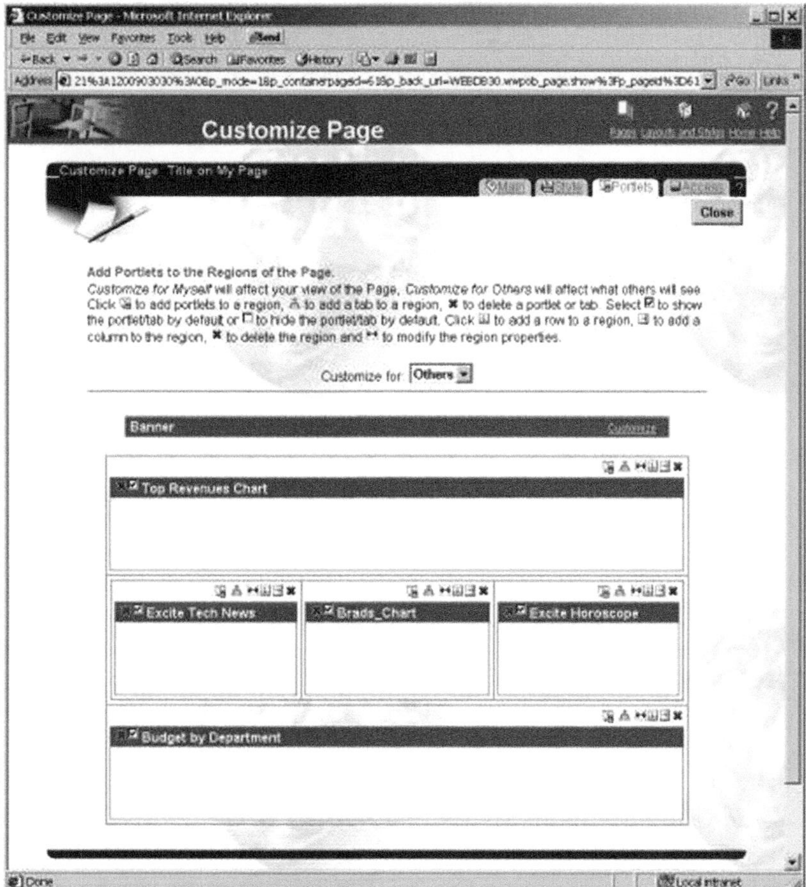

Exhibit 16.22 Final Result of Formatting for "MySelf"

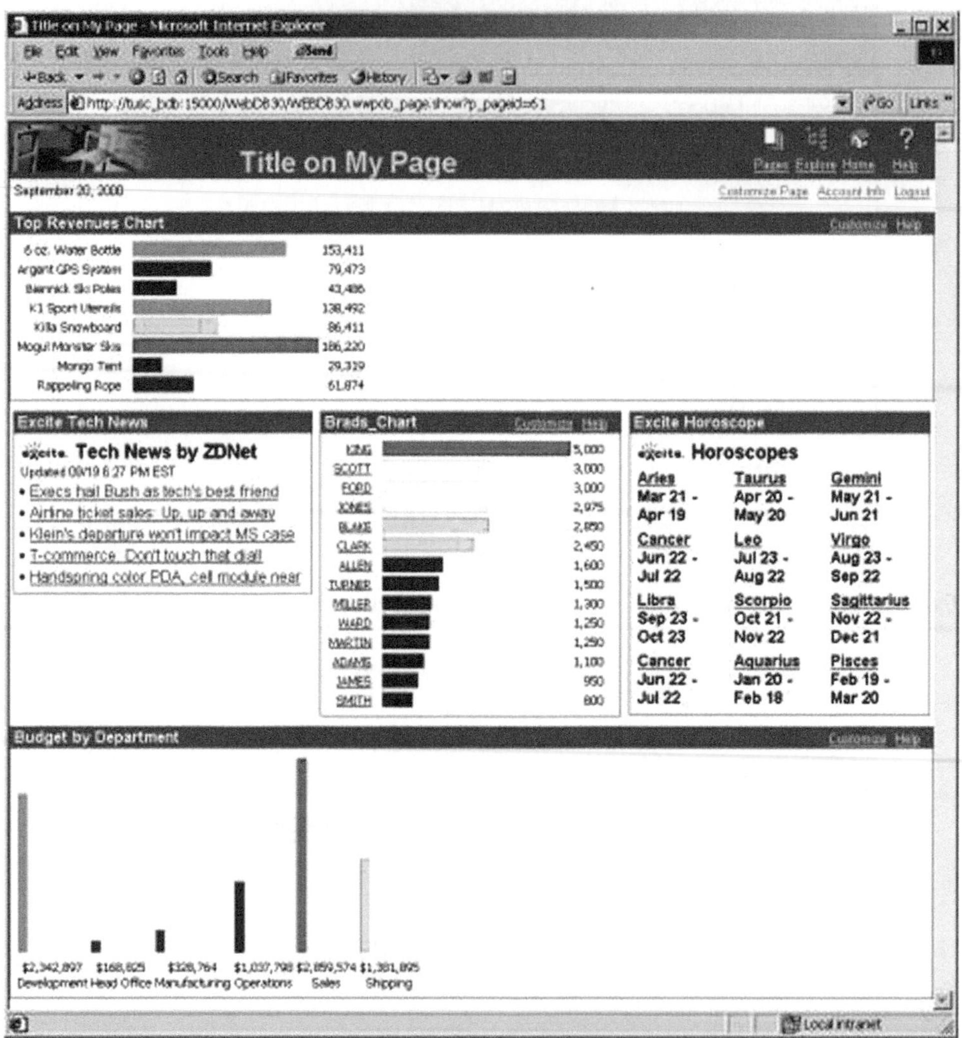

JAVA AND ORACLE

The introduction of the Java language into the Oracle engine has had a very important impact on applications development. Due to the high degree of portability of Java, as well as its interpretive nature, Java becomes an ideal language for the dynamic generation of information being accessed by Oracle. Whether we are discussing Java applets, Java servlets, the JVM Java virtual machine, or Java within PL/SQL, it is indispensable for the Oracle professional to understand the importance of Java in applications development.

Chapters 17 and 18 introduce a great conceptual overview of Java and demonstrate how Java can be used to create portable and robust Oracle applications.

Chapter 17

The Fast Track to Java with Oracle

Bradley D. Brown

Wow, this was fun — NOT! After trying to figure out the whole Oracle Java thing, it is finally starting to come together. There are so many (Java) options available that it was confusing to me — I think rightfully so! To move from my Oracle world of the PL/SQL cartridge into the Oracle world of Java, I figured that Java stored procedures were the way to go. I was wrong.

Why are Java stored procedures wrong for what I hoped to accomplish? Java stored procedures run on the database server, not the application server — just like a PL/SQL procedure runs on the database server. I did not really think about this until I put all the pieces together — you get the benefit of realizing it now. In fact, that is the real issue with the PL/SQL cartridge: the PL/SQL cartridge is not really all that scalable (nor is it thread-safe) because every cartridge execution requires a database operation. Accessing the database every time is fine, if you NEED to access the database; but what if you do not? To run Java on the application tier, you will want to use the Java cartridge. Otherwise, the n-tier environment quickly becomes heavily dependent on the database tier — so we are back to a one-tier (terminal/host) or maybe two-tier (client/server) environment. The application server scalability is greatly affected by the lack of thread ability by the PL/SQL cartridges. Threads reduce the per-user memory required from megabytes (i.e., 6 MB) to kilobytes (28 to 200 KB).

But do not get me wrong; the PL/SQL cartridge is a very efficient cartridge. Oracle worked hard to tune the login/logout efficiency for the PL/SQL cartridge so that the overhead is minimal. Additionally, the PL/SQL cartridge is proven — the Java cartridge is far less proven. So I am not saying the PL/SQL cartridge is bad; it is just not as efficient as the Java cartridge has the potential to be. If you (and your developers) don't mind using Oracle's proprietary program-

0-8493-1139-X/02/$0.00+$1.50
©2002 by CRC Press LLC

ming language and you have a database-driven application, the PL/SQL cartridge is likely a better solution. Keep in mind that no matter what, you will want to use PL/SQL for the data-centric operations — at least today that is true. I still believe that PL/SQL is fast and easier for programmers (and non-programmers) to learn. PL/SQL does not use an object-oriented methodology, which can be easier to understand. If your developers only know PL/SQL, you are also more likely to retain those developers longer because Java developers tend to get more job offers than PL/SQL developers. Then again, Java reports the third-largest group of programmers educated in the world — which is amazing to me.

I will cover the Java Stored Procedures first. It took me a while to put these pieces together, but my hope is that this helps you understand these pieces with considerably less effort than I spent on this task.

You might wonder what Oracle Java options are available. They are numerous and include:

- Java Stored Procedures
- Servlets and the Java Cartridge (JWeb)
- PL2JAVA
- SQLJ
- JSP
- EJB

Is Java better or faster than PL/SQL? Someone recently told me that he had read that Java was 10 times faster than PL/SQL. The question you need to ask yourself is, "At what?" Here is the answer directly from Oracle:

> As with any benchmark, with a little effort, you can create results to give the results you want. The only true answer to this question is: "It depends on what you want your application to do."
>
> PL/SQL is completely seamless with SQL, sharing the same data types, and is therefore ideal for SQL intensive applications — there are no data type conversions necessary and the application logic is simply procedures extending SQL or massaging SQL tables. In a scenario with lots of database read/writes and very little computation, code written in PL/SQL will always run significantly faster than similar code written in Java.
>
> Java is a general-purpose programming language and is ideal for building component-based applications, such as CORBA services, Enterprise JavaBeans, and for computationally intensive stored procedural applications. By running Java in Oracle8i, we allow Java applications to perform compute-intensive operations quicker than PL/SQL could and to scale better than any other platform in the industry. In a scenario with lots of computation and few database read/writes, code written in Java will always run significantly faster than similar code written in PL/SQL.

Because PL/SQL and Java interoperate cleanly in Oracle8i, the best answer may in fact be to have a combination of both languages. This is possible because the high level of interoperability allows PL/SQL and Java to have a number of common facilities — common library management facilities, common purity model, common security model etc .— and thus interoperate extremely cleanly in the server. This consistency makes it much easier to combine PL/SQL and Java in building applications. This approach would certainly allow customers to avoid risky complete rewrites of applications by wrapping their existing PL/SQL code and not rewriting it completely. Completely rewriting applications could involve substantial project and technical risks; depending on the type of application and how it was implemented, the rewrite may run faster or slower than the original.

With Java now built into the Oracle database server, will Oracle stop supporting (or developing) PL/SQL?

Absolutely not.

Oracle Server Technologies is actively enhancing PL/SQL and Java support, both in Oracle8i and beyond 8i. For example, PL/SQL is significantly faster in 8i than in 8.0, both transparently (from internal optimizations) and via new features (e.g., bulk SQL).

Java simply provides an alternative way to develop procedures in the server — it opens the server platform to another, broader set of application developers and ISVs. This does not mean that all other languages supported on the server should be dropped. In an analogous manner, Oracle supports IIOP as an alternate communication protocol into 8i but has no plans to desupport Net8.

Java Stored Procedures

JSP does not stand for Java stored procedures, but we will talk about JSP shortly. To write Java stored procedures, you must first write your Java program. Writing Java code can be done in a standard editor (e.g., Notepad or vi) or with a Java editing tool (e.g., JDeveloper or JBuilder). To get started, I recommend using a simple text editor. JDeveloper is great for a complete Oracle/Java development environment. Java is like C or C++, but I don't really know either of these languages. Although I found Java pretty easy to pick up, a Java programmer would likely say that my programs look like a hack at programming. I would agree — at least today.

I started with one of the stored procedure examples provided by Oracle and hacked my way from there. For my test case, all I wanted to do was select all the records from the employee (*emp*) table and display them back to the user in the browser. Seems easy enough, right? It certainly is with the

PL/SQL cartridge (if you know PL/SQL, that is). As I learned, Java stored procedures should not be used for this purpose. The reasons are many. The database cannot call a Java stored procedure without your wrapping the class into a PL/SQL procedure. "Wrapping" isn't really a good word. You are really just defining the Java stored procedure (that you've already loaded into the database) so that you can call the Java class from any place in Oracle. This is a goofy step, but it is required. I can only imagine that this goofy requirement will go away (or will be automated) at some future date.

Appendix 17.1 shows the Java class that I wrote. I documented the code so that you can figure out what each piece of the code is actually doing.

The example routine was saved as emp.java. As noted in the code itself, I had to pass the information (HTML) through a PL/SQL packaged variable — using htp.prn. This isn't pretty, but it worked. Next, you will want to make sure that your code compiles. You could just attempt to load your code into the database, but this will not usually work too well. *javac* is used to compile your Java code — this will create a class file. After installing OAS, *javac* is on your machine automatically; it is installed with OAS. The *javac* program is located in the ORACLE_HOME/ows/4.0/jdk/bin directory. You will need to set the *classpath;* this is where the Java compiler looks to find the files that you import (or include). For the above program, I had to use the following *classpath* statement:

```
set classpath=d:\oracle\ora81\sqlj\lib\translator. zip;d:\oracle\ora81\
  ord\ts\jlib\thindriver. lib;d:\oracle\ora81\jdbc\lib\classes111.zip;
  d:\oracle\oas\ows\cartx\jweb\classes\jweb.jar;a:\;
```

I would recommend putting the above statement into a batch script, or you could set the environmental parameter at the operating system level. To compile your Java program, all you need to do is type:

```
javac emp.java
```

If your program compiles, you can then load it into the database. However, I would recommend that you test the program first. Your program must have a "main" unit to be run in this manner. To change your program, just change the following line:

```
public static void pullemp () throws SQLException {
```

Simply change the program name (i.e., *pullemp*) to *main* and add *String args[ ]* to the parameter list as follows:

```
public static void main (String args []) throws SQLException {
```

This will allow you to test your program from the operating system. You can run the Java program at the operating system by typing:

```
java emp
```

When you are ready to load your tested Java program unit into the database, type the following command at the operating system prompt:

```
loadjava -u examples/examples@tuscl:1521:ORC1 -v -t -r emp.java
```

The *loadjava* module is well-documented in Oracle's online documentation. Note that the syntax for your connect string is the same as the connect string used for JDBC, which includes the username/password@host:port:sid.

If you attempt to load the above code with the oracle.html import uncommented, you will get an error because those routines do not already exist in the database. Although you will not need to do this for this example, you will likely need to load another library at some point. To load a missing library such as the oracle.html library, you will need to use the *loadjava* command (from the operating system prompt), which can load not only Java files, but zip and jar files (that are not compressed — as discussed in the documentation). Here is the syntax to load the oracle.html class files into the database:

```
loadjava -u examples/examples@tuscl:1521:ORC1 -v -r
d:\oracle\oas\ows\cartx\jweb\classes\jweb.jar
```

Next, you will need to do that goofy step that was mentioned above…you will need to declare the Java program to PL/SQL as follows:

```
CREATE OR REPLACE PACKAGE emp_java AS
   outbuff varchar2(32000);
   PROCEDURE pullemp;
END emp_java;
/

CREATE OR REPLACE PACKAGE BODY emp_java AS
   PROCEDURE pullemp
   AS LANGUAGE JAVA
   NAME 'emp.pullemp()';
END emp_java;
/
```

As you can tell, this is not a practical method of using Java stored procedures, but Exhibit 17.1 shows the result of executing the emp_java Java stored procedure.

So why show this example? Because this is what I believe people will want to use Java stored procedures for. Then after spending many, many hours attempting to make it work, you will get to this point. Hopefully, I have saved you hours of work.

Java database procedures are useful for programs that are light database users and heavy operating system users, heavy string parsing procedures, or are computationally intensive — all things that PL/SQL is not particularly good at. Although Java and PL/SQL appear to have the same disadvantages, in that they are both interpreted and are running in the database kernel, Java does

Exhibit 17.1 Java Procedure Sample Calling Oracle Database

EMPNO	ENAME	JOB	MGR	HIREDATE	SAL	COM	DEPTNO
8786	ADAMS	CLERK	7788	1983-01-12 00:00:00.0	1100		20
7499	ALLEN	SALESMAN	7698	1981-02-20 00:00:00.0	1600	300	30
7698	BLAKE	MANAGER	7839	1981-05-01 00:00:00.0	2850		30
7782	CLARK	MANAGER	7839	1981-06-09 00:00:00.0	2450		10
7902	FORD	ANALYST	7566	1981-12-03 00:00:00.0	3000		20
7900	JAMES	CLERK	7698	1981-12-03 00:00:00.0	950		30
7566	JONES	MANAGER	7839	1981-04-02 00:00:00.0	2975		20
7839	KING	PRESIDENT		1981-11-17 00:00:00.0	5000		10
7654	MARTIN	SALESMAN	7698	1981-09-28 00:00:00.0	1250	1400	30
7934	MILLER	CLERK	7782	1982-01-23 00:00:00.0	1300		10
7788	SCOTT	ANALYST	7566	1982-12-09 00:00:00.0	3000		20
7369	SMITH	CLERK	7902	1980-12-17 00:00:00.0	800		20

run faster for these types of operations. Java stored procedures would generally be occasional-use processes as opposed to persistent Java cartridges. One difference between Java servlets and Java stored procedures is simply the tier where they run. Java stored procedures would tend to fatten the data server layer, and Java servlets would tend to fatten the middle tier.

Don't get me wrong; Java stored procedures are useful. In fact, they are VERY useful. Often times, people will ask, which language — PL/SQL or Java — is better. The answer is that it depends on the operation that you are performing. If you wish to perform truly intense database operations, PL/SQL is likely better. If you wish to perform complex calculations (like you would in a C program), Java is likely better. Next, you need to decide where you wish to execute your code. Typically, the preference would be on the application server, in which case you need to use the Java cartridge, which is covered next.

Servlets and the Java Cartridge (JWeb)

Servlets (also called JServlets in OAS) are typically used to output HTML or XML, as there are lots of XML classes available in Java. One can think of them as being very similar to the other CGI flavors (Perl and C). These programs are commonly used to perform operating system type functions, opening sockets, starting and stopping processes, searching directories and copying files, and generally doing things one might alternately find in a C function.

Java cartridges (also called JWeb) can be used for the same purpose, but are generally things that run as persistent, multiple instance programs. A sample use might be to implement a Java program for use as a payment server. The Java program could run as a listener that interfaces with a credit card processing server (i.e., First Data Corp.) over a persistent 56K line. Interprocess communications and process monitors are other examples of good uses of Java cartridges.

Now convert the above example to use the Java cartridge (Appendix 17.2). This is how it should have been done the first time. It is actually pretty simple to convert the program. As you can see, the oracle.html toolkit was used to output the HTML back to the page. In fact, anything that is written to standard output will be sent to the browser. The JDBC driver was used to access the

Exhibit 17.2 The Output from Using the Java Cartridge

EMPNO	ENAME	JOB	MGR	HIREDATE	SAL	COM	DEPTNO
8786	ADAMS	CLERK	7788	1983-01-12 00:00:00.0	1100		20
7499	ALLEN	SALESMAN	7698	1981-02-20 00:00:00.0	1600	300	30
7698	BLAKE	MANAGER	7839	1981-05-01 00:00:00.0	2850		30
7782	CLARK	MANAGER	7839	1981-06-09 00:00:00.0	2450		10
7902	FORD	ANALYST	7566	1981-12-03 00:00:00.0	3000		20
7900	JAMES	CLERK	7698	1981-12-03 00:00:00.0	950		30
7566	JONES	MANAGER	7839	1981-04-02 00:00:00.0	2975		20
7839	KING	PRESIDENT		1981-11-17 00:00:00.0	5000		10
7654	MARTIN	SALESMAN	7698	1981-09-28 00:00:00.0	1250	1400	30
7934	MILLER	CLERK	7782	1982-01-23 00:00:00.0	1300		10
7788	SCOTT	ANALYST	7566	1982-12-09 00:00:00.0	3000		20
7369	SMITH	CLERK	7902	1980-12-17 00:00:00.0	800		20

Oracle database. This Java routine runs on the application server (i.e., OAS Server) as a database client, and the database server is used only for accessing the data from the *emp* table.

JWeb is a powerful solution for your Java and OAS needs. Exhibit 17.2 shows the output that results from executing the above Java routine.

PL2Java

The *pl2java* program simply generates Java wrapper classes for PL/SQL procedures and functions in PL/SQL packages. Like *javac, pl2java* is a part of the OAS product. After creating these classes, you can call the wrapper classes from your Java applications to invoke the PL/SQL program units. This method allows you to implement database logic in PL/SQL to ensure proper control of data in your databases and to invoke existing PL/SQL code from Java applications. Before you can run *pl2java,* you must install the DBMS_PACKAGE package in the SYS schema. The installation script can be found in the $ORACLE_HOME/ows/cartx/jweb/sql/ directory. The file to execute is named *dbpkins8.sql.*

pl2java is not as executable as I thought it might be. On NT, it is a command (*cmd*) file. The command file can be found in the $ORACLE_HOME/ows/cartx/jweb/bin directory. You may wish to add this directory to your path. The syntax to run *pl2java* is:

```
pl2java username/password@connect-string plsql_package
```

After executing *pl2java,* you will find a class file has been created for your package. For example, Assist.class was created after I executed the following statement (note the case of Assist, because this is the case in which the class file will be created):

```
pl2java examples/examples@tcp-loopback Assist
```

Each of the procedures and functions in the Assist package can now be called from the Assist class file. It is that easy! You cannot call the PL/SQL packaged routine's class file directly from the browser; you need to call the class file from another Java program. So let's take a look at how you might call a procedure (or function) from another Java program.

Below is an example that calls a PL/SQL procedure from the Assist class. The Assist package contains a procedure with the following definition:

```
procedure ask_quest
(in_question in varchar2)
```

Note that to call this procedure, we must first define Oracle Home and then log into the database. The procedure is called with ease. Functions are called in much the same manner; they simply return a variable. This is also well-documented.

```
import java.sql.*;          // Needed for SQL routines
import java.io.*;           // Needed for input/output
import oracle.rdbms.*;      // import Oracle classes that deal with database
                               session
import oracle.plsql.*;      // import Oracle classes that deal with PL/SQL
                               data types

public class assist_user {
   public static void main (String args [])  throws SQLException {

        try {
       // Define ORACLE_HOME
       Session.setProperty("ORACLE_HOME", System.getProperty("oracleHome"));

       // Create a new database session and logon
       Session session = new Session();
       session.logon("examples", "examples", "tcp-loopback");

       // Instantiate Assist wrapper class:
       Assist assist_user = new Assist(session);

       PStringBuffer myQuestion = new PStringBuffer(100);
       myQuestion.setValue("What is the color of money?");

       // Call the ask_question procedure
       assist_user.ask_quest(myQuestion);

   } catch (Exception e) {e.printStackTrace(System.out);
   }}
}
```

Once I learned about *pl2java,* I got to thinking. How about attempting to run *pl2java* for the *htp* and *htf* packages and then calling the respective packages and functions from my Java stored procedure? So like an excited kid, I stayed up almost all night trying to make this work. I was able to get the *htp* and *htf* packages run through and turned into classes. This was not a problem. Then I changed my above Java stored procedure HTML calls to use the *htp* and *htf* classes similar to this:

```
PStringBuffer strng = new PStringBuffer(100);
strng.setValue("Java Example using Java Procedure and htp");
htp.title(strng);
```

As hard as I tried to make this work, I simply fell one step short. The closer I got, the farther away I seemed to be. I ran into problems because classes cannot have default values like procedures can, so I had to supply a value for every procedure and function. This was fine; I changed the code to make this work. However, Java stored procedures use the JDBC default connection, while the classes created use the session object type. I could not get these two data types to work with each other. When dawn approached, I slept for a few hours and then went right back at it. I finally gave in and decided it simply was not meant to be.

SQLJ

SQLJ is yet another way to write Java code to access Oracle databases. SQLJ is a Java precompiler option for embedding SQL calls within a piece of Java code. My assessment is that SQLJ is for the Java programmer who doesn't come from the database world. There are tons of papers on this topic at technet.oracle.com.

JSP

OAS supports Java Server Pages (JSP). The HTML within the page is static, and Java is embedded within the HTML code. This approach is similar to ASP (Active Server Pages that are used by Microsoft to embed Visual Basic within HTML) and the new PL/SQL Server Pages. LiveHTML is really Perl Server pages in that LiveHTML uses Perl as its scripting language. WebDB has a feature called "Dynamic Pages," which are simply PL/SQL Server pages. My feeling about xSPs (whatever Server Pages) is that they were developed for the HTML developers who are moving into the dynamic world and might already know a programming language (e.g., Java, Visual Basic, Perl, or PL/SQL). Allaire (developers of Cold Fusion) has a JSP solution as well.

EJB

Beans are simply a method of developing your Java code in a standardized method where the units are called a bean. Enterprise JavaBeans (EJB) are server-side beans. This is yet another method of using Java with Oracle.

Performance

Now for the bad news. When I researched everything about Oracle and Java, everything seemed to indicate that Java was going to be the best/fastest/most scalable long-term solution for my needs. However, this did not prove to be true. Remember: this test is simply selecting all the data from the *emp* table

Exhibit 17.3 The Results after 100 Executions of Each Program Type

	PL/SQL	*Perl*	*LiveHTML*	*Java Cartridge*	*JavaStored Procedure*
Total Time	86.4	154.2	449	785.5	236.5
Avg Time per Execution	0.864	1.542	4.49	7.855	2.365
	Best time			Worst time	

and displaying it back to the browser. I wrote the same piece of code in PL/SQL, Perl, LiveHTML, Java (cartridge), and using a Java stored procedure. I had all three tiers (client, application server, and database server) running on the same physical machine (my laptop). So, this test is not absolute living proof that this will be faster in your environment. By no means is this proof that PL/SQL is **always** faster than Java. Remember that different languages have different advantages. PL/SQL is fast at selecting data from a table. If you are interested in these queries or my performance monitor, it is available on our Web site (under the "3 Kings" presentation). Exhibit 17.3 shows the results after 100 executions of each program type.

Summary

For scalable Oracle applications that must use Java, although the above results don't reflect my recommendation, I would recommend using the JWeb cartridge for maximum scalability and performance. For operations on the database server, I would recommend Java stored procedures. People often ask, "Now that Java is built into the Oracle database server, will Oracle stop supporting (or developing) PL/SQL?" The short answer is no. So what would I recommend if you are accessing the Oracle database and wish to do this as quickly as possible? PL/SQL for sure!

Sites Worth Checking Out

http://technt.oracle.com
http://www.jars.com
http://javasoft.com

Appendix 17.1 Java Class

```
/* Comments are either slash slash (single line) or slash star ended by star
slash. The import statements below are simply include statements — they
include other libraries of Java classes that allow you to write your program
by calling other functions. Note that I thought I needed to include the
oracle.html routines so that I could output HTML back to the browser. However,
Java procedures standard output does NOT go back to the browser. The only
way I could get information back to the browser was to send a long string
via a PL/SQL package variable — this is not a cool way to handle this. This
resulted in my conclusion that this way NOT the way to handle this. I could
pass parameters to the Java procedures, but I could not seem to get parameters
(e.g., a PL/SQL table) back from Java. This could be my inexperience, but I
couldn't find any documentation — anywhere — on this either.
*/

import java.sql.*;              // Needed for SQL routines
import java.io.*;               // Needed for input/output
// import oracle.html.*;        // thought I needed for the HTML output
                                     routines
import oracle.jdbc.driver.*;    // Needed for JDBC

public class emp {
   public static void pullemp () throws SQLException {
   // Change pullemp () to main (String args []) to test via command line
      String sql =
         "select * from scott.emp order by ename" ; // Here is the data
                                                        I wanted to select
      String connString;         // the connection string
      HtmlPage hp;               // Defines the HTML page - but can't be used
                                      here
      String buffer = "";        // Defines the buffer that will be sent back
                                      via package variable
      try {
         // register the jdbc driver
         DriverManager.registerDriver(new oracle.jdbc.driver.OracleDriver());
         System.out.println("Registered the Oracle JDBC driver.");

         /* Get connection with thin driver - this is explicit. I used this
            when testing in a standalone fashion. This would connect to my
            database (rather than using the existing connection).

         Connection conn = null;// the jdbc connection - needed if explicitly
            connecting
         connString = new String("jdbc:oracle:thin:examples/
            examples@tusc1:1521:ORC1");
         System.out.println("connection string: " + connString);
         conn = DriverManager.getConnection(connString);
         System.out.println("Connected to DB.");
         */

         // Used when used as a Java stored procedure (connect is already there)
         Connection conn = new OracleDriver().defaultConnection();

         PreparedStatement pstmt = conn.prepareStatement(sql);
         System.out.println("Prepared SQL Statement.");
         ResultSet rset = pstmt.executeQuery();
         System.out.println("Executed statement.");
```

(continues)

Appendix 17.1 Java Class (continued)

```
    /* This builds the HTML page, but in a Java stored procedure
       there is no way to send it back to the browser.

    hp = new HtmlPage("Java Example using Java Procedure");
    hp.getBody( ).addItem("Java Example using Java Procedure");
    hp.printHeader( );// Prints the content-type tag
    hp.print( );

       I had hoped I could do something like this:
  buffer = hp.print( );
       but that didn't work because I'm trying to assign a string to a
       program (not a function). There may be a way to do this, but I
       couldn't figure out how.
       */

    // Returns the meta data (column names and info)
    ResultSetMetaData meta = rset.getMetaData( );
    System.out.println("Got MetaData");

    // Retrieves the number of columns returned
    int cols = meta.getColumnCount( ), rows = 0;
    System.out.println("Columns reteived "+cols);

    // Set up the header information for the HTML
    buffer = "<HTML><HEAD><TITLE>Java Example using Java Procedure"+
"</TITLE></HEAD><BODY><TABLE BORDER=1><H1>Java Procedure Sample "+
"calling Oracle Database</H1><HR>";

    // Loop through and print the column names
    for (int i = 1; i <= cols; i++) {
       int size = meta.getPrecision(i);
       String label = meta.getColumnLabel(i);
       System.out.println("Column Label "+i+": "+label);
       if (label.length( ) > size) size = label.length( );
       while (label.length( ) < size) label += " ";
       buffer = buffer + "<TH>" + label + "</TH>";
    }

    // Now read through the rows
    while (rset.next( )) {
       rows++;
       buffer = buffer + "<TR>";
       System.out.println("Row: "+rows);
       for (int i = 1; i <= cols; i++) {
         int size = meta.getPrecision(i);
         String label = meta.getColumnLabel(i);
         String value = rset.getString(i);
         if (value == null) value = " ";          // For null values
         if (label.length( ) > size) size = label.length( );
         while (value.length( ) < size) value += " ";
         System.out.println("Got here!");
         buffer = buffer + "<TD>" + value + "</TD>";
       }
       buffer = buffer + "</TR>";
    }
    buffer = buffer + "</TABLE>";

    // If we didn't process any data, then say so...
    if (rows == 0) buffer = "No data found!\n";
```

Appendix 17.1 Java Class (continued)

```
        // Close up the record set
        System.out.println(buffer);
        rset.close();
        pstmt.close();

        // Now set the PL/SQL package variable - cheesy way to handle this...
        PreparedStatement pstmt2 = conn.prepareStatement("begin
emp_java.outbuff:='"+buffer+"';end;");
        ResultSet rset2 = pstmt2.executeQuery();
        rset2.close();
        pstmt2.close();

      } catch (SQLException e) {System.err.println(e.getMessage());}
   }
}
```

Appendix 17.2 Using the Java Cartridge

```
/* Note that I include the oracle.html routines so that I can output HTML
back to the browser. You could do this on your own by printing to standard
output too - this library just makes it easier for you.
*/
import java.sql.*;              // Needed for SQL routines
import java.io.*;               // Needed for input/output
import oracle.html.*;           // Needed for the HTML output routines
import oracle.jdbc.driver.*;    // Needed for JDBC

public class emp_cart {
public static void main (String args []) throws SQLException {
// Note that previously we had a routine name called pullemps, whereas here
   we have a "main" - this is a requirement of the Java cartridge
      String sql =
         "select * from scott.emp order by ename" ; // Here is the data I
                                                       wanted to select
      String connString;         // the connection string
      HtmlPage hp;               // Defines the HTML page - by can't be used
                                    here
      String buffer = "";        // Defines the buffer that will be send back
                                    via package variable
      try {
         // register the jdbc driver
         DriverManager.registerDriver(new oracle.jdbc.driver.OracleDriver());

         /* Get connection with thin driver — this is explicit. The java
            cartridge does not have a "default connection" to the database,
            so you must connect on your own — remember that this program is
            running on the app server, not the database server.
         */

         Connection conn = null;
         connString = new String("jdbc:oracle:thin:examples/
            examples@tuscl:1521:ORC1");
         conn = DriverManager.getConnection(connString);

         PreparedStatement pstmt = conn.prepareStatement(sql);
         ResultSet rset = pstmt.executeQuery();
```

(continues)

Appendix 17.2 Using the Java Cartridge (continued)

```
      // This builds the HTML page
      hp = new HtmlPage("Java Example using Java Cartridge");
      hp.getBody().addItem("<H1>Java Example using Java Cartridge</H1>");
      hp.printHeader();      // Prints the content-type tag

      // Returns the meta data (column names and info)
      ResultSetMetaData meta = rset.getMetaData();

      // Retrieves the number of columns returned
      int cols = meta.getColumnCount(), rows = 0;
      DynamicTable tab = new DynamicTable(cols);
      TableRow row[] = new TableRow[100];

      // Loop through and print the column names
      row[0] = new TableRow();
      for (int i = 1; i <= cols; i++) {
        int size = meta.getPrecision(i);
        String label = meta.getColumnLabel(i);
        if (label.length() > size) size = label.length();
        while (label.length() < size) label += " ";
        row[0].addCell(new TableHeaderCell(label));
      }
      tab.addRow(row[0]);

      // Now read through the rows
      while (rset.next()) {
        rows++;
        row[rows] = new TableRow();
        for (int i = 1; i <= cols; i++) {
          int size = meta.getPrecision(i);
          String label = meta.getColumnLabel(i);
          String value = rset.getString(i);
          if (value == null) value = " ";// For null values
          if (label.length() > size) size = label.length();
          while (value.length() < size) value += " ";
          row[rows].addCell(new TableDataCell(value));
        }
        tab.addRow(row[rows]);
      }
      hp.addItem(tab);

      // If we didn't process any data, then say so...
      if (rows == 0) buffer = "No data found!\n";

      // Close up the record set
      rset.close();
      pstmt.close();

      hp.print();

    } catch (SQLException e) {System.err.println(e.getMessage());}
  }
}
```

Chapter 18

Building a Java Applet for Monitoring Oracle

Serg Shestakov

One successful example of Java and Oracle integration is the monitoring applet. It is relatively easy to implement and can be very useful for monitoring production systems. This chapter considers all the steps to take in building and running this simple monitoring tool. The first part of the chapter covers the data schema definition, the applet's core structure, and methods, while the second part discusses how the applet displays runtime statistics. All scripts mentioned in this chapter and the code for the applet is available for downloading from *Oracle Internal's* Code Depot at www.auerbach-publications.com/scripts/monitor.html.

The primary goal of this applet is to demonstrate how to write effective code for Oracle database access using a thin JDBC connection. Assume the following server environment: JDK 1.1, Oracle Thin JDBC Driver 7.3.4, SPARC Solaris 2.6, Oracle RDBMS Server 7.3.4, SQL*Net Listener 2.3, SQL*Plus 3.3. The client machine should have a browser that supports JDK 1.1 — Netscape Navigator 4.x/Internet Explorer 4.x or higher. Having a sound card and dynamics on the client machine for playing sound alarms is optional but strongly recommended when monitoring systems are discussed.

Data Schema Definition

Before implementing the Java applet, it is necessary to define the data schema for network monitoring. Suppose we have several network modules. Each has its own name and unique number. Store this information in the MODULE table, which you create using the following SQL statement:

0-8493-1139-X/02/$0.00+$1.50
©2002 by CRC Press LLC

```
CREATE TABLE MODULE
   (MODULE_ID NUMBER (5),
   MODULE_NAME VARCHAR2 (20));
```

Next, define the data structure for storing the module's statistics. You want to store the following information: (1) statistics gathering time, (2) module ID, and (3) module status: whether module is up (status 1) or down (status –1). The corresponding SQL statement is:

```
CREATE TABLE STAT
   (STAT_TIME DATE,
   MODULE_ID NUMBER (5),
   MODULE_STATUS NUMBER (1));
```

Finally, add primary and foreign keys to your schema to guarantee data integrity. For the MODULE table, create a primary key on MODULE_ID field. And for the STAT table, create a foreign key on MODULE_ID field referencing parent table MODULE. Note that foreign keys are added with the ON DELETE CASCADE option so that when we delete a row from the MODULE table, this constraint will automatically refine rows with this module's statistics from the STAT table. To speed up data manipulation operations, index some fields in the data schema. Index the MODULE_ID field of the STAT table to speed up joins with the MODULE table, the STAT_TIME field of one STAT table to speed up manipulations with history data, and one MODULE_NAME field of the MODULE table to speed up name sorting operations.

```
ALTER TABLE MODULE ADD PRIMARY KEY (MODULE_ID);
ALTER TABLE STAT ADD FOREIGN KEY (MODULE_ID)
   REFERENCES MODULE ON DELETE CASCADE;
CREATE INDEX IND_STAT_MODULE_ID
   ON STAT (MODULE_ID);
CREATE INDEX IND_MODULE_NAME
   ON MODULE (MODULE_NAME);
CREATE INDEX IND_STAT_TIME
   ON STAT (STAT_TIME);
```

To demonstrate how to call stored procedures from the applet, define a simple PL/SQL stored procedure calculating network availability given a starting time. The CALC_AVAILABILITY procedure has one IN and one OUT parameter. It takes the starting date in string format (MON DD YYYY) as its first parameter and converts the string to date. Next, it sums all statistic records indicating that the module was running and then divides it by a number of all statistic records since a given time. Finally, it returns the resulting value as a second parameter. This stored procedure is as follows:

```
CREATE OR REPLACE PROCEDURE CALC_AVAILABILITY
     (STR_START IN CHAR, AVAIL OUT REAL) IS

   START_DATE DATE;
   SUM_UP NUMBER;
   SUM_DOWN NUMBER;
```

```
BEGIN
  START_DATE := TO_DATE(STR_START, 'MON DD YYYY');
  SELECT COUNT(*)
    INTO SUM_UP FROM STAT
    WHERE STAT_TIME>=START_DATE AND MODULE_
    STATUS=1;

  SELECT COUNT(*)
    INTO SUM_DOWN FROM STAT
    WHERE STAT_TIME>=START_DATE AND MODULE_
    STATUS=-1;
  IF (SUM_UP+SUM_DOWN = 0) THEN
    AVAIL := -1;
  ELSE
    AVAIL := ROUND(SUM_UP*100/(SUM_UP+SUM_
    DOWN),2);
  END IF;
END;
```

Now we have the data schema for storing statistics. The Java applet will access this schema and get all the necessary data. But how can we implement the statistics collection procedure? Usually, network control systems have some command or macros that produce a plaintext file where the module states are listed. To simplify the applet's logic, we assume that each batch load of statistics is performed with the fixed STAT_TIME value. The Oracle SQL*Loader utility is a perfect tool for appending new statistics to the STAT table. The best way to implement the statistics gathering utility on UNIX systems is to write a shell that produces a plaintext file with module states and runs Oracle SQL*Loader to append new statistics to database. This script can be scheduled for automatic execution as a cron job.

Another important procedure to implement is the collection refinement. We can set the history limit to, say, 30 days and periodically delete old statistics from the STAT table. An Exemplar Bourne shell script stat_ref.sh doing this job is available from www.auerbach-publications.com/scripts/monitor.html. The first section of this script defines the Oracle environment variables, and the second section runs the SQL*Plus utility with a predefined connect string. Do not forget to restrict access to this script using the chmod 700 stat_ref.sh command.

Note that statistics refinement should be scheduled for batch execution each day to avoid excessive growth of the STAT table. On UNIX systems, this can be done with the cron utility. To schedule the above-mentioned script for daily execution at 23:30, run crontab -e command and add the following line:

```
30 23 * * * stat_ref.sh
```

Applet's Core Structure

Now we will discuss how to implement the Java applet for network monitoring. A Java applet is a program in Java language designed for a Web browser. Remember that the primary goal of this applet is to demonstrate how to work effectively with Oracle data using a thin JDBC connection.

Using any text editor, we write the netmon.java file containing the program code. In the very beginning of our applet, we should put import statements for all the Java classes we want to use. First we will need the basic class java.applet.Applet to run a Java program in a browser. Next we will use classes included in the java.sql package to get access to data stored in Oracle database. And, of course, we will need graphical user interface components provided in java.awt.Color and java.awt.Graphics classes.

```
import java.applet.Applet;
import java.sql.*;
import java.awt.Color;
import java.awt.Graphics;
```

Because we are writing an applet for monitoring purposes, it should run nonstop. The following section of code defines our netmon class as a subclass of an applet designed to run in a Java-enabled browser. We use a runnable interface to provide our applet with run method instead of subclassing the thread because we already subclassed another one (that's applet). We compose class of eight code sections. In the first code section, we declare class variables. In the next three code sections, we define the applet life cycle overwriting the default methods of the applet class — start, run, and stop, respectively. In Section 5, we define the application logic of the runQuery method. This method is responsible for database access using the Oracle thin JDBC driver. Next come three code sections responsible for representing Oracle data. These are the addItem method, which fetches data we want to display; the paint method, which overwrites the standard method of awt.Graphics class; and the myplay method, which plays sound files. Note that sound-playing functionality makes our applet really useful for monitoring tasks.

```
public class netmon extends Applet implements Runnable
{
   <Section #1. variables declaration>
   <Section #2. start method>
   <Section #3. run method>
   <Section #4. stop method>
   <Section #5. runQuery method>
   <Section #6. addItem method>
   <Section #7. paint method>
   <Section #8. myplay method>
}
```

Variables Declaration: Section 1

First we will discuss section one, which declares the most important applet variables. It is good practice to run JDBC code in a separate thread. For this purpose, we declare the netmonThread variable. Because we will run the thread continuously and it is no use to refresh the same monitoring statistics from the Oracle database, we set a sleep interval for the applet — the timeout variable.

```
Thread myThread;
int timeout=5000;
```

Now it is time to define variables for the Oracle thin JDBC driver. This driver connects directly to Oracle using Java sockets. It can be downloaded to the browser and supplies the applet with methods to access Oracle data. With this driver, we can run SQL statements (both DDL and DML), call PL/SQL procedures, and do many other things. The connect_string is composed of the driver description, Oracle username/password, server name, port number for SQL*Net Listener, and Oracle SID name. For security reasons, it is better to keep Java source files in a separate directory protected from Web access. The driver_class variable will store the JDBC driver name. It will be used later to load this driver into the browser. The conn variable will be used as a connection to Oracle. Note that we want to optimize resources allocation, so we will issue all SQL statements with a single connection to Oracle.

```
String connect_string = "jdbc:oracle:thin:user/
  password@myhost:1521:ORCL";
String driver_class = "oracle.jdbc.driver.OracleDriver";
Connection conn = null;
```

Moreover, because our applet will run continuously and periodically refresh data, all SQL statements will run many times. The Oracle thin JDBC driver, like any other JDBC driver, has a PreparedStatement object, which is convenient for repetitive execution because it precompiles an SQL statement. To speed up access to the database, we must first define SQL queries and declare variables for corresponding precompiled statements. Another important reason to use PreparedStatement is its support for input parameters. These are represented with question mark placeholders. For the network monitoring, we will need to select queries for the following information: the last time statistics were gathered into the database (get_max_time), time of previous statistics gathering (get_prev_time), list of module names and its IDs (get_module_data), current module status and its previous status (get_status and get_old_status, respectively). Note that we convert data type fields to strings in SQL statements explicitly using the PL/SQL TO_CHAR function. This helps to work around some of the complexity associated with the date type in Java. For example, the lack of a Date.compareTo method (it appears only in JDK 1.2.), which is necessary to work with both the java.sql.Date and the java.sql.Time types because the first stores only day, month, and year, and the second stores only hours, minutes, and seconds. (When we do monitoring, we have to take into account days as well as seconds.) Of course, we can use the java.sql.Timestamp type, which has both date and time fields but also has a nanoseconds field, which we do not need at all; so for our purposes, it is less efficient. We prefer to work with the java.sql.String object rather than the java.sql.Date object and to do all format conversions in the Oracle database using the TO_CHAR and TO_DATE functions.

```
String get_max_time="SELECT TO_CHAR(MAX(STAT_
   TIME),'MON DD YYYY HH24:MI:SS') FROM STAT";
String get_prev_time="SELECT TO_CHAR(MAX(STAT_
   TIME),'MON DD YYYY HH24:MI:SS') FROM STAT WHERE STAT_TIME <
   TO_DATE(?,'MON DD YYYY HH24:MI:SS')";
String get_module_data = "SELECT MODULE_ID, MODULE_NAME FROM MODULE ORDER
   BY MODULE_
   NAME";
String get_status = "SELECT MODULE_STATUS FROM STAT WHERE STAT_TIME =
   TO_DATE(?,'MON DD YYYY HH24:MI:SS') AND MODULE_ID=?";
String get_old_status = "SELECT MODULE_STATUS FROM STAT WHERE STAT_TIME
   = TO_DATE(?,'MON DD YYYY HH24:MI:SS') AND MODULE_ID=?";
```

For each of these queries, we define a variable of the PreparedStatement type. Note that in the declaration section, we cannot precompile the statements at once — it should be done when we have an established connection to the Oracle database.

```
PreparedStatement stmt_max_time;
PreparedStatement stmt_prev_time;
PreparedStatement stmt_module_data;
PreparedStatement stmt_status;
PreparedStatement stmt_old_status;
```

To call our stored procedure calculating average network availability, we define the get_avg_avail call and declare a CallableStatement object to precompile the call upon establishing the connection to Oracle. Input and output parameters of our stored procedure are denoted with question mark placeholders. Later we will see how to pass bind variable from the applet to the stored procedure and read the results.

```
String get_avg_avail="{call CALC_AVAILABILITY
   (?, ?)} ";
CallableStatement stmt_avg_avail;
```

Now we declare three time-related variables. First we declare the max_time variable to store the result returned by get_max_time query. Next we need the last_time to save the results returned by get_prev_time query. To simplify the applet logic, we will need one more variable — the last_time. It keeps the last time of statistics gathering when the applet sleeps.

```
String max_time;
String prev_time;
String last_time;
```

It is interesting not only to read from the database and display the current status of each network module, but also to track how the module status changed since the previous statistics gathering. So when the applet reads statistics from Oracle, it reads for each network module's two values: current status and previous status. Having these two values helps the applet track module status changes. Current status can be either up or down. Previous status can also be either up or down. Thus, there are four possible situations:

(1) module status will change from up to down, (2) module will go from down to up, (3) module will stay up, or (4) module will stay down. For clarity of reading, we will define four codes that indicate module status change: down_to_up, up_to_down, up_to_up, and down_to_down, respectively. Also, our applet will use one more constant, none, to indicate the situation when the module status was not read from the database.

```
int down_to_up=2;
int up_to_down=3;
int up_to_up=1;
int down_to_down=4;
int none=0;
```

When we read the network module name and status from the Oracle database, we want to display this information in the browser's window. Our applet will fetch module names and additional messages (headers, footers, error codes) from the str_buffer array and information on module status changes from the stat_buffer array. To fetch data, the applet needs to know the current row number for both arrays. We will keep this row number in the cur_row variable.

```
String [] str_buffer;
int [] stat_buffer;
int cur_row;
```

Life Cycle — Start, Run, and Stop Methods: Sections 2–4

Now we discuss the three sections defining the core of our applet: its life cycle. This life cycle is defined by start, run, and stop methods. Section 2 defines the start method. This method is called whenever the applet receives control from a browser, that is, when the user visits or revisits the URL with the HTML document pointing to the applet. Later we will discuss how to write an HTML document calling our applet. The start method is responsible for creating and starting the applet's thread, the netmonThread. Before we create and start the thread, we want to play a sound indicating that the network monitoring applet is starting. We do this by calling the myplay method; this is a custom method for playing sounds, which is defined in Section 8. All that we need to know about this method now is that it takes the file name as a first parameter and the delay in milliseconds as a second parameter. Files are expected to be in .au format (the only audio format supported by JDK 1.1) and should be placed in the same directory with the netmon.class file. In our example, we play a computer.au file, which can be found on Solaris 2.6 systems under the /usr/demo/SOUND/sounds/ directory and copied to .class file location. Note that sound-playing functionality is important for monitoring the applet and playing a sound when the applet starts can help the operator make sure that dynamics are turned on and adjust the sound volume.

```
public void start()
   {
      if(netmonThread==null)
      {
         myplay("computer.au",3000);
         netmonThread=new Thread(this);
         netmonThread.start();
      }
}
```

When we start the thread, the applet executes its run method, the only method of Runnable interface. We define the run method in Section 3 of our applet as follows: initialize two arrays used for storing module names and text messages to display and the changes of module status, the str_buffer and the stat_buffer, respectively. Next, some initial values to the time-related variables (max_time, prev_time, and last_time) with some initial values in the format corresponding to Oracle's "DD MON YYYY HH24:MI:SS". Remember that we work with string representations of dates. Then the run method initializes this Thread variable, pointing to the current thread, and starts a loop. Within this loop the applet sequentially does three operations. First, it calls the runQuery method, which connects to Oracle database and fetches statistics on network monitoring. Second, it suspends the thread, freeing the processor for the timeout number of milliseconds using the sleep method. Third, it refreshes the picture in the browser's windows by calling the repaint method. The applet will exit this loop (and leave the run method) when the current thread is not equal to the thisThread. This will be true if the user leaves the page with applet. This will call the stop method, which will set the netmonThread to null. Note that if the user leaves the page and quickly returns to it, the start method will initiate a different thread, the exit condition becomes true, and the current loop will exit anyway. Because the run method calls sleep, we need to catch the InterruptedException.

```
public void run()
   {
      str_buffer = new String [80];
      stat_buffer = new int [80];
      max_time ="OCT 01 1990 00:00:00";
      prev_time="OCT 01 1990 00:00:00";
      last_time="OCT 01 1990 01:01:01";

      Thread thisThread=Thread.currentThread();
      while (thisThread == netmonThread)
      {
         try
         {
            runQuery();
            Thread.currentThread().sleep(time out);
            repaint();
         }
         catch(InterruptedException e) {}
      }
   }
```

Take a closer look at the stop method. It is defined in Section 4 of our applet. This method receives control when the user leaves the applet's page. By that time, we may have an established connection to the Oracle database and may have one or more of our statements opened. If we simply set the thread to null, the Java garbage collector will automatically free all opened JDBC resources. But we want to optimize our applet, so we explicitly free all the JDBC resources calling the appropriate close methods. For our convenience, we set the conn variable to null. (We want to be sure the applet will know it has to reopen the connection when the user revisits the applet's page.) Then we tell the thread to stop, and we set the netmonThread variable to null. Because we work with methods of the java.sql package, we need to catch the corresponding exception — that is, the SQLException. Note that we do nothing in the exception handling block, but we may want to display the error message to diagnostic output (using System.out.println method) for debugging purposes. To print the error message as it is, we can simply call the System.out.println(e). Listed below is the code implementing the stop method:

```
        public void stop()
  {
    try
    {
      if(netmonThread!=null)
      {
        stmt_max_time.close();
        stmt_prev_time.close();
        stmt_avg_avail.close();
        stmt_module_data.close();
        stmt_status.close();
        stmt_old_status.close();
        conn.close();
        conn=null;
        netmonThread.stop();
        netmonThread=null;
      }
    }
    catch (SQLException e) {}
  }
```

Working with Oracle

The runQuery method does all the work with Oracle: it establishes a connection to the database, fetches statistics, and tracks changes in network modules status. This method is defined in Section 5. Look at the code. First we put the try token, indicating we intend to catch Java exceptions. The runQuery method has a rather complex logic; so to simplify the code, we catch all Java exceptions.

```
public void runQuery ()
  {
    try
    {
```

Next, the applet checks whether it needs to open a connection to the Oracle database. If the conn variable is null, then the connection was either closed by the stop method or it was never established at all. In both cases we need to open a new connection. This is done with basic service for managing JDBC drivers, the DriverManager. First we register the Oracle thin JDBC driver using the registerDriver method. Then try to connect to Oracle using the getConnection method. Note that in Java terminology the connect string indicating the precise location of the database, username, and password is called a database URL. Remember that we defined the Oracle database URL in the connect_string variable (Section 1). The JDBC management layer tries to locate a registered driver, which can connect to a given URL. If the DriverManager fails to open a new connection, it raises an exception. To implement this logic, we write the following lines:

```
if (conn == null)
{

DriverManager.registerDriver (new oracle.jdbc.driver.OracleDriver ());
conn = DriverManager.getConnection (connect_string);
```

We can use one more method of the DriverManager service to print the JDBC trace information. To direct the trace messages to diagnostic (standard) output, we call the setLogStream method as follows:

```
DriverManager.setLogStream(java.lang.System.out);
```

If we successfully establish the connection, it will be useful to precompile all our statements. It will speed up requests processing when we enter the loop next time. We precompile select queries with the prepareStatement method and precompile call queries with the prepareCall method; both are from the Connection class. Recompilation is done on the server side. These methods are especially useful for precompiling parameterized SQL statements. When we have all the statements precompiled, we close the if block.

```
    stmt_max_time = conn.prepareStatement (get_max_time);
    stmt_prev_time = conn.prepareStatement (get_prev_time);
    stmt_module_data = conn.prepareStatement (get_module_data);
    stmt_status = conn.prepareStatement (get_status);
    stmt_old_status = conn.prepareStatement (get_old_status);
    stmt_avg_avail = conn.prepareCall (get_avg_avail);
}
```

The monitoring applet reads periodically from the Oracle database the time when the latest refresh of statistics happened. Now it is the first time when we run a query, so let us discuss this mechanism in detail. To run a select query against the Oracle database, we create a ResultSet object by calling the executeQuery method of a PreparedStatement object (in our case, the statement is precompiled so we don't need to pass a string to executeQuery). The ResultSet object has several methods to access columns of different types. These get* methods (getString, getFloat, etc.) work with the current row. The ResultSet object also has a method for moving between the rows: the next method. When this method succeeds in moving to the next row, it returns true. We can scroll the result set using the while (next( )) loop. Because the get_max_time query will return exactly one row, we put inside the while block only one statement storing value returned by our query to the max_time variable. To extract this value, we use the getString method, passing to it a column index. We can also specify columns by name, but indexes are preferred because that method is more efficient.

```
ResultSet rset = stmt_max_time.executeQuery();
while (rset.next())
  max_time=rset.getString(1);
```

When the max_time value is read, the applet needs to decide whether it should read the statistics or just redraw the picture showing the network status in the browser's window. We keep the last time when the applet scanned the statistics in last_time variable. The applet compares max_time variable with last_time; and if they are different, it prepares to read new statistics from the database. First it overwrites the last_time with the new value, the max_time. Next, it sets the rows counter to nil, indicating we have not yet processed any network modules.

```
if (!last_time.equals(max_time))
  {
    last_time=max_time;
    cur_row=0;
```

The applet needs to know when the previous statistics gathering happened. The select query returning this value was precompiled in the stmt_prev_time statement. But this is a parameterized SQL statement, so we have to pass it to a parameter, the max_time. This can be done with the setString method of the PreparedStatement object. It takes two parameters: the index of a column and value to bind. We execute a precompiled select query, create the result set, navigate through it, and read the query results into the prev_time variable exactly as we did for the max_time.

```
stmt_prev_time.setString(1,max_time);
rset = stmt_prev_time.executeQuery();
while (rset.next())
  prev_time=rset.getString(1);
```

Now we will discuss how the applet can pass parameters to a stored procedure, make a call, and read the results. Remember that our exemplary PL/SQL procedure, the CALC_AVAILABILITY, has one IN mode parameter and one OUT mode parameter. It takes a string representation of a date in "MON DD YYYY" format, calculates, and returns the average network availability since that time. The returned value is numeric and has REAL type. Note that there is a mapping between SQL data types and Java data types. According to this mapping, Oracle's REAL type corresponds to the float type of Java language. To store the resulting network availability, we need to declare a variable of float type, the avg_avail.

To define input and output parameters for our call, we will use two methods of the CallableStatement object. The first one, the setString, does exactly this — it binds the IN parameter to the substring extracted from the max_time variable. To get the string representation of a current date, we cut off hours, minutes, and seconds and leave only month, day, and year. According to the passed IN parameter, our stored procedure will return average availability for today, since there are 0 hours and 00 minutes. This indicator is very sensitive, and it changes noticeably when even a minor part of our network goes up or down. The second method of CallableStatement object, the registerOutParameter, defines another parameter as a number of REAL type. To call the stored procedure, we use the executeUpdate method of CallableStatement. This method is a more general case of working with the database as compared with the runQuery because it can be used for any kind of modification statement. When the call is executed, we retrieve results using the getFloat method. (Remember, the REAL type in Oracle corresponds to the float type in Java.) To this method we pass the index of question mark placeholder corresponding to the output parameter of our stored procedure (i.e., 2).

```
float avg_avail;
stmt_avg_avail.setString (1, max_time.substring(0,11));
stmt_avg_avail.registerOutParameter (2, java.sql.Types.REAL);
stmt_avg_avail.executeUpdate();
avg_avail= stmt_avg_avail.getFloat(2);
```

Indicators such as the average availability are useful for monitoring applications because operators quickly get tired of the monotonous job and need rather general metrics indicating the overall picture of a network. But indicators are tricky. When we define such indicators, we should be careful because it is known that it is difficult for an operator to analyze even seven to ten indicators, and it could cause information overload and slow down the reaction. In certain situations, an operator can ignore even significant deviations from the norm. Moreover, in stress situations, a large number of indicators (ten or more) could lead to wrong decisions and actions. We also have to take into account stress situations when we design a monitoring system. On average, three to five carefully chosen indicators can be enough for high-quality monitoring. If necessary, other metrics should be placed on secondary monitoring screens and used for in-depth analysis.

Now we have detected that the statistics on the server were refreshed and we want to read these statistics and renew them in the browser's window. First we take care of the header, representing new refresh time and new network availability indicator — both values were already retrieved from the Oracle database. We compose and fetch the messages to the str_buffer and stat_buffer arrays, calling the addItem method. Later information from both arrays will be interpreted and displayed with the applet's paint method. Caching all messages to arrays is a good way to the lower system resources required by the applet to repaint the monitoring information when it wakes up from sleep. The addItem method we will explain later; all we need to know now is that it takes two parameters: status change and message text.

We pass the none status change indicator because it is just a header we want to display.

```
addItem(none,"Refresh:      " +last_time);
addItem(none,"----------------------------");
addItem(none,"Today's availability: " +avg_avail+"%");
addItem(none,"----------------------------");
```

Practice shows that we can bring more useful information to operators if we track not only average availability, but also how it changes over time, and use colors to indicate positive and negative changes. But here we want to concentrate on the mechanism of interaction with Oracle rather than on the applet's functionality enhancements.

Before we start scrolling the record set, we declare the total_records counter and set it to nil. The applet increments this counter with every processing of the next network module (i.e., tracing its status change). Note that the total_records counter is different from the cur_row counter because the first one counts rows in the record set with network modules from the MODULE table and the second one points to the current index in arrays and is used for fetching network module names, states, and additional messages such as the average network availability. We run the select query and scroll the resulting record set like we did before: we call the executeQuery method of the precompiled select query, returning two columns with module IDs and module names, respectively. We navigate between rows using the next method of the RecordSet object. To read the columns, we call the getInt method for the first column (MODULE_ID) and the getString method for the second column (MODULE_NAME), passing to it the column indexes instead of names for better efficiency. The corresponding code is shown below.

```
int total_records = 0;
rset = stmt_module_data.executeQuery();
while (rset.next())
   {
   total_records = total_records + 1;
   int MODULE_ID = rset.getInt(1);
   String MODULE_NAME = rset.getString(2);
```

Now we have the module name to display. But we want to know its current status. There is a precompiled statement, stmt_status, with select query returning current status given time and unique module ID. The module name column can also be declared as unique, but working with numbers is more efficient. We reserve a MODULE_STATUS variable to keep the current network module status and initialize it with nil (remember that we negotiated to code up-and-running module status with 1 and down status with –1). If the MODULE_STATUS will still keep the nil value after the reading attempt, we can be sure that statistics for this particular module at a given time are not available for some reason. We pass the numeric parameter to statement exactly as we did before for select queries, using the setString method to pass the first parameter, max_time and setInt method to pass the second parameter, that is

MODULE_ID. As usual, we prefer column indexes to column names. We call the executeQuery method to execute a prepared statement, but now we have to place the result set into a new ResultSet object, the rset2, to avoid overwriting the results of get_module_data query. We still need to scroll through the rest rows of its rset. As usual, we move through the result set rows with the next method and retrieve the column value of numeric type with the getInt method.

```
int MODULE_STATUS = 0;
stmt_status.setString(1,max_time);
stmt_status.setInt(2,MODULE_ID);
ResultSet rset2 = stmt_status.executeQuery();
while (rset2.next())
  MODULE_STATUS = rset2.getInt(1);
```

To track changes in the network module status, the applet needs to know the previous status of each module. To keep this status, we declare and initialize with nil value the OLD_MODULE_STATUS variable. To retrieve the old status from the Oracle database, we use the precompiled stmt_old_status statement. We will pass to it two parameters: time of previous statistics gathering and MODULE_ID. Like the previous query, this one should be run with methods of RecordSet object — executeQuery, next, and getInt. Note that we can reuse the previously declared record set, rset, because we will not need the previous result set and it will be recreated when we reenter the loop.

```
int OLD_MODULE_STATUS =0;
stmt_old_status.setString(1,prev_time);
stmt_old_status.setInt(2,MODULE_ID);
rset2 = stmt_old_status.executeQuery();
while (rset2.next())
  OLD_MODULE_STATUS = rset2.getInt(1);
```

Now the applet already has information on both the previous and current status of the network module, so it can track the status changes. The difficulty is handling situations with an undefined status — when for some reason the applet receives no information on current and, often also, previous status of some network module. We will detect the status change code and store it to the status_change variable. Before we start determining what status change actually took place, we assign a none value to the status_change. Next we assume that if the previous status was down (–1) and the current status is unknown to applet (0) or also is down, the network module has no status change and we assign the down_to_down code to the status_change variable. When the old status was up (1) and it changed to down, we assigned the up_to_down code to the status_change. And when it was up (1) and it changed to down, we set the status_change to the down_to_up code. Finally, we assume that if the previous status was up, the new status of network module is unknown to the applet or also up. The network module keeps running, and we set status_change to up_to_up. The lines below define if statements doing this tiresome but important job:

```
int status_change=none;
if (MODULE_STATUS==-1 && OLD_MODULE_STATUS<=0)status_change=down_to_down;
```

```
if (MODULE_STATUS==-1 && OLD_MODULE_STATUS==1)status_change=up_to_down;
if (MODULE_STATUS==1 && OLD_MODULE_STATUS==-1)status_change=down_to_up;
if (MODULE_STATUS==1 && OLD_MODULE_STATUS>=0)status_change=up_to_up;
```

We considered all possible situations, and status_change now keeps the result of consideration. The most important situation to track is the one when the status changes from up to down. This means the module is not in service anymore, and we want to deliver the alarm to the operator. This demo applet will play the alarm sound — the crash.au file from the /usr/demo/SOUND/sounds/ directory (for Solaris 2.6 systems). We call the myplay method of this applet and pass to it two parameters: the sound file name and delay in milliseconds. The latter is required to pause the applet a little and helps to avoid conflicts with playing sounds when several modules change state.

```
if (status_change==up_to_down)
  myplay("crash.au",1700);
```

For real-world applications, it is useful to record sounds for each module and thus make sound alarms more informative for operators. We can play these sound files like this:

```
myplay(MODULE_NAME+".au",3100)
```

If modules have unique numbers (e.g., IP addresses), we can record sound files for numbers (1.au, 2.au, etc.) and easily synthesize a sound alarm as its sequence. These sound alarms help operators detect the problem module early without even having to look at the monitoring screen. Equipped with a simple speech-synthesizing mechanism, our applet turns into a useful agent, helping operators monitor complex networks of many nodes.

Another situation when we may want to play a sound is when a network module status changes from down to up. It is good news for operators, so we choose an appropriate sound file. (In our example, that is the spacemusic.au file, which can be found under the /usr/demo/SOUND/sounds/ in Solaris 2.6 systems.) And, in any situation where we want to display a list of network modules, using now the applet's addItem method we fetch the status change code and module name to the corresponding arrays for displaying information. We put several white spaces before the module name because we want to reserve a place for color marks indicating current module status. When we have fetched the data, we can close the scanning loop for a list of modules retrieved with the get_module_data statement.

```
   if (status_change==down_to_up)
     myplay("spacemusic.au",5000);
   addItem(status_change, "  "+MODULE_NAME);
}
```

There can possibly be a situation when we exit a loop and still have no rows encountered (i.e., total_records still keeps a nil value). This situation is alarming because we have no statistics, although we should have. So the applet plays an alarm to draw an operator's attention. Next we fetch the footer to the messages array and close the if block that we entered when we wanted to retrieve fresh statistics from the database.

```
        if (total_records==0)
          myplay("crash.au",1700);
        addItem(none,"-------------------------");
    }
```

In real-world monitoring processes, there may be other possible pitfalls that we should detect and take into account if we want to design a good monitoring tool. In a way, we have to monitor the monitoring system. This may lower the risks associated with those unforeseen blind spots in a state transition diagram of monitoring software. The more constraints we have in our system, the fewer risks we will have.

Now we should close our try block opened at the very beginning of the runQuery method. If we have an exception raised, it is important to reset the cur_row counter to nil, indicating that the information we had to display is obsolete (because of the exception), and set the current connection to null to try to reconnect when the applet awakes next time. As already mentioned, one important thing to do is to report problems not to blind diagnostic output, but to the browser's window. The runQuery method works with the Oracle database, so most common exceptions are ORA — messages that may indicate a situation when access to the Oracle database was denied because of the wrong username/password, a situation when the applet's session was killed, a situation when database shutdown/start-up was in progress, etc. We want to bring this information to the operators, so we retrieve the Java exception message with the getMessage method of the Exception object and fetch this message to the display array using applet's addItem method.

```
        }
        catch (Exception e) {
          cur_row=0;
          conn=null;
          addItem(none, "------- Error encountered.
          See message:");
          addItem(none, e.getMessage ());
        }
    }
```

Presenting the Results

To display the results, we create a custom addItem method for caching display information to the applets' arrays and redefine the default paint method of applet class. Section 6 listed below describes the addItem method used for fetching information we want to display in the browser's window with the paint method. The addItem method is called with two parameters — status change code for network module, the StatusChange, and message text, the newString. The status change code is fetched to the stat_buffer array, and the message text is fetched to the str_buffer array. We interpret the cur_row variable as an index for both arrays. When we are done fetching, we increment the index. Then we call the applet's default repaint method, which refreshes the picture, adding next the information string which can be one of the following: header, module name with status change indicator, footer, or error message.

```
void addItem(int newStatusChange, String newString)
{
   stat_buffer[cur_row]=newStatusChange;
   str_buffer[cur_row]=newString;
   cur_row++;
   repaint();
}
```

The paint method is described in Section 7. It takes one input parameter, the default Graphics object of java.awt package. Remember that we imported the Graphics class in the very beginning of our applet. We start the paint method with initializing pointers to the current row and column in the applet's window. Its values are given in pixels. Next we define a loop for all rows fetched to the applet's display arrays (str_buffer and stat_buffer) according to the cur_row index. Each time we enter the loop, we increment the cur_y pointer by 15, moving it to the next row. Next we store the message text to the tmpstr variable and the status change code to the stat variable.

```
public void paint(Graphics g)
{
   int cur_y=15;
   int cur_x=15;
   for (int m=0;m<cur_row;m++)
      {
      cur_y=cur_y+15;
      String tmpstr = str_buffer[m];
      int stat=stat_buffer[m];
```

If the status change code is different from none, the applet has some painting to do. Before we draw an alarm, we have to choose the color. This can be done with the setColor method of the Graphics object. It takes one input parameter indicating the color we want to set. This is a foreground color, so later we will have to return the default black color for messages printing. If the status change code indicates that the current state is down, we choose red. If the status change code indicates that the current state is up, we choose green.

```
if(stat!=none)
{
   if(stat==up_to_down || stat==down_to_down )
      g.setColor(Color.red);
   if(stat==down_to_up || stat==up_to_up)
      g.setColor(Color.green);
```

Now we have the color and want to draw a mark indicating status change. There are two situations: when the status does not change because of old refresh (up_to_up and down_to_down codes correspond to this state) and when the status changes to the opposite (up_to_down and down_to_up codes correspond to this state). In the first case, we want to draw just a small filled rectangle against each module name. (That is why we earlier left some space before the module name.) In the second case, we paint the entire line with the alarm color. In both cases, we do painting by calling the fillRect method of the Graphics object. Rectangle coordinates can be adjusted to fit a particular user's needs. What is more, for each network module, we can collect statistics on module availability, display this indicator, and put a color mark indicating whether today's module availability decreases or grows. For example, this may help operators find out quickly what modules are now OK but nonetheless have had some problems.

```
if(stat==up_to_up || stat==down_to_down)
  g.fillRect(cur_x,cur_y-9,12,10);
if(stat==up_to_down || stat==down_to_up)
  g.fillRect(cur_x,cur_y-9,150,10);
```

When we are done drawing color alarms, we should return the foreground color to the default (black). Next we can close if the block opened to process situations with status change code is different from none. Then we print the message to the browser's window, calling the drawString method of the Graphics object and passing to it three parameters: message text, current row, and current column.

```
      g.setColor(Color.black);
      }
    g.drawString(tmpstr, cur_x, cur_y);
    }
}
```

The last piece of code is Section 8 defining the myplay method, which in fact is a handy wrapper to Java's play method for playing sound files in .au format. (This is true for JDK 1.1; in later versions, more audio formats are supported.) The myplay method takes two input parameters — audio file name and delay in milliseconds. First we read from the current directory and play the sound file using the standard play method. (To read the current directory name, we call the getCodeBase method.) Then we suspend the applet's thread according to the delay parameter. This (1) helps to avoid conflicts when we have to play several sound alarms in a row and (2) improves the quality of sound alarms, making it clearer to understand. To suspend the current thread, we call the sleep method, which requires the InterruptedException to be caught, so we put the method code inside the try block.

```
void myplay (String aufile, long pausetime)
{
  try
  {
    play(getCodeBase(), aufile);
    Thread.currentThread().sleep(pause time);
  }
  catch(InterruptedException e) {}
}
```

Compiling and Running the Applet

At last we come to the point where we can put together all the code segments into the netmon.java file and use the javac netmon.java command to create a file of bytecodes. The resulting file will have the .class extension. Next we should copy the netmon.class file to a directory accessible by an HTTP daemon. To the same directory we can copy .au files if we intend to use the sound alarms mechanism. Remember that, for security reasons, we should keep Java sources in a separate directory with restricted permissions (not viewable on the Web).

To put the Java applet into the browser we write the netmon.html file. We create this file using any text editor. The netmon.html file defines window title and contains a special applet tag that tells the browser where to get .class file and the frame's height and width (in pixels):

```
<html>
<title> Network monitoring applet</title>
<body>
<applet code=netmon.class width=500 height=500>
</body>
</html>
```

To try our new applet, we need a statistics-gathering system. But at least we can just pretend we already have one. To fill the Oracle schema with test data, issue the SQL statements listed below. This will imitate a network of two modules and the results of two statistic-gathering processes. Both statistic gatherings reported the first module status was up and that the second module status was down.

```
INSERT INTO MODULE (MODULE_ID, MODULE_NAME)
   VALUES (1, 'Demo module 1');
INSERT INTO MODULE (MODULE_ID, MODULE_NAME)
   VALUES (1, 'Demo module 2');

INSERT INTO STAT (STAT_TIME, MODULE_ID, MODULE_STATUS)
   VALUES(TO_DATE('OCT 01 1999 14:00','MON DD YYYY HH24:MI'),1,1);
INSERT INTO STAT (STAT_TIME, MODULE_ID, MODULE_STATUS)
   VALUES(TO_DATE('OCT 01 1999 14:00','MON DD YYYY HH24:MI'),2,-1);

INSERT INTO STAT (STAT_TIME, MODULE_ID, MODULE_STATUS)
   VALUES(TO_DATE('OCT 01 1999 14:30','MON DD YYYY HH24:MI'),1,1);
INSERT INTO STAT (STAT_TIME, MODULE_ID, MODULE_STATUS)
   VALUES(TO_DATE('OCT 01 1999 14:30','MON DD YYYY HH24:MI'),2,-1);

COMMIT;
```

Now we can test the applet. The best way to do this is to issue an appletviewer netmon.html command on the server. The appletviewer is a graphical tool, and it can be very useful for debugging purposes because we can read diagnostic messages from its standard output.

When the applet is thoroughly tested, we can try to load and run it in the browser's window. We start the browser on a client machine, go to the URL of the netmon.html file, and run the applet. Given test data, our applet will display a header saying that the last refresh happened on October 1, 1999, at 14:30:00; the average network availability is 50 percent; and the list of two modules indicates that the first module is up and the second module is down with green and red marks, respectively. We can manually insert rows to the STAT table and see how the applet will track the changes in network availability and module status.

Conclusion

We have implemented a simple but very useful monitoring tool. We thoroughly discussed how to write efficient Java code for working with Oracle database. Our applet can run on any Web browser that supports JDK 1.1. We considered how to use a thin JDBC driver to access Oracle, what problems can arise, and the workarounds.

One problem with deploying applets integrated with databases is delays. In particular, it is important for geographically distributed networks. We have to think of making our applet more user-friendly. For example, we can print messages in the browser's window reporting to the operator when a connection takes too long. Another problem is security. This problem can be solved only if we protect all hardware and software components of our information system.

The strength of our monitoring applet is in its access to a statistics database. The more statistics we have, the better we can control the network. So we'll need to store and process large volumes of data. And we need thin-client software with a graphical interface and support for multimedia. An Oracle server is the best database — robust and scalable. Java applets can run from any browser, and using JDBC we can efficiently interact with one database. The future looks good for Oracle–Java in tandem.

ORACLE AND UNIX

Because more than 80 percent of all Oracle applications run under the UNIX platform, it is important for practicing Oracle professionals to get as much information regarding the interaction between the Oracle database in the UNIX operating system. Chapters 19 through 22 are taken from *Oracle Internals* and contain some invaluable tips and tricks regarding the use of the different dialects of UNIX to communicate with the database. These tips and tricks will improve the Oracle administrator's ability to manage Oracle for Unix.

It is important for Oracle administrators to understand that Oracle does not run in a vacuum. Rather, Oracle has tight integration with the operating system. This type of interaction includes the archiving of the redo log files, the physical interaction with the UNIX files, as well as the location off the various Oracle initialization files, log files, and trace files. Hence, it is very important that Oracle administrators have a very good knowledge and understanding of the details of the UNIX operating environment.

Tip: Compressing and Splitting a Huge Export File

Here is a hot tip from my latest book. (I have the publishers' permission to reproduce.)

With most tables growing into many gigabytes, few Oracle professionals know how to use the Oracle export utility for large SAP tables. One of the real drawbacks of the Oracle export utility is the set of restrictions imposed by the UNIX operating system. As you probably know, some UNIX systems limit an individual file to two gigabytes. Fortunately, with a few tricks, very large tables can also be exported using the Oracle utility, and with the use of the UNIX *split* and *compress* commands, we can easily export a ten-gigabyte table. The listing below shows an example of a parameter file for an Oracle/SAP export parameter file.

```
file=compress_pipe
direct=y
rows=y
indexes=y
tables=(vbep)
buffer=1024000
log=exp_vbep.lst
```

Notice that the output of this export is being directed to a file called COMPRESS_PIPE. The first step in running a split, compressed export is to create a named pipe for the compress and the split.

```
rm -f compress_pipe
rm -f spilt_pipe
mknod compress_pipe p
mknod split_pipe p
chmod g+w compress_pipe
chmod g+w split_pipe
```

Now that the pipes are in place, we can submit our export, using the parameter file from the following listing. Note that the export job must be submitted from the directory where the pipes exist and in the directory that will contain the exported dump files.

```
Nohup split -b500m < split_pipe > /tmp/exp_tab &
nohup compress < compress_pipe > split_pipe &
nohup exp parfile=export_tab.par file=compress_pipe > exp_tab.list 2>&1 &
```

Note that the UNIX *split* command will place the output from the export into files called *XAA, XAB, XAC*, each in 500-megabyte chunks.

Now that we have the file exported into manageable pieces, we can import the file by reversing the process, piping the import utility through the *uncompress* and *cat* UNIX commands. Below, the first statement concatenates the file back together into the *SPLIT_PIPE* file. The second command uncompresses the data from *SPLIT_PIPE* and places the uncompressed, unsplit file into *EXPORT_PIPE*. The third statement runs the import utility using *EXPORT_PIPE* as the input file.

```
nohup cat xaa xab xac xad > split_pipe &
nohup uncompress -c split_pipe > export_pipe &
nohup imp file=export_pipe
```

Tip: Using the UNIX iostat Utility to Find Disk Bottlenecks

One little-used free UNIX utility can be very valuable for identifying disk I/O bottlenecks. The utility is iostat, and here is the command:

```
prompt> iostat 15
```

The "iostat 15" says to display one line of output for every disk that we have attached to our database server. In this case we get output every 15 seconds, each showing the amount of I/O for each disk.

Here is a sample of the output:

```
Disks:     % tm_act   Kbps    tps     Kb_read    Kb_wrtn
hdisk6        1.0     73.8    4.2     8999945    3314136
hdisk7        0.7     86.4    3.1    13790876     629660
hdisk8        0.0      0.6    0.0       90469       2176
hdisk9        0.8     74.4    3.1     9875281    2532636
hdisk10       0.5     54.6    1.7     9108228       3616
hdisk11       0.1     13.7    0.4     2279793        244
```

Here are descriptions for the columns:

- % tm_act: the percentage of time that the disk was physically active.
- Kbps: the number of K-bytes transferred per second.
- tps: the number of I/O requests to the disk. (Note that multiple logical I/O requests can be merged into a single physical request.)
- Kb_read: the number of Kilobytes read during the interval.
- Kb_wrtn: the number of Kilobytes written during the time interval.

The "% tm_act" shows the percentage of active time for the disk, and this output, when used in conjunction with a utlestat report (report.txt) can show you disk bottlenecks.

Chapter 19

UNIX Scripts for Oracle Administration

Serg Shestakov

Many Oracle DBAs rely on UNIX scripts running repeating administrative tasks. There are two important advantages of UNIX shells: (1) they are simple, and (2) they are reliable. Adding up some scripts really makes the difference. This chapter considers a pack of utilities for Oracle administration implemented in Bourne shell. These scripts track and report problems with mission-critical Oracle processes — database instances, SQL*Net listeners, and Oracle Web Server listeners. Yet another script from this pack analyzes Oracle export log files, verifies if backup was successful, and reports status to DBAs. We will schedule these scripts in a crontab file for automatic execution.

We will consider how to monitor Oracle processes and how to send DBAs early warnings if something goes wrong. We assume the following environment: Solaris 2.6, Oracle Server 7.3, SQL*Net 2.3, and Oracle Web Server 2.1. Before we talk about scripts implementation, notice that our goal is to give DBAs flexible structures. We will discuss how DBAs can enhance a script's functionality to meet their particular needs.

Oracle Database Server Monitoring

The inst_mon.sh script tracks database instances. To have elegant and easily managed implementation, we will define configuration files to store tunable script parameters. Our goal is to demonstrate building blocks for Oracle monitoring. We want this script to monitor two situations: first, if the time required to establish connection to Oracle does not exceed some limit, and second, if the numeric value returned by SQL script does not exceed some threshold. For example, set the connection time limit to ten seconds and analyze

0-8493-1139-X/02/$0.00+$1.50
©2002 by CRC Press LLC

average dispatchers utilization (assume Oracle instance is running in multi-threaded configuration). Execute an SQL statement returning average dispatchers utilization and compare this value with a 50 percent utilization threshold.

We have to take some preliminary steps. To establish direct connection to Oracle, we need to know Oracle SID, Oracle username, and Oracle password. For remote databases, we need the SQL*Net service name, username, and password. To simplify script management, store this information in plain text file instances.cfg. The format of each line is: <SID> <connect string>, where <connect string> for direct connection is: <user>/<password>. To monitor instances running on remote machines, append @<service-name> to the end of the connect string. To distinguish between local and remote instances, we can write SIDs from remote hosts in the form <SID@hostname>.

We store SQL script in the session.cfg file. In our example, we put into this file the SQL statement calculating average dispatchers utilization followed by the EXIT command. Note that we add the prefix time_busy: to numeric value returned by the SQL query. We do this because we will need to extract a line with numeric value from the SQL log file. And by adding the time_busy keyword, we uniquely identify this line:

```
SELECT 'time_busy: '||
  round(avg(busy/(busy + idle)),2)*100
FROM v$dispatcher;
EXIT
```

We can add more SQL statements into our session to read other monitoring parameters from Oracle. We need one more configuration file, admins.cfg, to store e-mails of those Oracle DBAs who should be notified if script will detect problems with Oracle processes. The file contains a list of e-mails that are separated by space characters.

This set of plain configuration files makes it easier for a DBA to reconfigure the script if necessary. It is good practice to create a special directory for utilities and put all scripts and their configuration files there, and also put our files in /opt/ora/utils. Do not forget to restrict access to these files. For example, to make sure only the owner can access configuration files, use the following command: chmod 600 *cfg. To make sure only the owner can access and execute scripts, issue: chmod 700 *sh.

After the configuration files are prepared, return to the script body. Look at the code (see Appendix 19.1). The first line identifies one Bourne shell as the program to execute the script, and next follows a comment:

```
#!/bin/sh
# inst_mon.sh – utility for
# database instances monitoring
```

We need to assign values to some environment variables — ORACLE_HOME, NLS_LANG, PATH, and LD_LIBRARY_PATH. To access these environment variables from child processes, issue an export command. Reference the following section as <DEFINE ENVIRONMENT> because this code will be needed in other utilities.

```
ORACLE_HOME=/opt/ora/app/oracle/product/7.3.4
export ORACLE_HOME
NLS_LANG=AMERICAN_AMERICA.WE8ISO8859P1
export NLS_LANG
PATH=$ORACLE_HOME/bin:$PATH
export PATH
LD_LIBRARY_PATH=$LD_LIBRARY_PATH:$ORACLE_HOME/lib
export LD_LIBRARY_PATH
```

Let us now discuss how to implement the desired functionality. We change the working catalog because we want to use short file names. For security reasons, we change umask to 177 — this grants read and write permissions for newly created files only to its owner. Then we set the time limit for connecting to Oracle and set threshold for average dispatchers utilization:

```
cd /opt/ora/utils
umask 177
timeout=10
threshold=50
```

We are now ready to start a cycle for all instances. We extract the list of SID names from the instances.cfg file. For this purpose, we use a tiny program in nawk language {print $1}, which returns the first field in line, i.e., SID name:

```
for SID in `cat instances.cfg|nawk '{print $1}'`
do
```

The next section of code assigns a current SID value to the ORACLE_SID variable, extracts the appropriate connect string from the instances.cfg file, and stores it in the connect_string variable. We use a grep command to catch a line starting with the current SID. This section also defines a log file as <SID>.log and an alarm file as <SID>.alarm.

```
ORACLE_SID=$SID
export ORACLE_SID
connect_string=`grep "^$SID" instances.cfg|nawk '{print $2}'`
af=$SID.alarm
log_file=$SID.log
```

Below we run the Oracle SQL*Plus utility with a connect string extracted from the instances.cfg file. We log SQL*Plus output to <SID>.log file for further analysis. To log diagnostic messages, we add diagnostic output to a standard one using 2>&1 file descriptor association. We start SQL*Plus in the background and wait for the operation to complete in a fixed number of seconds:

```
sqlplus $connect_string < session.cfg 2>&1 > $log_file &
sleep $timeout
```

Once we reach the time limit, we scan the SQL*Plus log file and set two flags. We use a grep command with -c option to print the number of lines containing Connected keyword and store this number to is_conn variable. And if there is a line containing the time_busy keyword, we set the is_time_busy flag.

```
is_conn=`grep -c Connected $log_file`
is_time_busy=`grep -c time_busy $log_file`
```

In the following section, we analyze the is_conn flag. If its value differs from 1, the connection was not established within the time limit, and we prepare and send an alarm to the DBAs. When we write the alarm file, we first write a line starting with the Subject: field. The string following this field will be interpreted by the mail command as the subject of the e-mail message. The next lines will compose the message body. Note that command > file overwrites file with standard output of command. When we use command >> file, we append the standard output to the end of the file.

```
if test $is_conn -ne 1
then
  echo "Subject: Problems with " $SID "
  instance!" > $af
  echo "No connection in " $timeout "
  seconds." >> $af
mail `cat admins.cfg` < $af
fi
```

In a similar manner, we can append other useful system information to our alarm message. For example, we can append the output of the uptime command to show the current load and append the contents of the SQL*Plus log to help DBAs detect why connection failed.

If the is_time_busy flag equals 1, we store the number returned by SQL statement to time_busy variable. Program {print $2} is in nawk language and returns second field in line, i.e., average dispatchers utilization:

```
if test $is_time_busy -eq 1
then
  time_busy=`grep time_busy $log_file |
  nawk '{print $2}'`
```

Let us analyze the time_busy variable. If its value is greater than the threshold, the average dispatchers utilization is too high, and we prepare and send an alarm to the DBAs as we did before. First we compose Subject: field; next we append the message body and issue a mail command to distribute the alarm. Finally, we need to mark the end of the cycle for all instances and exit the script:

```
    if test $time_busy -gt $threshold
    then
      echo "Subject: Problems with " $SID "
      instance!" > $af
      echo "Dispatchers utilization:"
      $time_busy "%" >> $af
      echo "Tune MTS_MAX_DISPATCHERS!" >>
      $af
      mail `cat admins.cfg` < $af
    fi
  fi
done
exit 0
```

See Appendix 19.1.

It is easy to add other SQL statements to the session.cfg file and track other Oracle parameters in a similar manner. Another interesting way to enhance functionality is to scan Oracle ALERT files and analyze messages. When we discuss the SQL*Net monitoring utility, we will see how to implement the log file analysis.

The script for database instances monitoring was designed to act as an autonomous agent on behalf of DBAs. Let us schedule inst_mon.sh for automatic execution. We will do this by putting inst_mon.sh in the crontab file so it can be started as a cron job each 15 minutes. To edit a crontab file, run crontab -e command.

```
05,20,35,50 * * * * utils/inst_mon.sh
```

If we do not want automatic mailing of the script output to its owner, we can redirect diagnostic output and standard output of this script to the log file using "2>&1 > log_file" association.

SQL*Net Listeners Monitoring

We already know how to track the connection time and how to analyze SQL statement results. Now let us try something different but also very useful: we will try to analyze log files for SQL*Net listeners. The sqlnet_mon.sh script will do this. Before we discuss the script body, we have to define data structures to work with.

The SQL*Net listener names we want to monitor will be stored in the sqlnet_lsnr.cfg file, one listener name per line. Log files for SQL*Net listeners are usually located in $ORACLE_HOME/network/log/ and named <LISTENER>.log. Let us focus on error messages stored in these files. Each line with an error message has the format: <Message Code>: <Message text>. Sometimes, messages include a stack of errors. In this case, message code can be preceded by one or more space characters. We put message codes and their descriptions to sqlnet_msg.cfg file, each line in the form <Mask> <Description>, where <Mask> can be any subset of message code. In our example, the following errors will be tracked:

```
ORA-12535 Operation timed out. See
   CONNECT_TIMEOUT in listener.ora.
TNS- TNS error. See log file for details.
```

Because we want script monitoring to be revoked periodically and do not want to scan the same lines in the log file more than once, we will store the number of the last scanned line in sqlnet_<LISTENER>.line files. To distribute alarms to DBAs, the utility will use the already-mentioned admins.cfg file, containing a list of e-mails separated by space characters.

We begin sqlnet_mon.sh as we did for database instances monitoring: assign the Bourne shell to execute this script, put in some comment, define environment variables, set our working catalog, and restrict permissions for the newly created files (see Appendix 19.2).

```
#!/bin/sh
# sqlnet_mon.sh - script for SQL*Net listeners monitoring
<DEFINE ENVIRONMENT>
cd /opt/ora/utils
umask 177
```

Let us start a loop for all listeners stored in our sqlnet_lsnr.cfg. Once we enter the loop, we define the names of the configuration files to work with: listener log file to scan (if it does not exist, we print the error and go to the next listener), alarm file to create, and file with maximum line number to refresh. Also, we set the msg_found flag to zero, denoting that we still found no problems with the SQL*Net listener.

```
for LISTENER in `cat sqlnet_lsnr.cfg`
do
   listener_log=$ORACLE_HOME/network/log/
   $LISTENER.log
   if test ! -f $listener_log
   then
      echo "Not found: " $listener_log
   else
      af=sqlnet_$LISTENER.alarm
      lastline_file=sqlnet_$LISTENER.line
      msg_found=0
```

Now it is time for the most interesting part of the script: log file scanning. The next code section stores the maximum number of lines to total_lines variable and writes zero to .line file if it does not exist. Then it reads from .line file the maximum number of lines from a previous scan and rewrites the file with a new value.

```
total_lines=`cat $listener_log|wc -l`
if test ! -f $lastline_file
then
   echo "0" > $lastline_file
fi
last_line=`cat $lastline_file`
echo $total_lines > $lastline_file
```

First, we must scan the new log file from the beginning:

```
if test $last_line -gt $total_lines
then
   last_line=0
fi
```

Because the script will use a tail command to scan the log file, it calculates the offset in lines from the end of the file using the expr command and stores it to the delta variable. Also, we prepare a header of the alarm file — it will be used only if we encounter one or more error codes in the log file.

```
delta=`expr $total_lines - $last_line`
echo "Subject:Problems with SQL*Net (" $LIS-TENER ")" > $af
echo "Scanning $listener_log:" >> $af
echo "lines from $last_line to $total_lines" >> $af
```

We open a loop for all message codes extracted from the sqlnet_msg.cfg file. To filter message descriptions, we use nawk language. When the message code and offset are known, scanning is relatively straightforward. We store a number of message code occurences to msg_count variable, and if it is greater than zero, set the msg_found flag to 1 and append the message description and the number of occurences to the alarm file. The procedure repeats for all message codes:

```
for MSG in `cat sqlnet_msg.cfg | nawk '{print $1}'`
do
   msg_count=`tail -$delta $listener_log | grep
   -c $MSG `
   if test $msg_count -gt 0
   then
      msg_found=1
      echo "----------------------------" >> $af
      grep "^$MSG" sqlnet_msg.cfg >> $af
      echo "encountered $msg_count times" >> $af
   fi
done
```

Upon completing the loop for all message codes, we analyze the msg_found flag, and if it equals 1, we deliver the alarm to the DBAs listed in the admins.cfg file. When we are finished with all SQL*Net listeners, it is time to exit the script (see Appendix 19.2).

```
   if test $msg_found -eq 1
   then
      mail `cat admins.cfg` < $af
   fi
fi
done
exit 0
```

Let us schedule sqlnet_mon.sh for automatic execution every 15 minutes as a cron job, like we did for instances monitoring:

```
00,15,30,45 * * * * utils/sqlnet_mon.sh
```

Oracle Web Listeners Monitoring

When it is necessary to Web-enable an Oracle database, security is very important. Security will be the primary concern for our Oracle Web Server monitoring utility. What is a suspicious activity and how can we detect it? It is alarming when someone makes multiple unsuccessful attempts to log in or requests several nonexistent pages. The Oracle Web Listener (OWL) logs these attempts along with successful ones to a listener's log file. Log files for OWLs are commonly located in the $ORACLE_HOME/ows21/log directory. The file name has format: sv<Port number>.log. Let us name a new utility for OWLs monitoring oraweb_mon.sh. Because this script will focus on log file analysis, we will compose a script by enhancing the functionality of the sqlnet_mon.sh.

First, let us talk about data structures for the oraweb_mon.sh (Appendix 19.3). To provide the script with information on listeners, we create an oraweb_lsnr.cfg file, each line in format: <Listener name><Port number>. The log file format for OWL complies with the National Center for Supercomputing Applications logging standard for Web servers. Each unsuccessful attempt to log in/request a page produces a line, the last two fields of which have format: <Error code> <Number of bytes>. Error codes and their descriptions script will take from the owl_msg.cfg file each line in format: <Error Code> <Description>. In our example, we track the following errors:

```
400 Bad Request – Malformed syntax.
401 Unauthorized – Authorization is required or was refused.
403 Forbidden – The server refused to fulfill the request.
404 Not Found – Nothing matches the request by the client.
```

We store the maximum number of scanned lines in owl_<LISTENER>.line files as we did for SQL*Net listeners monitoring, and we use the admins.cfg file for alarm distribution. Now let us discuss the differences between oraweb_mon.sh and sqlnet_mon.sh. We do several replacements: change sqlnet_lsnr.cfg file for oraweb_lsnr.cfg, change sqlnet_msg.cfg file for owl_msg.cfg, and change sqlnet_<LISTENER>.line file for owl_<LISTENER>.line.

The loop for all listeners we define slightly different because there are two fields in each line of oraweb_lsnr.cfg, and we need the first field:

```
for LISTENER in `cat oraweb_lsnr.cfg | nawk '{print $1}'`
do
```

In the beginning of the loop we extract the line starting with current listener from the configuration file, read the port number as the second field, and define the OWL log name:

```
PORT=`grep "^$LISTENER" oraweb_lsnr.cfg|nawk '{print $2}'`
listener_log=$ORACLE_HOME/ows21/log/sv$PORT.log
```

Of course, the Subject: field of the alarm message now should represent the OWL name:

```
echo "Subject:Suspicious activity! OWL:$LISTENER" > $af
```

The last but most important difference between scripts is the way we set and analyze the msg_count flag. Remember that error code comes after varying number of fields separated by space characters, but it is preceded by exactly one field (denoting bytes count). To filter only the error code field, use the nawk program {print $(NF-1)}, which returns last but one field of each passed line. Note that backslash (\) is used to tell the Bourne shell to escape new line character and continue command string reading.

```
msg_count=`tail -$delta $listener_log | \
nawk '{print $(NF-1)}' |grep -c $MSG`
```

Because users sometimes unintentionally fail to log in/request a page, we set a threshold of attempts indicating suspicious activity. In our example, we set it to 15 times. We assume scans to be scheduled each 15 minutes, normal users activity to be low, and 15 failed logins/requests per 15 minutes to be alarming:

```
if test $msg_count -gt 14
```

Similarly, we can monitor suspicious activity coming from authorized users accessing Oracle PL/SQL procedures. When an authorized user attempts to run a known PL/SQL procedure with the wrong parameters or tries to call nonexistent packages/procedures within current database connection, the Oracle Web Agent (OWA) logs error messages to <OWA name>.err file usually located in $ORACLE_HOME/ows21/log directory. Error messages to track are

```
OWS-05111 No stored procedure matches this call
OWS-05101 Execution failed due to Oracle error
```

We can store a list of Oracle Web Agents to oraweb_agents.cfg file, error messages to owa_msg.cfg file, and scan OWA log files as we did for the Oracle Web Listeners log. We can enhance functionality relatively easily because the script structure is based on configuration files processing. Like sqlnet_mon.sh, the Oracle Web Server monitoring utility should be scheduled for automatic execution every 15 minutes using crontab -e command:

```
00,15,30,45 * * * * utils/oraweb_mon.sh
```

Oracle Exports Monitoring

Verifying Oracle export logs automatically is a good idea, and this can easily be done with a Bourne shell script. To make exports monitoring flexible and keep script configuration simple, we will use configuration files. There are two common situations with log verification: (1) when we check if some keywords combinations can be found in the log, and (2) when we check if some keyword combinations cannot be found. If a check succeeds, we raise an alarm. Let us assign type 1 for messages with the former processing logic, and type 2 for messages with the latter processing logic. Use the exp_msg.cfg file to store these user-defined export messages. Each line of exp_msg.cfg has the format: <Code>:<Type>:<Key-words>:<Description>. The <Code> field defines custom message code in form: ORAEXP-<number>. The next field, <Type>, describes processing logic — type 1 or 2, and the <Keywords> field defines what phrase uniquely identifies a custom message in the Oracle export log. Because keywords as a rule are not informative enough, we add the <Description> field to tell DBAs the message meaning. Note that we use an alternative field separator (:) because we want to process keywords and descriptions with space characters. In our example we verify the Oracle export log for the following messages, tracking common problems:

```
ORAEXP-1:1:No space left:Export failed – no space left on device
ORAEXP-2:2:WE8ISO8859P1:Export was in wrong character set
ORAEXP-3:1:EXP-:Export terminated with errors
ORAEXP-4:1:with warnings:Export terminated with warnings
```

Note that the Oracle export log should be written with 2>&1 association to catch a “No space left” message from diagnostic output. If we assign exp_db.sh as an export script, it should be logged like this:

```
exp_db.sh 2>&1 > exp.log
```

Now start the exp_mon.sh, our utility for Oracle exports monitoring (Appendix 19.4). First, analyze the number of parameters passed to it. We assume this script to be used with a single parameter — export log file name. So if the number of parameters differs from 1, we just print a help message and exit:

```
#!/bin/sh
# exp_mon.sh – utility for
# Oracle export log verification
if test $# -ne 1
then
   echo "Oracle export log verification."
   echo "Usage: exp_mon.sh <log file>"
   exit 0
fi
```

One more check: If a passed log file does not exist, we print an error message and exit the script:

```
if test ! -f $1
then
   echo "Not found: " $1
   exit 0
fi
```

The next section of code sets the current directory and permissions for new files, stores the first parameter (log file name) to exp_log variable, and defines the alarm file name:

```
cd /opt/ora/utils
umask 177
exp_log=$1
af=exp.alarm
```

It is time to open a loop for all message codes stored in the configuration file. When we enter the loop, we set the msg_found flag to zero and read message type, keywords, and description. We use nawk with -F option to override the default field separator with a colon. The following lines demonstrate it:

```
for MSG in `cat exp_msg.cfg | nawk -F : '{print $1}'`
do
   msg_found=0
   msg_type=`grep "^$MSG" exp_msg.cfg | nawk -F : '{print $2}'`
   msg_keywd=`grep "^$MSG" exp_msg.cfg|nawk -F : '{print $3}'`
   msg_desc=`grep "^$MSG" exp_msg.cfg | nawk -F : '{print $4}'`
```

Now scan the Oracle export log file for keywords. Scan and store the count to msg_count variable. Then analyze msg_count according to the type of processing logic: if a message has type 1 and keywords were found, or a message has type 2 and keywords were not found, we set the msg_found flag to 1.

```
msg_count=`grep -c "$msg_keywd" $exp_log`
if test $msg_type -eq 1 && test $msg_count -gt 0
then
  msg_found=1
fi
if test $msg_type -eq 2 && test $msg_count -eq 0
then
  msg_found=1
fi
```

If the msg_found flag equals 1, we have to generate an alarm and deliver it to the DBAs. Finally, having gone through all message codes, it is time to close the loop and exit the script:

```
if test $msg_found -eq 1
  then
    echo "Subject: " $msg_desc > $af
    echo "See log file $exp_log:" >> $af
    cat $exp_log >> $af
    mail `cat admins.cfg` < $af
  fi
done
exit 0
```

When and how to schedule exp_mon.sh depends on frequency of backups and log file naming conventions. Assume that a backup for the TEST database is scheduled every day at midnight. It should be finished by 4 a.m. and produces a log file called /exp/TEST.log. Then we can schedule the Oracle exports monitoring utility to run each day at 5 a.m. as follows:

```
00 05 * * * utils/exp_mon.sh /exp/TEST.log
```

What else can be done with the Bourne shell scripts for Oracle administration? Lots of useful things. We can check if an application runs in memory, monitor an application's running time and CPU utilization, log monitoring information to an Oracle database, and restart hanging processes. What is more, we can implement interactive utilities for Oracle administration — in particular it is useful for administering multiple database instances. These issues are challenging for a DBA to manage. And Bourne shell scripting is a good way to build simple and reliable solutions.

Appendix 19.1 Database Instances Monitoring Utility

inst_mon.sh

```
#!/bin/sh
# inst_mon.sh - utility for
# database instances monitoring
ORACLE_HOME=/opt/ora/app/oracle/product/7.3.4
export ORACLE_HOME
NLS_LANG=AMERICAN_AMERICA.WE8ISO8859P1
export NLS_LANG
PATH=$ORACLE_HOME/bin:$PATH
export PATH
cd /opt/ora/utils
umask 177
timeout=10
threshold=50
for SID in `cat instances.cfg | nawk '{print $1}'`
do
    ORACLE_SID=$SID
    export ORACLE_SID
    connect_string=`grep "^$SID" instances.cfg| nawk '{print $2}'`
    af=$SID.alarm
    log_file=$SID.log
    sqlplus $connect_string < session.cfg 2>&1 > $log_file &
    sleep $timeout
    is_conn=`grep -c Connected $log_file`
    is_time_busy=`grep -c time_busy $log_file`
    if test $is_conn -ne 1
    then
       echo "Subject: Problems with " $SID "instance!" > $af
       echo "No connection in " $timeout " seconds." >> $af
       mail `cat admins.cfg` < $af
    fi
    if test $is_time_busy -eq 1
    then
       time_busy=`grep time_busy $log_file | nawk '{print $2}'`
       if test $time_busy -gt $threshold
       then
          echo "Subject: Problems with " $SID "instance!" > $af
          echo "Dispatchers utilization:" $time_busy "%" >> $af
          echo "Tune MTS_MAX_DISPATCHERS!" >> $af
          mail `cat admins.cfg` < $af
       fi
    fi
done
exit 0
```

Appendix 19.2 SQL*Net Listeners Monitoring Utility

sqlnet_mon.sh

```
#!/bin/sh
# sqlnet_mon.sh - script for
# SQL*Net listeners monitoring
ORACLE_HOME=/opt/ora/app/oracle/product/7.3.4
export ORACLE_HOME
NLS_LANG=AMERICAN_AMERICA.WE8ISO8859P1
export NLS_LANG
PATH=$ORACLE_HOME/bin:$PATH
export PATH
cd /opt/ora/utils
umask 177
for LISTENER in `cat sqlnet_lsnr.cfg`
do

listener_log=$ORACLE_HOME/network/log/$LISTENER.log
   if test ! -f $listener_log
   then
     echo "Not found: " $listener_log
   else
     af=sqlnet_$LISTENER.alarm
     lastline_file=sqlnet_$LISTENER.line
     msg_found=0
     total_lines=`cat $listener_log|wc -l`
     if test ! -f $lastline_file
     then
       echo "0" > $lastline_file
     fi
     last_line=`cat $lastline_file`
     echo $total_lines > $lastline_file
     if test $last_line -gt $total_lines
     then
       last_line=0
     fi
     delta=`expr $total_lines - $last_line`
     echo "Subject:Problems with SQL*Net (" $LISTENER ")" > $af
     echo "Scanning $listener_log:" >> $af
     echo "lines from $last_line to " $total_lines >> $af
     for MSG in `cat sqlnet_msg.cfg | nawk '{print $1}'`
     do
       msg_count=`tail -$delta $listener_log | grep -c $MSG `
       if test $msg_count -gt 0
       then
         msg_found=1
         echo "--------------------" >> $af
         grep "^$MSG" sqlnet_msg.cfg >> $af
         echo "encountered " $msg_count " times" >> $af
       fi
     done
     if test $msg_found -eq 1
     then
       mail `cat admins.cfg` < $af
     fi
   fi
done
exit 0
```

Appendix 19.3 Oracle Web Listeners Monitoring Utility

oraweb_mon.sh

```
#!/bin/sh
# oraweb_mon.sh - script for
# Oracle Web Listeners monitoring
ORACLE_HOME=/opt/ora/app/oracle/product/7.3.4
export ORACLE_HOME
NLS_LANG=AMERICAN_AMERICA.WE8ISO8859P1
export NLS_LANG
PATH=$ORACLE_HOME/bin:$PATH
export PATH
cd /opt/ora/utils
umask 177
for LISTENER in `cat oraweb_lsnr.cfg | nawk '{print $1}'`
do
   PORT=`grep "^$LISTENER" oraweb_lsnr.cfg | nawk '{print $2}'`
   listener_log=$ORACLE_HOME/ows21/log/sv$PORT.log
   if test ! -f $listener_log
   then
     echo "Not found: " $listener_log
   else
     af=sqlnet_$LISTENER.alarm
     lastline_file=owl_$LISTENER.line
     msg_found=0
     total_lines=`cat $listener_log|wc -l`
     if test ! -f $lastline_file
     then
       echo "0" > $lastline_file
     fi
     last_line=`cat $lastline_file`
     echo $total_lines > $lastline_file
       if test $last_line -gt $total_lines
     then
       last_line=0
     fi
     delta=`expr $total_lines - $last_line`
     echo "Subject:Suspicious activity! OWL:$LISTENER" > $af
     echo "Scanning $listener_log:" >> $af
     echo "lines from $last_line to " $total_lines >> $af
     for MSG in `cat owl_msg.cfg | nawk '{print $1}'`
     do
       msg_count=`tail -$delta $listener_log | \
         nawk '{print $(NF-1)}' |grep -c $MSG`
       if test $msg_count -gt 14
       then
         msg_found=1
         echo "--------------------" >> $af
         grep "^$MSG" owl_msg.cfg >> $af
         echo "encountered " $msg_count " times" >> $af
       fi
     done
     if test $msg_found -eq 1
     then
       mail `cat admins.cfg` < $af
     fi
   fi
done
exit 0
```

Appendix 19.4 Exports Monitoring Utility

exp_mon.sh

```
#!/bin/sh
# exp_mon.sh - utility for
# Oracle export log verification
if test $# -ne 1
then
   echo "Oracle export log verification."
   echo "Usage: exp_mon.sh <log file>"
   exit 0
fi
if test ! -f $1
then
      echo "Not found: " $1
  exit 0
fi
cd /opt/ora/utils
umask 177
exp_log=$1
af=exp.alarm
for MSG in `cat exp_msg.cfg | nawk -F : '{print $1}'`
do
   msg_found=0
   msg_type=`grep "^$MSG" exp_msg.cfg | nawk -F :'{print $2}'`
   msg_keywd=`grep "^$MSG" exp_msg.cfg|nawk -F :'{print $3}'`
   msg_desc=`grep "^$MSG" exp_msg.cfg | nawk -F :'{print $4}'`
   msg_count=`grep -c "$msg_keywd" $exp_log`
   if test $msg_type -eq 1 && test $msg_count -gt 0
   then
     msg_found=1
   fi
   if test $msg_type -eq 2 && test $msg_count -eq 0
   then
     msg_found=1
   fi
   if test $msg_found -eq 1
   then
     echo "Subject: " $msg_desc > $af
     echo "See log file $exp_log:" >> $af
     cat $exp_log >> $af
     mail `cat admins.cfg` < $af
   fi
done
exit 0
```

Chapter 20

UNIX Tips and Tricks for the Oracle DBA

Donald K. Burleson

While Oracle DBAs are supremely charged with managing their Oracle databases, Oracle DBAs in the UNIX environment must also possess the knowledge to control how Oracle interacts with the external environment. This chapter examines the essential UNIX commands that every Oracle DBA must know.

What About "Root"?

In many cases, this involves using commands that are only available with the "root" UNIX user. Very often, the Oracle DBA requires root privileges to perform tasks outside the domain of the Oracle UNIX user, such as killing a user process, mounting a remote file system, or changing file permissions. Root privileges are also required to sign-on to UNIX as another UNIX user without knowing the user password. Most shops allow their DBA access to the root user, but some naïve shops require the DBA staff to see a systems administrator to issue all root commands. This approach is unproductive and often results in serious errors.

The Basic Areas of Commands

Before exploring the basic UNIX commands, we need to mention that there are several dialects of UNIX. There is HP/UX, AIX, Solaris, IRIX, DECUNIX, Linux, and a host of other implementations of UNIX, each with their own variants in command syntax. Hence, it is impossible to mention all possible command variations in this forum. The following UNIX commands will be addressed in this chapter:

0-8493-1139-X/02/$0.00+$1.50
©2002 by CRC Press LLC

- *Process management.* Process management commands are used for identifying and killing Oracle processes and for monitoring Oracle processes on the server.
- *Server values.* The server value display commands are used to show server values that impact the Oracle database, such as semaphore values and memory segment regions.
- *Server monitoring.* This class of UNIX commands is used to visualize server statistics. These include the use of utilities such as vmstat, iostat, and the `w` command. In addition, some dialects of UNIX support more sophisticated monitors such as the "top" and "glance" tools.
- *File and DASD management.* The file management commands are used to display file system characteristics, strings in binary files, and files with specific characteristics. These commands are used to find large files or recently used files in the Oracle file domain; they include the `grep` and `egrep` commands.
- *UNIX programming.* These commands include the remote mount commands and commands that are used to write shell scripts, including techniques for looping and testing condition codes.

Remember the Man Pages

One of the best ways to find the command syntax for your dialect of UNIX is to utilize the man pages. The systems administrator should install the man pages for all Unix commands so that help is easily available. To see the man pages for a command, enter `man commandname`.

Process Management Commands

The basic process management command is the `ps` command. The `ps` command is commonly used to display active processes and the characteristics of active processes.

Display Commands

The `ps -ef` command has the following values:

```
> ps -ef

UID          PID    PPID  C      STIME   TTY     TIME           CMD
oracle     13168     1    0    05:33:06   -      3:15  oracleprod (LOCAL=NO)
oracle     26164     1    0    12:57:10   -      4:54  oracleprod (LOCAL=NO)
UID  = The user ID that owns the process
PID  = The process ID for the task
PPID = The parent process. If the parent is "1", the process was created
        by root.
TIME = The current CPU time used by the process. This value will increase
        until the process is completed.
CMD  = The UNIX command that is being executed
```

Display top CPU consumers. The following command can be used to display the top CPU consumers on a server. Note that the `sort +6` displays the CPU column (columns are counted from left-to-right, with the first column being column 0).

```
>ps -ef|sort +6|tail
   oracle  55676     1    0    03:06:16 - 0:36     oracleprod (LOCAL=NO)
   oracle  24876     1    0    02:52:56 - 0:40     oracleprod (LOCAL=NO)
   oracle  41616     1    0    07:00:59 - 0:44     oracleprod (LOCAL=NO)
   oracle  43460     1    0    02:45:05 - 0:53     oracleprod (LOCAL=NO)
   oracle  25754     1    0    08:10:03 - 1:01     oracleprod (LOCAL=NO)
   oracle  17402     1    0    07:27:04 - 2:06     oracleprod (LOCAL=NO)
   oracle  14922     1    0    01:01:46 - 2:54     oracleprod (LOCAL=NO)
   oracle  13168     1    0    05:33:06 - 3:15     oracleprod (LOCAL=NO)
   oracle  26164     1    0    12:57:10 - 4:54     oracleprod (LOCAL=NO)
```

In some cases, column 5 is the CPU column:

```
>ps -ef|sort +5|tail
   root      5440   2094   0    Nov 21   - 0:47     /usr/sbin/syslogd
   root      9244      1   0    Nov 21   - 3:26     ./pcimapsvr.ip -D0
   root     10782      1   0    Nov 21   - 4:41     ./pciconsvr.ip -D0
   root      5990   2094   0    Nov 21   - 5:33     /usr/sbin/snmpd
   root      4312      1   0    Nov 21   - 7:14     /usr/sbin/cron
   root      4448   2094   0    Nov 21   - 9:25     /usr/sbin/rwhod
   root         1      0   0    Nov 21   - 198:59   /etc/init
   root      2450      1   0    Nov 21   - 438:30   /usr/sbin/syncd 60
```

Once you find the appropriate column (5 or 6), you can repeat the command to watch CPU consumption change for the offending process.

Another approach is to use the `ps auxgw` command. This has the following values:

```
  USER  PID  %CPU  %MEM  SZ     RSS    TTY    STAT    STIME    TIME COMMAND
```

The third column of this listing (%CPU) shows the percentage of CPU used. Hence, the following command will display the top CPU users:

```
>ps auxgw|sort +2|tail
   oracle 14922 0.6 1.0 8300 5720 - A 01:01:46 2:57 oracleprod (LOCAL=NO)
   oracle 22424 0.6 1.0 8328 6076 - A 07:48:43 0:21 oracleprod (LOCAL=NO)
   oracle 44518 0.8 1.0 8080 5828 - A 08:47:47 0:02 oracleprod (LOCAL=NO)
   oracle 20666 1.0 1.0 8304 6052 - A 08:15:19 0:22 oracleprod (LOCAL=NO)
   oracle 13168 1.6 1.0 8196 5760 - A 05:33:06 3:15 oracleprod (LOCAL=NO)
   oracle 17402 2.5 1.0 8296 6044 - A 07:27:04 2:06 oracleprod (LOCAL=NO)
   oracle 25754 2.5 1.0 8640 6388 - A 08:10:03 1:03 oracleprod (LOCAL=NO)
   oracle 41616 4.5 1.0 8312 6052 - A 07:00:59 4:57 oracleprod (LOCAL=NO)
   USER PID  %CPU  %MEM  SZ     RSS TTY STAT          STIME TIME        COMMAND
   root 516  78.9   0.0  16       4  -   A    Nov 21  194930:41         kproc
```

Yet another approach uses the `egrep` command to display the top CPU consumers. Below we see a root process called `kproc` using 78.9% of the CPU:

```
>ps augxww|egrep "RSS| "|head
   USER       PID %CPU %MEM   SZ    RSS TTY  STAT STIME        TIME       COMMAND
   root       516 78.9 0.0    16     4   -   A    Nov 21       194932:05  kproc
   oracle 41616  4.4 1.0 8312  6052   -  A    07:00:59     4:57
   oracle 20740  2.7 1.0 8140   5888      -   A            08:52:32   0:02
   oracle 17402  2.4 1.0 8296  6044   -   A    07:27:04     2:06
   oracle 25754  2.4 1.0 8640  6388   -   A    08:10:03     1:03
   oracle 13168  1.6 1.0 8196  5760   -   A    05:33:06     3:15
   oracle 20666  1.0 1.0 8304  6052   -   A    08:15:19     0:22
   oracle 14922  0.6 1.0 8300  5720   -   A    01:01:46     2:57
   oracle 44518  0.6 1.0 8080  5828   -   A    08:47:47     0:02
```

Show Load Averages

Another way of showing Oracle process usage is to monitor the "load average." The load average is a metric that shows overall resource consumption of the server. Note that there are three values for the load average: the load averages for the past minute, the past 5 minutes, and the past 10 minutes. Whenever the value exceeds "1," there is a CPU overload problem.

```
>w
10:02AM up 60 days, 18:46, 3 users, load average: 0.32, 0.39, 0.43
User       tty     login@     idle     JCPU    PCPU    what
oracle     pts/0   08:17AM       0    80:18   80:16    w
oracle     pts/1   09:15AM       5        2       0    ftp
milteerv   pts/2   01May00   9days        0       0    -ksh
```

Show Number of Active Oracle Dedicated Connection Users

This will not show MTS connections.

```
>ps -ef|grep $ORACLE_SID|grep -v grep|grep -v ora_|wc -l

   23
```

Killing Processes

There are times when it is necessary to kill all Oracle processes, or a selected set of Oracle processes. The Oracle DBA will want to kill all Oracle processes when the database is "locked" and he or she cannot enter server manager. (Note that when you kill Oracle processes, you must also issue the `ipcs` command to ensure that all memory segments are removed.)

The basic format of the `kill` command is:

```
Kill -9 PID1 PID2 PID3
```

To kill all Oracle processes, issue the following command:

```
ps -ef|grep "ora_"|grep -v grep|awk '{print $2}'|xargs -i kill -9 {}
```

Let's look at how it works:

1. The `ps -ef` displays all processes.
2. The `grep "ora_"` removes all but the Oracle background processes:

```
>ps -ef|grep "ora_"
   oracle 13022      1    0      May 07       -    0:18    ora_db02_vald
   oracle 14796  42726    0    09:00:46  pts/0    0:00    grep ora_
   oracle 17778      1    0      May 07       -    0:14    ora_smon_devp
   oracle 18134      1    0      May 07       -    0:37    ora_snp1_vald
   oracle 19516      1    0      May 07       -    0:24    ora_db04_prod
   oracle 21114      1    0      May 07       -    0:37    ora_snp0_devp
   oracle 28436      1    0      May 07       -    0:18    ora_arch_prod
```

3. The `grep -v grep` removes our `grep` command so that we don't kill our own process:

```
>ps -ef|grep "ora_"|grep -v grep
   oracle 13022      1    0      May 07       -    0:18    ora_db02_vald
   oracle 17778      1    0      May 07       -    0:14    ora_smon_devp
   oracle 18134      1    0      May 07       -    0:37    ora_snp1_vald
   oracle 19516      1    0      May 07       -    0:24    ora_db04_prod
   oracle 21114      1    0      May 07       -    0:37    ora_snp0_devp
   oracle 28436      1    0      May 07       -    0:18    ora_arch_prod
```

4. We now use the `awk` command to get the PID for these processes. The `awk '{print $2}'` command only displays the PID column:

```
>ps -ef|grep "ora_"|grep -v grep|awk '{ print $2 }'

13022
17778
18134
19516
21114
28436
28956
```

5. Finally, we "pipe" the list of PIDs to the `kill` command with `xargs -i kill -9 { } \;` Note that the xargs command is very useful for doing the same thing to a list. For example, if you want to `grep` for a string in a file list, just enter `find.-print|xarge grep mystring`.

But what if you want to leave the background processes running and only kill other Oracle processes? You could amend the above command to change the `grep "ora_"` to `grep -v "ora_"` (remember that `grep -v` EXCLUDES lines while `grep` INCLUDES lines). The following command will only kill "ksh" processes, leaving the basic Oracle processes running.

```
kill -9 `ps -fuoracle|grep ksh|awk '{print $2}'`
```

There are times when even the `kill -9` command fails to remove the process. This problem can be overcome by piping `/dev/null` to the ttyname as a part of the kill command. The following command is indispensable for killing stubborn tasks:

```
cat /dev/null > /dev/ttyname kill -9 pid#
```

Displaying Server Values

UNIX has a wealth of values that can be displayed that are important to the Oracle DBA.

The basic command to display server values is the lsdev -C command. This command will display all of the attached components, including disk, memory, CPUs, buses, and other hardware components:

For HP/UX:

```
>lsdev
   Character      Block       Driver        Class
       0            -1        cn            pseudo
       3            -1        mm            pseudo
      16            -1        ptym          ptym
      17            -1        ptys          ptys
      27            -1        dmem          pseudo
      28            -1        diag0         diag
      46            -1        netdiag1      unknown
      52            -1        lan2          lan
```

For AIX:

```
>lsdev -C

sys0        Available  00-00             System Object
sysplanar0  Available  00-00             System Planar
pci0        Available  00-fef00000       PCI Bus
pci1        Available  00-fed00000       PCI Bus
isa0        Available  10-58             ISA Bus
sa0         Available  01-S1             Standard I/O Serial Port
sa1         Available  01-S2             Standard I/O Serial Port
siokma0     Available  01-K1             Keyboard/Mouse Adapter
fda0        Available  01-D1             Standard I/O Diskette Adapter
scsi0       Available  10-60             Wide SCSI I/O Controller
pci2        Defined    20-78             PCI Bus
sioka0      Available  01-K1-00          Keyboard Adapter
sioma0      Available  01-K1-01          Mouse Adapter
hdisk0      Available  10-60-00-0,0      16 Bit SCSI Disk Drive
hdisk1      Available  10-60-00-1,0      16 Bit SCSI Disk Drive
lvdd        Available                    LVM Device Driver
mem0        Available  00-00             Memory
proc0       Available  00-00             Processor
proc1       Available  00-01             Processor
proc2       Available  00-02             Processor
```

```
proc3        Available  00-03              Processor
L2cache0     Available  00-00              L2 Cache
pmc0         Available  00-00              Power Management Controller
tty0         Available  01-S1-00-00        Asynchronous Terminal
rootvg       Defined                       Volume group
inet0        Available                     Internet Network Extension
en2          Defined                       Standard Ethernet Network
et0          Defined                       IEEE 802.3 Ethernet Network
lo0          Available                     Loopback Network Interface
pty0         Available                     Asynchronous Pseudo-Terminal
gxme0        Defined                       Graphics Data Transfer Assist
rcm0         Defined                       Rendering Context Manager
aio0         Available                     Asynchronous I/O
ssa0         Available  10-70              IBM SSA 160 SerialRAID Adapter
ssa1         Available  20-60              IBM SSA 160 SerialRAID Adapter
ssar         Defined                       SSA Adapter Router
pdisk0       Available  10-70-3070-09-P    SSA160 Physical Disk Drive
pdisk1       Available  10-70-34D0-12-P    SSA160 Physical Disk Drive
hdisk2       Available  10-70-L            SSA Logical Disk Drive
hdisk3       Available  10-70-L            SSA Logical Disk Drive
pdisk8       Available  20-60-34D0-13-P    SSA160 Physical Disk Drive
pdisk9       Available  20-60-34D0-15-P    SSA160 Physical Disk Drive
hdisk10      Available  20-60-L            SSA Logical Disk Drive
hdisk11      Available  20-60-L            SSA Logical Disk Drive
enclosure0   Available  00-00-3070         SSA Enclosure
enclosure1   Available  00-00-34D0         SSA Enclosure
loglv03      Defined                       Logical volume
lv04         Defined                       Logical volume
loglv04      Defined                       Logical volume
scsi1        Available  20-68              Wide SCSI I/O Controller
rmt0         Available  20-68-00-4,0       Differential SCSI DLT Tape Drive
rmt1         Available  20-68-00-5,0       Differential SCSI DLT Tape Drive
lus          Available                     Legato SCSI User Interface Release
```

AIX Only:

```
>lsattr -El sys0
keylock      normal       State of system keylock at boot time              False
maxbuf       20           Maximum number of pages in block I/O BUFFER CACHE True
maxmbuf      0            Maximum Kbytes of real memory allowed for MBUFS   True
maxuproc     200          Maximum number of PROCESSES allowed per user      True
autorestart  false        Automatically REBOOT system after a crash         True
iostat       true         Continuously maintain DISK I/O history            True
realmem      3137536      Amount of usable physical memory in Kbytes        False
conslogin    enable       System Console Login                              False
fwversion    IBM,L99071   Firmware version and revision levels              False
maxpout      0            HIGH water mark for pending write I/Os per file   True
minpout      0            LOW water mark for pending write I/Os per file    True
fullcore     false        Enable full CORE dump                             True
rtasversion  1            Open Firmware RTAS version                        False
modelname    IBM,9076-WCN Machine name                                      False
systemid     IBM,010013864 Hardware system identifier                       False
```

To see the base values for the server, you can enter the `lsattr -El sys0` command. This is useful for displaying system variables that are used by Oracle, such as maxuproc and maxbuf.

Memory Management

Here is how to see how much RAM memory exists on a server. We can use `grep` with the `lsdev` command (AIX version is shown) to isolate the memory for a processor:

```
>lsdev -C|grep mem
mem0        Available        00-00         Memory
```

Here we see that `mem0` is the name of the memory device. Now we can issue the `lsattr–El` command on `mem0` to see the amount of memory on the server. In the following AIX code snippet, we see that this server has 3 gigabytes of RAM memory attached.

```
>lsattr -El mem0

size        3064     Total amount of physical memory in Mbytes     False
goodsize    3064     Amount of usable physical memory in Mbytes    False
```

To see all allocated memory segments on your server, enter `>ipcs -pmb`:

```
IPC status from /dev/mem as of Thu May 11 09:40:59 EDT 2000
T       ID  KEY          MODE          OWNER    GROUP          SEGSZ  CPID  LPID
Shared Memory:
m     4096  0x670610c5  --rw-r--r--   root     system            12  45082 37386
m     4097  0x680610c5  --rw-r--r--   root     system        106496  45082 37386
m     4098  0x78041249  --rw-rw-rw-   root     system      16777216  47010 81312
m     4099  0x78061865  --rw-rw-rw-   root     system          7536  47880 81312
m        4  0x0d05014f  --rw-rw-rw-   root     system          1440  16968 72314
m   368645  0x0fe2eb3d  --rw-r-----   oracle   dba         35610624  17760 62118
m   401414  0x0f97693e  --rw-r-----   oracle   dba        229863424  61820 58340
m   274439  0x0fefeae2  --rw-r-----   oracle   dba         35610624  21992 72804
m   184328  0x0fefeb6e  --rw-r-----   oracle   dba         35610624  46690 76098
m   151561  0x0fe2eb03  --rw-r-----   oracle   dba          4972544  71116 24048
m     8202  0x0f956d88  --rw-r-----   oracle   dba         31117312  72448 76258
m   143371  0x0f96e941  --rw-r-----   oracle   dba         21200896  83662 58636
m   135180  0x78041185  --rw-rw-rw-   root     system          2656  81312 81312
```

This command shows the actual memory segments that are associated with the Oracle System Global Area (SGA). To see the specific memory segments, you can enter `svrmgrl` and issue the `oradebug ipc` command. Following we see that memory segment 401414 is the allocated SGA memory.

```
SVRMGR> oradebug ipc
-------------- Shared memory --------------
Seg Id      Address     Size
401414      40000000    229863424
Total: # of segments = 1, size = 229863424
-------------- Semaphores ----------------
Total number of semaphores = 200
Number of semaphores per set = 0
Number of semaphore sets = 0
Semaphore identifiers:
```

When Oracle crashes, sometimes these memory segments are held by the server and must be manually deallocated. We could clobber the SGA memory for this instance.

```
ipcrm -m 401414
```

Note: We only do this when the background processes have abnormally died.

Display Swap

Here is why having root is nice:

```
>swapon -a
ksh: swapon: 0403-006 Execute permission denied.
```

Display Number of CPUs

The `lsdev` command can be used to see the number of CPUs on a server. This is very important to an Oracle DBA because it shows the number of parallel query processes (i.e., parallel degree xx) that can be used on the server. The following command shows a server that this has four CPUs:

```
>lsdev -C|grep Process|wc -l 4
```

Showing Semaphores

The -s option of the `ipcs` command can be used to display semaphores. Semaphores are used by Oracle to serialize transactions.

```
>ipcs -s

IPC status from /dev/mem as of Thu May 11 09:51:12 EDT 2000
T    ID        KEY          MODE          OWNER   GROUP
Semaphores:
s     4096     0x0105ea85   --ra-ra-r--   root    system
s        1     0x620500fb   --ra-r--r--   root    system
s     4098     0x58061118   --ra-ra-r--   root    system
s     4099     0x690610c5   --ra-ra-ra-   root    system
s     4100     0x58061114   --ra-ra-r--   root    system
s    16389     0x01050088   --ra-------   root    system
s   344071     0x0101c6e7   --ra-ra-ra-   root    system
```

Showing System Log Messages

The following commands are used to display the OS error logs. This can be useful for detecting transient disk I/O problems and memory failures.

HP/UX:

```
>grep error /var/adm/syslog/syslog.log|more
May 1 20:30:08 sprihp01 syslog: NetWorker media:
   (warning) /dev/rmt/c5t6d0BESTn reading: I/O error
```

AIX:

```
>errpt -a|more
```

```
LABEL:              CORE_DUMP
IDENTIFIER:         C60BB505
Date/Time:          Tue May 9 10:34:47
Sequence Number:    24908
Machine Id:         000138644C00
Node Id:            sp2k6n03
Class:              S
Type:               PERM
Resource Name:      SYSPROC
```

Server Monitoring

It is critical for Oracle DBAs to first check their server when they see a performance problem. The server must be ruled out as the source of the performance problem before any Oracle tuning can happen. This chapter section shows how to monitor the server.

The `vmstat` *Utility*

The `vmstat` utility, also called `osview` on IRIX, is used for monitoring virtual memory. See Exhibit 20.1 for an example of this utility's use. Following are key values displayed by it:

- `r` = runqueue: When this value exceeds the number of CPUs (`lsdev -C|grep Proc|wc -l`), then the server is experiencing a CPU bottleneck.
- `pi` = Page in: any non-zero value indicates that the server is short on memory and RAM memory is being sent to the swap disk.

The following CPU values are percentages and will sum to 100:

- `us` = user CPU percentage
- `sy` = system CPU percentage
- `id` = idle CPU percentage
- `wa` = wait CPU percentage

When `us+sy` approaches 100, the CPUs are busy, but not necessarily overloaded. Only the runqueue values determine CPU overload. When `wa` values exceed 20, then 20 percent of the processing time is waiting for a resource, usually I/O. It is common to see high `wi` values during backup and exports, but high `wa` values can also indicate an I/O bottleneck.

Using the `iostat` *Utility*

The `iostat` utility shows elapsed I/O against each of the physical disks. An example of `iostat` is presented in Exhibit 20.2. The "3" is the time interval in seconds between snapshots, and all numbers are those accumulated between the 3-second interval. The important columns are:

- Kb_read = the amount of K-bytes read during the elapsed interval
- Kb_wrtn = the amount of K-bytes written during the elapsed interval

The iostat utility is great for finding busy disks. When the wa column of vmstat indicates an I/O bottleneck, the iostat utility should be your next stop. Once you have found the offending physical disk, identify the corresponding mount point (get the mapping of disk to mount points from your SA). You can then run the utlbstat-utlestat utility to see the specific Oracle data files that are causing the bottleneck. Once identified, these can be moved onto a "cooler" disk or striped across several devices.

Note: If you are using OS-level striping (i.e., RAID 0+1 or RAID 10), you should never see excessive I/O bottlenecks because all data files are spread across all spindles.

Exhibit 20.1 Using the vmstat Utility

```
>vmstat3
    kthr       memory                page                    faults              cpu
    ----     -----------     -------------------------    ------------     ---------------
    r  b        avm  fre      re pi  po  fr  sr cy         in   sy  cs      us  sy  id wa
    0  0      84283 207        0  1   1  59 174  0        178   40 142      18   4  75  4
    0  0      84283 187        0  4   0   0   0  0        144  294  70       2   1  91  6
    0  0      84283 184        0  0   0   0   0  0        171  740  99       5   2  89  4
    0  0      84283 165        0  0   0   0   0  0        173  193  98       1   8  52 40
    0  0      84283 150        0  3   0   0   0  0        205  615 136       4   2  87  6
    0  0      84283 141        0  1   0   0   0  0        281  935 192       5   0  91  4
```

Exhibit 20.2 Using the iostat Utility

```
> iostat 3
tty:            tin     tout    avg-cpu:     % user      % sys   % idle   % iowait
                0.0    306.7                   10.3        0.7     81.7        7.3
Disks:     % tm_act     Kbps          tps   Kb_read    Kb_wrtn
hdisk5          0.0      0.0          0.0         0          0
hdisk6          0.0      0.0          0.0         0          0
hdisk0          4.7     20.0          5.0        60          0
hdisk1          0.0      0.0          0.0         0          0
hdisk2          0.0      0.0          0.0         0          0
hdisk3          0.0      0.0          0.0         0          0
hdisk4          2.7     12.0          3.0        36          0
hdisk7          0.0      0.0          0.0         0          0
```

Bdf cpommand with hp/ux:

```
>bdf
Filesystem               kbytes        used         avail      %used    Mounted on
/dev/vg00/lvol3           86016       31833         50828        39%    /
/dev/vg00/lvol1           47829       22369         20677        52%    /stand
/dev/vg00/lvol8          716800      416758        282595        60%    /var
/dev/vg00/lvol7          536576      369184        156950        70%    /usr
/dev/vg02/lvol12        9216000        3365       8636853         0%    /u18
/dev/vg02/lvol11        4096000        2104       3838035         0%    /u17
```

Show Mount Points for a Physical Disk

The DBA should know the mapping between physical disk, logical volumes, and mount points. Without this information, it is very difficult to find an I/O problem. Now that you know the offending hdisk, you can use the following command to find the corresponding mount point:

```
>lspv -l hdisk7

hdisk7:
LV NAME   LPs   PPs   DISTRIBUTION          MOUNT POINT
loglv05   1     1     00..01..00..00..00    N/A
lv06      275   275   00..107..108..60..00  /u06
```

File and DASD Management

Let's begin with basic filesystem commands. The DBA often needs to see the most recent files in a filesystem that have been "touched." This is done with the command shown in Exhibit 20.3.

Exhibit 20.3 Determining Most Recently Touched Files in a Filesystem

```
>ls -alt|head
-rw-r---   1   oracle   dba   52429312   May 11 07:00   archlog272.arc
-rw-r---   1   oracle   dba   393829     May 10 20:20   archlog271.arc.Z
-rw-r---   1   oracle   dba   19748689   May 10 20:03   archlog270.arc.Z
-rw-r---   1   oracle   dba   16018687   May 10 08:05   archlog269.arc.Z
```

Note that "touched" is different from "changed." A file is touched anytime it is read by a process, but a file is only changed when it has been written.

Exhibit 20.4 displays the most recently changed files. Note that the -c option displays in reverse order, and we must pipe to "tail" to see the most recent values.

To display file size in 512-byte blocks, issue the following:

```
>du -s * |sort -n|tail
```

Exhibit 20.4 Determining Most Recently Changed Files

```
>ls -alc|tail
-rw-r---   1   oracle   dba   19176419   May 09 05:02   archlog263.arc.Z
-rw-r---   1   oracle   dba   15091191   May 09 05:03   archlog264.arc.Z
-rw-r---   1   oracle   dba   15850030   May 10 05:02   archlog265.arc.Z
-rw-r---   1   oracle   dba   571115     May 10 05:02   archlog266.arc.Z
-rw-r---   1   oracle   dba   20091443   May 10 05:02   archlog267.arc.Z
-rw-r---   1   oracle   dba   2364298    May 10 05:02   archlog268.arc.Z
```

Locating a File that Contains Certain Strings

This is a great command for finding all files that contain a specified string. For example, assume that you are trying to locate a script that queries the `v$session` table. Issue the `find` command, as shown in Exhibit 20.5, and UNIX will search all subdirectories, looking in all files for the `v$session` table.

Exhibit 20.5 An Example of the `find` Command

```
>find . -print|xargs grep v\$session

grep: 0652-033 Cannot open ./.sh_history.
./repfix/sp2_mig_test/log/PAUR.log:select username,sid,serial# from v$session
./repfix/sp2_mig_test/log/PUK.log:select username,sid,serial# from v$session
./repfix/sp2_mig_test/res.sql:from v$session
./repfix/sp2_mig_test/res.sql:select username,sid,serial# from v$session
./repfix/pcr/pcr491.log:SQL> select user, global_name, machine from v$session, g
./repfix/pcr/prosit_load/killusr.sql:from v$session
./repfix/pcr/pcr570d.log:SQL> select user, global_name, machine from v$session,
./repfix/pcr/pcr595.log:SQL> select user, global_name, machine from v$session, g
./repfix/presmp/afiedt.buf:select username, sid, serial# from v$session
./repfix/presmp/kill_sess_script.sql:from v$session
./repfix/presmp/run_start.sql:select username, sid, serial# from v$session
./rich/B1_scripts/create_kill_users.sql:from v$session
```

Finding Recently Created Files

The following command is great for finding files that have been recently added to your server. DBAs use this most commonly when a file system is nearly full and they need to identify the most recently added files. The following command lists all files that were created in the past day:

```
>find . -mtime -1 -print
```

Finding Large Files

When a filesystem becomes full, the DBA must quickly find all large files on the filesystem. The following command will cascade through the subdirectories and display all files that are greater than the specified size. In the following example, we find all files greater than 10K.

```
>find . -size +10000 – print
./repfix/presmp/stdy_plan_task.dmp
```

Deleting Files

As discussed, the DBA sometimes needs to remove older files from file systems. For example, the DBA may want to remove older archived redo logs from the redo log file system. The following command will identify all files that are more than 7 days old:

```
>find . -mtime +7
```

We can ignore all the `rm` commands to this syntax to automatically remove all files that are more than 7 days old. The `–exec` command functions similarly to the `xargs` command.

```
find . – mtime +7 -exec rm {} \;
```

Listing Volume Groups

The three commands (AIX only) shown in Exhibit 20.6 can be used to pair volume groups with UNIX mount points. The third command is a fancy version that uses the `xargs` command to directly display the volume groups.

Exhibit 20.6 Using the `lsvg` Command

```
>lsvg -o

appvg16
appvg15
appvg11

>lsvg -l appvg01

appvg01:
LV NAME        TYPE      LPs     PPs     PVs     LV STATE       MOUNT POINT
loglv00      jfslog        1       1     1       open/syncd     N/A
lv01            jfs      123     123     1       open/syncd     /u01
lv17            jfs       62      62     1       open/syncd     /legato

>lsvg -o|xargs lsvg -l

appvg16:
LV NAME        TYPE      LPs     PPs     PVs     LV STATE       MOUNT POINT
loglv15      jfslog        1       1     1       open/syncd     N/A
lv16            jfs      489     489     1       open/syncd     /u16
appvg15:
LV NAME        TYPE      LPs     PPs     PVs     LV STATE       MOUNT POINT
loglv14      jfslog        1       1     1       open/syncd     N/A
lv15            jfs      489     489     1       open/syncd     /u15
appvg14:
```

Replacing Default `tnsnames.ora` with a Soft Link to a Master Location

For Oracle DBA administration, it is important to have a single `tnsnames.ora` file of each server. The search order is:

```
$TNS_ADMIN
/etc
$ORACLE_HOME/network/admin

>ls -s $TNS_ADMIN/tnsnames.ora

$ORACLE_HOME/network/admin/tnsnames.ora

>ls -al t*
lrwxrwxrwx 1 oracle dba 39 May 16 09:00
   tnsnames.ora -> /uol/app/oracle/admin/tnsnames.ora
```

UNIX Programming

Once the Oracle DBA is comfortable with UNIX programming, there are many great DBA utilities that can be made by combining UNIX commands into scripts.

IF Testing

```
# Ensure that the parms have been passed to the script
if [ -z "$1" ]
  then
    echo "Usage: mon_purge.ksh <ORACLE_SID> <#_days_data_to_keep>
      (where value is > 100)"
    exit 99
  fi
if [ -z "$2" ]
  then
    echo "Usage: mon_purge.ksh <ORACLE_SID> <#_days_data_to_keep>
      (where value is > 100)"
    exit 99
  fi
# Exit is parm is not at least 100 days to keep data
tmp=`expr $2`
if [ $tmp -lt 100 ]
  then
    echo
    echo "Purge is less than 100 days. Aborting Purge."
    echo
    exit 99
  fi
```

Looping

The loop construct can be used to loop through all entries in a file. In the following example, we loop through /etc/oratab, visiting each database with an SQL*Plus command:

```
# Loop through each host name . . .
    for host in `cat ~oracle/.rhosts|cut -d"."
    -f1|awk '{print $1}'|sort -u`
do
  echo " "
  echo "************************"
  echo "$host"
  echo "************************"
  # Loop through each database name on the host. . .
  for db in `rsh $host "cat /etc/oratab|egrep
    ':N|:Y'|grep -v \*|cut -f1 -d':'"`
  do
    # Get the ORACLE_HOME for each database
    home=`rsh $host "cat /etc/oratab|egrep
     ':N|:Y'|grep -v \*|grep ${db}|cut -f2 -d':'"`
    echo " "
    echo "database is $db"
    done
done
```

Now we can use this technique to visit SQL*Plus on each database and execute the same command:

```
# loop from database to database for db in `cat /etc/oratab|egrep ':N|:Y'|grep
   -v \*|grep ${db}|cut - f1 -d':'"`
do
      echo " "
      echo "database is $db"
      rsh $host "
      ORACLE_SID=${db}; export ORACLE_SID;
      ORACLE_HOME=${home}; export ORACLE_HOME;
      ${home}/bin/sqlplus -s /<<!
      set pages 9999;
      set heading off;
      select value from v"\\""$"parameter where name='optimizer_mode';
      exit
      !"
done
```

Sending UNIX Files to cc:mail

```
cat /root/oracle/mon/dba_cmd.lst|mailx -s "Secret DBA Activity Report"
   michael.dugan@spcorp.com
```

Incrementing a Counter

```
count="`expr $count+1`"
```

Adding Two UNIX Variables

```
TOT=`expr $SYS + $USR`
```

Changing All Files in a Directory

This script changes the old string to the new string in all files in the directory. A backup of the prior contents is placed in a tmp directory.

```
#!/bin/ksh

tmpdir=tmp.$$

mkdir $tmpdir.new

for f in $*
do
   sed -e 's/sum/avg/g' < $f > $tmpdir.new/$f
done

# Whoops
mkdir $tmpdir.old
mv $* $tmpdir.old/
# Whoops

cd $tmpdir.new
mv $* ../

cd ..
rmdir $tmpdir.new
```

We execute the script, passing the file mask as an argument:

```
> chg_all.sh *.sql
```

Submitting Jobs in the Background

```
nohup filename > listingfilename 2>&1 &
```

UNIX Command Summary

Kill all Oracle	ps -ef|grep "ora_"|grep -v grep|awk '{print $2}'|xargs -i kill -9 {}
Kill all Oracle wo BG	kill -9 `ps -fuoracle|grep ksh|awk '{print $2}'`
Kill stubborn task	cat /dev/null > /dev/ttyname kill -9 pid#
Shutdown server	shutdown -r0
remote copy	rcp hostname:/file/name
remote mount file	mount host:/hostpath /alias/pathname
remote command	rsh host "ps -ef"
remount a lost file	mount -a
Show semaphores	ipcs -s
Show UNIX errors(AIX)	errpt -a|more
Show UNIX sys parms	lsattr -El sys0
Show memory	lsdev -C|grep mem followed by: Lsattr -El mem_name
See held memory segs	ipcs -pmb (note svrmgrl oradebug ipc command)
Remove memory segs	ipcrm -m xxxxx
Show swap info	swapinfo or swapon -a
Show paging space	lspa -a
Show top CPU%	ps auxgw|sort +2
Show total CPU usage	ps augxww|egrep "RSS| "
Show # CPU's	lsdev -C|grep Process|wc -l
OS CPU, paging stats	vmstat (osview on IRIX)
Show load avgs	w or "top w HP/UX, SGI & DEC"
OS I/O stats	iostat
Watch file writes	tail -f filename
search binary for string	strings filename|grep string
See recent chg	ls -alc|head
See recent touch	ls -alt|head
Hex dump file	od -x filename
Most active tasks	ps -ef|sort +6|tail

(continues)

UNIX Command Summary (continued)

Files < 3dys old	`find . -mtime -3 -print`
Files > 10k	`find . -size +10000 -print`
Find strings in dir hier	`find . -print|xargs grep -I string`
Del files > 20 dys old	`find . -mtime +20 -exec rm {} \;`
display return code	`echo $?`
Increment a counter	`count="`expr $count+1`"`
Add two UNIX variables	`TOT=`expr $SYS + $USR``
rows w col4=x or y	`egrep '^...(x,y)' < inputfile`
Show file usage	`du -s * |sort -n`
Create soft link	`ln -s destination_name file_name`
Display LVM	`vgdisplay -v`
Mount points for disk	`lspv -l diskname`
Show volume groups	`lsvg -o|xargs lsvg -I`

```
**************************************************************************
Enable backspace     ky stty erase (press backspace key)

Vi - Del to EOF      dG
V I -Read-in file    :r filename

In "set -o vi"

   <esc> \           = file completion
   <esc> k /string   = find a string
   editing    l=forward 1 char
              h=back I char

filename completion    set -o emacs <esc><esc>   or in csh: set filec <esc>
```

Chapter 21

File Exchange Solutions: SQL*Loader, PL/SQL, and Pro*C

Serg Shestakov
Dmitry Petrov

A very important aspect of any large information system is how it handles diverse and complex file exchange procedures. Interfaces to external files can play a key role in many areas (for example, when migrating to Oracle from legacy systems or supporting international standards such as Visa or Europay). In addition to the complexity associated with application logic, there are strong requirements for file exchange solutions to be fast, secure, and reliable. When data is stored in Oracle database, developers can rely on three basic Oracle tools when designing and implementing file exchange solutions: SQL*Loader, PL/SQL, and Pro*C. This chapter discusses how these powerful tools can be used in file exchange procedures; in particular, how to develop robust and reliabile file exchange solutions. Also shown is how to develop a safe file exchange daemon. Assume that Oracle database server is running on the UNIX platform and has Pro*C Precompiler software installed and is configured to work with the GNU version of C compiler.

SQL*Loader

The SQL*Loader utility loads data from external files into Oracle tables. It is very reliable and fits best when loading large amounts of data without complex processing. If one needs to implement complex logic, there is a way to bypass limitations of SQL*Loader functionality by writing data to a temporary table and then processing it with PL/SQL block. Despite some functional disadvantages,

0-8493-1139-X/02/$0.00+$1.50
©2002 by CRC Press LLC

SQL*Loader has a very flexible performance tuning mechanism to boost its performance. Properly tuned SQL*Loader outperforms both Pro*C and PL/SQL on most common tasks.

Now we will outline the most important parameters influencing SQL*Loader performance. We can choose between two load methods — conventional and direct. The conventional method uses the SQL INSERT command to move data and the COMMIT command to save changes. It supports concurrent access and applies all validation rules, but actively uses SGA and can slow down other applications running against the database. The direct method gives significant performance gains because it creates data blocks and writes directly to database using asynchronous I/O and addressing SGA only to maintain extents. The main disadvantages of the direct method are that it locks tables during load — users cannot change data (except other direct loads running in parallel); it supports only PRIMARY KEY, UNIQUE, and NOT NULL constraints; and it does not support in control file useful SQL functions such as REPLACE. The conventional method is the default; to change this behavior, specify DIRECT=TRUE in the parameter file or command line.

Let's focus on performance tuning for direct load. First of all, to speed up the direct load for databases running in ARCHIVELOG mode, we can turn off logging specifying UNRECOVERABLE in the SQL*Loader control file or temporarily switch database to NOARCHIVELOG mode. Next, we can calculate average/exact line length of input file line and prompt it to SQL*Loader along with number of asynchronous buffers. For example, if the line length for input file `TRANS.DAT` is 29 bytes and we want use 16 I/O buffers, we specify `INFILE 'TRANS.DAT' "RECSIZE 120 BUFFERS 16"`. If all lines have equal length, starting with SQL*Loader 1.1, we can indicate `"FIX 120"` and if it is an average length, we specify `"VAR 120"`. Note that double-quoted parameters are operating system specific. By default, SQL*Loader writes lots of messages. If discards are frequent and large files must be loaded despite the errors, we can suppress error messages by setting the SILENT parameter to (DISCARDS) and setting ERRORS=999999 to overwrite the default threshold of 50 errors when SQL*Loader aborts. In this case, the total number of errors will be printed anyway, so we can scan log and raise the alarm.

There are several other ways to boost direct load performance. We can try to reduce data saves, increasing ROWS parameter. We can presort data in external files by largest index; this will reduce temporary segment space usage and preallocate space for a new table specifying large INITIAL or MINEXTENTS value in the CREATE TABLE command. As mentioned, direct loads can even be run in parallel. It gives much better performance, but parallel direct load has limitations that may require some manual work, such as dropping each index before loading and creating it after loading (indexes are not supported), temporarily disabling referential integrity constraints. Parallel direct load works faster if we create and specify a separate data file for each load. In many cases, a combination of these performance-tuning practices can dramatically reduce the average load time.

As stated earlier, direct load does not support all the constraints. Most importantly, it disables triggers. So, for complex processing there are only two options left: (1) to load into temporary table and process data later or (2) to apply the conventional load method. Consider an example of complex conventional load using the triggers mechanism. In this example, we load a transactions file, a common task for electronic payments processing. We will see how to define a data schema, how to write PL/SQL code (package and triggers) to process data being loaded, and how to adjust the SQL*Loader configuration for a given task.

Let's start with the input file format. Each section in the transactions file has several lines. Section starts with header indicated by `001` prefix code and describing a 16-digit card number, date in 'DD.MM.YYYY' format and followed by several lines indicated by `002` prefix code and describing transactions made — sales point, sum, sign of operation (0 for minus, 1 for plus), currency. Sums are padded with whitespaces. The section below says that on Jan 01, 2000, there were two transactions with card number `0123000000000001`. Each transaction is a withdrawal (code `0`) in USD (code `840`). Withdrawals were made from terminals `POS0001` and `POS002` for $345.44 and $15.10, respectively:

```
001000123000000000000101.01.2000
002POS0001      345.440840
002POS0002      15.1  0840
```

The most difficult problem here is to track what transaction belongs to what card number — there are no unique IDs given in input file. Now we design data schema to store transactions. Because of the complex file structure, we need two tables: (1) temporary for headers and (2) permanent for all transactional data. We plan to tell SQL*Loader to choose what line is a header and what line is a transaction using the prefixes (`001` and `002`, respectively). Here goes the loader table called `L_TRX`, to store the card number, transaction date, and an additional counter to track the records:

```
REC_ID field:
   CREATE TABLE L_TRX
      (CARD_NUM          VARCHAR2(16),
        TRX_DATE         DATE,
        REC_ID           NUMBER);
```

The next task is to define the target TRX table to store all transactional data described above, plus an additional REC_NUM field — the number of the logical record from which the row will be loaded; its value is filled using the RECNUM keyword of SQL*Loader:

```
CREATE TABLE TRX
   (CARD_NUM          VARCHAR2(16),
     TRX_DATE         DATE,
     TRX_POINT        VARCHAR2(10),
     TRX_AMOUNT       NUMBER,
     TRX_SIGN         NUMBER(1),
     CURRENCY         VARCHAR2(3),
     REC_ID           NUMBER,
     REC_NUM          NUMBER);
```

Having defined the data structure, let's implement processing logic. Bypass SQL*Loader limitations using the power of Oracle PL/SQL language; then create a package in PL/SQL not to implement some logic but rather to store headers and service data in memory. For this purpose, declare two tables, keeping card numbers and transaction dates — CARD_NUM and TRX_DATE, respectively. Note that both tables are allocated dynamically and have unlimited memory quotas. Also declare two service number variables: TRX_rec_id and TRX_rec_num_prev that will help track a moment when we start reading transactions data related to the next card.

```
CREATE OR REPLACE PACKAGE SQLload AS
  TYPE CARD_NUM_type IS TABLE OF VARCHAR2(16)
    INDEX BY BINARY_INTEGER ;

  TYPE TRX_DATE_type IS TABLE OF DATE
    INDEX BY BINARY_INTEGER ;

  CARD_NUM CARD_NUM_type;
  TRX_DATE TRX_DATE_type;

  TRX_rec_idNUMBER(10);
  TRX_rec_num_prevNUMBER(10);
END SQLload;
```

The following piece of PL/SQL code creates the TBI_l_trx trigger that fetches header data being loaded into the in-memory tables, CARD_NUM and TRX_DATE. We will need this information when loading data into the main table (i.e., TRX).

```
CREATE OR REPLACE TRIGGER TBI_l_trx
BEFORE INSERT ON L_TRX FOR EACH ROW
BEGIN
  SQLload.CARD_NUM(:new.REC_ID) := :new.CARD_NUM;
  SQLload.TRX_DATE(:new.REC_ID) := :new.TRX_DATE;
END;
```

See Appendix 21.1.

Now we have come to the most important point: the TBI_trx trigger that populates the main TRX table with all the transaction details. We break the trigger's code into two parts. In the first part listed below, we target this trigger to run before inserts and assign initial values to service counters of our SQLload package when the trigger runs for the first time; that is, when TRX.REC_ID (which we write using the SEQUENCE function) equals 1.

```
CREATE OR REPLACE TRIGGER TBI_trx
BEFORE INSERT ON TRX FOR EACH ROW
BEGIN
    IF :new.rec_id = 1 THEN
      SQLload.TRX_rec_id := 0;
      SQLload.TRX_rec_num_prev := :new.rec_num;
    END IF;
```

The second part is responsible for detecting the moment when we start loading the first transaction of the next input file section. We track this moment using the TRX_rec_num_prev service counter; later we will show how this mechanism works. Once we have detected this moment, we need to increment another service counter (TRX_rec_id); that is, we generate the next unique ID linking the card number with its transactions. Next we refresh counters with new values so that we will be able to detect the first transaction related to the next card. Finally, we read the card number and transaction date from memory tables, store information to the main table, and end the trigger.

```
    IF (:new.rec_num-SQLload.TRX_rec_num_prev) >1 THEN
      SQLload.TRX_rec_id := SQLload.TRX_rec_id+1;
    END IF;

    SQLload.TRX_rec_num_prev := :new.rec_num;
    :new.rec_id := SQLload.TRX_rec_id;

    :new.CARD_NUM := SQLload.CARD_NUM(:new.REC_ID);
    :new.TRX_DATE := SQLload.TRX_DATE(:new.REC_ID);
END;
```

Now we define the SQL*Loader control file to move rows starting with 001 code into the L_TRX table and rows starting with 002 code into the TRX table. The corresponding control file (trans.ctl) is listed below. Note that we overwrite the temporary table with the REPLACE clause. To distinguish between the former and latter, we use WHEN- clause criteria. For each table field, we point to exact positions in the external file according to the format listed above. To fill REC_ID fields in both tables, we use the SEQUENCE function:

```
LOAD DATA REPLACE
INTO TABLE L_TRX
WHEN (1:3) = '001'
     (REC_ID              SEQUENCE (1,1),
     CARD_NUM             POSITION (4:19),
     TRX_DATE             POSITION (20:29)
  )

  INTO TABLE TRX
  WHEN (1:3) = '002'
     (REC_ID              SEQUENCE (1,1),
     REC_NUM              RECNUM,
     TRX_POINT            POSITION (4:10),
     TRX_AMOUNT           POSITION (11:25),
     TRX_SIGN             POSITION (26:26),
     CURRENCY             POSITION (27:29)
  )
```

Let's discuss, step-by-step, how the TBI_l_trx and TBI_trx triggers work together when we run load with our control file. When the loader reads transactions (excluding the first transaction), each line has 002 code and the logical record number of current transaction differs from those of previous transactions by 1. When the loader moves data from the section header, it puts data to the L_TRX table, triggering TBI_L_TRX. Note that at this point, the TRX_rec_num_prev variable of the SQLload package is not incremented and the line number differs from TRX_rec_num_prev by more than one. That is why we use this threshold to detect the moment when we start reading transactions related to the next card. We show how to run SQL*Loader in the chapter section describing file exchange daemons. If complex processing is required, we have to enhance SQL*Loader functionality with PL/SQL, but we can also read and write files directly from PL/SQL. We will discuss this mechanism in the next chapter section.

PL/SQL

Before we start working with files from within PL/SQL, we need to set the UTL_FILE_DIR parameter in init<SID>.ora file and restart the database. The path format is operation-system-specific. The asterisk means Oracle is allowed to work with any catalog. For example, to work only with /opt/oracle/FILES, we should specify:

```
UTL_FILE_DIR=/opt/oracle/FILES
```

Remember that a very important issue when interacting with external files is security. We work with external files using the utl_file package. Use a dedicated Oracle user for file exchange and make sure it has the EXECUTE privilege for the utl_file package. Let us assume Oracle database processes run under oracle8 OS user that belongs to dba group. Thus, files will be created under oracle:dba. It is a good practice to configure the oracle8 profile with the umask 640 command to restrict access rights for newly created files. Moreover, to run file exchange daemons safely, it is better to create another OS user (e.g., filex) and add it to the dba group. File exchange daemons are very interesting, and we will later take a closer look at them. You may also want to create an Oracle user called filex to log in from scripts automatically. Note that in daemon scripts it is useful not to keep open usernames and passwords, but rather apply OS-level authentication. Just to name one good reason — passwords should be changed periodically, and manual fixing of numerous scripts each time is a time-overkill. For security reasons, change the access rights for the file exchange catalog issuing:

```
chown filex:dba†/opt/oracle/FILES
chmod 770†/opt/oracle/FILES
```

This configuration lets both oracle8 and filex users create their own files in file exchange catalog and read each others' files. So, PL/SQL procedures can now be run under filex user. Working with files from PL/SQL is pretty straightforward and it's the most important advantage of this approach. Developers need very little training — if any — to start a project. Another plus is that, with PL/SQL, we can implement very sophisticated data processing. But PL/SQL works slowly as compared with SQL*Loader and Pro*C; thus, it is not recommended for working with large files.

With all its advantages and disadvantages, PL/SQL is the best solution for pilot projects that must be rapidly implemented. Now we will illustrate how we can work with files using PL/SQL. For this purpose, we will create a procedure named `Test_File`, the first section of which is given below (see Appendix 21.2). In this section, we declare the file handler and character buffer to fetch data from file `myFile` and `buf`, respectively. First we open the `outfile.dat` file for writing calling the `fopen` function that returns file handler given path, file name, and access mode ('r' - read, 'w' - write, or 'a' - read/write). Then we write the output file using the `put_line` function of the `utl_file` package that takes two parameters (file handler and a string). Once we have finished writing, we close the file with the `fclose` function.

```
CREATE OR REPLACE PROCEDURE Test_File IS
  myFile UTL_FILE.FILE_TYPE;
  buf VARCHAR2(2000);
BEGIN
  myFile := utl_file.fopen('/opt/oracle/FILES',
    'outfile.dat', 'w');

  utl_file.put_line(myFile, 'Test line 1');
  utl_file.put_line(myFile, 'Test line 2');

  if utl_file.is_open(myFile) then
    utl_file.fclose(myFile);
  end if;
```

The second code section illustrates how to read a file. In a similar way, we open the input file (infile.dat) for reading, and read each line in a loop with the `get_line` function until we raise the `no_data_found` exception and will be forced to close the external file. We print each line using the `put_line` function of the `dbms_output` package. Before calling the `Test_File` procedure from SQL console, do not forget to issue the `SET SERVEROUTPUT ON` command to see the `infile.dat` contents printed.

```
MyFile := utl_file.fopen('/opt/oracle/FILES',
    'infile.dat', 'r');

BEGIN
  LOOP
    utl_file.get_line(myFile,buf);
  dbms_output.put_line(buf);
  END LOOP;
EXCEPTION
  WHEN no_data_found THEN
    utl_file.fclose(myFile);
END;
```

The last code fragment listed defines user error messages for different exceptions that may arise when working with files from PL/SQL. Note that when the `utl_file.invalid_path` exception is raised and the path seems to be correct, this may be caused by a wrong UTL_FILE_DIR configuration (for example, DBA may not have restarted it yet with a new parameter); inappropriate access rights for file exchange catalog; whitespaces; or the wrong case in path or file name.

```
EXCEPTION
   WHEN utl_file.invalid_path THEN
      raise_application_error(-20001,
         'file location or name was invalid');
   WHEN utl_file.invalid_mode THEN
      raise_application_error(-20001,
         'the open_mode string was invalid');
   WHEN utl_file.invalid_operation THEN
      raise_application_error(-20001,
         'file could not be opened as requested');
   WHEN utl_file.invalid_filehandle THEN
      raise_application_error(-20001,
         'not a valid file handle');
   WHEN utl_file.write_error THEN
      raise_application_error(-20001,
         'OS error occured during write operation');
   WHEN no_data_found THEN
      raise_application_error(-20001,
         'reached the end of file');
   WHEN utl_file.read_error THEN
      raise_application_error(-20001,
         'OS error occurred during read');
   WHEN value_error THEN
      raise_application_error(-20001,
         'line to long to store in buffer');
END;
```

Thus far, we have discussed SQL*Loader and PL/SQL. Neither tool can be used to rapidly move large amounts of data from Oracle tables to external files. Pro*C is the best solution that fits here. We will discuss this next.

Pro*C

Pro*C/C++ is a precompiler that wraps ANSI C/C++ code and hides from the developer the complexity of working with OCI (Oracle Call Interface). Although in general it is possible to work with OCI directly, in most cases it is not required. With Pro*C, we can build very robust file exchange programs that show best performance moving data from Oracle tables to files and even can outperform SQL*Loader; in particular, when we cannot apply the direct load method. On UNIX platforms, Pro*C can be configured using `vi` to edit the `pcscfg.cfg` configuration file located under the `$ORACLE_HOME/precomp/admin` directory. Using Pro*C, we can implement very complex processing logic. The main precompiler drawback is its language; many Oracle developers need time to become comfortable with Pro*C — except those familiar with C/C++. We'll discuss a typical Pro*C application, transferring data from an Oracle table to an external file. Let's suppose a table called `Destination` has two columns storing source file names and target directories, `src` and `dst`, respectively, along with day of the week. The following SQL code creates the table and fills it with sample data:

```
CREATE TABLE Destination
   (Src VARCHAR2(20),
     Dst VARCHAR2(20),
     Day VARCHAR2(3));
INSERT INTO Destination (Src, Dst, Day) VALUES
       ('/opt/oracle/FILES/trans_mon.dat', 'E:\TRANS', 'mon');
INSERT INTO Destination (Src, Dst, Day) VALUES
       ('/opt/oracle/FILES/rep_mon.dat', 'D:\REPORTS', 'mon');
```

We want our program for a given day of the week to generate an output file named `list.dat`, storing in each line the source and destination separated by the # character. Take a look at the example file below that maps UNIX files to NT directories for Monday:

```
/opt/oracle/FILES/trans_mon.dat#E:\TRANS
/opt/oracle/FILES/rep_mon.dat#D:\REPORTS
```

A similar output file can be used as a parameter for some file exchange daemons. Let's call the Pro*C program `proc_test.pc` and see how it implements the desired behavior. First, we include a library to support I/O (`stdio.h`). We can also include the Pro*C library (`sqlca.h`), but it is better to use `EXEC SQL INCLUDE` for this purpose. The latter works in general — even when the file being included contains `EXEC SQL` commands, it will be precompiled. Now it is time to define variables. We will need one variable to keep a parameter (day of the week), one variable for a source name concatenated with target directory (it will be used to form rows in the output file), and one variable for connect information. Also as agreed, here we copy SQLCA; this data structure will keep the results of SQL commands (see Appendix 21.3).

```
#include <stdio.h>
EXEC SQL BEGIN DECLARE SECTION;
   char day[10];
   char line[41];
   char conn[2];
EXEC SQL END DECLARE SECTION;
EXEC SQL INCLUDE sqlca;
```

Here we define SQLerror function that prints error messages, if any, rolls back changes, and exits:

```
void SQLerror()
{ EXEC SQL WHENEVER SQLERROR CONTINUE;
   printf ("\nError found: %70s \n",
   sqlca.sqlerrm.sqlerrmc);
   EXEC SQL ROLLBACK WORK RELEASE;
   exit(1); }
```

From the code below you notice that we start the main program by declaring the external file handler (`outfile`) and opening the output file with the `fopen` function. The file name is indicated directly as the first argument of `fopen`. If file open fails, the program prints message and returns some error code:

```
int main(int argc, char *argv[])
{ FILE *outfile;
  outfile = fopen("list.dat", "wt");
  if ( outfile == NULL )
    { printf("\nError opening file.\n");
      return -5; }
```

Now we automatically log on to the Oracle database using the OS-level authentication mechanism. Remember that we discussed that it is better not to put user names and passwords in daemon scripts because otherwise we'll need to edit scripts each time the password changes. This rule also works for Pro*C programs. Moreover, each Pro*C program must be recompiled each time its source changes.

```
strcpy(conn, "/");
EXEC SQL WHENEVER SQLERROR DO SQLerror();
EXEC SQL CONNECT :conn;
```

Once the connection to Oracle is established, we define and open a cursor reading from the `NextDest` table source file names concatenated with target directories for a given day of the week. The first command line parameter is referred to as `argv[1]` and indicates the day of the week (`mon`, `tue`, etc.).

```
strcpy(day, argv[1]);
EXEC SQL DECLARE NextDest CURSOR FOR
  SELECT Src || '#' || Dst as Line
  FROM Destination WHERE Day = :day;
EXEC SQL OPEN NextDest ;
```

Next we start a loop scanning all rows returned by the cursor. The loop breaks upon receiving an ORA-01403 error, indicating that the fetch is complete. For each row, we read a source file name concatenated with destination and print this line to output file.

```
for ( ; ; )
{ EXEC SQL FETCH NextDest INTO :line;
  if (sqlca.sqlcode == 1403) break;
  fprintf(outfile, "%s\n", line); }
```

When the program leaves the loop, it closes the file and cursor, commits changes, and exits with normal status:

```
fclose(outfile);
EXEC SQL CLOSE NextDest;
EXEC SQL COMMIT WORK RELEASE;
exit(0); }
```

Probably the most tricky task when working with Pro*C is to configure it properly. This procedure strongly depends on the platform and C/C++ compiler being used. We recommend GNU C compilers. Once we have configured Pro*C, we can try to run our program. To run our `proc_test.pc` program, we must (1) precompile it, calling the Oracle executable `proc` that produces the C file (`proc_test.c`) with OCI codes substituted instead EXEC macros, (2) call the C compiler for `proc_test.c` file to create object file `proc_test.o`,

(3) create executable calling UNIX `make` command, and (4) run the executable with a parameter. In the simplest case, we need to run the four commands listed below (making sure that `PATH` points to `gcc`). First, one precompiles the source and makes a `.c` file; second, one produces the object file; third, one makes `proc_test` executable using library and path as explicitly indicated (to ease compilation); and (5) the last command runs our program to create a file for Monday.

```
proc iname=proc_test.pc
gcc -c proc_test.c
gcc -o proc_test proc_test.o -
  L$ORACLE_HOME/lib -lclntsh
proc_test mon
```

In general for complex Pro*C applications, `gcc` and `make` may require lots of options to be specified. Developers usually prepare a `make` configuration file (e.g., `myproc.mk`) by modifying one that comes with Oracle Pro*C demos and then simply issuing a UNIX command such as those listed below. Before we run it, we should configure `<target>` within `myproc.mk` and, by default, it is called `cppsamples` for C++ and `samples` for ANSI C. In our case, the `make` configuration file entry might look like this: `cppsamples proc_test`. Now at last we can create and run the executable:

```
make -f myproc.mk <target>
proc_test mon
```

By this time we have considered how to move data between Oracle tables and external files. But it is often required to implement complex file exchange procedures to move files between different systems using some application-specific scenarios. We will discuss how to move files between different systems using daemons written in UNIX shell. In particular, we will focus on how to make file exchange daemons secure and reliable.

File Exchange Daemons

Suppose our daemon receives files from another application. How do we ensure that we will read the most recently uploaded files and lock those files from other possibly running instances of our daemon? The signal files mechanism is an answer to this question. Signal files will help make a file exchange session more reliable. Now we will discuss the file exchange scenario in detail. Usually, the file exchange program runs from crontab once and tries to read some signal file. However, in a real-time environment, we had better use a daemon that also runs from crontab but does not exit at once and hang in memory for some time. We start daemon according to the file exchange schedule, and it waits for a signal file to appear in a predefined catalog. If the signal file does not appear until time-out, the daemon aborts and raises the alert. If it manages to detect the signal file within time limits, it logs normal status and does all the application-specific logic.

The following script, `filex_daemon.sh`, is a typical file exchange daemon written in UNIX Bourne shell (see also Appendix 21.4). We start the daemon script by declaring time-related variables. The `d0` and `n0` variables indicate the date and time until the daemon should stay in memory (we specify current date and 9:00, respectively). The `d0` and `n0` variables will keep the current date and time.

```
d0=`date '+%d'`
n0=900
d1=`date '+%d'`
n1=`date '+%H%M'`
```

Now we print a first message to the daemon log file (`filex_daemon.log`) and start a waiting cycle. To distinguish between different tasks that daemon executes, we reference the unique task number using an environment variable called `$TASK`. This is done to ease log analysis. To enter the loop, we check if the time limit has not been reached yet (for example if current time is less than 9:00 and if the date has not changed). The first thing we do upon entering the loop is to check whether the signal file, called `SignalCard<Date>.sf`, exists in the current directory and, if yes, we break the loop to do final preparations for the application-specific section of the daemon script. Otherwise, we suspend the daemon for some time, refresh current date/time variables, and return to time check.

```
echo 'Waiting for signal file, task #' $TASK
   > filex_daemon.log
while [ n1 -lt n0 -a d1 -eq d0 ]
do
      if [ -f SignalCard`date '+%m%d'`.sf] ; then
      echo "Signal file OK." >> fxd.log
      break
   fi
   sleep 600
   n1=`date '+%H%M'`
   d1=`date '+%d'`
done
```

The code section listed below checks once more whether the signal file exists and, if it does, removes it and goes to do application-specific processing; otherwise, it raises an alarm, sending an e-mail message to the administrator (`admin@hostname`) and exits.

```
if [ -f SignalCard`date '+%m%d'`.sf] ; then
   rm -f SignalCard*
else
   mail admin@hostname <<EOF
Subject:Signal file not found. Failed to
   execute $TASK.
EOF
   echo "Timeout reached." >> fxd.log
   exit 0
fi
```

The next part of the daemon does application-specific processing. We will see how to implement several typical tasks. The first task uses ftp service in a background. To keep ftp service silent, we can write a scenario using the `expect` utility, or we can create an ftp parameter file and send it to ftp via standard input. We will discuss the latter approach in detail. The example code is listed below. We want to receive several files from the remote NT server called `NT_HOST` and put those files into the Oracle directory for further processing. First, we check for the old ftp batch file called `get_trans.ftp` and, if it exists, remove it. Next, we put the desired session commands to the ftp batch file. We tell ftp to use binary transfer mode, turn on upper/lower case mapping, change to target UNIX file exchange directory (local), set source NT directory (remote), and do the actual file transfer — to get two files. Note that file names and source directory are specified via environment variables to ease script administration. Once we have the batch file, we involve the ftp; turn off interactive prompting (`i` option), and turn on remote server responses logging (`v` option).

```
if [ -f get_trans.ftp ] ; then
  rm -f get_trans.ftp
fi
echo "bin" > get_trans.ftp
echo "case" >> get_trans.ftp
echo "lcd /opt/oracle/FILES " >> get_trans.ftp
echo "cd ${SOURCE_DIR}" >> get_trans.ftp
echo "get ${FILE_1}" >> get_trans.ftp
echo "get ${FILE_2}" >> get_trans.ftp
echo "quit" >> get_trans.ftp
ftp -iv NT_HOST < get_trans.ftp
```

Earlier, we created the `Test_File` procedure reading from one file and writing to another file. Here, we will discuss a common task of calling a PL/SQL procedure from daemon. To execute a procedure, we invoke the `svrmgrl` utility and write commands to its standard input:

```
svrmgrl <<EOF
CONNECT /
EXECUTE Test_File;
EXIT
EOF
```

Another common task is calling SQL*Loader from daemon, analyzing if the load was successful, and logging the results. The code listed below illustrates how we can implement this task for our SQL*Loader sample control file (`trans.ctl`) to load the file called `TRANS.DAT`. First, we print a status message to log file for our task (`trans_<TASK>.log`). Next, we run the SQL*Loader executable (`sqlldr`) and supply it with some parameters: connect string (we log on to the database automatically using the UNIX account), control file, data file, bad records file, and log file; specify silent mode for discarded rows; and overwrite default value for the errors threshold. Finally, we check if there is a file with bad records. If it exists, then SQL*Load has failed and we give its bad file and log file unique names, indicating a failed task number, and raise an alarm like we did before — by sending an e-mail to the administrator.

```
echo 'Start loading TRANS.DAT' > trans_${TASK}.log
sqlldr USERID=/ CONTROL=trans.ctl DATA=TRANS.DAT \
   BAD=trans.bad LOG=trans.log \
   SILENT=(DISCARDS) ERRORS=999999
if [ -f trans.bad ] ; then
   mv -f trans.log trans${TASK}.log
   mv -f trans.bad trans${TASK}.bad
   echo 'Errors during load.' >>
      trans_${TASK}.log
mail admin@hostname <<EOF
Subject:Errors during load. Failed to execute
   $TASK.
EOF

else
   echo 'Load was OK. >> trans_${TASK}.log
fi
```

It is good practice to keep file exchange daemon logs in plaintext files. If we raise an alarm, it will be easier to analyze a plaintext file than to connect to Oracle and extract log data from its tables. *Note:* If problems are really serious, Oracle may not even be available.

Conclusion

We have discussed basic building blocks for fast, secure, and reliable file exchange solutions integrated with Oracle. SQL*Loader is the fastest tool to move data from external files to a database, and it has a very flexible performance-tuning mechanism. The direct load method gives strong performance benefits. SQL*Loader functionality can be greatly enhanced with the trigger mechanism — for the sequential load method. PL/SQL with its `UTL_FILE` package is easy to learn and can be used for pilot projects. Pro*C is difficult to configure, but it is a very powerful tool to access the database via OCI. It can implement complex business logic and shows its best performance when we need to move data from Oracle to external files. To make file exchange procedures secure and reliable, use daemons written in UNIX shell and rely on signal files. Do not cling to one particular tool. Detect bottlenecks and find solutions using the entire spectrum of technologies available.

Appendix 21.1 Trigger to Load Transactions: TBI_trx:

```
CREATE OR REPLACE TRIGGER TBI_trx
BEFORE INSERT ON TRX FOR EACH ROW
BEGIN
IF :new.rec_id = 1 THEN
    SQLload.TRX_rec_id := 0;
    SQLload.TRX_rec_num_prev := :new.rec_num;
END IF;
IF (:new.rec_num-SQLload.TRX_rec_num_prev) >1
THEN
    SQLload.TRX_rec_id := SQLload.TRX_rec_id+1;
END IF;

SQLload.TRX_rec_num_prev := :new.rec_num;
:new.rec_id := SQLload.TRX_rec_id;

:new.CARD_NUM := SQLload.CARD_NUM(:new.REC_ID);

:new.TRX_DATE := SQLload.TRX_DATE(:new.REC_ID);

END;
```

Appendix 21.2 PL/SQL Procedure Working with Files

```
Test_File:
    CREATE OR REPLACE PROCEDURE Test_File IS myFile
    UTL_FILE.FILE_TYPE; buf VARCHAR2(2000);
    BEGIN
        myFile := utl_file.fopen('/opt/oracle/FILES', 'outfile.dat', 'w');

        utl_file.put_line(myFile, 'Test line 1');
        utl_file.put_line(myFile, 'Test line 2');

        if utl_file.is_open(myFile) then
            utl_file.fclose(myFile);
        end if;

    MyFile := utl_file.fopen('/opt/oracle/FILES', 'infile.dat', 'r');

    BEGIN
        LOOP
            utl_file.get_line(myFile,buf); dbms_output.put_line(buf);
        END LOOP;
    EXCEPTION
        WHEN no_data_found THEN
            utl_file.fclose(myFile);
    END;

    EXCEPTION
        WHEN utl_file.invalid_path THEN
            raise_application_error(-20001,
                'file location or name was invalid');
        WHEN utl_file.invalid_mode THEN
            raise_application_error(-20001,
                'the open_mode string was invalid');
        WHEN utl_file.invalid_operation THEN
            raise_application_error(-20001,
                'file could not be opened as requested');

        WHEN utl_file.invalid_filehandle THEN
            raise_application_error(-20001,
                'not a valid file handle');
```

(continues)

Appendix 21.2 PL/SQL Procedure Working with Files (continued)

```
        WHEN utl_file.write_error THEN
            raise_application_error(-20001,
                'OS error occured during write
        operation');
        WHEN no_data_found THEN
            raise_application_error(-20001,
                'reached the end of file');
        WHEN utl_file.read_error THEN
            raise_application_error(-20001,
                'OS error occurred during read');
        WHEN value_error THEN
            raise_application_error(-20001,
                'line to long to store in buffer');
    END;
```

Appendix 21.3 Pro*C Program to Upload File `proc_test.pc`

```
#include
EXEC SQL BEGIN DECLARE SECTION;
    char day[10];
    char line[41];
    char conn[2];
EXEC SQL END DECLARE SECTION;
EXEC SQL INCLUDE sqlca;

void SQLerror()
{ EXEC SQL WHENEVER SQLERROR CONTINUE;
    printf ("\nError found: %70s \n",
sqlca.sqlerrm.sqlerrmc);
    EXEC SQL ROLLBACK WORK RELEASE;
    exit(1); }

int main(int argc, char *argv[])
{ FILE *outfile;
    outfile = fopen("list.dat", "wt");
    if ( outfile == NULL )
        { printf("\nError opening file.\n");
            return -5; }

strcpy(conn, "/");
EXEC SQL WHENEVER SQLERROR DO SQLerror();
EXEC SQL CONNECT :conn;

strcpy(day, argv[1]);
EXEC SQL DECLARE NextDest CURSOR FOR
    SELECT Src || '#' || Dst as Line
    FROM Destination WHERE Day = :day;
EXEC SQL OPEN NextDest ;

for ( ; ; )
{ EXEC SQL FETCH NextDest INTO :line;
    if (sqlca.sqlcode == 1403) break;
    fprintf(outfile, "%s\n", line); }

fclose(outfile);
EXEC SQL CLOSE NextDest;
EXEC SQL COMMIT WORK RELEASE;
exit(0); }
```

Appendix 21.4 File Exchange Daemon fxd.sh

```
d0=`date '+%d'`
n0=900
d1=`date '+%d'`
n1=`date '+%H%M'`

echo 'Waiting for signal file, task #' $TASK >
fxd.log
while [ n1 -lt n0 -a d1 -eq d0 ]
do
    if [ -f SignalCard`date '+%m%d'`.sf] ; then
        echo "Signal file OK." >> fxd.log
        break
    fi
    sleep 600
    n1=`date '+%H%M'`
    d1=`date '+%d'`
done

if [ -f SignalCard`date '+%m%d'`.sf] ; then
    rm -f SignalCard*
else
    mail admin@hostname <Subject:Signal file not
found. Failed to execute $TASK.
EOF
echo "Timeout reached." >> fxd.log
exit 0
fi

if [ -f get_trans.ftp ] ; then
    rm -f get_trans.ftp
fi
echo "bin" > get_trans.ftp
echo "case" >> get_trans.ftp
echo "lcd /opt/oracle/FILES " >> get_trans.ftp
echo "cd ${SOURCE_DIR}" >> get_trans.ftp
echo "get ${FILE_1}" >> get_trans.ftp
echo "get ${FILE_2}" >> get_trans.ftp
echo "quit" >> get_trans.ftp
ftp -iv NT_HOST < get_trans.ftp

svrmgrl <<EOF
CONNECT /
EXECUTE Test_File;
EXIT
EOF
echo 'Start loading TRANS.DAT' >
trans_${TASK}.log
sqlldr USERID=/ CONTROL=trans.ctl
DATA=TRANS.DAT \
    BAD=trans.bad LOG=trans.log \
    SILENT=(DISCARDS) ERRORS=999999
if [ -f trans.bad ] ; then
    mv -f trans.log trans${TASK}.log
    mv -f trans.bad trans${TASK}.bad
    echo 'Errors during load.' >>
trans_${TASK}.log
mail admin@hostname <Subject:Errors during
load. Failed to execute $TASK.
EOF

else
echo 'Load was OK. >> trans_${TASK}.log
fi
```

Chapter 22

Gauging How Linux May Change the DBMS Market

Paul Korzeniowski

Linux is only the kernel of an operating system, the part that controls hardware, manages files, and separates processes. Third-party companies can add multiple install methods, applications, and other add-ons to the Linux systems they ship, which are called Linux distributions. These companies can combine utilities and applications to differentiate their offerings. However, between these products, the actual Linux kernel has remained almost completely the same.

Linux History

Linux is the brainchild of Linus Torvalds, who created the operating system as a hobby while a student at the University of Helsinki in Finland in 1991. While studying, he developed an interest in Minix, a compact version of UNIX and set out to build a better variation of the operating system. In 1994, he delivered version 1.0 of Linux, and the operating system has been gaining popularity ever since.

The reason for the rise is the way Torvalds distributed the operating system. Linux does not really belong to any one company. Instead, the emerging operating system is available at no charge to developers who are encouraged to improve it (as long as any changes are available to all licensees) and then free to sell it to customers.

Because it is open-source software, a worldwide community of Linux engineers continually updates the operating system, and users can add modules as they choose. The result is that the operating system is constantly upgraded and bugs are quickly fixed.

0-8493-1139-X/02/$0.00+$1.50
©2002 by CRC Press LLC

This model is antithetical to commercial versions UNIX or Windows NT. In these cases, customers have little say about the operating system because the vendors believe they understand the operating system best — knowledge they charge customers for.

The engineering community transformed Linux from a student's technical toy into an operating system with increasing appeal. The software is now available as a shrinkwrapped packaged, and many find it to be simple to install, reliable, and easy to maintain.

The timing for Torvalds' new operating system model was fortuitous. The Internet changed the way large companies view and purchase software and offered the infrastructure needed to make Linux so accessible — and ultimately popular. Using technology via the World Wide Web is not considered as big a risk as it once was; freeware, once a no-no in corporate IT departments, has become part and parcel of many companies' operations.

A stronghold for Linux is the Internet service provider market, where the freeware Web server Apache has proven very popular. Momentum is growing among small to mid-sized businesses. The new operating system has been used for applications such as airplane design, firewalls, telescope control, and Web servers. A handful of small companies have been building new businesses based on marketing their iterations of Linux, with Caldera, Inc. and Red Hat Software, Inc. having two of the more popular versions.

International Data Corp., a Framingham, Massachusetts market research firm, reported that in 1998, 240,000 Linux servers were shipped. That represents 6.3 percent of the total market. Because users can download the operating system for free, as much as ten times that many persons may now rely on Linux.

Because of the growing level of support, the operating system is starting to attract attention from third parties, including top database management system (DBMS) suppliers. One reason is that the operating system promises to deliver on past UNIX promises of application portability that failed as various UNIX initiatives splintered. Supporting multiple iterations of an operating system can be expensive for vendors. The Linux Standard Base (LSB) defines a common core that ensures that compliant applications will run on all distributions of Linux. Gradually, the UNIX operating system variation that does not cost customers a dollar is gaining respect from big companies. In addition to DBMS vendors, IBM, Intel, and Netscape have promised or delivered products that run under Linux.

Linux Advantages

Corporations turn to new technology for two reasons: (1) lower costs and (2) increased functionality. Linux has the potential to offer both benefits.

Cost savings start with the fact that the operating system is basically free — although companies will have to make a modest payment from a third party that will deliver items such as documentation and technical support. In addition, the operating system runs on the Wintel architecture, so the underlying hardware requires a minimal investment.

Other savings are linked to the operating system's functionality. Like the IBM OS/2 and the SCO UnixWare, Linux is an operating system that advocates view as technically superior to Microsoft's Windows product line, which has not been as reliable, stable, or easy to implement as corporations desire. Because it is more reliable, Linux should require less maintenance. While the difference in support requirements will vary by company, it can be great; rather than having to spend two to four hours maintaining a single Windows 95 machine per week, technicians may need to work only 15 minutes for every Linux machine.

Linux's distribution model helps to ensure that the operating system will only get better with timely updates. Engineers can simultaneously work on needed enhancements, and only the best entries make their way into the operating system.

The emerging operating system also helps vendors cut costs. They no longer have to support an expensive research and development staff because any interested engineer is able to submit an enhancement. Although building a business on contribution from unseen engineers may seem risky, to date, engineers have delivered high-quality work. Engineers have focused on areas where they have expertise and have been able to add a wide range of functions to Linux.

Linux Weaknesses

Although Linux has made a great deal of progress since its inception, the operating system still has a long way to go until it meets supporters' expectations. The primary issues revolve around support. With traditional operating systems, users have a clear idea of which vendor to call when an operating system fails. With Linux, the issue is not as clear because anyone can download the software. Although the Linux community exists and a company can get support on the Internet, it is not the kind of guaranteed 24-hour-a-day response an enterprise customer needs.

In select cases, this will not be a major concern. Large corporations have sophisticated in-house staff and may be willing to take on the support chores themselves. But in most instances, small and mid-size corporations are looking to off-load support to third parties rather than add work for their in-house staff.

Third parties, such as Red Hat and Caldera, offer companies documentation and technical support for a nominal fee. Because Linux suppliers are small and have smaller-than-average research and development staffs, corporations may be leery in adopting the operating system; IT managers worry about ongoing enhancements and legal departments are concerned about who to sue if the operating system fails.

Recently, established PC suppliers have started to assuage these fears. In January of 1999, IBM announced it would support Linux on its NetFinity servers alongside Microsoft's Windows NT. If more well-known vendors follow the same course, Linux use may spread.

Another issue is long-term developments for the operating system. Because no single vendor is in charge, companies have no assurances that Linux will deliver on its write-once, run everywhere portability claims. Currently, Torvalds — who founded Transmeta, Inc., a Santa Clara, California, start-up working on its first product — determines which enhancements will be incorporated in the operating system. Although it has worked to date, there are concerns as to whether this approach will be viable if acceptance grows in the future.

Proponents promote the operating system as simple to use, but that is the case only to those already familiar with Linux. The operating system is much different than Windows NT, and getting Linux up and running can be a challenge. There are many differences from Windows, starting with the jargon (hard drives are not "C:" or "D:"; they are "hda" or "hdb") to the operating system's underlying concepts (Red Hat Linux is based on packages, a particular way of delivering and installing software).

Manually setting up hardware in Linux can be as arcane as it was in the old days of Microsoft's MS-DOS. To install Linux, a company needs to create anywhere from one to nine hard drive partitions. Red Hat recommends that new users read its 300-page manual before starting. Also, application installations present speed bumps.

As much as Linux supporters would like it to be, the general consensus is the operating system is not strong enough or mature enough for the enterprise. Scalability is an issue. The emerging operating system has not proven that it can support large complex applications on multiprocessing machines.

To make inroads into broader markets, operating systems need attractive applications. While thousands of commercial products operate on Windows, only somewhat recently have a few established software vendors shown any interest in Linux. In addition to DBMS supplier interest, Corel ported its WordPerfect suite to Linux, and Netscape is working on versions of its Communicator browser, messaging server, and directory server to the operating system. But support is still lacking from key players such as enterprise application vendors Baan, PeopleSoft, and SAP.

The same holds true with Linux hardware. Although IBM has moved to offer hardware support, most PC vendors are still sitting on the sidelines. To get into the corporate mainstream, Linux needs to have a few leading PC hardware vendors step up to the plate and deliver products optimized for it.

Add-on components support is also an issue. Linux has only a fraction of the video, printer, sound card, and network card support of Windows. The Red Hat setup offers some plug-and-play support, but it is spotty.

Linux's Impact on the DBMS Market

Microsoft's shadow hovers over DBMS vendors. Through a series of product enhancements, the company now offers a robust DBMS application server, its

SQL Server. To increase its market share, the company has been bundling the product as part of its Back Office suite and increasing the level of integration with other top-sellers. The strategy has worked well, so the firm is vying to become the market's top supplier.

Competitors would like to differentiate their wares, and Linux offers them that opportunity. Although Microsoft has said little about any plans to support the operating system, it would be surprising if the company moved quickly to port SQL Server to that platform. Historically, Microsoft has left non-Windows development work to partners. Thus, there is an opportunity for another supplier to emerge as the leading Linux DBMS vendor, and many are moving into that space.

In March 1996, Software AG became the first major DBMS vendor to line up in support of Linux. The company tailored its ADABAS D to run on Caldera's Network Desktop, a version of Linux augmented with client and server Internet and network tools, backup utilities, and a graphical user interface shell.

Other vendors were slower to make their move. In the summer of 1998, Informix outlined plans to develop a version of the Informix Dynamic Server for Linux. The company made the change because its international user group listed Linux support as its number-one priority. In keeping with Linux's roots, the company offered free user licenses, free technical support, and free e-mail support through a "try and buy" evaluation period. The Informix Dynamic Server, Linux Edition Suite, is composed of Informix Dynamic Server, Linux Edition; Informix Client Software Development Kit, which offers customers a single package of several application programming interfaces, including Open Database Connectivity, and Java Database Connectivity needed to develop applications for Informix servers; Informix-Connect, a runtime connectivity product; and an Apache integration document, because approximately 75 percent of all Apache Web servers run on Linux.

In July 1999, Oracle Corp. announced that it would port Oracle8 and Oracle Applications to Linux. The products will be available on Intel server platforms, and Oracle positioned its wares as an alternative to those running on Windows NT. The database vendor said that in addition to being easy to maintain, Linux will catch up to the functionality in commercial UNIX over the next few years.

InterBase Software Corp., a division of Inprise, started off offering a freeware version of its InterBase version 4.2 DBMS for Linux in May 1998. In August, the company announced the availability of InterBase 5 for the operating system.

At the end of 1998, Computer Associates unveiled Ingres II Linux Edition. The DBMS features a complete copy of the Ingres II database engine, along with core database functions such as variable page size, row-level locking, support for binary large objects (BLOBs), interfaces for C, compatibility with IngPerl (database access from the Perl scripting language), and Internet publishing capabilities that allow for application development using the Apache Server. The Ingres II Linux Edition is also compatible with other versions of Ingres II; thus, code written for the Ingres II Linux Edition will be fully portable to other platforms.

Linux Quick Facts

Web sites of some vendors selling Linux software include:

- Caldera: www.caldera.com
- MkLinux (linux for Apple machines): www.mklinux.apple.com
- Red Hat Software: www.redhat.com
- SuSe: www.suse.com

Other general Linux-related Web sites include:

- General Linux Information: http://metalab.unc.edu/LDP/links.html
- Linux BBS Service: http://www.komm.hdk-berlin.de/~rasca/linuxbbs.html
- Linux Users Group: http://lugww.nllgg.nl/

Supported hardware configurations such as Intel 386SX/16 with 1 MB RAM can scale to work with more than 1GB of RAM. The operating system has been ported to run on 386/486/Pentium machines with ISA, EISA, PCI, and VLB buses; Motorola 68020 with an MMU, a 68030, 68040, or a 68060; Compaq Alpha CPUs; and Sun Microsystems Inc. SPARC stations. (*Note:* There is no difference between client and server configurations. Developers have tailored the operating system to work on several chips, but the work is free, so there are not the speeds and feeds that come with commercial packages.)

Conclusion

Linux is the latest in a long list of emerging technologies with the potential to loosen the vise-like grip Microsoft holds on desktop computers. Proponents claim that the operating system's technical superiority, ease of distribution, and ongoing enhancements will lead to mass market acceptance.

In addition, many network and systems administrators do not like monopolies, which Windows NT is threatening to become. With IBM's OS/2 no longer a major player and Apple Computer Inc. sputtering during the past few years, administrators see a need for another alternative to Microsoft's products.

However, the freeware operating system is far behind the market leader; Linux has at most 5 million users worldwide, while companies and consumers have purchased more than 200 million copies of Windows.

History has not been kind to those who have tried to battle with the Goliath. After severing its relationship with Microsoft, IBM tried to win the desktop with OS/2; Novell attempted to defeat Windows with UnixWare; and Netscape tried to bypass the operating system and make the browser the focus of application development. Each initiative failed.

Linux supporters understand the challenge: Microsoft may be the 20th century's greatest marketing firm, and it will not surrender any of its business without a fight. To fulfill its grandiose potential, Linux will need to gain corporate and consumer acceptance during the next few years. To date, the emerging operating system has garnered only niche acceptance. While techies have been promoting it, most IT managers have yet to fully bless it. Many corporate cultures dictated that companies choose big, viable system vendors for IT solutions, and that is not likely to change due to global market fluctuations.

In addition, there is also the feeling that Linux supporters are bonded more by an aversion to Microsoft than by the operating system's benefits. The key backers have been companies with antipathy for Microsoft: Netscape, Oracle, and IBM.

Rather than dethrone Windows, a more realistic scenario has Linux overtaking SCO's OpenServer or UnixWare 7 as the leading UNIX operating system on Intel platforms. The emerging operating system could make a push into data centers and battle with IBM's AIX, HP's HP-UX, and Sun's Solaris.

Because of its progress and potential, Linux should be a technology that companies monitor and maybe trial for select applications. Once Linux has equal market share to what Apple's Macintosh enjoys at the desktop market, then the talk about it overtaking Windows may be justified. For now, the operating system is an interesting product that IT managers should track rather than rush out and deploy.

ORACLE BACKUP AND RECOVERY

V

Oracle backup and recovery has become increasingly sophisticated since Oracle 7. Starting with the Enterprise Backup Utility (EBU), and culminating in Oracle's Recovery Manager (RMAN), Oracle backup and recovery has become a very important topic for Oracle shops that are faced with keeping the Oracle systems continuously available, while at the same time ensuring quality backup and recovery capability.

Chapters 23 through 27 are extracted from *Oracle Internals*' experts to discuss some of the in-depth technical nuances of the EBU and RMAN products. With the introduction of Oracle hot backups, Oracle backup and recovery remains one of the most complex and challenging areas of Oracle administration.

Chapter 23

Strategies for an Archives Management Program

Michael J.D. Sutton

Few professionals have navigated through few archives management (AM) projects, teams, successes, and failures. Why? Because there have been few successes to point to, and because there has been no poignant business reason to proceed with such initiatives (at least until recently). Nonetheless, many corporations and public sector organizations are now experiencing significant pain and financial liability from the loss of their corporate memory. The lack of archives management strategies is holding back "well-intentioned" but untrained project directors and managers from coming to grips with the issues, concerns, problems, and obstacles associated with an archive repository (AR). The overall strategy outlined here could well be an important reference document for one's next initiative.

Foundational Concepts

Why does one need a strategy? One needs a strategy because the AM initiative one has been asked to embark upon has no anchors to hold anyone to the *present*. Archives management is about time, and the effect time has on artifacts created in the *present*. Archives management is, paradoxically, about the *future* (which most people cannot see unless they profess to be prophets), but only when that *future* has become the *past*. AM does not incorporate in its conceptual model a classical linear timeline; it presents a reverse timeline where the *past* only becomes valuable again when it is many years old.

Suppose one is asked to plan an archives repository in such a way that information objects created in the *present* can be "read" (or at least understood) in the *future*, within their original, rich context. However, someone (or some

0-8493-1139-X/02/$0.00+$1.50
©2002 by CRC Press LLC

automated system) in the *future* must, at its *present* moment, contend with information objects from the *past*. The information objects at that point in the *future* never seem to have enough context or content to permit their proper understanding.

Archives management, especially as it is defined in digital terms, is a very young discipline. The key business drivers and benefits are not yet well-defined or clearly mapped. The project director has no means of testing whether information objects created as an output to an AM initiative will be usable in the future, other than through simulated testing. This testing cannot take into account software product or system evolution over a five- to ten-year period, or even worse, over a 25- to 100-year period. The best a project director can do is make an educated guess and hope that when five or more years have passed, he may have been a prophet in his own land.

Although there is little to go on at this time to justify an AM initiative, there is anecdotal material that points to business drivers and benefits. There are **key business drivers** that can justify an AM initiative, including:

- An antiquated or traditional records management system that cannot cope with the emerging challenges and requirements of a digital workspace
- Increasing online space requirements for current operational databases, datamarts, and data warehouses
- Short- and long-term technological obsolescence
- An enterprise's drive to harmonize all systems onto a heterogeneous environment
- An inability to find, locate, catalog, and use current or historical digital information objects
- New uses for "old" data from sales, human resources, marketing, facilities, engineering, and financial databases

There are also numerous potential benefits in implementing an archives management program that may apply to an organization, including:

- Decreased corporate exposure during audits or legal inquiries
- Increased compliance with various levels of laws and regulation (international, federal, state/province, county/region, and city/municipal)
- Improved records management and control
- Appropriate retention and timely destruction of business records
- Streamlined and rationalized processes where business owners do not have to be concerned with archiving information objects from their current systems

Take, for example, the Year 2000 issues and problems that most organizations were contending with. These were a significant archives management problem. As automated systems grew in the 1960s and 1970s, no one could predict how memory costs would fall or how software would handle date-related information.

In fact, most people who worked on such systems never expected COBOL, PL/I, RPG, or even Assembler compilers to last more than five years. Alas, one is now in the *future*, and trying to cope with the professional inability to plan for legacy applications that were just too poorly documented to re-write, and too integral to the business to throw away.

An AM initiative differs substantially from a contemporary information system project. The AM initiative can be described by a number of characteristics:

- Generally five to seven years in length
- An average team size of five members for an enterprise of 1000 client users
- Historical focus on record and file structures that are not currently in vogue
- Primarily concerned with the disposition of the digital records of the enterprise after they are at least seven years old

Contrast this with the characteristics of a contemporary information system project:

- Generally less than two years in duration (and preferably less than one year)
- An average team size of seven to ten members for an enterprise of 1000 client users
- *Avant garde* focus on record and file structures that are just currently in use
- Primarily concerned with the creation and use of digital records of the enterprise created in the *present*, less than two years from their date of creation

There is a significant difference in the business goals and objectives of the two projects. In addition, the owners and technology supporters of the current system projects have been allocated no time or budget to worry about or plan for the eventual retirement or disposition of the systems, data, or documents. These *present-focused* business and technology leaders have incentives, i.e., bonuses, dividends, or stock options, based on what they help the company accomplish *today* or *tomorrow* — not five to seven years from now.

The tools used within an AM project must contend with both old and new technologies, software, media devices, methods, file structures, record formats, etc. The tools of an AM initiative are Janus-like in their employment. (Janus was the classical Roman god who had two faces: one looked into the past while the second looked into the future. Janus was identified with doors, gates, and beginnings and endings). The AM project team must contend with having one foot in the *past* and one in the *future*, while the *present* passes them by.

Information management professionals — at the behest of private and public sector leaders — have worked for over 40 years to automate (digitize) less than 20 present of the enterprise information assets and intellectual capital. Regretfully, in doing so, they have forced most enterprises to be short-term in their vision of the value of information objects and systems, to rely too heavily on the digital nature of the information. Thus, many organizations almost ignore the digital as well as the hardcopy storage and long-term retrieval value of information. These enterprises may not have "lost their minds," but they have lost their corporate memory. When an audit or legal discovery process tries to contend with digital information that is five to ten years old (or even three years old), there are significant problems in reconstructing these information objects and their context. And for many enterprises today, this "corporate amnesia" results in hefty legal costs, fines, and lost revenue.

Archives Management Problem Statement

Most organizations that wish to survive in today's aggressive business climate must continually improve, evolve, and reposition their market, products, and services, and aggressively maintain their profitability. The enterprise must create and achieve short-term business goals, objectives, and strategies. Many businesses have invested heavily in automated legacy systems. These systems may be nearing or have already passed their retirement date. The valued corporate memories in these systems may be incorporated into new, emerging corporate systems; or, alternatively, the digital information objects may be stored offline to comply with legal and regulatory requirements. The worst case is that these out-of-date systems, data, and document objects are ignored until it is too late to determine how they could be migrated to physical media or logical format to be useful.

All enterprises are facing a challenge to preserve digital systems, data, and documents over short-, medium-, and long-term periods of time. Some companies have lost significant income from audits because substantiating data and documents (stored digitally) were lost years earlier; but not discovered until it was too late. The business owners of current operational information systems are generally preoccupied with operational challenges, issues, and concerns surrounding applications performance and availability. Managers are asked to contend with short-term business objectives and present problems, not with hypothetical problems that might emerge in the distant future.

The oversimplified diagram shown in Exhibit 23.1 might help to illustrate the preservation challenge that one faces. Current information systems create or acquire information objects that have immediate corporate value. This is the operational stage of a corporate information value life cycle. The operational stage may encompass one to two fiscal years. The requirement during this stage for instant retrieval dictates that the information objects are stored online. This stage might also encompass data marts and data warehouses that require relatively quick access and retrieval response times.

The corporate value of the information will decrease over time because it simply is no longer current; and current information is very important when generating profits or increased stock price value. The information objects

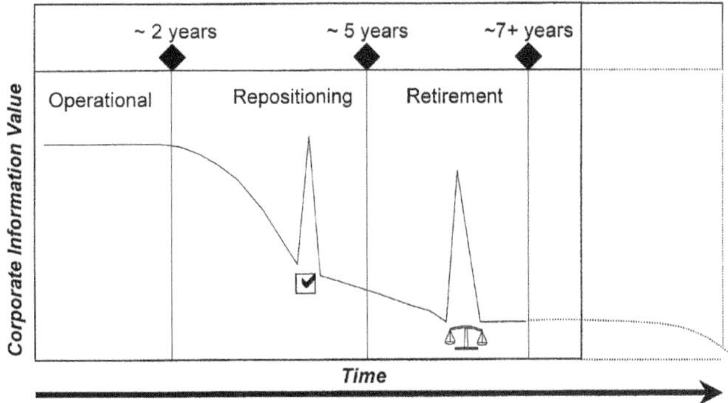

Exhibit 23.1 Information Preservation Stages

migrate to the repositioning stage of the corporate information value life cycle. The repositioning stage can incorporate three to five fiscal years of information objects. The use of near-line or offline storage media (optical disks, CD-ROMs, QIC tapes, etc.) generally applies at this stage, and may continue for up to five or six years. Instantaneous retrieval is not as critical at this juncture in the life cycle. Nonetheless, during this period of time, external audits by regulatory or tax agencies may take place; this creates a peak in the perceived corporate value of the information where its value may be as much or more than its original corporate value.

Generally, information objects during this period of time exhibit certain characteristics of aging, including:

- The loss of the original information and its context
- The original media may be unreadable or devices to read it are no longer manufactured
- The original file and record structure may be unknown, foreign, or undocumented
- Any significant business rules stored in the software programs are unreadable, unusable, or unknowable
- Any individuals who may have worked on the original system or database have moved on to other opportunities

In short, corporate amnesia exists.

Finally, the corporate information moves into the retirement stage of the corporate information value life cycle. Information objects can remain dormant here for six to 20 years, depending on legal, historical, and archival requirements. The information objects are loaded onto offline media such as magnetic tapes, DAT (digital archive tapes), or possibly CD-ROMs. Historians, social scientists, or lawyers are the expected users for these seldom-accessed information objects. Nonetheless, the information objects must retain enough content, logical structure, and context to be more useful than just a historical artifact.

A business framework or archival facility has rarely existed in present-day enterprises to accommodate the corporate information life cycle as described above. Thus, a digital archives repository rarely exists or is available in today's public and private sector institutions to use as a model. A digital archives repository is required to contextually preserve the database objects, document objects, business rules, system documentation, and other descriptive data (metadata). Such a repository must accommodate information objects over a medium- to long-term period of time (i.e., from five to 20 years) in a software- and hardware platform-neutral format (e.g., that proposed in ISO Reference Model of the Consultative Committee for Space Data Systems White Paper, *Open Archival Information System* (*OAIS*)). The archives management strategy might help to position this commitment to a repository.

Foundational Definitions

Before describing an archives management strategy (AMS), some basic vocabulary intrinsic to archives management is required. An archives management program consists of specific information objects, facilities, processes, and preservation domains. One can start with the information objects.

At the fore of a good AMS is the *business record* — a by-product of a business transaction preserved for future use as evidence of transacting business. A business record must maintain a number of preservation characteristics. Charles Dollar, in *Ensuring Access over Time to Authentic Electronic Records: Strategy, Alternatives, and Best Practices,* proposes a number of preservation characteristics that help preserve the legal integrity of a business record while stored and archived; these characteristics include:

- *Authentic:* the measure of the reliability of a record (i.e., its ability to remain unaltered, unchanged, and uncorrupted)
- *Encapsulated:* the measure of the self-referential linkage of logical components in a record
- *Identifiable:* the measure of the specification of unique identification boundaries in a record
- *Intelligible:* the measure of the integrity of the bit stream represented in a record
- *Readable:* the measure of the integrity of the bit stream device processing of a record
- *Reconstructable:* the measure of the quality of rebuilding the same structure and intellectual content of a record
- *Retrievable:* the measure of the capability to locate objects and parts of a record
- *Understandable:* the measure of the quality of the context of creation of a record

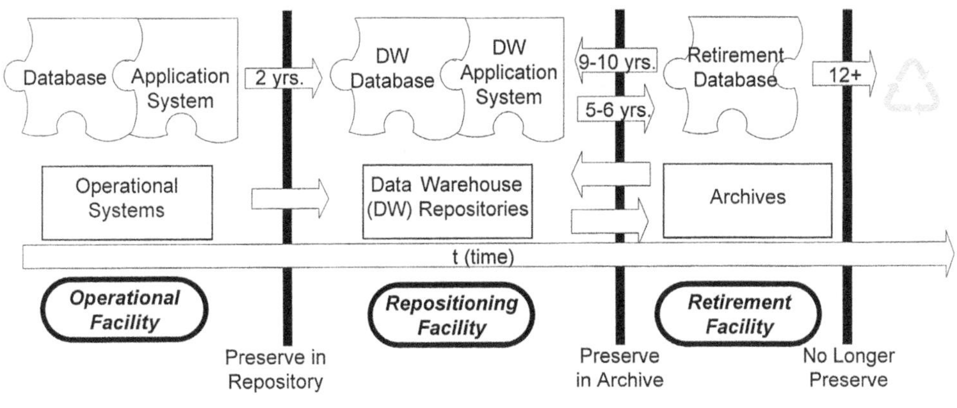

Exhibit 23.2 Time-Based Migration of Information Between Current and Successive Stages

Business records are aggregated into files. An *operational file* is an information object that contains information of immediate, instantaneous interest to a reader. Digital copies of operational files are normally created in the course of data management procedures, and are referred to as *backup files.* A *repositioned file* is a specially formatted copy of an original operational file that can be retrieved through near-line storage media instead of online storage media. For longer-term storage, repositioned files are migrated to retired files.

A *retired file* contains information objects that would be the foundation for reconstructing an authentic instance of a file in its original format and context. A retired file can encompass system, data, and document objects. The information content can be conveyed to the user or another computer as audio data, bitmap data, data fragments and databases, spatial (geographical) data, spreadsheets, text, vector data, and video data.

The files are managed by different facilities (as illustrated in Exhibit 23.2). An *operational facility* is accountable for managing the current information assets of an enterprise. The information assets are digital and are stored online for immediate access. A *repositioning facility* manages the nearly current information assets (i.e., information that may be between two and five years old). The information objects are stored on near-line media for near-instant access. A *retirement facility* manages the dormant information assets (i.e., information that may be between six and 25 or more years old). The retirement facility can store the information objects in a hardware- and software-neutral format to diminish the problems of technological obsolescence. All the facilities execute specific processes upon the information objects under their control (see Exhibit 23.3).

A number of specific processes can be executed on the operational and repositioning environments to move them into an archival environment, including:

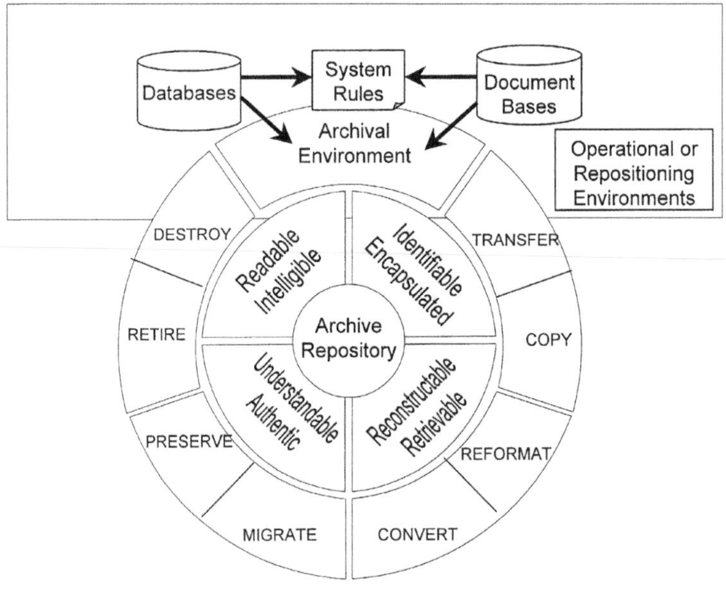

Exhibit 23.3 Archival Management Processes

1. *Convert:* importing or exporting of records from one software-dependent environment to another while ensuring the preservation of structure, content, and context
2. *Copy:* the creation of a digital binary twin of the original file
3. *Destroy:* physically disposing of the media and information objects so as to make them totally unreadable (i.e., degaussing, crushing, melting, etc.)
4. *Migrate:* moving authentic electronic records from legacy information systems in online systems to another storage media, such as near-line or offline storage, while preserving the logical view of the original records
5. *Reformat:* transferring records from one medium to another without alteration of the bit stream of a record (e.g., with no change in appearance, content, or logical structure)
6. *Retire:* moving information objects to very dormant offline storage to protect and preserve records from corruption and make them relatively inaccessible
7. *Transfer:* repositioning electronic records from online or near-line storage to offline storage for infrequent retrieval

Finally, there is *metadata*. This is specific descriptive data about particular data objects which increases the precision in recalling information objects from a search of a repository of data, document, or systems. *Metadata* can describe an information object with fields such as author, business unit of the author, creation date, modification date, security classification, or subject. This overview of the emerging vocabulary of AM will serve as a foundation for subsequent discussion.

Strategies for an Archives Management Initiative

The following set of strategies and guiding principles are proposed for constructing a framework to design and successfully engineer an archives management program.

Strategy 1: Develop a Repositioning Facility

The repositioning facility will depend on available budget as well as corporate technical resourcing, knowledge, and support. In addition, the enterprise will require skills in data mart and data warehouse design, and an informed and experienced digital records management group. The repositioning facility will ensure the availability of a corporate memory for between two and five years. The operational facility feeds the repositioning facility after two or three fiscal years have elapsed for the operational data.

Strategy 2: Develop a Retirement Facility

The retirement facility must construct a long-term program, which most enterprises are not willing to fund. This retirement facility will need long-term financing so that it is not cut from the budget during lean times. This is a corporate commitment to preserve the memory of the institution. This business unit will be responsible for the archival activities associated with appraisal, collection, migration, protection, reformation, retention, and, finally, the destruction of digital information assets. The retirement facility will warrant that valuable corporate memory is available and accessible. A corporate records management program may already handle many of these functions for hardcopy records. But beware, most records management staff are ill-equipped to cope with managing digital records, especially over such a long term; a new business unit may need to be defined in the organization.

Strategy 3: Employ Guiding Principles in Architecture and Design

The following guiding principles are proposed to jump-start the design and deployment of an AMS.

Principle 1: Manage long-term information assets in the same way one manages short-term information assets. Most organizations ignore the problems and challenges of storing information assets over the long term. This is metaphorically similar to the problems that industrial and manufacturing sectors are experiencing with pollution. If ignored in planning and design, it will cost 100 times as much to reconstruct information assets or pay the fines and costs of mismanaged archival data.

Principle 2: Business owners of the information assets are concerned with the present — not the future. Business owners should not be made responsible for ensuring medium-term repositioning and long-term preservation of their information objects. They hardly have enough time to keep their current, operational systems performing within acceptable operational limits and backed up for disaster recovery. If the enterprise forces the operational facility to worry about repositioning and retiring, then these activities will never be done. (How many people have omitted backing up their hard disks when they first started on a PC? — my point exactly.) A separate set of facilities (with their own goals and incentives) must be brought into play to relieve the stress and pressure exhibited in the operational facility. This can even be outsourced to companies that are starting to sell services for digital records and archives management facilities.

Principle 3: Aggressively pursue the preservation of critical information assets. A digital retirement facility must be mandated to proactively collect and acquire the critical information objects that need to be preserved. Otherwise, corporate amnesia is guaranteed. Corporate amnesia increased as companies expended incredible budgets on the Y2K problem instead of on more significant areas such as enterprise document management systems. Neglect and incompetence invalidate any warranty for corporate survival.

Principle 4: Destroy archived information assets in a timely manner. Maintaining access and availability of all digital objects over a long-term period is both impractical and expensive. Assets must be categorized according to their records retention schedule to facilitate their timely destruction. Periodically evaluate the retention periods of archival information assets and destroy the records according to their legal requirements before they can be used against the institution in legal proceedings. The only thing worse than corporate amnesia is "photographic recall" — very risky in any court proceeding. Nonetheless, there may be corporate records of a historical nature that should be preserved longer than their normal destruction date. Make sure that only the historical records are preserved.

Principle 5: Assess compliance with all legal and statutory rules and regulations. Some business unit must be made responsible for maintaining a comprehensive checklist of relevant laws, statutes, and regulations. Often, the knowledge about retention is scattered among different business units; no one is really accountable for knowing or enforcing the legal and statutory requirements. This must change, and accountability must be assigned. There are too many financial liabilities that can cost an institution if these requirements are ignored.

These guiding principles should help in creating a firm foundation for AM activities.

Recap

This chapter has presented a vocabulary, broad strategies, and guiding principles for embarking on an archives management program. The strategies revolve around the creation and staffing of a repositing facility and a retirement facility. The existence of these two facilities will relieve the operational facility of the stress and pressure to try and find a short-term solution for a long-term problem. The solution is not really within their mandate or skill set to achieve. Separate business units must be "anointed" with these tasks.

Beware of the lack of funding and commitment when starting an AM initiative. Because of the short-term thinking prevalent in most organizations, these would be the types of facilities that would be cut from the organization when times get tough. If the enterprise sees corporate value and the substantial benefits of an AM program, then it must be committed to keep that program intact. An archives repository with gaps is a corporate memory with missing fragments — it may take a great deal of effort to understand and there will be gaps that could leave out important or legally required data. Can the enterprise afford that?

Bibliography

Barry, R., *Best Practices for Document Management in an Emerging Digital Environment,* http:/www.rbarry.com/UKRMS1/UKRMS1.html.

Barry, R., Electronic Records And Objects Circa 2001, *University College London, School of Library, Archive and Information Studies Conference Proceedings — 75th Anniversary Celebration,* 1994 http:/www.rbarry.com /CON-PAP2/CON-PAP2.html.

Barry, R., Electronic Document and Records Management Systems: Towards a Methodology for Requirements Definition, *Information Management & Technology,* 27, 6, 1994.

Beagrie, N. and Greenstein, D., *A Strategic Policy Framework for Creating and Preserving Digital Collections* (Arts and Humanities Data Service: London, 7/14/98).

Bennett, J., *A Framework for Data Types and Formats, and Issues Affecting the Long Term Preservation of Digital Material* (British Library Research and Innovation Centre: West Yorkshire, U.K., 1997).

Commission on Preservation and Access, Research Libraries Group, *Preserving Digital Information: Report of the Task Force on Archiving Digital Information* (Yale University, May 1, 1996).

Consultative Committee for Space Data Systems, *Open Archival Information System (OAIS) White Book,* CCSDS 650.0-W-4.0, 08/17/1998.

Dollar, C., *Ensuring Access over Time to Authentic Electronic Records: Strategy, Alternatives, and Best Practices* (Manuscript: Vancouver, BC: Nov., 1998) [available soon as a digital book from www.cohasset.com].

Dollar, C. and Williams, R., New Strategy for Migrating Long-Term Electronic Records: Meeting Operational Needs with Less Risk and at Lower Cost, *Cohasset Associates, Inc. Managing Electronic Records Conference Proceedings,* 1995.

Getty Conservation Institute and Getty Information Institute, *Time & Bits, Managing Digital Continuity.*

Haynes, D., et al., *Responsibility for Digital Archiving and Long Term Access to Digital Data* (British Library Research and Innovation Centre: West Yorkshire, U.K., 1997).

Hedstrom, M., From Practice to Theory: Applying Archival Theory to Electronic Records Management, *Cohasset Associates, Inc. Managing Electronic Records Conference Proceedings,* 1996.

Jones, M., *Bibliography of Materials Relating to the Preservation of New Technology and Preservation Using New Technology* (National Library of Australia: Canberra ACT, 1994), http://www.nla.gov.au/1/pres/pubs/bibmj.html.

Kahle, B., Preserving the Internet, *Scientific American,* March 1997, http://www.sciam.com/0397issue/0397kahle.html.

Kelly, K., et al., *Models for Action: Practical Approaches to Electronic Records Management and Preservation,* Center for Technology in Government: Albany, NY, 1998.

Kowlowitz, A. and Kelly, K., *Functional Requirements to Ensure the Creation, Maintenance, and Preservation of Electronic Records,* Center for Technology in Government: Albany, NY, 1998.

Long Now Foundation, Clock/Library, http://www.longnow.org/library/library.html.

MacCarn, D., *Toward a Universal Data Format for the Preservation of Media,* WGBH Educational Foundation: Boston, undated.

McGovern, T. and Samuels, H., Our Institutional Memory at Risk: Collaborators to the Rescue, *Cause/Effect,* 20(3), 19–21 and 49–50, 1997.

Rasmussen, D., *Digitization — The Issues, Projects and Technology: A Selective Bibliography,* National Library of Canada: Ottawa, 1995.

Ross, S., Acting to Avoid Loss, but When Disaster Strikes — Relying on Digital Archeology, *Cohasset Associates, Inc. Managing Electronic Records Conference Proceedings,* 1998.

Rothenberg, J., Ensuring the Longevity of Digital Information, *Scientific American,* 272(1), 24–29.

Rothenberg, J., Metadata to Support Data Quality and Longevity, *IEEE Metadata Computer Conference Proceedings,* 1996, http://computer.org/conferen/meta96/rothenberg_paper/ieee.data-quality.html.

Shepard, T., Universal Preservation Format Update, *D-Lib Magazine,* Nov. 1997, http://www.dlib.org/dlib/november97/11clips.html.

Skupsky, D., Legal Requirements for Optical Disk Records and Electronic Imaging Systems, *AIIM Show and Conference Proceedings,* March 31–April 3, 1996.

Sutton, M., *Document Management for the Enterprise: Principles, Techniques, and Applications,* John Wiley & Sons: NY, 1996.

Williams, R., Managing the New Corporate Memory, *International Council on Archives — Section of International Organizations Workshop,* June 1998.

Williams, R., The Seven Key Legal Issues for Managing Electronic Records, *Cohasset Associates, Inc. Managing Electronic Records Conference Proceedings,* 1995.

Chapter 24

Scripting Oracle Backups with RMAN and EBU

Howard Fosdick

Over the past several years, Oracle has evolved to better automate, control, and manage backup and recovery tasks. In Oracle8, the component to accomplish this is the Recovery Manager (RMAN). Its equivalent in Oracle7 is the Enterprise Backup Utility (EBU).

The conceptual architectures of RMAN and EBU are extremely similar. Backup and recovery operations at sites that use them often appear to be similar as well. But, ultimately, the two are different, incompatible products. RMAN exclusively manages Oracle8 databases, while EBU covers only Oracle7 databases from release 7.1.6 onward. The backups taken by one component may not be utilized by the other.

This chapter describes one way to automate backup and recovery procedures using RMAN or EBU. It describes how to write scripts (in languages such as Rexx, Perl, or Korn) to drive the facilities of RMAN and EBU and to develop the kinds of fully automated, "lights-out" backup and recovery procedures typically required at large sites.

But first some background. We start with a highly simplified description of the underlying architecture of RMAN and EBU. After this, we explore the specifics of how to design and code RMAN and EBU automation scripts. Note that this chapter is *not* intended to address all the issues of backup and recovery that must be considered in order to define a site's backup–recovery strategy. These decisions involve more than this chapter can address. (Ultimately, unique site and application requirements drive an organization's backup and recovery strategy.) The intent here is to discuss the infrastructural underpinnings required to automate a backup–recovery strategy, whatever it might be, through scripts.

0-8493-1139-X/02/$0.00+$1.50
©2002 by CRC Press LLC

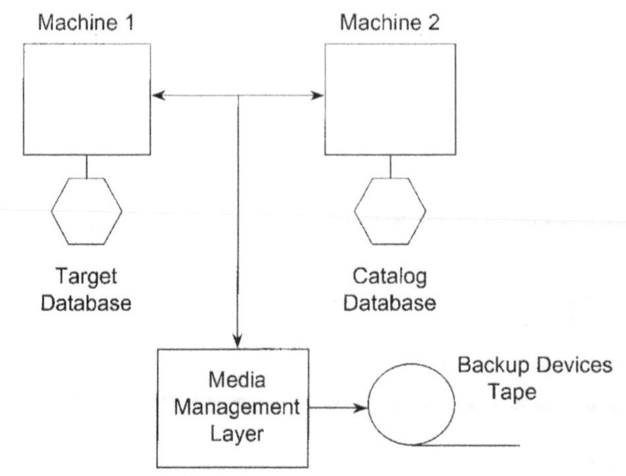

Exhibit 24.1 The RMAN/EBU Architecture

The RMAN–EBU Architecture

Exhibit 24.1 diagrams the conceptual architecture common to both RMAN and EBU. A "recovery catalog" manages and controls backup and recovery operations. (The "recovery catalog" is variously referred to as the "backup catalog," the "RMAN catalog," or the "EBU catalog" in Oracle literature.) At large sites, the "recovery catalog" commonly resides in a different Instance, on a different machine than the databases to be backed up. RMAN or EBU combines information from a database's Control File with the repository of information in the recovery catalog to oversee and manage backup and recovery operations. This allows RMAN or EBU to determine which files are needed in a recovery situation, intelligently recover to a point in time, report on the status of recent backups, and perform similar functions.

Using the information in the recovery catalog, the various processes of RMAN or EBU interface with a Media Management Layer (MML) to perform backup or recovery operations. The MML is a tape-management product supplied by a vendor other than Oracle (Legato System, Inc. products are one example). This third-party product performs actual tape operations, such as reading, writing, labeling, or verification. (If backups are written to disk, RMAN or EBU can do this work itself and does not require a third-party tape-management product.)

The same basic architecture applies to recoveries as well as backups. In recovery situations, RMAN or EBU gets coordinating information from the recovery catalog and directs the third-party tape-management product via the MML interface. The intelligence RMAN or EBU supplies simplifies the task of the DBA in typical recovery situations and reduces the risk of error.

To initially make a database eligible for backup via RMAN or EBU, "register" that database with the recovery catalog via the `REGISTER` command. The recovery catalog must subsequently be kept in sync with the databases it manages. When structural (DDL) changes are made to a database, or when many archive logs have been generated, the recovery catalog needs to be resynchronized with the subject database. This is done via a single `RMAN` command (`RESYNC CATALOG FROM BACKUP CONTROLFILE`). EBU automatically resync's outdated configurations before online backups; or use the `REGISTER` command for this purpose. A parameter allows the user to specify whether configuration should be verified prior to an offline or "cold" backup.

Another architectural issue is how to back up the recovery catalog itself. Large sites typically have two RMAN catalogs, each backing up the other. For greatest reliability, these catalogs may reside on different Oracle Instances on different machines.[1]

For Oracle7 databases, the situation may be simpler. EBU automatically backs up the catalog's contents by writing it to tape immediately following the backup data of the target database. The `RESTORE CATALOG` command can be used to restore the most recent EBU Catalog backup, if necessary.

Using RMAN and EBU Facilities

Both RMAN and EBU have their own "command language." These commands direct RMAN or EBU operations, for example, to request backup or recovery, or simply to list information about backups from the recovery catalog. While the RMAN and EBU command languages exist for the same purpose (and indeed feature many similarities), they are actually two different languages. The EBU command language contains only a half dozen commands (`BACKUP`, `BACKUP CATALOG`, `REGISTER`, `RESTORE`, and `RESTORE CATALOG`), plus the catalog utility `EBUTOOL` with its two dozen operands. The RMAN command language is more sophisticated and extensive. The RMAN manual lists some 40-odd commands and subclauses.

Using either RMAN or EBU, there are several ways to enter and execute commands. The most basic approach is to interactively enter commands via the products' Command Line Interface (CLI). The CLI is conveniently accessed; but given the length and complexity of typing in many of the commands, its usefulness is limited.

Another approach is to use "command files." Enter the commands into a file with any editor; then refer to that file when running RMAN or EBU. Command files effectively allow us to run commands in batch mode. They are best for saving lengthy commands in a convenient format, plus this method can be used to invoke commands from scripts written in languages such as Rexx, Perl, or Korn. Scripting in this manner allows automation and production backup and recovery operations for scheduled batch and off-hours execution.

Oracle Enterprise Manager (OEM) offers Window's point-and-click strengths through its "backup manager" and "recovery manager" icons. The GUI generates the underlying code of equivalent line commands: this requires the least expertise of the various ways to issue RMAN and EBU commands. It is quick and a great learning vehicle, but may not be appropriate for managing large or mission-critical databases. Because it is interactive, its use requires on-the-spot expertise. Even when such operations can be scheduled, the approach lacks the comprehensive environmental analysis, error-checking, and automated problem-handling required in critical production environments.

RMAN offers one new technique that EBU lacks, called "stored scripts." Here you enter commands (interactively or via the command-file technique) and save them as a "stored script" in the RMAN recovery catalog. Then invoke them at will. Each script can refer to only one database. Under UNIX, RMAN includes a number of example stored scripts in the `$ORACLE_HOME/rdbms/demo` directory. They address many kinds of backup, restore, and recovery, including incomplete recovery, disaster recovery, and consistent backup.

Stored scripts allow us to build tried-and-true backup and recovery procedures. They lend themselves to the batch mode operations often required when large databases are involved, and are a sound method to productionalizing backup and recovery procedures. We can then write our own scripts (in Rexx, Perl, or Korn) that invoke RMAN stored scripts. To distinguish these two kinds of scripts, we refer to those written in Rexx, Perl, or Korn as "OS scripts," while scripts that consist solely of RMAN commands are stored scripts. OS scripts invoke stored scripts in order to use RMAN facilities.

Should we use the command-file technique or stored scripts as the input for the OS scripts we wrote? For EBU, there is only one choice: the command-file approach, because EBU does not support stored scripts. For RMAN, the choice comes down to whether we want to control the RMAN scripts through the RMAN catalog or in the same manner as the source code of our OS scripts. Some sites prefer to keep their command files with their OS scripts, using the same source code control system or procedures for both. Command files can be accessed without having to go through the RMAN interface, using its commands, and some prefer this approach. RMAN OS scripts can also more closely match what was coded for EBU OS scripts because they take the same approach to executing command files.

Other sites view the RMAN stored scripts as an important benefit of the recovery catalog. Keep everything in the catalog, consolidated and controlled from there, and use the catalog properly in its intended role. Either approach works fine: the choice will have little impact on either the purposes or logic of any OS scripts written to manage RMAN backup and recovery.

Developing OS Scripts

Once we decide whether OS scripts should utilize stored scripts or command files, we face a basic decision as to how many OS scripts to develop. Some sites prefer distinct programs for backups versus recoveries. Others go so far as to have separate OS scripts for each purpose: online backups, offline backups, archivelog-only backup, recovery to the most recent state, point-in-time recovery, etc.

The RMAN and EBU command languages are small enough to allow a simpler approach. A single OS script can be developed that analyzes the command language input, carries out the proper error-handling and set-up procedures, and then executes the RMAN or EBU command(s). If both Oracle7 and Oracle8 databases are supported, just two basic OS scripts are needed: one for RMAN, another for EBU. Each would be an input-driven, generic "command file" executor, capable of analyzing and then properly executing any command in the RMAN or EBU command language, respectively.

With this approach, OS scripts need to do some limited analysis of the command-file input. Embedding intelligence in the RMAN or EBU script to understand these command languages is not difficult. It requires no more than a single parsing routine. Alternatively, OS scripts can be made even simpler by telling them what command they will execute in any particular run via command line parameters or input flags. This avoids "reverse-engineering" the RMAN or EBU command language in OS scripts. It also avoids having to change the RMAN OS script if Oracle alters the RMAN command language in future releases of Oracle8.

Exhibit 24.2 Which Language Should You Script In?

Which language should you use to develop your OS scripts? Many organizations already have standards that dictate this decision independent of the need to write OS scripts to automate RMAN or EBU. And many developers simply use the language they know or prefer. The information provided here is not intended to challenge your standards (or even promote one language over another, as technicians are often extremely sensitive on this subject!), but merely to list some considerations for those who face this decision.

Rexx is easiest to learn, write, debug, and maintain. It is part of the NT Resource Kit and has become somewhat of a *de facto* scripting standard for NT. You can also buy it very inexpensively for any flavor of UNIX; but for whatever reason, few sites do.

The Korn shell dominates UNIX scripting: most UNIX sites already use it. It comes free with every UNIX variant and UNIX professionals are most likely to know it already. But while Korn is powerful, its difficult syntax hampers those who do not already know it and renders Korn shell scripts difficult to maintain. Korn leads to high programmer productivity among those who know it intimately, but low productivity for casual programmers. Syntax errors are extremely common in Korn programs.

Most view Perl as the next logical evolution beyond Korn. It has more features and power, and seems to be gaining adherents under both UNIX and NT. But it continues the Korn tradition of arcane syntax and lack of mneumonics. It is relatively difficult to learn, use on a casual basis, and maintain. Like the Korn shell, Perl is highly productive for those who know it intimately and work in it all the time, but reveals low productivity for those who use it on a casual basis.

Whichever method is used, the goal is to tailor script actions to the preliminaries necessary to execute specific RMAN or EBU commands. Under RMAN, for example, most commands execute with the database open and available. But offline or cold backups, and backups for databases in `NOARCHIVELOG` mode, require the database in "mount state" before the backup, while various kinds of restores and recoveries have their own database status requirements. The OS script either needs to recognize the RMAN command it intends to execute, or be told what to do via input arguments, in order to handle these commands properly.

EBU imposes similar requirements. For offline or cold backups, OS script must cleanly shut down the Oracle database prior to executing the `BACKUP OFFLINE` command. The following steps are one way to do this. These steps are based on a sample OS script that Oracle Corporation provides for offline backups, called the "lights-out script."

1. `SHUTDOWN IMMEDIATE` (as a background command)
2. Sleep for a user-given time period to give Step 1 a chance to complete
3. `SHUTDOWN ABORT` (if the `SHUTDOWN IMMEDIATE` of Step 1 worked, this fails and has no ill effect; if the `SHUTDOWN IMMEDIATE` of Step 1 did *not* work, this aborts the database Instance)
4. `STARTUP RESTRICT`
5. `REGISTER` the database with the EBU catalog
6. `SHUTDOWN NORMAL` (this shuts down the Instance as required, prior to a cold backup; it will do any necessary transaction cleanup if the database had to be shut down in Step 2, `SHUTDOWN ABORT`)
7. Execute the EBU script to backup the database under control of the EBU catalog
8. `STARTUP` (restart database after backup is done)

If the database is operating in `ARCHIVELOG` mode, the current online redo log file must be archived in order to back it up with the other datafiles.

In like manner, the `RESTORE` command requires that the target database or objects being restored be offline prior to execution. Finally, the `BACKUP CATALOG` and `RESTORE CATALOG` commands must be "single-threaded." No other EBU jobs can run while either of these commands execute.

Features Checklist

What other logic should scripts contain? If the goal is total automation, the OS scripts should identify and correct all possible error conditions and address all forseeable circumstances. The OS script must handle any error conditions, as opposed to requiring human intervention (and the night-time paging that it likely entails).

A few organizations like their scripts to identify all possible problems, but prefer to have staff manually correct problems. These sites usually have large data centers and 24/7 scheduling staffs. This approach certainly may be appropriate for critical or unusual recovery situations. But in most other cases, OS scripts offer higher success rates by reducing human error even while making better use of scarce staff.

In either case, here are some issues RMAN and EBU OS scripts should address:

- Register previously unregistered databases.
- Resynchronize the target database in the recovery catalog (as necessary).
- Ensure the recovery catalog database and its listener are up and accessible.
- Ensure the target database and its listener are up and accessible; or that they are placed into the appropriate state for the specific RMAN or EBU commands to be executed.
- Where the target database status was changed from "open state" prior to executing a command, after executing the command, the database should be brought back "up" and its state verified as accessible. This may be useful even in cases where a backup command failed, for example. But it would not be applicable after other kinds of failure, such as a failed recovery.
- On systems where there are time-shared terminal users, sending a shutdown message is appropriate prior to the database shutdown.
- Handle the differences between `ARCHIVELOG` and `NOARCHIVELOG` mode databases. For example, NOARCHIVELOG mode databases do not support hot backups and must follow a clean database shutdown.
- For Oracle7 databases only, ensure that no tablespace is errantly in "hot backup mode" from a previously aborted run of the script when the job starts.[2]
- Output trace information to a log sufficient to trace critical backup and recovery procedures. A clever idea is two output logs: one logging high-level, simple messages for quick reference, and a second containing detailed debugging information should it be required.
- Report or list appropriate results information from the recovery catalog upon completion.
- For Oracle8, RMAN stores any information on corrupt data blocks in its recovery catalog. The script may interrogate this to verify the state of the database and the validity of the backup.
- Both Oracle7 and Oracle8 have an offline utility that performs physical data structure integrity checking. `DB_VERIFY` cannot detect all kinds of corruption, but it does identify many; it is advisable to run it from certain of scripts, especially under Oracle7.
- For fatal errors, contact support personnel as per site standards (usually by direct paging or console messages to schedulers or, more rarely, via e-mail or computer-controlled telephony).
- For Oracle8, RMAN does not back up INIT.ORA, SQLNET.ORA, CONFIG.ORA, LISTENER. ORA, TNSNAMES.ORA, and the password file, so OS script should handle this.

- For Oracle8, the script should catalog and manage user-created backups, if this is part of the backup strategy.
- Detect possible conflicts from duplicate submissions. For example, a backup can easily verify whether another is running on the same Oracle Instance at the same time. Normally, the job submitted second should simply terminate itself with an appropriate warning message.

There may be other criteria to add, but this basic list covers the features most sites require.

Return Code Handling

One very important feature of OS scripts is proper verification of the success or failure of the RMAN or EBU commands. There are a few cases where RMAN or EBU return codes are misleading. For example, EBU will sometimes give a return code of 0, although corrupt database blocks forced the utility to skip backing up a file. OS script can inspect the textual output from EBU looking for messages starting with "EBU-" and identify cases where the backup is invalid although EBU returned a 0 return code.

If a job is run to back up archive logs under RMAN and there are no archive logs to back up, RMAN yields a failing return code of 1. OS script can intercept this return code, write out a warning message, and send a backup job return code of 0. No one wants to be paged simply because a backup script did not find any archived logs to back up!

Performance

Performance can be measured in any number of ways. How long do backups run? What is the time-to-recover? What is the performance impact of online backups on other jobs? What resources do backups consume? All are legitimate performance questions.

The first step in achieving "good performance" is to precisely define the term. There are often trade-offs between the different performance criteria. For example, minimizing nightly backup speed may require a different backup–recovery strategy than one that minimizes time-to-recover. The management team must share a common definition of what "good performance" is before spending time and effort trying to achieve it.

In achieving most performance goals, the OS scripts are a minor piece of the puzzle. More often, maximizing performance concerns (1) hardware architecture and (2) effective RMAN/EBU command file scripts.

For example, from the standpoint of hardware architecture, minimizing communications links and keeping the architecture homogeneous often increase backup reliability and speed. A system design that spans multiple communications links and backs up NT machines to UNIX and then mainframe tape silos is likely to provide less performance and reliability than one that backs up across a single, fast communication link in a homogeneous machine configuration.

This is but a single example, but it embodies the key concept: carefully design hardware architecture with fast, reliable components because this is a key area that OS scripts cannot themselves address.

When using either the command file or stored script techniques, it's easy to isolate and improve RMAN or EBU commands. Plus, we can easily measure and compare their relative performance. Keeping operations parallel and tape drives busy are fundamental to fast RMAN or EBU backups.

For Oracle8, recovery manager maintains parallel operations by creating multiple backup sets and file copies in parallel. Making `BACKUP`, `COPY,` and `RESTORE` commands parallel requires specifying multiple `ALLOCATE CHANNEL` commands. For `BACKUP`s, ensure the number of files specified or implied in the backup is greater than the `FILES-PERSET` operand. For `COPY`s, specify multiple datafiles in a single `COPY` command. Under certain conditions, RMAN can shorten recovery time as well through parallelization.

EBU and Oracle7 provide several techniques to ensure that backup tapes are kept streaming (continuously writing). "Multiplexing" interlaces blocks from different database files stored on different physical disk drives onto a single backup fileset. The MUX specifier of the `BACKUP` command enables this feature. EBU will also attempt to sustain high disk transfer rates by using asynchronous I/O and sharing memory among its I/O processes.

The allure of these performance techniques, of course, is that we only need change the stored script or command file executed by OS script to take advantage of them. Generic OS scripts need not be altered.

Conclusion

In designing performant, reliable backup and recovery procedures, large sites with critical applications face significantly different issues than smaller organizations and sites with smaller databases. Often, large companies will need to develop their own scripts to implement fast, reliable backup and recovery mechanisms. OS scripts that drive RMAN and EBU make a potent combination in achieving these goals.

Notes

1. Both RMAN and EBU are flexible in the number and location of their catalogs. We have described a typical scenario for large RMAN sites: two recovery catalogs, each backing up the other. Each exists in a different Instance on a different machine. Some sites place their catalogs in existing databases with other production applications, while others prefer to isolate them in single-purpose "backup/recovery control" Instances. RMAN does not require a recov-

ery catalog; but without one, we lose fundamental features of the product. These include point-in-time recovery, stored scripts, and recovery with lost or damaged control files. Few sites use RMAN without a recovery catalog.

2. Use a query such as this to determine if any tablespaces are still in hot backup mode from an aborted previous run of an EBU backup script:

   `SELECT TABLESPACE_NAME, V$BACKUP.STATUS FROM SYS.DBA_DATA_FILES, V$BACKUP WHERE FILE_ID = FILE#` and `V$BACKUP.STATUS = 'ACTIVE;` RMAN and Oracle8 do not put tablespaces in hot backup mode because an Oracle server process reads the datafiles being backed up. RMAN thus does not issue the `ALTER TABLESPACE BEGIN BACKUP` statement.

Recommended Reading

Oracle8 Server Backup and Recovery Guide, A54640 (Oracle Corp., Redwood City, CA). *Oracle7 Enterprise Backup Utility Administrator's Guide,* A48522 (Oracle Corp., Redwood City, CA).

Chapter 25

Alert Mechanisms for RMAN Backups

Guang Sheng Wan

Recovery Manager (RMAN) is an Oracle utility used by the database administrator (DBA) to back up, restore, and recover database files. RMAN manages the processes of creating backups of database files, archived redo log files and control files, and restoring or recovering from backups. It greatly simplifies the tasks DBAs perform during these processes. It can detect many types of corruption problems, and makes sure that the backup does not include corrupted blocks. RMAN provides true incremental backups and automatic parallelization of backups and restores. Its efficiency is very important for any 24 × 7 database environment.

To make use of RMAN functionality and ease normal operations, Oracle DBAs normally automate resync (resynchronize) catalog operations and daily backup operations based on their backup strategies. For DBAs to ensure their jobs have been successfully completed, they check messages in the log files. There are many RMAN messages in the log files, and DBAs need to identify which are informational messages and which are error messages. This process tends to be tedious, especially when there are a considerable number of database servers to manage.

Is there any way to automate the process? Is it possible to build an Oracle database package that tells the DBA if there was any problem on the RMAN backup? The alert mechanisms introduced below provide one possibility. Before going into detail, it is necessary to discuss the RMAN recovery catalog.

RMAN Recovery Catalog

The recovery catalog is a repository of information used and maintained by RMAN. RMAN uses the information in the recovery catalog to determine how

0-8493-1139-X/02/$0.00+$1.50
©2002 by CRC Press LLC

to execute requested backup and restore actions. RMAN can work without the recovery catalog under certain conditions, but the usage of RMAN is limited without the recovery catalog. For example, RMAN cannot run stored scripts; it is not possible to perform tablespace point-in-time recovery and recovery when the control file is lost or damaged. To utilize the full functionality of RMAN, the use of the recovery catalog is strongly recommended.

The recovery catalog contains the following information:

- The recovery catalog version and all checkpoints
- Registered target databases and their incarnations (database incarnation is used by RMAN to identify the different "versions" of the same physical database)
- Data file, archive log, and control file backup sets and backup pieces
- Data file and control file copies
- Archived redo logs, redo log ranges, and all redo log history
- Tablespace and data file attributes
- Redo log files, data files, and tablespaces at the target database
- Corrupted block ranges in data file backups or datafile copies
- RMAN stored scripts (a sequence of RMAN commands stored in the recovery catalog)

The recovery catalog table definitions and their primary/unique keys are listed in Exhibit 25.1. For the column definitions and their descriptions, please refer to *Oracle 8 Backup and Recovery Guide, Release 8.0* (December 1997).

The RMAN Backup Alert System

Because RMAN recovery catalog stores all data for database backups and recoveries, it is not difficult to obtain an answer on the status of a specific database backup. The package CHECK_RMAN_BACKUP (to be discussed in detail) is the product of this idea, and with the package, it is easy to set up an alert system for RMAN backups. Exhibit 25.2 shows the architecture of the RMAN backup alert system.

Oracle DBAs can schedule daily RMAN backup jobs and resync catalog jobs using RMAN stored scripts in the recovery catalog (i.e., in the table SCR and SCRL). These jobs are controlled by RMAN and performed by the target database server processes. An incremental level 0 backup performs backup for all blocks that have ever been used. Incremental backups at levels greater than 0 back up only blocks that have been changed since previous incremental backups. Typically, level 0 database backups are scheduled once a week; level 1 database backups are scheduled twice a week; level 2 database backups are scheduled three times a week or more. While resync catalog jobs are scheduled more often than the backup jobs, it does depend on the number of archived redo log files generated each day. For example, they may run every 15 to 30 minutes. Note that the DBAs should manually resynchronize the recovery catalog whenever structural changes have been made to the target database. It is critical for the DBAs to be alerted if anything unexpected happens.

Exhibit 25.1 RMAN Recovery Catalog Tables and Their Primary/Unique Keys

Table Name	Primary Key Column(s)	Unique Key Column(s)	Information Stored in the Table
AL	AL_KEY	DBINC_KEY AL_RECID AL_STAMP	Archived redo logs. It corresponds to the V$ARCHIVED_LOG fixed view in the control file.
BCB		BDF_KEY BCB_RECID BCB_STAMP	Corrupted block ranges in data file backups. It corresponds to the V$BACKUP_CORRUPTION fixed view in the control file.
BCF	BCF_KEY	1. DBINC_KEY BCF_RECID BCF_STAMP 2. BS_KEY	Control file backups in backup sets. (A backup data file record with file# 0 is used to represent the backup control file in the V$BACKUP_DATAFILE view.)
BDF	BDF_KEY	DBINC_KEY BDF_RECID BDF_STAMP	All data file backups in backup sets.
BP	BP_KEY	BS_KEY BP_RECID BP_STAMP	All backup pieces of backup sets. (A backup piece is a physical file in an RMAN-specific format that belongs to one and only one backup set.)
BRL	BRL_KEY	DBINC_KEY BRL_RECID BRL_STAMP	Backup redo logs. It corresponds to the V$BACKUP_REDOLOG fixed view in the control file.
BS	BS_KEY	1. DB_KEY BS_RECID BS_STAMP 2. DB_KEY SET_STAMP SET_COUNT	All backup sets for all database incarnations. (An RMAN-specific logical grouping of one or more backup pieces.)
CCB		CDF_KEY CCB_RECID CCB_STAMP	Corrupt block ranges in data file copies. It corresponds to the V$COPY_CORRUPTION fixed view in the control file.
CCF	CCF_KEY	DBINC_KEY CCF_RECID CCF_STAMP	Control file copies. (A data file copy record with file# 0 is used to represent the control file copy in the V$DATAFILE_COPY view.)
CDF	CDF_KEY	DBINC_KEY CDF_RECID CDF_STAMP	All data file copies.
CKP	CKP_KEY	DBINC_KEY CKP_SCN CKP_TYPE CKP_CF_SEQ CF_CREATE_TIME	All recovery catalog checkpoints.

(continues)

Exhibit 25.1 (continued)

Table Name	*Primary Key Column(s)*	*Unique Key Column(s)*	*Information Stored in the Table*
DB	DB_KEY	DB_ID	All target databases that have been registered in this recovery catalog.
DBINC	DBINC_KEY	DB_KEY RESET_SCN RESET_TIME	All incarnations of the target databases registered in this recovery catalog.
DF	DBINC_KEY FILE# CREATE_SCN	1. DBINC_KEY FILE# DROP_SCN 2. DBINC_KEY TS# TS_CREATE_SCN FILE#	All data files of all database incarnations.
DFATT		DBINC_KEY FILE# CREATE_SCN END_CKP_KEY	Data file attributes that change over time.
OFFR	OFFR_KEY	1. DBINC_KEY OFFR_RECID OFFR_STAMP 2. DBINC_KEY FILE# OFFLINE_SCN CF_CREATE_TIME	Data file offline ranges.
ORL	DBINC_KEY FNAME		All redo log files for all database incarnations.
RCVER			Recovery catalog version.
RLH	RLH_KEY	1. DBINC_KEY THREAD# SEQUENCE# LOW_SCN 2. DBINC_KEY RLH_RECID RLH_STAMP	All redo log history for all threads.
RR	RR_KEY		Redo log ranges for all database incarnations.
RT	DBINC_KEY THREAD#		All redo threads for all database incarnations.
SCR	SCR_KEY	DB_KEY SCR_NAME	RMAN stored scripts.
SCRL		SCR_KEY LINENUM	RMAN stored script lines.

Exhibit 25.1 (continued)

Table Name	*Primary Key Column(s)*	*Unique Key Column(s)*	*Information Stored in the Table*
TS	DBINC_KEY TS# CREATE_SCN	1. DBINC_KEY TS# DROP_SCN 2. DBINC_KEY TS_NAME CREATE_SCN	All tablespaces of all database incarnations.
TSATT		DBINC_KEY TS# CREATE_SCN END_CKP_KEY	Tablespace attributes that change over time.

By installing or creating the CHECK_RMAN_BACKUP package in the RMAN database under the recovery catalog schema, adding a few lines for calling the functions of the package in an ALERT program (for example, alrtpatrol.tcl, which was written in Oratcl, and performs checking on all database servers' exceptions and performance measurements. It is used in Highmark Life & Casualty Group), and the DBA will be alerted or paged if any exception occurs. It is also possible to build a small Tcl script in Oracle Enterprise Manager, and schedule it to run periodically. Because DATAFILE_BACKUP, REDOLOG_BACKUP, and CTRLFILE_BACKUP are inline functions in the CHECK_RMAN_BACKUP package, SQL*Plus or any other Oracle program interfaces can be used for retrieving the return values. The following is an example:

```
SELECT check_rman_backup.datafile_backup ('sig','02:30:00', 0),
  check_rman_backup.redolog_backup ('sig', '02:30:00', 0),
  check_rman_backup.ctrlfile_backup ('sig', '02:30:00', 0)
FROM DUAL;
```

where `'sig'` refers to the target database name; `'02:30:00'` refers to the backup start time; 0 means the checking is for the current date.

CHECK_RMAN_BACKUP Package

CHECK_RMAN_BACKUP is a stored package that performs checking on RMAN backup and resync catalog operations based on the data stored in the RMAN recovery catalog. It was developed on Oracle 8.0.5 for Windows NT, and implemented on Oracle 8.0.5.1.0 for IBM AIX. There are four main functions in the package:

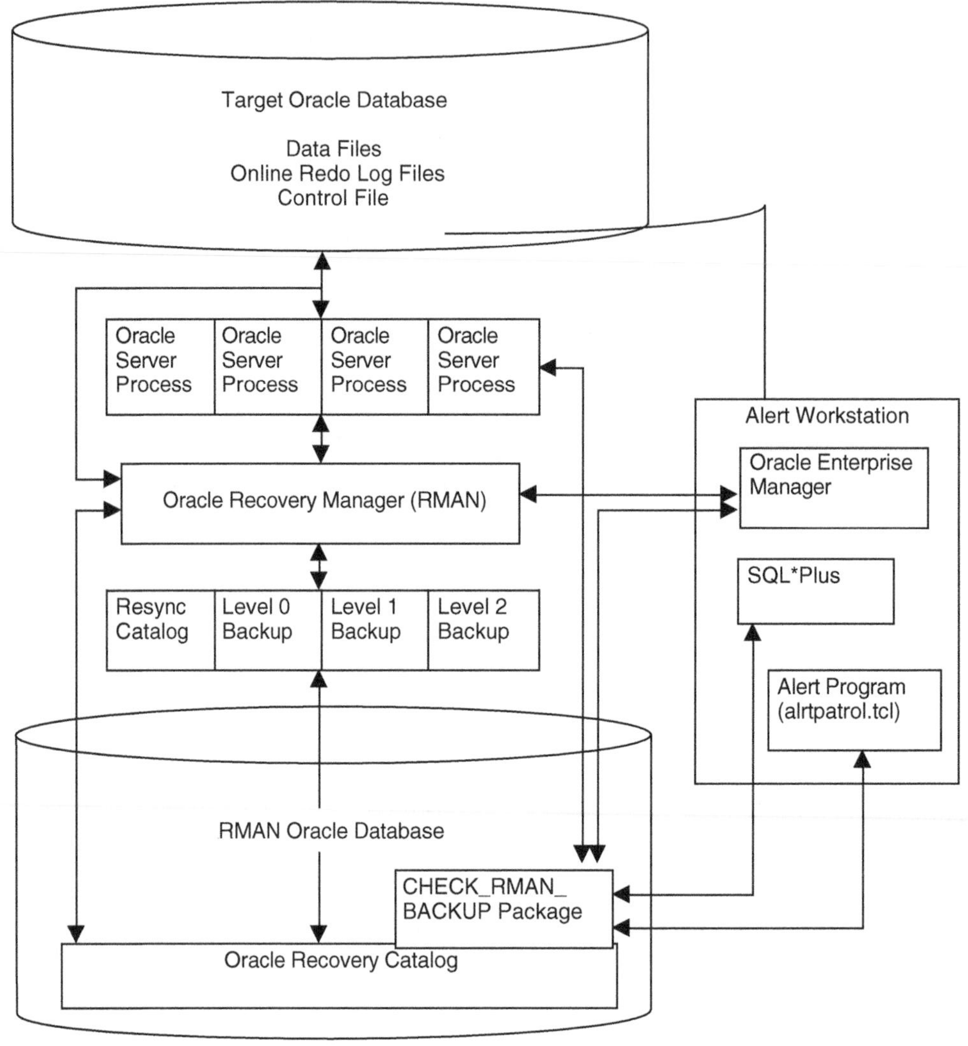

Exhibit 25.2 The Architecture of the RMAN Backup Alert System

1. DATAFILE_BACKUP
2. REDOLOG_BACKUP
3. CTRLFILE_BACKUP
4. RESYNC_RCVCAT

Each of the first three functions accepts the database name, backup start time, and offset (to system date) as input parameters, and returns "1" if the specific backup has been successfully completed. If the backup has not been completed or there was no backup at all, the function will return "0." The resync_rcvcat function accepts database name and database link as input parameters, and returns "1" if the recovery catalog and the control file of the target database are in synchronization; otherwise, it returns "0."

First of all, it is important to be certain that the recovery catalog and the control file of the target database are in synchronization. Once that has been confirmed, it makes sense to verify if the backup has been completed successfully. There are two types of resync catalog operations performed by RMAN. One is partial resynchronization and the other is full resynchronization. Partial resynchronizations transfer information to the recovery catalog about archived redo logs, backup sets, and data file copies. They will not transfer information such as new data files, new or removed tablespaces, and new or removed online log groups and members. Partial resynchronizations are initiated by RMAN before performing backup, copy, restore, recovery, list, and report operations if RMAN determines that resynchronization is necessary. They are also initiated by RMAN after performing backup, copy, restore, switch, register, reset, and catalog operations. A full catalog resynchronization is an RMAN operation that refreshes the recovery catalog with all changed information in the database's control file. They are normally initiated by DBAs, and can also be initiated by RMAN if it determines this action is necessary before executing certain commands.

To verify if the recovery catalog is up-to-date, the most important thing is to ensure that the information about archived redo log files in the AL table are the same as those in the target database's control file (i.e., in V$ARCHIVED_LOG view). In addition, it is also important to verify the data files, tablespaces, and online redo log files if they are tallied with those in the control file of the target database. RESYNC_RCVCAT accesses DF and V$DATAFILE for comparing data files, TS and V$TABLESPACE for comparing tablespaces, and ORL and $LOGFILE for online redo log files comparison. If any of the comparisons fails, it means the recovery catalog is not up-to-date.

To check if the data file RMAN backup was successful, it is necessary to verify that all "normal" (not read-only or not dropped) data files have been backed up. In other words, the data files listed in the DF table should be included in the backup data file list (i.e., in the BDF table) for the checking period. DATAFILE_BACKUP, REDOLOG_BACKUP and CTRLFILE_BACKUP use a one-day period (from the specified backup start date and time) as the checking period.

It is a little tricky to verify that the archived redo log backup was successfully completed because the names or sequence numbers and the numbers of the archived redo log files are changing every day. Function REDOLOG_BACKUP_DATE is used to get the latest successful archived redo log backup date based on the specified backup start time. To do so, it retrieves the last two different dates based on the backup start time specified (from the BS table), and obtains the maximum redo log sequence number backed up in the previous backup (if considering the later date is the current one from the BRL table). The BS table contains the completion time for each backup set. Then it counts the number of archived redo log files to be backed up in the current backup based on the maximum redo log sequence number and the current backup completion time (from the AL table). Finally, it gets the number of archived redo log files backed up during the period of time from the BRL table under the above conditions. If they are the same, it means the archived redo log files have been successfully backed up. The function returns the backup date to the caller. The REDOLOG_BACKUP function figures out whether the backup was successful or not using the date and time in question and the date returned by REDOLOG_BACKUP_DATE.

Note that as long as FILE #1 has been backed up, the control file was backed up too. It is easy for CTRLFILE_BACKUP to find out the control file backup records from the BCF and BS tables (the latter contains the backup time) for the specified database and the backup start time.

As mentioned earlier, RMAN uses the term "database incarnation" to identify the different "versions" of the same physical database. The incarnation of the database changes once it has been opened with the RESETLOGS option. To be certain the accessed data is related to the current database version, GET_DBINC function can be used for returning the current database incarnation according to the database name specified.

For flexibility, some functions in the CHECK_RMAN_BACKUP package accept an input parameter, which is called "offset" (to the current date). Zero (0) indicates the current date or SYSDATE; 1 indicates one day ago, and so on.

For the detailed logic, please refer to the PL/SQL source code in Appendix 25.1. The RMAN recovery catalog column definitions and descriptions are given in Appendix 25.2.

Conclusion

By plugging in the CHECK_RMAN_BACKUP package, the DBA does not need to manually check the RMAN backup log files, nor to manually verify if the RMAN recovery catalog is up-to-date. It does make sense to change the way in which the DBA handles the RMAN backup verifications too. Instead of pulling the messages from the backup log files, the DBA can run the package and get the results from the RMAN database. Furthermore, by constructing a small program, an alert system for RMAN backups can be set up so that the DBA can be alerted only if there is anything that needs attention. It is especially helpful if there are many database systems in a 24 × 7 database environment.

Acknowledgment

I would like to thank Daniel Clamage for his contributions and comments.

Appendix 25.1 PL/SQL Source Code

```
REM Program Name: Check RMAN backup and resync catalog
REM Module Name : chkrmanbkup.sql
REM Written By : Guang Sheng Wan
REM Description :
REM    1. Verify if the daily RMAN backup was successful based on
REM       the input values: database name, backup start time and
REM       offset to the current date
REM    2. Verify if the recovery catalog was up to date based on
REM       the input values: database name and database link name
REM Log in as : The RMAN recovery catalog owner
REM Modification:
REM    V1.0 28-NOV-1999 - Initial release.
REM    V1.1 25-DEC-1999 - Second release.

CREATE OR REPLACE PACKAGE CHECK_RMAN_BACKUP IS

-- Check if the datafile backup was successful
-- Returns 1 if all datafiles have been successfully backed up
-- Returns 0 if no datafile or not all datafiles have been backed up
-- Returns SQLCODE if there is any error
FUNCTION DATAFILE_BACKUP (p_db_name IN VARCHAR2,
       p_backup_start_time IN VARCHAR2,   -- in 'HH24:MI:SS' format
       p_offset IN NUMBER DEFAULT 0)
RETURN NUMBER;
PRAGMA RESTRICT_REFERENCES (DATAFILE_BACKUP, WNDS, WNPS);

-- Check if the archived redo log backup was successful
-- Returns 1 if all archived redo logs have been successfully backed up
-- Returns 0 if no archived redo log or not all archived redo logs
--     have been backed up
-- Returns SQLCODE if there is any error
FUNCTION REDOLOG_BACKUP (p_db_name IN VARCHAR2,
       p_backup_start_time IN VARCHAR2,   -- in 'HH24:MI:SS' format
       p_offset IN NUMBER DEFAULT 0)
RETURN NUMBER;
PRAGMA RESTRICT_REFERENCES (REDOLOG_BACKUP, WNDS);

-- Get the archived redo log backup date
-- Returns archived redo log backup date for successful backup
-- Returns 'The redo log backup failed.' for unsuccessful backup
-- Returns SQLCODE (in VARCHAR2 format) if there is any error
FUNCTION REDOLOG_BACKUP_DATE (p_db_name IN VARCHAR2,
       p_backup_start_time IN VARCHAR2,   -- in 'HH24:MI:SS' format
       p_offset IN NUMBER DEFAULT 0)
RETURN VARCHAR2;
PRAGMA RESTRICT_REFERENCES (REDOLOG_BACKUP_DATE, WNDS);

-- Check if the control file backup was successful
-- Returns 1 if control file has been successfully backed up
-- Returns 0 if control file has not been backed up
-- Returns SQLCODE if there is any error
FUNCTION CTRLFILE_BACKUP (p_db_name IN VARCHAR2,
       p_backup_start_time IN VARCHAR2,   -- in 'HH24:MI:SS' format
       p_offset IN NUMBER DEFAULT 0)
RETURN NUMBER;
PRAGMA RESTRICT_REFERENCES (CTRLFILE_BACKUP, WNDS, WNPS);
```

(continues)

Appendix 25.1 (continued)

```
-- Check if the recovery catalog was up to date
-- Returns 1 if the recovery catalog and the target database's control
--     file are in synchronization
-- Returns 0 if they are not in synchronization
-- Returns SQLCODE if there is any error
FUNCTION RESYNC_RCVCAT (p_db_name IN VARCHAR2,
                        p_db_link IN VARCHAR2)
RETURN NUMBER;

-- Get the database incarnation
-- Returns a number if it is okay
-- Returns 0 if no database incarnation found
-- Returns SQLCODE if there is any error
FUNCTION GET_DBINC (p_db_name IN VARCHAR2)
RETURN NUMBER;
PRAGMA RESTRICT_REFERENCES (GET_DBINC, WNDS, WNPS);

END CHECK_RMAN_BACKUP;
/

CREATE OR REPLACE PACKAGE BODY CHECK_RMAN_BACKUP IS

-- Returns 1 if all datafiles have been successfully backed up
-- Returns 0 if no datafile or not all datafiles have been backed up
-- Returns SQLCODE if there is any error
FUNCTION DATAFILE_BACKUP (p_db_name IN VARCHAR2,
       p_backup_start_time IN VARCHAR2,    -- in 'HH24:MI:SS' format
       p_offset IN NUMBER DEFAULT 0)
RETURN NUMBER IS

    pl_no_of_files     NUMBER := 0;
    pl_no_of_bdfs      NUMBER := 0;
    pl_dbinc           NUMBER := 0;
    pl_completion_from DATE := TO_DATE(TO_CHAR(SYSDATE-p_offset,
                              'MM/DD/YYYY')||' '||p_backup_start_time,
                              'MM/DD/YYYY HH24:MI:SS');
    -- always 24 hours after from date
    pl_completion_toDATE := TO_DATE(TO_CHAR(SYSDATE+1-p_offset,
                              'MM/DD/YYYY')||' '||p_backup_start_time,
                              'MM/DD/YYYY HH24:MI:SS');

BEGIN

-- Get the database incarnation first
pl_dbinc := GET_DBINC (p_db_name);

-- Get the number of the data files for the database incarnation
BEGIN
    SELECT COUNT(file#) no_of_dfs
      INTO pl_no_of_files
    FROM df
    WHERE dbinc_key = pl_dbinc
      AND read_only = 0
      AND NVL(drop_time, pl_completion_from) >= pl_completion_from
      AND create_time < pl_completion_from;

EXCEPTION
    WHEN OTHERS THEN
```

Appendix 25.1 (continued)

```
        RETURN (SQLCODE);
END;


-- Get the number of the data files that have been backed up
BEGIN
SELECT COUNT(file#) no_of_bdfs
     INTO pl_no_of_bdfs
FROM bdf b
WHERE completion_time BETWEEN pl_completion_from AND pl_completion_to
        AND dbinc_key = pl_dbinc
        AND EXISTS (SELECT 'X'
           FROM df d
           WHERE d.dbinc_key = pl_dbinc
              AND d.read_only = 0
              AND NVL(d.drop_time, pl_completion_from) >=
                 pl_completion_from
                    AND d.create_time < pl_completion_from
                       AND d.dbinc_key = b.dbinc_key
                       AND d.file# = b.file#
                    AND d.create_scn = b.create_scn);

EXCEPTION
     WHEN OTHERS THEN
        RETURN (SQLCODE);
END;

-- Compare the two numbers, and return the comparison result
IF pl_no_of_files = pl_no_of_bdfs OR
     (pl_no_of_files < pl_no_of_bdfs AND-- cater for more backups
        MOD(pl_no_of_bdfs, pl_no_of_files) = 0) THEN
     RETURN (1);
ELSE
     RETURN (0);
END IF;

END DATAFILE_BACKUP;

-- Returns 1 if all archived redo logs have been successfully backed up
-- Returns 0 if no archived redo log or not all archived redo logs
--      have been backed up
-- Returns SQLCODE if there is any error
FUNCTION REDOLOG_BACKUP (p_db_name IN VARCHAR2,
           p_backup_start_time IN VARCHAR2, -- in 'HH24:MI:SS' format
           p_offset IN NUMBER DEFAULT 0)
RETURN NUMBER IS

     pl_rl_backup_date    VARCHAR2(30) := NULL;
     pl_backup_sets       NUMBER := 0;

     pl_completion_from DATE := TO_DATE(TO_CHAR(SYSDATE - p_offset,
                              'MM/DD/YYYY')||' '||p_backup_start_time,
                              'MM/DD/YYYY HH24:MI:SS');
     -- always 24 hours after from date
     pl_completion_to DATE := TO_DATE(TO_CHAR(SYSDATE+1 - p_offset,
                              'MM/DD/YYYY')||' '||p_backup_start_time,
                              'MM/DD/YYYY HH24:MI:SS');
```

(continues)

Appendix 25.1 (continued)

```
BEGIN
pl_rl_backup_date := REDOLOG_BACKUP_DATE
                         (p_db_name, p_backup_start_time, p_offset);
IF pl_rl_backup_date = 'The redo log backup failed.' THEN
    RETURN (0);
-- Error or some other DATE
ELSIF SUBSTR(pl_rl_backup_date, 5, 1) = '/' THEN
    BEGIN
      SELECT COUNT(bs_key)
        INTO pl_backup_sets
      FROM bs
      WHERE bck_type = 'L'
        AND TO_CHAR(completion_time, 'YYYY/MM/DD') = pl_rl_backup_date
        AND completion_time BETWEEN pl_completion_from
              AND pl_completion_to;
      IF pl_backup_sets > 0 THEN
        RETURN (1);
      ELSE
        RETURN (0);
      END IF;

      EXCEPTION
        WHEN OTHERS THEN
          RETURN (SQLCODE);
    END;
ELSE
    -- SQLCODE from REDOLOG_BACKUP_DATE
    RETURN (TO_NUMBER (pl_rl_backup_date));
END IF;

END REDOLOG_BACKUP;

-- Returns archived redo log backup date for successful backup
-- Returns 'The redo log backup failed.' for unsuccessful backup
-- Returns SQLCODE (in VARCHAR2 format) if there is any error
FUNCTION REDOLOG_BACKUP_DATE (p_db_name IN VARCHAR2,
          p_backup_start_time IN VARCHAR2,  -- in 'HH24:MI:SS' format
          p_offset IN NUMBER DEFAULT 0)
RETURN VARCHAR2 IS

pl_completion_to DATE := TO_DATE(TO_CHAR(SYSDATE+1 - p_offset,
                         'MM/DD/YYYY')||' '||p_backup_start_time,
                         'MM/DD/YYYY HH24:MI:SS');

-- For getting the completion time of the previous backup set
-- Backup type - 'L' for archived redo log
CURSOR c_bs IS
    -- Format 'YYYY/MM/DD' is used for ORDER BY DESC
    SELECT DISTINCT TO_CHAR(completion_time,
                         'YYYY/MM/DD') completion_time
    FROM bs
    WHERE bck_type = 'L'
      AND completion_time < pl_completion_to
    ORDER BY completion_time DESC;
c_bs_rec c_bs%ROWTYPE;
pl_prev_bs_date VARCHAR2(10) := NULL;
pl_curr_bs_date VARCHAR2(10) := NULL;
pl_max_log_no   NUMBER := 0;
```

Appendix 25.1 (continued)

```
pl_no_of_logs     NUMBER := 0;
pl_brl_count      NUMBER := 0;
pl_dbinc          NUMBER := 0;
pl_sqlcode_c      VARCHAR2(10) := NULL;

BEGIN

-- Get the database incarnation first
pl_dbinc := GET_DBINC (p_db_name);

-- Get the completion time of the previous backup set
BEGIN
     OPEN c_bs;

     -- Get the last two backup dates
     FOR i IN 1..2 LOOP
        FETCH c_bs INTO c_bs_rec;
        EXIT WHEN c_bs%NOTFOUND;
        IF i = 1 THEN
           pl_curr_bs_date := c_bs_rec.completion_time;
        ELSIF i = 2 THEN
           pl_prev_bs_date := c_bs_rec.completion_time;
        END IF;
     END LOOP;
     CLOSE c_bs;

     EXCEPTION
        WHEN OTHERS THEN
           pl_sqlcode_c := TO_CHAR(SQLCODE);
           IF c_bs%ISOPEN THEN
              CLOSE c_bs;
           END IF;
           RETURN (pl_sqlcode_c);
END;

-- Get the maximum archived redo log number of the previous backup set
BEGIN
     SELECT MAX(b.sequence#) sequence#
        INTO pl_max_log_no
     FROM brl b
     WHERE b.dbinc_key = pl_dbinc
        AND EXISTS (SELECT 'X'
           FROM bs s
           WHERE TO_CHAR(s.completion_time, 'YYYY/MM/DD') =
              pl_prev_bs_date
              AND s.bck_type = 'L'
              AND s.bs_key = b.bs_key);

     EXCEPTION
        WHEN OTHERS THEN
           RETURN (TO_CHAR(SQLCODE));
END;

-- Get the number of archived redo log files to be backed up
BEGIN
     SELECT COUNT(sequence#) cnt
        INTO pl_no_of_logs
     FROM al a
```

(continues)

Appendix 25.1 (continued)

```
     WHERE sequence# > pl_max_log_no
        AND completion_time < (SELECT min(start_time)
           FROM bs
           WHERE TO_CHAR(start_time, 'YYYY/MM/DD') =
              pl_curr_bs_date
           AND bck_type = 'L')
        AND dbinc_key = pl_dbinc;

     EXCEPTION
        WHEN OTHERS THEN
           RETURN (TO_CHAR(SQLCODE));
END;

-- Get the number of archived redo log files which have been backed up
BEGIN
     SELECT COUNT(sequence#) cnt
        INTO pl_brl_count
     FROM brl b
     WHERE bs_key IN (SELECT bs_key
        FROM bs
        WHERE TO_CHAR(completion_time, 'YYYY/MM/DD') =
           pl_curr_bs_date
        AND bck_type = 'L')
        AND (thread#, sequence#) IN
           (SELECT thread#, sequence#
           FROM al
           WHERE sequence# > pl_max_log_no
           AND completion_time <
              (SELECT min(start_time)
              FROM bs
              WHERE TO_CHAR(start_time, 'YYYY/MM/DD') =
              pl_curr_bs_date
              AND bck_type = 'L')
              AND dbinc_key = pl_dbinc)
        AND dbinc_key = pl_dbinc;

     EXCEPTION
        WHEN OTHERS THEN
           RETURN (TO_CHAR(SQLCODE));
END;

-- Compare the two numbers, and return the comparison result
IF (pl_brl_count = pl_no_of_logs AND pl_curr_bs_date IS NOT NULL) THEN
     RETURN (pl_curr_bs_date);
ELSE
     RETURN ('The redo log backup failed.');
END IF;

END REDOLOG_BACKUP_DATE;

-- Returns 1 if control file has been successfully backed up
-- Returns 0 if control file has not been backed up
-- Returns SQLCODE if there is any error
FUNCTION CTRLFILE_BACKUP (p_db_name IN VARCHAR2,
           p_backup_start_time IN VARCHAR2, -- in 'HH24:MI:SS' format
           p_offset IN NUMBER DEFAULT 0)
RETURN NUMBER IS
```

Appendix 25.1 (continued)

```
pl_completion_from DATE := TO_DATE(TO_CHAR(SYSDATE-p_offset,
          'MM/DD/YYYY')||' '||p_backup_start_time,
          'MM/DD/YYYY HH24:MI:SS');
-- always 24 hours after from date
pl_completion_to DATE := TO_DATE(TO_CHAR(SYSDATE+1-p_offset,
          'MM/DD/YYYY')||' '||p_backup_start_time,
          'MM/DD/YYYY HH24:MI:SS');
pl_cf_count NUMBER := 0;

BEGIN
     SELECT DECODE(COUNT(bcf_key), 0, 0, NULL, 0, 1) cnt
        INTO pl_cf_count
     FROM bcf, bs
     WHERE bcf.dbinc_key = GET_DBINC(p_db_name)
        AND bs.completion_time BETWEEN pl_completion_from
             AND pl_completion_to
        AND bs.bs_key = bcf.bs_key;
     RETURN (pl_cf_count);

     EXCEPTION
        WHEN OTHERS THEN
           RETURN (SQLCODE);

END CTRLFILE_BACKUP;

-- Returns 1 if the recovery catalog and the target database's control
--     file are in synchronization
-- Returns 0 if they are not in synchronization
-- Returns SQLCODE if there is any error
FUNCTION RESYNC_RCVCAT (p_db_name IN VARCHAR2,
                        p_db_link IN VARCHAR2)
RETURN NUMBER IS

pl_dbinc          NUMBER := 0;
pl_prod_stmt      VARCHAR2(200);
pl_prod_max_no    NUMBER := 0; -- Max archived redo log sequence no.
                               -- from target DB
pl_rman_max_no NUMBER := 0;    -- Max archived redo log sequence no.
       -- from RMAN
pl_prod_no_dfs NUMBER := 0;    -- Number of datafiles from target DB
pl_rman_no_dfs NUMBER := 0;    -- Number of datafiles from RMAN
pl_prod_no_tss NUMBER := 0;    -- Number of tablespaces from target DB
pl_rman_no_tss NUMBER := 0;    -- Number of tablespaces from RMAN
pl_prod_no_rls NUMBER := 0;    -- Number of online redo log files
                               -- from target DB
pl_rman_no_rls NUMBER := 0;    -- Number of online redo log files
                               -- from RMAN

     -- Helping function for dynamic SQL needed, so any database link
     --   can be supplied
     -- Returns a positive number if it is okay
     -- Returns SQLCODE if it fails
     FUNCTION GET_NUMBER (p_sql_stmt IN VARCHAR2)
     RETURN NUMBER IS

     pl_c          NUMBER := 0;
     pl_rc         NUMBER := 0;
     -- pl_stmt    VARCHAR2(200) := NULL;
```

(continues)

Appendix 25.1 (continued)

```
    pl_number     NUMBER := 0;
    pl_sqlcode_n  NUMBER := 0;

BEGIN
    -- pl_stmt := p_sql_stmt;
    pl_c := DBMS_SQL.OPEN_CURSOR;
    -- return (pl_c);
    DBMS_SQL.PARSE (pl_c, p_sql_stmt, DBMS_SQL.NATIVE);
    DBMS_SQL.DEFINE_COLUMN (pl_c, 1, pl_number);
    pl_rc := DBMS_SQL.EXECUTE_AND_FETCH (pl_c);
    IF pl_rc > 0 THEN
      DBMS_SQL.COLUMN_VALUE (pl_c, 1, pl_number);
    END IF;
    DBMS_SQL.CLOSE_CURSOR (pl_c);
    RETURN (pl_number);
    EXCEPTION
      WHEN OTHERS THEN
        pl_sqlcode_n := SQLCODE;
        IF DBMS_SQL.IS_OPEN(pl_c) THEN
          DBMS_SQL.CLOSE_CURSOR (pl_c);
        END IF;
        RETURN (pl_sqlcode_n);
END GET_NUMBER;

BEGIN

-- Get the database incarnation first
pl_dbinc := GET_DBINC (p_db_name);

-- Partial resync comparison
-- Get the maximum archived redo log number from the target database
BEGIN
    pl_prod_stmt := 'SELECT MAX(sequence#) FROM V$ARCHIVED_LOG@'
      ||p_db_link;
    pl_prod_max_no := GET_NUMBER(pl_prod_stmt);
    IF pl_prod_max_no < 0 THEN
      RETURN (pl_prod_max_no);          -- Error condition; abort.
    END IF;
END;

-- Get the maximum archived redo log number
-- from the RMAN recovery catalog
BEGIN
    SELECT MAX(sequence#) max_no
      INTO pl_rman_max_no
    FROM AL
    WHERE dbinc_key = pl_dbinc;

    EXCEPTION
      WHEN OTHERS THEN
        RETURN (SQLCODE);
END;

-- Compare the two archived redo log numbers, and return 0 if not equal
IF pl_prod_max_no != pl_rman_max_no THEN
    RETURN (0);
END IF;
```

Appendix 25.1 (continued)

```
-- Full resync comparison
-- Get the number of datafiles from the target database
BEGIN
    pl_prod_stmt := 'SELECT COUNT(file#) FROM V$DATAFILE@'||p_db_link;
    pl_prod_no_dfs := GET_NUMBER(pl_prod_stmt);
    IF pl_prod_no_dfs < 0 THEN
       RETURN (pl_prod_no_dfs);           -- Error condition; abort.
    END IF;
END;

-- Get the number of datafiles from the RMAN recovery catalog
BEGIN
    SELECT COUNT(file#) cnt
       INTO pl_rman_no_dfs
    FROM DF
    WHERE dbinc_key = pl_dbinc;

    EXCEPTION
       WHEN OTHERS THEN
          RETURN (SQLCODE);
END;

-- Compare the two datafile numbers, and return 0 if not equal
IF pl_prod_no_dfs != pl_rman_no_dfs THEN
    RETURN (0);
END IF;

-- Get the number of tablespaces from the target database
BEGIN
    pl_prod_stmt    := 'SELECT COUNT(ts#) FROM V$TABLESPACE@'||p_db_link;
    pl_prod_no_tss  := GET_NUMBER(pl_prod_stmt);
    IF pl_prod_no_tss < 0 THEN
       RETURN (pl_prod_no_tss);           -- Error condition; abort.
    END IF;
END;

-- Get the number of tablespaces from the RMAN recovery catalog
BEGIN
    SELECT COUNT(ts#) cnt
       INTO pl_rman_no_tss
    FROM TS
    WHERE dbinc_key = pl_dbinc;

       EXCEPTION
          WHEN OTHERS THEN
             RETURN (SQLCODE);
    END;

-- Compare the two tablespace numbers, and return 0 if not equal
IF pl_prod_no_tss != pl_rman_no_tss THEN
    RETURN (0);
END IF;

-- Get the number of online redo log files from the target database
BEGIN
    pl_prod_stmt := 'SELECT COUNT(group#) FROM V$LOGFILE@'||p_db_link;
    pl_prod_no_rls := GET_NUMBER(pl_prod_stmt);
    IF pl_prod_no_rls < 0 THEN
```

(continues)

Appendix 25.1 (continued)

```
        RETURN (pl_prod_no_rls);          -- Error condition; abort.
     END IF;
END;

-- Get the number of online redo log files from
-- the RMAN recovery catalog
BEGIN
     SELECT COUNT(fname) cnt
        INTO pl_rman_no_rls
     FROM ORL
     WHERE dbinc_key = pl_dbinc;

     EXCEPTION
        WHEN OTHERS THEN
           RETURN (SQLCODE);
END;

     -- Compare the two online redo log file numbers,
     -- and return the comparison result
     IF pl_prod_no_rls != pl_rman_no_rls THEN
        RETURN (0);
     ELSE
        RETURN (1);                       -- 1 means all okay
     END IF;

END RESYNC_RCVCAT;

-- Returns a number if it is okay
-- Returns 0 if no database incarnation found
-- Returns SQLCODE if there is any error
FUNCTION GET_DBINC (p_db_name IN VARCHAR2)
RETURN NUMBER IS

     pl_max_dbinc_no NUMBER := 0;

BEGIN

     SELECT MAX(dbinc_key) dbinc_key
        INTO pl_max_dbinc_no
     FROM dbinc
     WHERE db_name = UPPER(p_db_name);

     IF pl_max_dbinc_no IS NOT NULL THEN
        RETURN (pl_max_dbinc_no);
     ELSE
        RETURN (0);
     END IF;

     EXCEPTION
        WHEN OTHERS THEN
           RETURN (SQLCODE);

END GET_DBINC;

END CHECK_RMAN_BACKUP;
/
```

Appendix 25.2 RMAN Recovery Catalog Column Definitions and Their Descriptions

Table Name	*Column Name (P for Primary Key, U for Unique key)*	*Null?*	*Data Type*	*Description*
AL	AL_KEY (P)	NOT NULL	NUMBER	Archived log key
AL	DBINC_KEY (U)	NOT NULL	NUMBER	Database incarnation key
AL	AL_RECID (U)	NOT NULL	NUMBER	Archived log recid (record id) from control file
AL	AL_STAMP (U)	NOT NULL	NUMBER	Archived log stamp from control file
AL	THREAD#	NOT NULL	NUMBER	Archived log thread number
AL	SEQUENCE#	NOT NULL	NUMBER	Archived log sequence number
AL	LOW_SCN	NOT NULL	NUMBER	System Change Number (SCN) generated when switching in
AL	LOW_TIME	NOT NULL	DATE	Timestamp when low SCN allocated
AL	NEXT_SCN	NOT NULL	NUMBER	SCN generated when switching out
AL	NEXT_TIME	NULL	DATE	Timestamp when next SCN allocated
AL	FNAME	NULL	VARCHAR2(1024)	Archived log file name
AL	FNAME_HASHKEY	NULL	VARCHAR2(20)	Hashed file name for indexing
AL	ARCHIVED	NOT NULL	VARCHAR2(1)	Archived flag ('Y' for archived redo log, 'N' for inspected online redo log)
AL	BLOCKS	NOT NULL	NUMBER	Number of blocks written
AL	BLOCK_SIZE	NOT NULL	NUMBER	Block size in bytes
AL	COMPLETION_TIME	NOT NULL	DATE	Time when the log was archived or copied
AL	STATUS	NOT NULL	VARCHAR2(1)	Availability status code ('A' for available, 'U' for unavailable, 'D' for deleted)

(continues)

Appendix 25.2 (continued)

Table Name	Column Name (P for Primary Key, U for Unique key)	Null?	Data Type	Description
BCB	BDF_KEY (U)	NOT NULL	NUMBER	Data file backup or copy key
BCB	BCB_RECID (U)	NOT NULL	NUMBER	Recid from control file
BCB	BCB_STAMP (U)	NOT NULL	NUMBER	Stamp from control file
BCB	PIECE#	NOT NULL	NUMBER	Backup piece to which block belongs
BCB	BLOCK#	NOT NULL	NUMBER	Starting block number in the file
BCB	BLOCKS	NOT NULL	NUMBER	Number of blocks in the corrupt range
BCB	CORRUPT_SCN	NULL	NUMBER	SCN at which corruption was detected
BCB	MARKED_CORRUPT	NOT NULL	VARCHAR2(1)	Flag to indicate could not read from disk ('Y' for yes)
BCF	BCF_KEY (P)	NOT NULL	NUMBER	Backup control file key
BCF	BS_KEY (U2)	NOT NULL	NUMBER	Backup set key
BCF	DBINC_KEY (U1)	NOT NULL	NUMBER	Database incarnation key
BCF	BCF_RECID (U1)	NOT NULL	NUMBER	Backup control file recid from control file
BCF	BCF_STAMP (U1)	NOT NULL	NUMBER	Backup control file stamp from control file
BCF	CKP_SCN	NOT NULL	NUMBER	Control file checkpoint SCN
BCF	CKP_TIME	NOT NULL	DATE	Time when control file checkpoint occurred
BCF	CREATE_TIME	NOT NULL	DATE	Control file creation time
BCF	MIN_OFFR_RECID	NOT NULL	NUMBER	Recid of the oldest offline range
BCF	BLOCK_SIZE	NOT NULL	NUMBER	Block size in bytes
BDF	BDF_KEY (P)	NOT NULL	NUMBER	Data file backup key
BDF	DBINC_KEY (U)	NOT NULL	NUMBER	Database incarnation key

Appendix 25.2 (continued)

Table Name	Column Name (P for Primary Key, U for Unique key)	Null?	Data Type	Description
BDF	BDF_RECID (U)	NOT NULL	NUMBER	Data file backup recid from control file
BDF	BDF_STAMP (U)	NOT NULL	NUMBER	Data file backup stamp from control file
BDF	BS_KEY	NOT NULL	NUMBER	Backup set key
BDF	FILE#	NOT NULL	NUMBER	Database file number
BDF	CREATE_SCN	NOT NULL	NUMBER	Creation SCN
BDF	INCR_LEVEL	NULL	NUMBER	Incremental backup level (null, 0 to 4)
BDF	INCR_SCN	NOT NULL	NUMBER	SCN since backup contains changes
BDF	CKP_SCN	NOT NULL	NUMBER	SCN of the last data file checkpoint
BDF	CKP_TIME	NOT NULL	DATE	Time when the last data file checkpoint occurred
BDF	ABS_FUZZY_SCN	NULL	NUMBER	Absolute fuzzy SCN
BDF	RCV_FUZZY_SCN	NULL	NUMBER	Media recovery fuzzy SCN
BDF	RCV_FUZZY_TIME	NULL	DATE	Timestamp for media recovery fuzzy SCN
BDF	DATAFILE_BLOCKS	NOT NULL	NUMBER	Number of blocks in the data file
BDF	BLOCKS	NOT NULL	NUMBER	Number of blocks written to backup
BDF	BLOCK_SIZE	NOT NULL	NUMBER	Block size in bytes
BDF	COMPLETION_TIME	NULL	DATE	Data file backup completion time
BP	BP_KEY (P)	NOT NULL	NUMBER	Backup piece key
BP	BS_KEY (U)	NOT NULL	NUMBER	Backup set key
BP	DB_KEY	NOT NULL	NUMBER	Database key
BP	BP_RECID (U)	NOT NULL	NUMBER	Backup piece recid from control file
BP	BP_STAMP (U)	NOT NULL	NUMBER	Backup piece stamp from control file

(continues)

Appendix 25.2 (continued)

Table Name	*Column Name (P for Primary Key, U for Unique key)*	*Null?*	*Data Type*	*Description*
BP	PIECE#	NOT NULL	NUMBER	Backup piece number
BP	TAG	NULL	VARCHAR2(32)	User specified tag
BP	DEVICE_TYPE	NOT NULL	VARCHAR2(255)	Backup device type ('DISK')
BP	HANDLE	NOT NULL	VARCHAR2(1024)	Backup piece handle
BP	HANDLE_HASHKEY	NOT NULL	VARCHAR2(30)	Indexed hashkey on handle
BP	COMMENTS	NULL	VARCHAR2(255)	Comments on the backup piece
BP	MEDIA	NULL	VARCHAR2(80)	Backup media handle
BP	CONCUR	NOT NULL	VARCHAR2(1)	Concurrent access support ('Y' for yes, 'N' for no)
BP	START_TIME	NOT NULL	DATE	Time when the backup piece started
BP	COMPLETION_TIME	NOT NULL	DATE	Time when the backup piece completed
BP	STATUS	NOT NULL	VARCHAR2(1)	Backup piece status code ('A' for available, 'U' for unavailable, 'D' for deleted)
BRL	BRL_KEY (P)	NOT NULL	NUMBER	Backup redo log key
BRL	DBINC_KEY (U)	NOT NULL	NUMBER	Database incarnation key
BRL	BRL_RECID (U)	NOT NULL	NUMBER	Backup redo log recid from control file
BRL	BRL_STAMP (U)	NOT NULL	NUMBER	Backup redo log stamp from control file
BRL	BS_KEY	NOT NULL	NUMBER	Backup set key
BRL	THREAD#	NOT NULL	NUMBER	Redo log thread number
BRL	SEQUENCE#	NOT NULL	NUMBER	Redo log sequence number
BRL	LOW_SCN	NOT NULL	NUMBER	SCN generated when switching in
BRL	LOW_TIME	NOT NULL	DATE	Time when low SCN allocated

Appendix 25.2 (continued)

Table Name	*Column Name (P for Primary Key, U for Unique key)*	*Null?*	*Data Type*	*Description*
BRL	NEXT_SCN	NOT NULL	NUMBER	SCN generated when switching out
BRL	NEXT_TIME	NOT NULL	DATE	Time when next SCN allocated
BRL	BLOCKS	NOT NULL	NUMBER	Number of blocks written to backup
BRL	BLOCK_SIZE	NOT NULL	NUMBER	Block size in bytes
BS	BS_KEY (P)	NOT NULL	NUMBER	Backup set key
BS	DB_KEY (U1) (U2)	NOT NULL	NUMBER	Database key
BS	BS_RECID (U1)	NOT NULL	NUMBER	Backup set recid from control file
BS	BS_STAMP (U1)	NOT NULL	NUMBER	Backup set stamp from control file
BS	SET_STAMP (U2)	NOT NULL	NUMBER	Set_stamp from control file
BS	SET_COUNT (U2)	NOT NULL	NUMBER	Set_count from control file
BS	BCK_TYPE	NOT NULL	VARCHAR2(1)	Backup type code ('D' for full data file, 'I' for incremental data file, 'C' for incremental cumulative data file, 'L' for archivelog)
BS	INCR_LEVEL	NULL	NUMBER	Incremental backup level (0 to 4)
BS	PIECES	NOT NULL	NUMBER	Number of backup pieces in the backup set
BS	START_TIME	NOT NULL	DATE	Time when the backup started
BS	COMPLETION_TIME	NOT NULL	DATE	Time when the backup completed
BS	STATUS	NOT NULL	VARCHAR2(1)	Backup set status code ('A' for available, 'D' for deleted)
CCB	CDF_KEY (U)	NOT NULL	NUMBER	Data file copy key
CCB	CCB_RECID (U)	NOT NULL	NUMBER	Recid from control file

(continues)

Appendix 25.2 (continued)

Table Name	Column Name (P for Primary Key, U for Unique key)	Null?	Data Type	Description
CCB	CCB_STAMP (U)	NOT NULL	NUMBER	Stamp from control file
CCB	BLOCK#	NOT NULL	NUMBER	Block number in the file
CCB	BLOCKS	NOT NULL	NUMBER	Number of blocks in corrupt range
CCB	CORRUPT_SCN	NULL	NUMBER	SCN at which corruption was detected
CCB	MARKED_CORRUPT	NOT NULL	VARCHAR2(1)	Flag to indicate could not read from disk
CCF	CCF_KEY (P)	NOT NULL	NUMBER	Control file copy key
CCF	DBINC_KEY (U)	NOT NULL	NUMBER	Database incarnation key
CCF	CCF_RECID (U)	NOT NULL	NUMBER	Control file copy recid from control file
CCF	CCF_STAMP (U)	NOT NULL	NUMBER	Control file copy stamp from control file
CCF	FNAME	NOT NULL	VARCHAR2(1024)	Control file copy file name
CCF	FNAME_HASHKEY	NOT NULL	VARCHAR2(20)	Hashed file name for indexing
CCF	TAG	NULL	VARCHAR2(32)	Control file copy tag
CCF	CKP_SCN	NOT NULL	NUMBER	Control file checkpoint SCN
CCF	CKP_TIME	NOT NULL	DATE	Control file checkpoint time
CCF	CREATE_TIME	NOT NULL	DATE	Control file creation time
CCF	MIN_OFFR_RECID	NOT NULL	NUMBER	Recid of the oldest offline range
CCF	BLOCK_SIZE	NOT NULL	NUMBER	Block size in bytes
CCF	COMPLETION_TIME	NOT NULL	DATE	Time when the copy was taken
CCF	STATUS	NOT NULL	VARCHAR2(1)	Status code ('A' for available, 'U' for unavailable, 'D' for deleted)

Appendix 25.2 (continued)

Table Name	Column Name (P for Primary Key, U for Unique key)	Null?	Data Type	Description
CDF	CDF_KEY (P)	NOT NULL	NUMBER	Data file copy key
CDF	DBINC_KEY (U)	NOT NULL	NUMBER	Database incarnation key
CDF	CDF_RECID (U)	NOT NULL	NUMBER	Data file copy recid from control file
CDF	CDF_STAMP (U)	NOT NULL	NUMBER	Data file copy stamp from control file
CDF	FILE#	NOT NULL	NUMBER	Database file number
CDF	CREATE_SCN	NOT NULL	NUMBER	Creation SCN
CDF	FNAME	NOT NULL	VARCHAR2(1024)	Data file copy file name
CDF	FNAME_HASHKEY	NOT NULL	VARCHAR2(20)	Hashed file name for indexing
CDF	TAG	NULL	VARCHAR2(32)	Data file copy tag
CDF	INCR_LEVEL	NULL	NUMBER	Incremental backup level (null or 0)
CDF	CKP_SCN	NOT NULL	NUMBER	SCN of the last data file checkpoint
CDF	CKP_TIME	NOT NULL	DATE	Time when the last data file checkpoint occurred
CDF	ONL_FUZZY	NOT NULL	VARCHAR2(1)	Online fuzzy ('Y' for yes)
CDF	BCK_FUZZY	NOT NULL	VARCHAR2(1)	Backup fuzzy ('Y' for yes)
CDF	ABS_FUZZY_SCN	NULL	NUMBER	Absolute fuzzy SCN
CDF	RCV_FUZZY_SCN	NULL	NUMBER	Media recovery fuzzy SCN
CDF	RCV_FUZZY_TIME	NULL	DATE	Timestamp for media recovery fuzzy SCN
CDF	BLOCKS	NOT NULL	NUMBER	Number of blocks
CDF	BLOCK_SIZE	NOT NULL	NUMBER	Block size in bytes
CDF	COMPLETION_TIME	NOT NULL	DATE	Time when the copy completed
CDF	STATUS	NOT NULL	VARCHAR2(1)	Data file copy status code ('A' for available, 'U' for unavailable, 'D' for deleted

(continues)

Appendix 25.2 (continued)

Table Name	*Column Name (P for Primary Key, U for Unique key)*	*Null?*	*Data Type*	*Description*
CKP	CKP_KEY (P)	NOT NULL	NUMBER	Checkpoint key
CKP	CKP_SCN (U)	NOT NULL	NUMBER	Control file checkpoint SCN
CKP	CKP_TIME	NULL	DATE	Control file checkpoint timestamp
CKP	CKP_CF_SEQ (U)	NOT NULL	NUMBER	Control file sequence
CKP	CF_CREATE_TIME (U)	NOT NULL	DATE	Control file version time
CKP	DBINC_KEY (U)	NOT NULL	NUMBER	Database incarnation key
CKP	CKP_TYPE (U)	NOT NULL	VARCHAR2(7)	Resync Type ('FULL' or 'PARTIAL')
CKP	CKP_DB_STATUS	NULL	VARCHAR2(7)	Database status ('OPEN' or 'MOUNTED')
CKP	RESYNC_TIME	NOT NULL	DATE	Resync time
CKP	PREV_CKP_KEY	NULL	NUMBER	Previous checkpoint key
CKP	HIGH_DF_RECID	NOT NULL	NUMBER	Data file recid at control file checkpoint SCN
DB	DB_KEY (P)	NOT NULL	NUMBER	Database key
DB	DB_ID (U)	NOT NULL	NUMBER	Database ID
DB	CURR_DBINC_KEY	NULL	NUMBER	Current database incarnation key
DBINC	DBINC_KEY (P)	NOT NULL	NUMBER	Database incarnation key
DBINC	DB_KEY (U)	NOT NULL	NUMBER	Database to which this incarnation belongs
DBINC	DB_NAME	NOT NULL	VARCHAR2(8)	Current database name
DBINC	RESET_SCN (U)	NOT NULL	NUMBER	SCN of last resetlogs
DBINC	RESET_TIME (U)	NOT NULL	DATE	Timestamp of last resetlogs
DBINC	PARENT_DBINC_KEY	NULL	NUMBER	Parent database incarnation
DBINC	CF_CREATE_TIME	NULL	DATE	Control file version time at last resync

Appendix 25.2 (continued)

Table Name	*Column Name (P for Primary Key, U for Unique key)*	*Null?*	*Data Type*	*Description*
DBINC	CKP_SCN	NOT NULL	NUMBER	Control file checkpoint SCN at last full resync
DBINC	FULL_CKP_CF_SEQ	NOT NULL	NUMBER	Control file sequence at last full resync
DBINC	JOB_CKP_CF_SEQ	NOT NULL	NUMBER	Control file sequence at last partial resync
DBINC	HIGH_TS_RECID	NULL	NUMBER	Tablespace recid
DBINC	HIGH_DF_RECID	NULL	NUMBER	Data file recid
DBINC	HIGH_RT_RECID	NULL	NUMBER	Redo log thread recid
DBINC	HIGH_ORL_RECID	NULL	NUMBER	Online redo log recid
DBINC	HIGH_OFFR_RECID	NOT NULL	NUMBER	Offline range recid
DBINC	HIGH_RLH_RECID	NOT NULL	NUMBER	Log history recid
DBINC	HIGH_AL_RECID	NOT NULL	NUMBER	Archived log recid
DBINC	HIGH_BS_RECID	NOT NULL	NUMBER	Backup set recid
DBINC	HIGH_BP_RECID	NOT NULL	NUMBER	Backup piece recid
DBINC	HIGH_BDF_RECID	NOT NULL	NUMBER	Backup data file recid
DBINC	HIGH_CDF_RECID	NOT NULL	NUMBER	Data file copy recid
DBINC	HIGH_BRL_RECID	NOT NULL	NUMBER	Backup redo log recid
DBINC	HIGH_BCB_RECID	NOT NULL	NUMBER	Backup data file corruption recid
DBINC	HIGH_CCB_RECID	NOT NULL	NUMBER	Data file copy corruption recid
DBINC	HIGH_DO_RECID	NOT NULL	NUMBER	Deleted object recid
DF	DBINC_KEY (P) (U1) (U2)	NOT NULL	NUMBER	Database incarnation key
DF	FILE# (P) (U1) (U2)	NOT NULL	NUMBER	Database file number
DF	CREATE_SCN (P)	NOT NULL	NUMBER	Data file creation SCN
DF	CREATE_TIME	NULL	DATE	Data file creation time
DF	TS# (U2)	NOT NULL	NUMBER	Tablespace id in target database
DF	TS_CREATE_SCN (U2)	NOT NULL	NUMBER	Tablespace creation SCN

(continues)

Appendix 25.2 (continued)

Table Name	Column Name (P for Primary Key, U for Unique key)	Null?	Data Type	Description
DF	BLOCK_SIZE	NOT NULL	NUMBER	Block size in bytes
DF	CLONE_FNAME	NULL	VARCHAR2(1024)	Clone data file name
DF	DROP_SCN (U1)	NULL	NUMBER	Data file drop SCN
DF	DROP_TIME	NULL	DATE	Data file drop time
DF	STOP_SCN	NULL	NUMBER	Data file offline clean or read only SCN
DF	READ_ONLY	NOT NULL	NUMBER	Data file read only flag (1 or 0)
DFATT	DBINC_KEY (U)	NOT NULL	NUMBER	Database incarnation key
DFATT	FILE# (U)	NOT NULL	NUMBER	Database file number
DFATT	CREATE_SCN (U)	NOT NULL	NUMBER	Data file creation SCN
DFATT	START_CKP_KEY	NOT NULL	NUMBER	Checkpoint when first observed
DFATT	END_CKP_KEY (U)	NULL	NUMBER	Checkpoint when changed (null means current)
DFATT	FNAME	NULL	VARCHAR2(1024)	Data file name
DFATT	BLOCKS	NULL	NUMBER	Data file size in blocks
OFFR	OFFR_KEY (P)	NOT NULL	NUMBER	Offline range key
OFFR	DBINC_KEY (U1) (U2)	NOT NULL	NUMBER	Database incarnation key
OFFR	OFFR_RECID (U1)	NULL	NUMBER	Offline range recid
OFFR	OFFR_STAMP (U1)	NULL	NUMBER	Offline range stamp
OFFR	FILE# (U2)	NOT NULL	NUMBER	Data file number
OFFR	CREATE_SCN	NOT NULL	NUMBER	Data file creation SCN
OFFR	OFFLINE_SCN (U2)	NOT NULL	NUMBER	Data file offline SCN
OFFR	ONLINE_SCN	NOT NULL	NUMBER	Data file online checkpoint SCN
OFFR	ONLINE_TIME	NOT NULL	DATE	Data file online checkpoint time
OFFR	CF_CREATE_TIME (U2)	NULL	DATE	Control file creation time
ORL	DBINC_KEY (P)	NOT NULL	NUMBER	Database incarnation key

Appendix 25.2 (continued)

Table Name	Column Name (P for Primary Key, U for Unique key)	Null?	Data Type	Description
ORL	THREAD#	NOT NULL	NUMBER	Redo log thread number
ORL	GROUP#	NOT NULL	NUMBER	Redo log group number
ORL	FNAME (P)	NOT NULL	VARCHAR2(1024)	Redo log file name
RCVER	VERSION	NOT NULL	VARCHAR2(12)	Recovery catalog version
RLH	RLH_KEY (P)	NOT NULL	NUMBER	Redo log history key
RLH	DBINC_KEY (U1) (U2)	NOT NULL	NUMBER	Database incarnation key
RLH	RLH_RECID (U2)	NOT NULL	NUMBER	Redo log history recid from control file
RLH	RLH_STAMP (U2)	NOT NULL	NUMBER	Redo log history stamp from control file
RLH	THREAD# (U1)	NOT NULL	NUMBER	Redo log thread number
RLH	SEQUENCE# (U1)	NOT NULL	NUMBER	Redo log sequence number
RLH	LOW_SCN (U1)	NOT NULL	NUMBER	SCN generated when switching in
RLH	LOW_TIME	NOT NULL	DATE	Timestamp when switching in
RLH	NEXT_SCN	NOT NULL	NUMBER	SCN generated when switching out
RLH	STATUS	NULL	VARCHAR2(1)	Status code ('C' for cleared)
RR	RR_KEY (P)	NOT NULL	NUMBER	Redo log range key
RR	DBINC_KEY	NOT NULL	NUMBER	Database incarnation key
RR	LOW_SCN	NOT NULL	NUMBER	Low SCN of the range
RR	HIGH_SCN	NOT NULL	NUMBER	High SCN of the range
RT	DBINC_KEY (P)	NOT NULL	NUMBER	Database incarnation key
RT	THREAD# (P)	NOT NULL	NUMBER	Redo log thread number
RT	SEQUENCE#	NOT NULL	NUMBER	Last redo log sequence number allocated
RT	ENABLE_SCN	NULL	NUMBER	SCN of last enable
RT	ENABLE_TIME	NULL	DATE	Timestamp of last enable

(continues)

Appendix 25.2 (continued)

Table Name	*Column Name (P for Primary Key, U for Unique key)*	*Null?*	*Data Type*	*Description*
RT	DISABLE_SCN	NULL	NUMBER	SCN of last disable
RT	DISABLE_TIME	NULL	DATE	Timestamp of last disable
RT	STATUS	NOT NULL	VARCHAR2(1)	Status code ('D' for disabled, 'E' for enabled, 'O' for open)
SCR	SCR_KEY (P)	NOT NULL	NUMBER	RMAN stored script key
SCR	DB_KEY (U)	NOT NULL	NUMBER	Database key
SCR	SCR_NAME (U)	NOT NULL	VARCHAR2(100)	RMAN stored script name
SCRL	SCR_KEY (U)	NOT NULL	NUMBER	RMAN stored script key
SCRL	LINENUM (U)	NOT NULL	NUMBER	Line number
SCRL	TEXT	NOT NULL	VARCHAR2(1024)	Text of the line
TS	DBINC_KEY (P) (U1) (U2)	NOT NULL	NUMBER	Database incarnation key
TS	TS# (P) (U1)	NOT NULL	NUMBER	Tablespace id in target database
TS	TS_NAME (U2)	NOT NULL	VARCHAR2(30)	Tablespace name
TS	CREATE_SCN (P) (U2)	NOT NULL	NUMBER	Tablespace creation SCN (from the first datafile)
TS	CREATE_TIME	NULL	DATE	Tablespace creation time
TS	DROP_SCN (U1)	NULL	NUMBER	Tablespace drop SCN
TS	DROP_TIME	NULL	DATE	Tablespace drop time
TSATT	DBINC_KEY (U)	NOT NULL	NUMBER	Database incarnation key
TSATT	TS# (U)	NOT NULL	NUMBER	Tablespace id in target database
TSATT	CREATE_SCN (U)	NOT NULL	NUMBER	Tablespace creation SCN
TSATT	START_CKP_KEY	NOT NULL	NUMBER	Checkpoint when first observed
TSATT	END_CKP_KEY (U)	NULL	NUMBER	Checkpoint when changed (null means current)
TSATT	RBS_COUNT	NULL	NUMBER	Number of rollback segments in this tablespace (null means unknown)

Chapter 26

Tips and Scripts for Implementing RMAN

Guang Sheng Wan

Backup and recovery are among the most important tasks performed by database administrators (DBAs). Sometimes, these tasks can be time-consuming and erroneous. It is critical for the DBA to set up a proper backup and recovery strategy and put it in place.

Before Oracle8, the Oracle DBA normally used customer-written scripts, Oracle7's Enterprise Backup Utility, or third-party tools to perform the physical Oracle database backup and restore process. Oracle8's Recovery Manager (RMAN) comes with Oracle8 versions and provides a better solution for an Oracle8 database's backup and recovery.

RMAN manages the processes of creating backups of database files and restoring or recovering from backups. It greatly simplifies the tasks DBAs perform during these processes. It can detect many types of corruption blocks, and makes sure that the backup does not include corrupted blocks. RMAN provides true incremental backups and automatic parallelization of backups and restores. It is also efficient and robust.

Implementing RMAN takes time because all RMAN scripts must be tested thoroughly. The following tips and scripts (tested on Oracle8.0.5 for AIX version 4.3.2, running in ARCHIVELOG mode) may help you to implement RMAN on your Oracle8 databases.

Tip 1: Use Recovery Catalog for Performing a Wider Variety of Automated Backup and Recovery Functions

Although a Recovery Catalog schema and its associated space are required for using Recovery Catalog, it is still advisable to have it in a separate database residing on different hard disk drives from the target database you will be

0-8493-1139-X/02/$0.00+$1.50
©2002 by CRC Press LLC

backing up so that you can perform tablespace point-in-time recovery, create stored RMAN scripts, and recover the target database when the control file is lost or damaged.

To set up Recovery Catalog, you can run $ORACLE_HOME/rdbms/admin/catrman.sql while connected to the RMAN database.

Tip 2: Set Up a Small Test Database for Testing

To speed up your testing processes, a small test database with similar physical database structures of your production database is required. It is also advisable to use "disk" rather than "tape" as your backup medium during the test stage.

Exhibit 26.1 displays RMAN scripts that are used for allocating or releasing one or more I/O channels. (A channel is required for the backup, copy, restore, or recover command.) You can invoke RMAN and connect to the target and recovery catalog database, then run the following scripts after you register the target database.

Exhibit 26.1 Allocating or Releasing One or More I/O Channels

```
# Allocates one channel
replace script alloc_1_disk {
allocate channel d1 type disk;
setlimit channel d1 kbytes 2097150 maxopenfiles 36 readrate 200;
}

# Releases one channel
replace script rel_1_disk {
release channel d1;
}

# Allocates more channels
replace script alloc_all_disks {
allocate channel d11 type disk;
allocate channel d12 type disk;
allocate channel d13 type disk;
setlimit channel d11 kbytes 1572864 maxopenfiles 32 readrate 200;
setlimit channel d12 kbytes 1572864 maxopenfiles 32 readrate 200;
setlimit channel d13 kbytes 1572864 maxopenfiles 32 readrate 200;
}

# Releases all channels
replace script rel_all_disks {
release channel d11;
release channel d12;
release channel d13;
}
```

Tip 3: Back Up Control File, Archived Log Files, and Data Files, But Not Online Redo Log Files

The control file should be backed up any time there are structural changes to the database. It must be included in whole database backups.

You should never back up (copy) online redo logs. The best way to back up the contents of the online redo logs is to archive them, then back up the archived redo log files.

All data files must be backed up so that when a data file is damaged, RMAN can recover the database using the backup for the damaged file. You can specify that if any corruption is found in the system tablespace's files, the backup of these files should be aborted.

RMAN does not take care of parameter files, instance password file, or export file; you have to handle the backup of them separately (see Exhibit 26.2).

Exhibit 26.2 Backing Up the Control File

```
# Backs up the control file
replace script backup_cf_disk {
execute script alloc_1_disk;
backup
format '/bkup/SID/%d_cf_t%t_s%s_p%p'
(current controlfile);
execute script rel_1_disk;
}

# Backs up the archived redo log files, and deletes them
# once the backup has successfully completed.
replace script backup_al_all_disk {
execute script alloc_all_disks;
backup
filesperset 50
format '/bkup/SID/%d_al_t%t_s%s_p%p'
(archivelog all delete input);
execute script rel_all_disks;
}

# Backs up the whole database. The database must be mounted and
# closed. It should be the first backup of the target database.
replace script backup_db_mount_full_disk {
execute script alloc_all_disks;
# It is assumed that the datafile 1 is the only file in the system
# tablespace. No corruption is allowed in this file.
set maxcorrupt for datafile 1 to 0;
backup
full
tag backup_db_mount_full
filesperset 8
format '/bkup/SID/%d_mf_t%t_s%s_p%p'
(database);
execute script rel_all_disks;
sql 'alter database open';
sql 'alter system archive log current';
execute script backup_al_all_disk;
}
```

Tip 4: Create a Suitable Backup Strategy

A proper plan must be made to protect your production database against potential failures based on the service requirements and the database size. It

Exhibit 26.3 Multiplexed Online Redo Log

Backup	Sunday	Monday	Tuesday	Wednesday	Thursday	Friday	Saturday
Level 0	2:00 PM						
Level 1				2:00 AM		2:00 AM	
Level 2			2:00 AM		2:00 AM		2:00 AM

may not be acceptable to lose any data in a production environment if a disk failure damages some of the files that constitute a database. Therefore, the database may have to be operated in ARCHIVELOG mode, ideally with a multiplexed online redo log. Exhibit 26.3 shows an example.

Level 0 backup: Backs up the whole database. This backup is part of the incremental strategy. It means that it can have incremental backups of levels greater than 0 applied to it.

Level 1 backup: This backup will only back up the blocks which have been modified since the last level 0 backup was performed. Otherwise, it is exactly the same backup as the level 0 above.

Level 2 backup: This backup will only back up the blocks which have been modified since the last level 0 or 1 backup was performed. Otherwise, it is exactly the same as the level 0 or 1 backups above.

The scripts in Exhibit 26.4 describe how to do the three levels' backups.

Tip 5: Plan Your Test Cases and Start the Testing From Single Failures

As you know, statement and process failure are automatically undone by Oracle; instance failure is automatically recovered by Oracle when the database opens; user and application error requires a database to be recovered to a point in time before the error occurred (point-in-time recovery is not covered in this chapter). Media (disk) failure is a major concern to the Oracle DBA. To recover a database from media failure, the following cases must be tested for recovery purposes:

- Damaged control file(s)
- Damaged online redo log files
- Damaged data files
- Damaged archived redo log files

To simplify the test cases, you can ignore the case of damaged archived redo log files. You may have to immediately back up all data files so that you have a complete backup that does not require the damaged archived redo log group.

If some of the control files (not all) are lost, you can immediately abort the instance and use an intact copy of the control file to copy over the damaged control files. But the case of losing all control files must be tested.

Exhibit 26.4 Three Levels' Backups

```
# Incremental level 0 (whole) database backup
# The control file is automatically included each time file 1 of the
# system tablespace is backed up.
replace script backup_db_level_0_disk {
execute script alloc_all_disks;
set maxcorrupt for datafile 1 to 0;
backup
incremental level 0
tag backup_db_level_0
# The skip inaccessible clause ensures the backup will continue
# if any of the datafiles are inaccessible.
skip inaccessible
filesperset 9
format '/bkup/SID/%d_0_t%t_s%s_p%p'
(database);
execute script rel_all_disks;
sql 'alter system archive log current';
execute script backup_al_all_disk;
}

# Incremental level 1 database backup
replace script backup_db_level_1_disk {
execute script alloc_all_disks;
set maxcorrupt for datafile 1 to 0;
backup
incremental level 1
# You can use the 'skip readonly' and 'skip offline' clauses
# to omit backing up these files if you have already had
# valid backups of them.
skip offline
skip readonly
skip inaccessible
tag backup_db_level_1
filesperset 9
format '/bkup/SID/%d_1_t%t_s%s_p%p'
(database);
execute script rel_all_disks;
sql 'alter system archive log current';
execute script backup_al_all_disk;
}

# Incremental level 2 database backup
replace script backup_db_level_2_disk {
execute script alloc_all_disks;
set maxcorrupt for datafile 1 to 0;
backup
incremental level 2
skip offline
skip readonly
skip inaccessible
tag backup_db_level_2
filesperset 9
format '/bkup/SID/%d_2_t%t_s%s_p%p'
(database);
execute script rel_all_disks;
sql 'alter system archive log current';
execute script backup_al_all_disk;
}
```

If the online redo log of a database is mirrored, and at least one member of each online redo log group is not affected by the media failure, Oracle allows the database to continue functioning as normal. You should at least test the following cases:

- Loss of all members of active online redo log files
- Loss of all members of inactive online redo log files
- Loss of all members of the current online redo log files

If a media failure affects the data files of the SYSTEM tablespace or any data files that contain active rollback segments, the database becomes inoperable. If it affects only other data files, then the affected data files are unavailable, but the database can continue to operate. Therefore, three cases (SYSTEM tablespace data files, rollback segment tablespace data files, and other tablespace data files) should be properly tested.

Start testing from single failures and construct all RMAN scripts to cover all combinations of the single failures and run the scripts on different backup scenarios (from Monday to Sunday). The RMAN scripts in Exhibit 26.5 are used for recovering the database from losing all control files, online redo log files, SYSTEM/ROLLBACK tablespace data files and other tablespace data files, as well as the worst case — all of them.

If you lose the control file(s), all online redo log files, or the current redo log file(s), the database must be opened with the RESETLOGS option after being recovered (see Exhibit 26.6). After opening the database with the RESETLOGS option, the backup is no longer valid. You have to take a full database or level 0 incremental database backup immediately. Remember that it is necessary to register the new incarnation of the database with the RESET DATABASE command in RMAN.

Tip 6: Conduct a Performance Benchmark When Implementing RMAN on a Production Database

Once all scripts and scenarios have been tested, your RMAN scripts are logically ready for implementing in your production system. Before doing that, you may change "allocate channel d11 type disk" to "allocate channel t1 type SBT_TAPE," and so on, and use different "format" commands for your tape backups. Do not forget to use script alloc_1_disk for those commands which need a DISK channel to be allocated, such as REPLICATE, RECOVER, etc. You can maintain some sort of naming convention for your RMAN scripts. Make sure that the new RMAN scripts work fine with the test database, then port them over to the production system, and start to do a benchmark on the backup performance. Script alloc_all_disks (or alloc_all_tapes) and alloc_1_disk may have to be changed to obtain better performance in your production environment

Exhibit 26.5 Restoring Control Files

```
# Restores control files
replace script restore_cf_disk {
execute script alloc_1_disk;
restore
controlfile to '/bkup/SID/ctrl01.ctl.res';
replicate
controlfile from '/bkup/SID/ctrl01.ctl.res';
execute script rel_1_disk;
}

# Recovers the database from losing all control files
# The instance must be started, but the database cannot be mounted
# The replicate command requires a device of type disk to be allocated.
replace script restore_recover_cf_disk {
execute script restore_cf_disk;
sql 'alter database mount';
recover database;
# The following command may be performed separately
# sql 'alter database open resetlogs';
}

# Recovers the database from losing the current redo log file
# You have to shutdown the instance using ABORT option
# The 'set until' command dictates at which log sequence recovery
# will stop. It is critical that this command is issued BEFORE
# data files are restored, Otherwise RMAN will attempt to restore
# the most recent set of data files, which could be ahead of the
# specified log.
replace script restore_recover_current_log_disk {
execute script alloc_all_disks;
# set until logseq=<the current redo log sequence number> thread=1
# if 'resync catalog' has been issued timely
set until logseq=8 thread=1;
restore database;
sql 'alter database mount';
recover database;
execute script rel_all_disks;
}
```

To maintain the RMAN backup and recovery strategy in a production environment, it is important to follow up with the tasks below:

- Automate resynchronize (resync) catalog operations. (Try to shorten the time between two "resync catalog" operations.)
- Automate everyday backup operations (based on your backup plan).
- Set up a strategy for backing up the RMAN database.

Once you have done the above tasks, you will be confident with your RMAN implementation.

Exhibit 26.6 Database Recovery

```
# Recovers the database if SYSTEM and
# ROLLBACK (RBS) tablespaces'
# data files are damaged.
replace script restore_recover_ts_
# sysrbs_disk {
sql 'alter database mount';
execute script alloc_all_disks;
restore tablespace 'system' ;
restore tablespace 'rbs' ;
recover tablespace 'system' ;
recover tablespace 'rbs' ;
sql 'alter database open';
sql 'alter tablespace system online';
sql 'alter tablespace rbs online';
execute script rel_all_disks;
}

# Recovers the database if other
# tablespaces' data files are damaged,
# while the database is open.
replace script
  restore_recover_ts_users_disk {
sql 'alter tablespace users offline
  immediate';
execute script alloc_1_disk;
restore tablespace 'users' ;
recover tablespace 'users' ;
sql 'alter tablespace users online';
execute script rel_1_disk;
}

replace script restore_db_disk {
# Restores all data files to their
# current locations.
execute script alloc_all_disks;
restore (database);
execute script rel_all_disks;
}

# Recovers all datafiles.
replace script recover_db_disk {
execute script alloc_1_disk;
recover database;
execute script rel_1_disk;
}

# Recovers the database if all
  database
# related files are damaged.
replace script
  restore_recover_all_cld_disk {
execute script restore_cf_disk;
# As long as the current online redo
# log file is damaged, it is not
# possible to recover the database
# completely.
set until logseq=366 thread=1;
sql 'alter database mount';
execute script restore_db_disk;
execute script recover_db_disk;
sql 'alter database archivelog';
# sql 'alter database open
  resetlogs';
}
```

Chapter 27

Paging People with Oracle8i Out of the Box

Hervé Deschamps

This chapter provides a step-by-step method to use Oracle8i Release 2's UTL_SMTP package, DBMS_JOB package, and a simple subscription model to send e-mails to those people subscribed to specific events that may occur in the database.

Remember how complicated it used to be to send e-mails to people from an Oracle database? It used to require programming in C (or other third-party language), knowing about daemons, using dbms_pipe, etc. These overly complicated techniques disheartened many developers from adding to their application this fairly trivial and essential functionality. And when they did build it, maintenance was an issue because most code developed in our industry is poorly documented and people change jobs frequently.

Why should users periodically check with the system for given events? Take the example of the CDC (Centers for Disease Control) organization in the United States. Should people working for the CDC periodically check their multi-hospital database for specific symptom groups that indicate the presence of dangerous diseases? Should people working for the CDC have to run a number of reports daily for that purpose? Of course not. The system should be able to alert them when certain events occur in the system. By enabling people to work by exception, many organizations could reduce operation costs.

It is now very easy to send pages to people. You can even send text messages on average cell phones. No need for special Web-enabled ones, although it does not hurt. This chapter shows you how to do all that — and more.

Step 1: The E-Mail Package

With the e-mail package documented in Exhibits 27.1 and 27.2, sending an e-mail to a pager only takes one command:

0-8493-1139-X/02/$0.00+$1.50
©2002 by CRC Press LLC

```
mail.send (
   p_sender=> 'noReply@nomail.com',
   p_recipient=> 'joe.smith@myPager.com',
   p_subject=> 'System Alert',
   p_message=> v_alert_message
);
```

Exhibit 27.1 Mail Package Header

```
Package mail is
--
-- Purpose: Send email messages
--
-- modification history
-- Person    Date      Comments
-- ------    ------    -----------------------------------------
-- hdd       000913    Creation

   g_smtp_server        varchar2(2000);
     g_smtp_server_port pls_integer;

   function get_sys_parameter (p_name in varchar2) return varchar2;

   procedure send (
       p_sender       in   varchar2,
       p_recipient    in   varchar2,
       p_message      in   varchar2,
       p_subject      in   varchar2
                      );
     end; -- Package Specification mail
```

Exhibit 27.2 Mail Package Body

```
package body mail is

--
-- Purpose: Send email messages
--
-- modification history
-- Person    Date      Comments
-- ------    ------    -----------------------------------------
-- hdd       000913    Creation

   function get_sys_parameter (p_name in varchar2) return varchar2 is v_return
     varchar2(2000);
       begin
         select distinct value
         into v_return
         from system_parameters
         where name = p_name;
```

Exhibit 27.2 Mail Package Body (continued)

```
   return v_return;
       end;

procedure send (
        p_sender        in   varchar2,
        p_recipient     in   varchar2,
        p_message       in   varchar2,
        p_subject       in   varchar2
                             )
      is
        mail_conn       utl_smtp.connection;
      begin
        mail_conn := utl_smtp.open_connection (g_smtp_server,
             g_smtp_server_port);
        utl_smtp.helo (mail_conn, g_smtp_server);
        utl_smtp.mail (mail_conn, p_sender);
        utl_smtp.rcpt (mail_conn, p_recipient);
        utl_smtp.data (
             mail_conn,
             'Subject : '||p_subject ||
             CHR (13) ||
             CHR (10) ||
             'To : ' ||
             p_recipient ||
             CHR (13) ||
             CHR (10) ||
             p_message
        );
        utl_smtp.quit (mail_conn);
      end send;
--
      -- Mail package init
      --
      begin
           g_smtp_server := get_sys_parameter ('smtp_server');
           if g_smtp_server is null then
             raise_application_error(-20031, 'Could not find system parameter
               smtp_server
      in table system_parameters.');
           end if;

g_smtp_server_port := cast(get_sys_parameter('smtp_server_port') as number);
           if g_smtp_server_port is null then
             raise_application_error(-20031, 'Could not find system parameter
      smtp_server_port in table system_parameters.');
           end if;

end; -- Package body mail
```

Since Oracle8.1.6, Oracle Corp. kindly provided us with the built-in package utl_smtp. This is what we use in this chapter to send an e-mail. To open a connection with an SMTP server, utl_smtp requires a server name and a port. These values are stored in global variables g_smtp_server and g_smtp_server_port that are declared in the header part of our mail package. These two variables are initialized by the mail package body, as shown in Exhibit 27.2.

We chose to store the SMTP server name and port in a table called system_parameters (see Exhibit 27.3) to make our mail package more easily portable from our development environment to the client's production environment. We grouped all system parameters into one table so that there is only one place to go at install time.

Exhibit 27.3 System_parameters Table Description and Content

```
SQL> desc system_parameters

Name                   Null?           Type
----------------       ----------      ---------------
ID  NOT  NULL          NUMBER(11)
NAME                   NOT  NULL       VARCHAR2(40)
VALUE                  NOT  NULL       VARCHAR2(2000)
COMMENTS                               VARCHAR2(4000)
CREATE_USER_ID                         VARCHAR2(10)
CREATE_DATE                            DATE
LAST_CHANGE_USER_ID                    VARCHAR2(10)
LAST_CHANGE_DATE                       DATE
UPDATE_STAMP                           NUMBER(5)

SQL> select name, value
     2 from system_parameters;

NAME                   VALUE
----------------       --------------------
smtp_server            smtp05.us.oracle.com
smtp_server_port       25
```

Step 2: The Alert Table

All that is required to send an e-mail to somebody is to call the mail package documented above. Such a call can be put in a number of database triggers in a number of tables. Such a call could also be placed in the code of a number of application modules.

In our environment, we wanted to follow a structured and encapsulated method to manage alerts. Many people may be subscribed to receive pages for many types of alerts. It was necessary to divorce the process of sending batches of alert pages from the database transactions that trigger these pages. The triggering transaction commit process should not have to wait synchronously for the page sender process to complete.

Thus, we first created a database table called "alerts" to keep a log of all alerts generated by the system. This table is shown in Exhibit 27.4. Note that this table does not keep track of who the alert was sent to. There is only one record per event that triggered an alert.

Columns ALERT_TS_START and ALERT_TS_END are used to specify a datetime range when the alert should be sent. Under certain conditions, we can choose to use this to delay the time when people should be paged or to make the alert expire very quickly. We can even document an alert in the past without having it ever sent by the system.

Exhibit 27.4 Alerts Table Description and Content

```
SQL> desc alerts

Name                     Null?           Type
-------------------      --------        --------------
ID NOT NULL              NUMBER(11)
ALERT_MESSAGE                            VARCHAR2(2000)
ALERT_TS_START                           DATE
ALERT_TS_END                             DATE
CREATE_USER_ID                           VARCHAR2(10)
CREATE_DATE                              DATE
LAST_CHANGE_USER_ID                      VARCHAR2(10)
LAST_CHANGE_DATE                         DATE
UPDATE_STAMP                             NUMBER(5)
CLE_ID                   NOT NULL        NUMBER(11)
```

The column CLE_ID is a foreign key to a generic list-of-value application table called code_list_values. CLE_ID establishes the type of alert message. Examples of types are "syndrome" and "new incident." Users can subscribe to any or several types of alerts. For example, Sylvia may only need to be paged when a "syndrome" alert is produced by the system. Nasir may need to be paged whenever either a "syndrome" or a "new incident" alert is produced by the system.

Step 3: Building the Alert Package

The second step to build the alert mechanism is to group as much of the functionality in our package. The only part of alerts that we cannot include in this package is the event-specific functionality, such as the format of the actual message (see Exhibit 27.5).

Exhibit 27.5 Alert Package Header

```
package alert is
-- Purpose: Schedule and send alert messages
-- modification history
-- Person    Date     Comments
-- ------    ------   ------------------------
-- hdd       000913   Creation

   procedure prepare (p_message in varchar2 default 'No message supplied',
     p_alert_type in varchar2 default 'SYNDROME',
     p_ts_start in date default sysdate,
     p_ts_end in date default sysdate+20);

   procedure send; -- Internal only, do not use. (had to be made public
     though...)

end; -- Package Specification alert
```

We felt it necessary to divorce the process of sending batches of alert pages from the database transactions that trigger these pages. The triggering transaction commit process should not have to wait synchronously for the page sender process to complete. Only procedure "prepare" should be used by database triggers or application modules that send alerts. The procedure "prepare" submits a queued job using dbms_job that runs procedure "send" later in a separate transaction. So there is no need to call procedure "send."

Programming style: for the sake of brevity we have not included the exception handling code in any of Exhibit 27.6. For example, we do not show how we more elegantly handle a situation where the alert type "SYNDROME" has not been loaded in the database like it should be during the install.

```
package body alert is
```

Exhibit 27.6 Alert Package Body

```
package body alert is
   procedure prepare (p_message in varchar2 default 'No message supplied',
        p_alert_type in varchar2 default 'SYNDROME',
        p_ts_start in date default sysdate,
        p_ts_end in date default sysdate+20) is

     v_cle_id     number;
     v_jobno      binary_integer;
   begin
     select  id
     into    v_cle_id
     from    code_list_values
     where   value = p_alert_type;

   insert into alerts (alert_message, alert_ts_start, alert_ts_end, cle_id)
     values
       (p_message, p_ts_start, p_ts_end, v_cle_id);

     -- submit a job to send the alerts
     dbms_job.submit(v_jobno, 'alert.send;', sysdate+1/24/60/2);
     end; -- procedure prepare

procedure send is
     cursor alert_pages is
        select email_address,
               alert_message,
               alt.id alt_id
        from   persons psn,
               alerts alt,
               person_paging_subscriptions pps
        where  alt.cle_id = pps.cle_id and                      -- same alert_type
               sysdate >= alert_ts_start and
               sysdate <= alert_ts_end and
               pps.psn_id = psn.id and
               psn.email_address is not null;
```

Exhibit 27.6 Alert Package Body (continued)

```
        begin
          for  cur_alert in alert_pages loop
               mail.send (
                 p_sender=> 'herve.deschamps@oracle.com',
                 p_recipient=> cur_alert.email_address,
                 p_subject=> 'x',
                 p_message=> cur_alert.alert_message
          );

      if v_old_id != 0 and v_old_id != cur_alert.alt_id then
                                                          -- update same alert
        only once
          update alerts
          set alert_ts_end = sysdate
          where id=v_old_id;
        end if;
        v_old_id := cur_alert.alt_id;
      end loop;
      commit;
   end; -- procedure send

end; -- package body alert
```

Procedure "prepare" has defaults for all its parameters, although in practice the first two parameters will be used by most of the programs calling it. In contrast, the default value of the two timestamp parameters is almost never overwritten.

All procedure "prepare" does is to insert a record in table "alerts" defined in the previous step and to submit a job to dbms_job that will run procedure 'alert.send' in 30 seconds from the present time.

Procedure "send" scans the "alerts" table for active records (i.e., not expired by the value of alert_ts_end) and sends e-mails to all the people who are subscribed to that type of alert (CLE_ID column defined in Step 2). Once the alerts are sent, their end timestamps are set to the current time so that they are never sent again.

Step 4: Using the Alert Package

When a new incident is recorded in table "incidents," the system must send an alert to all people who are subscribed to the "new incident" alert type. We do this with a database pre-insert trigger on table "incidents" as shown in Exhibit 27.7.

All that is left to do is insert a record in table "incidents" and a message will be sent to all people subscribed to the alert type "new incident."

Exhibit 27.7 Pre-Insert Trigger on Table "Incidents" to Kick Off an Alert

```
declare
   v_incident_name     varchar2(2000);
   v_location_name     varchar2(2000);
begin
   v_incident_name := :new.name;
   v_location_name := :new.site_location;

   alert.prepare (p_message => 'LEADER ALERT: New incident:
     '||v_incident_name||' was initiated. Location: '||
          v_location_name||' at '||to_char(sysdate,'mm/dd/rrrr hh24:mi')
||'.',
          p_alert_type => 'NEW INCIDENT');
     end;
```

ORACLE SQL TUNING

Oracle SQL tuning is one of the most overlooked areas of Oracle tuning. The individual SQL statements that comprise the requests to the database engine can be tuned — often with dramatic results.

Unfortunately, Oracle SQL tuning is one of the most complex areas of Oracle administration. Any individual Oracle SQL statement can have an execution plan that is quite complex, and it is never intuitive to the Oracle administrator which execution plan will lead to the greatest response time. *Oracle Internals* has solicited a wealth of information from Oracle tuning experts on maximizing the performance of SQL statements within Oracle's library cache and ensuring that your Oracle database runs at optimal levels.

The following chapters from *Oracle Internals* are drawn from some of the best Oracle experts in the industry. John Beresniewicz of Precise Software has a landmark presentation entitled "Piranhas in the Pool: ..." (Chapter 30), in which he discusses the reusability of SQL and Oracle's implementation of the cursor sharing option in order to alleviate excessively parsing within Oracle's library cash. Also included are chapters from noted authors Rick Greenwald (Chapter 28) and Jonathan Gennick (Chapter 31) that discuss the intricacies of Oracle's cost-based optimizer and what the Oracle professional can do to ensure the fastest response time for all SQL statements.

In addition to being extremely complex, Oracle SQL tuning is also quite tedious. The Oracle professional must be able to fish through the library cash, identify high-usage SQL statements, and at the same time ensure that the tuning remains in place, regardless of what might happen to the Oracle statistics and initialization parameters.

Chapter 28

Cost-Based Optimization: Whys and Hows

Rick Greenwald

One of the founding notions of relational databases is the basic concept that no one needs to define an explicit navigation path to retrieve data. This does not mean that no explicit path is used to retrieve data, but rather that the database itself will determine the optimal way to get the data requested by a query.

In most production scenarios, much of the data in an Oracle database can be retrieved by a number of possible paths. The Oracle query optimizer performs the valuable task of determining which potential path should be used to execute a query.

Rule-Based Optimization

In its history, the Oracle database has actually had two different optimizers. Oracle's first query optimizer was a rule-based optimizer. As its name implies, the rule-based optimizer used a set of rules to determine the optimal retrieval path. With a limited set of rules, a database developer could count on how the rule-based optimizer would resolve the retrieval path for a particular query.

The bad thing about the rule-based optimizer was that no simple set of rules could effectively resolve all potential query scenarios. In addition, a rule, by its very nature, cannot differentiate between shades of grey in the database. A rule resolves to a binary result — yes or no. But, for instance, the mere presence of an index can mean different things in different situations.

Take the case of a simple join. The join uses two indexes to accomplish the operation. To a rule-based optimizer, each index is equivalent — whether the join is implemented by joining Index A to Index B is irrelevant. But imagine that Index A has 100 entries and Index B has 10,000 entries. It would be much faster to use Index A as the starting point for the join, since this

0-8493-1139-X/02/$0.00+$1.50
©2002 by CRC Press LLC

would mean 100 logical reads and then finding the matching row in Index B. If the join were performed with Index B as the starting point, the operation would perform 10,000 logical reads and matches.

In another scenario, an index is being used to select unique rows in a table. It is much faster to use an index to find a specific value. But what if the index only contains a few distinct values? Because retrieval through an index requires twice as many reads — one for the index and one for the associated row — using an index with only a few unique values could take more resources than reading the table directly.

The Cost-Based Optimizer

Both of the scenarios described above point to the same problem — the *cost* of using different retrieval paths can vary widely. Because of this, Oracle introduced the cost-based optimizer. Once again, as the name implies, the cost-based optimizer takes into account the potential cost of using any particular retrieval path as it determines the optimal path.

The cost-based optimizer takes into account a set of basic statistics that reflect the state of the various tables and indexes within the database. These statistics primarily relate to the size of these database entities and to the cardinality, or uniqueness, of the entries in an index. The greater the percentage of distinct values in an index, the better that index is for selecting specific values. The statistics also reflect the overall depth of the index, which can also affect the cost of using the index for certain operations.

You can also create a histogram for data where values are not evenly distributed. You might have an index with 10,000 entries and 5000 unique values. With the standard statistics, the cost-based optimizer would assume that there are approximately two entries for each unique value. But the reality could be one value with 5001 entries and one entry each for the other 4999 entries. A histogram can help the cost-based optimizer to recognize this situation and react appropriately.

Collecting Statistics

You collect statistics with the ANALYZE SQL command or with one of the procedures in the DBMS_STATS PL/SQL package, which is one of the built-in packages. There are specific procedures to gather statistics on a table, index, schema, or the entire database. The DBMS_STATS procedures use the ANALYZE command to collect statistics, but also run these commands in parallel and can perform additional tasks associated with collecting statistics.

When you collect statistics, you can collect statistics on the entire target entity or on a random sampling of the data in the entity. Collecting statistics on the entire target will be absolutely correct, but could take significantly longer.

You should consider gathering statistics as a part of your regular database maintenance routine. You probably want your statistics to reflect the accurate state of your data, since even the best optimizer is totally dependent on the view of the database offered by the statistics. Keep in mind that whenever the statistics for a particular database object change, any query that references that object will be re-optimized when it is initially executed.

Which Optimizer to Use

Since the Oracle database used the rule-based optimizer for many years, you still have the choice of using either one of the two optimizers.

You can set the optimizer mode as an initialization parameter, which affects the operation of the entire database, or with the ALTER SESSION command for a particular session. For both of these methods, you can set the optimizer mode to RULE to force the use of the rule-based optimizer or CHOOSE, which will use the rule-based optimizer if there are statistics for any table used in the query. The default optimizer mode for Oracle8i is CHOOSE.

So you can use either optimizer, but which one should you use? It makes sense to use the cost-based optimizer unless you have a compelling reason not to. Oracle has stopped putting support for new features, such as recognizing and using star schemas or materialized views, into the rule-based optimizer. In fact, the Oracle documentation warns that the rule-based approach may not be supported in future versions of the database.

If you are refraining from moving to the cost-based optimizer because you have finely tuned SQL statements based on the rule-based optimizer, you can always use stored outlines, which are described in the final section of this chapter.

Overriding the Decision of the Optimizer

There may be times when the performance of the database leads you to believe that the optimizer has not chosen the proper retrieval path. Before even starting to discuss the topic of overriding the decision of the optimizer, I feel compelled to strongly caution you against ever taking this course of action. There are a few good reasons for accepting the retrieval path suggested by the optimizer:

- The optimizer is continually being improved. As mentioned above, new features in the Oracle database are continually being added to the cost-based optimizer, and the cost-based optimizer itself is constantly being refined. Once you override the cost-based optimizer, your query cannot benefit from these changes.
- The optimizer reacts to changes in the database environment. If you force your own decision onto a query, Oracle will always follow your direction, regardless of changes in the database. What may have been a better decision today may also turn out to be a poor decision based on the state of the database next month. You could keep revisiting the decisions you force on the database, but this can rapidly become a maintenance headache.

- Everyone likes to think that they know how their database works better than any old optimizer. But a comforting thought does not necessarily reflect reality. If you can conclusively determine that the cost-based optimizer is not coming up with the right decision for your particular query, then, and only then, should you proceed to override the decision of the optimizer. Remember, a perceived mistake by the optimizer could be due to a bug in the optimizer, which can be fixed, or it could be due to your less-than-absolute understanding of the database.

You should only consider overriding the decision of the optimizer once you have specifically investigated the queries and their paths. But if you have conclusively determined that the optimizer is not making the correct decision for a query, you can add a hint. A hint is essentially a comment within a query that directs the optimizer to use a specific path or technique to optimize a query. Of course, you will also have to test the versions of the query with their hints to guarantee that the new optimization is superior.

You can also use stored outlines to pre-optimize your SQL statements and store the result of the optimization. In effect, a stored outline is saved as a series of hints. When you use stored outlines and the cost-based optimizer encounters an SQL query that matches one of the stored outlines, the optimizer simply retrieves the outline rather than optimize the statement. Stored outlines give you a fixed optimization path, so they will have to be periodically recreated. For an OLTP application, where the same SQL queries are being constantly reused, stored outlines can reduce the overhead of query optimization.

Stored outlines can also be useful when moving to a new version of the database, or when gathering a new set of statistics. Either one of these situations can cause an SQL query to be optimized in a different way. By creating a set of stored outlines, you always have the option of using the "old" optimizations if the new ones result in reduced performance.

The Oracle8i database gives you a way to check out the affect that a new set of statistics might have on your SQL operations. With some of the procedures in the DBMS_STATS package, you can export statistics to another table in your Oracle database. You can use this table to preserve the previous statistics while you collect a new set of statistics and determine their effect on your SQL. If it turns out that your applications worked better with the old statistics, you can simply drop the new statistics and import the old ones.

The art and science of query optimization is one of the most complex areas in your Oracle database. This chapter has attempted to give you an overview of your optimization options so that you can move into your really challenging task — exploring the way that your own Oracle database works with your own set of SQL queries.

Chapter 29

Analytic Functions

Jonathan Lewis

In Oracle version 8.1.6, Oracle Corp. introduced a whole new layer of functionality to its implementation of SQL: the analytic functions. This chapter provides a brief introduction to these functions, describing their use and then demonstrating the benefit in clarity and brevity of the code that they offer. This chapter is based on material previously presented to the U.K. Oracle User Group at their annual conference in December 2000.

The Way Things Were

Assume you have a data warehouse describing the sales for a chain of shops selling computer games. One of your main data tables, describing sales by location and title sold per week, may look something like the following:

```
create table game_sale (
    title          varchar2(30),
    store          varchar2(30),
    sales          number(10,2),
    week_ending    date
);
```

How would you deal with the requirement for an end-user report showing the two best-selling games in each store this week? There are two traditional approaches: procedural and non-procedural.

In the procedural case, we simply write a piece of SQL that sorts the data for a given week by store and period, then use a 3GL to walk through it one row at a time, making sure we print only the first two rows for each store. Consider, for example, this very simple PL/SQL solution that produces output which is correct but perhaps not entirely aesthetically satisfactory:

0-8493-1139-X/02/$0.00+$1.50
©2002 by CRC Press LLC

```
declare
   cursor c1 is
      select    store, title, sales
      from      game_sale
      where     week_ending = '21-Jan-2001'
      order by  store, sales desc
   ;
   m_last_row   c1%rowtype;
   m_out_ct     number := 0;

begin
for r1 in c1 loop
      if (m_last_row.store != r1.store) then
         m_out_ct := 0;
         dbms_output.new_line;
      end if;

      if m_out_ct != 2 then
         dbms_output.put_line (
            r1.store || ' - ' ||
            r1.title || ' - ' || r1.sales
         );
         m_out_ct := m_out_ct + 1;
      end if;

   m_last_row := r1;
end loop;
end;
/

Glasgow - Crash Simulator - 1934
Glasgow - Manic the Gerbil - 913

London - Dome - 2167
London - Portal Combat - 1824

PL/SQL procedure successfully completed.
```

The following non-procedural solution is rather more compact. On the plus side, if we are using SQL*Plus, it does allow us to produce a much tidier output without resorting to more fiddly little bits of code. On the minus side, the style of thinking required to produce this code is not really "natural"; thus, it is not immediately obvious that the SQL is appropriate to the requirement. More significantly, perhaps, this second solution requires Oracle to perform a correlated subquery for each row we examine to check how many items sold more than the current item in the current store this week — this could be a very resource-intensive query.

```
select    store, title, sales

from      game_sale gs1
where     week_ending = '21-Jan-2001'
and  2 > (
   select    count(*)
   from      game_sale gs2
```

```
    where     gs2.week_ending = gs1.week_ending
    and       gs2.store = gs1.store
    and       gs2.sales > gs1.sales
      )
order by
    store, sales desc;

STORE           TITLE                        SALES
----------      --------------------     ---------
Glasgow         Crash Simulator               1934
                Manic the Gerbil               913

London          Dome                          2167
                Portal Combat                 1824
```

In fact, both solutions also suffer from logical defects, partly because the requirement was not specified with sufficient precision, but also because the code in both cases is too simplistic.

Look at the PL/SQL code and ask yourself what would happen if `Glasgow` happened to sell 913 copies of `Dome` — it would not be reported although it appears to qualify for second place. (In fact, two users running the same query with a different set of `init.ora` parameters might get different answers, depending solely on a minor variation in their `init.ora` parameters, such as `sort_area_size`). Anyway, if there is a draw for second place, should both items be reported or should neither item be reported? The requirement was for the **two** best-selling games — we have no indication of how we should handle draws that result in more than two candidate titles.

The SQL option suffers from similar problems. Take the same scenario where `Dome` ties with `Manic` in `Glasgow`. As it stands, the SQL solution will automatically return three lines for Glasgow. At least there is no risk of the results changing randomly and you can choose to control the result by changing the inequalities in the SQL, substituing '>' for `'>='`, but you do need to think very carefully about how you are supposed to handle tied places.

One final point to consider with these solutions is the next, simple, refinement of the requirement. The top two sales in `London` total 3,991 whereas the top two sales in `Glasgow` total 2,847 - surely the marketing director will want to see the stores sorted in descending order by volume of sales. How do you do that in PL/SQL or SQL ?

An Analytic Solution

The analytic functions offer a cleaner and simpler solution at the SQL level. We can solve (one version of) our requirement using the `rank()` function. This function behaves like all the other analytic functions: after any initial selection, manipulation, and grouping of the data, but before applying an `order by` clause, it will:

- Break the data into partitions (nothing to do with partitioned tables or partition views)
- Optionally sort the data within each partition for further processing
- Optionally define "windows" within each partition (not shown in this example)
- Add value to the output based on the partitions and windows.

All this extra processing is cued by the `over()` clause as follows:

```
select store, title, sales, in_store_rank ranked
from (
select
store, title, sales,
     rank() over (
        partition by store
        order by sales desc
     ) as in_store_rank
  from game_sale
where week_ending = '21-Jan-2001'
   )
where in_store_rank <= 2
order by
store, in_store_rank;

STORE        TITLE                    SALES   IN_STORE_RANK
----------   --------------------   ---------  -------------
Glasgow      Crash Simulator           1934               1
             Manic the Gerbil           913               2

London       Dome                      2167               1
             Portal Combat             1824               2
```

You will note that I have used an in-line view as part of the query. There are two reasons for this. First, you cannot use an analytic function in a `where` clause but we want to test the value of the generated rank, so we have wrapped our SQL in a pair of parentheses and made it an in-line view. The second reason is for clarity: if you use a complex SQL statement to generate the basic solution, it is convenient to improve clarity by pushing it into an in-line view before applying the analytic functions to something that now looks like a simple table. I frequently use in-line views when applying analytic views. (Be warned, however, that I have found a few exotic cases in which this causes dramatic changes to execution paths; in particular, when mixing partitioned tables with partition views. The current status of this problem is "possibly a bug".)

In examining the highlighted (boldfaced) code that demonstrates the use of the `rank()` function, we see the `partition` clause that breaks the data set into separate sections. Each section is then sorted in descending order by the `sales` column. When this phase of sorting is complete, Oracle applies a ranking to the intermediate data and the job is nearly finished. Because we want to report only the top two rows for each `store (partition)` we wrap the query into an in-line view, and restrict our selection to those rows in which the generated rank is less than or equal to 2. Note that we then sort the final result set; it is likely, but not guaranteed, that the data for this example would coincidently appear in the correct order, but it is important to remember that any application of analytic functions takes place before, and independently of, the final `order by` clause. Do not rely on side-effects; always include an explicit closing `order by` if you want your output sorted.

In case you are wondering about tied places, the `rank()` function leaves gaps. If sales of `Dome` in the `Glasgow` store had matched those of `Manic`, then both games would have been ranked 2, and the next placed game would have been ranked 4, with no game in third place. There is an alternative ranking function, `dense_rank()`, that would give the results 1,2,2,3,4..., but no there is no function for generating the ordering 1,3,3,4,5....

We can be a lot more fanciful than this simple example, however. We note that `London` clearly sells more games than `Glasgow`. Perhaps we would like to list the store not alphabetically, but by total sales. We can do this by introducing another style of analytic function, partitioning the data again by store, and sorting on the result of that function.

```
select store, title, sales
from (
   select
      store, title, sales,
      rank() over (
         partition by store
         order by sales desc
      ) as in_store_rank,
      sum(sales) over (
         partition by store
      ) as store_totals
   from game_sale
   where week_ending = '21-Jan-2001'
   )
where
   in_store_rank <= 2
order by
   store_totals desc, in_store_rank;
```

In the highlighted (boldfaced) code this time, we have taken the familiar `sum()` function and used it in its new analytic form, demonstrating that analytic functions can use existing columns as parameters and are not restricted to generating new values as the paremeterless `rank()` function does. In this case, we only have a `partition` clause, which splits the data by `store` again, and thereby sums the `sales` by `store` without the need for the "traditional" `group by` clause. In this way, we can get "raw data" and summaries on the same line of a report without having to run two versions of the query or joining a table to itself. By the way, the example above sorts the store by total sold in each store; it is left as a useful and interesting exercise to sort the stores by the totals of just the games listed in the report.

The savings in processing can be significant, but do remember that each time we do any partitioning we are introducing more work, typically sorting.

However the v$sysstat and v$sesstat views do not appear to report in all the work that Oracle is doing, so be a little cautious as you investigate the possibilities on offer from analytic functions.

There are numerous functions, old and new, that can be used in this analytic way. The existing functions, like sum() above are count(), avg(), min(), max(), variance(), and stddev(). Apart from the rank() function introduced above, we have the new dense_rank(), percent_rank(), and row_number(). There are also a number of new statistical functions, such as corr(), var_pop(), var_samp(), covar_pop(), covar_samp(), stddev_pop(), stddev_samp(), and an entire host of regression functions. There are also the cume_dist() and ntile() functions (the latter allowing data to be split into percentiles, quartiles, etc.). Finally, under the heading of "miscellaneous but useful," we have the functions first_value(), last_value(), ratio_to_report(), lead(), and lag().

Common Requirements

Let's look at a couple of the new functions and see how they answer some of the most commonly asked questions about SQL. How do I report the difference between one row and the next? How do I report a figure as the percentage of the total for a report? How do I make one column report a running total of the figures in another column?

First, the lead() function can be used to return the data from the *following* row in the output. lead() and lag() take as their parameters the name of the column you want to report, and the distance (expressed as a number of rows) between the current row and the row you want to report alongside it. In my case, the distance is just one row; hence, the value 1 appearing in the function in this example.

```
select
  title, this_sale, next_sale,
  this_sale - next_sale delta
from (
  select title, sales this_sale,
    lead(sales,1) over (
      partition by store
      order by sales desc
    ) as next_sale
  from game_sale
where week_ending = '21-Jan-2001'
);

TITLE                THIS_SALE NEXT_SALE DELTA
----------------     -------------------------
Crash Simulator           1934       913  1021
Tonic the Gerbil           913       482   431
Dome                       482       315   167
Portal Combat              315        72   243
Age of Umpires              72
```

Next, to report one column as a percentage of the total data, we use the `ratio_to_report()` function. This function is named somewhat modestly, as it can be used not only to report the data as a percentage of the report total, but can also be used to report the data as a ratio of a partition. I demonstrate this by showing how a query can be simultaneously partitioned in many ways (bear in mind that this does mean more sorting, however).

Note how this report does not need to use an in-line view because I am not using the result of an analytic function as the basis for a subsequent `where` clause. Note also how an empty `over()` clause shows that I am treating the entire data set as the partition.

```
select
  store, title, sales,
  ratio_to_report(sales) over (
    partition by store
  ) store_ratio,
  ratio_to_report(sales) over (
  ) country_ratio
from game_sale
where week_ending = '21-Jan-2001'
order by
  store, sales desc;

Store     Title              Sale  St %   Co %
--------  -----------------  ----  ----  -----
Glasgow   Crash Simulator    1934   .52    .24
          Tonic the Gerbil    913   .25    .11
          Dome                482   .13    .06
          Portal Combat       315   .08    .04
          Age of Umpires       72   .02    .01

London    Dome               2167   .49    .27
          Portal Combat      1824   .41    .22
          Crash Simulator     247   .06    .03
          Age of Umpires      110   .03    .01
          Tonic the Gerbil     52   .01    .01
```

Finally we come to the example of a running total, which also introduces the final feature of analytic functions, and the `over()` clause, which is the `range` or `rows` clause. Thus far, our analytic functions have been associated with either a single row from a partition (e.g., `rank()`) or with the entire set of data within the partition (e.g., `ratio_to_report()`). It is possible, however, to specify that a function should be applied to a range within the partition. There are several types of range specification, such as *"within 3 rows of the current row," "within 10 days of the date in the current row," "the week* (yes, analytic functions do know what a week is) *preceding the date in the current row,"* etc. In this example, we use one of the simplest options, which is *"this row and all the preceding rows in the partition,"* to make a function produce the running total of the partition. Note that if you use the `range` or `rows` clause, you must have an `order by` clause in the `over()` clause to allow the ranging calculation to have a consistent, reproducible, meaning.

```
select
   store, week_ending, sales,
   sum(sales) over(
      partition by store
      order by week_ending
      range unbounded preceding
   ) running
from game_sales
where store = 'Glasgow'
order by store, week_ending;
```

```
STORE      WEEK ENDING    SALES  RUNNING
--------   -----------    -----  -------
Glasgow    07-May-2000    4,000    4,000
           14-May-2000    5,000    9,500
           21-May-2000    6,000   15,000
           28-May-2000    7,000   22,000
           04-Jun-2000    8,000   30,000
           11-Jun-2000    7,802   37,802
           18-Jun-2000    7,636   45,438
           25-Jun-2000    8,134   53,572
            2-Jul-2000    7,815   61,387
            9-Jul-2000    8,023   69,410
```

This is a wonderful demonstration of how a very clean and simple piece of SQL can now be used to produce a result that previously required some heavy-duty calculation from the database engine, or a carefully tested piece of procedural code. In this particular case, we also have an example where the analytic function appears to be applied with virtually no overhead to produce a commonly requested form of output.

Conclusion

Analytic functions are very powerful and allow you to produce useful tabular results with very little programming, but it helps to use in-line views to increase the clarity of code.

Be careful about performance; some of the function available clearly require Oracle to do a lot of sorting. But because the sort statistics are not reported, you should only apply analytic functions to relatively small result sets.

One final warning. PL/SQL does not yet recognize the syntax of analytic functions in static code, so you will need to resort to `ref cursors` and dynamic SQL to implement analytic functions inside PL/SQL packages.

Chapter 30

Piranhas in the Pool: Investigations into Literal SQL and Oracle Shared Pool Performance

John Beresniewicz

The Oracle shared pool is a highly sophisticated mechanism designed to improve performance generally through the sharing of SQL statements, stored PL/SQL, and other objects among users. The shared pool's library cache is designed to conserve both CPU and memory resources by avoiding redundant parsing, optimization, and memory allocation steps for commonly executed SQL. These efficiencies are based on storing execution information in complex data structures for subsequent reuse by identical SQL.

Unfortunately, it is also possible for application SQL to be particularly troublesome for the shared pool to manage. The very mechanisms designed to improve performance for sharable SQL introduce additional overhead when SQL is non-sharable; and in sufficient volume, such non-sharable SQL can severely compromise database performance.

This chapter investigates the effects of non-sharable SQL on Oracle performance and presents quantitative results of controlled testing of the issue. Oracle shared pool internals are also discussed, as well as DBA strategies for managing performance of high-volume non-sharable SQL.

The Problem: Non-Sharable SQL

The Oracle shared pool was first created in Oracle v7 to improve application performance by creating and managing sharable data structures to hold

0-8493-1139-X/02/$0.00+$1.50
©2002 by CRC Press LLC

execution information for SQL and PL/SQL.[1] OLTP applications in particular are characterized by embedded SQL that is essentially identical for all users and thus executed by Oracle many times. The efficiencies of sharing execution information accrue in both memory and CPU: less memory required for a single shared copy of execution information and less CPU consumed developing execution information (parsing and optimizing) once versus many times.

The Oracle library cache is the shared pool component responsible for managing the shared execution data structures for SQL and PL/SQL (as well as other objects).

Literal SQL versus Bind Variables

Consider a generic OLTP application in which data is inserted into and (often) queried essentially one row at a time. The application may issue statements resembling the following:

```
INSERT INTO Emp (empID, Name, MgrID) VALUES (123, 'Arlene', 123);
INSERT INTO Emp (empID, Name, MgrID) VALUES (456, 'John B', 123);
SELECT Name, MgrID FROM Emp WHERE empID = 123;
SELECT Name, MgrID FROM Emp WHERE empID = 456;
```

There are clearly similarities between statements: each of the INSERTs is inserting a single row into the database and each of the SELECTs is querying a row. We would expect Oracle to develop identical execution plans for the two INSERTs and likewise for the SELECTs. The statements differ, however, in specific column values that are referenced in the statements, and these values appear as numeric and character literals in the statements themselves. We refer to such SQL statements as "literal SQL."

Oracle provides application developers with an alternative method to literal SQL through which the same SQL statement can be used multiple times, referencing different specific column values each time. The technique involves the use of placeholders, called bind variables, in the SQL statements themselves. Bind variable versions of the above SQL would resemble the following:

```
INSERT INTO Emp (empID, Name, MgrID) VALUES (:bv1, :bv2, :bv3);
SELECT Name, MgrID FROM Emp WHERE empID = :bv1;
```

Prior to each statement, execution-specific values are attached, or bound, to the placeholder variables so that the statements will reference the correct data. The bind variable SQL exhibits a notational efficiency in that a single textual representation of each statement suffices for all specific variable combinations, whereas each literal SQL statement is textually different from its logical clones.

SQL Processing

When an SQL statement is received by Oracle, a number of steps take place before actual execution. The specific steps depend on whether a sharable version of the statement is located in the library cache. A general outline of these steps is:

1. Library cache handle (identifier) is computed from text of the statement.
2. Handle is used to check for library cache object (LCO) of a matching statement.
3. If usable library cache object found (cache hit), it is pinned and executed. Done.

If no usable LCO found (cache miss):

4. Call shared pool memory manager to obtain memory.
5. Hard parse and optimize the SQL and create LCO.
6. Pin and execute LCO. Done.

Steps 2 through 6 all involve various latching and pinning activities. In particular, the library cache latches protect a number of activities and the shared pool latch is required to accomplish step 4.

Oracle is designed so that only steps 1, 2, and 3 are required when users execute SQL that is identical to previously executed SQL and for which a library cache object can be located. Finding a matching object depends on matching library cache handles. These handles are rapidly computed from the pure text of the statement in step 1; no parsing is done at this point. Similarly, steps 2 and 3 are designed to support rapid and concurrent execution through the use of multiple library cache latches mapped to an array of hash chains.[1]

Steps 4 and 5 are required when no matching library cache object is found, so Oracle creates one for subsequent reuse by the same or other users. In step 4, the shared pool's generic memory manager is tasked to supply chunks of memory to hold the various components of the library cache object. This happens under protection of the single shared pool latch, where free lists of available memory chunks are searched for correctly sized pieces. If sufficient memory chunks cannot be located, unpinned chunks of re-creatable shared pool memory will be LRU flushed to make room.[2] Step 5 involves the development of the library cache object contents required to execute the statement. The SQL is parsed and optimized, and various privilege and dependency information is looked up and captured. This step involves considerable code path and can be CPU intensive. In the sense that the library cache is designed to avoid step 5 as much as possible, it can be thought of as a kind of CPU cache (as opposed to the buffer cache where data is saved to avoid physical I/O).

The Literal SQL Problem

We have seen that the library cache is designed to efficiently share and execute SQL that is textually identical to previously executed SQL. With literal SQL, however, the embedded literal values result in textually unique statements and the library cache search will not result in a hit. Thus, steps 1 through 6 will be required for each literal SQL statement, including the expensive shared pool memory allocation, parsing, and optimization steps. For literal SQL, the code path overhead of the library cache is purely that — overhead — and no savings of CPU or memory are realized.

When the volume of literal SQL is small, the extra CPU cycles and memory are usually not enough to impact performance. However, when applications rapidly generate large volumes of literal SQL, additional overhead can be incurred as follows:

- Additional pressure on library cache latches
- Fragmentation of shared pool free memory causes longer free list searches, increasing contention for shared pool latch
- Significant CPU consumption due to extra parsing, optimization, and latch spinning

Thus, we see that the very mechanisms designed to improve OLTP performance and scalability are effectively compromised and become a performance drag when presented with high volumes of literal SQL. An insidious aspect of the problem is that it often goes overlooked or undetected during application development and testing, surfacing only after production deployment under full transaction loads. Of course, this is the worst possible scenario for a business because repairing an application after deployment is the most costly and risky time to do so.

Oracle8.1.6 introduced a new initialization parameter, called CURSOR_SHARING, which was intended to provide the DBA with a "silver bullet" for the literal SQL problem. This parameter can be set to force Oracle to parse literals out of the SQL in step 1, replacing it with a bind variable version of the statement. The bind versions will compute identical library cache handles and locate a sharable LCO in step 2.

Where Does It Come From?

Because the shared pool and library cache have been part of Oracle since version 7, it is fair to wonder why this problem is still a concern today. My sense is that traditional client/server tools, applications, and developers have for the most part adopted the widespread use of bind variables. Today, however, we are confronted with a new computing paradigm and a barrage of new tools and languages to support it: the World Wide Web.

Applications written for the Web (using Visual Basic, Java, etc.) often dynamically generate SQL in response to click-streams using literal values captured in browser HTML pages. The result is literal, non-sharable SQL. In addition, these Web applications have an essentially limitless potential user community and thus are capable of generating large volumes of literal SQL.

Although I cannot prove the above theory beyond the several cases of which I am aware, anecdotal evidence suggests that applications with literal

SQL problems became much more common during 1999. Ask yourself what happened in 1999 that could cause a tidal shift in application characteristics? There is only one logical answer: the Web.

Performance Effects

Oracle performance can be severely compromised by large volumes of literal SQL. Some of the symptoms that may be noticed include:

- The system is CPU bound and exhibits an insatiable appetite for CPU.
- The system appears to "hang" after some period of normal operation.
- There is latch contention on shared pool and library cache latches.
- Increasing the shared pool size delays the problem but it re-occurs more severely.

Identifying the Problem

An Oracle instance suffering from too much literal SQL will likely exhibit some of the symptoms above. There are several investigations the DBA can use to help confirm that this is indeed happening in the instance.

Library Cache Hit Ratio

The library cache hit ratio should be very high (98%) when SQL is being shared and will remain low regardless of shared pool sizing adjustments when SQL is chronically non-sharable. Use the following query to determine the hit ratios by namespace in the library cache.

```
SELECT namespace
      ,(100*gethitratio ) hit_ratio
   FROM v$librarycache;
```

The "SQL AREA" namespace will be the one affected by literal SQL.

SQL Parse-to-Execute Ratio

The following query displays the percentage of SQL executed that did not incur an expensive hard parse. Literal SQL will always be fully parsed, so a low percentage may indicate a literal SQL or other SQL sharing problem.

```
SELECT 100 * (1 - A.hard_parses/B.executions) noparse_ratio
   FROM
      (select value hard_parses
             from v$sysstat
        where name = 'parse count (hard)' )
   A
      ,(select value executions
             from v$sysstat
        where name = 'execute count' )
   B;
```

Again, when this ratio is high, Oracle is sparing CPU cycles by avoiding expensive parsing; when this ratio is low, there may be a literal SQL problem.

Latch Free Waiters

A telltale sign that the instance is suffering library cache and shared pool problems is active latch contention with sessions waiting on the "latch free" wait event. The following query will select all current sessions waiting for either the shared pool or library cache latches.

```
SELECT sid, event, name latch
  FROM v$session_wait w
    ,v$latch  l
  WHERE w.event = 'latch free'
    AND l.latch# = w.p2
    AND l.name IN ('shared pool','library
  cache');
```

When this query selects more than 5 to 10 percent of total sessions, there is likely a very serious performance degradation taking place and literal SQL may be the culprit.

Finding Literal SQL

We can attempt to locate literal SQL in the V$SQL fixed view by grouping and counting statements that are identical up to a certain point based on the observation that most literal SQL becomes textually distinct toward the end of the statement (e.g., in the WHERE clause). The following query returns SQL statements having more than ten statements that textually match on leading substring.

```
SELECT S.sql_text
  FROM v$sql S
    ,(select substr(sql_text,1,&&size) sqltext,
      count(*)
          from v$sql
        group by substr(sql_text,1,&&size)
      having count(*) > 10
    ) D
  WHERE substr(S.sql_text,1,&&size) = D.sqltext;
```

The SQL*Plus substitution variable `&&size` can be adjusted to vary the text length used to match statements, as can the value 10 used to filter by level of duplication. Note that this query is expensive and should not be executed frequently on production systems.

Initialization Parameters

The following Oracle initialization parameters have an important impact on library cache and shared pool performance.

shared_pool_size

The total size of the shared pool, this parameter is most often adjusted in response to poor library cache hits-to-gets or reloads-to-pins ratios. In fact,

Exhibit 30.1 Hash Buckets for `_kgl_bucket_count` Index Values

_kgl_bucket_count	*Hash Buckets*
0	509
1	1021
2	2039
3	4093
4	8191
5	16381
6	32749
7	65521
8	131071

many Oracle instances are probably configured with `shared_pool_size` set too large when application SQL is not highly sharable. Optimally, this setting should be large enough to retain all the reusable library cache objects, plus enough to accommodate the maximum total of concurrent non-sharable object sizes.

_kgl_bucket_count

This parameter is an index that can be used to set the initial size of the library cache's hash bucket array to a prime number. The array is automatically resized dynamically by Oracle in response to demand for more library cache objects. However, this resizing operation can negatively impact performance while it takes place.[1] This performance interruption can be avoided by setting `_kgl_bucket_count` in advance. Exhibit 30.1 shows the size of the hash bucket array corresponding to `_kgl_bucket_count` values.[3]

An additional advantage of setting this parameter is that the hash bucket array size will remain a prime number when resizing is avoided. According to Steve Adams,[3] the resizing operation simply doubles the current size of the array, which will result in non-prime array sizes. Library cache handles are assigned to hash buckets using a simple modulo hash function[1] that works best when applied using primes.

Steve Adams supplies a nice script called `kgl_bucket_count.sql` that can be used to determine an appropriate setting for this index. Run the script after a normal production transaction load has developed on the instance. See Reference 4 to obtain this script.

_kgl_latch_count

This parameter is the number of child library cache latches. Each latch serializes access to a group of the hash buckets determined by simple modulo function[1] as follows:

```
latch# = ( bucket#(object handle) MOD _kgl_latch_count )
```

As always, when modulo hashing is involved, prime numbers provide the best assurance of an even distribution of assignments. Therefore, it is probably best if `_kgl_latch_count` is a prime number; that is, if the current setting is 4, then perhaps 3 or 5 is a better choice. Note also that on single-CPU systems, there is no gain from setting this value away from the default of 0 (one library cache latch and no child latches).

cursor_sharing

`cursor_sharing` is a new initialization parameter in Oracle8.1.6 that is designed to help manage the kinds of problems with non-sharable SQL investigated in this chapter. `cursor_sharing` can take the following values:

- EXACT = Library cache object matching based on exact SQL (or PL/SQL) text match as in pre-8.1.6 Oracle
- FORCE = Oracle automatically substitutes bind variables to replace literals in SQL statements before library cache object matching takes place, causing increased sharing of literal SQL

When `cursor_sharing` is set to FORCE, Oracle adds an extra layer of parsing that identifies statements as equivalent if they differ only in the values of literals, hashing them to identical library cache objects. We will see that, under the right circumstances, this setting can help solve the performance problems of literal SQL. However, not all applications will benefit from forced cursor sharing. See Reference 5 for a discussion of the appropriate use of this new initialization parameter.

Testing the Performance of High-Volume Literal SQL

The problem of high-volume literal SQL and the explanation provided above are all well and good; however, I became interested in demonstrating and quantifying these issues under controlled circumstances. Anecdotal evidence suggests that a number of DBAs have been wrestling with this issue in relation to specific applications they are charged with supporting. I wanted to implement a generic test environment in which the problem could be replicated and studied. This experimental and quantitative approach had the following objectives:

- Demonstrate that the problem is generic and not application specific.
- Quantify the severity of the problem.
- Corroborate the explanation of the problem's root causes.
- Investigate the effectiveness of different strategies for managing the problem.

Testing Requirements

The test environment had to satisfy a number of requirements to meet these objectives. Some of the most important are discussed below.

Literal and Non-literal SQL

The tests must measure performance of both literal and non-literal versions of the SQL for comparison purposes. The non-literal SQL should use bind variables and bind/execute the same variable values as used for the literal SQL.

Reproducible Results

The test environment should be completely controlled by and dedicated to the testing process. There should be no user SQL activity other than the test SQL. Multiple test runs using the same parameters should yield close to identical results.

Adjustable Execution Rates

The rate at which SQL is generated and issued to Oracle should be adjustable so that performance under different transaction volumes can be studied.

Multi-user Simulation

Because latch contention is a major symptom of the problem under investigation, multiple user sessions must be simulated to induce and study this contention.

NDS or DBMS_SQL

Oracle8 provides two methods for dynamically generating and submitting SQL using PL/SQL, and there may be performance differences between them. Therefore, the tests should allow for SQL generation using either of these mechanisms.

The SQLSlammer Procedure

I developed a PL/SQL package called LibC with routines to facilitate the generation of controllable parse rates of literal and non-literal SQL. The core component of this package is a procedure called SQLSlammer, the specification of which is listed in Exhibit 30.2.

Exhibit 30.2 SQLSlammer Procedure Specification

```
PROCEDURE SQLslammer
   (stmts_per_slam_IN IN POSITIVE
   ,total_slams_IN IN POSITIVE
   ,slam_sleeptime_IN IN NUMBER
   ,stmt_size_IN IN POSITIVE
   ,TFuse_rand_comment_IN IN BOOLEAN := TRUE
   ,TFuse_bindvars_IN IN BOOLEAN := FALSE
   ,TFuse_NDS_IN IN BOOLEAN := TRUE
   ,rand_seed_IN IN INTEGER := rand_seed
   );
```

The parameters for SQLSlammer can be used to control the volume and kind of SQL that is generated, as well as the method used to generate the SQL. The routine uses a pseudo-random number generator to create random-like but repeatable tests. An explanation of each of the parameters follows.

- **stmts_per_slam_IN:** The procedure generates batches of SQL statements, and each batch is called a "slam." This parameter controls the number of statements in each batch.
- **total_slams_IN:** The procedure loops until this many batches have been processed.
- **slam_sleeptime_IN:** The procedure will "sleep" between batches for this many seconds. Adjustable sleep times are necessary to better simulate user-generated SQL where there is latency between statements.
- **stmt_size_IN:** The procedure will pad the statement out to this length using an embedded comment, allowing investigation of the impact of larger and smaller statements on the shared pool.
- **TFuse_rand_comment_IN:** The statement will be padded with a randomized comment, making it unique.
- **TFuse_bindvars_IN:** Boolean that when TRUE causes the procedure to generate statements using bind variables in the WHERE clause; otherwise, the statements are literal SQL and effectively unique.
- **TFuse_NDS_IN:** Boolean that when TRUE causes the procedure to generate SQL using Native Dynamic SQL (NDS); otherwise, the DBMS_SQL built-in package is used.
- **rand_seed_IN:** A seed for the pseudo-random number generator used to make the literal SQL unique.

Test SQL

The SQL generated by SQLSlammer is extremely simple — purposefully so. I did not want the statement to be particularly difficult to parse or optimize, nor to require significant buffer cache resources or the potential to induce physical disk I/O. The objective was to isolate the stress on Oracle to the library cache and shared pool memory management mechanisms as much as possible.

Bind Variable Version

```
SELECT /* comment: $$$$$ */ "DUMMY" FROM dual WHERE dummy = :HV;
```

Literal SQL Version.

```
SELECT /* comment: $$$$$ */ "DUMMY" FROM dual WHERE dummy = '12345';
```

The pseudo-random number generator that produced values for the literal had a cycle length of over 1 million values.

Test Script

A critical requirement of the testing framework was to simulate multiple users, as latch contention was one of the main issues under investigation. I enlisted the Oracle job queue to help meet this requirement and devised an SQL*Plus script that does the following:

- Shuts down and restarts Oracle to pick up any initialization parameter changes and begins each test identically
- Disables the Oracle job queue background processes
- Submits a number of identically configured SQLSlammer jobs to the Oracle job queue; SQL*Plus variables are defined to hold SQLSlammer parameter values and simplify test configuration changes
- Collects before-test performance metrics
- Enables enough job queue processes to run all the jobs simultaneously
- Executes an identical SQLSlammer procedure in the foreground and measures elapsed time
- Collects after-test performance metrics

This testing framework allowed for a controllable number of identical processes to be initiated, each generating the same workload in the background as done by the foreground process. A subtle yet critical element was that each of the SQLSlammer jobs was forced to generate its own stream of literal SQL by initializing the random number generator with the job number.

It was helpful that in Oracle8, the instance can be stopped and restarted from SQL*Plus and also that both JOB_QUEUE_PROCESSES and CURSOR_SHARING can be set using the ALTER SYSTEM command. This allowed the entire test to be controlled from a single SQL*Plus script. The actual test script is listed in Appendix 30.1.

Performance Metrics

The test script (Appendix 30.1) captures a number of relevant performance data points before and after each test run. Some of the more important metrics captured include:

- **Elapsed time:** The elapsed time in seconds of the foreground run. The symmetric nature of the transaction load across all sessions in a test makes this a good measure of overall system response time.
- **Latch free wait time:** The total time waited (in seconds) on the latch free wait event across all sessions during the test run.
- **Latch impact:** A metric proposed by Steve Adams[2] to estimate the "relative impact of latch sleeps on overall performance." The experimental procedure focused on the impact of both library cache and shared pool latches.
- **Latch sleep rate:** The ratio of latch sleeps to latch gets, indicating the amount of contention for the latch.[2] The sleep rate of the library cache and shared pool latches was monitored.
- **Flushed chunks, pins, and releases:** Several measures of shared pool LRU list activity as discussed in Reference 2. Pinned chunks are removed from the list, and released chunks are added to the MRU end of the list. Chunk flushes take place when new library cache objects cannot allocate sufficient space from the free lists and must age out chunks to make room.
- **Executions:** Total number of SQL statements executed during the test as reported by V$SYSSTAT.
- **Parse count (hard):** Total number of hard parses performed during the test as reported by V$SYSSTAT. Hard parses involve creation of a new library cache object for the SQL or PL/SQL.
- **CPU used:** Total CPU consumption by all Oracle processes during the test as reported by V$SYSSTAT.
- **Parse time CPU:** Total CPU consumed parsing by all Oracle processes during the test as reported by V$SYSSTAT.

APT Scripts

Many of the above performance metrics were collected using APT scripts supplied by Steve Adams on the Ixora Web site.[4] In particular, the following scripts proved very useful:

1. `kgl_bucket_count.sql`
2. `shared_pool_free_lists.sql`
3. `shared_pool_lru_stats.sql`
4. `latch_sleeps.sql`
5. `resource_waits.sql`

Experienced DBAs with difficult performance tuning issues are well-advised to pay an occasional visit to this site for the latest tips and techniques from Adams.

Oracle8.1.5 Tests

The first series of tests were conducted on an Oracle8.1.5 database running under Windows NT. The testing objectives were as follows:

- Confirm and quantify the inverse relationship between shared pool size and performance under severe pressure from literal SQL.
- Verify that latch contention for shared pool and library cache latches are involved in the performance degradation of larger shared pools.
- Investigate literal SQL performance differences between using DBMS_SQL and Native Dynamic SQL.
- Quantify the scalability differences between applications using literal SQL versus bind variables.

Shared Pool Size and Performance

On the surface, it is counter-intuitive that under pressure from large volumes of literal SQL, Oracle performance can degrade as the shared pool size is increased. Normally, more memory is better in all things computer related, so why should this be different? The explanation is that memory usually assists performance by eliminating physical disk access. However, in the case of the shared pool and literal SQL, an inverted CPU–memory trade-off develops where more memory actually results in larger data structures to manage with more management overhead due to the non-sharing of library cache objects. This overhead is CPU intensive, so with enough SQL pressure, the system becomes CPU bound and performance suffers drastically.

One of the main purposes of this experimental investigation was to verify this unusual phenomenon under controlled conditions. There is certainly plenty of anecdotal evidence from DBAs that this inverse relationship between shared pool memory and performance exists for some applications, but others without these problems may remain skeptical in the absence of hard facts.

The first series of tests was simply to record response time variations under pressure from a fixed transaction volume of literal SQL as the shared pool size was progressively increased. Separate test runs using Native Dynamic SQL (NDS) and the DBMS_SQL built-in package were made to evaluate any performance differences between these methods of dynamically generating SQL.

Exhibit 30.3 shows the results of this test series. Both DBMS_SQL and NDS revealed significant degradation in response time performance as the shared pool size was increased from 10 to 50 megabytes (25 percent and 31 percent worse, respectively).

Also, NDS consistently outperformed DBMS_SQL for dynamic SQL processing. This is probably because of the additional latching and pinning overhead associated with the package-based DBMS_SQL implementation. This result is good news for developers because NDS is also much easier to use.

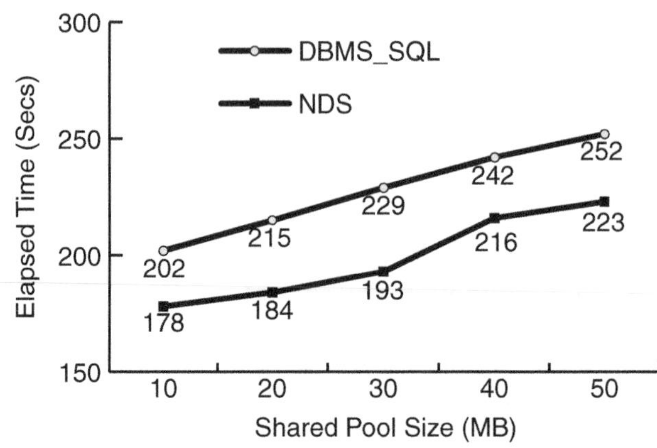

Exhibit 30.3 Performance of Literal SQL Using NDS and DBMS_SQL Versus Shared Pool Size

Shared Pool Size and Latch Impact

In addition to measuring response time, metrics on the shared pool and library cache latches were collected to help confirm the explanation that much of the performance degradation of larger shared pools was due to increased contention for these latches and, in particular, the single shared pool latch.

Exhibit 30.4 illustrates that increasing shared pool size can exacerbate latching problems under high parse rates of literal SQL.

These results are consistent with the explanation in Reference 2 that rapid escalation of shared pool latch contention is due to longer free list searches under the latch resulting from an increased volume of small free chunks in the pool.

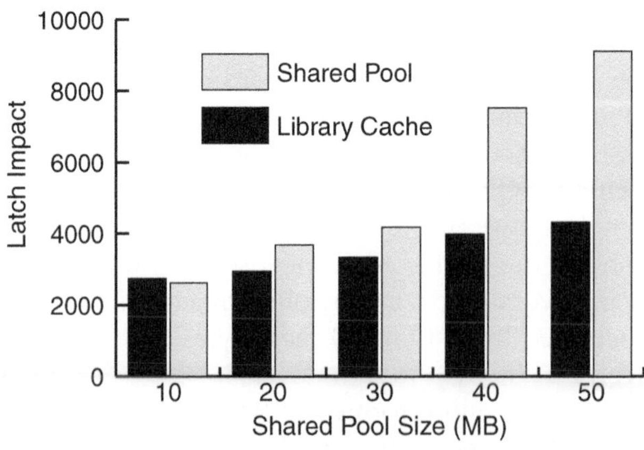

Exhibit 30.4 Relationship of Shared Pool Size to Latching Problems Under High Literal SQL Parse Rates

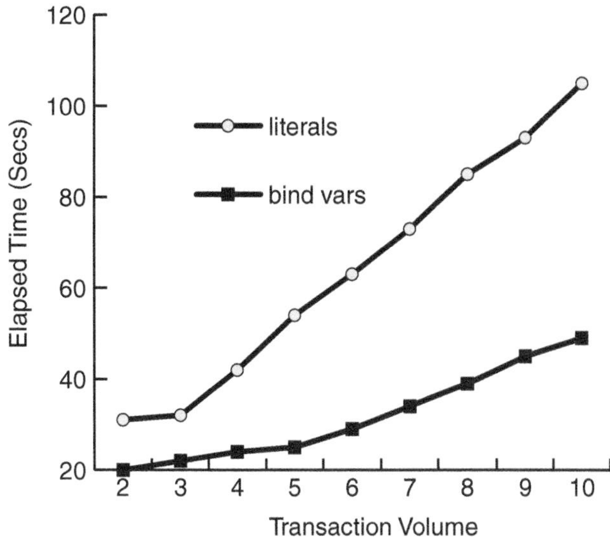

Exhibit 30.5 Scalability of Literal SQL Versus Bind Variables

Scalability Testing

System scalability is a big concern these days, especially for Web-based applications where the potential (and hoped-for) user community is essentially limitless. One symptom of the literal SQL problem is that it can severely throttle application scalability. This is primarily due to the great appetite for CPU cycles exhibited by high-volume literal SQL applications. Once the system becomes CPU bound, additional transactions will bog down response time.

Exhibit 30.5 displays the relationship of response time to transaction volume under Oracle8.1.5 for transactions using both literal SQL and bind variables. One can see that both the literal and bind variable SQL showed some scalability under increased transaction volume. The literal SQL showed relatively constant response time up to three transaction volume units, whereas the bind variable SQL did not begin degrading until five volume units, after which there was linear degradation in performance for increased volume. Thus, the bind variable implementation scaled to more than twice the transaction volume as the literal SQL. The eventual linear degradation in performance was also less severe in the case of bind variables. This is also an indication of much better scalability properties; the system can sustain a much higher transaction volume for a given response time tolerance.

Oracle8.1.6 Tests

To test the new CURSOR_SHARING system parameter, it was necessary to upgrade the test environment to version 8.1.6 of Oracle. The entire 8.1.5 test suite was not re-executed; however, some comparison runs were made and interesting differences noted between the versions.

8.1.6 Test Configurations

The testing regimen consisted of running five different SQLSlammer configurations against an 8.1.6 database on Windows NT. The following initialization parameter settings were common across all the tests:

```
SHARED_POOL_SIZE = 15M
_KGL_BUCKET_COUNT = 4
_KGL_LATCH_COUNT = 0
```

The shared pool was modestly sized but not oversized so as to avoid severely stressing the shared pool for the literal SQL runs. The KGL bucket count was fixed in advance to avoid incurring performance bumps due to hash bucket resizing. The test machine was a single-CPU Pentium, so multiple KGL latches would not be helpful (this was confirmed by some preliminary testing).

Exhibit 30.6 shows the SQLSlammer parameter settings for the five test configurations. The transaction rate and number of users were the same for all tests, while the variations were in the use of CURSOR_SHARING, bind variables, and Native Dynamic SQL or DBMS_SQL. The transaction volume was sufficient to cause the system to become CPU-bound during each of the tests; thus, the results represent relative performance under duress.

Finally, an additional test not noted in the table was executed to compare performance of the shared pool under stress from literal SQL when the pool is oversized. For this test, the shared pool was sized at 50 MB and the same SQLSlammer parameter values were used as in the 8.1.5 testing.

8.1.6 Test Results

The test suite certainly produced a lot of interesting data to consider. There were significant differences between the tests in a number of key performance indicators. Exhibit 30.7 summarizes the 8.1.6 test results.

Exhibit 30.6 8.1.6 SQLSlammer Test Configurations

Test #	*Binds?*	*NDS?*	*Cursor Sharing*	*Jobs (Users)*	*STMTS*	*Slams*	*Sleep (Secs)*
0	FALSE	FALSE	EXACT	10	5	1000	0.02
1	FALSE	TRUE	EXACT	10	5	1000	0.02
2	TRUE	TRUE	EXACT	10	5	1000	0.02
3	FALSE	TRUE	FORCE	10	5	1000	0.02
4	FALSE	FALSE	FORCE	10	5	1000	0.02

Exhibit 30.7 8.1.6 Test Results

	Test 0	*Test 1*	*Test 2*	*Test 3*	*Test 4*
Elapsed time (sec)	121	100	51	45	60
Latch free wait time (sec)	222.3	183.2	24.6	9.7	25.4
Library cache latch impact	5222	4244	1609	590	801
Library cache latch sleep rate	0.28%	0.24%	0.10%	0.09%	0.12%
Shared pool latch impact	1299	1418	0	0	0
Shared pool latch sleep rate	0.07%	0.08%	0.00%	0.00%	0.00%
Flushed chunks	150,912	144,904	0	0	0
Pins and releases	742,949	736,368	100,215	37,203	23,651
Library cache load lock wait time	0	62.1	0	0	0
Executions	52,920	53,077	52,709	52,665	52,708
Parse count (hard)	50,242	50,274	195	189	194
CPU used	230.3	194.5	103.9	91.7	121.4
Parse time CPU	58.5	59.8	9.1	12.1	11.8

Analysis of 8.1.6 Results

The 8.1.6 test results confirm several conclusions drawn from the 8.1.5 testing and provide quite definitive proof of the value of CURSOR_SHARING. In addition, interesting new questions are raised by some unexpected observations.

Effect of Bind Variables

The advantage of using bind variables rather than literal SQL is observed by comparing Test 1 and Test 2 results:

- Test 2 elapsed time improved 100 percent over Test 1.
- Test 2 library cache latch impact was much reduced versus Test 1.
- Test 2 had no shared pool latch impact versus significant impact for Test 1.

- Test 1 had many more shared pool pins and chunk flushes.
- Test 1 used more CPU for parsing and overall.

The use of bind variables (resulting in identical SQL) creates many fewer library cache objects and rapid hashing to the matching object. The library cache latch is thus released more quickly, reducing the latching impact of the library cache latch.

Increased sharing of library cache objects reduced the demand for shared pool memory allocations to the point that contention for this latch was eliminated by the use of bind variables. The negligible pressure on the shared pool is reflected in the fact that no chunk flushing was induced in Test 2.

As expected, CPU utilization was considerably reduced through the use of bind variables, confirming an original design objective of the library cache.

Effect of CURSOR_SHARING

A primary purpose of the 8.1.6 testing was to assess the impact of the new CURSOR_SHARING system parameter and its potential for helping DBAs manage ill-behaved applications with high parse rates of literal SQL. Comparing Test 1 to Test 3, and also Test 0 to Test 4, serves this goal.

In comparing these test results, CURSOR_SHARING exhibits advantages similar to those obtained using bind variables in Test 2:

- Reduced library cache impact
- Negligible shared pool activity
- Reduced CPU demands

In fact, Test 3 produced the best elapsed time of all tests despite the fact that all the SQL was literal. Thus, it is clear that CURSOR_SHARING can be used to significantly enhance the performance of high-volume literal SQL and is a great boon to the DBA saddled with such applications.

CURSOR_SHARING Versus Bind Variables

Comparing Test 2 and Test 3 reveals that CURSOR_SHARING = FORCE showed significantly better performance than bind variables in both elapsed time and reduced library cache latching impact. This surprising result deserves further investigation to produce an adequate explanation. Library cache latch impact was significantly reduced as were shared pool pins and releases. Parsing CPU time increased some, but overall CPU time was reduced. Perhaps the additional parsing involved in forced cursor sharing also enables increased sharing of shared pool memory heaps.

Native Dynamic SQL Versus DBMS_SQL

The tests also allow some comparison of Native Dynamic SQL (NDS) versus the DBMS_SQL built-in package to implement dynamic SQL processing. Under both exact (Test 0 versus Test 1) and forced (Test 3 versus Test 4) cursor sharing, NDS significantly outperformed DBMS_SQL. This result is the same as that observed under the 8.1.5 testing discussed above.

Latch Impact Improvements

Another surprise result of the 8.1.6 investigation was that shared pool and library cache latching are significantly reduced in impact over 8.1.5 when the shared pool is oversized and literal SQL is parsed in volume. Exhibit 30.8 shows comparative results for a 50-MB shared pool using DBMS_SQL to generate literal SQL with `cursor_sharing = exact`.

Exhibit 30.8 Latch Impact of Literal SQL in Oversized Shared Pool under 8.1.5 and 8.1.6

Impact	*8.1.5 Result*	*8.1.6 Result*
Library cache latch sleep rate	0.17%	0.09%
Shared pool latch sleep rate	0.24%	0.05%
Latch free wait time (sec)	162.2	53.3
Elapsed time (sec)	252	195

Clearly, there have been improvements in the 8.1.6 code in addition to those implemented for forced cursor sharing. Reliable sources[3] indicate that library cache latching modifications have been made in 8.1.6 as well as improvements in shared pool free list management.

Conclusion

The library cache and shared pool memory manager are integral components of the Oracle server designed to create efficiencies and thereby improve performance through the caching and reuse of CPU-intensive steps during SQL processing. Applications characterized by high volumes of literal (non-sharable) SQL can compromise these efficiencies, induce additional overhead, and degrade performance. Experimental results confirm that this is the case and support the explanation that contention for the shared pool and library cache latches plays a major role in this problem.

The DBA should not assume that poor library cache performance is curable by increasing the shared pool size. Experimental results confirm anecdotal reports that this can exacerbate problems caused by non-sharable SQL. Rather, developers should be educated in the use of bind variables, and these techniques should be brought to bear on the new generation of Web applications.

Finally, the new CURSOR_SHARING initialization parameter introduced in Oracle8.1.6 addresses and corrects the performance impact of literal SQL by converting it to bind variable format before library cache object matching is undertaken. Results show that this new feature does indeed correct for the performance penalty of literal SQL and promises to be a "silver bullet" for DBAs burdened with pathologically non-sharable SQL. Production 8.1.5 instances supporting Web applications generating dynamic SQL should be expeditiously upgraded to take advantage of this feature.

References

1. To, Lawrence and Manalac, Roderick, *Shared Pool Internals,* Center of Expertise, Oracle Worldwide Customer Support, 1996.
2. Adams, Steve, *Oracle8i Internal Services,* O'Reilly & Associates, 1999.
3. Personal correspondence with Steve Adams.
4. Adams, Steve, Ixora Web site, www.ixora.com.au/.
5. Oracle Corporation, *Oracle8i Designing and Tuning for Performance, Release 2 (8.1.6),* 1999.

Additional References

Ault, Michael, Diving into the Shared Pool, *Oracle Internals,* 1999.

Feuerstein, Steven, *Guide to Oracle8i Features,* O'Reilly & Associates, 1999.

Feuerstein, Steven, Dye, Charles, and Beresniewicz, John, *Oracle Built-in Packages,* O'Reilly & Associates, 1998.

Oracle Metalink (support.oracle.com), *Main Issues Affecting the Shared Pool on Oracle 7 and 8,* Bulletin ID 62143.1, 1999.

Oracle Worldwide Customer Support, *Internal Latch Contention,* Document ID 107963.963, 1995.

Appendix 30.1 Library Cache and Shared Pool Testing Script

The following script is the SQL*Plus script to stress test library cache and shared pool. It shows the SQL*Plus script used to execute tests and gather performance statistics. Different testing scenarios are achieved by changing values of the test control variables.

```
rem ***************************************************
rem * Exercises the library cache and shared pool using
rem * multiple identical SQLslammer procedures running
rem * under the Oracle job queue as well as in foreground.
rem * Gathers performance stats using various scripts,
rem * mostly from Steve Adams (www.ixora.com.au/)
rem ***************************************************
rem **
rem ** reinitialize by bouncing instance
rem **
connect internal
startup force nomount;
alter database mount;
alter database open;
connect jmb/jmb

rem **
rem ** test control parameters
rem **
DEFINE numjobs             = 9
DEFINE lowjob              = 100
DEFINE stmts_per_slam      = 5
DEFINE total_slams         = 1000
DEFINE slam_sleeptime      = .02
DEFINE stmt_size           = 50
DEFINE TFuse_rand_comment  = FALSE
DEFINE TFuse_bindvars      = FALSE
DEFINE TFuse_NDS           = FALSE
DEFINE CURSOR_SHARING      = EXACT

rem **
rem ** initial SQL*Plus settings
rem **
set verify off
set timing off
set serveroutput on size 100000
set numwidth 12

rem **
rem ** disable job queue
rem **
ALTER SYSTEM SET job_queue_processes = 0;

rem **
rem ** remove previous jobs
rem **
DECLARE
   lowjob INTEGER := TO_NUMBER(&&lowjob);
   hijob  INTEGER := TO_NUMBER(&&lowjob)+TO_NUMBER(&&numjobs);
```

(continues)

Appendix 30.1 Library Cache and Shared Pool Testing Script (continued)

```
BEGIN
   FOR jobrec IN (select job from user_jobs)
   LOOP
      BEGIN
         DBMS_JOB.REMOVE(jobrec.job);
      EXCEPTION
         WHEN OTHERS THEN NULL;
      END;
   END LOOP;
END;
/

rem **
rem ** set NLS date format for implicit date conversion
rem **
ALTER SESSION SET NLS_DATE_FORMAT='YYYY:MM:DD:HH24:MI:SS';

rem **
rem ** submit jobs
rem **
DECLARE
   lowjob  INTEGER := TO_NUMBER(&&lowjob);
   hijob   INTEGER := TO_NUMBER(&&lowjob)+TO_NUMBER(&&numjobs);
BEGIN
   FOR jobno IN lowjob..hijob
   LOOP
      DBMS_JOB.ISUBMIT
            (job  => jobno
            ,what => 'BEGIN libC.SQLslammer'||
                          ' (stmts_per_slam_IN => &&stmts_per_slam'||
                          ' ,total_slams_IN => &&total_slams'||
                          ' ,slam_sleeptime_IN => &&slam_sleeptime'||
                          ' ,stmt_size_IN => &&stmt_size'||
                          ' ,TFuse_rand_comment_IN => &&TFuse_rand_comment'||
                          ' ,TFuse_bindvars_IN => &&TFuse_bindvars'||
                          ' ,TFuse_NDS_IN => &&TFuse_NDS'||
                          ' ,rand_seed_IN => job'||
                          ' ); END;'
            ,next_date => TO_CHAR(SYSDATE,'YYYY:MM:DD:HH24:MI:SS')
            ,interval => null
            );
   END LOOP;
-- modify next_date for low and hi job, will run these in foreground
DBMS_JOB.NEXT_DATE(TO_NUMBER(lowjob),TO_CHAR(SYSDATE+1,
   'YYYY:MM:DD:HH24:MI:SS'));
--DBMS_JOB.NEXT_DATE(TO_NUMBER(hijob),TO_CHAR(SYSDATE+1,
   'YYYY:MM:DD:HH24:MI:SS'));
   --
   SYS.DBMS_SHARED_POOL.KEEP('LIBC','P');
   SYS.DBMS_SHARED_POOL.KEEP('SYS.DBMS_SQL','P');
   SYS.DBMS_SHARED_POOL.KEEP('SYS.STANDARD','P');
   SYS.DBMS_SHARED_POOL.KEEP('SYS.DBMS_STANDARD','P');
   SYS.DBMS_SHARED_POOL.KEEP('SYS.DBMS_LOCK','P');
   SYS.DBMS_SHARED_POOL.KEEP('SYS.DBMS_UTILITY','P');
   COMMIT;
END;
/
```

Appendix 30.1 Library Cache and Shared Pool Testing Script (continued)

```
rem
rem set cursor_sharing
rem
ALTER SYSTEM SET CURSOR_SHARING = &&CURSOR_SHARING;

spool libCrpt.txt

prompt .SQL Slammer test run report
prompt .
prompt .  Total SQLslammer jobs:  &&numjobs
prompt .          Stmts per slam:  &&stmts_per_slam
prompt .             Total slams:  &&total_slams
prompt . Sleeptime between slams:  &&slam_sleeptime
prompt .          Statement size:  &&stmt_size
prompt .    Use random comments?  &&TFuse_rand_comment
prompt .          Use bind vbls?  &&TFuse_bindvars
prompt .                Use NDS?  &&TFuse_NDS
prompt .        cursor_sharing?  &&CURSOR_SHARING
show sga

col KGL_parm_setting format a40

SELECT name||' : '||value KGL_parm_setting
   FROM  sys.all_parms
   WHERE name IN ('_kgl_latch_count','_kgl_bucket_count');

rem **
rem ** gather stats and reports for begin of run
rem **
SELECT name, value
      FROM v$sysstat
   WHERE name IN ('recursive cpu usage'
                ,'CPU used by this session'
                ,'parse time cpu'
                ,'parse time elapsed'
                ,'parse count (total)'
                ,'parse count (hard)'
                ,'execute count'
                );

@@SA_shared_pool_free_lists.sql
@@SA_shared_pool_lru_stats.sql

rem **
rem ** enable job queue to start test
rem **
ALTER SYSTEM SET job_queue_processes = &&numjobs;
BEGIN
   DBMS_LOCK.SLEEP(10);
END;
/

col RUN_DATE new_value begin_date
SELECT TO_CHAR(SYSDATE) RUN_DATE
   FROM dual;
```

(continues)

Appendix 30.1 Library Cache and Shared Pool Testing Script (continued)

```
set timing on
prompt
prompt Running foreground test...
rem **
rem ** run the low and high jobs in foreground
rem **
DECLARE
   lowjob INTEGER := TO_NUMBER(&&lowjob);
   hijob  INTEGER := TO_NUMBER(&&lowjob)+TO_NUMBER(&&numjobs);
BEGIN
   null;
   DBMS_JOB.RUN(lowjob);
   --DBMS_JOB.RUN(hijob);
END;
/

SELECT  TO_CHAR(SYSDATE) END_DATE
        ,86400*( SYSDATE - TO_DATE('&&begin_date') ) RUN_SECONDS
   FROM dual;

rem **
rem ** gather stats and reports for end of run
rem **
SELECT name, value
      FROM v$sysstat
   WHERE name IN ('recursive cpu usage'
                 ,'CPU used by this session'
                 ,'parse time cpu'
                 ,'parse time elapsed'
                 ,'parse count (total)'
                 ,'parse count (hard)'
                 ,'execute count');

@@SA_kgl_bucket_count.sql
@@SA_shared_pool_free_lists.sql
@@SA_shared_pool_lru_stats.sql
@@SA_latch_sleeps.sql
@@SA_resource_waits.sql

spool off
set timing off
```

Chapter 31

Managing Database Objects in Sets

Jonathan Gennick

When I first began my career, I was a programmer operating in a mainframe COBOL environment. We wrote procedural code. Our typical programs were batch programs that read records from a file and processed those records in a read-loop. The read-loop contained program logic to identify records of interest and to perform operations on those records. I worked in that environment for several years and I was happy.

In the early 1990s, I was introduced to relational databases and SQL. SQL allows you to work in terms of sets. Suddenly, rather than processing one record at a time, I could process an entire set of records with one statement. This led to a completely different way of thinking about data that I found exhilarating. The challenge now was to write a WHERE clause that precisely identified the set of records (or rows) that I needed to work with, and then to use the SQL statement, expressions, and subqueries necessary to accomplish my task.

Eventually, I moved from programming to database administration. Instead of writing programs to deal with large amounts of records, I was managing databases containing large numbers of objects such as tables and indexes. Somewhere along the line, I saw a script written by another DBA that used an SQL query to generate Data Definition Language (DDL) commands that were then executed against the database. I realized then what the other DBA already knew — that I could apply SQL's power to manipulate data in terms of sets to many of my database administration tasks.

Using SQL to Write SQL

The technique I'm writing about is frequently referred to as using SQL to write SQL. Every Oracle database contains within it a set of data dictionary views.

0-8493-1139-X/02/$0.00+$1.50
©2002 by CRC Press LLC

These views return information about all the objects in the database. If you have an operation to perform on a large number of database objects, instead of writing a large number of DDL statements yourself, you can automate the process using SQL to generate the DDL statements that you want to execute. The process for doing that is as follows:

1. Write a SELECT statement that returns the value of an expression, where that expression ends up being the DDL statements that you want to execute.
2. Using SQL*Plus, spool the output from the SELECT statement to a file.
3. Using SQL*Plus', @ command, execute the statements in the file that you just created.

The first key to this technique is that you need to be able to write a WHERE clause that precisely restricts your SELECT query to just those database objects on which you want to operate. The second key to this technique is that you must be able to write an expression that returns the DDL statements that you wish to execute. Sometimes this is easy, and sometimes it is not. Naming conventions — and your adherence to them — can sometimes come into play here.

Rebuilding Indexes: An Example

Recently, I was faced with the task of moving some 800+ indexes from one set of tablespaces to another. These indexes were owned by seven different users, and the problem was that all the tables and indexes for each user had been created in each user's default tablespace. My task was to create an index tablespace for each user and then move each user's indexes to that new tablespace.

Creating the new tablespaces was easy. I did that by hand because there were only seven of them, and I adopted the rather simple naming convention of *USERNAME*_INDEXES for the tablespace name. For example, for the user named UIMSMGR, I created a tablespace named UIMSMGR_INDEXES. The next task was a bit more difficult. I needed to move each index to one of the new tablespaces. To do that, I decided to use the ALTER INDEX REBUILD command. For each index, I would need to issue a command such as:

```
ALTER INDEX index_name REBUILD TABLESPACE username_indexes;
```

I wanted to issue the same command against all 800+ indexes for the seven users in question, so that made this a good time to think about operating on the entire set at once. Information about indexes can be found in the ALL_INDEXES data dictionary view. First, I needed to identify the set of indexes to be moved. I did that using the WHERE clause shown in the following SELECT statement:

```
SELECT owner, index_name
FROM all_indexes
WHERE owner in ('UIMSMGR','UIMSUSR',…)
```

This query gave me the owner name and index name for all indexes that I wanted to rebuild in order to change their tablespace assignments. The problem now was to generate the necessary ALTER INDEX REBUILD statements. To do that, I came up with the expression in the following SQL SELECT statement:

```
SELECT 'ALTER INDEX '
       || owner || '.' || index_name
       || ' REBUILD TABLESPACE '
       || owner || '_INDEXES;'
  FROM all_indexes
WHERE ((owner in ('UIMSMGR', 'UIMSUSR'...)));
```

This SELECT statement returns a computed expression that evaluates to the command that I wanted to execute. The OWNER and INDEX_NAME columns from the view are used in the expression to build up a fully qualified index name. The OWNER column is also used to generate the appropriate tablespace name for each index. This is where my adherence to a naming convention comes into play. In all cases, the index tablespace name consisted of the index owner's username followed by the string '_INDEXES;'. Had I not followed a consistent naming convention, it might not have been possible to operate on all 800+ indexes at one time; I might have been forced to deal separately with each user's indexes separately. It did take me a couple of tries to get the expression just right so that it would generate syntactically correct DDL statements.

Once I had the statement figured out, I only needed to spool the output to a file and then execute that file. This I did from SQL*Plus using the following commands:

```
SET PAGESIZE 0
SET LINESIZE 1000
SPOOL rebuild_indexes.sql
SELECT'ALTER INDEX '
     || owner || '.' || index_name
     || ' REBUILD TABLESPACE '
     || owner || '_INDEXES;'
  FROM all_indexes
WHERE ((owner in ('UIMSMGR', 'UIMSUSR'...)));
SPOOL OFF

--Execute the generated script
@rebuild_indexes.sql
```

Setting PAGESIZE to 0 eliminated column and page headings that might otherwise clutter up the script file I was generating. These headings would result in syntax errors when I executed the file. While such syntax errors are only a mere annoyance — you can just ignore them when you run the script — I prefer to keep my scripts clean. That way, I know that any errors I see are real.

The reason I set the LINESIZE to 0 was to prevent wraparound in my generated DDL statements. SQL*Plus' default line width is 80 characters. Lines longer than 80 characters are wrapped at that point, and sometimes the line breaks are inserted in such a way as to cause syntax errors in generated SQL statements. To prevent problems, I set the LINESIZE to a value high enough to accommodate the statements that I was generating.

Now, in truth, I didn't really want to execute the same command on all 800+ indexes. There were 40 or 50 that were so large that I did not want them lumped in with the others. But it was a simple matter to edit my generated script file and delete the ALTER INDEX commands for those indexes. Then I executed the script.

One caveat that is relevant to this example: you might want to think twice about unleashing 800 ALTER INDEX REBUILD commands against your database. At least think about *when* you want to do it and *how long* it will take. In my case, I was preparing a database for production. It wasn't being used yet and it contained minimal data.

So that's it. Instead of dealing with 800 indexes one at a time, I was able to deal with 800 indexes all at once — a much more manageable task. This worked so well that I even wrote a script in case I ever need to do this again. You can grab a copy of that script, if you like, at http://gennick.com/rebuild_index_article.html.

Learning about the Data Dictionary

There are several sources of information about the data dictionary; and if you are an Oracle DBA, it behooves you to become familiar with it. The *Oracle8i Reference* manual is the primary source of information about the Oracle data dictionary. Another, often convenient source of information is a data dictionary poster, such as those handed out at Oracle conferences and trade shows.

If you do not have a manual or a poster handy, you can obtain information about the data dictionary from the data dictionary itself. Two views — DICTIONARY and DICT_COLUMNS — document all the other data dictionary views.

The DICTIONARY view returns one row describing each data dictionary view. For example:

```
SQL> SELECT table_name, comments
   2 FROM dictionary
   3 ORDER BY table_name;

TABLE_NAME         COMMENTS
---------------- ------------------------
ALL_ALL_TABLES     Description of all object and relational tables accessible
                     to the user

ALL_ARGUMENTS      Arguments in object accessible to the user

ALL_ASSOCIATIONS   All associations available to the user
ALL_CATALOG        All tables, views, synonyms, sequences accessible to the user
```

If you are looking for views relating to a specific type of object such as a table, you can restrict the query using a LIKE predicate such as the one used in the following example:

```
SQL> SELECT table_name, comments
  2 FROM dictionary
  3 WHERE table_name LIKE '%TABLE%';

TABLE_NAME         COMMENTS
---------------- ------------------------
ALL_ALL_TABLES     Description of all object and relational tables accessible
                    to the user

ALL_NESTED_TABLES Description of nested tables in tables accessible to the user

ALL_OBJECT_TABLES Description of all object tables accessible to the user
```

The DICT_COLUMNS view describes the contents of each data dictionary column. Once you find a view of interest, you can query DICT_COLUMNS for descriptions of all the columns in that view. Remember the DICTIONARY and DICT_COLUMNS view names. With these two views at your disposal, information about the data dictionary is only a query away.

Chapter 32

Oracle's Joins

Richard Earp
Sikha Bagui

There is often a need to select data from columns from more than one table. A join combines columns and data from two or more tables (and in some cases, of one table with itself). The tables are listed in a FROM clause of a SELECT statement, and a join condition between the two tables is specified in a WHERE clause.

For example, suppose we create a table called `Emp` with an employee number (`Empno`) and a job code (`JobCode`) as follows:

Emp

Empno	JobCode
101	cp
102	ac
103	de

And then we create a second table called `Job`, which contains the job code (`JobC`) and a job title (`JobTitle`):

Job

JobC	JobTitle
de	dentist
cp	programmer
ac	accountant
do	doctor

We can use the following join command:

```
SELECT *
FROM job, emp
WHERE job.jobc = emp.jobcode;
```

0-8493-1139-X/02/$0.00+$1.50
©2002 by CRC Press LLC

This will display those resultant tuples that have `JobC` in `Job` equal to `JobCode` in `Emp`, as follows:

Empno	JobCode	JobC	JobTitle
102	ac	ac	accountant
101	cp	cp	programmer
103	de	de	dentist

Tuples from `Job` without a matching tuple in `Emp` are eliminated from the `JOIN` result. Tuples with nulls in the join attributes are also eliminated.

Cartesian Product

Joining two tables together without using a `WHERE` clause will produce a Cartesian product. A Cartesian product for the above example would be:

```
SELECT *
FROM job, emp;
```

The above command says to combine all of the data in both tables and make a new table. The result would be:

Empno	JobCode	JobC	JobTitle
101	cp	de	dentist
102	ac	de	dentist
103	de	de	dentist
101	cp	cp	programmer
102	ac	cp	programmer
203	de	cp	programmer
101	cp	ac	accountant
102	ac	ac	accountant
103	de	ac	accountant
101	cp	do	doctor
102	ac	do	doctor
103	de	do	doctor

Therefore, the result of a Cartesian join will be a relation, say Q, which will have n*m attributes (where n is the number of tuples from the first relation and m is the number of tuples from the second relation). In our example above, there is a result of 12 tuples (3 × 4) in the resulting set, with all possible combinations of tuples from `Emp` and `Job`. A Cartesian product can be called a `JOIN` with no join condition.

Oftentimes, the Cartesian product also gives data that has little meaning, and is usually a result of the user having forgotten to use an appropriate `WHERE` clause in the `SELECT` statement.

Equi-joins

The most common JOIN involves join conditions with equality comparisons. Such a join, where the comparison operator is '=', is called an equi-join (as in the example shown below):

```
SELECT *
FROM job, emp
WHERE job.jobc = emp.jobcode;
```

Examining the two resulting tables from above, one can see that the equi-join is actually a Cartesian product followed by a relational algebra equality selection and, in fact, the equi-join is defined in relational algebra as a Cartesian product followed by a relational algebra select (not to be confused with an SQL select).

Tables can also be joined using other relational operators such as >, >=, <, <=, and <>.

Natural Join

The term "natural join" in relational algebra refers to an equi-join without the duplicate column and with the obvious join condition. If one spoke of the natural join on Emp and Job, it would produce:

Empno	JobCode	JobTitle
102	ac	accountant
101	cp	programmer
103	de	dentist

The implied join condition is the equality of job code in the two tables.

Unfortunately, some authors also use the term "natural join" to mean a join between a table with a foreign key and the table that contains the referenced primary key. Because of this confusion and ambiguity, we will not refer to the natural join again in this chapter.

Joining More Than One Table

Multiple tables can be joined using join conditions. For example, if we create another table as follows:

EmpN

EmpName	Empno
John Smith	103
Sally Cox	101
George Pilcher	102

and then join the three tables as follows:

```
SELECT Jobc, JobTitle, Empno, EmpName
FROM job, emp, empn
WHERE job.jobc=emp.jobcode
AND emp.empno=empn.empno;
```

the result of the join will be:

Jobc	JobTitle	Empno	EmpName
ac	accountant	102	George Pilcher
cp	programmer	101	Sally Cox
de	dentist	103	John Smith

This join is a pairwise operation. This "triple join" is actually either (EmpN join Emp) join Job, or EmpN join (Emp join Job). The choice of how the join is executed is usually made by the database's optimizer.

Outer Joins

In an equi-join, tuples without matching tuples values are eliminated from the `JOIN` result. For example, in the following join example, we have lost the information on the "doctor" from the Job table because no employee is a doctor.

```
SELECT *
FROM job, emp
WHERE job.jobc = emp.jobcode;
```

Empno	JobCode	JobC	JobTitle
102	ac	ac	accountant
101	cp	cp	programmer
103	de	de	dentist

In some cases, it may be desirable to include rows from one table that have no matching rows in the other table. `Outer joins` are used when we want to keep all the tuples from the first relation, `Emp`, or all the tuples from the second relation, `Job`, whether or not they have matching tuples in the other relation. An `outer join` where we want to keep all the tuples from the first relation (or left relation) is called a `left outer join`. An `outer join` where we want to keep all the tuples from the second relation (or right relation) is called the `right outer join`. The term `full outer join` is used to designate the union of the left and right outer joins.

In Oracle, the (+) makes the join an outer join. Also in Oracle, the standard `left` and `right` designations are not used. Instead, Oracle uses the terms "driving table" and "driven table" to designate the outer join. In the expression

```
WHERE Job.Jobc = Emp.Jobcode(+)
```

`Job` is the driving table, and `Emp` is the driven table. Hence, in Oracle, what is left or right is irrelevant.

```
A right outer join
SELECT *
FROM Emp, Job
WHERE Emp.JobCode(+) = Job.Jobc;
```

Empno	JobCode	JobC	JobTitle
102	ac	ac	accountant
101	cp	cp	programmer
103	de	de	dentist
		do	doctor

This lists all the job codes available in the table Job, even if there are no employees using those codes in Emp yet. Here, Job is the driving table.

```
A left outer join
SELECT *
FROM Emp, Job
WHERE Emp.JobCode=Job.Jobc(+);
```

Empno	JobCode	JobC	JobTitle
102	ac	ac	accountant
101	cp	cp	programmer
103	de	de	dentist

This table shows all the Empno and JobCodes of the employees (from the Emp table), even if there is no corresponding JobCode or JobTitle in the Job table. Here, Emp is the driving table.

We will now look at some examples of "extended outer joins."

Outer Join with an AND

If we add an AND condition in the WHERE clause, we produce this result:

```
SELECT *
FROM Emp, Job
WHERE Emp.JobCode=Job.Jobc(+)
AND Job.Jobc='cp';
```

Empno	JobCode	JobC	JobTitle
102	ac		
101	cp	cp	programmer
103	de		

This table purports to show all the Empno and JobCodes of the employees (from the Emp table), even if there is no corresponding JobCode or JobTitle in the Job table and where the JobCode from the Job table is "cp." This result turns out to be the same as an ordinary join. The effect of the outer join in the WHERE clause is not apparent because no outer join has been included in the AND clause. To correct this, when using outer joins, the (+) must also be placed in the *other* conditions, as shown below:

```
Outer join in other conditions
SELECT *
FROM Emp, Job
WHERE Emp.JobCode=Job.Jobc(+)
AND Job.Jobc(+)='cp';
```

Empno	JobCode	JobC	JobTitle
102	ac		
101	cp	cp	programmer
103	de		

This table shows all the Empno and JobCodes of the employees (from the Emp table), even if there is no corresponding JobCode or JobTitle in the Job table, and includes all the Empnos and JobCodes from the Emp table including the Empno with a JobCode of "cp." But why did we get the other two rows with nulls? Because of the outer join in

```
AND Job.Jobc(+)='cp'.
```

This tells Oracle to include in the answer all rows where the outer join produces a 'cp' for Job.Jobc(+). No row matches Emp.JobCode= 'ac', so we get a null for that row because of the outer join. Also, no row matches Emp.JobCode='de', so we get a null row for that. There is, however, a match for Emp.JobCode='cp', so that row prints <101, cp, cp, programmer>.

Outer Joins and Nulls

Suppose we test for nulls in the outer join result table:

```
SELECT *
FROM Emp, Job
WHERE Emp.JobCode=Job.Jobc(+)
AND Job.Jobc(+) is null;
```

Empno	JobCode	JobC	JobTitle
102	ac		
101	cp		
103	de		

This result can be explained as follows. First, by putting a (+) on the Job.Jobc condition, we are telling Oracle to create a row for every Emp row, match or not. Then, by including

```
AND Job.Jobc(+) is null;
```

we are telling Oracle to include in the answer the rows where the outer join produces a null for Job.Jobc(+). The thing to remember is that during the process of creating an outer join, some rows match some values of JobCode, but some do not; hence, the "is null" condition is true for those cases.

Outer Join Not Included in the Null Condition

If we do not include a `(+)` on the null condition:

```
SELECT *
FROM Emp, Job
WHERE Emp.JobCode=Job.Jobc(+)
AND Job.Jobc is null;

no rows selected
```

Here, we are telling Oracle to create the outer join first, then report only those rows where there is a null for `Jobc` in `Job`. Because no rows have been selected, it shows that all employees have a matching job code.

```
SELECT *
FROM Emp, Job
WHERE Emp.JobCode=Job.Jobc(+)
AND (Job.Jobc is null or Job.Jobc = 'ac');
```

Empno	JobCode	JobC	JobTitle
102	ac	ac	accountant

Again, this becomes a simple equi-join because the `(+)` was not included in the

```
AND (Job.Jobc is null or Job.Jobc = 'ac');.
```

Outer Join with OR and IN

Changing the previous query to test the outer join condition, we might try:

```
SELECT *
FROM Emp, Job
WHERE Emp.JobCode=Job.Jobc(+)
AND (Job.Jobc(+) is null or Job.Jobc(+) = 'ac');
AND (Job.Jobc(+) is null or Job.Jobc(+) = 'ac');

                                               *
ERROR at line 4: outer join operator (+) not allowed in operand of OR
  or IN
```

As shown above, an outer join is not allowed in connection with `OR` and `IN`.

Inline Views and Outer Joins

If tables would be appropriate for an outer-join query, creating an inline view as a table (with an alias — we used exp as our table alias) may be the best way to handle outer joins. For example:

```
SELECT * FROM
(SELECT *
FROM Emp, Job
WHERE Emp.Jobcode=Job.jobc(+)) exp

WHERE exp.jobc='cp' or exp.jobc='ac';
```

The output would be:

Empno	JobCode	JobC	JobTitle
102	ac	ac	accountant
101	cp	cp	programmer

Using the inline view eliminates the problem of guessing the result of added conditions because once the outer join is created, it then behaves like an ordinary table when placed in the view.

Symmetric Outer Joins

An outer join cannot be symmetric. This means that two tables may not be outer joined to each other [the (+) cannot be on both sides of the condition at the same time] in Oracle. For example:

```
SELECT *
FROM job, emp
WHERE job.jobc(+)=emp.jobcode(+);

WHERE job.jobc(+)=emp.jobcode(+);

                                  *

ERROR at line 3: a predicate may reference only one outer-joined table
```

In this example, there is no driving table and, hence, Oracle disallows the double outer join. A way to work around this problem would be to UNION the left and right outer joins, which would produce the symmetric join.

Chaining Outer Joins

As with ordinary joins, several levels of an outer join are possible. If a table Z is outer joined to a table Y, and then the outer join result is outer joined to a table X, this is known as *chaining* on the outer join.

Below is an example of chaining of an outer join — the table Job is outer joined to `Emp`, which can then be thought of as being outer joined to `EmpN`:

```
SELECT *
FROM job, emp, empn
WHERE job.jobc(+)=emp.jobcode
AND emp.empno(+)=empn.empno;
```

And the result would be:

Jobc	JobTitle	Empno	JobCode	EmpName	Empno
ac	accountant	102	ac	George Pilcher	102
cp	programmer	101	cp	Sally Cox	101
de	dentist	103	de	John Smith	103

The important thing to note here is that the outer join has to be carried all the way through.

A table cannot be outer joined to more than one table at the same time, as in:

```
SELECT *
FROM job, emp, empn
WHERE job.jobc=emp.jobcode(+)
AND emp.empno(+)=empn.empno;

FROM job, emp, empn

                    *

ERROR at line 2: a table may be outer joined to at most one other table
```

Performance of Outer Joins

Outer joins are inherently not any different from inner joins. If only one of the tables being used in an outer join has an index, the optimizer usually chooses the table without the index as the driving table. If the outer join forces the indexed table to be the driving table [by including the (+) on the other table] and if this is the only index, the index cannot be used. If both tables have indexes on the join column, the outer join can be used to force which table should be the driving table [Note: The driving table would be the table without the (+)].

Self-Join

A self-join is where a table is joined to itself. In this case, the query "sees" two identical copies of the table and table aliases must be used to distinguish between the two tables. An example of a self-join would be if we included a supervisor's social security number (superssn) and an employee's social security number (ssn) in our EmpN table and there exists in our table some employees who supervise other employees. The table would look like:

EmpN

EmpName	EmpNo	SuperSSN	SSN
John Smith	103	1234090992	
Sally Cox	101	1234090992	1234090991
George Pilcher	102	1234090991	1234090995

From this table, we can see that John Smith is Sally Cox's supervisor, Sally Cox is George Pilcher's supervisor, and John Smith has no supervisor. A listing of employees and their supervisors could be shown by using a self-join of this table as follows:

```
SELECT e.empname employee_name, s.empname supervisor_name
FROM empn e, empn s
WHERE e.superssn=s.ssn;
```

EMPLOYEE NAME	SUPERVISOR NAME
George Pilcher	Sally Cox
Sally Cox	John Smith

An outer join can also be included in a self-join. For example, we could show all employees, whether or not they have a supervisor.

```
SELECT e.empname employee_name, s.empname supervisor_name
FROM empn e, empn s
WHERE e.superssn=s.ssn(+);
```

EMPLOYEE NAME	SUPERVISOR NAME
John Smith	
George Pilcher	Sally Cox
Sally Cox	John Smith

Joining Views

Views are joined just as tables are joined. The views to be joined would be listed in the `FROM` clause, and the relationships in the `WHERE` clause.

Joining More than Two Tables

When more than two tables are being joined, the optimizer treats the query as a set of binary joins. This means that if a query has to join three tables, the optimizer will first join two of the three tables, then join this result to the third table.

If the three tables to be joined are of different sizes, the order in which the joins are performed may affect the efficiency of the query. If the size of the resulting set from the first join is large, then many rows will have to be processed by the second join. So, it may be advisable to join the two smallest tables first, and then join this result to the larger table. The *Explain Plan* command shows how to interpret the order of the joins. The *Explain Plan* output is most easily obtained using `SET AUTOTRACE ON`, but be advised that the *Explain Plan* table has to be created before `SET AUTOTRACE ON` is executed. The *Explain Plan* table is best created by a utility supplied by Oracle called `UTLXPLAN.SQL`.

Tuning Issues and Processing of Joins

Oracle has three methods for processing joins: `MERGE JOIN`, `NESTED LOOP`, and `HASH JOIN`. Depending on the nature of the application and queries, one may sometimes want to force the optimizer to use a method different from its first choice by the optimizer of join methods. Below is an explanation of the different join operations available, and a summary of when each may be most useful.

Merge Join

In a MERGE JOIN operation, the tables to be joined are processed separately, sorted, and then merged (joined). MERGE JOIN operations are commonly used when there are no indexes available. Let us use the following join to further understand the MERGE JOIN:

```
SELECT /*+ ORDERED USE_MERGE */ *
FROM emp, job
WHERE emp.jobcode = job.jobc;
```

Output will be:

Empno	JobCode	JobC	JobTitle
102	ac	ac	accountant
101	cp	cp	programmer
103	de	de	dentist

```
Execution Plan
   0        SELECT STATEMENT Optimizer=CHOOSE
   1    0   MERGE JOIN
   2    1   SORT (JOIN)
   3    2   TABLE ACCESS (FULL) OF 'JOB'
   4    1   SORT (JOIN)
```

Note: The /*+ ORDERED USE_MERGE */ after the SELECT statement is called a "hint." A hint is used to force a join method to be used by the optimizer. Here, the optimizer is being forced to use a SORT MERGE JOIN.

In the above query, Job and Emp were joined, but no indexes were used. Because in a MERGE JOIN operation each table is preprocessed separately before being joined, Job and Emp were first read individually by a TABLE ACCESS FULL operation, and then the set of rows returned from the table scan of the Job table was sorted by a SORT JOIN operation. Then a set of rows was returned from the table scan of Emp, and sorted by a second SORT JOIN operation. Data from the two SORT JOIN operations was then merged by a MERGE JOIN operation. Because the MERGE JOIN operation has to wait for two separate SORT JOIN operations, it typically performs poorly for online users. MERGE JOIN operations are efficient when tables are of equal size; but as table sizes increase, the time required for the sorts to be completed increases dramatically.

Nested Loops

If an index is available for the join conditions, then Oracle may perform a NESTED LOOPS join. NESTED LOOPS join two tables by retrieving data from the first table, and then for each record retrieved, an access is performed on the second table (access by an index of the second table). For example, we will first create an index of Emp:

```
    ALTER TABLE Emp
    ADD CONSTRAINT Emps_ndx
PRIMARY KEY (Empno);

Table altered.
```

Then we will perform the following NESTED LOOPS operation:

```
SELECT /*+ ORDERED USE_NL */*
FROM emp,job
WHERE emp.jobcode=job.jobc;
```

Output will be:

Empno	**JobCode**	**JobC**	**JobTitle**
102	ac	ac	accountant
101	cp	cp	programmer
103	de	de	dentist

Execution Plan

```
0        SELECT STATEMENT Optimizer=CHOOSE
1    0   NESTED LOOPS
2    1   TABLE ACCESS (FULL) OF 'JOB
3    1   TABLE ACCESS (BY ROWID) OF 'EMP'
4    3   INDEX (UNIQUE SCAN) OF 'EMPS_NDX'
```

Note: The /*+ ORDERED USE_NL*/ hint is forcing the optimizer to use the NESTED LOOPS operation.

In our example, since an index has been created for the Emp table, and there is no index available for the Job table, the Job table will be used as the driving table for the query. A TABLE ACCESS FULL operation will select all of the records of the Job table, and for each record retrieved, the Emp table will be checked to determine if it contains an entry for the value of the current record from the Job table. If a match is found, then the RowID for the matching Emp row will be retrieved from the index.

Unlike the Merge Join operation, the NESTED LOOPS operation does not wait for the whole set of records to be selected before returning records to successive operations. NESTED LOOPS return records as soon as they are found, providing the first matching rows quickly to users; hence, NESTED LOOPS are more useful for online users. In NESTED LOOPS joins, the order in which the tables are joined is critical. A NESTED LOOPS join is most useful if the smaller table is used as the driving table, and the larger table is accessed by an index. If multiple indexes are available, then Oracle will select a driving table for the query, unless one is specifically mentioned in the hint.

Hash Joins

In a HASH JOIN, each table is first read into main memory separately by a TABLE ACCESS FULL operation, and then a hashing function is used to compare the second table to the first table. The rows that result in matches are then returned to the user. HASH JOINS use memory (because the two tables that are being compared are kept in the memory), so applications that make extensive use of HASH JOINS may need to increase the amount of memory available in the database's System Global Area (specified in the init.ora parameters). If tables are small and can be scanned quickly, then hash joins may be appropriate for queries executed by an online user. The order of execution for the hash join is:

```
SELECT /*+ ORDERED USE_HASH */*
FROM emp,job
WHERE emp.jobcode=job.jobc;
```

Output will be:

Empno	JobCode	JobC	JobTitle
102	ac	ac	accountant
101	cp	cp	programmer
103	de	de	dentist

```
    Execution Plan
0           SELECT STATEMENT Optimizer=CHOOSE
1    0      HASH JOIN
2    1      TABLE ACCESS (FULL) OF 'JOB'
3    1      TABLE ACCESS (FULL) OF 'EMP'
```

Note: The /*+ ORDERED USE_HASH*/ is hinting to the optimizer to use the HASH JOIN operation. Once a HASH JOIN is done, HASH JOIN will be performed by optimizer unless disabled with the initialization parameter HASH_JOIN_ENABLED=FALSE.

Summary

This chapter has introduced the outer join — an extension of the normal equi-join of two tables. In constructing outer joins, there are options that allow a programmer to display part or all of the rows in one table, whether or not there are matching rows in the other table. Oracle uses the term "driving table" to designate the table that will be wholly represented in the outer join, whereas the SQL standard uses the terms "left" and "right outer joins." (Driving table is actually more descriptive, more useful, and less ambiguous than "left" and "right.") Oracle disallows full outer joins (symmetric outer joins), but such a join can be had using a UNION workaround.

Outer joins seem to act strangely when other constraints are placed on the join in the `WHERE` clause. Although the "strange" behavior is explainable, the best advice might be to use the outer join in an inline (or other) view so that the outer join product can be handled in a more normal way without worrying about added conditions and syntax restrictions on the "ordinary" outer join.

Finally, a discussion of join tactics is presented. Merge-joins, nested-loops joins, and hashed joins are illustrated to show that Oracle (as would other database systems) chooses an internal method to return results from joins. The point in this chapter is that one can force which of the tables is the driving table in both inner (normal equi-joins) and outer joins, and that outer joins are not necessarily faster or slower than ordinary equi-joins.

Editor's Note: Beware of Cost-based joins in Oracle7. Beware of a known problem with Oracle cost-based optimizer in n-way joins in Oracle7. Whenever three or more tables are joined using `first_rows` or `all_rows`, Oracle will perform a full-table scan against one of the tables, even if indexes are available to alleviate the full-table scan. Hence, carefully check all n-way joins in Oracle7 and ensure that the execution plan only does a full-table scan on very small tables. Otherwise, change the execution plan with a `/+* rule */` hint.

Chapter 33

To_Format

Anunaya Shrivastava

Many of us have wondered why we cannot have a format function to format the alphanumeric character data on the lines of the DATATYPE conversion functions such as TO_DATE, TO_NUMBER, and TO_CHAR. These independent conversion functions are excellent instruments in datatype conversions as well as data formatting. However, the implicit premise with these conversion functions is that you are trying to convert the datatype of given data. For example, if we want to convert a number 99 into a format of 99.00, we can use the TO_CHAR function viz. TO_CHAR(99,'99.99') to yield a 99.00 as the data value. However, in the event of this use of the TO_CHAR function, the format mask supplied is "hard-coded." So, if a number larger than two digits comes as the data input, the resulting output is "#####" as the data value exceeds the format mask supplied for the purpose. There is a very practical requirement to format data in data interfacing and data conversion programs where the source data is emanating as a character datatype, whereas the contents of the data value are all numeric.

1. To format a data source column and store a telephone number with hyphens or the social security number. The effort to change a telephone number (2487400509) to (248-740-0509) via the approach of TO_CHAR (TO_NUMBER ('2487400509'),'999-999-9999')) errors out into ORA-01481 (invalid number format).
2. To convert a numeric digit amount into words. For example, we have a check amount and we want to spell out the amount viz. $123.45 to one hundred twenty three dollars and forty five cents. This conversion is also provided by the function with a format mask of NTW.

In this approach, I have written the TO_FORMAT function to take care of the aforesaid issues. This function will provide you with a tool that can be

0-8493-1139-X/02/$0.00+$1.50
©2002 by CRC Press LLC

Exhibit 33.1 Summary of Format Masks

Format Mask	*Mode*	*Description/Example*
NTW	Numbers To Words	TO_FORMAT('99','NTW')= NINETY NINE
ZIP	Zipcode	TO_FORMAT('435609898','ZIP')=43560-9898
TEL	Telephone number	TO_FORMAT('2487400509','TEL') =248-740-0509
SSN	Social security number	TO_FORMAT('248463456', 'SSN') =248-46-3456
DEC	Two digits after the decimal	TO_FORMAT('99','DEC')= 99.00

used to format the alphanumeric data and will save development time, as you do not have to reinvent the wheel for any of these programmatic chores.

Design of the TO_FORMAT Function

The nomenclature of the TO_FORMAT function is analogous to TO_DATE, TO_CHAR, and TO_NUMBER because it helps us to format data like these functions but is not a datatype conversion function. The name of the function to format alphanumeric data stored in the Varchar2 column is TO_FORMAT. The structure of the function TO_FORMAT is:

```
FUNCTION TO_FORMAT(instring in VARCHAR2 [ ,format_mask in Varchar2])
RETURN VARCHAR2;
```

where arguments instring is the source string and format_mask is the format picture. The default format mask is DEC. The format masks are described below and the summary of format masks is depicted in Exhibit 33.1.

- NTW — this mask stands for Numbers To Words. This mask helps to signal the function to convert the numbers into words. For example, a value of "33" gets converted to "Thirty Three."
- ZIP — this mask can be used to format the zipcode data.
- TEL — this mask can be used to format the telephone number data.
- SSN — this mask can be used to format the social security number data.
- DEC — this mask can be used to display the decimal notation.

Note : The format masks are based on data representation in the United States only. For other countries, please modify the function accordingly.

The processing logic of the function is displayed in Exhibit 33.2.

Using the TO_FORMAT Function in Development

The TO_FORMAT function can be used across the board of Oracle development tools viz. SQL, PL/SQL, FORMS 5.0 or FORMS 6i, or REPORTS 3.0 or higher. The usage is outlined in the following discussion.

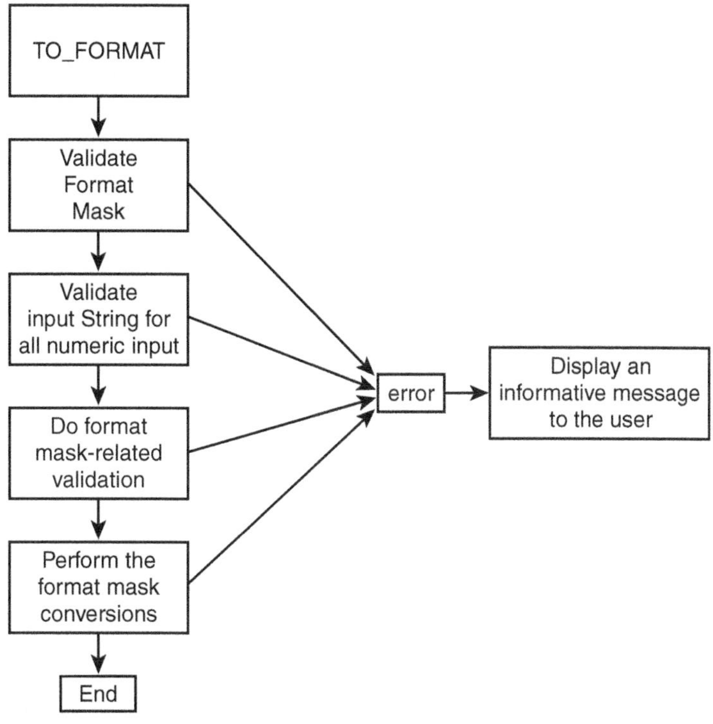

Exhibit 33.2 The Processing Logic Overview

```
SQL
SELECT TO_FORMAT ('99', 'NTW') FROM DUAL;
Output: Ninety-Nine.
```

For an invoice table storing invoice amount where we want all the invoice amount (NUMBER datatype) to be shown in words, we will do the following:

```
SELECT TO_FORMAT(invoice_amount, 'NTW') FROM Invoice_table;
PL/SQL
```

In our PL/SQL programs, we can call this function to assign a formatted value to the column inside a cursor of a program. The variable can be assigned a formatted value, viz:

```
National_identifier := TO_FORMAT(people_cur.ssn,'SSN');
```

We can similarly use the function in Forms and Reports to accomplish our objectives. In Forms, we can write the following code in case of a When-Button-Pressed trigger in block called check having two items, Amount and Amount_words:

```
:Check.Amount_words := TO_FORMAT(:Check.amount);
```

The usage in Reports is analogous to that in SQL.

Conclusion

The TO_FORMAT function (see Appendix 33.1) is a useful tool to format the varchar2 or a numeric column in any database manipulation. It provides us with validation and allows us to do very useful formatting operations. The utility of the function can be enhanced with a combination of standard functions (like Upper function to return the words for number in Upper Case) provided by Oracle. Many practical format masks have been added and one can expand on this by adding more format masks arising from business requirements. The TO_FORMAT function will find tremendous use in conversions and interface programs dealing with PL/SQL or SQL languages.

Acknowledgment

The author would like to acknowledge and thank Suganthi Natarajan for help in content development and Nanette Sommers for help in editing.

Appendix 33.1 Create or Replace Function TO_FORMAT

```
Create or replace Function TO_FORMAT ( instring in Varchar2,
   format_mask in Varchar2 default 'DEC')
RETURN VARCHAR2
/*****************************************************************
Purpose : To create a function to format alphanumeric character data
   and numeric data with help of the TO_CHAR function
Author : Anunaya Shrivastava
Acknowledgements:Suganthi Natarajan
Creation Date : 15-MAR-1999
*****************************************************************/
IS
------------user defined exceptions that will occur in the program------------
invalid_format_mask exception;
non_numeric_entry exception;
wrong_input_format exception;
wrong_tel_no exception;
wrong_ssn_no exception;
wrong_zip_no exception;
exp_too_long exception;

---------------variables to do data manipulation in the program---------------
v_format varchar2(3);
v_valid_significant varchar2(17);
v_significant_digits Varchar2(15);
v_Decimal_digits Varchar2(2);
v_length_significant Number;
v_input NUMBER(15);
v_length NUMBER(15);
v_repeat Number(13);
v_short number(13);
v_Dummy NUMBER(13);
v_output Varchar2(2000);

BEGIN
/* check format mask. This step checks whether the format mask supplied by
   the user is amongst the valid format masks for the function*/
begin
v_format:=UPPER(format_mask);
IF v_format not in ('NTW','ZIP','TEL','SSN','DEC')
   then
      raise invalid_format_mask;
end if;
exception
   When invalid_format_mask then
      RETURN 'You entered an invalid format mask';
end;

---------****** validate digits in the string *******---------
/* This step checks whether all the alphanumeric characters are indeed numbers.
   This is done by looping through the string character by character and
   finding whether the ASCII value of the string characters lies in the
   number set of ( 0,1,2,3,4,5,6,7,8,9)*/
begin
   FOR i in 1.. LENGTH(replace(instring,'.'))
      LOOP
         IF ASCII(substr(replace(instring,'.'),i-1,1))>47 and
            ASCII(substr(replace(instring,'.'),i-1,1))<58
```

Appendix 33.1 Create or Replace Function TO_FORMAT (continued)

```
        THEN
          v_valid_significant:=v_valid_significant ||substr(instring,i-1,1);
        else
          raise non_numeric_entry;
        END IF;
      END LOOP;
EXCEPTION
   When non_numeric_entry then
     RETURN (' The valid input for the function is between 0..9');
   End;

-----------------------****** split the string *********---------------------
/* this step spilts the input string into the left hand side of the decimal
   and right hand side of the decimal*/
begin
v_significant_digits := instring;
   IF (instr(instring,'.')>=1) and v_format in ('NTW','DEC') then
     v_significant_digits:=substr(instring,1,instr(instring,'.')-1);
     v_Decimal_digits:=substr(instring,instr(instring,'.')+1,2);
   end if;
exception
   When others then
     RETURN 'Please enter the correct input format for the format mask';
   end;

-----------------*** TEL number validation and display****------------------
/* If the telephone number mask is input by the user then format the string
   into 3-3-4 format*/
begin
   IF v_format='TEL' and LENGTH(v_significant_digits)=10 then
     RETURN substr(v_significant_digits,0,3)||'-'||
        substr(v_significant_digits,4,3)||'-'||
        substr(v_Significant_Digits,7,4);
     elsif v_format ='TEL' and LENGTH(v_significant_digits) <> 10 then
        raise wrong_tel_no;
   end if;
Exception
   When wrong_tel_no then
     RETURN ('Wrong telephone number');
   end;

---------------------*** SSN validation and display****----------------------
/* If the SSN number mask is input by the user then format the string into
   3-3-4 format*/

begin
   If v_format = 'SSN' and LENGTH(v_significant_digits)=9 then
     RETURN substr(v_significant_digits,0,3)||'-'||
        substr(v_significant_digits,3,2)||'-'||
        substr(v_significant_digits,5,4);
     elsif format_mask ='SSN' and LENGTH(v_Significant_digits)<>9 then
        raise wrong_ssn_no;
   end if;
exception
   When wrong_ssn_no then
     RETURN ('Wrong social security number');
   end;
```

Appendix 33.1 Create or Replace Function TO_FORMAT (continued)

```
---------------------*** ZIP validation and display-------------------------
/* If the zip mask is input by the user then format the string into 5 or
   5-4format*/
begin
   If v_format= 'ZIP' and LENGTH(v_significant_Digits) = 5
      then return v_Significant_digits;
      elsif format_mask ='ZIP' and LENGTH(v_Significant_Digits)=9
         then return substr(v_Significant_digits,0,5)||'-'||
            substr(v_Significant_digits,5,4);
      elsif format_mask ='ZIP' and (LENGTH(v_Significant_digits) NOT IN (5,9))
then
         raise wrong_zip_no;
   end if;
exception
   When OTHERS then
      RETURN ('Wrong zip code number');
   End;
----------------------*** Decimal representation *******---------------------
/* this step just adds a decimal point and two zeros to the input-
   a reportingrequirements in many places*/
Begin
   IF v_format='DEC' then
      RETURN v_significant_digits||'.'||nvl(v_decimal_digits,'00');
   end if;
EXCEPTION
   When others then
      RETURN 'Not correct decimals';
end;
-------------**** Number to words validation &representation****-------------
/* this step converts the numbers to words. It utilizes the to_char and
   to_date function's compound ability to convert Julian days into words. So
   we trick the to_char,to_date function to actually convert number into
   words. "Julian" - days since December 31,4713 B.C. This step can take a
   number that is 15 characters long*/
BEGIN
IF v_format ='NTW' then
   if LENGTH(v_significant_digits)>15 or v_significant_digits='0' then
      Raise Exp_too_long;
   end if;
v_input := v_significant_digits;
v_length:=LENGTH(to_char(v_input));
v_repeat:=CEIL(v_length/3);
v_dummy :=nvl(v_dummy,0);

For i in 1..v_repeat
LOOP
   if (v_length-v_dummy)>=3 then
      v_Short:=TO_NUMBER(substr(v_Significant_digits,
         (v_length-v_dummy-2),3));
      ELSE
         v_short:=TO_NUMBER(substr(v_significant_digits,1,
            (v_length-v_dummy)));
   end if;
      declare
         v_current varchar2(1000);
         v_temp varchar2(250);
```

Appendix 33.1 Create or Replace Function TO_FORMAT (continued)

```
      begin
         if v_dummy=3 then
            v_temp:='thousand';
         elsif v_dummy=6 then
            v_temp:='million';
         elsif v_dummy=9 then
            v_temp:='billion';
         elsif v_dummy=12 then
            v_temp:='trillion';
         end if;

   if v_short <> 0 then
         select to_char(to_date(v_short,'j'),'Jsp') INTO V_current
         FROM DUAL;
         v_output:=v_current||' '||v_temp||' '||v_output;
      end if;
   end;
      v_dummy :=nvl(v_dummy,0)+3;
   END LOOP;
END IF;

IF v_decimal_digits is null or v_decimal_digits='00' then
      RETURN rtrim(v_output)||' dollar';
   ELSE
      RETURN rtrim(v_output)||' dollar and
'||to_char(to_date(v_decimal_digits,'j'),'Jsp')||' cents';
end if;

exception
   When exp_too_long then
      RETURN 'Please enter a value between 1 .. 999999999999999';
   When value_error then
      RETURN 'Please enter a new value between 1 .. 999999999999999';
END;

-------------------** This is it**************************-----------------

END;
/
```

ORACLE DISK MANAGEMENT

All Oracle professionals recognize that the I/O against the physical disk is the most intense component of Oracle processing. In fact, the majority of all Oracle tuning is done with the direct intent of reducing physical disk I/O. Physical disk I/O is the major contributor to all Oracle performance problems, and anything the Oracle administrator can do to understand the I/O subsystems of the Oracle database will have a direct and immediate impact on the performance of the database.

With today's sophisticated disk arrays such as EMC disks, Oracle administrators are challenged more than ever before to understand the internal architectures of these disk I/O subsystems and ensure that they make proper usage of Oracle's RAM buffers in order to minimize disk I/O.

Chapter 34

Exploring Disk Size and Oracle Disk I/O Performance

Bruce D. Rodgers

The purpose of this chapter is to re-visit the continuing argument that application performance (often measured in disk I/O) is optimized by deploying a large number of smaller-capacity disk drives in the database storage array. As storage requirements continue to grow exponentially, the drive capacity issue remains central to application performance.

The issues surrounding disk capacity/performance persist because of the notion that in random read/write environments more disks moving simultaneously is optimal. The notion of striping data (RAID 1) to initiate concurrent disk drive read/writes has been an effective means of generating disk performance gains. The notion also persists because of the fear that large-capacity drives have longer latency periods as the drive heads locate desired disk positions.

The Great Debate

Those favoring smaller capacity drives argue that:

- Smaller capacity drives (9GB, 18GB) have been upgraded to match the spindle speeds (10,000 rpm) and faster access times of the larger disks.
- Areal densities (a product of track density and the number of bits per track) have exploded, so that the time needed to access a given gigabyte of data has deteriorated. Densely packed bits can mean fewer disks for a given amount of storage to be located and retrieved.

0-8493-1139-X/02/$0.00+$1.50
©2002 by CRC Press LLC

Exhibit 34.1 Disk Storage/Footprint Impact

1 Terabyte Example	*Average Access Times*	*Internal Transfer Rate*	*Vertical Inches of Rack Space (or U)*	*Number of 9-Bay Rackmount Enclosures*
112 × 9GB	9.9 msec	7–10MBs	112 in. (64U)	13
56 × 18GB	7.7 msec	11–17MBs	56 in. (32U)	7
28 × 36GB	5.4 msec	17–29MBs	28 in. (16U)	4
14 × 73GB	5.6 msec	26–40MBs	14 in. (8U)	2
6 × 180GB	N/A	N/A	7 in. (4U)	1

The large-capacity drive camp counter-argues

- Larger-capacity drives (36GB, 73GB) are individually faster than their smaller brethren.
- Increasing areal densities are more than offset by improvements in the hardware technology (processors, intelligent caching).

There are a number of issues that should be reviewed together to determine how disk capacity affects application performance.

Disk Technology Changes

Disk capacities have changed dramatically in the last couple of years: storage providers have been supporting 36GB and 73GB drives for some time, and larger-capacity drives are expected by the end of 2001. The drive manufacturers have created faster spindle speeds (7200, 10K, and 15K rpm) and created shorter latency periods. Access times are down. Transfer speeds are up and seek times are down. See Exhibit 34.1 for some representative disk drive performance variables.

The Fibre Channel and SCSI camps continue their respective arguments about which general technology class is best for the user. While fibre drives have some inherent speed advantages (in terms of throughput), they can also be considerably more expensive.

Completing disk I/O instructions involves several variables, including disk access or seek times, read/write times, and transfer rates. While transfer rates have increased dramatically, the greatest percentage of the disk I/O time is still related to the seek times (as in moving the heads to find the data). The seek times can consume 70 to 80 percent of the clock time needed to complete the disk I/O. It is these seek times that storage systems providers are attacking with improved hardware technology (in the server and the storage controller).

Changing Processor Technology

In Exhibit 34.2, the upper slope represents the relative rate of change in CPU technology, while the lower slope represents the relative rate of change in

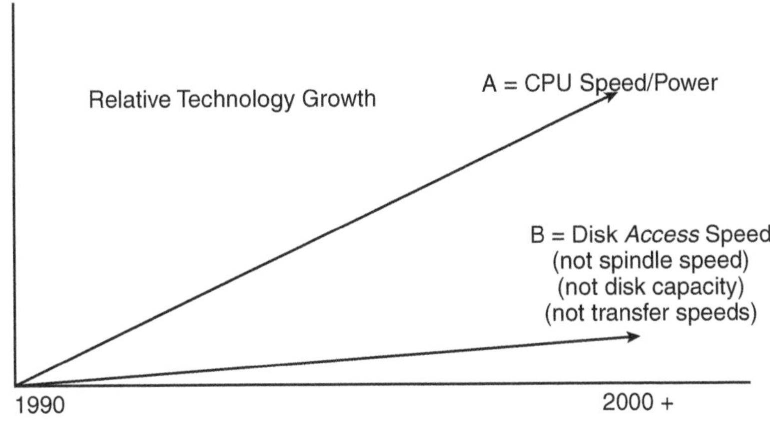

Exhibit 34.2 Technology Change in Processors and Hard Disk Drives

disk drive technology (including spindle speeds, capacity, and access times). The area between the two curves represents the time needed to complete the I/O activity. Note that the curves are diverging and more time can be spent by faster and more powerful CPUs waiting for the I/Os to complete. As disks have become bigger and faster, so has the potential for the server(s) to wait for the disk drives to complete their I/Os — especially in interactive applications (e.g., database queries).

Server manufacturers have achieved huge gains in the performance of the processor, the presence of multiple processors, and the availability of large memory buffers in the server (for staging the I/O instructions). You can consume your entire IT budget stuffing memory into your servers.

Application Content: The Secret to Understanding Storage Performance

Application content is most often the critical issue in resolving disk performance. Application content refers to the read/write mix as well as the random versus repetitive content of the application. All applications are not created equal. Some applications are write intensive, while others are read intensive. Users should know their application content mix to assist in selecting their storage array.

The process of determining application activity is fairly simple. Most operating systems contain the necessary utilities, such as SARs (system activity reports), IOSTATs (I/O statistics), or performance monitors, that present the application activity at a given point in time. These statistics are more meaningful when derived during known periods of application intensity.

The majority of applications are not random in content (which would benefit from several small-capacity drives). While much of the raw data may in fact be randomly stored, there are many repetitive functions present in the database application (e.g., look-up tables, log files, temp files). Some amount of time in the database application is always spent in repetitive disk activity.

Caching Technology

The most common approach for compressing these two technology development curves (to minimize wait states) has been for server and storage providers to load the hardware with cache. In addition to improved server processor technology, more memory has been introduced — on the disk drives, in the storage controller, and in the server. Most often, the memory in the hardware configuration is implemented as an FIFO buffer for staging the I/O instructions.

How the memory scheme is implemented can be more important in dealing with the application content than simply stuffing the hardware with a huge (and perhaps expensive) buffer. More recent advances in memory platforms have included intelligence that can actually reduce the actual frequency of disk reads/writes.

Managing the I/O Cycles

Who manages the disk I/O cycles? The CPU or the external controller? Storage providers continue to add intelligence (in the form of software programs and search algorithms) to the RAID controllers. The net effect can be the migration of the I/O management from the server to the external controller (thus reducing the number of CPU cycles needed to manage the storage array).

Some storage providers have integrated SSD and RAID technologies to provide the best of both worlds (safety and performance). In recent years, some RAID controllers have emerged with cache that "adapts" to changes in the application read/write activity. One example of such an "adaptive" cache is a retentive scheme that holds frequently used read/write data in memory rather than going to the disk drives for each I/O — and does so *without* user intervention.

System Reliability and Economics

The original impetus for RAID was to add data protection in the event of misbehaving disk drives by writing the data in multiple locations. If a given disk misbehaves, then a hot spare disk can rebuild the data stripes so there is no loss of continuity in operating the system.

The growth in disk capacity has provided the opportunity to re-visit the basic economics and safety (price, footprint, and MTBF) of the array.

As databases (and the related number of disk drives needed to store the data) continue to grow, the older notion of lots of little drives is questionable from the simple point of reliability. Given that newer, larger-capacity drives are faster than older, smaller drives, the issue of reducing the number of active devices in a system also provides for improved MTBFs — the long-proven logic of system reliability dictates that a system with fewer components will produce longer MTBFs because there are fewer devices to misbehave.

Cabinet footprint has also become more of a pressing issue as users find their facilities space outgrown (cabinet footprint size, weight, and heat). In addition, co-location companies may charge their clients in terms of floor space or rack space consumed. A terabyte of 18-GB drives consumes seven 9-bay racks, while a terabyte of 73-GB drives consumes two 9-bay racks — a savings of 35 vertical inches (or 20 U) in the rack, not to mention the savings in heat generation.

The Bottom Line

While both camps continue their arguments and individual data points, what matters most in determining performance is the application content. Given repetitive and intensive disk activity in the application (confirmed in the IOSTATs), an optimal approach lies in a combination of intelligent controller cache and large-capacity drives. Not all application content is created equal (in its randomness). New-generation, large-capacity drives are faster than their smaller (older generation) brethren. The presence of cache in the storage system sub-assemblies can provide substantial performance gains, but *how* the memory platform is implemented (FIFO buffer versus intelligent or "adaptive" cache) can have greater impact on application performance.

Users should use the available system utilities to know their application content. Vendors should know which mix of storage technology best fits the users' application.

Chapter 35

Adaptive Strategies for Disk Performance in Oracle

Bruce D. Rodgers

During the past couple of years, we have witnessed an explosion in the use of database engines (e.g., Oracle) at both the enterprise and department level of a wide range of businesses. The Internet environment has provided additional impetus for more dependence on these engines.

As user loads grow and data storage demands expand, a primary issue for many DBAs has been extracting maximum performance from the application, especially as performance relates to disk drive I/O. Increases in disk drive densities and spindle speeds have not kept pace with user demands to satisfy ever-changing performance demands. Database applications viewed as a necessary discipline of business management have evolved for many into a primary tool for competitive advantage.

As the use of the database engines has evolved, there are a number of behavioral issues that arise when maximizing system performance. Common problems include:

- Underestimating the size of the data storage needs
- Underestimating the rate of growth of the data storage needs
- DBAs often get little help in predicting the growth of their user community (translation = increased load on the application)
- Users typically do not throw anything away — there are also legal reasons for data retention
- DBAs often do not know their read/write mix
- DBAs often do not know the random/repetitive application content

The software approach — a fair number of offerings have been made in position papers as well as software utilities to assist DBAs in indexing disk drive activity and load balancing the application to squeeze more performance.

0-8493-1139-X/02/$0.00+$1.50
©2002 by CRC Press LLC

Application tuning by the DBA (focusing on changing the application software) has long fueled a growing consultative marketplace. Tuning can be an effective approach to gaining I/O performance, but the process can be long and tedious and requires thoughtful documentation.

The traditional hardware approach — for many years, solid-state disk (SSD) platforms have existed, first for mainframe environments and subsequently for server environments. SSDs (implemented purely in silicon) have provided the greatest performance leverage but at a very high price. In addition, using SSD platforms has required the DBA to have accurate knowledge of what data to migrate to the SSD platform in order to generate the desired performance gains.

Traditional SSD platforms have not been "adaptive" in managing the content of what data is resident in the silicon — if the application content changes, the SSD content also needs to change to continue to maximize the performance benefit.

Many users do not know what specific application content changes during a "normal" business day; this shifts the burden back to the DBA to continually isolate and migrate frequently used data to the SSD platform.

The other traditional hardware approach has been to stuff prodigious quantities of cache memory into the server to enlarge the staging buffer for I/O instructions. Such an approach can be effective in the short term but can also prove to be quite expensive.

CPU vendors often suggest buying more main memory. This additional memory is dedicated to internal data caching in the hopes of improving performance of I/O-intensive applications. The theory is that data will be available at high main memory throughput rates. Performance gains are realized *if the correct or "hot data" is available* from main memory. The actual hit ratio for main memory must be high or the improvement will be marginal.

Common pitfalls of main memory caching include:

- RDBMS caching schemes may not cache some files key to performance increases.
- Large main memory support is needed for OLTP systems. Some database servers can exceed a 32 bit system's memory-address-space-limit of 2GB or 4GB.
- CPU Memory caching may have *limited tunability* and may not adapt to dynamic changes in system requirements.
- OS and application demands for main memory are not static. Performance suffers if pageout is invoked. Swapping does not use aging to determine which pages are moved to disk. Hot data may be moved back to disk, or worse, less critical data may be held in memory while data more critical to system performance is moved to the paging device.
- Some CPU vendors map main memory to disk in case of a shutdown. Additional overhead, incurred by mapping large memory cache, consumes extra CPU cycles and I/O resources.

- Hot data can be flushed from CPU main memory during large reads leaving the main memory cache full of inactive data.

There Is Another Way...

Adaptive caching technology represents a new approach to the management of data. A combination of unique architectural design and advanced algorithms, adaptive caching, and dynamic RAID assignment delivers exceptional disk I/O performance improvements for database applications at a fraction of the cost of conventional SSD. Adaptive caching technology — without user intervention — automatically adjusts its contents to always contain the most frequently used information.

Cache Management and Dynamic RAID Level Assignment

(Cache here, cache there, everywhere cache, cache...)

Most storage providers have stuffed their systems with cache because of the potential performance leverage and relative cost position. Users will find cache on the disk drives, cache on the servers, and cache in the external RAID controllers (some as small as 32 megabytes, some as large as 8 gigabytes). The *presence* of cache is far less important than *how* the cache is implemented for the user.

Exhibit 35.1 illustrates how data patterns and block sizes in SEEK Systems' architecture are identified for cache retention. The dynamic space serves as a FIFO buffer, while the protected space section is where frequently used data is relocated and retained until more frequently used data bumps previously held information from the hierarchy.

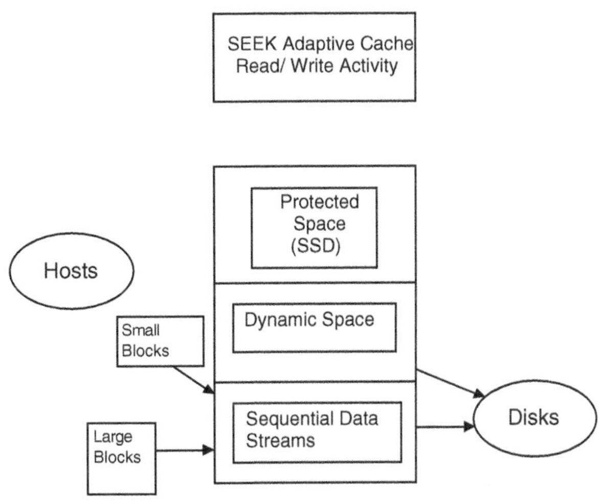

Exhibit 35.1 SEEK Systems' Architecture

The superior performance of adaptive caching can be traced to advanced memory management algorithms. Data in solid state memory can be retrieved 20 times faster than data on magnetic disk, so it is critical that active data stays in memory and inactive data is moved to magnetic disk. To accomplish this, SEEK's adaptive caching technology uses a combination of *least recently used* and *least frequently used* algorithms to maximize performance.

Normal Space: Least Recently Used Data

SEEK's controller architecture divides solid-state memory into *normal* (or *dynamic*) *space* and *protected space.* Similar to the operation of host-based cache, normal space uses a least recently used algorithm; as memory is needed for reads and writes, it replaces the least recently used data in the normal space with this new data. The operation can be compared to a stack of cafeteria trays, in which trays are added to the top and removed from the bottom.

The least recently used approach is the most common type of caching, and for buffering I/O, it is highly effective. However, this approach suffers from a problem known as *cache pollution.* Cache pollution results when reads or writes come through with data that is only to be used once, or perhaps a few times. This replaces data in cache that is being used repeatedly by the host — data that is much more important to keep in solid-state memory.

Protected Space: Least Frequently Used Data

To eliminate the problem of cache pollution, SEEK's RAID controller uses protected space. Whereas normal space uses a least *recently* used caching algorithm, the protected space uses a least *frequently* used caching algorithm. The controller actually tracks how much each data block is being accessed and moves the most heavily used data from normal space to protected space.

At any given moment, protected space looks just like conventional SSD. The data is safe from any cache pollution and will remain in solid-state memory until the controller algorithms detect that there is data that has become more active. By continually monitoring data activity, only the most active data is kept in protected space, ensuring SSD performance for most I/O operations regardless of application activity.

A common question about dynamic RAID assignment concerns the overhead needed to manage the process. Because of the efficiency of the architecture, adaptive technologies approach 90+ percent of the raw performance of traditional SSDs, which is of very high value given that the price points are 50 percent of traditional SSDs.

Other Acceleration Techniques

SEEK's RAID controller uses protected space and normal space to make sure that only active data is kept in solid-state memory. It also employs algorithms to optimize performance for disk reads and writes. For read operations, a common caching algorithm known as a *prefetch* is performed. When the host requests data not in memory, the controller not only reads the requested data from disk, but the data that immediately follows as well. This is because there is a good chance that the host will request this data next, and one large operation to disk is much more efficient than two smaller ones.

Prefetch can also be easily adjusted during operation for optimal performance. For online transaction processing, a value of two is generally optimal (for every block of data requested, an additional two prefetch blocks are returned); while for more sequential operations (backups, decision support), a prefetch multiple of four or five is preferred.

For writes to disk, a method known as *concatenation of writes* increases performance in much the same way that prefetch works with reads. When the controller writes information to disk, it pre-organizes data according to where it resides on the physical disk, and writes out data accordingly. The result is fewer, larger, and more efficient writes to disk. Every time disk writes are obviated, precious milliseconds of disk seek time are saved for the user. Carried to the extreme, the logic of this architecture says never go to the drives if possible — perform as many operations in silicon as economically possible.

Actual Acceleration Results

Relational database applications recognize some of the most impressive performance gains from adaptive caching and dynamic RAID assignment. Standard files that are moved into protected space include temporary tablespace (or workspace), transaction log files, and heavily used indexes and tablespaces.

Temporary tablespaces are where intermediary processing is carried out. For complex queries the activity to these tempspaces is particularly write intensive, as data is written and updated repeatedly. Table sorts, updates, joins, and similar commands are particularly taxing on this tempspace. Following are some of the performance improvements seen with various relational database benchmarks, by moving tempspace behind the adaptive SSD platform.

Exhibit 35.2 displays a benchmark that was a create/sort of 100,000 records, with one primary key and five alternate keys. There were three simulated users performing this concurrently, with over 62,000 operations per user. The application performance increased by 78 percent.

The benchmark in Exhibit 35.3 consists of a complex update involving three tables and over 72,000 operations. Adaptive caching increased performance by 98 percent.

Transaction log files can also be fairly I/O-intensive files, with a large percentage of writes. These files are where the database engine records transactions so that it can rollback tables to previous states should complications arise. How these files are used varies by database engine, but queries utilizing such commands as Rollback, Begin, Save, and Commit are particularly heavy in their use of the transaction log files.

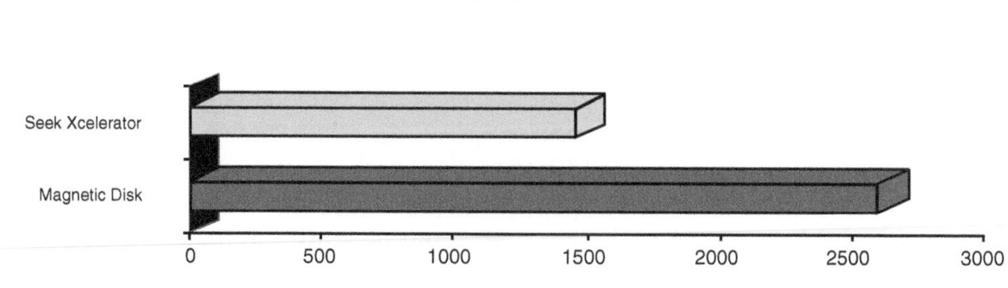

Exhibit 35.2 Create/Sort of 100,000 Records

The example in Exhibit 35.4 shows the performance gain for a particular database when the transaction log files were executed on the SEEK RAID platform. Performance gain was 25 percent for this benchmark, but jumped to 170 percent when a truncate was initially performed.

More Performance in Less Memory

The advanced algorithms of SEEK's adaptive caching architecture ensure that active data is kept in solid-state memory, where it can be accessed 20 times faster than if it resided on magnetic disk. In addition, I/O for inactive data on magnetic disk benefits from prefetch of reads and concatenation of writes.

Dynamic RAID Level Assignment — How It Works

RAID disk array systems suffer from a number of well-understood and fairly well-publicized problems. These problems include difficulties with customer education, configuration, and storage management, as well as a price premium over raw disk capacity. Additional performance penalties, such as multiple write updates to maintain redundancy and double copies of data through the array controller memory, compound these problems. Existing disk array controllers add complications because they are expensive and not very scalable. One way to resolve this problem is with a platform thrust comprised of RAID and intelligent caching technologies.

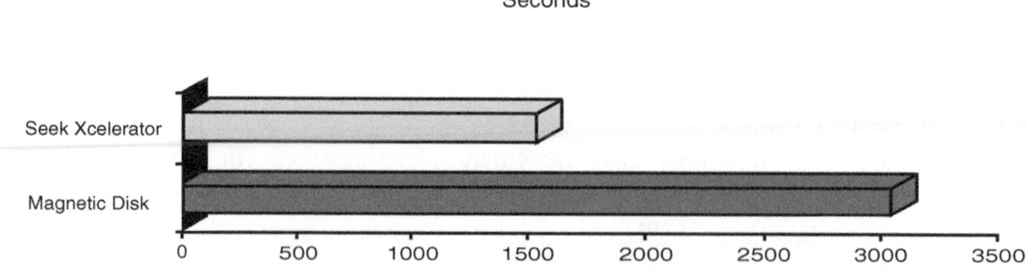

Exhibit 35.3 A Complex Update Involving Three Tables and Over 72,000 Operations

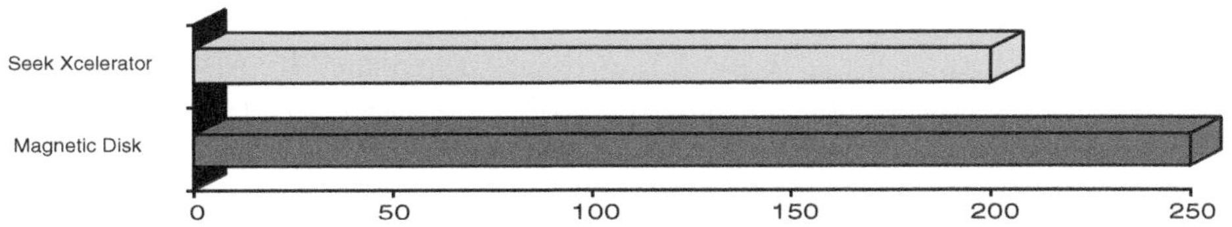

Same Benchmark Performed with a Truncate

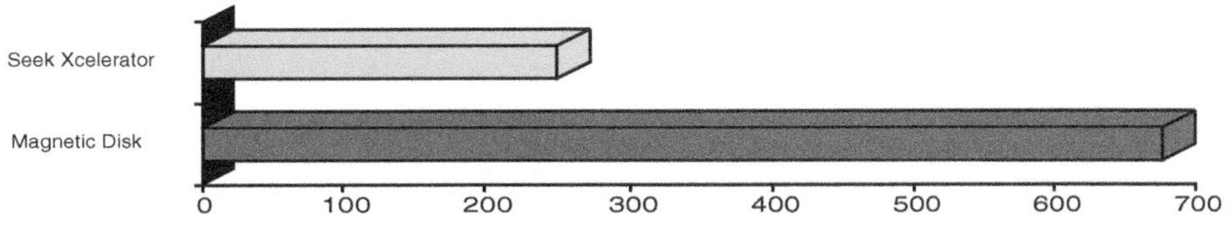

Exhibit 35.4 Transaction Log Benchmark

Within the last few years, disk systems based on RAID technology have proliferated to the point of becoming commonplace. Significant problems still exist in terms of education, configuration, and management of these disk array systems. Effective deployment and use of a RAID array require an understanding of system parameters such as I/O rates and request sizes under normal and maximized conditions. These parameters are generally either unknown or vary so widely that there exists no "typical" load for system tuning.

RAID manufacturers often do not allow dynamic changes to the RAID configuration once the disk array is initialized and in operation. Changing the number of disks used and the levels of protection provided at each target address often requires that data be copied to a backup device before the configuration changes. After the configuration changes, the managed disks must be re-initialized and the data copied again from the backup device. This process takes many hours or even days, and while in progress, the disk array is offline and the host data is not available.

Adaptive caching technology provides an ongoing dynamic balance between the demands for maximum I/O performance and for minimum disk capacity lost to RAID data protection. It allows the online addition of disk capacity to an existing disk array without backing up and restoring the existing data. By hiding configuration details from the user, it also allows the user to view the disk array as if it were just a bunch of disks (JBOD).

Adaptive caching technology exists primarily to minimize and, in most cases, eliminate the infamous RAID 5 write penalty. Because RAID 5 is the most frequently implemented and commercially successful of the basic RAID variations, this write penalty has caused customers great disappointment. The disk array software dynamically adjusts the storage method used for each host write request in order to eliminate the write penalty. The controller chooses the best RAID format for a request based on proprietary heuristics involving a number of variables. The architecture utilizes a block pool, with a section of reserved disk space, on three or more of the managed disks, available strictly to the memory manager. The controller allocates sections from the block pool to hold write data in temporary storage. The block pool allocation produces a holding area for the write data formatted for the optimum RAID performance for a particular request. The memory manager uses the allocated space to perform the write operation at optimal speed.

Write operations from the host that would normally result in a RAID 5 write (with a write penalty) take place in this allocated space in the most efficient manner without changing the host's logical space. By choosing a block from the block pool with the correct depth and width parameters, the write takes place without a write penalty. As the memory manager allocates block from the block pool and inserts them into the mapped logical space, it adds the replaced disk blocks to the block pool for subsequent use (see Exhibit 35.5).

The block pool is a limited resource (the dynamic and protected spaces together can share memory from 128MB to 1024MB). The block pool allocation manager constantly evaluates the state of the block pool, and it acts to free entries based on garbage collection and least-recent-access. In essence, the block pool manager acts very much like a secondary cache memory manager between the RAM cache and the RAID 5 disk space.

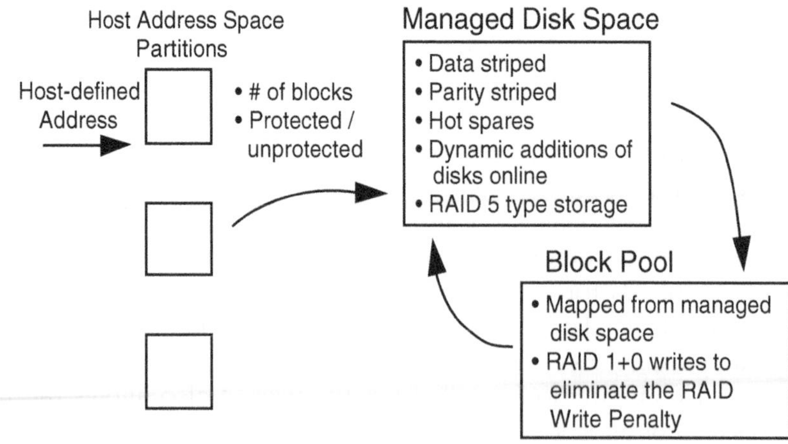

Exhibit 35.5 SEEK Systems' Controller Technology Maps Correctly Sized Blocks into the Existing Logical Host Space

Memory Management

One hundred percent memory storage is the purest form of I/O performance (e.g., SSDs). But it is very expensive — $70 per megabyte, versus $1 per megabyte for rotating media. Adaptive technologies optimize this trade-off by analyzing how frequently the host or hosts need data. Requested data is cached. To eliminate cache pollution, the algorithm separates active cache and stores it in protected space. This discrimination technique bridges the disk/memory barrier. Users receive memory storage performance but a significantly reduced price. The process of dynamically staging "hot data" is known as adaptive caching.

Other traditional cache techniques are used — write thru and write back. Both offer performance improvement from all peripherals on the SCSI bus. However, write-back cache delivers the most significant I/O performance improvement. The difference between the two occurs in the role the CPU plays. When writing to disk, a controller with write-back cache holds the write in a cache buffer, but signals to the CPU that the write has already been completed.

This frees the CPU to go on to other tasks instead of waiting for the write to actually be written to the disk. With write-thru cache, the controller stores the write in a cache buffer but the CPU still knows the write has not been completed. In this case, the efficiency comes from the write concatenation process, in which writes going to the same sector of the disk are accumulated and sent as a larger block transfer.

The Bottom Line

The combination of adaptive caching and dynamic RAID assignment provides an easy-to-install alternative strategy for improving database disk I/O performance.

The technology is host independent (attaching to UNIX, NT, AIX, Linux, SCO, and other operating systems) and application independent (no code changes are needed in the application software). This powerful hardware technology has proven to be a very cost-effective strategy for immediately improving disk performance in database applications. Because of the unique caching architecture, the net effect of implementing the technology is increased CPU utilization (as I/O tasks are offloaded to the external controller) and decreased disk I/O activity.

Chapter 36

RAID and Oracle

David C. Sisk

There is significant confusion and debate in many organizations that use Oracle over when and what RAID technologies should be used, and under what circumstances. In reality, this is a fairly complicated topic that requires a broad understanding of many technical characteristics, so it is no big surprise that there is some confusion and debate. This chapter attempts to make this information clear and understandable. There is no single answer that works best for every installation and suite of applications. However, by learning the cold, hard facts, you will know how to design a solution that meets the necessary objectives.

Because of the complexity of this particular topic, this chapter is presented in two sections. The first section discusses the characteristics of commonly available RAID levels, and the second section discusses which RAID levels are appropriate for which Oracle files.

Characteristics of Commonly Available RAID Levels

The Typical Objectives

There are three objectives that RAID can potentially satisfy. The first is, of course, the most obvious: to establish fault-tolerance. All RAID levels except RAID0 satisfy this objective well. The second objective depends more on the RAID configuration selected: to improve performance. Specifically, this objective can be divided into improving read performance, improving write performance, or improving both. Of course, every good feature has its price, and RAID is no different. The third objective is a monetary concern: to satisfy the previous objectives in a cost-effective manner. Notice that these three are (of course) primarily conflicting objectives. The first step in selecting the appropriate RAID technologies is not yet a technical decision. The organization must rank the

0-8493-1139-X/02/$0.00+$1.50
©2002 by CRC Press LLC

objectives in order of importance. If fault-tolerance is a big concern but performance is not, then there is an easy answer to the question. If performance outweighs fault-tolerance, the necessary approach is also self-evident. If fault-tolerance and performance are both crucial, then be prepared to pay the extra bucks to satisfy those needs.

Common Flavors of RAID

Quite a few RAID algorithms have been constructed over the years. However, there is a subset that vendors normally offer. These choices and their characteristics are examined and compared with single disks below:

1. *RAID0: Disk stripping.* RAID0 requires at least two physical disks. Data is read and written across multiple drives, so disk I/O is relatively evenly spread. Writes can occur in a block or streaming manner (similar to non-RAIDed disks) as requested by the operating system or application software. Disk failure results in lost data. Compared with a single disk drive, RAID0 has the following attributes:
   - Better read performance
   - Better write performance
   - Inexpensive in cost
   - Not fault-tolerant
   - Storage equivalent to sum of physical drive storage in the array
   - Readily available from most vendors implemented in hardware or software
2. *RAID1: Disk mirroring.* RAID1 requires two physical disks. Logical writes are done by physically writing the data to both disks simultaneously and typically can be done in a block manner or streaming manner, as requested by the operating system or application software. Reads can be done using either disk. In the event of disk failure, data can still be retrieved and written to the surviving disk. Compared with a single disk drive, RAID1 has the following attributes:
   - Better read performance
   - Similar write performance
   - Expensive
   - Fault-tolerant
   - Storage equivalent to one-half the sum of the physical drive storage in the mirrored set
   - Readily available from most vendors implemented in hardware or software
3. *RAID5: Disk stripping with parity.* RAID5 requires at least three physical disks. On a logical write, a block of data is physically written to disk; parity information is calculated using the block just written plus blocks already existing on disk, and then the parity information is written to disk. For each logical write, four physical I/Os are required. In RAID5, the parity information is rotated among the physical disks to prevent

bottlenecks caused by a dedicated parity disk. Note that writes occur in a block manner regardless of whether the operating system sends a stream of data to be written or requests to write whole blocks. On a logical read, data is read from multiple disks in a manner very similar to RAID0. In the event of a disk failure, data can be reconstructed on-the-fly using the parity information, although performance will of course degrade. Compared with a single disk drive, RAID5 has the following attributes:

- Data is striped across multiple physical disks, and parity data is striped across storage equivalent to one disk
- Better read performance
- Poorer write performance
- Inexpensive
- Fault-tolerant
- Storage equivalent to N – 1 times the number of physical drives in the array
- Readily available from most vendors implemented in hardware or software

4. *RAID10 (or RAID0+1): Mirrored stripe sets.* RAID10 requires at least four physical drives and combines the performance gains of RAID0 with the fault-tolerance and expense of RAID1. Data is written simultaneously to two mirrored sets of striped disks in blocks or streams. Reads can be performed against either striped set. If a disk drive fails in one striped set, data can be written to and read from the surviving striped set. Compared with a single disk drive, RAID10 has the following attributes:
   - Better read performance
   - Better write performance
   - Expensive
   - Fault-tolerant
   - Storage is one-half of the sum of the physical drives' storage
   - Available from only a few vendors (at the time of this writing)

Hardware or Software?

Now that the RAID level algorithms have been described and some of their characteristics illustrated, there is a second consideration to discuss: Should RAID be done at the hardware level, software level, or some combination of both? In general, the best choice is to implement RAID at the hardware level. In most cases, all of the necessary logic and data transfers are handled locally on the array controller or RAID adapter without saturating the bus portions of the server's I/O systems and without requiring additional CPU cycles.

These devices, like the hardware they plug into, vary quite a bit in capability from vendor to vendor. Most RAID adapters will support RAID0, RAID1, and RAID5 configurations per channel and will vary in cache size from no cache up to 16 or 32 MB, with some current models approaching several hundred megabytes of cache. The cache will typically be used to balance improved read performance (by read-ahead of data) and improved write performance by caching physical writes. Most RAID adapters will have a setting that specifies whether the write cache is set to "write-through" (physically writing the information on disk before acknowledging the write to the operating system) or "write-cache" (providing acknowledgment to the operating system after the data has been cached for write but before it has been physically written to disk). Oracle Corp. recommends setting this parameter to "write-through." If a power outage occurs after the write acknowledgment is received by the operating system (and the database instance) but before the data is written to disk, then a datafile error will be encountered on the next start-up of the instance. There are a few RAID adapters that reliably overcome this problem by battery backup of the cache contents. In this case, even if the power fails, the contents of the cache that is not written to disk will be maintained by the battery until the power is restored and the server hardware restarted. If this feature is used to provide better write performance, then its resilience should be thoroughly tested prior to placing a database server configured with "write-cache" settings into production use. If the "write-cache" setting does not absolutely guarantee protection from data loss, do not use it. Check with your specific hardware vendor for detailed information regarding the functionality of the selected array controllers and their specific settings.

So what about software RAID? Obviously, if your budget does not allow hardware RAID, then software RAID is an option. Software RAID is least desirable for write-intensive applications; read-intensive apps are much less sensitive to its effects. In general, software RAID0 tends to be the least expensive in terms of operating system resources. The same volume of data is sent to the drives, with minor CPU resources required to decide where to split the data for striping. Software RAID1 tends to be much more resource-intensive. Again, minor CPU resources are required to provide the instructions to duplicate the data, but twice as much data must be sent through the I/O bus to the disk subsystems. The worst possible choice for operating system or software-level implementation is RAID5. Recalling that each logical write requires two physical writes and two physical reads, plus calculation of parity information, software RAID5 can easily saturate the I/O bus and spin the CPU into infinity. Avoid software RAID5 if at all possible. As an additional note, there may be some shortcomings in the fault-tolerance of some software RAID implementations. Although the operating system will protect itself as well as other files, low-level items such as boot loaders, master boot records, and other parts of boot partitions may be somewhat invisible to the operating system. For example, parts of the boot partition may not be mirrored when doing software RAID1. If the drive containing the boot partition fails, it may be very difficult to boot the server hardware. In most cases, hardware RAID eliminates this concern.

Finally, are there situations where some combination of hardware and software RAID might be sensible? Surprisingly, the answer is "yes." Only a handful of system vendors offer array controllers that support RAID10 (or RAID0+1). If RAID10 is strongly desired under this circumstance, a possible solution is to perform RAID1 mirroring at the hardware level, then RAID0 striping at the operating system or software level. This approach accomplishes the goal while placing a minimum of strain on the operating system resources.

Workload Considerations

Individual disk drives have a rather interesting characteristic. Disks are much less sensitive to the rate of data transfer (throughput) than they are to the volume of discrete I/O requests (workload). Disk throughput is very close to constant; the drive always spins at the same rotational speed. For highly random I/O, it will likely take longer for the data to be found than to read or write it. The disk arm can be in only one position at a time. For this reason, the number of I/Os per second will typically have a greater impact on disk access time than will the sheer volume of data. Most modern disk drives, regardless of their data transfer rating, rotational speed, or any other characteristic, will support 60 to 80 random I/Os per second or 80 to 100 sequential I/Os per second. This varies by vendor and model, so check with your specific hardware vendor to verify these numbers.

Identifying performance bottlenecks based on the workload of individual disks is fairly straightforward. If your application grossly exceeds the rated transfers per second capacity of a particular disk, then the disk I/O times (in seconds per transfer) will climb from the tens of milliseconds to hundreds of milliseconds, and the disk transfer queue will grow to double-digit size. Most operating systems provide utilities to examine this behavior and the statistics can be retrieved from the Oracle V$FILESTAT dynamic view as well.

When RAID technologies are used, this characteristic becomes a bit clouded and more complicated to analyze. However, use this simplifying assumption: the Oracle instance and the operating system will recognize a disk array as a single disk. With that in mind, you need to know the composite workload capacity of the disk array rather than the individual disk drives. Luckily, this composite workload is a reasonably straightforward calculation, based on what we already know about RAID algorithms. Below are the equations that will provide the theoretical read and write workloads as a function of the individual workload capacites of the disk drives, the number of drives in the disk array, and the RAID level used.

1. *RAID0:* All disks are available for read and write activity. The workload threshold of the array is essentially the sum of the workload thresholds of the individual disks. For consistency, the equation is presented with read and write activity separated.
   - RAID0 array max transfers/sec = (% reads) × (max transfers/sec/disk) × (# disks) + (% writes) × (max transfers/sec/disk) × (# disks)
2. *RAID1:* Both disks are written simultaneously, but data can be read from either disk. The read workload threshold is essentially twice the write workload threshold. The number of disks will always be 2, of

course, but the equation includes that parameter for consistency's sake. This equation provides the workload capacity for a RAID10 array.

- RAID1 array max transfers/sec = (% reads) × (max transfers/sec/disk) × (# disks) + (% writes) × (max transfers/sec/disk) × (# disks/2)

3. *RAID5:* All disks are available for logical reads (minus one disk's worth of storage used for parity information), but a logical write requires one physical write for the data, two physical reads to retrieve existing data to use in the parity calculation, then another physical write to store the parity block. In other words, a logical write requires four physical I/Os. Recall that these writes occur only at the block level. (Note that specific vendors may have variations on this algorithm, so check with your hardware vendor to verify its exact implementation of RAID5, then modify the given equation to reflect the specific algorithm used if it is different. The equation given below assumes the default algorithm, thus providing the most conservative estimate of workload threshold.)
   - RAID5 array max transfers/sec = (% reads) × (max transfers/sec/disk) × (# disks – 1) + (% writes) × (max transfers/sec/disk) × (# disks/4)

If you use only software RAID instead of hardware RAID, decrement the final numbers by 10 to 15 percent. If you use software RAID0 with hardware RAID1, decrement the final number by approximately 5 percent. It should be noted that these calculations are approximations and that workload information provided by the vendor will typically be the result of laboratory testing. As such, the true workload threshold of a disk array will vary with each installation, the specific mix of accesses, etc. However, these approximations will provide reasonably dependable information necessary to identify and alleviate disk-related bottlenecks and to perform the necessary planning to select a particular RAID configuration. In the exhibits below, a series of sample calculations have been performed to help provide insight into the characteristics of each type of RAID configuration. Assumptions for the first chart include four physical disks of size 4 GB each, having a vendor-reported workload threshold of 60 transfers per second. The second chart examines the same scenario using six physical disks. Both charts assume hardware-level RAID.

Possible configurations using four physical disks are displayed in Exhibit 36.1 and possible configurations using six physical disks are displayed in Exhibit 36.2.

Exhibit 36.1 Possible Configurations Using Four Physical Disks

Configuration	*Number of Disks*	*Available Space (GB)*	*Max Reads/Sec*	*Max Writes/Sec*
Single disk	1	4	60	60
RAID0	4	16	240	240
RAID1	4	8	240 (two arrays)	120 (two arrays)
RAID5	4	12	180	60

Exhibit 36.2 Possible Configurations Using Six Physical Disks

Configuration	*Number of Disks*	*Available Space (GB)*	*Max Reads/Sec*	*Max Writes/Sec*
Single disk	1	4	60	60
RAID0	6	24	360	360
RAID1	6	12	360 (three arrays)	180 (three arrays)
RAID5	6	20	300	90

As can be seen from Exhibits 36.1 and 36.2, RAID0 offers good read and write performance, but no fault-tolerance. RAID1 offers good read performance and half as much write performance, but provides fault-tolerance. RAID5 reclaims most of the space lost to RAID1, provides fault-tolerance, and offers reasonably good read performance but provides poor write performance. (In fact, RAID5 requires four disks to regain the same write performance as a single disk.) Also note that streaming logical writes, as well as block-level logical writes, to RAID5 arrays are handled as block-level physical writes. Finally, read or write workload capacity can be increased in any RAID configuration by adding physical disks.

Conclusion

We've essentially covered every practical aspect that you could possibly need to know about RAID characteristics, short of delving into operating system and vendor-specific implementations. The following chapter section discusses what all this means to an Oracle instance. Specifically, these RAID configurations are examined in the context of the Oracle files that live on them.

RAID Configurations

Redo Logs

Assume that redo log members are written to in a sequential streaming manner. Ideally, redo log members should be placed on dedicated non-RAID drives or dedicated RAID0 arrays consisting of a single drive in each array. Members mirrored at the Oracle software level should be placed on different drives or arrays to provide fault-tolerance. Redo log members should theoretically be the only files on these sets of drives. Recalling that a non-RAID drive (or a RAID0 "array" consisting of only one drive) will typically support 80 to 100 sequential writes per second. All but the highest intensity installations should find that workload capacity more than adequate. Ideally, each drive or array holding redo log members should be connected to physically separate disk controllers, or at least different channels on the same controller, to improve fault-tolerance. We mentioned single-drive RAID0 arrays above. Why create

RAID0 arrays consisting of single drives? There are hardware array controllers that will not permit any attached drive to be configured as non-RAID. One option in this case is to configure a RAID0 array consisting of only a single drive (if the array controller allows it). If you "stripe" data across a single drive, it is the same as writing to a non-RAID drive. Another option is to connect the non-RAID drives to non-RAID drive contollers. Do what works best for your particular hardware, but remember that a non-RAID drive and a single-drive RAID0 array are essentially the same thing. If necessary, ask your hardware vendor for help in making this decision.

Keep in mind that it is crucial to mirror redo log members at the Oracle software level. It is well-known that redo logs are required for instance and media recovery, as well as instance operation in general. If the Oracle instance has any doubt that it made a "good write" to any particular redo log member, it will mark this member as "STALE." If the Oracle instance knows there are multiple copies of this redo log, it will simply archive one of the "good" copies and clear the stale copy. If the Oracle instance knows there is only one copy of this particular stale redo log, it will halt until a DBA performs the necessary corrective procedure. This halt will happen regardless of whether the redo log member is mirrored at the hardware level or at the operating system level. In either case, both copies are stale and cannot be used because the Oracle instance "sees" only one copy. Use Oracle-level mirroring for redo logs and forget about other means of mirroring these particular files. Make sure there are at least two members of each redo log group, or even three if your installation has extremely high availability requirements.

Is placing redo logs on hardware RAID1 arrays bad? Theoretically, no. But in practice, the answer is, in fact, yes. If you are using Oracle-level mirroring, as any good DBA would, you are simply wasting disk space and workload capacity. It can also be very difficult to explain to nontechnical decision-makers why redo logs must be mirrored at the software level even if they are mirrored at the hardware or operating system level. The best choice in practice is avoidance. The fault-tolerance gained from RAID1 arrays is unnecessary if one uses Oracle-level redo log mirroring. RAID5, whether done via hardware or the operating system, is typically the worst choice for redo logs given its write penalty and its block-oriented write algorithm.

What do you do if your installation is so write-intensive that redo logs on single dedicated drives are indeed a bottleneck? In other words, how would you scale up this configuration? Rather than using single drives, place the redo log members on RAID0 arrays with two or more drives each, keeping the mirroring at the Oracle level. Recall that for each drive added to each RAID0 array, you gain 80 to 100 sequential writes per second of workload capacity.

How would you scale down this configuration? If a workload capacity of 80 to 100 sequential writes per second is not needed, place the redo logs on arrays with other database files. Of course, still maintain the Oracle-level redo log mirroring by placing the members on different disk arrays or physical drives.

Data and Index Files

If performance is a big concern and availability is not, then just about all tablespace-related data files can be placed on RAID0 arrays. However, a situation where availability is not a big concern will seldom be encountered in our modern world of global commerce. Consider fault-tolerant configurations such as RAID1, RAID5, or RAID10 (or RAID0+1). Any of these configurations can be made to work well, particularly in a read-intensive environment, given one crucial requirement: enough drives in the array. Can a RAID5 array be made to handle writes faster than a RAID10 array? Yes, although it may require more drives to accomplish this goal with RAID5 than it does with RAID10, assuming the hardware supports that many drives in an array. In our age of technology, the question often becomes "should we?" rather than "can we?" There is one advantage in the Oracle software that is often overlooked: data files are, in general, written to only during checkpoints, and these writes are done at the block level. Checkpoint frequency and buffer cache size can be adjusted to accommodate all but somewhat extreme situations in many cases, softening the expense of less-than-ideal write capacity. The dollars saved on disk drives, however, may well be absorbed by additional memory required to allow the large buffer size necessary to hold a huge number of dirty blocks. Again, the question becomes "should we?" rather than "can we?"

In general, when a system must have an extremely high write capacity, data files should be placed on RAID10 arrays. As we saw in the first section, RAID10 provides fault tolerance and the best write (and read) performance. If RAID10 is not available as a hardware-based option, then perform RAID1 at the hardware level and stripe these RAID1 arrays using O/S-level RAID0. Using RAID10 or "RAID0+1" would typically be preferred over "striping" data at the Oracle level, as this approach requires extents to be manually allocated in data files on different disk arrays. An entire extent will typically be a "stripe" size that is a bit too large to adequately accomplish the intended goal. If done at the hardware or O/S level, the stripe size will be much smaller (typically the same size as or smaller than the database block size), thus providing the desired benefit of spreading writes across multiple physical drives.

RAID1 also provides good write performance. However, any database of modern size that supports a high volume of insert activity will surely require more than a single RAID1 disk array. If multiple RAID1 arrays are needed, why not keep life simple and stripe these into larger RAID10 arrays? Let the hardware or operating system do the majority of the "disk balancing" work.

In general, for a system with moderate write requirements and heavy read requirements, RAID5 is not a bad choice if it can be done at the hardware level. RAID5 provides fault-tolerance and is more cost-effective than RAID10. And with larger numbers of disk drives in the array, it will closely approximate the read performance of a similar RAID10 array. Recalling that writes to data files are done at the block level during asynchronous checkpoints, a large RAID5 array will accommodate a reasonable write workload. Recall also that one RAID5 array made up of ten disk drives will perform better than two

RAID5 arrays made from five disk drives each. Keep in mind that RAID0 will almost always provide the best write performance for data files. It does not provide any fault tolerance, but if budgets are limited, performance is crucial, and availability commitments are minimal, RAID0 will get the job done in a cost-effective manner.

SYSTEM Tablespace, Rollback Segments, and Temp Segments

Up to this point, we have focused primarily on data and index data files, but there are others to consider. In general, the same rules apply to data files for the SYSTEM tablespace, rollback tablespaces, and temp tablespaces. Specifically, it is crucial for data files for the SYSTEM tablespace and rollback segments to be placed on fault-tolerant arrays if availability is a concern. The instance cannot function if these tablespaces are inaccessible. In the modern world of large Enterprise Resource Planning (ERP) systems, data warehouses, and Web-based commerce systems, the SYSTEM tablespace is likely to be one of the smallest and most lightly used tablespaces in the database. Rollback segments typically will not be used more than data and index tablespaces, so apply rules similar to those for data and index tablespaces. Temp segments, however, can be handled a bit differently in some cases. If temp segments are crucial to the operation of a particular system (meaning crucial functionality is not available without the ability to perform large sorts, build indexes, etc.), then follow the same rules as for other database files. If little functionality is impacted without temp segments available for sorts, place them on a RAID0 array or even a single disk drive if the requirements are minimal. Even if these drives fail, the temp segments can be dropped and recreated in a temporary location with no loss of permanent data.

Archive Logs, Control Files, Oracle Software and Configuration Files

Ideally, the archive log destination should be fault tolerant. If it becomes unavailable, the database will halt until the condition is corrected. Archive logs are written asynchronously as whole files, so with the exception of extremely high change activity, RAID5 can be a good choice. If the particular system needs to handle an extremely high rate of change activity, then RAID10 may be required, although this requirement would be unusual. There are several instance-level settings to adjust how archive logs are written, so in most cases any write penalties can be overcome without exceptional difficulty.

Control files are rarely a performance concern but they are an availability concern. Because they will typically be quite small compared with other database files, these can go onto fault-tolerant disk arrays or single drives almost without being noticed. Always mirror control files at the Oracle level regardless of any other fault tolerance because it will certainly be noticed if they are lost or inaccessible. The Oracle software and configuration files should ideally be placed on fault-tolerant arrays. These files will typically have insignificant read requirements compared with other database files and essentially no write requirements. However, the Oracle instance cannot function without them. Fault-tolerant disk arrays for datafiles are useless if the software or configuration files are sitting on a failed drive.

A Sample Configuration Model

Exhibit 36.3 depicts a sample configuration model based on the information discussed above. Because RAID5 offers fault-tolerance, good read performance, and the all-important cost-effectiveness, we will start with that configuration and discuss the steps to take when RAID5 simply will not meet the necessary requirements.

Examine Exhibit 36.4 to get a feel for the approximate workloads that can be supported without performance degradation.

Note that this model assumes that fault-tolerance for redo logs is established through Oracle software-level mirroring, and all other fault-tolerance is established through hardware-level RAID.

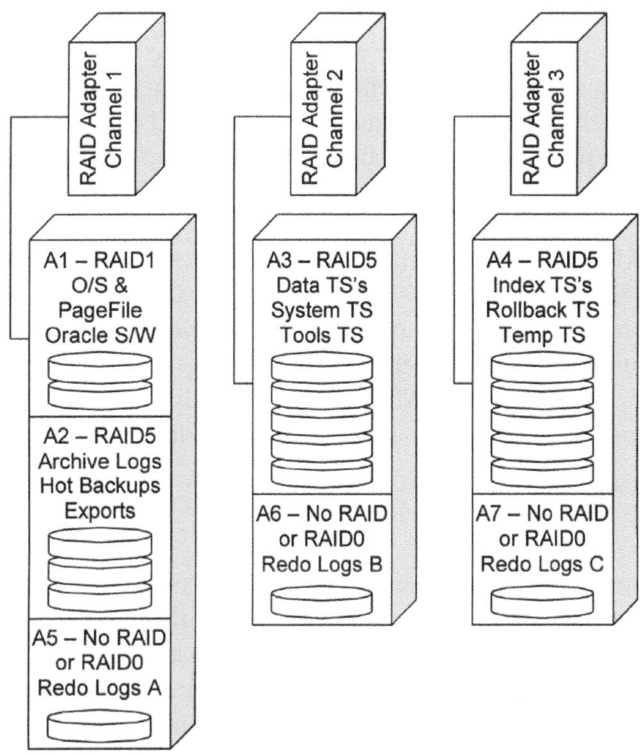

Exhibit 36.3 Sample Configuration Model

Exhibit 36.4 Approximate Workloads

Array	*RAID Level*	*Number of Disks*	*Workload Capacity (empty): Writes per second*	*Workload Capacity (empty): Reads per second*	*Primary Use*
A1	RAID1	2	60	120	O/S and software
A2	RAID5	3	45	120	Archive logs
A3	RAID5	5	75	240	Data
A4	RAID5	5	75	240	Index
A5	RAID0	1	80	80	Redo logs
A6	RAID0	1	80	80	Redo logs
A7	RAID0	1	80	80	Redo logs
Sum		18	495	960	

Scaling Up or Down

In general, scaling down would involve simply removing disk drives and consolidating disk arrays. In its most scaled-down form, this model would consist of all files stored on a single RAID5 disk array. This would be far from ideal, but it should work quite well for small installations and low-volume applications.

Scaling up this configuration while retaining the fault-tolerance is much more interesting, as there are essentially three distinct approaches that could be taken, although the approach may be determined by the limitations of the hardware in question. Below are three possible approaches in the order of least difficult and expensive to most difficult and expensive:

1. Add additional drives to the disk arrays, up to the maximum supported by the hardware.
2. Add additional disk arrays and array controllers, again up to the maximum supported by the hardware.
3. Change the RAID5 to RAID10, or the equivalent as supported by the hardware, and adjust the number of disk drives.

Conclusion

As stated earlier, there is no single configuration that will satisfy the requirements of every installation. Ideally, a solution that meets the availability, performance, and fault-tolerance needs of each installation should be individually engineered. The author hopes that the information presented in this chapter is sufficient to allow that process to occur with minimal guesswork. In all likelihood, however, this information leads to yet another question that is not possible to answer in this chapter (or several volumes of books, for that matter): How many database-level reads and writes are required to process one transaction? Obviously, it depends quite heavily on the application and its characteristics. In most cases, the only way to answer that question is to monitor a production system and extrapolate the numbers. This task is certainly possible for an existing production system, but it is a bit more difficult when planning a new system.

Chapter 37

Visualizing the I/O Signature

Gary E. Sharpe

Using new visualization technology, it is now possible to observe the "I/O signature" of a production Oracle database, averaged over intervals of several hours to a week of workshifts or longer. Analysis carried out on some of the best-managed production servers in leading enterprises results in the conclusion that the logical I/O generated by users and applications is usually poorly matched to the capability of the disk storage resources on which the database and system files reside.

As a natural consequence of the relational architecture, sets of schema-related objects become mutually active under the influence of applications and queries. Over any given work-shift interval a small number of such sets will, on average, be much more active than all other sets. This means that logical I/O activity over that interval is concentrated in a small percentage of the logical volumes of the database. In an active production system, the result is a tendency for the physical disks on which these "hot volumes" reside to become loaded beyond their efficient capacity. When this happens, queuing of I/O transactions will occur on these devices, disk-access service time will increase geometrically, and processor I/O wait time will consume a higher than appropriate percentage of server processing capacity. Faced with performance degradation, management may decide to invest in a processor upgrade, a solution that may not significantly improve response and throughput. The server has become I/O bound and will not scale in performance. Such a condition is unnecessary and can be avoided. This is because, as can be easily observed, perhaps two-thirds of the remaining disks (on average) are barely being utilized during this same interval and are available to handle a large share of the I/O load.

0-8493-1139-X/02/$0.00+$1.50
©2002 by CRC Press LLC

Overloaded disks are often referred to as "hot disks," a reflection of their inability to deliver efficient performance beyond fixed physical limits. The nonlinear and highly skewed nature of Oracle object activity is revealed in its physical I/O signature. The same "hockey stick" characteristic is reflected in all activity parameters as the visualization process drills from the physical to the logical domain.

Techniques have been developed for relocating Oracle's logical components so as to extract the maximum performance from the disk resources on which they reside. This is called "optimal physical placement of database objects," and the methodology can be referred to as "placement tuning." In a well-tuned system, three conditions are met:

1. Oracle's logical I/O signature generates physical I/O that is distributed across available storage resources; the result is that the average activity of each disk device is maintained well within its capacity for efficient work.
2. Where necessary, a logical entity or group of entities is striped across several disks so that their physical I/O bandwidth adds to support the logical I/O generated by the application load.
3. The database schema is specifically designed to best facilitate a state optimal placement to be attained (referred to as "placement-aware" schema design).

Historically, in pursuing performance management in order to maintain contracted service levels, most Oracle DBAs have been able to operate solely in the logical domain, ignoring their relationship with the physical platforms. This is no longer an acceptable practice. The first section of this chapter discusses the industry and technology trends that are driving the need for new awareness about the way Oracle interacts with, and is limited by, available server resources. It then reviews related requirements and methodology. The second section presents three examples showing the benefits that can accrue when attention is paid to physical placement tuning.

Industry and Technology Trends

Storage and User Growth

In the world of information technology, nothing is growing faster than the Internet and the volumes of data stored on enterprise servers. In fact, forces driving these two trends have something in common. The complexity of managing this massive store of information so that it is responsively accessible to desktop clients grows in proportion to its volume and competitive value to business. IDC estimates that, in 1997, UNIX enterprise users installed more attached storage than in the prior 30 years combined. Sun Microsystems recently announced that it shipped 1.6 petabytes of storage in the past year, or about six-and-a-half terabytes each business day. Even this trend is accelerating.

International Data Corp. (IDC) said that, in 2000, suppliers shipped ten times the storage capacity shipped in 1997. By 2002, UNIX and NT growth will dwarf mainframe storage, which will by then account for little more than two percent of the total server storage market.

Static Disk Performance

Gains in disk technology continue unabated. However, that development has succeeded only in yielding ever-higher areal data densities for the same OEM cost per drive. Vendor competition for user dollars therefore focuses on offering the lowest possible cost per megabyte by reducing the number of disks, accomplished by employing the highest possible capacity per individual drive. This is unfortunate because, for a given capacity, it results in a small number of devices being available to meet the access requirements of applications.

Worse, while end-user price per megabyte has plummeted, the disks on which a database is stored are not significantly faster than a decade ago. The disk drive remains the only component in today's computing systems to which Moore's law does not apply. Mechanical disk latencies now consume 95 percent of the time required to execute each physical I/O — a massive 13,000 microseconds on average — especially significant considering that each Oracle I/O generates hundreds of physical I/Os. Improvements in I/O interconnect technology are largely swamped by huge mechanical disk rotation and seek latencies. Disk cache helps mask these delays, but only if important data can be maintained resident, an increasing challenge for databases trending toward terabyte territory.

Increasing Need to Mask Disk Latency

By its nature, an RDBMS like Oracle generates a large number of physical I/Os during each data-base transaction. For example, a single transaction resulting from a mail-order operator's depression of the *enter* key could result in 100 files being accessed or updated before control is returned to that operator less than one second later. Simultaneously, several hundred other operators may require similarly efficient access to these same files. Since an individual disk drive can efficiently perform no more than 50 to 70 random (or 200 to 400 sequential) physical I/O operations per second, pains must be taken to ensure that the mechanical capabilities of many disk drives working together are applied to the workload. Note that a disk drive can be pushed beyond this level of work, but service time and queue length will escalate rapidly.

Traditionally, the DBA has sought to tune a database system for appropriate performance by operating entirely within the logical regime. The methodology governing Oracle parameter tuning and schema design, and for optimizing application SQL for fast execution, is both widely practiced and documented. However, neither the need for placement tuning nor its principles are well understood. The techniques are seldom taught and little has been written on the subject.

Rapidly growing databases and heavily loaded applications now make lack of proactive placement tuning the critical "missing link" in many Oracle shops, and an increasing source of systemic server performance loss. To correct this situation, the DBA must conscientiously develop strategies for masking storage latencies, effectively making them invisible to applications, through "optimal physical placement" of database objects — parallelizing physical I/O as it relates to the mutual activity of Oracle objects. Physical placement is a difficult, time-consuming job because hot disks are difficult to detect and nearly impossible to predict.

Further, true optimization requires that the Oracle schema itself must be designed to facilitate physical placement of objects. This raises important new issues, especially with the introduction of table and index partitioning in Oracle8. Also, Oracle8's integration of traditional and complex datatypes, each having distinctly different I/O signatures, further complicates the matching of logical requirements to physical resources.

Oracle's I/O Signature

Production systems employ very large numbers of logical entities, including tables and indexes, tablespaces, logs, and many other system files and volumes. Groups of entities are mutually related by schema design, and therefore become mutually active, depending on the nature of each transaction or query being executed. Over a given workshift interval, database activity typically appears concentrated in a small subset of mutually related entities. Because logical activity directly generates corresponding physical I/O activity, the same characteristic also appears naturally among the physical disks on which the logical entities reside, unless specific action is taken to intervene. Exhibit 37.1 shows the Oracle physical I/O signature that can be observed on a typical, hard-driven production server.

Exhibit 37.1 shows the load imposed on individual disk drives in the system. Note that this is not a short-term instantaneous phenomenon, but rather the average condition over the interval being analyzed — in this case an entire workshift. A similar pattern is seen both for shorter and longer intervals. The dashed line indicates the maximum rated physical I/O capacity of an individual disk drive (that is, the point beyond which service time becomes unacceptable). The striking fact illustrated is that, while a significant proportion of the disks in the system are loaded beyond their efficient capacity, and therefore queuing, an even larger number are virtually idle on average.

Effect on Processor Performance

The impact of these systemic performance losses, resulting from I/O-bound processes, can be seen by observing the distribution of server activity over the same interval represented in Exhibit 37.2.

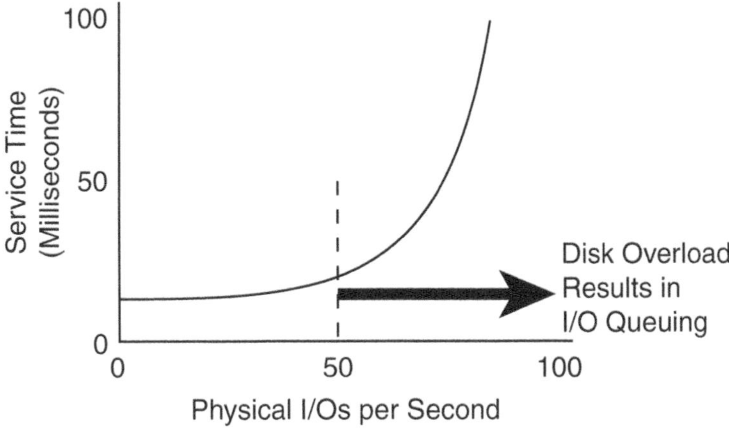

Exhibit 37.1 Application Service Time, Relative to a Single Disk

Note that the server is reporting that roughly 50 to 60 percent of its capacity is being consumed in I/O wait time over the entire workshift. In fact, idle time — spare capacity — is less than one percent averaged over the period. This server has become severely I/O bound due to improper physical placement of critical and active volumes. At the same time, the majority of available storage resources are nearly idle (see Exhibit 37.3).

Faced with lagging transaction response and throughput performance, management may be tempted to add more memory or CPU nodes to the server, but this is not the answer. Performance cannot be made to scale and the investment will be wasted because the system cannot use additional processing capacity. In his book, *Oracle Performance Tuning and Optimization with CD-ROM* (Macmillan Computer Publishing, 1996), Edward Whalen,

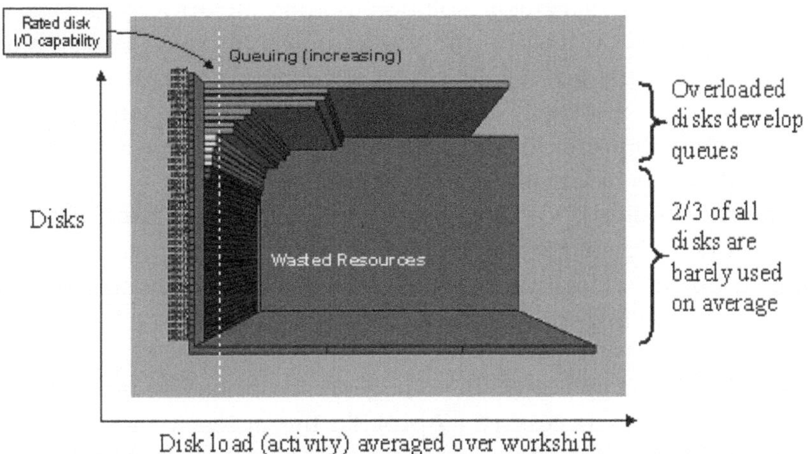

Exhibit 37.2 Typical Oracle I/O Signature with Respect to Available Disk Resources

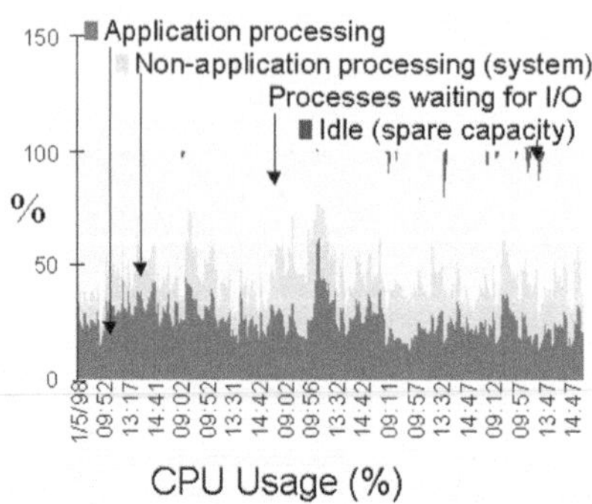

Exhibit 37.3 Distribution of Processor Cycle Related to this I/O Signature

of Performance Tuning Corporation, defines a well-tuned Oracle server as one that is CPU-bound. This condition clearly cannot exist when processes are waiting for I/O.

Placement Tuning Methodology

When we visualize the situation in this manner, and with additional subsequent analysis, it becomes a straightforward matter to develop the required solution to remove the source of performance loss. The goal is to make sufficient I/O bandwidth available to the processor so it will burn fewer cycles waiting and expend more time doing productive work. This requires intervention in the distribution of disk workload, to relocate highly active volumes and files from disks which are building queues to those which are largely idle during the interval assessed. The key point is to be able to measure or predict which entities are rendered mutually active by Oracle during application execution. The optimal physical placement solution is thus inextricably linked to both the database schema design and the workgroup transaction or batch application loads. Further, any given solution must be optimized with respect to one or more particular workshift intervals of greatest importance to business operations, and compromised across the application mix prevailing at the time.

Placement is fundamentally governed by the available budget of random and sequential physical I/Os associated with each disk device. These values should never be exceeded in the average condition for the interval being dealt with. Based on this principle, optimizing physical placement involves three discrete steps, as follows:

1. Individual volumes and files, in general, should be striped across as many drives as necessary to provide the access bandwidth required, plus an additional safety factor for peak loads and growth within the interval. Thus, if an application file or volume requires an average of 200 random reads and writes to maintain service-level adherence during a critical interval, it should be initially striped across at least five or six

drives. As activity grows, the stripe width can grow to employ additional drives; however, it is usually better to avoid stripe widths of more than a few drives, as they are unnecessarily cumbersome, and focus instead on separation of entities and their relocation to new dedicated disk stripesets.

2. The second step is to distribute files and volumes that are mutually related to one another by virtue of the Oracle schema design, and therefore become mutually active under application loads. It is only necessary to relocate those that are seen to be highly active — the so-called hot objects during the interval being optimized. Starting with the most active and working down, a point will be reached where further relocation ceases to improve performance. At this point, placement may be judged optimal, and all physical devices will be safely loaded. For example, consider how the hot objects in a mutually active entity set might be properly distributed. A table and a related index are each assigned to separate dedicated tablespaces, each of which in turn is assigned to a separate two-disk stripeset. Each entity generates an average of 80 physical I/Os per second during a critical interval, well within the I/O capacity of a two-disk stripeset. A total of four disks is used to achieve maximum performance. A total of ten I/Os remains on each disk device to allow for growth, or for use by entities of low or periodic activity.
3. The third step is to maintain proper distribution among two or more sets of mutually active entities that may be loading the server. Consider that a financial batch program and a manufacturing application may be simultaneously undergoing heavy use by departments. Each application generates its own I/O signature, in which there are active entities that must be striped and distributed. It is therefore necessary to ensure that, even as each individual set is properly distributed, co-location of entities from each set is not allowed to occur in a manner that would produce unwanted device overloads.

Clearly, while these steps are simple and even obvious, their application in real-life systems is another matter. Determining exactly which entities and which disks are hot, how they are related, and then solving the problem of what to do about it is made complex by the sheer number of logical and physical components in modern systems.

A typical Oracle Financials application has been observed to comprise 7500 tables and 11,000 indexes; this does not include system files or other files and volumes that may be co-resident and loading the same physical devices. Optimally distributing related files and volumes is a daunting task.

Non-Oracle file activity is extremely important in considering a solution. While the DBA tends to think in Oracle space alone, adequate for standard Oracle and SQL tuning, the entire logical and physical environment must be analyzed and understood when placement tuning. For example, if a non-Oracle system file is consuming an interval-average of 100 I/Os from a two-disk stripeset, that stripeset cannot be a relocation destination for an Oracle file requiring bandwidth of 70 I/Os. (In fact, in this case, the system file itself should be restriped to three disks to provide additional headroom for growth and peak loads.)

RAID and EMC Systems

The discussion to date has not made a distinction between placement on storage systems comprised of large numbers of individual channel-connected disks, and cached controller-based systems employing RAID or other architectures. Some differences should be noted.

Modern RAID systems, originating with OEM manufacturers like CLARiiON, Symbios, and Compaq's StorageWorks unit, usually configure five-drive disk groups as RAID-5 stripesets. This means that all volumes, although striped by default across five disks, appear resident on a single large disk of four times the size (parity consumes one-fifth of the capacity) and five times the read bandwidth (write bandwidth is less because the need to record parity consumes an extra write and read). The principles of optimal placement still apply; however, striping is less of an issue, although volumes are sometimes striped across two disk groups when greater bandwidth is required. Also, placement opportunity is actually decreased by the presence of hard-wired disk grouping.

EMC storage systems present a special case in which the need and opportunity for optimizing physical placement remains undiminished. EMC also supports what is called "RAID-S" but, instead of striping the physical disks to create a large system disk, it creates logical disks called hypervolumes that map only to the disk drive on which they reside. Using this technique, the systems administrator can control which logical entity resides on each disk. The administrator can also command the VM (volume manager) to enable striping to increase I/O bandwidth.

Curiously, some administrators choose not to stripe at all, which means that all the I/O of a busy volume can be concentrated in a single disk. This can have detrimental performance characteristics and indicates a lack of understanding of the principles of storage tuning.

RAID systems invariably include moderate to very large disk caches, partially compensating for massive disk latency and inadequate striping. But if the database is very large, the cache may represent only a percent or less of its volume, and cache pollution may result when hot entities are displaced by the far larger volume of less active entities. Vendors have various strategies for mitigating this tendency, but none significantly reduces the need for optimizing physical placement.

Volume Managers

Today, virtually all UNIX servers are delivered with a volume manager (VM) and it is impossible to go very far in optimizing physical placement without using one. The VM provides vital information about volume activity and the means, through a graphical interface or scripted procedures, to carry out volume relocation solutions. A VM also facilitates adding and removing physical disks, logical volumes, and file systems. Volumes can be performance optimized, mirrored, or striped in RAID groups for redundancy and higher access bandwidth, or expanded and shrunk in size, by the systems administrator. However, the VM also works autonomously to add physical space as volumes grow, and this means that it can also create poor placement if allowed to do its work without manual intervention for performance management.

A volume is seen by Oracle as a logical disk. A few years ago when a two-gigabyte database was considered typical, a single disk could be dedicated to a file system. Often the first disk would be partitioned into slices for multiple file systems, such as *root, usr, tmp,* etc. There were always constraints as to number of slices, and once a disk was partitioned, as the database grew, it could not be changed without great difficulties.

The VM was originally invented to allow growing file systems to span more than one disk drive. As larger physical drives became available, the VM began to be used to partition the disk into smaller "sub-disks," but in a manner that allowed those partitions to be mirrored or moved from disk to disk in real-time for system management purposes.

Ironically, VMs were designed to make it easy to forget about the physical domain in fast-growing enterprise systems but, as we have shown, this is inconsistent with maintaining high performance. A VM can be a powerful tool in the hands of an expert who knows how to use it — but it is often ignored as an aid in Oracle performance tuning, specifically for physical placement. In a fast-growing system, an uncontrolled volume manager may actually generate poor placement and systemic server performance loss. The well-thought-out and orderly logical structure of the database schema can be reduced to spaghetti-like entanglements and hotspots at the physical level as the VM seeks free space for growing volumes, unseen and undetected by the DBA.

Case Studies on Placement Tuning

New Issues Governing Oracle Performance

The release of Oracle8 brings powerful new technological enablers into play. For the first time, there are few architectural limitations to database size; the new release has been advertised as supporting ten times the users, transactions, and capacity of Oracle7. It is also designed to combine traditional and complex data types like binary objects, each of which will load the storage systems with distinctly different I/O signatures. Bigger transaction loads will place a premium on striping for high I/O bandwidth. Finally, the popular table and index partitioning feature, which enables objects to span tablespaces, adds a new abstraction layer between the logical and physical regimes, adding to the challenge as well as the importance of achieving optimal physical placement.

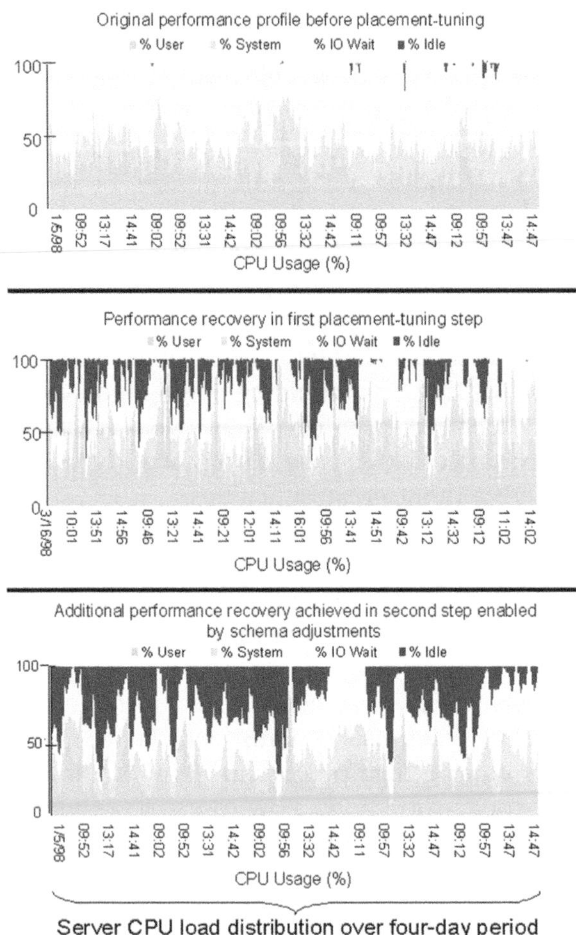

Exhibit 37.4 Relocating a Small Subset of Active Entities in a Production Server

Examples from the Real World

Several case studies are presented, demonstrating how leading Oracle users have dealt with placement tuning in optimizing the performance of production systems.

Example 1: Placement Tuning Recovers Lost Server Capacity, Increases Throughput

Exhibit 37.4 shows how significant gains in throughput and processing capacity can be made, merely by relocating a small subset of active entities in a production server. The server is a large processor with 16 nodes supporting more than a half terabyte of storage. The application is Oracle Financials. The charts show the process time distribution. As can be seen in the top chart, the system was originally severely I/O bound and reporting less than one percent average idle time over the four-day sampling period. Even worse, the processor is reporting a state of I/O wait more than 50 percent of the time.

The problem stems from disk overloads that are generating high service times in the five most active stripesets. Note that the top stripeset is generating service times that average 400 percent of optimal uncached value of 13 milliseconds averaged over four days, even though 2 GB of cache is available in the storage system. Drilling into this stripeset shows it to be comprised of 11 disk drives, and executing an average of about 500 I/Os per second. Drilling further into the logical volumes resident on this stripeset clearly shows that this heavy I/O load is being generated by some of the most important Oracle objects in the application. The user has made the stripeset unusually wide to handle the combined I/O load of many active volumes and files, yet unacceptable latency is still accumulating.

With this visual evidence, and with a total of 90 disks available, two-thirds of which are barely used on average, the DBA staff decided that a far better solution was to relocate the volumes on this stripeset to five new stripesets of four drives each, using the volume manager to carry out the action. The benefit gained from this is immediately evident in the second chart, which shows that an average of 17.5 percent in idle time was gained as a result, due to the corresponding reduction in I/O wait time. At the same time, an average increase of about 40 percent was seen in total I/Os per second for the volumes originally resident in the top stripeset. This resulted in a reduction of more than 60 percent in execution time for certain batch jobs.

With this success, the DBA team attempted a further optimization by creating several additional tablespaces, to permit separation of active tables and indexes that had been part of the same tablespace. This permitted additional volume relocation, increasing average idle time over the workshift interval to 22 percent.

In summary, nearly one-quarter of a large server's capacity was recovered, deferring any requirement for an upgrade costing several hundred thousand dollars. Simultaneously, the critical logical I/O throughput increased by an average of 60 percent. All this was achieved with only a few hours of effort. Once appropriate insight was gained, opportunities and solutions became obvious.

Example 2: Placement Tuning to Eliminate Undetected Conflict Between Critical Oracle and System Entities

Exhibit 37.5 explores an unsatisfactory situation that remained undetected in a multi-terabyte Oracle data warehouse. Exploration of a week's worth of production with drill-down visualization technology revealed periods of swapping that correlated with severe I/O wait-induced performance loss.

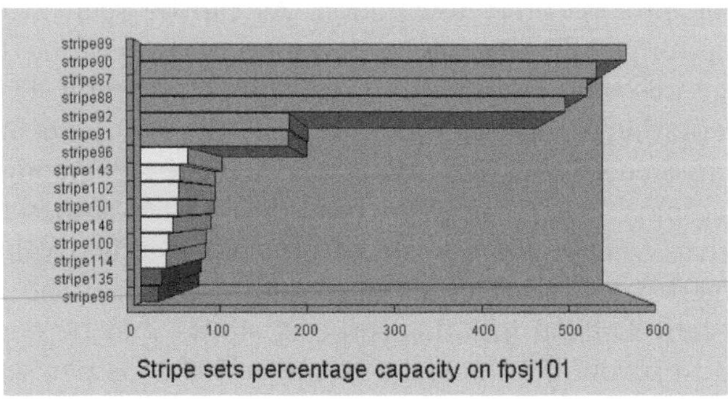

Exhibit 37.5 Four Very Hot Stripesets

Analysis started by looking at average service time for stripesets. Exhibit 37.5 shows four very hot stripesets. The default value for 100 percent service time is 13 msec. The graph shows that these four stripesets exhibit maximum average values of 500 to 600 percent of optimum, or 65 msec. Although the average is very high, peaks can be observed to range into the hundreds of milliseconds when the data is revealed in a chronological view (not shown).

Drilling into the four most active stripesets shows that they are, in fact, single disks. Further exploration reveals that resident swap files are the source of heavy I/O to two of these disks during critical intervals.

The read portion of the activity for two swap volumes is shown in Exhibit 37.6, each on a separate disk drive. Combined with write activity, it is clear that swapping is using most of the efficient I/O capacity of these drives.

This periodic swapping clearly correlates with CPU statistics during the same time period. Exhibit 37.7 shows that a large percentage of processor

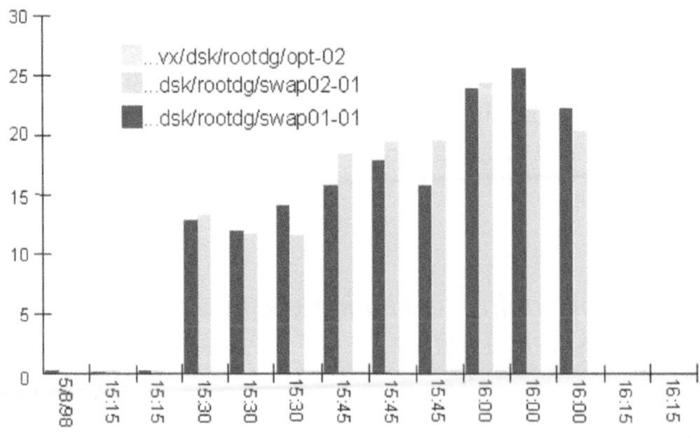

Exhibit 37.6 Activity for Two Swap Volumes

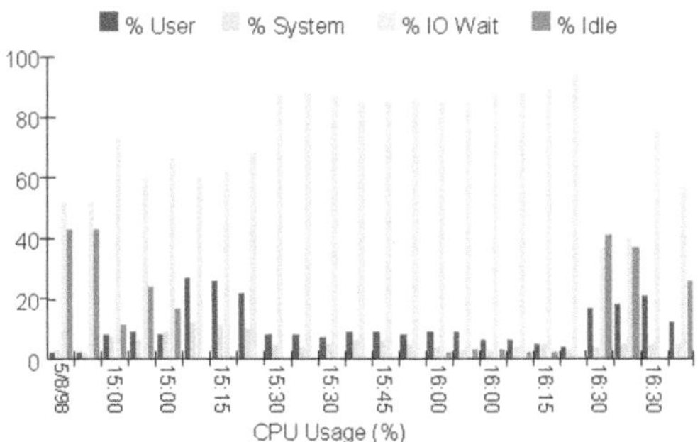

Exhibit 37.7 Service Time as Percent of Optimum for Top Fifteen Most Active Stripesets

capacity in the interval is being consumed in wait–I/O cycles, seriously affecting the performance experienced by users.

Ideally, enough memory should be available to avoid swapping, but this is difficult to achieve. In this case, the result was exacerbated by adverse placement of critical objects, making the impact of swapping far worse than it should have been. The precise cause is easily seen when we drill to view the co-resident volumes (Exhibit 37.8). Note that volumes containing Oracle redo logs are co-resident with the swap volumes, which are consuming most of the available device bandwidth. Because Oracle is only as fast as its redo logs, all related applications are being doubly impacted by swapping, specifically because of poor physical placement. This is confirmed when we look at the top-ten highest service times by volume in Exhibit 37.9.

One may well ask how situations like this can exist in a system administered by some of the best Oracle practitioners in the industry. The answer is that such circumstances are common because of the tens of thousands of logical entities that must be distributed across dozens or hundreds of disks, the

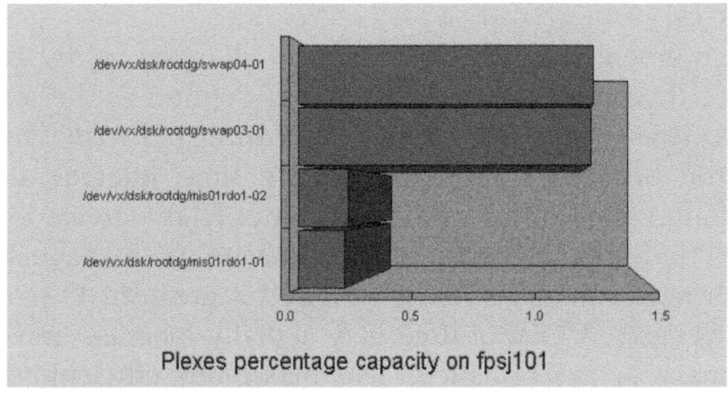

Exhibit 37.8 Co-Resident Volumes

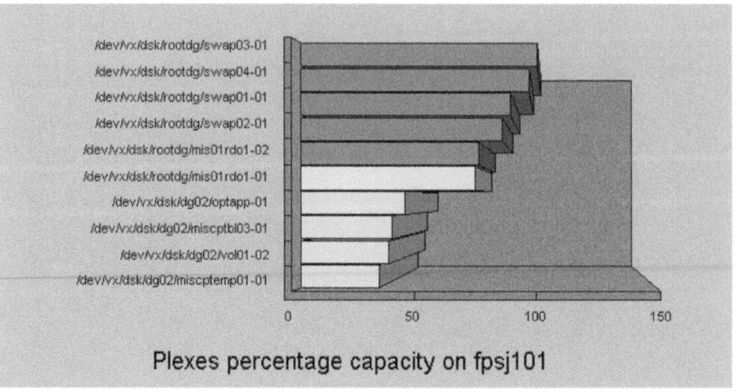

Exhibit 37.9 Top-Ten High Service Times Resulting from Co-Residency

absence of software with which to manage the interface between logical and physical domains, and the frequently crisis-driven nature of database administration. Under these conditions, oversights, inability to visualize conflicts, and even failure to detect performance losses are to be expected.

Example 3: Using Placement Tuning to "Cache with Finesse"

An OLTP server was analyzed and shown to have its most active Oracle tables and indexes well distributed in separate tablespaces for placement purposes. This provided administrators with the means to distribute related, mutually active tables and indexes on separate disk drives in order to parallelize I/O and prevent disk latency from accumulating. As a result, no Oracle database stripesets were seen to be overloaded during the sample period, as shown in Exhibit 37.10.

For example, peak I/O for *Stripe9,* a stripeset hosting active Oracle volumes and comprising six disks, was measured at 126 I/Os per second, or 21 I/Os per second for each of the drives, about one-third their individual capacity. No problems were thus found in the Oracle space, yet the IT staff remained concerned about periods of degraded performance that correlated with high I/O wait statistics.

The problem emerged when the view was changed to display the top-ten stripeset service time rankings. Service time is defined as the *total time taken by a process to execute an I/O request, including I/O wait time.* This is an important metric because during the service time interval, the requesting process is waiting and work is not being done. High service times, resulting in poor OLTP performance, sometimes motivate IT managers to purchase more processor nodes than would be required if greater I/O parallelism were present. In such cases, I/O wait time may actually increase and there may be little improvement in performance. The maximum efficient service time is about 13 milliseconds for a non-cached RAID or disk I/O, and around 3 msec when cache residency precludes a physical I/O. Exhibit 37.11 normalizes service time statistics with reference to 13 msec. Stripesets exceeding this value indicate performance loss due to I/O waits and queue development.

Exhibit 37.10 I/O Activity of Swap Files and Redo Logs Resident on the Same Physical Devices

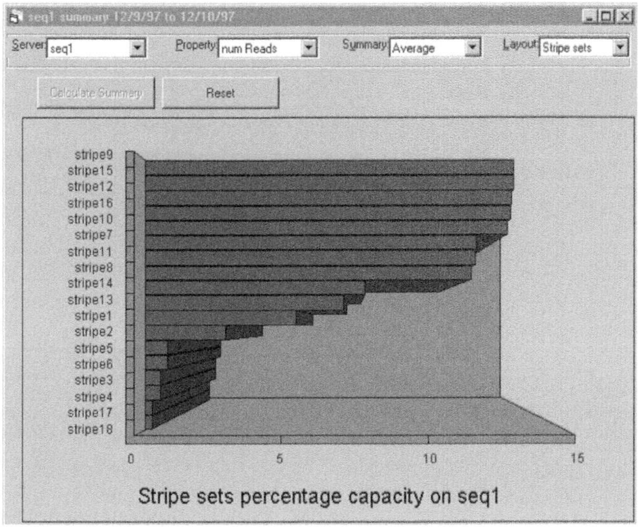

With service time selected as the property, this graph shows a different picture, with *Stripe1* and *Stripe2* indicating unacceptably high service times, 300 to 400 percent of the desired maximum. This is not a transient condition, but rather the average situation over a seven-hour period for two consecutive days. If the volumes on these stripesets are important in the execution of business applications, we have detected a serious source of performance loss.

Exhibit 37.11 Normalized Service Time Statistics to 13 msec

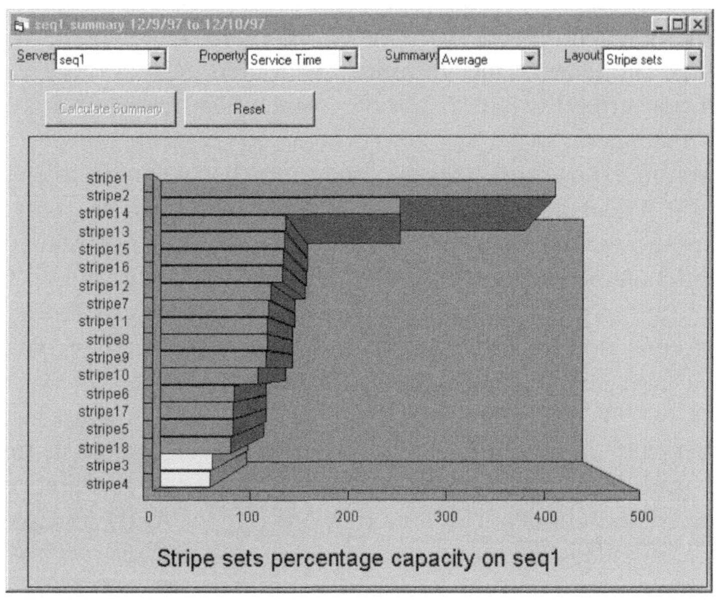

Exhibit 37.12 Selecting *Stripe1* and Drilling to Its Disks

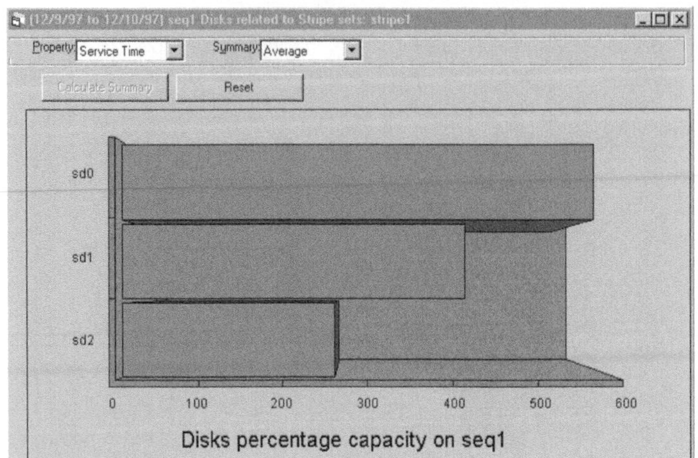

The questions are: What resides on these stripesets? and What is the activity of each disk within a stripeset?

The next step is to search for overloaded disks within each stripeset that may be displaying high average service times due to interference within other stripesets (that is, crossed stripesets), or other Oracle or non-Oracle files. This is done by drilling down on the heavily loaded stripesets to determine both disk load balance and volume usage.

Selecting *Stripe1* and drilling to its disks shows its disk loads are not balanced, with varying service times. It is important to find the reason for this; only one disk need be overloaded to make the entire stripeset, and all its other disks, appear similarly overloaded — even if, individually, they are not. In Exhibit 37.12, the service time for the entire *Stripe1* is that of disk *sd0*. This disk either contains one or more additional active logical entities not shared by *sd1* and *sd2*, or the volumes distributed across *Stripe1* are concatenated and not striped at all, a mistake sometimes made through misuse of the volume manager.

This question can be resolved by drilling to the plexes in this stripeset. In Exhibit 37.13, it can be seen that the highest I/O load is *rootvol.* Further investigation shows that most of the I/O is writes and not reads. Note also that the third busiest plex is *SWAPVOL,* which is accessed when the system is forced to resort to paging, a prime indicator of inefficiency. These are critical system files and, although not part of the Oracle space, they have a fundamental impact on Oracle application performance.

Note that two of the plexes are pinstriped rather than solid in color. This indicates that they are each part of a striped volume that is, in turn, part of a stripeset. Solid bars indicate non-striped entities or, if resident on multiple disks, concatenated entities. (Entities that are part of RAID groups would be shown as cross-hatched.)

Exhibit 37.13 Drilling to the Plexes in the Stripeset

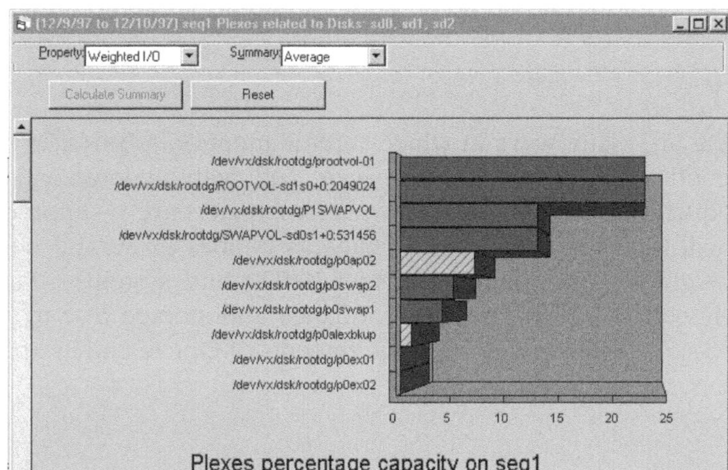

In concluding the investigation, it was determined that six non-Oracle system disks, including those discussed above, were all exhibiting very high write levels and unacceptable service times, and contributing to processor I/O wait time for all processes. Two of these were mirrored and included the root file system and swap space. To eliminate the resulting performance losses, it was decided to relocate the active volumes resident on these disks to a small, cached disk array. A cached disk array converts short sequential writes to long block disk writes, resulting in better disk utilization. In addition, a cached disk array provides a low service time on writes (until write cache gets filled, which would occur only on very heavy random writes).

It was also recommended that volumes containing redo log files be placed on the disk array. These were resident on two other high-service-time disks. The database can only update as fast as synchronous writes to the log file can occur. It was judged that with cache the physical writes would complete in 2 to 3 msec, compared with up to 13 msec or more in the prior placement configuration.

Two key points related to the vital importance of optimal physical placement in tuning Oracle for maximum performance are made in this example. Note that neither deals directly with Oracle itself, and yet both have everything to do with Oracle performance. First, the performance and placement of non-Oracle system files important to database execution are critical, doubly so if they share the same physical resources. Second, there may be no performance-based rationale for converting the entire storage system to a cached disk array. On the contrary, significant benefits can be achieved by relocating important, especially write-intensive files and volumes to an array of limited capacity based on optimal placement methodology. It can be theorized that a small array, dedicated to servicing a small but active subset of the logical system and database entities, can actually offer better performance, since its cache does not become polluted by the total volume of I/O generated by a far larger number of less active objects.

Summary

Clearly, there are many ways in which careful attention to physical placement of active entities can benefit performance. Left without intervention of this kind, load distribution is — and performance impacts are — unpredictable at best, and will tend to degrade into chaos as entities grow and needed free space is sought by the volume manager. DBAs and systems administrators must closely collaborate for total performance and storage resource management, based specifically on the I/O requirements of Oracle and its applications.

DISTRIBUTED ORACLE SYSTEMS

Due to the volatile nature of corporate computing in the twenty-first century, many corporations are faced with the challenges of managing widely distributed Oracle systems, systems that span geographical areas, hardware platforms, and database architectures.

While some Oracle managers deliberately plan distributed Oracle networks, others are forced into distributed databases because of changes in corporate structure. Managers who are embracing "downsizing" and "rightsizing" migrations have created situations in which many diverse "islands" of information are spread across many computer networks.

"Open systems" has become one of the foremost buzzwords but very little has been written about the issues involved with managing a diverse network of Oracle databases and how to make disparate Oracle systems behave as a part of an integrated enterprise.

It is the responsibility of the Oracle database manager to ensure that all of the information resources within the organization communicate with each other. This "bridge-building" function is very foreign to the traditional manager who is accustomed to the centralized mainframe environment. The recent popularity of Web-based Oracle systems has also affected the expectations of the end-user community. Users now expect systems that possess sophisticated HTML and Java interfaces, and they demand multiplexing capabilities that can simultaneously access information from many Oracle databases.

There is more to distributed Oracle management than mastering the Net8 and replication technology. Successful managers are also aware of the psychological issues involved in distributing Oracle resources.

It is also the role of the system manager to ensure that all of the distributed Oracle systems remain intact — both from a physical and logical view. The Oracle manager must be able to ensure the same seamless connections and security that they were accustomed to in the mainframe days, and they must also ensure that the Oracle database performs at acceptable levels.

Chapters 38 and 39 explore issues surrounding distributed Oracle systems, specifically techniques for automating the distribution of Oracle client software and tools for Net8 and SQL*Net performance tuning.

Chapter 38

Automating Distribution of Oracle Client Software

Charles Mansfield

In today's client/server environment, Oracle administrators face the challenge of maintaining thousands of PCs that contain Oracle client software. Automating the distribution of Oracle software on each desktop is a formidable challenge, and most companies hire a staff of PC technicians whose job it is to manually distribute Oracle software to the PCs.

This chapter presents a solution to the time-consuming task of software distribution. With current technology, it is possible to automate the distribution using batch scripts and imports of Registry files in the Windows 95 and NT environment. Instead of requiring a visit to each PC to run the Oracle installer, the software can be installed on a central server, then shared by the entire enterprise. Only a subset of the Oracle client software must reside on the PC, and the distribution of these items can be automated with a log-on batch script that copies in the files.

While the concept of automating distribution of client software is simple, there are numerous details. This chapter briefly examines issues involved in automating client software distribution and outlines the necessary steps for the alternative described. The discussion begins by reviewing the potential product components for installation and client configurations, and then moves on to discuss distribution methods, alternatives, and Registry update methods.

Product Components

Oracle Client Software

Oracle has a host of software that resides on PC clients, and the Oracle installer (Exhibit 38.1) provides a list of some available and installed products in a

0-8493-1139-X/02/$0.00+$1.50
©2002 by CRC Press LLC

Exhibit 38.1 Oracle Asset Manager with Client Products

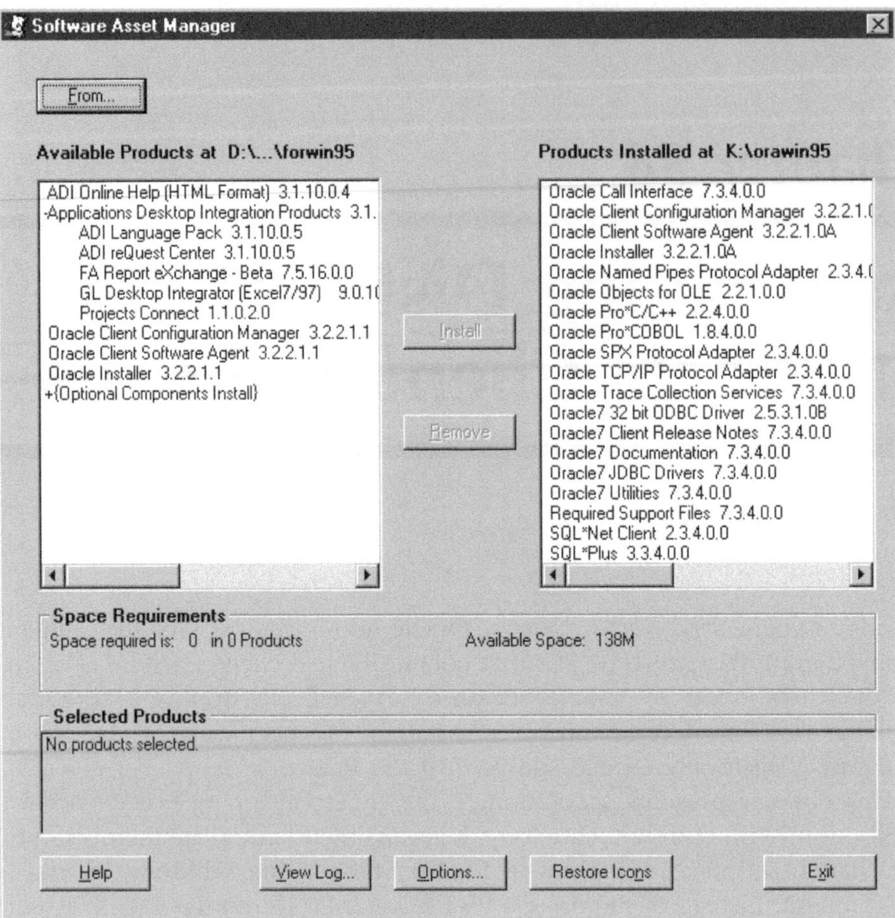

prototypical environment. On the simpler end of the spectrum, the software may be the SQL*Net Client and the TCP/IP Adapter products, along with SQL*Plus. Other potential products include the Oracle ODBC Driver, the Oracle Call Interface (OCI), OLE, and a host of other client software. Oracle Financials requires the Application Desktop Interface Client (ADI 3.1) and the General Ledger Desktop Interface (GLDI) to be considered for automated distribution.

PC Operating Environments

There are numerous PC operating systems in the workplace today, the most popular being Windows 95, 98, and NT. For simplicity, our example uses Windows 95 and Oracle 7.3.4 client software. While the Windows 3.1 client is not considered in this discussion of Oracle 7.3.4 client software, it is worth mentioning that the .INI files in 3.1 have generally been replaced by the Registry in Windows 95.

The Oracle server can reside on any number of platforms, such as UNIX or Windows NT. For sharing Oracle client software within an NT server shop, we generally utilize a domain server. However, not every shop uses domain servers and, where a workgroup configuration is being used in the office, the distribution method is more limited.

So, what are the choices regarding distribution methods? Potentially, we are deploying Oracle software to hundreds or even thousands of clients. We must avoid physically visiting the desktop!

What are some of the distribution options?

There are software distribution products, but many have significant shortcomings. Most companies choosing to buy a distribution package will spend thousands of dollars on software to distribute Oracle software. In addition to the high cost, the expertise required to configure the software is considerable. Also, the timeframe is a big issue — evaluating and selecting the distribution software, configuration, and implementation can take a great deal of time. One such product is the Oracle Client Software Manager (OCSM). This is an Oracle-supplied option for software distribution, but it will work only with a properly configured network. OCSM is actually comprised of two components, the Oracle Client Configuration Manager (OCCM) and the Oracle Client Software Agent (OCSA). OCCM can define a configuration that will determine a user's access to Oracle software; it also defines a set of products each user group will have available, whether loaded on a client or a shared pool on a file server.

Nevertheless, Oracle still recommends the complete installation of all files to the client machine. For Oracle Financials, Oracle states "ADI products will not work unless all product components are replicated to each client." (This is more interesting in light of the emerging network computing concept.)

For OCSM, there are two requirements. First, OCSM requires that client machines belong to an NT domain, which not all installations have. Even with NT servers, an installation could still be using a workgroup versus domain authentication. Second, OCSM requires that Microsoft Remote Registry Services be installed on both the OCSM host and client machines. Again, if this is not already in place, OCCM may not be an option.

Automated Distribution

Clearly, when faced with the task of updating hundreds of PCs, automated software distribution becomes the best solution. Some of the up-front work may appear intensive, but through methodical steps it is possible to alleviate thousands of hours of tedious, repetitive work.

Automating software distribution requires working with the Windows Registry to a limited degree so that background information on the Registry will be useful. However, if one considers that through a few steps one can automate distribution, it is worth examining. The steps for loading software onto a client PC include:

- Copying DLLs and files off the network
- Copying in a directory of icons for Oracle client executables that actually points to a central application server location
- Registry subtrees pertaining to the Oracle software must be imported

The Windows Registry

Before there was a registry, Windows 3.1 used .INI files to store application-specific information, and this made software distribution simple. For example, information for Oracle and ODBC was stored in the ORACLE.INI and ODBC.INI files. Now, with the Registry, we no longer need these .INI files.

In simple terms, the registry is the central information database for Windows 95. While there is much that can be done with the Registry, beware: there is a huge potential for damage if the Registry is manipulated incorrectly. However, with care it is a fairly easy repository of information to manipulate. The Registry was designed to be hierarchical and was originally designed to simplify the operating system. It eliminated the need for initialization (INI) files (except for legacy applications). Incidentally, the Registry also eliminates the need for autoexec.bat.

The Registry should contain all the values necessary to run an application. Unfortunately, Oracle client applications such as ADI 3.1 still read the PATH from autoexec.bat to locate executables. This becomes a problem when, for example, the application server is running Novell 4.11 and the client is running Windows 95. Novell 4.11 overwrites the PATH with its drive mappings. As a result, Windows 95 client software installed to a Novell application server will not show up in the PATH and Oracle consequently cannot find the software.

An interesting point about the Registry is that an administrator can access the Registry information on any computer across the network, when used in conjunction with remote procedure call (RPC) mechanism and Win32-based Registry APIs. This is useful when checking the settings for installed client software. As is the case with OCCM, viewing the Registry on a remote computer requires Microsoft Remote Registry Service on the administrator's computer and the remote computers. Bear in mind that information for multiple users and configurations can be stored in one computer. This allows flexibility but is also another item to check when ensuring proper setup.

The changes needed in the Registry for software distribution do not require a lot of space. Nevertheless, bear in mind that the Registry has no size restriction and can include binary and text values.

Values in the Registry are commonly viewed from the editor. However, the Registry can also be viewed as a text file, and this is especially useful for creating subtree Registry files for later import. Beware, however, when editing the Registry files. It is a common practice in Windows to double-click on a file — for example, a Power Point, Word, or text file — and to have its associated application start up. *Do not* double-click on a Registry file to view it; this will result in importing the values in the file into the Registry, something not intended. For example, double-clicking on any *.reg (.REG) file in Explorer

Exhibit 38.2 Registry View of Oracle Subtree under Hkey_Local_Machine

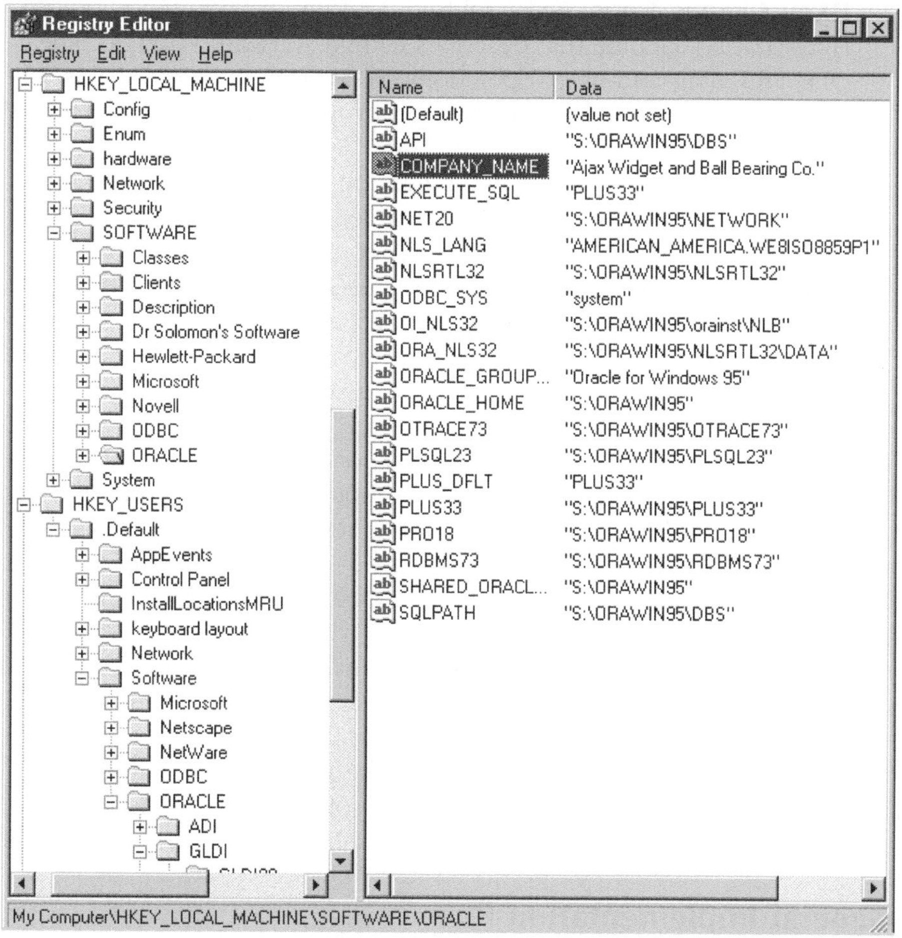

or File Manager immediately imports the contents into the machine's Registry. Open a .REG file carefully through Notepad or Wordpad and then proceed with viewing or editing.

To invoke the Registry editor from the Start menu, click Run and type `regedit`. (In Windows-NT, you can also use `regedt32`). To find a particular item within the Registry, click Find under the Edit menu. Exhibit 38.2 shows a view of the Registry editor.

As previously mentioned, the Registry contains a hierarchical structure. There are six major subtrees with subtrees or subkeys under each branch, similar to the structure viewable in Windows Explorer. Of the six subtrees, four are of particular interest:

1. **Hkey_Local_Machine.** This subtree contains specific information about the type of hardware on the machine, software settings. All users who log on use this information. The Software subkey holds data about specific software installed on the computer that can write to the Registry

and configuration data. It includes information added when registering an application to use a specific filename extension.

2. **Hkey_Classes_Root.** This subtree actually points to a branch of Hkey_Local_Machine that describes certain software settings, especially OLE and drag-and-drop operations. It is useful to know this is out there, although distribution can occur without exporting from this subtree.
3. **Hkey_Users.** This subtree holds generic and user-specific data about all the users who log on to the computer. Information includes default settings for applications and desktop configurations.
4. **Hkey_Current_User.** This subtree points to a branch of Hkey_Users for the currently logged-on user. Hkey_Local_Machine is a key, with a subkey of SOFTWARE and a subkey under that called ORACLE. The subkeys can contain values that have a name and data.

The Registry can be imported, exported, or recreated; but by using the export capability of the Registry editor, the specific Oracle subtrees can be saved in the .REG file text format. Running regedit.exe Sample.reg, where Sample.reg is the name of a file containing a subkey, will import the text subkey back into the Registry. This will be essential for creating a batch file to automate the process.

For automating distribution of Oracle client software, it is best to find a machine that we can use as a baseline for Registry editing. Installed client software will result in additional Registry entries that will be isolated for export to the distribution clients. Having discussed the Registry, we can now turn to an implementation plan for automated client software distribution.

A General Implementation Plan

For Windows 95, there is a simple plan that can be used to automate the distribution of Oracle client software. Exhibit 38.3 gives an overview of the plan's topology. With appropriate modifications, this same general plan could be adapted for NT software distribution. The plan has two phases: determining the files needed and accomplishing the distribution of those files.

Phase 1: Establish a Baseline of Files

Step 1: Establish a directory on the network to hold the files to be used later for distribution, including subdirectories to hold .EXE and .DLL files for \windows\system.

Step 2: As noted before, finding an "empty" test environment is essential. Find a "clean" test machine without the Oracle client installed. This base machine will be known as PC_A.

- Run regedit. To remove all traces of Oracle, check that hkey_local_machine\software should not have an entry for Oracle. If it does, run the installer to view any Oracle products that can be deinstalled.
- Remove the Oracle home (e.g., c:\orawin95), and delete the Oracle subtree with regedit.
- Ensure that there is no directory "\Windows\ Start Menu\Programs\Oracle for Windows 95" (or, for NT, "\Windows\Profiles\All Users\Start Menu\Programs\Oracle for Windows NT") which holds the icons for the client executables. As we shall see later, this directory can be copied to the network for download later on.

Step 3: Determine size and date of files in \windows\system for later comparison.

- Open an MS-DOS window. (A "command" window can be opened with Start, Run.)
- Change directory with "cd" to \windows\system.
- Use "dir/oen > list1.txt" from DOS in \windows\system to get a baseline of files. This lists the files by group and then sorts by name. This list will be needed for comparison against the directory file listing that will be gathered after the distribution ("dir/oen/b would list the files without the dates, but dates are needed.)

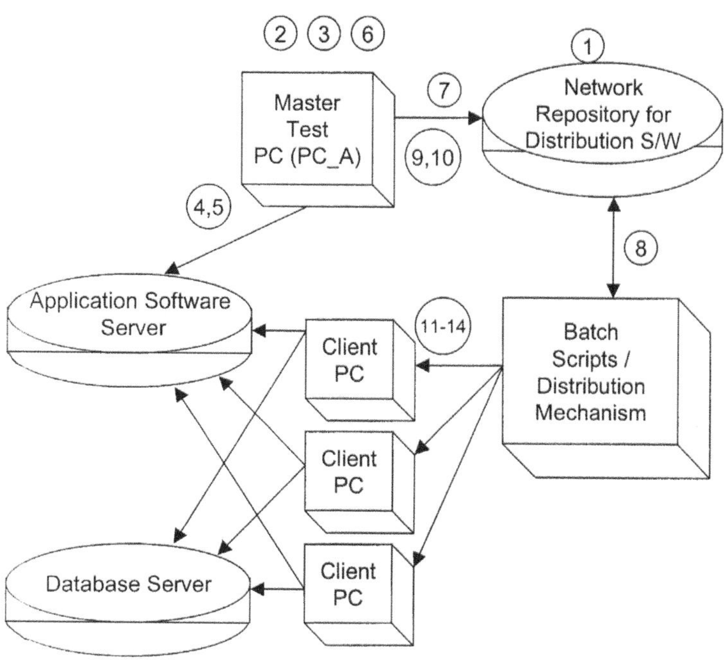

Exhibit 38.3 Implementation Diagram

Step 4: Install the Oracle client software on a "clean" client machine but use the network drive for the Oracle home — not a local drive. Use the Oracle Installer to install the desired client software to the central network drive. For example, install the software (versus C:) to S:\ORAWIN95. The network drive Oracle home should be added to autoexec.bat by updating the "SET PATH=" statement within that file. There should be no spaces around the "=" sign. The path should now include s:\orawin95\bin.

Step 5: Configure Oracle client software and ensure that it works properly. For example, new machine data sources can be created within the ODBC 32-bit administrator using the newly installed Oracle ODBC driver. This will be especially useful when including ODBC subkeys in Registry exports.

Step 6: Get the new baseline of files in \windows\system and run "dir/oen > list2.txt" from DOS on PC_A. Now compare the files that have been added or changed (look at the dates and byte counts). The sorted lists (list1.txt and list2.txt) can be compared manually or, if UNIX is accessible, ftp the files over and use *diff* (e.g., "diff list1.txt list2.txt > diff1and2.txt") to get a list of the differences.

Step 7: Using the difference list from Step 6, create a batch file to copy the new files to the holding area. An example of lines from a batch file might simply be:

```
copy c:\windows\system\ODBC16GT.DLL   k:\dba\registry\proto\wsysdlls
copy c:\windows\system\ODBC32GT.DLL   k:\dba\registry\proto\wsysdlls
copy c:\windows\system\ODBCINT.DLL    k:\dba\registry\proto\wsysdlls
copy c:\windows\system\ODBCJI32.DLL   k:\dba\registry\proto\wsysdlls
copy c:\windows\system\ODBCJT32.DLL   k:\dba\registry\proto\wsysdlls
copy c:\windows\system\ODBCSTF.DLL    k:\dba\registry\proto\wsysdlls
copy c:\windows\system\ODBCTL32.DLL   k:\dba\registry\proto\wsysdlls
copy c:\windows\system\ODBCTRAC.DLL   k:\dba\registry\proto\wsysdlls
copy c:\windows\system\ODDBSE32.DLL   k:\dba\registry\proto\wsysdlls
copy c:\windows\system\ODEXL32.DLL    k:\dba\registry\proto\wsysdlls
copy c:\windows\system\ODFOX32.DLL    k:\dba\registry\proto\wsysdlls
copy c:\windows\system\ODTEXT32.DLL   k:\dba\registry\proto\wsysdlls
copy c:\windows\system\OIADM400.DLL   k:\dba\registry\proto\wsysdlls
copy c:\windows\system\OICOM400.DLL   k:\dba\registry\proto\wsysdlls
copy c:\windows\system\OIDIS400.DLL   k:\dba\registry\proto\wsysdlls
copy c:\windows\system\OIFIL400.DLL   k:\dba\registry\proto\wsysdlls
copy c:\windows\system\OIGFS400.DLL   k:\dba\registry\proto\wsysdlls
copy c:\windows\system\OIP21.DLL      k:\dba\registry\proto\wsysdlls
copy c:\windows\system\OIPRT400.DLL   k:\dba\registry\proto\wsysdlls
copy c:\windows\system\OISLB400.DLL   k:\dba\registry\proto\wsysdlls
copy c:\windows\system\OISSQ400.DLL   k:\dba\registry\proto\wsysdlls
copy c:\windows\system\OITWA400.DLL   k:\dba\registry\proto\wsysdlls
copy c:\windows\system\OIUI400.DLL    k:\dba\registry\proto\wsysdlls
copy c:\windows\system\OLEMSG.DLL     k:\dba\registry\proto\wsysdlls
copy c:\windows\system\OLEMSG32.DLL   k:\dba\registry\proto\wsysdlls
```

Step 8: Using a batch script format similar to Step 7, reverse the direction of the copy and create a batch script to copy the files from the network location to the local drive's\windows\system.

Step 9: Export key registry subtrees. Using regedit, use the option to export a registry file. Export the following subtrees to the network repository (e.g., S:\auto_ora):

```
HKEY_LOCAL_MACHINE\SOFTWARE\ORACLE to S:\auto_ora\hlmora.reg
HKEY_LOCAL_MACHINE\SOFTWARE\ODBC\ODBCINST.INI
   to S:\auto_ora\hlmodbc.reg
HKEY_CURRENT_USER\Software\ORACLE to S:\auto_ora\hcuora.reg
HKEY_CURRENT_USER\Software\ODBC\ODBC.INI to S:\auto_ora\hcuodbc.reg
HKEY_USERS\.Default\Software\ORACLE to S:\auto_ora\huora.reg
HKEY_USERS\.Default\Software\ODBC\ODBC.INI to S:\auto_ora\huodbc.reg
```

Also, create a batch script to import the Registry entries. The script could simply contain:

```
regedit s:\auto_ora\hlmora.reg
regedit s:\auto_ora\hlmodbc.reg
regedit s:\auto_ora\hcuora.reg
regedit s:\auto_ora\hcuodbc.reg
regedit s:\auto_ora\huora.reg
regedit s:\auto_ora\huodbc.reg
```

Step 10: Copy the icon directory "C:\Windows\Start Menu\Programs\Oracle for Windows 95" to S:\auto_ora or the network repository.

Phase 2: Distribute Files to Client

Step 11: Check the autoexec.bat on PC_B or create a batch script to add, for example, S:\orawin95\bin (or the appropriate Oracle home location) to the PATH.

Step 12: On PC_B, the client, use the batch script created in Step 8 to copy down the necessary files that must reside in \windows\system.

Step 13: Run the batch script to import the Registry entries in Step 9.

Step 14: Copy, for example, "s:\auto_ora\Oracle for Windows 95" to "C:\Windows\Start Menu\Programs;" this, too, can be automated.

Use logon scripts or work with the network administrator to automate the process.

This approach does not work with some networks. For example, mentioned earlier was the problem encountered with Novell 4.11 on Windows 95, overwriting of the path (as defined in autoexec.bat) by the Novell drive mappings. In the case of trying to get ODBC to work from a central server, the directory S:\ORAWIN95 (where 'S' is a network drive on the server) must be in the path in autoexec.bat. Unfortunately, S: as a mapping overwrites the path that includes S:\ORAWIN95. Consequently, anything beyond the simplicity of SQL*Net or SQL*Plus ceases to function in this configuration under Novell. The only way to overcome the problem is to install all of the executables (EXEs) and dynamic linked library files (DLLs) locally, as opposed to a few, defeating the purpose and using up space. This is further compounded in trying to install ADI 3.1 and GLDI and was abandoned. If the client is running NT, however, the path can be explicitly set in the environment and the problem with Novell potentially overcome. Another consideration is that the *.SET files for ADI 3.1 and GLDI, if stored on the server, cannot be written to; thus, all users will have to have the same desktop configuration.

Conclusion

While Oracle has not sanctioned these procedures, they nonetheless provide an idea of how an organization might tailor an automated process to avoid the pain of visiting every Oracle desktop. Oracle technical support has acknowledged these concepts and it appears that this approach will become even more popular as Oracle customers roll out thousands of Oracle clients.

Chapter 39

SQL*Net Diagnostics and Performance Tuning

Serg Shestakov
Dmitry Petrov

Network diagnostics and performance tuning are important issues to consider for savvy administrators managing complex distributed Oracle installations. Oracle has many powerful features for SQL*Net diagnostics, such as logging and tracing mechanisms, explanation tools, and statistics collection. To optimize network performance, administrators should accurately tune Oracle SQL*Net services. There are many external and internal factors influencing SQL*Net performance. This chapter considers how to tune SQL*Net buffer size, how to speed up connections for dedicated and multi-threaded servers, what is listeners load balancing; and we will also learn new Net8 features affecting SQL*Net diagnostics and performance. We use the SQL*Net term to describe both Net8 software and older versions, starting with SQL*Net 2.3.x. We also use Oracle utility names for UNIX systems.

SQL*Net is a transparent network interface provided for Oracle applications to connect to Oracle DBMS server software. Oracle SQL*Net hides the complexity of Underlying Network Protocol (UNP) and takes care of managing connections over distributed heterogeneous networks. Consider the protocol stack in detail. UNP consists of upper layer protocol (ULP) and lower layer protocol (LLP). To better understand the overall picture, take a look at the protocol stack in terms of the Open System Interconnection (OSI) model (see Exhibit 39.1).

Oracle applications can be Oracle Forms, SQL*Plus, etc. Oracle server software can be Oracle7 or Oracle8 DBMS servers. SQL*Net software consists of several major components: Oracle Call Interface/User Program Interface (for client side), Oracle Program Interface (for server side), Two Task Common, Transparent Network Substrate, and Oracle Protocol Adapters. The most popular

0-8493-1139-X/02/$0.00+$1.50
©2002 by CRC Press LLC

Exhibit 39.1 Mapping Oracle Network Architecture to OSI Model

Oracle Network Architecture	*OSI Layers*
Oracle applications, Oracle server software	Application layer
SQL*Net	Presentation layer, Session layer
ULP	Transport layer, Network layer
LLP	Data link layer
Physical layer	Physical layer

ULPs are TCP/IP, and DECnet, IPX/SPX; and common LLPs are FDDI, Ethernet, Token Ring, and ARCNET. The physical layer deals with hardware sending and receiving data on a carrier.

Before starting the analysis, let's define what factors affect network performance and select evaluation criteria. We considered network stack and saw that SQL*Net performance is strongly influenced by underlying UNP parameters. On the other hand, SQL*Net performance is affected by upper-level Oracle software characteristics such as administrator's choice on using multi-threaded server versus dedicated server, number of active server processes, time required to scan large tnsnames.ora files, level of SQL*Net tracing configured on client side and server side, security mechanisms used to authenticate connections, encrypt data being transferred, and checksumming models. And, of course, SQL*Net performance is influenced by external network factors like topology, throughput, domain name service configuration, etc. It is important to remember that the basic characteristics of SQL*Net performance for processing Oracle transactions are connect time and query time. We will see how to reduce network traffic and make data transfer fast and reliable by synchronizing UNP parameters with SQL*Net parameters.

Let's highlight some of the network problems related to SQL*Net software. Among these are: broken connections, bad load-balancing, too long response times at peak workloads, and automatic adjustment of Oracle server software causing excessive resources utilization. If an error arises, it affects many network components and error codes spread like wildfire through the protocol stack. It is difficult to locate the true reason causing the network problem; but fortunately, there are tools to help with SQL*Net diagnostics.

SQL*Net Diagnostics

To reduce administrator headaches because of network problems, Oracle offers tracing and logging features of SQL*Net and Trace Assistant tool to explain the trace codes. Tracing can provide very detailed information and should be turned on to solve serious problems that cannot be resolved by analyzing standard log messages. To locate what network component causes the problem, one should systematically run checks to reduce the search scope. First, check if the server node is accessible from the client machine. Then, make sure on the server side that the database is up and running. Third, check if the client has the appropriate network adapter installed. After that, run the Listener Control utility and see if the listener required by client is running and can handle requests for target database. A good way to make sure that Oracle can establish client/server connection is `tnsping` utility. This utility takes the TNS service name as a first parameter, and the number of attempts as a second (optional) parameter. This utility returns response time if it manages to establish the connection. The `tnsping` utility can also be used to measure network throughput between client and server. If `tnsping` fails, check the configuration files syntax. If a problem persists, you can use logging and tracing mechanisms to get in-depth information.

Let's show how to turn on the SQL*Net logging and tracing. On the client side, one can define the directory where to put log and trace files in the `sqlnet.ora` file using the `LOG_DIRECTORY_CLIENT` and `TRACE_DIRECTORY_CLIENT` parameters, respectively. One can also define the log and trace file names with the `LOG_DIRECTORY_CLIENT` and `TRACE_DIRECTORY_CLIENT` parameters of the `sqlnet.ora` file. By default, trace on UNIX systems is written to `$ORACLE_HOME/network/trace/sqlnet.trc`, and log is written to `sqlnet.log` file under the same directory. On the server side, one can define log and trace destinations with the following parameters: `LOG_DIRECTORY_<lsnr>`, `LOG_FILE_<lsnr>`, `TRACE_DIRECTORY_<lsnr>`, and `TRACE_FILE_<lsnr>`.

All these parameters should be configured in the `listener.ora` file. By default, server logs and traces are stored in `listener.log` and `listener.trc` files under the `$ORACLE_HOME/network/trace` directory. Note that, by default, logging is turned on and one can change this behavior with the `LOGGING_<lsnr>` parameter of the `listener.ora` file. One can switch between different trace standards on the client side using the `TRACE_LEVEL_CLIENT` parameter of `sqlnet.ora`. At the server side, the trace level parameter is called `TRACE_LEVEL_<lsnr>` and it should be included into the `listener.ora`. Valid trace levels are: `OFF`, `USER`, `ADMIN`, and `SUPPORT` for Oracle8.

Now let's discuss how to analyze network problem using log messages. First, scan the tail of SQL*Net log file and detect what is the latest error number caused by the application. It usually corresponds to the last line of log file. Remember that log files can grow to very large sizes, which makes it difficult to read. One should carefully filter the log information. For example, on UNIX systems, one can see the last 40 log lines issuing a `tail -40 <log file name>` command. The last non-empty message in the error stack usually indicates actual problem cause. If log analysis does not help to remove the problem, turn on the tracing at the desired level and repeat the sequence of events triggering the error. Trace information is generated according to the network layers participating in the data transfer. Do not forget to turn off the tracing once the problem is solved. Excessive tracing may slow down the overall network performance.

The mission-critical component of SQL*Net software is the listener. Let's take a closer look at the most common listener error codes and workarounds for the corresponding problems. The ORA-12541 error "No listener," which appears at some client's logs while the listener is up and running, denotes that incoming connection requests are received too quickly and listener cannot handle it. To avoid this problem, increase the `QUEUESIZE` parameter at `listener.ora` file, restart the listener, and see if the new value is sufficient. Another listener-related error is ORA-12224 "TNS: No listener." It indicates that connection cannot be completed because listener is not running. One can try to bypass the problem by verifying if the client connects to the same address the listener actually uses and that version compatibility is OK. One of the most frequent listener errors is ORA-12545 "TNS: Name lookup failure." This error indicates that the client cannot make contact with remote node. Check the correctness of the `ADDRESS` keyword syntax on the server and client. Next, make sure that the listener process on the remote node has been started. Log on to the server and run the Listener Control utility. Within this utility, issue a `STATUS <lsnr>` command; and if there are no listeners, run it with the `START` command. Common practice among administrators is to copy service descriptions on a client machine when target database changes or one more database should be added to those listed in the `tnsnames.ora` file. This can raise the ORA-12154 error "TNS: Could not resolve service name." Upon receiving this error, check if the service name supplied for connection exists in the configuration file and if all its parameters are correct. To avoid such problems, the administrator should take care of configuration files version control.

When turning on SQL*Net tracing, Oracle writes errors and warnings along with internal parameters and hex packet representations to trace files, which are not that easy to read and analyze. For better presentation and explanation of trace messages, you can use Trace Assistant. Run Trace Assistant from the operating system environment, issuing a `trceval` command for SQL*Net 2.3.x or the `trcasst` command for Net8. Trace Assistant can evaluate SQL*Net packets; it can also present summary and detailed reports. Summary shows the total number of sent and received packets, and detailed report displays a bit-level picture. Valuable command-line options for Trace Assistant include summary connectivity information (c), detailed connectivity information (d), detailed TTC information (t), summary Two-Task Common information (u), and SQL commands (q) — which should be used together with (u) and overall trace statistics (s). Command syntax is slightly different for SQL*Net 2.3.x and Net8.

To monitor network traffic carried by SQL*Net without resource-intensive tracing, you can use a third-party network analyzer that will collect statistics on SQL*Net listener ports. Another way is to use native Oracle statistics that can be accessed using the `V_$SYSSTAT` view. There are six major parameters related to SQL*Net traffic statistics; these are number of bytes sent to client and database link via SQL*Net, number of bytes received from client and database link via SQL*Net, and total number of SQL*Net roundtrips between client and database link. You can read current values by issuing the following SQL statement:

```
SELECT name, value FROM v_$sysstat
  WHERE name LIKE '%SQL*Net%';
```

To avoid manual typing and get a better picture of network traffic dynamics you can decide to design a data schema for cumulative statistics, write a statistics collection procedure, and schedule it for regular execution. The entire process is described below in the "Optimizing Connect Time with MTS" section where a similar problem is solved.

Optimizing Query Time with SDU Buffer Size

SDU is an acronym for Session Data Unit. The SDU parameter can be included in the SQL*Net configuration files `tnsnames.ora` and `listener.ora`. SDU defines SQL*Net buffer size and it is a most important factor influencing SQL*Net query time. SDU buffer size varies from 2 K to 32 K. The goal is to synchronize SDU with buffer sizes of underlying UNP protocols and application-level buffer size. A wrong guess for SDU parameter may lead to traffic overhead and fragmentation, which may cause longer query times. If the SDU buffer size is insufficient for the application fetching mechanism, this causes fragmentation. And, of course, if the ULP buffer size is smaller than the SDU buffer size, this also causes fragmentation. Following is an example on how one can overwrite the default SDU parameter in `listener.ora` file:

```
SID_LIST_LISTNER=
  (SID_LIST=
    (SID_DESC=
      (SDU=4096)
        .......
    )
  )
```

And an example of configuring SDU buffer size for the tnsnames.ora file is:

```
oracle.world=
  (DESCRIPTION=
    (SDU=4096)
      ........
  )
```

Let's show how to tune the SDU buffer size. Assume that ULP, LLP, and application fetch buffer sizes and header sizes are known. The best network performance will be gained if the buffer size for each underlying layer plus its header size is slightly greater than the data buffer size of the current layer. The administrator can model the data transmission for a wide range of SDU parameters. The goal is to detect situations in which fragmentation occurs. Once fragmentation is detected, the data buffer should be split into parts according to the buffer sizes and header sizes of the underlying layer. Ideally, the SDU buffer size should include the maximum application fetch size possible and be less than or equal to the UNP buffer size minus SQL*Net header size.

Optimizing Connect Time with Dedicated Server

When working with a dedicated server, the SQL*Net connect time can be reduced using prespawned (prestarted) server processes. Thus, one can gain better performance during peak workloads. One can adjust the number of prespawned processes with `listener.ora` parameters: `PRESPAWN_MAX`, `POOL_SIZE`, and `TIMEOUT`. The first parameter restricts maximum number of prestarted Oracle server processes, the second parameter limits the number of prestarted server processes the listener can create for the selected protocol, and the third parameter can be used to make the server process wait for the net connect request before shutting down. Thus, one can get better connection times for next requests by increasing server resources utilization. The example below illustrates corresponding `listener.ora` syntax:

```
(SID_LIST=
   (SID_DESC=
      (SID_NAME=ORCL)
      (ORACLE_HOME=/opt/oracle)
      (PRESPAWN_MAX=70)
      (PRESPAWN_LIST=
         (PRESPAWN_DESC=
            (PROTOCOL=TCP)
            (POOL_SIZE=10)
               (TIMEOUT=2)))))
```

To tune the number of prespawned servers, one needs a thorough understanding of the connection request processing mechanism. When listeners process a request, it can either spawn a new server process and pass connection to it, or redirect the connection to an already allocated process. This mechanism is transparent to the user, but affects the connection time. One way to process the request is called a Bequeath session method, and a second method is called a Redirect session. When prespawned processes are not configured, the default method is Bequeath session. However, if one has configured the `PRESPAWN_MAX` parameter, Oracle can use a Redirect session method. The client passes the request to the listener and the listener checks if any of prespawned processes are available. If yes, the listener returns a prespawned address to client, the client disconnects from listener and starts working with the prespawned process directly. If no prespawned processes are available, the listener refuses to process the client request. Best results can be achieved by experimenting with the parameters that control the prespawned processes' behavior and measuring connect time at different workloads.

Optimizing Connect Time with MTS

The multi-threaded server (MTS) has a major impact on overall SQL*Net performance — connect time first of all. The most important issues to consider when optimizing response times for a multi-threaded server are balancing the number of shared server processes and number of dispatchers running. Oracle system dictionary views hold current performance indicators and values gathered since start-up; but server and network loads change all the time and there is a need for detailed time distributions to make correct decisions on performance tuning (i.e., how often indicators reach peaks and what are the average values). So, because of the need for cumulative statistics, simple select statements addressing the system dictionary views are not enough. Thus, step by step, additional data structures will be created to hold cumulative statistics and write a statistics collection procedure.

Statistics Collection for MTS

There are two adjustable parameters in the `init.ora` file related to shared server processes: `MTS_SERVERS` and `MTS_MAX_SERVERS`. The first parameter regulates the initial number of shared servers created at start-up, and the second parameter limits the maximum number of shared server processes. If the administrator sets an insufficient initial number of shared servers, Oracle dynamically creates additional shared servers up to `MTS_MAX_SERVERS` and de-allocates when processes idle time exceeds a predefined threshold. If the administrator sets too high a number of initial shared servers, Oracle never de-allocates these processes created at start-up. This may cause excessive usage of system resources. So, to optimize network performance without server overhead, one needs to set the `MTS_SERVERS` according to the calculated average number of active shared server processes. To avoid low connection times at peak server workloads, one needs to set the `MTS_MAX_SERVERS` parameter to not less than maximum number of required server processes. One way to tune these parameters is to experiment with different values and tracking the performance gains.

Now one can discuss how to collect, store, and view the statistics related to shared server processes. The Oracle system dictionary holds the current number of shared servers running at `V_$SHARED_SERVER` view. (We prefer to directly address the `v_$` views to avoid addressing its public synonyms.) To hold the history of this performance indicator, the `MTS_Server_Statistics` table is defined by:

```
create table MTS_Server_Statistics (
  Timepoint DATE,      -- When statistics was collected
Server_count INTEGER   -- Number of shared servers running
 );
```

To regulate the number of dispatchers running, there are parameters in the `init.ora` file — `MTS_DISPATCHERS` and `MTS_MAX_DISPATCHERS` — that set the initial and maximum number of dispatchers, respectively. To tune these parameters, one needs to calculate the dispatchers load ratio (i.e., the busy time divided by overall running time). One can monitor these statistics by querying the `V_$DISPATCHER`. To store cumulative statistics on dispatcher load, create the `MTS_Dispatcher_Statistics` table. The corresponding DDL command is:

```
create table MTS_Dispatcher_Statistics (
   Timepoint DATE,                  -- When statistics was collected
   Disp_name VARCHAR2 (5),          -- Dispatcher name
   Disp_network VARCHAR2 (128),     -- Dispatcher Protocol
   Cumu_busy REAL,                  -- Cumulative busy time
   Cumu_idle REAL,                  -- Cumulative idle time
   Cumu_ratio REAL                  -- Cumulative dispatcher load ratio
);
```

Now we'll show how the administrator can fetch statistics to the tables using a PL/SQL procedure; call it `MTS_Statistics`. First, declare the procedure. Because one wants this procedure to gather cumulative statistics, there needs to be two parameters — the number of runs and the time delay between runs. (Assume that the time delay is indicated in minutes.) The corresponding code is:

```
CREATE OR REPLACE PROCEDURE MTS_Statistics
   (Runs IN INTEGER, Time_delay IN INTEGER) AS
```

Now declare all the necessary variables. It is easy to gather cumulative statistics for shared servers because one must only fetch and store the number of running servers. No additional variables are necessary. But one needs several variables to calculate cumulative statistics on dispatcher loads. The `Prev_busy` and `Prev_idle` variables are used to keep information from the previous run — dispatcher busy time and idle time, respectively. The `Intrv_busy` and `Intrv_idle` will be used to store changes of corresponding parameters since the last run, and the `Intrv_ratio` will be used to calculate the indicator of current dispatcher load. Once finished with the declarations, start procedure body defining the main loop, which calculates cumulative statistics several times as specified in the `Runs` parameter.

```
   Prev_busy    REAL;
   Prev_idle    REAL;
   Intrv_busy   REAL;
   Intrv_idle   REAL;
   Intrv_ratio  REAL;
BEGIN
FOR Counter IN 1 .. Runs LOOP
```

First, fetch statistics on the number of shared servers running from the corresponding system view and store it into the `MTS_Server_Statistics` table along with current time. (Note that shared servers with `QUIT` status are not taken into account.

```
INSERT INTO MTS_Server_Statistics
   (Timepoint, Server_count)
   (SELECT SYSDATE, Count(*)
     FROM SYS.V_$SHARED_SERVER
     WHERE Status != 'QUIT');
```

The next section of code starts a loop for cursor `Cur_Status`, calculating the dispatcher load ratio for each network protocol being used. One obtains the dispatcher name, network protocol, total busy time, and total idle time from the `V_$DISPATCHER` system view. Once a loop starts, there are two possible situations. When the procedure is invoked for the first time, cumulative load ratio does not make any sense; thus, the situation is processed by analyzing the Counter variable.

```
FOR Cur_Status IN (SELECT Name, Network, Busy, Idle
    FROM SYS.V_$DISPATCHER)
  LOOP

  IF Counter = 1 THEN
    INSERT INTO MTS_Dispatcher_Statistics
    VALUES(SYSDATE, Cur_status.name, Cur_status.network,
    Cur_status.Busy, Cur_Status.Idle, NULL);
  ELSE
```

However, each next time one enters the loop, one already has previous statistics; thus, one can calculate the current cumulative load ratio. The previous values are stored in the MTS_Dispatcher_Statistics table; so one first needs to fetch previous values into memory variables Prev_busy and Prev_idle. To get these values, select a last recent row from the MTS_ Dispatcher_Statistics table:

```
SELECT Cumu_busy, Cumu_idle INTO Prev_busy, Prev_idle
  FROM MTS_Dispatcher_statistics
  WHERE Disp_name = Cur_Status.Name AND Timepoint = (SELECT max(Timepoint)
    FROM MTS_Dispatcher_Statistics
    WHERE Disp_name = Cur_Status.Name);
```

Detect changes in busy time and idle time since last run and store it into Intrv_busy and Intrv_idle variables. Then calculate the cumulative dispatcher load ratio as the percentage of busy time since last run divided by the time elapsed since last run. Now one can store the cumulative ratio into the MTS_Dispatcher_Statistics table along with system time, dispatcher name, network protocol, total busy, and total idle time. The processing of statistics for dispatchers is over, so the inner loop is closed.

```
Intrv_busy := Cur_Status.Busy - Prev_busy;
Intrv_idle := Cur_Status.Idle - Prev_idle;
Intrv_ratio := Intrv_busy / (Intrv_busy + Intrv_idle) * 100;
INSERT INTO MTS_Dispatcher_Statistics
  VALUES(SYSDATE, Cur_status.name, Cur_status.network,
    Cur_status.Busy, Cur_Status.Idle, Intrv_ratio);
END IF;
END LOOP;
```

To save the inserted statistics, issue a COMMIT statement and then call the SLEEP procedure from the DBMS_LOCK package to suspend the procedure execution for a given period, thus converting the parameter Time_delay given in minutes to seconds. Now, at last, one can close the main loop and end the procedure body. The corresponding statements are:

```
    COMMIT;

    DBMS_LOCK.SLEEP(Time_delay*60);

  END LOOP;
END MTS_Statistics;
```

One can run the statistics collection procedure manually from the SQL*Plus console, issuing the EXECUTE statement, or schedule it for regular execution in crontab file (on UNIX systems). If the statistics collection procedure is to be run under an Oracle user different from SYS, do not forget to grant necessary access rights for system views and DBMS_LOCK package.

Tuning Methodology Based on MTS Statistics

Remember that the multi-threaded server performance indicators discussed above are strongly related to SQL*Net connection times. Now we show the tuning methodology based on statistics collected into the MTS_Dispatcher_statistics and MTS_Server_Statistics tables using the MTS_Statistics procedure. The methodology consists of three major steps.

1. *Initialization.* We need to assign initial values to the MTS parameters influencing SQL*Net performance. A good starting point for MTS_DISPATCHERS is one integer higher than the maximum number of concurrent sessions, divided by the number of connections per dispatcher. The number of connections per dispatcher can be extracted from the MAXIMUM_CONNECTIONS field of the V_$MTS system view. The initial MTS_SERVERS value should be set so that each shared server is related to 20 users. Oracle recommends setting MTS_MAX_DISPATCHERS and MTS_MAX_SERVERS to the upper limit applicable for your particular system.
2. *Statistics collection.* We need to run our MTS_Statistics procedure issuing the below listed SQL*Plus command. Note that, to reduce the influence on statistics being collected, the procedure should be run via dedicated session:

```
EXECUTE MTS_Statistics(<Number of runs>, Time delay>);
```

Ideally, the number of runs multiplied by the time delay should be equal to the application running time — 24 hours for non-stop systems. Statistics should be collected each working day for at least one week. To improve the statistics quality, one can run the collection procedure according to the following recommendations. First-day statistics collection should be run as frequently as possible because parameters are not tuned. Each evening, statistics should be analyzed and parameters should be adjusted (according to Step 3). Each next day, increase the time delay and decrease the number of runs. If by the end of the tuning period, the analysis shows that no changes are necessary, then one has a well-tuned multi-threaded server. Otherwise, tuning should be continued.

3. *Analysis.* This step is broken into two parts:
   a. *Servers performance analysis.* To see the overall distribution, one can select the last recent rows, filtering by collection time; thus one

can screen peak workloads. To adjust the shared server tuning parameters, issue the following SQL statement:

```
SELECT avg(Server_count), max(Server_count)
  FROM MTS_Server_Statistics
  WHERE Timepoint like SYSDATE;
```

We recommend setting the MTS_SERVERS equal to the average number of shared servers running. Respectively, we recommend setting the MTS_MAX_SERVERS equal to the maximum number of shared servers running.

b. *Dispatchers load analysis.* One can analyze overall distribution as done for the shared servers. But now we need to detect the average dispatcher's workload ratio and its standard deviation:

```
SELECT Disp_name,
    avg(Cumu_ratio) "Avg ratio",
    stddev(Cumu_ratio)"Std.dev."
  FROM MTS_Dispatcher_Statistics
  WHERE Timepoint like SYSDATE GROUP BY Disp_name;
```

If the average workload is greater than 50 percent, we significantly increase the number of MTS_DISPATCHERS. If the average workload is less than 50 percent, this means that there are too many dispatchers; thus, one should decrease MTS_DISPATCHERS and MTS_MAX_DISPATCHERS. Standard deviation indicates how often the workload changes. The closer the standard deviation is to zero, the better the statistics obtained. Note that the administrator can add more dispatchers and shared servers running the appropriate ALTER SYSTEM command.

Improving the Interface

The best way to avoid manual typing of SQL commands to view the statistics gathered into our data structures is to build a Web interface. For example, one can use the Oracle application server and write PL/SQL procedures, generating dynamic HTML pages on-the-fly. Thus, information can be presented in a very convenient way; for example, one can highlight performance indicators exceeding the threshold.

Listener Load Balancing

One good way to increase SQL*Net performance is listener load balancing. This has major impact on connection time for heavily loaded systems. With several listeners configured for a single database or several database instances and load balancing, there are more chances to bypass the bottlenecks when establishing a connection. This works for both dedicated servers and multi-threaded servers. One can configure multiple listeners configuring init.ora and listener.ora files on the server side, and tnsnames.ora on the client side. To enable load balancing between multiple listeners with multi-threaded server, one should assign TRUE to the MTS_MULTIPLE_LISTENERS parameter of the init.ora file. If we need to run several listeners for single multi-threaded server, we should add several addresses to init.ora file like shown below:

```
MTS_LISTENER_ADDRESS=
   (ADDRESS=(PROTOCOL=tcp)(HOST=myhost)
     (PORT=1521))
MTS_LISTENER_ADDRESS=
   (ADDRESS=(PROTOCOL=tcp)(HOST=myhost)
     (PORT=1522))
```

If each listener is to serve several ports, one should include the ADDRESS_LIST keyword. Note that, for dedicated servers, one does not need to change init.ora parameters at all. Now go to the client side and see how to configure the tnsnames.ora file. To gain the increased performance from load balancing, one should enable the random connection between listeners. This can be done by providing each listener coordinates with a separate DESCRIPTION keyword.

```
oracle.world=
(DESCRIPTION_LIST=
   (DESCRIPTION=(ADDRESS_LIST=
     (ADDRESS=PROTOCOL=tcp)(HOST=myhost)  (PORT=1521))))
   (DESCRIPTION=(ADDRESS_LIST=
     (ADDRESS=(PROTOCOL=tcp)(HOST=myhost)  (PORT=1522))))
(CONNECT_DATA=(SID=mysid)))
```

For many listeners to communicate with many database instances, one should indicate the CONNECT_DATA keyword for each description and skip the final CONNECT_DATA for all listeners. If there are equal replicated databases, one can create a service name that maps to several database instances with different global names.

To make sure that load balancing works, you can run the Listener Control utility (lsnrctl) and issue the SERVICES command. From its output, you will then learn current listener configuration. Also, turn on SQL*Net tracing and monitor how clients connect to database instances.

Net8 New Features

The administrator can use multiplexing and connection pooling. The connection pooling feature helps to maximize the number of physical links to MTS. To increase network performance by multiplexing sessions across a single physical link, one can install Connection Manager software. Another important feature of Net8 is Raw Transport — the ability of Net8 to work without headers whenever possible. Tracing functionality is also extended and supplied with better explanation capabilities. Trace Assistant for Net8 can display error information at three decoding levels.

Connection Pooling: How It Works

With connection pooling, Oracle opens up new connections to the multi-threaded server until a maximum number of connections is reached. Next connection requests will wait until the dispatcher temporarily disconnects some idle connection and becomes available. Note that when the idle session (disconnected temporarily) requests service from dispatcher, the connection will be reestablished as soon as possible. This mechanism gives significant SQL*Net performance gains for OLAP applications. To configure the connection pooling, one must specify four additional attributes for the `MTS_DISPATCHERS` parameter of the `init.ora` file. The first attribute is `POOL`. Valid values are `ON`, `OFF`, `IN`, and `OUT`. Simply turn on the pooling mechanism setting `POOL=ON`. The second attribute is `CONNECTION`; it controls the maximum number of connections to database per dispatcher in terms of pooling. The third attribute is `SESSIONS`; it regulates the maximum number of sessions per dispatcher. The fourth attribute is `TICKS`; it is given in 10-second ticks and defines the time limit for a connection to wait. One can use brief attributes to name up to three characters. An example for connection pooling configuration:

```
MTS_DISPATCHERS=
   "(PROT=tcp)(CONN=4)(DISP=1)(POOL=ON)(SESS=5)
    (TICKS=3)"
```

Now let's discuss how to make sure that connection pooling works. For the above listed configuration, upon restarting the database, we can sequentially open and leave idle five SQL*Plus sessions. If connection pooling works, we notice that the fifth connection will hang for 30 seconds according to the `TICKS` parameters.

Conclusion

To summarize, Oracle network problems can be caused by numerous internal and external factors. SQL*Net diagnostics are based on trace files analysis. Trace Assistant is a tool aimed to ease the diagnostic codes filtering and explanation. SQL*Net performance is measured by connection time and query time. The best query time obtains if we manage to synchronize SQL*Net buffer size with application fetching buffer and UNP buffers. We discussed how it could be tuned by adjusting the SDU parameter. Connection time can be decreased by tuning Oracle server software and configuring the SQL*Net client. We demonstrated how to enable load balancing between multiple listeners, how to prestart Oracle server processes for dedicated server, and how to tune a multi-threaded server by collecting and analyzing the statistics on shared servers and dispatchers. Finally, we outlined the Net8 new features affecting network performance and discussed how the connection pooling mechanism works.

ORACLE BUFFER AND SGA MANAGEMENT

This is one of the most technical areas of Oracle Internals, and also one of the most important to the Oracle professional. The proper configuration of the Oracle SGA and the buffer pools is critical to the performance of any Oracle database.

The Oracle data buffers are especially important. The data buffers exist to minimize disk I/O on the Oracle database and the proper sizing and configuration of the KEEP, RECYCLE, and DEFAULT pools can have a major impact on Oracle performance. The Oracle professional must be able to identify frequently referenced small tables and assign them to the KEEP pool, locate large-table, full-table scans and assign them to the RECYCLE pool, all while ensuring that the entire database is properly buffered.

The tuning of the library cache and shared pool is also very important. The Oracle DBA must constantly monitor the shared pool to ensure that Oracle is not experiencing any internal bottlenecks, and make sure that all SQL in the library cache is properly managed.

This is one of the most complex areas of Oracle tuning because of the complexity of the internal mechanisms that govern the behavior of the SGA. This section contains chapters by some of the foremost names in Oracle administration. Mike Ault, author of *Oracle8i Administration and Management,* presents his secrets of the shared pool. John Beresniewicz, one of the best Oracle internals experts and author of the *Q Diagnostic Center for Oracle* and co-author of *Oracle Built-in Packages* with Stephen Feuerstein, presents two in-depth chapters concerning data buffering in Oracle8i.

Chapter 40

Pinning Packages in the SGA

Donald K. Burleson

As more shops begin encapsulating their SQL into stored procedures, more application code will move away from external programs and into the database engine. Application vendors are delivering their PL/SQL in packages and more developers are encapsulating their SQL into stored procedures.

Oracle DBAs must be conscious of the increasing memory demands of stored procedures, however, and carefully plan for the days when all of the database access code resides within the database.

When a request is made to Oracle to parse an SQL statement or PL/SQL block, Oracle will first check the internal memory structures to see if the parsed object is already in the library cache buffer. In this fashion, Oracle avoids doing unnecessary re-parsing of SQL statements. In an ideal world, it would be wonderful if we could allocate memory to hold all SQL, thereby ensuring that Oracle would never re-parse a statement. However, the costs of memory in the real world make this prohibitive.

In Oracle8i, we see the concept of static binding where a pre-bound execution plan can be immediately loaded and executed. However, until Oracle8i becomes readily available, we must still manage the library cache.

Library cache objects are paged out based on a least recently used (LRU) algorithm. Once loaded into the RAM memory of the shared pool, procedures will execute very quickly, and the trick is to prevent pool thrashing as many procedures compete for a limited amount of shared-pool memory.

As databases evolve and the majority of processing SQL resides inside stored procedures, Oracle Server's shared pool becomes very important. As a review, the shared pool consists of the following subpools:

0-8493-1139-X/02/$0.00+$1.50
©2002 by CRC Press LLC

1. The dictionary cache: storage for data dictionary objects
2. Library cache: storage for procedures, triggers, etc.
3. Shared SQL areas
4. Private SQL area (exists during cursor open/cursor close); within the private SQL area are the "persistent" area and the "runtime" area

The shared pool uses an LRU algorithm to determine which objects get paged out of the shared pool. As this paging occurs, "fragments" or discontiguous chunks of memory are created within the shared pool.

Imagine SHARED_POOL being similar to a tablespace. Just as you may get an ORA-1547 error message when you cannot get sufficient contiguous free space in the tablespace, similarly, you will get ORA-4031 when you cannot get contiguous free space in the SHARED_POOL (sga).

With Oracle7 Release 7.2 and above, you no longer need a contiguous piece of memory to load a package, procedure, or function, so the chances of getting this message are reduced.

This means that a large procedure that fits into memory initially may not fit into contiguous memory when it is reloaded after paging out. Consider a problem that occurs when the body of a package has been aged out of the instance's SGA because of other more recent or frequent activity. Fragmentation then occurs, and Oracle Server cannot find enough contiguous memory to reload the package body, resulting in an ORA-4031 error.

Remember that an SQL statement must be placed into a package in order to be pinned.

Tuning the Library Cache

The shared SQL areas and the PL/SQL areas are called the library cache, which is a subcomponent of the shared pool. The library cache miss ratio tells the DBA whether or not to add space to the shared pool, and it represents the ratio of the sum of library cache reloads to the sum of pins. In general, if the library cache ratio is over 1, you should consider adding to the `shared_pool_size`. Library cache misses occur during the compilation of SQL statements. The compilation of an SQL statement consists of two phases: the parse phase and the execute phase. When the time comes to parse an SQL statement, Oracle first checks to see if the parsed representation of the statement already exists in the library cache. If not, Oracle will allocate a shared SQL area within the library cache and then parse the SQL statement. At execution time, Oracle checks to see if a parsed representation of the SQL statement already exists in the library cache. If not, Oracle will re-parse and execute the statement.

Within the library cache, hit ratios can be determined for all dictionary objects that are loaded. These include table/procedures, triggers, indexes, package bodies, and clusters. If any of the hit ratios fall below 75 percent, you should add to the `shared_pool_size`.

Exhibit 40.1 An Example of an SQL*Plus Query Interrogating the V$LIBRARYCACHE Table

```
library.sql - lists the library cache
PROMPT
PROMPT   ========================
PROMPT   LIBRARY CACHE MISS RATIO
PROMPT   ========================
PROMPT (If>1 then increase the shared_pool_size in init.ora)
PROMPT
COLUMN "LIBRARY CACHE MISS RATIO"         FORMAT 99.9999
COLUMN "executions"                       FORMAT 999,999,999
COLUMN "Cache misses while executing"     FORMAT 999,999,999
SELECT sum(pins) "executions", sum(reloads)
   "Cache misses while executing",
   (((sum(reloads)/sum(pins)))) "LIBRARY CACHE MISS RATIO"
FROM v$librarycache;

PROMPT
PROMPT   ========================
PROMPT     LIBRARY CACHE SECTION
PROMPT   ========================
PROMPT hit ratio should be>70, and pin ratio>70 ...
PROMPT

COLUMN "reloads" FORMAT 999,999,999
SELECT namespace, trunc(gethitratio * 100) "Hit ratio",
TRUNC(pinhitratio * 100) "pin hit ratio", RELOADS "reloads"
FROM V$LIBRARYCACHE;
```

The table `V$LIBRARYCACHE` is the `V$` table that keeps information about library cache activity. The table has three relevant columns: `namespace`, `pins`, and `reloads`. The first is the `namespace`, which indicates whether the measurement is for the SQL area, a table or procedure, a package body, or a trigger. The second value in this table is `pins`, which counts the number of times an item in the library cache is executed. The `reloads` column counts the number of times the parsed representation did not exist in the library cache, forcing Oracle to allocate the private SQL areas in order to parse and execute the statement.

Exhibit 40.1 shows an example of an SQL*Plus query to interrogate the `V$LIBRARYCACHE` table to retrieve the necessary performance information. Exhibit 40.2 shows the output of the SQL query displayed in Exhibit 40.1.

One of the most important measures a developer can take to reduce the use of the library cache is to ensure that all SQL is written within stored procedures. For example, Oracle library cache will examine the following SQL statements and conclude that they are not identical:

```
SELECT * FROM customer;
SELECT * FROM Customer;
```

While capitalizing a single letter, adding an extra space between verbs, or using a different variable name might seem trivial, the Oracle software is not sufficiently intelligent to recognize that the statements are identical. Consequently,

Exhibit 40.2 The Output of the Query in Exhibit 40.1

```
SQL> @temp
=========================
LIBRARY CACHE MISS RATIO
=========================
(If>1 then increase the shared_pool_size in init.ora)
executions          Cache misses while executing   LIBRARY CACHE MISS RATIO
----------          ----------------------------   ------------------------
   251,272                                 2,409                      .0096
=========================
LIBRARY CACHE SECTION
=========================
hit ratio should be > 70, and pin ratio > 70 ...
NAMESPACE           Hit ratiopin     Hit ratiopin     reloads
----------------    -------------    ------------    ---------
SQL AREA                       90              90        1,083
TABLE/PROCEDURE                93              93        1,316
BODY                           96              96            9
TRIGGER                        89              89            1
INDEX                           0               0            0
CLUSTER                        44              44            0
OBJECT                        100             100            0
PIPE                          100             100            0

8 rows selected.
```

Oracle will re-parse and execute the second SQL statement, although it is functionally identical to the first SQL statement.

Another problem occurs when values are hard-coded into SQL statements. For example, Oracle considers the following statements to be different:

```
SELECT COUNT(*) FROM CUSTOMER WHERE STATUS = 'NEW';
SELECT COUNT(*) FROM CUSTOMER WHERE STATUS = 'PREFERRED';
```

This problem is easily alleviated using an identical bind variable such as:

```
SELECT COUNT(*) FROM CUSTOMER WHERE STATUS = :var1;
```

The best way to prevent reloads from happening is to encapsulate all SQL into stored procedures, bundling the stored procedures into packages. This removes all SQL from application programs and moves them into Oracle's data dictionary. This method also has the nice side effect of making all database calls appear as functions. As such, a layer of independence is created between the application and the database. Again, by efficiently reusing identical SQL, the number of reloads will be kept at a minimum and the library cache will function at optimal speed.

The `cursor_space_for_time` parameter can be used to speed executions within the library cache. Setting `cursor_space_for_time` to `False` tells Oracle that a shared SQL area can be de-allocated from the library cache to make room for a new SQL statement. Setting `cursor_space_for_time` to `True` means that all shared SQL areas are pinned in the cache until all application cursors are closed. When set to `True`, Oracle will not bother to check the library cache on subsequent execution calls because it has already pinned the SQL in the cache. This technique can improve the performance for some queries, but `cursor_space_for_time` should not be set to `True` if there are cache misses on execution calls. Cache misses indicate that the `shared_pool_size` is already too small, and forcing the pinning of shared SQL areas will only aggravate the problem.

Another way to improve performance on the library cache is to use the init.ora `session_cached_cursors` parameter. As you probably know, Oracle checks the library cache for parsed SQL statements, but `session_cached_cursors` can be used to cache the cursors for a query. This is especially useful for tasks that repeatedly issue parse calls for the same SQL statement — for example, where an SQL statement is repeatedly executed with a different variable value. An example would be the following SQL request that performs the same query 50 times, once for each state:

```
SELECT SUM(sale_amount)
FROM SALES
WHERE
state_code = :var1;
```

How to Pin Oracle Packages

To prevent reparsing of SQL, you can mark packages as nonswappable, telling the database that after their initial load, they must always remain in memory. This is called "pinning" or "memory fencing." Oracle provides the procedure `dbms_hared_pool.keep` for pinning a package. You can unpin packages using `dbms_shared_pool.unkeep`.

Note: *In addition to pinning packages at database start-up time, the* `dbmspool.keep` *procedure can be called at runtime to pin a package of standalone stored procedure.*

The choice of whether to pin a procedure in memory is a function of the size of the object and the frequency of its use. Very large procedures that are called frequently might benefit from pinning, but you might never notice any difference in that case, because the frequent calls to the procedure will have kept it loaded into memory anyway.

In an ideal world, the init.ora `shared_pool` parameter would be large enough to accept every package, stored procedure, and trigger your applications might invoke. Reality, however, dictates that the shared pool cannot grow indefinitely, and you need to make wise choices regarding which objects you pin.

Note: *Only packages can be pinned. Stored procedures cannot be pinned unless they are placed into a package.*

As stated above, the choice of whether to pin a package in memory is a function of the size of the object and the frequency of its use, and very large packages that are called frequently might benefit from pinning, but any difference might go unnoticed because the frequent calls to the procedure have kept it loaded into memory anyway. Therefore, because the object never pages out in the first place, pinning has no effect. Also, the way procedures are grouped into packages can have some influence. Some Oracle DBAs identify high-impact procedures and group them into a single package, which is pinned in the library cache.

Also as stated above, in an ideal world, the `shared_pool` parameter of the init.ora should be large enough to accept every package, stored procedure, and trigger that can be used by the applications. However, reality dictates that the shared pool cannot grow indefinitely, and wise choices must be made in terms of which packages are pinned.

Because of their frequent usage, Oracle recommends that the STANDARD, DBMS_STANDARD, DBMS_UTILITY, DBMS_DESCRIBE, and DBMS_OUTPUT packages always be pinned in the shared pool. The following snippet demonstrates how a stored procedure called `sys.standard` can be pinned:

```
CONNECT INTERNAL;

@/usr/oracle/rdbms/admin/dbmspool.sql

EXECUTE dbms_shared_pool.keep('sys.standard');
```

A standard procedure can be written to pin all of the recommended Oracle packages into the shared pool. Here is the script:

```
EXECUTE dbms_shared_pool.keep('DBMS_ALERT');
EXECUTE dbms_shared_pool.keep('DBMS_DDL');
EXECUTE dbms_shared_pool.keep('DBMS_DESCRIBE');
EXECUTE dbms_shared_pool.keep('DBMS_LOCK');
EXECUTE dbms_shared_pool.keep('DBMS_OUTPUT');
EXECUTE dbms_shared_pool.keep('DBMS_PIPE');
EXECUTE dbms_shared_pool.keep('DBMS_SESSION');
EXECUTE dbms_shared_pool.keep('DBMS_SHARED_POOL');
EXECUTE dbms_shared_pool.keep('DBMS_STANDARD');
EXECUTE dbms_shared_pool.keep('DBMS_UTILITY');
EXECUTE dbms_shared_pool.keep('STANDARD');
```

Oracle Corporation recommends that you always pin the `STANDARD`, `DBMS_STANDARD`, `DBMS_UTILITY`, `DBMS_DESCRIBE`, and `DBMS_OUTPUT` packages in the shared pool.

Automatic Re-Pinning of Packages

UNIX users might want to add code to the /etc/rc file to ensure that the packages are re-pinned after each database start-up, guaranteeing that all packages are re-pinned with each bounce of the box. A script might look like this:

```
[root]: more pin
ORACLE_SID=mydata
export ORACLE_SID
su oracle -c "/usr/oracle/bin/svrmgrl /<<!
connect internal;
select * from db;
  @/usr/local/dba/sql/pin.sql
exit;
!"
```

The database administrator also needs to remember to run pin.sql whenever restarting a database. This is done by reissuing the `PIN` command from inside SQL*DBA immediately after the database has been restarted.

How to Measure Pinned Packages

Exhibit 40.3 shows a handy script to look at pinned packages in the SGA. The output from this listing should show those packages that are frequently used by your application. Exhibit 40.4 shows the output of memory.sql.

Exhibit 40.3 Looking at Pinned Packages in the SGA Using memory.sql

```
memory.sql - Display used SGA memory for triggers, packages, and procedures
SET PAGESIZE 60;
COLUMN EXECUTIONS          FORMAT 999,999,999;
COLUMN Mem_used            FORMAT 999,999,999;

SELECT SUBSTR(owner,1,10) Owner,
SUBSTR(type,1,12)          Type,
executions,
sharable_mem               Mem_used,
SUBSTR(kept||' ',1,4)      "Kept?"
FROM v$db_object_cache
WHERE TYPE IN ('TRIGGER','PROCEDURE','PACKAGE BODY','PACKAGE')
ORDER BY EXECUTIONS DESC;
```

Exhibit 40.4 The Output of memory.sql

```
SQL> @memory
OWNER    TYPE            NAME          EXECUTIONS   MEM_USED    KEPT
-----    --------------  ----------    ----------   -------     ------
SYS      PACKAGE         STANDARD      867,600      151,963     YES
SYS      PACKAGE BODY    STANDARD      867,275       30,739     YES
SYS      PACKAGE         DBMS_ALERT    502,126        3,637     NO
SYS      PACKAGE BODY    DBMS_ALERT    433,607       20,389     NO
SYS      PACKAGE         DBMS_LOCK     432,137        3,140     YES
SYS      PACKAGE BODY    DBMS_LOCK     432,137       10,780     YES
SYS      PACKAGE         DBMS_PIPE     397,466        3,412     NO
SYS      PACKAGE BODY    DBMS_PIPE     397,466        5,292     NO
HRIS     PACKAGE         S125_PACKAGE  285,700        3,776     NO
```

Chapter 41

Investigating the Multiple Buffer Pool Feature of Oracle8

John Beresniewicz

The Oracle buffer cache is critical to obtaining optimal database performance. Prior to Oracle8, there were few tuning options for the buffer cache, other than assigning buffers using the DB_BLOCK_BUFFERS initialization parameter. In most cases, the LRU algorithm governing the buffer cache works quite well; no other tuning is required. However, certain data access patterns have been identified that could benefit from alternative buffer aging algorithms. Oracle8 allows the buffer cache to be divided into as many as three separate buffer pools to accommodate multiple cache management strategies and assignment of objects to specific buffer pools. These new cache areas are known as the DEFAULT, RECYCLE, and KEEP buffer pools.

This chapter presents results of preliminary investigations into this new and little-utilized feature of Oracle8, including some experimental evidence that it can provide significant performance benefits under the right circumstances.

Buffer Cache Review

All Oracle data is obtained by users from the buffer cache. The basic purpose of the cache is to minimize physical disk I/O by holding (*buffering*) copies of requested data blocks in memory. Data that is buffered in the cache can be served to users at memory access speed, much faster than going to disk for it. The large performance penalty of disk I/O makes tuning the buffer cache an extremely important task for the DBA.

0-8493-1139-X/02/$0.00+$1.50
©2002 by CRC Press LLC

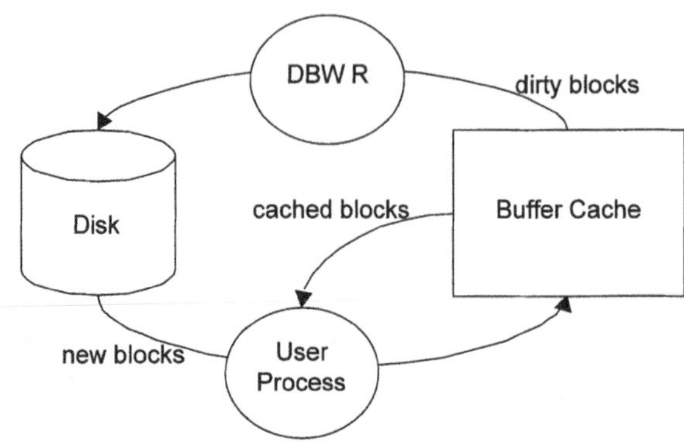

Exhibit 41.1 Block Movement Between Buffer Cache and Disk

Oracle data is stored on disk in identically sized units called *blocks*. Block size is determined at database creation by the DB_BLOCK_SIZE initialization parameter. The buffer cache is also divided into buffers of this same size, and each buffer can hold exactly one database block. Thus, the block is the basic unit of data transfer between disk and memory in Oracle.

Exhibit 41.1 shows a basic schematic of block movement between disk and the buffer cache through user processes and the DBWR background process. User processes obtain blocks from the cache if they can; otherwise, they read from disk into the cache. DBWR is responsible for writing dirty (modified) blocks out from the cache to disk.

Cache Hit Ratio

The buffer cache is a shared resource, accessible by all users. When a user process requests data, Oracle first looks for that data's block in the cache. If the data is buffered in the cache, it is returned to the requestor immediately. This is called a *cache hit.* When the data is not found, a *cache miss* occurs and the user process reads the data from disk into an available buffer in the cache. The *cache hit ratio* is the overall percentage of data requests that are served directly from the cache. In Oracle, the buffer cache hit ratio is normally computed using the following formula:

$$\text{Cache hit ratio} = 100 * (1 - \text{Physical reads/Logical reads})$$

In this formula, "physical reads" corresponds to cache misses and "logical reads" corresponds to total data requests.

Tuning the buffer cache for optimum performance usually involves adding buffers to the cache until the hit ratio has been maximized. The number of buffers in the cache is specified by the DB_BLOCK_BUFFERS initialization parameter.

Buffer Aging and LRU Lists

An Oracle database typically has many more data blocks on disk than memory buffers in the buffer cache. Since not all blocks can be buffered in the cache at once, new block requests (cache misses) must find room in the cache to be read in from disk. When this happens, another block in the cache is usually discarded because the cache is normally full (and fixed in size).

The buffer cache is carefully designed to favor keeping frequently requested blocks in memory and allow less popular blocks to be replaced by new block requests. Decisions about which blocks to replace are made using a *least recently used* (or LRU) algorithm. This algorithm uses a data structure called the *LRU list.* This list basically orders the buffers in the cache according to when they were last accessed by a user. When a block is accessed, it is moved to the most recently used (MRU) end of the list. Blocks in the cache that are not accessed for awhile will find more and more blocks ahead of them in the list, and they will be closer to the LRU end of the list. This is also known as buffer aging in the LRU list.

Buffers are replaced in the cache from the least recently used end of the LRU list. This helps ensure that frequently accessed buffers are not discarded, as they are regularly moved to the MRU list with each access. This mechanism of keeping the most requested blocks in the buffer cache is normally effective at minimizing disk I/O.

Managing a single LRU list can sometimes be a bottleneck in a heavily loaded database. The buffer cache can be divided into multiple working sets of buffers, each of which is effectively an individual LRU list. The number of *working sets* (LRU lists) used by Oracle is determined by the `DB_BLOCK_LRU_LATCHES` initialization parameter. This parameter is also important for configuring multiple buffer pools, as each pool must have at least one working set (and thus LRU latch).

DBWR and the Dirty List

In addition to the LRU list, Oracle keeps a list of buffers containing data that has been modified by users. This list is called the *dirty list.* Changed data committed by users must eventually be written to disk, as this is the permanent storage of the database. The DBWR background process is responsible for moving blocks from the dirty list to their permanent locations in disk files.

Dirty blocks cannot be replaced in the cache until they have been written to disk; otherwise, the changes would be lost. An overabundance of dirty buffers can negatively impact cache efficiency by reducing available slots for new blocks. This can happen when DBWR is unable to keep up with the volume of update activity. Multiple DBWR processes can be configured in this case to increase the capacity to write out dirty blocks.

Full Table Scans: `CACHE` and `NOCACHE`

The LRU aging algorithm of Oracle's buffer cache treats blocks accessed for full-table scans differently than blocks accessed randomly, based on the observation that full scans could flood the MRU end of the list with blocks that have low probability of reuse. To avoid the negative impact on cache performance that this could cause, Oracle places blocks from full scans at the LRU end of the list, allowing them to be quickly replaced rather than aging other blocks.

In certain cases (such as small lookup tables) full-table scan blocks may actually be good candidates for reuse and would be better placed at the MRU end of the list. Oracle7 classified tables as "small" or "large" based on the initialization parameter SMALL_TABLE_THRESHOLD and placed full scan blocks at the MRU or LRU end of the LRU list, depending on whether the scanned table was small or large, respectively.

Oracle provides the ability to override the default cache treatment of full table scans (for large or small tables) at the table level using the CACHE or NOCACHE clauses of the CREATE TABLE and ALTER TABLE statements. Specifying CACHE indicates that the table's blocks should be placed at the MRU end of the LRU list when read during a full-table scan.

Full scan LRU treatment of blocks can also be specified at the individual SQL statement level, using the CACHE and NOCACHE hints.

Note that, although CACHE and NOCACHE are supported in Oracle8, the SMALL_TABLE_THRESHOLD is no longer a visible or documented initialization parameter.

Buffer Cache Problems

The LRU algorithm of the Oracle buffer cache is normally very good at providing efficient minimization of physical disk I/O. However, there are some situations in which normal buffer cache aging may not be the best option for overall performance; for example:

- Blocks that should not go to the MRU end of the list
- Blocks that should be excluded from aging and stay in the cache

The first situation can occur when very large tables are accessed randomly by users with little block use overlap among users. In this case, the MRU end of the list is flooded by blocks that will not result in subsequent cache hits, yet age other blocks down to the LRU end of the list. These other blocks may be replaced when they could have resulted in cache hits had they been kept.

The second situation occurs when there are data blocks that will definitely be requested regularly and we want to ensure that physical disk I/O is not necessary to obtain their data. Examples might be small lookup tables or perhaps specific indexes.

The new multiple buffer pool feature of Oracle8 allows greater control over buffer cache usage to help address these problems and obtain even better cache performance.

Oracle8 Buffer Pools

The two situations noted above are cases in which the LRU aging algorithm of the Oracle8 buffer cache could be improved upon by treating certain types of blocks differently. The Oracle8 buffer cache can be divided into three separate pools of buffers to help segregate blocks with different LRU aging requirements. These pools are known as the `RECYCLE`, `KEEP`, and `DEFAULT` buffer pools.

The `RECYCLE` Pool

In the first case, random access blocks flooding the MRU end of the list will not have a high reuse rate, yet can age more desirable blocks out of the cache. Physical disk reads will be incurred when these other blocks are subsequently requested again. It would be better if these random access blocks could "age faster" in the cache and be quickly replaced, rather than pushing other blocks out. The Oracle8 `RECYCLE` buffer pool is specifically designed to provide working sets of buffers that can be rapidly aged out of the cache.

By isolating blocks from large, randomly accessed tables away from the rest of the buffer cache, the `RECYCLE` pool relieves the pressure these blocks can place on the LRU list. This allows buffers from other objects to age less quickly and increases the chances of subsequent cache hits.

The `RECYCLE` pool can also be used to place a strict upper bound on the number of buffers any particular object will consume in the buffer cache. Since blocks from objects assigned to the `RECYCLE` pool will not likely be needed again soon, the pool itself can often be far smaller than the number of buffers these objects would occupy in the `DEFAULT` pool. This results in more memory available for the other pools, thus increasing their efficiency.

The `KEEP` Pool

The second problem with the LRU aging algorithm noted that some blocks would be better off if they "aged more slowly" (or not at all) out of the cache. Imagine a transaction that randomly accesses a table and joins in data from five small lookup tables based on foreign keys. If the blocks from these lookup tables and their indexes are not in the cache, this transaction may incur an additional ten or more physical disk reads to get the data. When response time is critical, this extra overhead can cause a wide disparity between the best and worst cases. The Oracle8 `KEEP` buffer pool allows objects to be effectively "pinned" into the buffer cache and excluded from the LRU aging process.

The `KEEP` pool is used to ensure the presence of buffers in the cache, regardless of when they were last accessed. This feature should be used carefully, however, as pinning infrequently used objects into the pool can be a waste of memory that could be better used elsewhere.

Exhibit 41.2 Database Initialization Parameters for Configuring Oracle8 Buffer Pools

Parameter	*Description*
DB_BLOCK_BUFFERS	Total number of block buffers for all pools
DB_BLOCK_LRU_LATCHES	Total number of LRU latches for all pools
BUFFER_POOL_KEEP	Number of buffers and latches for the KEEP pool
BUFFER_POOL_RECYCLE	Number of buffers and latches for the RECYCLE pool

The DEFAULT Pool

The DEFAULT pool is for all objects not explicitly assigned to one of the other pools. There is always a DEFAULT pool and it will most likely be the largest of the pools under normal circumstances. When the RECYCLE and KEEP pools are not configured, the DEFAULT buffer pool operates the same as the Oracle7 buffer cache.

Configuring Multiple Buffer Pools

The DEFAULT, KEEP, and RECYCLE buffer pools are configured using the initialization parameters in Exhibit 41.2. The KEEP and RECYCLE pools are explicitly configured with buffers and LRU latches; the DEFAULT pool is allocated the remainder from the overall totals specified by DB_BLOCK_BUFFERS and DB_BLOCK_LRU_LATCHES.

For example, suppose we have 1000 total cache buffers to allocate. We can assign 700 to DEFAULT, 200 to KEEP, and 100 to the RECYCLE pools with one LRU latch per pool as follows:

```
db_block_buffers = 1000
db_block_lru_latches = 3
buffer_pool_keep = (buffers:200,lru_latches:1)
buffer_pool_recycle = (buffers:100,lru_latches:1)
```

Note the syntax for the two new parameters, BUFFER_POOL_KEEP and BUFFER_POOL_RECYCLE. The minimum size of an LRU working set is 50 buffers, so the number of buffers configured for any of the pools must be at least 50 times the number of LRU latches. Conversely, the number of LRU latches cannot exceed DB_BLOCK_BUFFERS divided by 50. Each LRU working set in a pool is equally sized at the number of buffers divided by the number of latches.

The maximum number of LRU latches that can be configured for all the pools is six times the number of CPUs.

Load Balancing Multiple DBWRs

When multiple buffer pools are used in combination with multiple DBWR processes, there is a potential for uneven load balancing to occur between the

DBWR processes. The DBWR processes are assigned to LRU working sets in round-robin fashion, and the working sets from different pools may be of different sizes. For example, a DBWR assigned to working sets from the KEEP and DEFAULT pools may have a much different workload than one assigned sets from the RECYCLE pool. Oracle recommends that such load imbalances can be avoided by allocating to each pool a number of LRU latches equal to a multiple of the number of DBWR processes. Under this strategy, each DBWR will draw the same number of working sets from each pool; thus, the load will be balanced.

Assigning Objects to Buffer Pools

Segments can be assigned to buffer pools using the new BUFFER_POOL option of the STORAGE clause. For example, a table can be created and assigned to the KEEP pool as follows:

```
CREATE TABLE new_table
   (col1 NUMBER
   ,col2 VARCHAR2(100)
   )
   TABLESPACE tablespace_name
   STORAGE (INITIAL 64K
     NEXT 128K
     BUFFER_POOL KEEP);
```

Other valid values are BUFFER_POOL RECY CLE and BUFFER_POOL DEFAULT.

The following statements accept this new STORAGE clause option:

```
CREATE TABLE
CREATE INDEX
CREATE CLUSTER
ALTER TABLE
ALTER INDEX
ALTER CLUSTER
```

When a pool is not explicitly specified, segments are assigned to the DEFAULT pool. Clustered tables inherit the pool of their cluster. Note also that pools can be specified at the partition level for partitioned segments.

If a segment is reassigned from one pool to another using an ALTER command, blocks in the cache from the segment stay in their current pool until aged out. New blocks from the segment will be loaded into the new pool.

Viewing Buffer Cache Information

There are several Oracle8 fixed tables and views that provide valuable information about the buffer cache and the new buffer pools.

The X$BH Fixed Table

Perhaps the most complete source of information about the Oracle8 buffer cache is the X$BH fixed table. This table contains one row for every buffer

Exhibit 41.3 Useful Columns from the X$BH Fixed Table

Column	Data Type	Description
ADDR	RAW	Address of buffer in SGA
BUF#	NUMBER	Sequential number of buffer in cache
OBJ	NUMBER	Object id of segment owning block in the buffer
TS#	NUMBER	Tablespace number owning block in the buffer
FILE#	NUMBER	File number owning block in the buffer
DBARFIL	NUMBER	Relative file number of the block in the buffer
DBABLK	NUMBER	Block number in file of block in the buffer
SET_DS	RAW	Joins to X$KCBWDS.ADDR to identify working set of buffer
CLASS	NUMBER	Block class (1 = data block, 4 = header block)
STATE	NUMBER	Used to determine status of block (e.g., FREE)
FLAG	NUMBER	Encodes various information about the block, including dirty status and whether read sequentially or randomly
NEXT_REPL	RAW	Address of next buffer on LRU list
PRV_REPL	RAW	Address of previous buffer on LRU list

in the buffer cache. There are more than 50 columns in this table, and they are not officially documented. Much of the information is relevant mostly to Oracle Parallel Server environments, where buffer cache coordination between instances introduces additional complexity. However, I have been able to dig up interesting and useful information on some of the columns in X$BH, as described in Exhibit 41.3.

As with the other internal fixed tables, X$BH can only be queried by the SYS user. Oracle provides a view called V$BH which externalizes X$BH; however, V$BH is designed specifically for Oracle Parallel Server installations and will not display information when queried from a non-OPS instance. This is unfortunate because X$BH has such interesting information.

We can overcome this shortcoming by creating our own view to externalize the useful X$BH information. The following code segment defines the view `Q$BUFFER_CACHE`, which does just that. It can be run as SYS and then SELECT privilege on the view granted out to other users requiring buffer cache information.

```
rem*******************************************
rem*Externalizes useful buffer cache information
rem*from the X$BH and X$KCBWBPD fixed tables
rem*******************************************
CREATE OR REPLACE VIEW q$buffer_cache
   (buf_addr
   ,buf_no
   ,dba_file
   ,dba_blk
   ,tbs_id
   ,obj_id
```

```
     ,blk_class
     ,status
     ,pool
     ,dirty
     ,io_type
     ,nxt_repl
     ,prv_repl
     )
AS
SELECT
       bh.addr
       ,bh.buf#
       ,bh.dbarfil
       ,bh.dbablk
       ,bh.ts#
       ,bh.obj
       ,bh.class
       ,DECODE(bh.state,0,'FREE',1,'XCUR',2,
       'SCUR', 3,'CR',4,'READ',5,'MREC',6,'IREC')
       ,bp.bp_name
       ,DECODE(BITAND(bh.flag,1),0,'N','Y')
       ,DECODE(BITAND(bh.flag,524288),0,'RANDOM',
       'SEQUENTIAL')
       ,nxt_repl
       ,prv_repl
  FROM
       x$kcbwbpd    bp
       ,x$bh        bh
WHERE
            bp.bp_size > 0
  AND       bh.buf# >= bp.bp_lo_bnum
  AND       bh.buf# <= bp.bp_hi_bnum;
```

The Q$BUFFER_CACHE view can answer all kinds of useful queries about the buffer cache and pools. For example, the following SQL shows buffer counts by pool, object owner, type, and I/O type:

```
SELECT pool
       ,owner
       ,object_type
       ,io_type
       ,count(*)
  FROM     q$buffer_cacheBC
           ,dba_objectsO
WHERE BC.obj_id = O.object_id
GROUP BY pool,owner,object_type,io_type;
```

V$BUFFER_POOL and V$BUFFER_POOL_STATISTICS

The V$BUFFER_POOL view supplies basic information about how many LRU working sets and buffers are assigned to each pool, and the range of buffers assigned to each. The underlying fixed table is X$KCBWBPD, which is joined to X$BH in the Q$BUFFER_CACHE view to associate each buffer with the pool it belongs to. Normally, V$BUFFER_POOL will not be useful except to verify the buffer pool configuration.

Exhibit 41.4 V$BUFFER_POOL_STATISTICS Columns

Column	Data Type	Description
ID	NUMBER	Buffer pool number
NAME	VARCHAR2(20)	Buffer pool name
SET_MSIZE	NUMBER	Maximum set size
CNUM_REPL	NUMBER	Total buffers on LRU lists
CNUM_WRITE	NUMBER	Total buffers on dirty lists
CNUM_SET	NUMBER	Total working set buffers
BUF_GOT	NUMBER	Total buffers gotten
SUM_WRITE	NUMBER	Total buffers written
SUM_SCAN	NUMBER	Total buffers scanned
FREE_BUFFER_WAIT	NUMBER	Total free buffer wait events (V$SYSTEM_EVENT)
WRITE_COMPLETE_WAIT	NUMBER	Total write complete wait events (V$SYSTEM_EVENT)
BUFFER_BUSY_WAIT	NUMBER	Total buffer busy wait events (V$SYSTEM_EVENT)
FREE_BUFFER_INSPECTED	NUMBER	Total free buffer inspected (V$SYSSTAT)
DIRTY_BUFFERS_INSPECTED	NUMBER	Total dirty buffers inspected (V$SYSSTAT)
DB_BLOCK_CHANGE	NUMBER	Total block changes (V$SYSSTAT)
DB_BLOCK_GETS	NUMBER	Total block gets (V$SYSSTAT)
CONSISTENT_GETS	NUMBER	Total consistent gets (V$SYSSTAT)
PHYSICAL_READS	NUMBER	Total physical reads (V$SYSSTAT)
PHYSICAL_WRITES	NUMBER	Total physical writes (V$SYSSTAT)

There is an interesting and useful new Oracle8 view called V$BUFFER_POOL_STATISTICS that contains lots of information about buffer cache performance. It is created by the CATPERF.SQL script located in the <ORACLE_HOME>/rdbms/admin directory. CATPERF.SQL is not executed automatically when the database is created, so it must be explicitly executed (as SYS) to create the view. Exhibit 41.4 lists the columns in V$BUFFER_POOL_STATISTICS.

The statistics in V$BUFFER_POOL_STATISTICS represent totals across all working sets for each pool. Many of the columns give performance statistics at the buffer pool level that were previously only available at the instance level in either V$SYSSTAT or V$SYSTEM_EVENT. Clearly, the V$BUFFER_POOL_STATISTICS view is key to analyzing the performance of multiple Oracle8 buffer pools. For example, we can calculate the individual buffer pool hit ratios using the following SQL:

```
SELECT name
     ,1-(physical_reads/(db_block_gets+
     consistent_gets))
        hit_ratio
FROM v$buffer_pool_statistics;
```

Exhibit 41.5 Buffer Pool Test Object Sizes

Object Name	*Object Type*	*Blocks*
LARGE_TBL	TABLE	14409
LARGE_TBL_PK	UNIQUE INDEX	142
LOOKUP_TBL	TABLE	505
LOOKUP_TBL_PK	UNIQUE INDEX	5

Testing the Multiple Buffer Pool Feature

I decided to experiment with the Oracle8 RECYCLE and KEEP buffer pools to validate their usefulness as described by Oracle. In particular, I was interested in simulating the situation where random access to a large table causes extreme pressure on the LRU list and degrades performance. This is described in the documentation as an ideal candidate for use of the RECYCLE pool. In addition, I decided to use a smaller lookup table to investigate the KEEP buffer pool.

Test Objects and Environment

Four schema objects were used for the tests: two tables and two indexes. The two tables each had a numeric identifier column serving as the primary keys (implemented by the two indexes). The tables also contained a VARCHAR2 data column. Rows were inserted into the two tables such that each row occupied exactly one block. This was an important part of the experimental design: it guaranteed that every unique row access corresponded to a unique block request. After object creation, ANALYZE statistics were computed to obtain the exact object sizes shown in Exhibit 41.5.

The database block size was 2048 bytes to conserve memory and disk space. The test machine was a single Pentium II 350 CPU with 96 MB of memory running Win NT 4.0 Workstation and Oracle8 v8.0.5.

The `Buffer_Stuffer` Procedure

I created a PL/SQL package called ECO99 with some procedures to help implement these buffer pool experiments. The main procedure in this package is called BUFFER_STUFFER. It is designed to "randomly" access rows (blocks) in LARGE_TBL without ever asking for the same row twice. This controlled and repeatable randomness (how's that for an oxymoron?) is accomplished using a specially selected linear congruential algorithm to generate primary key values for LARGE_TBL.

The main cursor in BUFFER_STUFFER and its EXPLAIN PLAN output (from TKPROF) are:

```
CURSOR large_tbl_cur
   (cur_id_col large_tbl.id_col%TYPE)
IS
SELECT A.data_col data1, B.data_col data2
   FROM large_tbl A, lookup_tbl B
   WHERE A.id_col = cur_id_col
      AND A.id_col2 = B.id_col;

Execution Plan
-----------------------------------------------
SELECT STATEMENT GOAL: CHOOSE
   NESTED LOOPS
   TABLE ACCESS   GOAL: ANALYZED (BY INDEX ROWID) OF 'LARGE_TBL'
      INDEX       GOAL: ANALYZED (RANGE SCAN) OF 'LARGE_TBL_PK'
      (UNIQUE)
   TABLE ACCESS   GOAL: ANALYZED (BY INDEX ROWID) OF 'LOOKUP_TBL'
      INDEX       GOAL: ANALYZED (UNIQUE SCAN) OF 'LOOKUP_TBL_PK'
      (UNIQUE)
```

Each cursor open and fetch touches all four of the test objects and retrieves data from a single row in LARGE_TBL joined to a single row in LOOKUP_TBL.

The BUFFER_STUFFER procedure has parameters that can vary the buffer get rate and total number of buffers gotten. The procedure signature looks like this:

```
PROCEDURE buffer_stuffer
   (buffs_per_stuff_IN IN INTEGER
   ,sleep_secs_IN IN NUMBER
   ,total_stuffs_IN IN INTEGER
   ,seed_IN IN INTEGER := rand_seed
   );
```

Each execution will get total_stuffs_IN batches of buffs_per_stuff_IN buffers, sleeping sleeps_secs_IN between batches. The seed_IN parameter can optionally be used to seed the primary key generator. BUFFER_STUFFER has proven to be a reliable utility for applying specific and repeatable amounts of pressure to the buffer cache LRU list.

Buffer Pool Configurations

The test script was executed against four different buffer pool configurations. All configurations allocated a total of 1000 buffers and three LRU latches, with different specific pool allocations and assignment of objects to pools. Briefly, the purpose of each test was the following (see Exhibit 41.6):

1. Establish a baseline, using DEFAULT pool only
2. Place LARGE_TBL in a small RECYCLE pool
3. Pin LOOKUP_TBL in the KEEP pool
4. Use RECYLE pool for LARGE_TBL and pin indexes in KEEP pool

Experimental Procedure

The experiments consisted of executing the following script under each configuration:

Exhibit 41.6 Buffer Pool Configurations Tested

Test ID	*DEFAULT*	*RECYCLE*	*KEEP*
TEST1	1000 buffers, 3 LRU latches All objects	n/a	n/a
TEST2	950 buffers, 2 LRU latches LOOKUP_TBL LOOKUP_TBL_PK LARGE_TBL_PK	50 buffers, 1 LRU latch LARGE_TBL	n/a
TEST3	500 buffers, 2 LRU latches LARGE_TBL LARGE_TBL_PK LOOKUP_TBL_PK	n/a	500 buffers, 1 LRU latch LOOKUP_TBL
TEST4	800 buffers, 1 LRU latch LOOKUP_TBL	50 buffers, 1 LRU latch LARGE_TBL	150 buffers, 1 LRU latch LOOKUP_TBL_PK LARGE_TBL_PK

```
set timing on
set serveroutput on size 1000000

SELECT name
     ,consistent_gets+db_block_gets logical_reads,physical_reads
     ,DECODE(consistent_gets+db_block_gets,0, TO_NUMBER(null)
       ROUND(1-physical_reads/(consistent_gets+db_block_gets),1) )
         hit_ratio

FROM
     sys.v$buffer_pool_statistics;

DECLARE
  physrds_before INTEGER := eco99.mystat ('physical reads');
  physrds_after INTEGER;

BEGIN
  eco99.set_rand(14406,967,3041);
  eco99.buffer_stuffer(100,.1,100);
  DBMS_OUTPUT.PUT_LINE('Phys Rds: '||
    TO_CHAR(eco99.mystat('physical reads')-physrds_before) );
END;
/

SELECT name
     ,consistent_gets+db_block_gets logical_reads ,physical_reads
     ,DECODE(consistent_gets+db_block_gets,0,TO_NUMBER(null)
       ,ROUND(1-physical_reads/(consistent_gets+db_block_gets),1) )
         hit_ratio

FROM
     sys.v$buffer_pool_statistics;
```

The script gathers buffer pool information from V$BUFFER_POOL_STATISTICS before and after the BUFFER_STUFFER procedure does 10,000 random accesses to LARGE_TBL joined to LOOKUP_TBL. Each test run requested 10,000 unique blocks from LARGE_TABLE, as well as every block from each of the other segments. Between tests, the database was stopped, reconfigured, and restarted. Tests were executed immediately after database start-up to ensure cache conditions were as identical as possible. Elapsed time was reported from SQL*Plus timing output.

Experimental Results

The tests yielded some interesting results, detailed in Exhibit 41.7. The most striking of these is the huge advantage gained by using a minimally configured RECYCLE pool, shown in TEST2. Real-locating just 5 percent of the cache (50 blocks) from the DEFAULT pool to the RECYCLE pool and placing the large random access table there reduced physical reads by 33 percent and improved elapsed time by 31 percent. The absolute minimum number of physical reads possible for a test run is 10,652. TEST2 generated just 58 extra disk reads above this minimum value, which I at first found hard to believe.

Pinning LOOKUP_TBL into the KEEP pool (TEST3) improved performance, but only about half as much as TEST2. The relatively large buffer allocation (500) needed to capture the table may have been too much: the DEFAULT cache had only 500 buffers to manage the extreme pressure applied by LARGE_TBL blocks in addition to the two indexes.

Exhibit 41.7 Detailed Experimental Results

Test ID Elapsed Time	*Buffer Pools*	*Physical Reads*	*Logical Reads*	*Hit Ratio (Percent)*
TEST1	DEFAULT	16,018	30,164	46.9
162.0 seconds	RECYCLE			
	KEEP			
	Total	16,018	30,164	46.9
TEST2	DEFAULT	706	20,164	96.5
112.3 seconds	RECYCLE	10,000	10,000	0.0
	KEEP			
	Total	10,706	30,164	64.5
TEST3	DEFAULT	12,845	20,164	36.3
139.4 seconds	RECYCLE			
	KEEP	500	10,000	95.0
	Total	13,345	30,164	55.8
TEST4	DEFAULT	553	10,364	94.7
112.2 seconds	RECYCLE	10,000	10,000	0.0
	KEEP	147	10,000	98.5
	Total	10,700	30,364	64.8

The TEST4 results were virtually identical to TEST2, demonstrating the dominance of the RECYCLE pool allocation. Presumably, the TEST4 configuration could have a positive effect on other transactions using the two indexes as they are pinned into the KEEP pool.

The experiment was designed principally to test the RECYCLE pool under extreme LRU pressure, and the results certainly bear out its value under these circumstances.

Conclusion

The new RECYCLE and KEEP buffer pools of Oracle8 appear to be very useful for enhancing buffer cache efficiency in specific situations. Large OLTP systems exhibiting chronically low hit ratios may be candidates for the RECYCLE buffer pool, as well as any database where randomly accessed objects are overly greedy for buffer cache space. The KEEP pool can be used to isolate and pin blocks to help guarantee performance of specific transactions consistently accessing the same relatively small objects. Smaller data warehouse dimension tables may be worth exploring for assignment to this pool.

It will be interesting to move beyond laboratory experiments and see actual field results using this powerful new Oracle8 feature to tune large-scale database buffer caches.

Bibliography

Oracle8 Concepts Release 8.0, Oracle Corporation, 1997.
Oracle8 Reference Release 8.0, Oracle Corporation, 1997.
Oracle8 Tuning Release 8.0, Oracle Corporation, 1997.
Oracle8 SQL Reference Release 8.0, Oracle Corporation, 1997.
Oracle Built-in Packages, O'Reilly & Associates, 1998.
Oracle PL/SQL Built-ins Pocket Reference, O'Reilly & Associates, 1998.
Numerical Recipes in C, Cambridge University Press, 1988.

Chapter 42

Diving into the Shared Pool

Michael R. Ault

Perhaps one of the least understood areas of Oracle Shared Global Area optimization is tuning the shared pool. The generally accepted tuning methodology involves throwing memory into the pool until the problem goes under. This chapter examines the shared pool and defines a method for tuning that uses measurement — not guesswork — to drive the tuning methodologies. This chapter shows you how to monitor and tune the shared SQL area of the shared pool, as well as what to pin, and looks at other areas such as multithreaded server, hashing, and the generalized tuning of the library and data dictionary cache areas.

Defining the Shared Pool?

Many people know that the shared pool is a part of the Oracle shared global area (SGA) but little else. What exactly is the shared pool? The shared pool contains several key Oracle performance-related memory areas. If the shared pool is improperly sized, then overall database performance will suffer — sometimes dramatically. Exhibit 42.1 diagrams the shared pool structure located inside the various Oracle SGAs.

As you can see from examining the structures in Exhibit 42.1, the shared pool is separated into many substructures. The substructures of the shared pool fall into two broad areas, the *fixed size areas* that for a given database at a given point in time stay relatively constant in size, and the *variable size areas* that grow and shrink according to user and program requirements.

Areas inside the library cache substructure in Exhibit 42.1 are variable in size, while those outside the library caches (with the exception of the request and response queues used with MTS) stay relatively fixed in size. The sizes are determined based on an Oracle internal algorithm that ratios out the fixed areas based on overall shared pool size, a few of the intialization parameters,

0-8493-1139-X/02/$0.00+$1.50
©2002 by CRC Press LLC

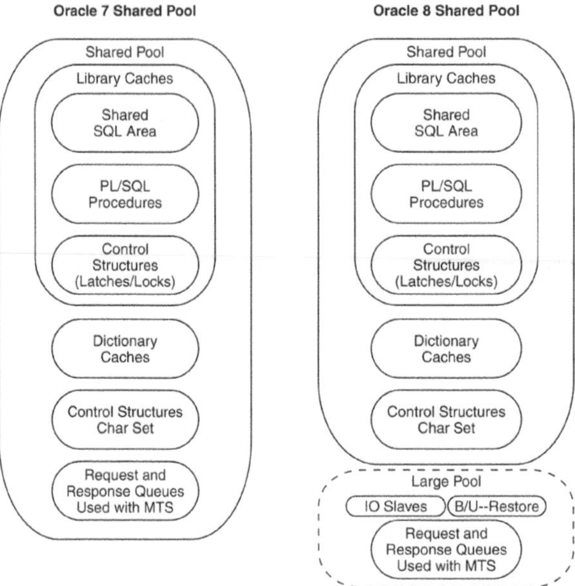

Exhibit 42.1 Oracle7 and Oracle8 Shared Pool Structures

and empirical determinations from previous versions. In early versions of Oracle (notably 6.2 and lower versions), the dictionary caches could be sized individually, allowing a finer control of this aspect of the shared pool. With Oracle7, the internal algorithm for sizing the data dictionary caches took control from the DBA.

The shared pool is used for objects that can be shared among all users, such as table definitions, reusable SQL (although nonreusable SQL is also stored there), PL/SQL packages, procedures, and functions. Cursor information is also stored in the shared pool. At a minimum, the shared pool must be sized to accommodate the needs of the fixed areas, plus a small amount of memory reserved for use in parsing SQL and PL/SQL statements or ORA-07445 errors will result.

Monitoring and Tuning the Shared Pool

Let me begin by stating that the default values for the shared pool size initialization parameters are almost always too small by at least a factor of four. Unless a database is limited to the basic scott/tiger type schema, and overall physical data size is *less* than a couple of hundred megabytes, even the "large" parameters are far too small. What parameters control the size of the shared pool? Essentially only one — `SHARED_POOL_SIZE`. The other shared pool parameters control how the variable space areas in the shared pool are parsed out, but not overall size. In Oracle8, a new area, the large pool, controlled by the `LARGE_POOL_SIZE` parameter is also present. Generally speaking, I suggest starting at a shared pool size of 40 megabytes and moving up from

Exhibit 42.2 Sample Script to Show SGA Use

```
REM Script to report on shared pool usage
REM
column shared_pool_used format 9,999.99
column shared_pool_size format 9,999.99
column shared_pool_avail format 9,999.99
column shared_pool_pct format 999.99
@title80 'Shared Pool Summary'
spool rep_out\&db\shared_pool
select
   sum(a.bytes)/(1024*1024) shared_pool_used,
   max(b.value)/(1024*1024) shared_pool_size,
   (max(b.value)/(1024*1024))-(sum(a.bytes)/(1024*1024))
      shared_pool_avail, (sum(a.bytes)/max(b.value))*100
shared_pool_pct
   from v$sgastat a, v$parameter b
where a.name in (
'reserved stopper',
'table definiti',
'dictionary cache',
'library cache',
'sql area',
'PL/SQL DIANA',
'SEQ S.O.') and
b.name='shared_pool_size';
spool off
ttitle off
```

there. The large pool size will depend on the number of concurrent users, number of multi-threaded servers and dispatchers, and the sort requirements for the application.

What should be monitored to determine if the shared pool is too small? For this, we need to wade into the data dictionary tables, specifically the V$SGASTAT and V$SQLAREA views. Exhibit 42.2 is a report that shows how much of the shared pool is in use at any given time the script is run.

The script in Exhibit 42.2 should be run periodically during times of normal and high database usage. The results will be similar to Exhibit 42.3. If our `shared_pool_pct` figures stay in the high nineties, then we may need to increase the size of the shared pool; however, this isn't always the case.

Too often, all that is monitored is how much of the shared pool is filled. No one looks at *how* it is filled, with "good" reusable SQL or "bad" throwaway SQL. Examine how the space is being used before deciding whether the shared pool should be increased in size, decreased in size, or perhaps a periodic

Exhibit 42.3 Sample Output from Exhibit 42.2 Script

```
Date: 11/18/98                                                    Page: 1
Time: 04:16 PM               Shared Pool Summary                  SYSTEM
                               ORTEST1 database
SHARED_POOL_USED    SHARED_POOL_SIZE    SHARED_POOL_AVAIL    SHARED_POOL_PCT
----------------    ----------------    -----------------    ---------------
            3.66               38.15                34.49               9.60
```

Exhibit 42.4 SQL Script to Create a View to Monitor Pool Use by User

```
rem FUNCTION: Creates summary of v_$sqlarea and dba_users for use in
rem           sqlmem.sql and sqlsummary.sql reports
rem
rem
create or replace view sql_summary as
  select
    username, sharable_mem, persistent_mem, runtime_mem
  from
    sys.v_$sqlarea a, dba_users b
  where
    a.parsing_user_id = b.user_id;
rem
```

flush schedule set up, with the size remaining the same. So how can we determine what is in the shared pool and whether it is being properly reused or not? Let's look at a few more reports.

The first report we examine shows how individual users are utilizing the shared pool. Before we can run the report, a summary view of the V$SQLAREA view must be created; I unimaginatively call this view the `SQL_SUMMARY` view. The code for the `SQL_SUMMARY` view is shown in Exhibit 42.4.

Once the `SQL_SUMMARY` view is created, the script in Exhibit 42.5 is run to generate a summary report of SQL areas used — by user. This shows the distribution of SQL areas and may show that some users are "hogging" a disproportionate amount of the shared pool area. Usually, such a user is not employing good SQL coding techniques, thereby generating a large volume of non-reusable SQL areas.

Sample output from the script in Exhibit 42.5 is shown in Exhibit 42.6. In the sample report, no single user is really hogging the SQL area. If a particular user is hogging SQL areas, the script in Exhibit 42.6 will show what SQL areas it has and what is in them. This report on the actual SQL area contents can then be used to help teach the user how to better construct reusable SQL statements.

In the example output, we see that SYSTEM user holds the most SQL areas and our application DBA user, GRAPHICS_DBA, holds the least. Because these reports were run on my small Oracle 8.0.5 database, this is normal; however, the application owner will usually hold the largest section of memory in a well-designed system, followed by ad hoc users using properly designed SQL. In a situation where users are not using properly designed SQL statements, the ad hoc users will usually have the largest number of SQL areas and show the most memory usage. Again, the script in Exhibit 42.7 shows the actual in memory SQL areas for a specific user. Exhibit 42.8 shows the example output from a report run against GRAPHICS_USER using the script in Exhibit 42.7.

One warning about the script in Exhibit 42.7: the report it generates can run to several hundred pages for a user with a large number of SQL areas. What things should you watch for in a user's SQL areas? First, watch for the non-use of bind variables; bind variable usage is shown by the inclusion of

Exhibit 42.5 SQL Script to Report on SQL Area Use by User

```
rem
rem FUNCTION: Generate a summary of SQL Area Memory Usage
rem FUNCTION: uses the sqlsummary view.
rem
rem
rem sqlsum.sql
rem
column areas                                      heading Used|Areas
column sharable      format 999,999,999     heading Shared|Bytes
column persistent    format 999,999,999     heading Persistent|Bytes
column runtime       format 999,999,999     heading Runtime|Bytes
column username      format a15             heading "User"
column mem_sum       format 999,999,999     heading Mem|Sum
start title80 "Users SQL Area Memory Use"
spool rep_out\&db\sqlsum
set pages 59 lines 80
break on report
compute sum of sharable on report
compute sum of persistent on report
compute sum of runtime on report
compute sum of mem_sum on report
select
  username,
  sum(sharable_mem) Sharable,
  sum( persistent_mem) Persistent,
  sum( runtime_mem) Runtime ,
  count(*) Areas,
  sum(sharable_mem+persistent_mem+runtime_mem) Mem_sum
from
  sql_summary
group by username
order by 2;
spool off
pause Press enter to continue
clear columns
clear breaks
set pages 22 lines 80
ttitle off
```

Exhibit 42.6 Output from Exhibit 42.5

```
Date: 11/18/98                                                  Page: 1
Time: 04:18 PM            Users SQL Area Memory Use              SYSTEM
                              ORTEST1 database
                       Shared  Persistent    Runtime   Used        Mem
User                    Bytes       Bytes      Bytes  Areas        Sum
--------------- ---------  ----------    -------   -----  ---------
GRAPHICS_DBA           67,226       4,640     30,512     10    102,378
SYS                   830,929      47,244    153,652     80  1,031,825
SYSTEM              2,364,314      37,848    526,228     63  2,928,390
--------------- ---------  ----------    -------   -----  ---------
sum                 3,262,469      89,732    710,392    153  4,062,593
3 rows selected.
```

Exhibit 42.7 Sample Script to Show Active SQL Areas for a User

```
rem
rem FUNCTION:  Generate a report of SQL Area Memory Usage
rem            showing SQL Text and memory catagories
rem
rem sqlmem.sql
rem
column sql_text          format a60   heading Text word_wrapped
column sharable_mem                   heading Shared|Bytes
column persistent_mem                 heading Persistent|Bytes
column loads                          heading Loads
column users             format a15   heading "User"
column executions                     heading "Executions"
column users_executing                heading "Used By"
start title132 "Users SQL Area Memory Use"
spool rep_out\&db\sqlmem
set long 2000 pages 59 lines 132
break on users
compute sum of sharable_mem on users
compute sum of persistent_mem on users
compute sum of runtime_mem on users
select
   username users, sql_text, Executions, loads, users_executing,
   sharable_mem, persistent_mem
from
   sys.v_$sqlarea a, dba_users b
where
   a.parsing_user_id = b.user_id
   and b.username like upper('%&user_name%')
order by 3 desc,1;
spool off
pause Press enter to continue
clear columns
clear computes
clear breaks
set pages 22 lines 80
```

variables such as ":1" or ":B" in the SQL text. Notice that in the example report in Exhibit 42.8 the first four statements use bind variables and, consequently, are reusable. Non-bind usage means that hard-coded values such as 'Missing' or '10' are used. Notice that for most of the rest of the statements in the report, no bind variables are used, although many of the SQL statements are nearly identical. This is one of the leading causes of shared pool misuse and results in useful SQL being drowned in tons of non-reusable garbage SQL.

The problem with non-reusable SQL is that it must still be looked at by any new SQL inserted into the pool (actually, its hash value is scanned). While a hash value scan may seem a small cost item, if your shared pool contains tens of thousands of SQL areas, this can be a performance bottleneck. How can we determine, without running the report in Exhibit 42.7 for each of possibly hundreds of users, if we have garbage SQL in the shared pool?

Exhibit 42.8 Report Output Example for a Users SQL Area

```
Date: 11/18/98
Time: 04:19 PM                    Users SQL Area Memory Use                                           SYSTEM
                                      ORTEST1 database

                                                                                          Shared Persistent
User         Text                                           Executions Loads  Used By   Bytes      Bytes
-----------  ---------------------------------              ---------- -----  --------  ------ ----------
GRAPHICS_DBA BEGIN dbms_lob.read (:1, :2, :3, :4); END;           2121     1        0   10251        488
             alter session set nls_language= 'AMERICAN' nls_territory=  7  1        0    3975        408
             'AMERICA' nls_currency= '$' nls_iso_currency= 'AMERICA'
             nls_numeric_characters= '.,' nls_calENDar= 'GREGORIAN'
             nls_date_format= 'DD-MON-YY' nls_date_language= 'AMERICAN'
             nls_sort= 'BINARY'
             BEGIN :1 := dbms_lob.getLength (:2); END;               6     1        0    9290        448
             SELECT TO_CHAR(image_seq.nextval) FROM dual             6     1        0    6532        484
             SELECT graphic_blob FROM internal_graphics WHERE        2     1        0    5863        468
             graphic_id=10
             SELECT RPAD(TO_CHAR(graphic_id),5)||':                  1     1        0    7101        472
             '||RPAD(graphic_desc,30)||' : '||RPAD(graphic_type,10) FROM
             internal_graphics ORDER BY graphic_id
             SELECT graphic_blob FROM internal_graphics WHERE        1     1        0    6099        468
             graphic_id=12
             SELECT graphic_blob FROM internal_graphics WHERE        1     1        0    6079        468
             graphic_id=32
             SELECT graphic_blob FROM internal_graphics WHERE        1     1        0    6074        468
             graphic_id=4
             SELECT graphic_blob FROM internal_graphics WHERE        1     1        0    5962        468
             graphic_id=8
***************                                                                     ------ ----------
sum                                                                                  67226       4640
```

Exhibit 42.9 Script to Create the SQL_GARBAGE View

```
REM
REM View to sort SQL into GOOD and GARBAGE
REM
CREATE OR REPLACE VIEW sql_garbage AS
SELECT
   b.username users,
   SUM(a.sharable_mem+a.persistent_mem) Garbage,
   TO_NUMBER(null) good
FROM
   sys.v_$sqlarea a, dba_users b
WHERE
   (a.parsing_user_id = b.user_id and a.executions<=1)
GROUP BY b.username
UNION
SELECT DISTINCT
   b.username users,
   TO_NUMBER(null) garbage,
   SUM(c.sharable_mem+c.persistent_mem) Good
FROM
dba_users b, sys.v_$sqlarea c
WHERE
(b.user_id=c.parsing_user_id and c.executions>1)
GROUP BY b.username;
```

The script in Exhibit 42.9 shows a view that provides details on individual users' SQL area reuse. The view can be tailored to individual environments if the limit on reuse (currently set at 1) is too restrictive. For example, in a recent tuning assignment, resetting the value to 12 resulted in nearly 70 percent of the SQL being rejected as garbage SQL; in DSS or data warehouse systems, where rollups are performed by the month, bimonthly or weekly values of 12, 24, or 52 might be advisable. Exhibit 42.10 shows a report script that uses the view created in Exhibit 42.9.

The report script in Exhibit 42.10 shows at a glance (well, maybe a long glance for a system with hundreds of users) which users aren't making good use of reusable SQL. A sample report output is shown in Exhibit 42.11.

Note in Exhibit 42.11 that the GRAPHICS_DBA user only shows 58.49 percent shared SQL use based on memory footprints. From the report in Exhibit 42.8, we would expect a low reuse value for GRAPHICS_DBA. The low reuse value for the SYSTEM user is due to its use as a monitoring user: the monitoring SQL is designed to be used once per day or so; it was not built with reuse in mind.

Putting It in Perspective

So what have we seen so far? We have examined reports that show both gross and detailed shared pool usage, and whether or not shared areas are being reused. What can we do with this data? Ideally, we will use the results to size our shared pool properly. Let's set out a few general guidelines for shared pool sizing.

Exhibit 42.10 Sample Report Script for SQL Reuse Statistics

```
REM
REM  Report on SQL Area Reuse by user
REM
column garbage        format 9,999,999,999   heading 'Non-Shared SQL'
column good           format 9,999,999,999   heading 'Shared SQL'
column good_percent   format 999.99          heading 'Percent Shared'
set feedback off
break on report
compute sum of garbage on report
compute sum of good on report
compute avg of good_percent on report
@title80 'Shared Pool Utilization'
spool rep_out\&db\sql_garbage
select
   a.users,
   a.garbage,
   b.good,
   (b.good/(b.good+a.garbage))*100 good_percent
from
   sql_garbage a, sql_garbage b
where
   a.users=b.users
and
   a.garbage is not null
and
   b.good is not null
/
spool off
set feedback off
clear columns
clear breaks
clear computes
```

Guideline 1

If gross usage of the shared pool in a *non* ad hoc environment exceeds 95 percent (rises to 95 percent or greater and stays there), establish a shared pool size large enough to hold the fixed size portions, pin reusable packages and procedures. Increase shared pool by 20-percent increments until usage drops below 90 percent on the average.

Guideline 2

If the shared pool shows a mixed ad hoc and reuse environment, establish a shared pool size large enough to hold the fixed size portions, pin reusable packages, and establish a comfort level above this required level of pool fill. Establish a routine flush cycle to filter nonreusable code from the pool.

Guideline 3

If the shared pool shows that no reusable SQL is being used, establish a shared pool large enough to hold the fixed size portions, plus a few megabytes (usually not more than 40) and allow the shared pool modified least recently used (LRU) algorithm to manage the pool.

Exhibit 42.11 Report from Showing SQL Reuse Statistics

```
Date: 11/18/98                                                    Page: 1
Time: 04:16 PM              Shared Pool Utilization               SYSTEM
                               ORTEST1 databas

USERS            Non-Shared SQL           Shared SQL      Percent Shared
-------------   ---------------          -----------     ---------------
GRAPHICS_DBA            27,117                38,207               58.49
SYS                    302,997               575,176               65.50
SYSTEM               1,504,740               635,861               29.70
-------------   ---------------          -----------     ---------------
avg                                                                51.23
sum                  1,834,854             1,249,244
```

INITIALIZATION PARAMETERS THAT AFFECT THE SHARED POOL

Name	Description
shared_pool_size	Size in bytes of shared pool (7 and 8)
shared_pool_reserved_size	Size in bytes of reserved area of shared pool (7 and 8)
shared_pool_reserved_min_alloc	minimum allocation size in bytes for reserved area of shared pool (7 and 8)
large_pool_size	Size in bytes of the large allocation pool (8 only)
large_pool_min_alloc	Minimum allocation size in bytes for the large allocation pool (8 only)
parallel_min_message_pool	Minimum size of shared pool memory to reserve for pq servers (8 only)
backup_io_slaves	Number of backup IO slaves to configure (8 only)
temporary_table_locks	Number of temporary table locks to configure (7 and 8)
dml_locks	Number of DML locks to configure (7 and 8)
sequence_cache_entries	Number of sequence numbers to cache (7 and 8)
row_cache_cursors	Number of row caches to set up (7 and 8)
max_enabled_roles	Number of role caches to set up (7 and 8)
mts_dispatchers	Number of MTS dispatcher processes to start with (7 and 8)
mts_max_dispatchers	Maximum number of dispatcher processes to allow (7 and 8)
mts_servers	Number of MTS servers to start with (7 and 8)
mts_max_servers	Maximum number of MTS servers to allow (7 and 8)
open_cursors	Maximum number of open cursors per session (7 and 8)
cursor_space_for_time	Hold open cursors until process exits (7 and 8)

VIEWS MENTIONED IN ARTICLE

View Name	Purpose
V$PARAMETER	Contains current settings for all documented initialization parameters
V$SGASTAT	Contains sizing information for all SGA areas
V$SQLAREA	Contains information and statistics on the SQL area of the shared pool
V$DB_OBJECT_CACHE	Contains information on all cached objects in the database shared pool area
V$LIBRARYCACHE	Contains statistics on the library caches
V$ROWCACHE	Contains statistics on the data dictionary caches
DBA_USERS	Contains database user information

Exhibit 42.11 Report from Showing SQL Reuse Statistics (continued)

SOFTWARE MENTIONED IN ARTICLE

Software	Manufacturer	Purpose
Oracle Administrator	RevealNet, Inc.	Administration Knowledge base
Q Diagnostic	Savant Corp.	Provide Oracle DB diagnostics

Under guidelines 1, 2, and 3, start at around 40 megabytes for a standard-size system. Not that in guideline 2, it is stated that a routine flush cycle should be instituted. This flies in the face of what Oracle support pushes in its shared pool white papers; however, it works from the assumption that proper SQL is being generated and the administrator wants to reuse the SQL present in the shared pool. In a mixed environment where there is a mixture of reusable and nonreusable SQL, the nonreusable SQL will act as a drag against the other SQL (I call this "shared pool thrashing") unless it is periodically removed by flushing. Exhibit 42.12 shows a PL/SQL package that can be used by the DBMS_JOB job queues to periodically flush the shared pool only when it exceeds a specified percent.

Exhibit 42.12 Script to Run a Shared Pool Flush Routine

```
PROCEDURE flush_it(p_free IN NUMBER) IS
--
CURSOR get_share IS
SELECT
   SUM(a.bytes)
FROM
   v$sgastat a
WHERE
      a.name in (
      'reserved stopper',
      'table definiti',
      'dictionary cache',
      'library cache',
      'sql area',
      'PL/SQL DIANA',
      'SEQ S.O.');
--
CURSOR get_var IS
   SELECT
value
   FROM
v$parameter
   WHERE
name = 'shared_pool_size';
--
CURSOR get_time IS
   SELECT
sysdate
   FROM
dual;
--
      todays_date    DATE;
      mem_ratio      NUMBER;
      share_mem      NUMBER;
      variable_mem   NUMBER;
```

Exhibit 42.12 Script to Run a Shared Pool Flush Routine (continued)

```
      cur INTEGER;
      sql_com         VARCHAR2(60);
      row_proc        NUMBER;
--
BEGIN
      OPEN get_share;
      OPEN get_var;
      FETCH get_share INTO share_mem;
      DBMS_OUTPUT.PUT_LINE('share_mem:  '||to_char(share_mem));
      FETCH get_var INTO variable_mem;
      DBMS_OUTPUT.PUT_LINE('variable_mem:  '||to_char(variable_mem));
      mem_ratio:=share_mem/variable_mem;
      DBMS_OUTPUT.PUT_LINE(TO_CHAR(mem_ratio,'99.999')||'
         '||TO_CHAR(p_free/100,'99.999'));
      IF mem_ratio>p_free/100 THEN
         cur:=DBMS_SQL.OPEN_CURSOR;
         sql_com:='ALTER SYSTEM FLUSH SHARED_POOL';
         DBMS_SQL.PARSE(cur,sql_com,dbms_sql.v7);
            row_proc:=DBMS_SQL.EXECUTE(cur);
         DBMS_SQL.CLOSE_CURSOR(cur);
         OPEN get_time;
         FETCH get_time INTO todays_date;
         INSERT INTO dba_running_stats VALUES ('Flush of Shared
Pool',mem_ratio,35,todays_date,0);
         COMMIT;
      END IF;
END flush_it;
```

The command set to perform a flush on a once-every-30-minute cycle, when the pool reaches 95 percent full, would be:

```
VARIABLE x NUMBER;
BEGIN
dbms_job.submit(
:X,'BEGIN
dbms_revealnet.flush_it(95);
END;',SYSDATE,'SYS-
DATE+(30/1440)');
END;
/
COMMIT;
```

Always commit after assigning a job, or it will not be run and queued.

There is always a discussion as to whether this really does help performance, so I set up a test on a production instance: on day one, I did no automated flushing; on day two, I instituted the automated flushing. Exhibit 42.13 shows the graphs of performance indicators, flush cycles, and users.

The thing to note about the graphs in Exhibit 42.13 is the overall trend of the performance indicator between day one and day two. On day one (the day with an initial flush as indicated by the steep plunge on the pool utilization graph, followed by the buildup to maximum and the flattening of the graph), the performance indicator shows an upward trend. The performance indicator is a measure of how long the database takes to do a specific set of tasks

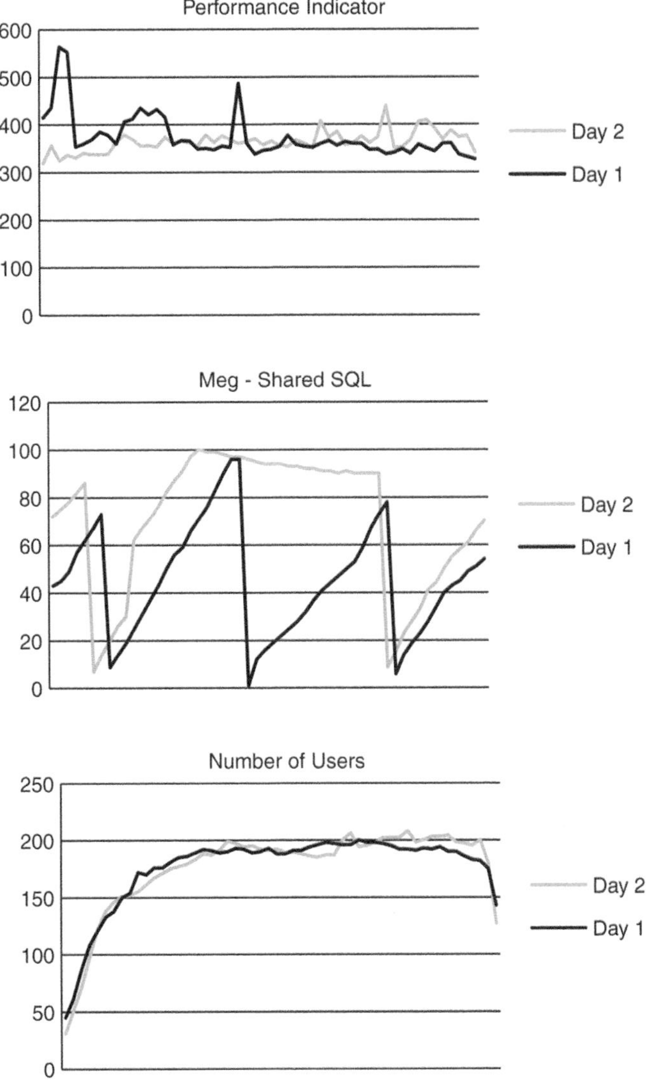

Exhibit 42.13 Graphs Demonstrating Effects of Flushing

(from the Q Diagnostic tool from Savant Corporation). Therefore, an increase in the performance indicator indicates a net decrease in performance. On day two, the overall trend is downward with the average value less than the average value from day one. Overall, the flushing improved performance by 10 to 20 percent. Depending on the environment, I have seen improvements as great as 40 to 50 percent.

One thing that made the analysis difficult was that on day two, there were several large batch jobs run that weren't run on day one. The results still show that flushing has a positive effect on performance when the database is a mixed SQL environment with a large percentage of non-reusable SQL areas.

Guideline 3 also brings up an interesting point: when the shared pool is already over-allocated, following guideline 3 may result in *decreasing* the size of the shared pool. In this situation, the shared pool becomes a cesspool filled with nothing but garbage SQL. After allocating enough memory for dictionary objects and other fixed areas, then ensuring that the standard packages and such are pinned, only maintain a few megabytes above and beyond this level of memory for SQL statements. Because none of the code is being reused, we want to reduce the hash search overhead as much as possible. Do this by reducing the size of the available SQL area memory so as few a number of statements are kept as possible.

Summary

We have covered a lot of territory thus far. We now understand that the old "just increase the shared pool" answer isn't good enough anymore when it comes to tuning problems. We must take an in-depth look at the shared pool and tune what needs to be tuned — not just throw memory at a problem until it submerges. Indeed, I have shown that in some cases increasing the size of the shared pool may harm performance and decreasing the size may be advisable. I have also presented three general guidelines for shared pool tuning. The shared pool is vital to the proper performance of an Oracle database; it must be properly tuned or drown in bad performance.

What to Pin

In all of the guidelines stated so far, I mention that the memory is usually allocated above and beyond that needed for fixed-size areas and pinned objects. How do you determine what to pin? Generally speaking, any package, procedure, function, or cursor that is frequently used by your application should be pinned into the shared pool when the database is started. I suggest adding a "null" startup function to every in-house generated package. It essentially looks like Exhibit 42.14.

The purpose of the null start-up function is to provide a touch point to pull the entire package into the shared pool. This allows you to create a start-up SQL procedure that pulls all of the application packages into the pool and pins them

Exhibit 42.14 Example Null Start-Up Function

```
FUNCTION start_up
RETURN number IS
Ret NUMBER:=1;
BEGIN
Ret:=0
RETURN ret;
END start_up;
```

using the DBMS_SHARED_POOL package. The DBMS_SHARED_POOL package may have to be built in earlier releases of Oracle. The DBMS_ SHARED_POOL package is built using the DBM-SPOOL. SQL and PRVTPOOL.PLB scripts located in (UNIX) $ORACLE_HOME/rdbms/admin or (NT) x:\orant\rdbms\admin (where x: is the home drive for your install).

How do you determine what packages, procedures of functions to pin? Actually, Oracle has made this easy by providing the V$DB_OBJECT_ CACHE view that shows all objects in the pool, and, more importantly, how they are being utilized. The script in Exhibit 42.15 provides a list of objects that have been loaded more than once and have executions greater than one. A rule of thumb is that if an object is being frequently executed and frequently reloaded, it should be pinned into the shared pool. Note that you only have to pin the package, not the package and package body.

Exhibit 42.15 Script to Show Objects that Should be Kept

```
rem
rem FUNCTION: Report Stored Object Statistics
rem
column owner          format a11       heading Schema
column name           format a30       heading Object|Name
column namespace                       heading Name|Space
column type                            heading Object|Type
column kept           format a4        heading Kept
column sharable_mem   format 999,999   heading Shared|Memory
column executions     format 999,999   heading Executes
set lines 132 pages 47 feedback off
@title132 'Oracle Objects Report'
break on owner on namespace on type
spool rep_out/&db/o_stat
select
      OWNER,
      NAMESPACE,
      TYPE,
      NAME,
      SHARABLE_MEM,
      LOADS,
      EXECUTIONS,
      LOCKS,
      PINS,
      KEPT
from
      v$db_object_cache
where
      type not in (
'NOT LOADED','NON-EXISTENT','VIEW','TABLE','SEQUENCE')
         and executions>0 and loads>1 and kept='NO'
order by owner,namespace,type,executions desc;
spool off
set lines 80 pages 22 feedback on
clear columns
clear breaks
ttitle off
```

Guideline 4

Determine usage patterns of packages, procedures, functions, and cursors and pin those that are frequently used.

The Shared Pool and MTS

The use of the multi-threaded server option (MTS) in Oracle requires a sometimes dramatic increase in the size of the shared pool. This increase in the size of the shared pool caused by MTS is due to the addition of the user global areas required for sorting and message queues. If you are using MTS, you should monitor the V$SGASTAT values for MTS-related memory areas and adjust the shared pool memory allocations accordingly.

Note that in Oracle8 you should make use of the large pool feature to pull the user global areas (UGA) and multi-threaded server queues out of the shared pool area if MTS is being used. This prevents the fragmentation problems that have been reported in shared pools when MTS is used without allocating the large pool.

Guideline 5

In Oracle7, when using MTS, increase the shared pool size to accommodate MTS messaging and queuing, as well as UGA requirements. In Oracle8, use the Large Pool to prevent MTS from affecting the shared pool areas.

A Matter of Hashing

We have discussed hashing in prior chapter sections. Essentially, each SQL statement is hashed and this hash value is then used to compare to already-stored SQL areas; if a matching hash is found, the statements are compared. The hash is only calculated based on the first 200 or so characters in the SQL statement, so extremely long SQL statements can result in multiple hashes being the same, although the stored SQL is different (if the first 100 or so characters in each statement are identical). This is another argument for using stored procedures and functions to perform operations and for the use of bind variables. There is hope, in 8i (or 8.1, if you prefer) that the hash value will be calculated on the first 100 and last 100 characters, reducing the chances of multiple identical hash values for different SQL statements.

If the number of large, nearly identical statements is high, then the number of times the parser has to compare a new SQL statement to existing SQL statements with the same hash value increases. This results in a higher statement overhead and poorer performance. You should identify these large statements and encourage users to rewrite them using bind variables, or to proceduralize them using PL/SQL. The report in Exhibit 42.16 will show if you have a problem with multiple statements being hashed to the same value.

Exhibit 42.16 Example Script to Report on Hashing Problems

```
Rem:
rem: FUNCTION: Shows by user who has possible
rem:           SQL reuse problems
rem:
column total_hash                          heading 'Total Hash|Values'
column same_hash                           heading 'SQL With|Same Hash'
column u_hash_ratio format 999.999         heading 'SQL Sharing|Hash'
start title80 'Shared Hash Value Report'
spool rep_out\&&db\shared_hash.lst
break on report
compute sum of total_hash on report
compute sum of same_hash on report
select
      a.username,
      count(b.hash_value) total_hash,
      count(b.hash_value)-count(unique(b.hash_value)) same_hash,
         (count(unique(b.hash_value))/count(b.hash_value))*100 u_hash_ratio
from
      dba_users a,
      v$sqlarea b
where
      a.user_id=b.parsing_user_id
group by
      a.username;
clear computes
```

The script in Exhibit 42.16 produces a report similar and shows which users are generating SQL that hashes to the same values. A faster way to find the hash values would be to do a self-join and filter out the hash values that are duplicate. Sounds easy enough; but remember, the V$ tables have no rowids, so you can't use the classic methods; you have to find another column that will be different when the HASH_VALUE column in V$SQLAREA is the same. Look at the select in Exhibit 42.17.

Once you have the hash value, you can pull the problem SQL statements from either V$SQLAREA or V$SQLTEXT very easily; see Exhibit 42.18.

Long statements require special care to see that bind variables are used to prevent this problem with hashing. Another help for long statements is to use views to store values at an intermediate state, thus reducing the size of the variable portion of the SQL. Notice in the example in Exhibit 42.18 that the only difference between the two identically hashed statements is that the "region_code" and "region_dealer_num" comparison values are different. If bind variables had been used in these statements, there would only have been one entry instead of two.

Exhibit 42.17 Example Select to Determine Duplicate Hash Values

```
select distinct a.hash_value from v$sqlarea a, v$sqlarea b, dba_users c
where a.hash_value=b.hash_value and
a.parsing_user_id = c.user_id
and c.username='DCARS' and ¬ change to user you are concerned about
a.FIRST_LOAD_TIME != b.FIRST_LOAD_TIME
```

Exhibit 42.18 Example of Statements with Identical Hash Values but Different SQL

```
DCARS:select sql_text from v$sqlarea where hash_value='441376718';

SQL_TEXT
-----------------------------------------------------------------------------
SELECT region_code, region_dealer_num, consolidated_dealer_num,
dealer_name, dealer_status_code, dealer_type_code, mach_credit_code,
parts_credit_code FROM dealer WHERE region_code = '32' AND
   region_dealer_num = '6433'

SELECT region_code, region_dealer_num, consolidated_dealer_num,
dealer_name, dealer_status_code, dealer_type_code, mach_credit_code,
parts_credit_code FROM dealer WHERE region_code = '56' AND
   region_dealer_num = '6273'
```

Guideline 6

Use bind variables, PL/SQL (procedures or functions), and views to reduce the size of large SQL statements to prevent hashing problems.

Monitoring Library and Data Dictionary Caches

Having spent a lot of time looking at the shared SQL area of the shared pool, let's wrap up with a high-level look at the library and data dictionary caches. The library cache area is monitored via the V$LIBRARYCACHE view and contains the SQL area, PL/SQL area, table, index, and cluster cache areas. The data dictionary caches contain cache area for all data dictionary-related definitions.

The script in Exhibit 42.19 creates a report on the library caches. The items of particular interest in the report generated by the script in Exhibit 42.19 (shown in Exhibit 42.20) are the various ratios.

Look at the example output from the script in Exhibit 42.19 in Exhibit 42.20. In Exhibit 42.20, we see that all Get Hit% (gethitratio in the view), except for indexes, are greater than 80 to 90 percent. This is the desired state; the value for indexes is low because of the few accesses of that type of object. Notice that the Pin Hit% is also greater than 90 percent (except for indexes); this is also to be desired. The other goals of tuning this area are to reduce reloads to as small a value as possible (this is done by proper sizing and pinning) and to reduce invalidations. Invalidations happen when, for one reason or another, an object becomes unusable. However, if you must use flushing of the shared pool, reloads and invalidations may occur as objects are swapped in and out of the shared pool. Proper pinning can reduce the number of objects reloaded and invalidated.

Guideline 7

In a system where there is no flushing, increase the shared pool size in 20 percent increments to reduce reloads and invalidations and increase hit ratios.

Exhibit 42.19 Example Script to Monitor the Library Caches

```
rem
rem Title: libcache.sql
rem
rem FUNCTION: Generate a library cache report
rem
column namespace                             heading "Library Object"
column gets              format 9,999,999    heading "Gets"
column gethitratio       format 999.99       heading "Get Hit%"
column pins              format 9,999,999    heading "Pins"
column pinhitratio       format 999.99       heading "Pin Hit%"
column reloads           format 99,999       heading "Reloads"
column invalidations     format 99,999       heading "Invalid"
column db format a10
set pages 58 lines 80
start title80 "Library Caches Report"
define output = rep_out\&db\lib_cache
spool &output
select
      namespace,
      gets,
      gethitratio*100 gethitratio,
      pins,
      pinhitratio*100 pinhitratio,
      RELOADS,
      INVALIDATIONS
from
      v$librarycache
/
spool off
pause Press enter to continue
set pages 22 lines 80
ttitle off
undef output
```

Exhibit 42.20 Example of the Output from Library Caches Report

```
Date: 11/21/98                                                   Page: 1
Time: 02:51 PM              Library Caches Report                 SYSTEM
                              ORTEST1 database

Library Object        Gets    Get Hit%     Pins   Pin Hit%  Reloads  Invalid
---------------- ------ --------- ------ -------- ------- -------
SQL AREA            46,044      99.17   99,139      99.36       24       16
TABLE/PROCEDURE      1,824      84.59    6,935      93.21        3        0
BODY                   166      93.98      171      91.23        0        0
TRIGGER                  0     100.00        0     100.00        0        0
INDEX                   27        .00       27        .00        0        0
CLUSTER                373      98.12      373      97.59        0        0
OBJECT                   0     100.00        0     100.00        0        0
PIPE                     0     100.00        0     100.00        0        0
```

Exhibit 42.21 Script to Monitor the Data Dictionary Caches

```
rem
rem title:      ddcache.sql
rem FUNCTION:   report on the v$rowcache table
rem HISTORY:    created sept 1995 MRA
rem
start title80 "DD Cache Hit Ratio"
spool rep_out\&db\ddcache
SELECT (SUM(getmisses)/SUM(gets)) RATIO
FROM V$ROWCACHE
/
spool off
pause Press enter to continue
ttitle off
```

The data dictionary caches used to be individually tunable through several initialization parameters; now they are internally controlled. The script in Exhibit 42.21 should be used to monitor the overall hit ratio for the data dictionary caches.

The ratio reported from the script in Exhibit 42.21 should always be less than 1. The ratio corresponds to the number of times out of 100 that the database engine sought something from the cache and missed. A dictionary cache miss is more expensive than a data block buffer miss; so, if your ratio gets near 1, increase the size of the shared pool because the internal algorithm is not allocating enough memory to the data dictionary caches.

Guideline 8

In any shared pool, if the overall data dictionary cache miss ratio exceeds one percent, increase the size of the shared pool.

Summary

We have discussed ways to monitor for what objects should be pinned, discussed multi-threaded servers, looked at hashing problems and their resolution, as well as examined classic library and data dictionary cache tuning. We have established eight guidelines for tuning the Oracle shared pool:

Guideline 1: If gross usage of the shared pool in a non-ad hoc environment exceeds 95 percent (rises to 95 percent or greater and stays there), establish a shared pool size large enough to hold the fixed size portions, pin reusable packages, and procedures. Gradually increase shared pool by 20 percent increments until usage drops below 90 percent, on the average.

Guideline 2: If the shared pool shows a mixed ad hoc and reuse environment, establish a shared pool size large enough to hold the fixed size portions, pin reusable packages, and establish a comfort level above this required level of pool fill. Establish a routine flush cycle to filter nonreusable code from the pool.

Guideline 3: If the shared pool shows that no reusable SQL is being used, establish a shared pool large enough to hold the fixed size portions plus a few megabytes (usually not more than 40) and allow the shared pool modified least recently used (LRU) algorithm to manage the pool (also see Guideline 8).

Guideline 4: Determine usage patterns of packages, procedures, functions, and cursors and pin those that are frequently used.

Guideline 5: In Oracle7, when using MTS, increase the shared pool size to accommodate MTS messaging and queuing, as well as UGA requirements. In Oracle8, use the Large Pool to prevent MTS from affecting the shared pool areas.

Guideline 6: Use bind variables, PL/SQL (procedures or functions), and views to reduce the size of large SQL statements to prevent hashing problems.

Guideline 7: In a system where there is no flushing, increase the shared pool size in 20 percent increments to reduce reloads and invalidations and increase object cache hit ratios.

Guideline 8: In any shared pool, if the overall data dictionary cache miss ratio exceeds one percent, increase the size of the shared pool.

Using these guidelines and the scripts and techniques covered in this chapter, you should be well on the way toward a well-tuned and well-performing shared pool.

Chapter 43

Managing Multiple Buffer Pools in Oracle8

Michael R. Ault

The buffer cache is the area in memory where data is stored from data tables, indexes, rollback segments, clusters, and sequences. No data can get to users from a disk unless it goes through the Oracle db block buffers (except for special types of sorts). By ensuring that enough buffers are available for transient storage of these data items, execution can be expedited by reducing required disk reads.

Oracle7 and early Oracle8 releases had only the "normal" buffer area to worry with. Now, Oracle8i has added the capability to subdivide this buffer area into KEEP and RECYCLE buffer areas. Later we examine how these areas interact and how they should be tuned and sized.

Classic db Block Buffer Tuning

The statistics "db block gets," "consistent gets" (their sum is logical reads), and "physical reads" from the V$SYSSTAT table show the relationship between "logical" or cache hits versus "physical" or disk hits, while retrieving the above type of data. The statistic called "hit ratio" is determined by the simple formula:

```
logical reads = db_block_gets + consistent_gets hit ratio(%) =
   ((logical reads - physical reads) / logical reads) * 100 .
```

If the hit ratio is less than 80 to 90 percent in a loaded and running database, this indicates that there may be insufficient buffers allocated. If the hit ratio is less than 80 to 90 percent, increase the INIT.ORA parameter DB_BLOCK_BUFFERS. However, a high hit ratio may not always indicate a healthy buffer area. Also, if a hit ratio during periods of high use is below 70 to 90 percent, increase the DB_BLOCK_BUFFERS INIT.ORA parameter.

0-8493-1139-X/02/$0.00+$1.50
©2002 by CRC Press LLC

If DB_BLOCK_BUFFERS is set too high, shared memory size may be exceeded on UNIX or NT, for instance. Another possible result is that the entire Oracle process could be swapped out due to memory contention with other processes. In either case, it is not a desirable condition. To avoid exceeding shared memory area size, be sure to set these operating system values (on UNIX) high when the instance is created. To avoid swapping, know how much memory is accessible; talk with the system administrator to determine this.

Tuning the Multipart Oracle8 Buffer Cache

In Oracle8 and Oracle8i, the database block buffer has been split into three possible areas: the default, keep, and recycle buffer pool areas. It is not required that these three pools be used; only one, the default pool configured with the DB_BLOCK_BUFFERS initialization parameter, must be present. The others are "sub" pools to this main pool. How are the various pools used?

Use of the Default Pool

If a table, index, or cluster is created by specifying that the keep or recycle pool be used for its data, then it is placed in the default pool when it is accessed. This is standard Oracle7 behavior and, if no special action is taken to use the other pools, then this is also standard Oracle8 and Oracle8i behavior. The initialization parameters DB_BLOCK_BUFFERS and DB_BLOCK_LRU_ LATCHES must be set if multiple pools are to be used:

```
DB_BLOCK_BUFFERS = 2000
DB_BLOCK_LRU_LATCHES = 10
```

Use of the Keep Pool

The keep database buffer pool is configured using the BUFFER_POOL_KEEP initialization parameter::

```
BUFFER_POOL_KEEP = ë100,2í
```

The two specified parameters are the number of buffers from the default pool to assign to the keep pool and the number of LRU (least recently used) latches to assign to the keep pool. The minimum number of buffers assigned to the pool is 50 times the number of assigned latches. The keep pool, as its name implies, is used to store object data that shouldn't be aged out of the buffer pool, such as lookup information and specific performance-enhancing indexes. The objects are assigned to the keep pool either through their creation statement or by specifically assigning them to the pool using the ALTER command. Any blocks already in the default pool are not affected by the ALTER command, only subsequently accessed blocks.

The keep pool should be sized so that it can hold all the blocks from all tables created with the buffer pool set to "keep."

Use of the Recycle Pool

The recycle database buffer pool is configured using the `BUFFER_POOL_RECYCLE` initialization parameter:

```
BUFFER_POOL_RECYCLE = ë1000,5í
```

The two specified parameters are the number of buffers from the default pool to assign to the recycle pool and the number of LRU (least recently used) latches to assign to the keep pool. The minimum number of buffers assigned to the pool is 50 times the number of assigned latches.The recycle pool, as its name implies, is used to store object data that should be aged out of the buffer pool rapidly, such as searchable LOB information. The objects are assigned to the recycle pool either through their creation statement or by specifically assigning them to the pool using the `ALTER` command. Any blocks already in the default pool are not affected by the `ALTER` command, only subsequently accessed blocks.

As long as the recycle pool shows low block contention, it is sized correctly.

With the above setpoints for the default, keep, and recycle pools, the default pool would end up with 900 buffers and three LRU latches.

Sizing the Default Pool

The default pool holds both the keep and recycle pools; it must be sized according to the following formula, as a minimum:

```
Default = (keep + recycle
  + (total_of_non-keep_or_recycle_object_
  sizes/100))/DB_BLOCK_SIZE
```

Each object not explicitly assigned to the keep or recycle pools will be placed into the default pool when it is accessed. As a general rule of thumb, the data currently in use will be equal to approximately one twentieth to one hundredth of the physical database objects such as tables, clusters, and indexes. I suggest starting at one hundredth and moving up from there.

Sizing the Keep Pool

The keep buffer pool should be sized to the total size of the data objects that are explicitly assigned to the pool. Remember, the keep pool is designed to hold objects that would have been cached in earlier versions of Oracle. Generally speaking, small indexes, lookup tables, and small active data tables are good candidates for the keep pool. To size the pool, move a good estimate of the size of the objects to be kept.

Sizing the Recycle Pool

Probably the most difficult pool to size will be the recycle pool. The reason is that it is designed to hold transient data objects (such as chunks of LOB data items). I suggest sizing the recycle pool according to the following formula:

```
Recycle = (SUM(size_non_lob_object(1-n)/20) +
   (lob_chunk_size_i(1-n)
      * No_simul_accesses_i))
```

The first part of this formula is for non-LOB objects that might be searched in large pieces, such as partitioned tables. Find the partition size, then exclude the division by 20, and just use the partition size.

The second half of the formula addresses `LOB` (`BLOB`, `CLOB`, `NCLOB`) type objects that will be accessed in chunks, such as for searching or comparing using piece-wise logic. The specified chunk size for each assigned object times the number of expected different simultaneous accesses is used to derive the area size required. The sum of the two numbers should give a size for the recycle pool.

Tuning the Three Pools

Since the classic method of tuning the shared pool is not available in Oracle8i, we must examine new methods to achieve the same ends. This involves looking at what Oracle has provided for tuning the new pools. A new script, `cat-perf.sql`, offers several new views for tuning the Oracle buffer pools. These views are:

`V$BUFFER_POOL`	Provides static information on pool configuration
`V$BUFFER_POOL_STATISTICS`	Provides pool-related statistics
`V$DBWR_WRITE_HISTOGRAM`	Provides summary information on DBWR write activities
`V$DBWR_WRITE_LOG`	Provides write information for each buffer area

Of the four new views, the `V$BUFFER_POOL_STATISTICS` view seems the most useful for tuning the buffer pool. The `V$BUFFER_POOL_STATISTICS` view contains statistics such as `buffer_busy_waits`, `free_buffer_inspected`, `dirty_buffers_inspected`, and physical write-related data for each of the pool areas.

If a buffer pool shows excessive numbers of `dirty_buffers_inspected` and high amounts of `buffer_busy_waits`, then it probably needs to be increased in size.

When configuring LRU latches and DBWR processes, remember that the latches are assigned to the pools sequentially and to the DBRW processes in round-robin fashion. The number of LRU processes should be equal to, or a multiple of, the value of DBWR processes to ensure that the DBRW load is balanced across the processes.

Summary

Oracle has provided multiple buffer pools to allow tighter control over how Oracle8 treats data objects. Through proper use of the default, keep, and recycle pools, a DBA should be able to improve overall database performance.

While some tools such as the `X$` tables that DBAs have used in the past to tune the Oracle buffer pool have been eliminated, several new views are now provided to allow multiple pool tuning.

Chapter 44

Oracle8i Buffer Cache: New Features

*John Beresniewicz**

Oracle8i continues to enhance the buffer cache management improvements begun in Oracle 8.0 with the introduction of more sophisticated buffer replacement algorithms. Recall that in Oracle 8.0 the buffer cache was partitioned into multiple disjoint pools (DEFAULT, RECYCLE, and KEEP) into which specific blocks could be placed to accommodate different buffer aging requirements. Oracle8i contains enhancements to the buffer aging and replacement algorithms in the form of midpoint LRU insertion and touch count MRU promotion. These new features should result in better buffer cache performance out of the box, that is, without complex tuning analysis.

This chapter discusses the midpoint insertion buffer replacement strategy and presents experimental results designed to test its effectiveness at protecting the DEFAULT pool from cold buffer flooding. In addition, it will introduce and investigate some interesting new columns in the X$BH fixed table that can help in identifying candidate objects for the KEEP and RECYCLE pools.

Multiple Buffer Pools

Last year in *Oracle Internals,*[1] I covered the multiple buffer pool feature introduced in Oracle 8.0 and presented experimental results into its usefulness at improving buffer cache performance under the stress of severe cold buffer flooding. The results were pretty compelling that under the right circumstances, the RECYCLE and KEEP buffer pools can provide significant performance advantages.

Briefly recalling the results of of that article,[1] it was seen that the RECYCLE pool is best used to temporarily house buffers from tables that are randomly

* ©2000 by John Beresniewicz and Sarant Corporation. Printed with permission.

accessed very frequently with little or no block sharing among users. Such block access scenarios can stress the traditional LRU replacement strategy by flooding the MRU end of the list with basically useless buffers, aging more useful (potentially reusable) buffers down to the LRU end, and perhaps out of the cache altogether. In this case, a very small RECYCLE pool for these high-volume, low-reuse buffers can provide great relief in the form of improved retention of more sharable buffers.

In addition, response time variances can potentially be smoothed out using the KEEP pool to pin key blocks into the cache that are needed for critical transactions.

Some difficulties noted in that article[1] are deciding whether to use multiple buffer pools, which segments to assign to which pools, and how to size and tune the pools. Also, while the multiple buffer pools present new tuning options for experienced DBAs with good knowledge of supported applications and time for analysis, most Oracle installations are not in such an advantageous position. The new features discussed here should help improve Oracle buffer cache performance without extensive analysis, in addition to providing better information for multiple pool analysis when it is undertaken.

While the Oracle8i documentation has not quite caught up with these new features, there is a good discussion of Oracle8i buffer cache operation in Morle's book.[2]

New INIT.ORA Parameters

The first indication of major changes to the Oracle8i buffer cache internal algorithms comes in the form of a number of new initialization parameters that, judging from their names and descriptions, are clearly involved with buffer cache aging in the various pools. These parameters are all of the "hidden" variety, indicating that they should not generally be modified from their default values except with extreme discretion and under instruction from Oracle Corporation. (Readers of Oracle Internals are not likely to be intimidated by undocumented initialization parameters.)

Exhibit 44.1 lists some of these new parameters.

Midpoint Insertion and Touch Count Promotion

One of the most significant changes to the Oracle8i buffer replacement algorithms involves the concept of midpoint insertion in the LRU lists of the buffer pools. In Oracle8i, when a buffer is first read into the cache from disk, it is not immediately placed at the MRU end of the list as in previous versions. Instead, the buffer is inserted into the middle of the LRU list and a "touch count" is kept on the buffer. The touch count is simply a count of the number of times the buffer has been accessed by a user. When the touch count reaches a threshold value, the buffer is promoted to the MRU end of the list. By default, it takes at least two touches to move to the MRU end of the list.

Exhibit 44.1 New Hidden INIT.ORA Parameters Affecting Buffer Pool Aging

INIT.ORA Parameter	*Default Value*	*Description*
`_db_percent_hot_default`	50	Percent of default buffer pool considered hot
`_db_percent_hot_keep`	0	Percent of keep buffer pool considered hot
`_db_percent_hot_recycle`	0	Percent of recycle buffer pool considered hot
`_db_aging_cool_count`	1	Touch count set when buffer cooled
`_db_aging_freeze_cr`	FALSE	Make CR buffers always be too cold to keep in cache
`_db_aging_hot_criteria`	2	Touch count that sends a buffer to head of replacement list
`_db_aging_stay_count`	0	Touch count set when buffer moved to head of replacement list
`_db_aging_touch_time`	3	Touch count that sends a buffer to head of replacement list

Midpoint insertion and the touch count threshold effectively divide the buffer pools into "hot" and "cold" regions. Buffers must be accessed multiple times to be placed into the hot region. The size of these hot regions is configured by the following parameters:

```
_DB_PERCENT_HOT_DEFAULT
_DB_PERCENT_HOT_KEEP
_DB_PERCENT_HOT_RECYCLE
```

Note from Exhibit 44.1 that only the DEFAULT buffer pool comes preconfigured with a hot region specified and that the midpoint is indeed in the middle of the LRU list (50 percent of the pool is hot).

Midpoint insertion should make the DEFAULT buffer pool much more resilient to MRU pressure by single-use blocks, discussed in Reference 1 as the classic case for using the RECYCLE pool. In essence, the cold region of the DEFAULT pool should absorb the LRU activity for these low usage blocks and keep them from aging more desirable blocks out of the hot region of the pool. The cold region will act, in effect, like a built-in RECYCLE pool. We should be able to test this theory by executing and measuring the cold buffer flooding tests performed in Reference 1 against a DEFAULT pool with varying hot region sizes.

Testing Midpoint Insertion

To test the effectiveness of midpoint insertion at protecting the DEFAULT pool from a flood of cold buffers, I created the testing environment used in Reference 1 in an Oracle8i database. Exhibit 44.2 shows the objects and their sizes in the Oracle8i test environment.

Exhibit 44.2 Buffer Pool Test Object Sizes under Oracle8i

Object Name	*Object Type*	*Blocks*
LARGE_TBL	TABLE	14409
LARGE_TBL_PK	UNIQUE INDEX	67
LOOKUP_TBL	TABLE	504
LOOKUP_TBL_PK	UNIQUE INDEX	2

One interesting point is that under Oracle8i, the two primary key indexes were approximately half their sizes under Oracle 8.0. This reduction in index size was a surprising result (to me) that deserves more investigation. The implication for the buffer cache tests is that fewer total blocks in the test schema containing the same amount of data should improve cache efficiency automatically in that fewer physical reads are required to read all index blocks into the cache.

Briefly recapitulating from Reference 1, the testing scenario involved 10,000 pseudo-random (non-repeated) primary key accesses of LARGE_TBL joined to LOOKUP_TBL through the PK-FK join. Each block in both tables contained exactly one row, so each test run performed 10,000 single block accesses from LARGE_TBL, combined with numerous repeated block accesses from LOOKUP_TBL, as well as the indexes.

The midpoint insertion tests were conducted by executing the test script in a database with a single 1000 buffer DEFAULT pool configured by adjusting the _DB_PERCENT_HOT_DEFAULT parameter as follows:

- Oracle 8.0 baseline test as previously performed in Reference 1
- 50, the default setting, should be enough to preserve all non-LARGE_TBL blocks
- 0, should behave similar to Oracle 8.0 baseline test
- 75, should be similar to having a small RECYCLE pool containing LARGE_TBL
- 25, should be better than 2 but worse than 1 as LOOKUP_TBL will not fit into hot region

Test Results

Each configuration was tested three times and the results averaged. It is interesting to note that the same technique was used under Oracle 8.0 with almost no variance between results in successive runs of the same test. Under Oracle8i, results between runs of the same test showed more variance, although they were still very close together. I am not sure exactly what to make of this, although it may be an indication that the new algorithms are "fuzzier" and less deterministic than the old ones.

Exhibit 44.3 gives results for the midpoint insertion tests. The baseline results for the Oracle 8.0 testing are reproduced for comparison purposes.

Exhibit 44.3 Oracle8i Midpoint Insertion Test Results

Test ID (Elapsed Time)	*_db_percent_hot_default*	*Physical Reads*	*Logical Reads*	*Hit Ratio*
TEST0 (162.0 seconds)	N/A	16,018	30,164	46.9%
TEST1 (124.0 seconds)	50	11,233	20,317	44.8%
TEST2 (145.5 seconds)	0	13,525	20,321	33.4%
TEST3 (125.8 seconds)	75	11,452	20,316	43.6%
TEST4 (131.8 seconds)	25	12,122	20,318	40.3%

The midpoint insertion test results are not as compelling as the multiple pool results. However, it is clear that adjusting the percentage of the cache considered "hot" has a measurable impact on performance under the stress of cold block pressure.

TEST2 should be compared first to TEST0, the baseline test under Oracle 8.0. The absence of a hot region in TEST2 should presumably have deprecated the buffer replacement algorithm to standard LRU behavior. The 10 percent gain in elapsed time performance over TEST0 can probably be attributed to the fewer number of index blocks in the Oracle8i version of the test schema.

Comparing TEST2 and TEST1 gives an indication of potential out-of-the-box performance gains due to midpoint insertion with the default parameter settings. In the scenario tested, the gain was a significant 14.8 percent. The combined gains of midpoint insertion and reduced index sizes were an impressive 23.5 percent. Note that this improvement was strictly due to kernel differences between Oracle 8.0 and Oracle8i under default cache parameter settings. This shows that the new and improved buffer cache algorithms can benefit all DBAs, not just those with the expertise and time to analyze and configure the multiple pools.

TEST3 and TEST4 also behaved more or less as predicted. TEST3 allocated 750 buffers to the hot region. Because the test scenario accesses LARGE_TBL blocks only once, whereas all other blocks get multiple touches, this is effectively like having LARGE_TBL assigned to a 250 buffer RECYCLE pool and 750 buffers for the other blocks. TEST4 allocated 250 buffers to the hot region — not enough to hold all the LOOKUP_TBL and index blocks which will end up there due to multiple touches. Thus, we expected TEST3 to outperform TEST4, which was indeed the case.

New X$BH Columns

While investigating these improvements to the Oracle8i buffer cache, I noticed the addition of the following columns to X$BH:

- LRU_FLAG
- TCH
- TIM

Clearly, the LRU_FLAG column contains some information about LRU treatment or state of the block, but I have not determined or discovered exactly what. Simple preliminary experiments reveal varying values and block counts for each value, indicating the column probably does contain meaningful information.

The TIM column is probably related to the new _DB_AGING_TOUCH_TIME initialization parameter. Again, I have not had sufficient time to investigate either the parameter or the new column, but they almost certainly play a role in the new buffer cache algorithms. Perhaps in addition to counting touches, Oracle also considers how long between touches when deciding on replacement and LRU movement of buffers.

I was able to correctly surmise and confirm that the TCH column represents the number of times a buffer has been touched by user accesses. This is the touch count that apparently relates directly to the promotion of buffers from the cold region to the hot, based on having been touched _DB_AGING_HOT_CRITERIA times. It occurred to me that this column could be extremely useful in solving some previously thorny tuning and buffer pool configuration issues, including:

- Identifying candidate segments for the RECYCLE pool
- Identifying candidate segments for the KEEP pool
- Identifying "hot" blocks and tables

Recycle Pool Candidates

The following query uses X$BH.TCH to identify objects in the buffer cache with single-touch buffer counts totaling more than five percent of the total cache. These segments are potentially good candidates for placement in the RECYCLE buffer pool as they are occupying significant cache space with blocks that have not yet been reused.

```
SELECT objobject
     ,COUNT(1) buffers
     ,100*(COUNT(1)/totsize) pct_cache
  FROM
     x$bh
     ,(select value totsize from v$parameter
     where name = 'db_block_buffers')
WHERE tch = 1
GROUP BY obj,totsize
HAVING 100*(COUNT(1)/totsize) > 5;
```

KEEP Pool Candidates

On the other hand, the KEEP buffer pool may be a good place to stash blocks from segments that are used frequently and occupy more than a trivial amount of space. The following query uses X$BH.TCH to identify those objects whose blocks average more than five touches and occupy more than 20 blocks in the cache.

```
SELECT objobject
      ,COUNT(1) buffers
      ,AVG(tch) avg_touches
   FROM
      x$bh
GROUP BY obj
HAVING AVG(tch) > 5
   AND COUNT(1) > 20;
```

Note that in this query, the values 5 and 20 are somewhat arbitrary and may be adjusted to provide more focused information for a particular installation.

Hot Blocks

Finally, the old conundrum of identifying hot blocks and tables becomes almost trivial with the aid of X$BH.TCH. This query displays object id and block addresses for blocks with more than 100 touches. Again, the value of 100 will be installation dependent, so adjust it to suit your needs.

```
SELECT objobject
      ,dbarfilfile#
      ,dbablkblock#
      ,tchtouches
   FROM
      x$bh
WHERE tch > 100
ORDER BY 1,2;
```

Conclusion

The Oracle8i database introduces newer and more sophisticated algorithms for buffer cache management, including midpoint LRU insertion and touch count-based aging. The initialization parameters controlling these new features are not intended for user modification; however, tests indicate they can have measurable impact on cache performance. Controlled testing demonstrated an impressive 23.5 percent performance gain due strictly to differences between Oracle 8.0 and Oracle8i using default settings for both caches.

Finally, new columns in X$BH related to the new buffer cache algorithms are proving useful for identifying tuning opportunities by giving greater insight into block access frequencies in the buffer cache.

References

1. Beresniewicz, Investigating the Multiple Buffer Pool Feature of Oracle8, *Oracle Internals*, August 1999.
2. Morle, *Scaling Oracle8i*, Addison-Wesley, 2000.
3. Feuerstein, Dye, and Beresniewicz, *Oracle Built-in Packages*, O'Reilly & Associates, 1998.

ORACLE TABLE MANAGEMENT

The management of objects within the Oracle database can have a huge impact on the performance of the Oracle system. Oracle maintains its own internal control structures within every Oracle object, including tables and indexes, and requires proper settings for all of the storage parameters, especially percent free, percent used, and free list parameter.

Prior to the development of employees object reorganizations in Oracle I, it was the challenge of the Oracle administrator to identify those tables and indexes which were functioning in some optimal levels and schedule those for reorganization. Object reorganizations are primarily used to clean up to and coalesce the Oracle free list, remove chained rows, and place the Oracle object within a single extent on the disk device.

Tip: Finding Chained-Row Tables to Reorganize

Here is the code that generates a report showing all tables with excessive chained rows. Note that the use of this script is predicated on the use of Oracle's ANALYZE command to populate the chain_cnt and num_rows columns of the DBA_TABLES data dictionary view.

```
-- © 1997 by Donald K. Burleson
spool chain.lst;
set pages 9999;

column c1 heading "Owner"     format a9;
column c2 heading "Table"     format a12;
column c3 heading "PCTFREE"   format 99;
column c4 heading "PCTUSED"   format 99;
column c5 heading "avg row"   format 99,999;
column c6 heading "Rows"      format 999,999,999;
column c7 heading "Chains"    format 999,999,999;
column c8 heading "Pct"       format .99;
```

```
set heading off;
select 'Tables with chained rows and no RAW columns.' from dual;
set heading on;

select
   owner                c1,
   table_name           c2,
   pct_free             c3,
   pct_used             c4,
   avg_row_len          c5,
   num_rows             c6,
   chain_cnt            c7,
   chain_cnt/num_rows   c8
from dba_tables
where
owner not in ('SYS','SYSTEM')
and
table_name not in
   (select table_name from dba_tab_columns
        where
   data_type in ('RAW','LONG RAW')
   )
and
chain_cnt > 0
order by chain_cnt desc
;
```

This will produce a nice report that shows a table that you will want to reorganize:

Owner	*Table*	*PCTFREE*	*PCTUSED*	*avg row*	*Rows*	*Chains*	*Pct*
SAPR3	ZG_TAB	10	40	80	5,003	1,487	.30
SAPR3	ZMM	10	40	422	18,309	509	.03
SAPR3	Z_Z_TBLS	10	40	43	458	53	.12
SAPR3	USR03	10	40	101	327	46	.14
SAPR3	Z_BURL	10	40	116	1,802	25	.01
SAPR3	ZGO_CITY	10	40	56	1,133	10	.01

6 rows selected.

Chapter 45

How I Reorganized a Large Database

Biju Thomas

Proper space management and less fragmentation is key to the performance of a database. Fragmentation happens over time. We call a tablespace fragmented when there is a lot of free space available, but they are in such small pieces that Oracle cannot use them. Whenever Oracle allocates next extent to an object, it looks for contiguous space. Coalescing the tablespace will only coalesce the free extents that are adjacent to each other. By querying the DBA_FREE_SPACE view, you can determine the extent of fragmentation in the tablespace. This chapter is a case study, encompassing the steps taken to reorganize a large application database. The idea here is to provide the steps and scripts that can be used to reorganize data and index (one table, many tables, or just indexes) with minimal modification to the scripts. The database used is Oracle 7.3.4 (in Oracle8i, there is the option to move tables from one tablespace to another).

The Scenario

This is a large application database with about 650 tables. Before reorganizing, the data tablespace was 160 GB and the index tablespace was 140 GB. All of the application data was on a single tablespace and all the indexes were on another tablespace. The tablespaces were fragmented a lot, and although there were about 20 GB free in each tablespace, the "unable to extent" error message was common. The fragmentation may have been caused for many reasons. The most obvious ones are:

- Production support developers had privilege on application data tablespace to create their temporary tables. Creating and dropping tables left a lot of space fragmented.

0-8493-1139-X/02/$0.00+$1.50
©2002 by CRC Press LLC

- The indexes were created in the data table space earlier, and later moved to an index tablespace, which caused a lot of fragmentation in the data tablespace.
- The indexes were not sized properly; when they reached a set extent threshold, they were rebuilt in the same tablespace, leaving a lot of small unusable extents.

The application has about 17 tables that are very large, rows in the range of 100 million to 350 million. Fragmentation and all data in one tablespace had a big impact on performance and resource usage. The database is about 700 GB, with five other related applications. This is a very critical application and it is very difficult to get a downtime. After explaining the benefits of performance, recovery time, and space saving, management agreed to a downtime of 48 hours to reorganize the data and indexes. The space was a big selling point as the disks were mirrored, and also using EMCs BCV, gaining 20 GB will really give 60 GB.

The Plan

1. Separate the large tables from the small ones. The six top tables have their own tablespaces.
2. Create corresponding index tablespaces.
3. Make the extent sizes uniform in tablespace to avoid fragmentation.
4. Get 160 GB of additional space to keep the data safe. The current data tablespace is 160 GB; after the new tablespaces are created and tested, the old ones can be dropped and the space allotted can be reclaimed.
5. Rename the old tables and create new tables in the new tablespaces. Tables are created using the `CREATE TABLE AS` syntax with `UNRECOVERABLE` (`NOLOGGING`, if using Oracle8) and `PARALLEL` clauses, which dramatically improves the table creation speed. Also, the number of archive logs generated during the process is less. This method of creating tables is much faster than export/import, using SQL*Load, or any other third-party utility.
6. Drop indexes and index-tablespaces on the old tables and create the new tablespaces and new indexes.

The Control Table

Because we had to move tables and indexes to different tablespaces and adjust their storage, we created a control table with all the necessary information to generate the DDL script. This table also had statistical information, just to see how much space was saved. The table structure is shown in Exhibit 45.1.

Exhibit 45.1 Control Table Structure

```
Table: APP_TAB_REORG
OBJ_NAME                 VARCHAR2(30)
   OBJ_TYPE              VARCHAR2(15)
   NEW_TSPACE            VARCHAR2(30)
   OBJ_BYTES_USED        NUMBER
   OBJ_BYTES_ALLOCATED   NUMBER
   OBJ_ROWS              NUMBER
   OBJ_EXTENTS           NUMBER
   NEW_BYTES_USED        NUMBER
   NEW_BYTES_ALLOCATED   NUMBER
   NEW_ROWS              NUMBER
   NEW_EXTENTS           NUMBER
```

By looking at the space usage in the DBA_SEGMENTS view, we decided to have ten data tablespaces and ten index tablespaces. The top six tables will have their own tablespaces; and there will be two tablespaces for medium-sized tables (less than 5 GB but above 1 GB; 11 tables) and two tablespaces for small tables (less than 1 GB; about 600 tables). The queries listed in Exhibit 45.2 were used to populate the control table.

Similarly, the control table was populated with the rest of the table information. Exhibit 45.3 gives the break-up of tablespace based on the table sizes. The table also gives the default INITIAL and NEXT extent sizes that will be used for all the objects in that tablespace.

The control table was populated with index information as well. The index tablespace names are similar to the data tablespaces, except that the "DAT" is replaced with "IND." Exhibit 45.4 displays the SQL that is used to populate.

Exhibit 45.2 Queries Used to Populate the Control Table

For the top six tables - above 5GB:

```
insert into app_tab_reorg
(obj_name, obj_type, new_tspace,
obj_bytes_allocated)
select segment_name, 'TABLE',
'APP_DAT_TABLE1', bytes
from dba_segments
where owner = 'APP'
and segment_type = 'TABLE'
and bytes > 5*1024*1024*1024;
```

Note: The NEW_TSPACE column was updated with appropriate tablespace for the five tables.

For the tables of size between 3 GB and 5 GB:

```
insert into app_tab_reorg
(obj_name, obj_type, new_tspace,
obj_bytes_allocated)
select segment_name, 'TABLE',
'APP_DAT_LARGE01', bytes
from dba_segments
where owner = 'APP'
and segment_type = 'TABLE'
       and bytes between 1024*1024*1024
          and 5*1024*1024*1024;
```

Exhibit 45.3 Table Space Based on Table Sizes

Data Tablespace Name	*Table Size*			*Extent Size*
APP_DAT_TABLE1 through APP_DAT_TABLE6	Top 6 tables,	above	5 GB	499 MB
APP_DAT_LARGE02	Between	1 GB and	5 GB	499 MB
APP_DAT_LARGE01	Between	100MB and	1 GB	100 MB
APP_DAT_SMALL02	Between	5 MB and	100 MB	5 MB
APP_DAT_SMALL01	Less than	5 MB		256 KB

Exhibit 45.4 SQL Used to Populate the Table

```
insert into app_tab_reorg (obj_name, obj_type, new_tspace)
select index_name, 'INDEX',
       replace(tr.new_tspace, 'DAT','IND')
from   dba_indexes di, app_tab_reorg tr
where  di.table_owner = 'APP'
and    tr.obj_type = 'TABLE'
and    tr.obj_name = di.table_name;

update app_tab_reorg tr
set obj_bytes_allocated = (select bytes from dba_segments ds
       where segment_name = tr.obj_name
       and segment_type = 'INDEX'
       and owner = 'APP')
where  obj_type = 'INDEX';
```

The control-table creation and the initial population script is `cr_table.sql`. Now we have all the table and index names that need to be reorganized and their new tablespace names in the control table.

Get the Scripts Ready

Before the actual reorganization starts, we can make most of the scripts ready. The following scripts were used.

1. To create new data and index tablespaces, separate script files were created for each tablespace with appropriate INITIAL, NEXT values. When creating the tables or indexes, we will not specify the storage parameters, so it is very important that we create the tablespaces with the appropriate default storage values.
2. To drop the foreign and primary keys and also the triggers, we will not generate a create script because we are going to use the export/import utility to create these objects and to reapply the grants. The script `gen_drop1.sql` will generate three script files: `drop_trig.sql` to drop triggers, `drop_fkeys.sql` to drop foreign keys, and `drop_pkey.sql` to drop the primary keys.

3. To drop the indexes and recreate the indexes in their new tablespaces, the script `gen_drop2.sql` will generate the script file (`drop_index.sql`) to drop indexes. The script `gen_crind.sql` will generate the index creation scripts (one script file for each new tablespace).
4. To define the column default values, when creating the table using CTAS (CREATE TABLE AS), column default values are not copied. The import utility also skips this because it is part of the table creation. The script `gen_default.sql` will generate the script file (`cr_tabdefault.sql`).
5. To rename the tables, the script `gen_rentab.sql` will generate the script file (`ren_tabs.sql`).
6. To create tables in the new tablespaces, the script `gen_crtab.sql` will generate two table creation script files: `cr_tab1.sql` to create the smaller tables and `cr_tab2.sql` to create the large tables in parallel mode.
7. To get the statistics, `calcspace_pre.sql` is used to populate the control table with the storage space information such as bytes allocated, bytes used, and total number of extents before the reorg. `calcspace_post.sql` is used to populate the control table with storage space information after the reorg. `findrows_pre.sql` is used to populate the control table with the current rows in each table, and `findrows_post.sql` is used to populate the control table after the reorg.
8. The script `counts.sql` is run before and after the reorg process to get the object counts.

The Steps

Before beginning the reorganization, the script to create the new tablespaces with appropriate default storage values was ready.

1. *Backup database.* Before we began the reorganization process, we made sure that we had a good cold backup. We also took a full structure export (export with ROWS=N), and an application (USER) level export (no rows) to create keys, constraints, and grants.
2. *Make data tablespace read-only.* Because the database has other applications and was up and running, we made our application data tablespace to read-only mode — just to make sure that no one updates any data during our reorg process.
3. *Create new data tablespaces.* We created the new data tablespaces using the scripts prepared earlier. Tablespace creation is a very time-consuming process (large tablespaces).
4. *Collect statistics.* When the tablespace creation was in progress, we ran scripts `calc-space_pre.sql` and `findrows_pre.sql`. After these two scripts were completed, we ran `counts.sql` and printed out the spool file.

5. *Script to create indexes.* Run script `gen_crind.sql` to generate script files to create indexes later. (Make sure to run this script before you drop the indexes and primary/unique keys!)
6. *Scripts to drop triggers, foreign keys, and primary/uniquekeys.* Run script `gen_drop1.sql`, which generates script files `drop_trig.sql`, `drop_fkeys.sql`, and `drop_pkey.sql`. Run scripts in order.
7. *Script to drop indexes.* Run script `gen_drop2.sql` after completing step 6, to drop the indexes (primary key indexes are dropped in step 5). Run `drop_index.sql`.
8. *Script to define column default values.* Run script `gen_default.sql` to generate script file.
9. *Rename tables.* After dropping the constraints and indexes, the tables are renamed with a 'ZZ_' prefix. Run script `gen_rentab.sql` to generate and run `ren_tabs.sql`.
10. *Create tables.* Run script `gen_crtab.sql` to create tables. The `cr_tab1.sql` script is run first to create the smaller tables. Break the `cr_tab2.sql` script file into multiple other smaller scripts to create the tables simultaneously (separate script for each tablespace).
11. *Drop index tablespace.* While the table creation was in progress, we dropped index tablespace to get space to create the new index tablespaces. We started to create the new index tablespaces using the scripts prepared earlier after all data tablespace creation was complete.
12. *Create indexes.* As and when the tables for a tablespace were completed, we started to build indexes for the corresponding tables using the scripts generated in step 5. There was one script for each tablespace.
13. *Monitor progress.* The following query can be used to monitor the progress of table creation (gives the list of tables that need to be created in the new tablespaces).

```
select  table_name  from  dba_tables  a
where   owner  =  'APP'  and
table_name  like  'ZZ%'  and
not  exists  (select  1  from  dba_tables  b
where   b.owner  =  'APP'
and     b.table_name  not  like  'ZZ%'
and     a.table_name  =  'ZZ_'||b.table_name);
```

Similarly for indexes, use the query:

```
select obj_name from app_tab_reorg
where obj_type = 'INDEX'
and obj_name not in
(select index_name from dba_indexes
where owner = 'APP');
```

14. *Object creation completed, create constraints and triggers.* When the table and index creation was completed, we started to import from the structure export taken in step 1. The parameters used were FROMUSER, TOUSER, IGNORE=Y. This step brings in the primary keys, unique keys (we already have created the indexes), check constraints, grants, comments, and triggers. This step also analyzes tables for the COST-based optimizer.

15. *Modify columns to have the default values.* Run script file `cr_tabdefault.sql` created in step 8.
16. *Recompile all invalid stored objects.* Use script `cinvobj.sql` to compile all the views, procedures, functions, triggers, and packages that are invalid after the reorg.
17. *Finally collect statistics.* Run scripts `calc-space_post.sql` and `findrows_post.sql` to populate the control table with statistics after the reorganization. After these two scripts were completed, we ran `counts.sql`, printed out the spool file, and compared it against the spool file printed out in step 4.

Exhibit 45.5 summarizes the scripts used in the process and their purpose. The scripts can be downloaded from the Oracle Internals Web site and are included here in Appendices 45.1 through 45.13.

Results

The reorganization was completed long before the expected time. Because we were creating the table using CTAS, the total table creation took only six hours (multiple tables were created at the same time as there were no TEMP space or rollback issues when using the UNRECOVERABLE clause), which was rather surprising to us. The index creation took about 20 hours. The space saved was very significant. Overall, in the database level, we saved about 70 GB (30 GB in data — on a single table, the saving was 20 GB! — and 40 GB in index space), which was very much worth the effort.

Summary

This chapter discussed a case study to reorganize data and indexes to new tablespaces. The scripts provided can be used when reorganizing the tables and indexes with minimal modifications. If you have got enough downtime for the application, you can drop the indexes after creating all the tables (instead of dropping the indexes to save space and time immediately after renaming the tables). Then you can use a hint or ORDER BY clause to SELECT the rows in the primary key order. Having the rows ordered helps Oracle to speed up the index reads. Also keep in mind that if you have objects like triggers, constraints, or indexes owned by users outside the application on the application tables, you need to save them and recreate them after the reorganization.

Exhibit 45.5 Scripts Used

Script Name	Purpose
`cr_table.sql`	Creates the control table and populates it with the table and index names that need to be reorganized. The script assumes that the schema owner name is APP.
`calcspace_pre.sql`	To find the space used by APP-owned tables: space allotted, space used, number of extents are updated to the control table. Run before the reorganization.
`calcspace_post.sql`	To find the space used by APP owned tables: space allotted, space used, number of extents are updated to the control table. Run after the reorganization.
`findrows_pre.sql`	To find the total number of rows in each table owned by the APP id, and updates the control table. Run before the reorganization.
`findrows_post.sql`	To find the total number of rows in each table owned by the APP id, and updates the control table. Run after the reorganization.
`counts.sql`	To find the object counts and free space available. Run this script before and after the reorganization and verify the results to make sure you have all the objects recreated.
`gen_crind.sql`	Script to generate index creation scripts. One script file is generated for each new tablespace. Uses utl_file package, which requires the parameter utl_file_dir in the init.ora file.
`gen_drop1.sql`	Generates scripts to drop triggers, primary keys, and foreign keys.
`gen_drop2.sql`	Generates scripts to drop indexes.
`gen_default.sql`	Generates script to create column default values.
`gen_rentab.sql`	Generates script to rename the APP-owned tables to ZZ_table_name. These tables are dropped after the reorganization is completed.
`gen_crtab.sql`	Generate table creation scripts from the control table using CTAS. Split the second script generated to multiple scripts so that they can be run in parallel.
`cinvobj.sql`	Compiles all INVALID objects in the database.

Appendix 45.1 cr_table.sql

```
REM Create Control Table
REM
CREATE TABLE APP_TAB_REORG (
   OBJ_NAME             VARCHAR2 (30),
   OBJ_TYPE             VARCHAR2 (15),
   NEW_TSPACE           VARCHAR2 (30),
   OBJ_BYTES_USED       NUMBER,
   OBJ_BYTES_ALLOCATED  NUMBER,
   NEW_INIT_BYTES       NUMBER,
   NEW_NEXT_BYTES       NUMBER,
   OBJ_ROWS             NUMBER,
   OBJ_EXTENTS          NUMBER,
   NEW_BYTES_USED       NUMBER,
   NEW_BYTES_ALLOCATED  NUMBER,
   NEW_ROWS             NUMBER,
   NEW_EXTENTS          NUMBER,
CONSTRAINT PK_APP_TAB_REORG PRIMARY KEY (OBJ_TYPE, OBJ_NAME))
PCTFREE 50;

REM Populate Table Information
REM Large tables - over 5GB
REM
insert into app_tab_reorg
   (obj_name, obj_type, new_tspace)
select segment_name, 'TABLE', 'APP_DAT_TABLE1'
from dba_segments
where owner = 'APP' and segment_type = 'TABLE'
and bytes > 5*1024*1024*1024;

REM Update each tablespace for the next four tables
REM
update app_tab_reorg
set    new_tspace = 'APP_DAT_TABLE2'
where  obj_name   = 'TABLE2';

REM Continue the updates....
REM

REM For the tables of size between 3GB to 5GB:
REM
insert into app_tab_reorg (obj_name, obj_type, new_tspace,
obj_bytes_allocated)
select segment_name, 'TABLE', 'APP_DAT_LARGE01', bytes
from dba_segments
where owner = 'APP' and segment_type = 'TABLE'
and bytes between 1024*1024*1024 and 5*1024*1024*1024;

REM Continue with different condition and tablespace name
REM for rest of the tablespaces.
REM Chage the following line in each of the new inserts.
REM bytes between 1024*1024*1024 and 5*1024*1024*1024;
REM

REM Insert Index Information
REM Indexes are broken down in tablespaces as in their data
REM tablespaces. The index tablespace names are similar to the data
REM tablespace name, 'DAT' changed to 'IND'.
```

(continues)

Appendix 45.1 cr_table.sql (continued)

```
REM
insert into app_tab_reorg (obj_name, obj_type, new_tspace)
select index_name, 'INDEX', replace(tr.new_tspace, 'DAT', 'IND')
from   dba_indexes di, app_tab_reorg tr
where  di.table_owner   = 'APP'
and    tr.obj_type      = 'TABLE'
and    tr.obj_name      = di.table_name;

update   app_tab_reorg tr
set      bytes = (select bytes from dba_segments ds
                  where  segment_name = tr.obj_name
                  and    segment_type = 'INDEX'
                  and    owner = 'APP')
where obj_type = 'INDEX';

REM End cr_table.sql
```

Appendix 45.2 calcspace_pre.sql

```
REM To find the actual space used by APP owned tables
REM Space allotted, space used, number of extents
REM updated to the control table.
REM Run before the reorganization
REM
Set serveroutput on
declare
      /* Indexes */
      cursor cind is
      select owner, index_name
      from   dba_indexes where
        table_owner = 'APP';

      /* Tables */
      cursor ctab is
      select owner, table_name
      from   dba_tables where
        owner = 'APP';

      wdate varchar2 (25) := to_char(sysdate,'Mon DD, YYYY HH:MI AM');

      wtotal_blocks              number;
      wtotal_bytes               number;
      wunused_blocks             number;
      wunused_bytes              number;
      wlast_used_extent_file_id  number;
      wlast_used_extent_block_id number;
      wlast_used_block           number;

      wextents number;

   begin
```

Appendix 45.2 `calcspace_pre.sql` (continued)

```
   for rind in cind loop

      -- Actual space used by the index
      --
      dbms_space.unused_space (rind.owner, rind.index_name, 'INDEX',
                               wtotal_blocks, wtotal_bytes,
                               wunused_blocks,
                               wunused_bytes, wlast_used_extent_file_id,
                               wlast_used_extent_block_id,
                               wlast_used_block);

      select  extents
      into    wextents
      from    dba_segments
      where   segment_type   = 'INDEX'
      and     owner          = 'APP'
      and     segment_name   = rind.index_name;

      update APP_tab_reorg set
      obj_bytes_allocated    = wtotal_bytes,
      obj_bytes_used         = wtotal_bytes - wunused_bytes,
      obj_extents            = wextents
      where   obj_type       = 'INDEX'
      and     obj_name       = rind.index_name;

   end loop;

   for rtab in ctab loop

      -- Actual space used by the index
      -- dbms_space.unused_space (rtab.owner, rtab.table_name, 'TABLE',
                                  wtotal_blocks, wtotal_bytes,
                                  wunused_blocks,
                                  wunused_bytes, wlast_used_extent_file_id,
                                  wlast_used_extent_block_id,
                                  wlast_used_block);

      select  extents
      into    wextents
      from    dba_segments
      where   segment_type   = 'TABLE'
      and     owner          = 'APP'
      and     segment_name   = rtab.table_name;

      update APP_tab_reorg set
      obj_bytes_allocated    = wtotal_bytes,
      obj_bytes_used         = wtotal_bytes - wunused_bytes,
      obj_extents            = wextents
      where   obj_type = 'TABLE'
      and     obj_name = rtab.table_name;

   end loop;

   end;
/
set serveroutput off feedback on verify on pages 999
REM End caclspace_pre.sql
```

Appendix 45.3 calcspace_post.sql

```
REM To find the actual space used by APP owned tables
REM Space allotted, space used, number of extents
REM updated to the control table.
REM Run after the reorganization
REM
Set serveroutput on
declare
      /* Indexes */
      cursor cind is
      select owner, index_name
      from   dba_indexes where
        table_owner = 'APP' ;

      /* Tables */
      cursor ctab is
      select owner, table_name
      from   dba_tables where
        owner = 'APP';

      wdate varchar2 (25) := to_char(sysdate,'Mon DD, YYYY HH:MI AM');

      wtotal_blocks               number;
      wtotal_bytes                number;
      wunused_blocks              number;
      wunused_bytes               number;
      wlast_used_extent_file_id   number;
      wlast_used_extent_block_id  number;
      wlast_used_block            number;

      wextents number;

   begin

   for rind in cind loop

      -- Actual space used by the index
      --
      dbms_space.unused_space (rind.owner, rind.index_name, 'INDEX',
                               wtotal_blocks, wtotal_bytes,
                               wunused_blocks,
                               wunused_bytes, wlast_used_extent_file_id,
                               wlast_used_extent_block_id,
                               wlast_used_block);

      select extents
      into   wextents
      from   dba_segments
      where  segment_type  = 'INDEX'
      and    owner         = 'APP'
      and    segment_name  = rind.index_name;

      update APP_tab_reorg set
      new_bytes_allocated   = wtotal_bytes,
      new_bytes_used        = wtotal_bytes - wunused_bytes,
      new_extents           = wextents
      where obj_type        = 'INDEX'
      and   obj_name        = rind.index_name;

   end loop;
```

Appendix 45.3 `calcspace_post.sql` (continued)

```
   for rtab in ctab loop

      -- Actual space used by the index
      --
      dbms_space.unused_space (rtab.owner, rtab.table_name, 'TABLE',
                               wtotal_blocks, wtotal_bytes,
                               wunused_blocks,
                               wunused_bytes, wlast_used_extent_file_id,
                               wlast_used_extent_block_id,
                               wlast_used_block);

      select  extents
      into    wextents
      from    dba_segments
      where   segment_type   = 'TABLE'
      and     owner          = 'APP'
      and     segment_name   = rtab.table_name;

      update APP_tab_reorg  set
      new_bytes_allocated    = wtotal_bytes,
      new_bytes_used         = wtotal_bytes - wunused_bytes,
      new_extents            = wextents
      where   obj_type       = 'TABLE'
      and     obj_name       = rtab.table_name;

   end loop;

   end;
/
set serveroutput off feedback on verify on pages 999
REM End of calcspace_post.sql
```

Appendix 45.4 findrows_pre.sql

```
REM To find the total number of rows in each table
REM owned by the APP id, and update the control table.
REM Run before the reorganization.
REM
Set serveroutput on
declare

      /* Tables */
      cursor ctab is
      select owner, table_name
      from   dba_tables where
         owner = 'APP';

      wrows number;
      cursor_handle integer;
      dummy integer;

   begin

   for rtab in ctab loop

      cursor_handle := dbms_sql.open_cursor;
      dbms_sql.parse(cursor_handle,'select count(*) from '
         || rtab.owner ||'.'||
         rtab.table_name,DBMS_SQL.V7);
      dbms_sql.define_column(cursor_handle,1,wrows);
      dummy := dbms_sql.execute_and_fetch(cursor_handle, true);
      dbms_sql.column_value(cursor_handle, 1, wrows);
      dbms_sql.close_cursor(cursor_handle);

      update APP_tab_reorg set
      obj_rows = wrows
      where obj_type = 'TABLE'
      and   obj_name = rtab.table_name;

   end loop;

   end;
/
set serveroutput off feedback on verify on pages 999
REM End of findrows_pre.sql
```

Appendix 45.5 indrows_post.sql

```
REM To find the total number of rows in each table
REM owned by the APP id, and update the control table.
REM Run after the reorganization.
REM
Set serveroutput on
declare

      /* Tables */
      cursor ctab is
      select 'APP' owner, obj_name table_name
      from   APP_tab_reorg where
      obj_type = 'TABLE' and
      new_rows is null;

      wrows number;
      cursor_handle integer;
      dummy integer;

   begin

   for rtab in ctab loop

      cursor_handle := dbms_sql.open_cursor;
      dbms_sql.parse(cursor_handle,'select count(*) from '
         || rtab.owner ||'.'||
         rtab.table_name,DBMS_SQL.V7);
      dbms_sql.define_column(cursor_handle,1,wrows);
      dummy := dbms_sql.execute_and_fetch(cursor_handle, true);
      dbms_sql.column_value(cursor_handle, 1, wrows);
      dbms_sql.close_cursor(cursor_handle);

      update APP_tab_reorg set
      new_rows = wrows
      where obj_type = 'TABLE'
      and   obj_name = rtab.table_name;

   commit;

   end loop;

   end;
/
set serveroutput off feedback on verify on pages 999
REM End of findrows_post.sql
```

Appendix 45.6 counts.sql

```
REM To find the object counts and free space available
REM Run this script before and after the reorganization
REM and verify the results to make sure you have
REM all the objects recreated.
REM
spool counts
col owner format a6
set feedback on pages 9999 echo off verify off
select To_char(sysdate, 'DD-MON-YYYY HH24:MI:SS') System_date
from dual
/
prompt Triggers owned on APP tables
select owner, TABLE_OWNER, count(*)
from dba_triggers
where (table_owner = 'APP' or
owner = 'APP')
group by owner, TABLE_OWNER
/
prompt Indexes owned on APP tables
select owner, table_owner, uniqueness, count(*)
from dba_indexes
where (table_owner = 'APP' or
owner = 'APP')
group by owner, table_owner, uniqueness
/
prompt Comments on APP Tables
select owner, table_type, count(*)
from   dba_tab_comments
where  owner = 'APP'
group by owner, table_type
/
prompt Comments on APP Columns
select owner, count(*)
from   dba_col_comments
where  owner = 'APP'
group by owner
/
prompt Foreign key constraints on APP tables
select owner, r_owner, count(*)
from dba_constraints
where (owner = 'APP'
or     r_owner = 'APP')
and    constraint_type = 'R'
group by owner, r_owner
/
prompt Object Counts for APP
select object_type, status, count(*)
from   dba_objects
where  owner = 'APP'
and object_name not like 'ZZ_%'
group by object_type, status
/
prompt Invalid Objects
col object_name format a40
col owner format a15
select owner, object_name
```

Appendix 45.6 `counts.sql` (continued)

```
from   dba_objects
where  status = 'INVALID'
/
prompt APP Table and Index Space Usage
col MB_SIZE format "999,999.9"
col extents format "999,999"
col wcnt format     "999,999"
select segment_type, tablespace_name, sum(bytes)/1048576
MB_size,
        sum(extents) extents, count(segment_name) wcnt
from   dba_segments
where owner = 'APP'
group by segment_type, tablespace_name
/

Prompt APP Tablespace free space
COLUMN tsname     FORMAT a17
COLUMN extents    FORMAT 9999
COLUMN bytes      FORMAT 999,999,999
COLUMN largest    FORMAT 999,999,999
COLUMN Tot_Size   FORMAT 9,999,999 HEADING "TOTAL (M)"
COLUMN Tot_Free   FORMAT 9,999,999 HEADING "FREE (M)"
COLUMN Pct_Free   FORMAT 999 HEADING "FREE %"
COLUMN Fragments  FORMAT 999,999
COLUMN Large_Ext  FORMAT 9,999,999
SELECT a.tablespace_name TSNAME, SUM(a.tots)/1048576 Tot_Size,
        SUM(a.sumb)/1048576 Tot_Free,
        SUM(a.sumb)*100/sum(a.tots) Pct_Free,
        SUM(a.largest)/1048576 Large_Ext, SUM(a.chunks)
Fragments
FROM (SELECt tablespace_name, 0 tots, SUM(bytes) sumb,
             MAX(bytes) largest, COUNT(*) chunks
           FROM dba_free_space a
           GROUP BY tablespace_name
           UNION
           SELECT tablespace_name, SUM(bytes) tots, 0, 0, 0
           FROM   dba_data_files
           GROUP BY tablespace_name) a
where   a.tablespace_name like 'APP%'
GROUP BY a.tablespace_name
/
spool off
REM End of counts.sql
```

Appendix 45.7 gen_crind.sql

```
REM Script to generate index creation scripts
REM One script file is generate for each new tablespace
REM Uses utl_file package, which requires the
REM Parameter utl_file_dir in the init.ora file
REM
set serveroutput on feedback off verify off pages 0
declare

   /* File name to save script */
   wtabindfile VARCHAR2 (34);
   wtabindftype utl_file.file_type;

   /* Tablespaces */
   cursor ctspace is
   select distinct new_tspace
   from   APP_tab_reorg
   where  obj_type = 'INDEX';

   /* Indexes */
   cursor cind (wtspace in varchar2) is
   select owner, table_owner, table_name, index_name,
        new_tspace tablespace_name, new_init_bytes initial_extent,
        new_next_bytes next_extent,
        decode(uniqueness,'UNIQUE','UNIQUE') unq
   from dba_indexes, APP_tab_reorg
   where owner     = 'APP' and
     index_name   = obj_name and
     obj_type     = 'INDEX' and
     new_tspace   = wtspace
   order by table_name, index_name;

   /* Index columns */
   cursor ccol (o in varchar2, t in varchar2, i in varchar2) is
   select decode(column_position,1,'(',',')||
        rpad(column_name,40) cl
   from dba_ind_columns
   where table_name  = upper(t) and
        index_name  = upper(i) and
        index_owner = upper(o)
   order by column_position;

begin

   for rtspace in ctspace loop

      wtabindfile   := lower(rtspace.new_tspace)|| '.sql';
      wtabindftype  :=
           utl_file.fopen('/ora_backup/demodb', wtabindfile, 'w');

      for rind in cind (rtspace.new_tspace) loop

      utl_file.put_line(wtabindftype, 'create '||rind.unq||' index '||
rind.owner || '.' || rind.index_name||' on '||rind.table_owner||'.'||
rind.table_name);

        for rcol in ccol
           (rind.owner, rind.table_name, rind.index_name) loop
           utl_file.put_line(wtabindftype, rcol.cl);
```

Appendix 45.7 gen_crind.sql (continued)

```
      end loop;
        utl_file.put_line(wtabindftype, ') pctfree 5 tablespace ' ||
          rind.tablespace_name);
        utl_file.put_line(wtabindftype, 'storage (initial ' ||
          rind.initial_extent || ' next ' || rind.next_extent || '
          pctincrease 0)');
        utl_file.put_line(wtabindftype, 'unrecoverable ');
        utl_file.put_line(wtabindftype, '/');

      end loop;

      utl_file.fclose(wtabindftype);

   end loop;
end;
/
set serveroutput off feedback on verify on pages 999
REM End of gen_crind.sql
```

Appendix 45.8 gen_drop1.sql

```
REM To drop the triggers on APP tables
REM
set pages 0 lines 200 trims on feedback off
spool drop_trig.sql
select 'drop trigger ' || owner||'.'|| trigger_name ||';'
from    dba_triggers
where   table_owner = 'APP';
spool off
REM
REM To drop the foreign key constraints
REM
spool drop_fkeys.sql
select 'alter table ' || owner ||'.'|| table_name ||
       ' drop constraint ' || constraint_name || ';'
from    dba_constraints
where   constraint_type = 'R'
and     owner = 'APP';
spool off
REM
REM To drop the Primary keys
REM
spool drop_pkeys.sql
select 'alter table ' || owner ||'.'|| table_name || ' drop primary key;'
from    dba_constraints
where   constraint_type = 'P'
and     owner = 'APP';
spool off
REM End of gen_drop1.sql
```

Appendix 45.9 **gen_drop2.sql**

```
REM To drop indexes (after dropping primary and unique keys)
REM
set pages 0 trims on feedback off
spool drop_index.sql
select 'drop index APP.' || index_name ||';'
from   dba_indexes
where  owner = 'APP';
spool off
REM End of gen_drop2.sql
```

Appendix 45.10 **gen_default.sql**

```
REM Alter tables to create default column values
REM
set pages 0 feedback off lines 200 trims on
spool cr_tabdefault.sql
select 'alter table APP.' || table_name || ' modify ' || column_name
       || ' default ' , data_default , ';'
from  dba_tab_columns
where owner = 'APP'
and   data_default is not null
order by table_name;
spool off
REM End of gen_default.sql
```

Appendix 45.11 **gen_rentab.sql**

```
REM Generate script to rename APP owned tables
REM to ZZ_table_name.
REM
set feedback off pages 0 lines 200 trims on
spool ren_tabs.sql
select 'rename ' || obj_name || ' to ZZ_' || obj_name ||';'
from  APP_tab_reorg
where obj_type = 'TABLE';
spool off
REM End of gen_rentab.sql
```

Appendix 45.12 gen_crtab.sql

```
REM Generate table creation scripts from the control table
REM using CTAS
REM Split the second script to multiple scripts so
REM that they can be run in parallel
REM
set pages 0 feedback off lines 80 trims on
spool crobj/cr_tabs1.sql
select 'create table APP.'|| obj_name,
'  tablespace ' || new_tspace || ' pctfree ' ||
decode(new_tspace, 'APP_DAT01_SMALL', 10, 5) || ' initrans 2',
'  storage (initial ' || new_init_bytes, ' next ' || new_next_bytes ||
' pctincrease 0 maxextents 5000) unrecoverable',
'  as',
'  select * from APP.ZZ_' || obj_name || ';'
from APP_tab_reorg
where obj_type = 'TABLE'
and   new_tspace like 'APP_DAT0__SMALL'
order by new_tspace, obj_name;
spool off
REM
REM
spool crobj/cr_tabs2.sql
select 'create table APP.'|| obj_name,
'  tablespace ' || new_tspace || ' pctfree ' ||
decode(new_tspace, 'APP_DAT01_SMALL', 10, 5) || ' initrans 2',
'  storage (initial ' || new_init_bytes, ' next ' ||new_next_bytes ||
' pctincrease 0 maxextents 5000) unrecoverable parallel (degree 6)',
'  as',
'  select * from APP.ZZ_' || obj_name || ';'
from  APP_tab_reorg
where obj_type = 'TABLE'
and   new_tspace not like 'APP_DAT0__SMALL'
order by new_tspace, obj_name;
spool off
REM End of gen_crtab.sql
```

Appendix 45.13 **cinvobj.sql**

```
REM script to compile all invalid objects in the database
REM
set termout off echo off pages 0 trims off lines 100
spool /tmp/cinv.sql
select 'alter '||decode(object_type,'PACKAGE BODY', 'PACKAGE'
,object_type)|| ' ' ||owner||'.'|| object_name ||' compile'||
decode(object_type, 'PACKAGE BODY', ' body;', ';')
from dba_objects
where status = 'INVALID'
/
spool off
set termout on feedback on echo on
spool /tmp/cinvobj.lis
@/tmp/cinv.sql

column owner format A6
column object_name format A30
column object_type format A20
select owner, object_name, object_type, status
from dba_objects
where status = 'INVALID'
/
spool off
REM End of cinvobj.sql
```

Chapter 46

Partition and Conquer

Raj Pande

With Oracle8, the lowest level of granularity for data storage has been lowered from tables to partitions. A table can have many partitions, each with the same logical attributes, but with different physical attributes. The concept of partitioning opens up new possibilities in terms of tuning and database administration. However, at least in the current release, partitioning comes with a lot of constraints that the DBA must be aware of. Partitions cannot be used, for example, with tables that use the object extension of `Oracle8`.

This chapter builds on a basic understanding of the partitioning concept and provides detailed examples.

Conceptual Terms

- *Partitioning keys.* The list of columns that are used to define the partitions. One partitioning key consists of an ordered list of up to 16 columns. This cannot contain `ROWID`, `LEVEL`, `MLSLABEL`, or other pseudocolumns. Both the tables and the indexes can be partitioned, and it is important to distinguish the partitioning keys from the indexing keys. It sometimes gets confusing, especially for tables with local partitioned indexes (see detailed examples later). The pseudovalue `MAXVALUE` is used to signify an undefined upper boundary for partitioning columns.
- *Equipartition.* Partitions that have partitioning keys identical in type and range are equipartitions. One never explicitly creates equipartitions. All local partitioned indexes are automatically created as equipartitions with the partitions of the underlying table. Equipartitioning makes maintenance and recovery of table partitions convenient because, with any maintenance of the table partitions, the associated index partitions are automatically maintained by Oracle. It also improves the execution plan when working with parallel query by speeding up access to the partition.

0-8493-1139-X/02/$0.00+$1.50
©2002 by CRC Press LLC

For the purpose of partitioning, NULL values are sorted higher than any other value (except MAXVALUE).

If MAXVALUE is defined as a partition bound for the nth element of the partition list, then any other higher range is irrelevant (and illegal) for values defined in the n+ partition element. For example, if a partition is defined as:

```
partition by range (flda, fldb, fldc, fldd)
partition pa values less than (v11, v21, v31, v41)
partition pb values less than (v12, v22, v32, v42)
partition pc values less than (v13, MAXVALUE, v33, v43)
partition pd values less than (v14, MAXVALUE, v34, v44)
```

then, having defined partition pc, partition pd is irrelevant and illegal. Partition pc might as well be

```
partition pc value less than (v13, MAXVALUE, MAXVALUE, MAXVALUE);
```

Partitioned tables with global indexes or nonpartitioned indexes cannot use the direct-load INSERT path; only the conventional path is supported for inserting into these tables.

Table Partitioning

A partitioned table can have unpartitioned or global indexes. Similarly, an unpartitioned table can have index partitions but these can only be global partitioned indexes. See Exhibit 46.1 and the examples later in this chapter.

A partitioned table cannot have LOB, LONG, LONG RAW, cannot be part of cluster, and should *not* be an index organized table. Partitioned tables cannot have columns with object, REF, nested table, or array datatypes.

In a partitioned table, an insert into the table with the value of the partitioning column being *greater than* or *equal* to the highest range value for the partition will fail. This effectively acts as a constraint on the table, although it is not recorded as a constraint in the data dictionary. Similarly, because nulls are sorted higher than any other value, if the fields that make up the partitioning key contain a NULL, then the range for that column should be defined as MAXVALUE; otherwise, the insert with null values will fail.

For example, if deptno in the EMP table can be null, then we need to create the partitioned table:

```
CREATE TABLE EMP (
empno number,
  ........)
partition by range (deptno)(partition emp_p1
     values less than (10), partition emp_p2
     values less than (20), partition emp_p3
     values less than (MAXVALUE));
```

Index Partitioning

There are two types of partitions related to indexes; each has two subtypes. Assume a table with columns PC1, PC2, PC3, IC1, IC2, IC3, and so forth. See Exhibit 46.1 for a summary of options for index partitioning.

Exhibit 46.1 Conditions for Using a Nonunique Index to Have a Unique Constraint

Index Type	*Table Partition Cols*	*Index Partition Cols*	If *Nonunique Index Cols*	Then *a Unique Constraint on*	*Condition*
Local nonprefixed	PC1, PC2, PC3	PC1, PC2, PC3	PC3,* PC2, PC1 [,IC1] [,..]	PC3, PC2, PC1 [,IC1] [,..]	Partitioning columns must be a subset of the unique index.
Local prefixed	PC1, PC2, PC3	PC1, PC2, PC3	PC1, PC2, PC3 [,IC1[,..]]	PC1, PC2, PC3 [,IC1[,..]]	No additional requirement on unique index because of the prefix.
Global prefixed	PC1, PC2, PC3	IC1, PC1	IC1, PC1 [,IC2[,..IC3]]	IC1, PC1 [,IC3[,PC2]]	No additional requirement on unique index because of the prefix.

* The partitioning keys must be a subset of the nonunique index and they must form a left prefix portion of the unique index.

For partitioned indexes, Exhibit 46.1 summarizes conditions under which a nonunique index can be utilized to satisfy a unique/pk constraint. In general, for a unique constraint to be satisfied from a nonunique index, the unique constraint must be a left prefix of the nonunique index. The following conditions must also be met.

Local. All the keys in a specific partition of an index point only to rows in a single underlying table partition. There are two types of local index partitioning:

1. Local prefixed indexes
2. Local nonprefixed indexes

Global. The keys in the index partitions are not constrained in any way. They can point to rows in any partition of the underlying table. In fact, the table may even be nonpartitioned. There are two types of global indexes, but only the global prefixed index is supported by Oracle; an unprefixed index is not supported.

For all practical purposes, nonpartitioned indexes are treated the same as global prefixed indexes. In the definitions, we are referring to the indexes that are partitioned. It is the index that is prefixed. If a partitioned index is a bitmap index, then it can only be a local partition.

As pointed out, we should be clear about the keys for the index partitions and the keys for the index because of the way some conditions exist for the partitioned indexes to be unique. These are explained later with the examples. For example, in Appendix 46.6,* the partitioning column list for both the table EMP6 and index J3 is (`EMPNO`), whereas the index J3 is made up of columns (`empno, deptno`).

Local Index Partitions

Local index partitions are created by specifying keyword `LOCAL` in the syntax. Oracle creates local index partitions so that they are always equipartitioned with the underlying table, that is, Oracle range partitions the indexes on the same columns, creates the same number of partitions with the same range values as the underlying table. The advantage is that Oracle automatically maintains the index partitions as the partitions, in the underlying table are added, dropped, or split, ensuring that the index partitions are always equipartitioned with the table partitions.

With local partitioned indexes, a maintenance operation on the underlying table (other than `SPLIT PARTITION`) always affects only one index partition. There is true partition independence, which helps in roll-in/roll-out of partitions; the maintenance time is only proportional to the data in the partition of the underlying table.

* For this example and others, see Appendices 46.1 through 46.6, or visit the *Oracle Internals* code repository on the Web at www.auerbach-publications.com/scripts.

Local Prefixed Index Partitions

A local prefixed index partition is created when the index is left prefixed with the column list of the partitioning columns. (The partitioning columns are a left subset of the indexed columns.) See Appendix 46.3. The table EMP3 has three partitions partitioned on (`empno`). The index J1 is created on (`empno, deptno`). The index is automatically partitioned on `empno`, as it is a local partitioned index. It is a local prefixed index partition; the index key is created left prefixed with the partitioning keys (`empno`). Note that to create local partitioned indexes, one need not define the partition ranges as they are taken from the table definitions. You only specify the partition names and any other physical attributes.

Local Nonprefixed Index Partitions

If the index column list is not left prefixed with the partitioning columns, then it is a nonprefixed index. For a local nonprefixed index to be unique, the partitioning columns must be a subset of the indexing columns. In the example in Appendix 46.5, the table (and the local index) are partitioned on (`deptno`). The index is created on (`empno, deptno`), which is not a left prefix on the partition keys. We can still create a unique index because the partitioning column (`deptno`) is a subset of the indexing columns (`empno, deptno`):

```
CREATE UNIQUE INDEX J1 ON EMP5 (EMPNO, DEPTNO)
   LOCAL (PARTITION JI1, PARTITION JI2, PARTITION JI3);
select a.index_name, a.locality, a.alignment,
   b.uniqueness from user_part_indexes a,
   user_indexes b where b.index_name =
   a.index_name;
INDEX_NAME     LOCALITY     ALIGNMENT        UNIQUENESS
----------     --------     ------------     ----------
J1             LOCAL        NON_PREFIXED     UNIQUE
J3             LOCAL        PREFIXED         NONUNIQUE
PK_DEPT        LOCAL        PREFIXED         UNIQUE
```

Global Index Partitions

When the partitioned index is created with a global keyword, then it is global. With global index partitions, the keys in one index partition normally point to more than one table partition. They can be manually created to be equipartitioned with the underlying table partitions, but the difference with respect to the local index partitions is: (1) the maintenance of these global equipartitions is not done automatically by Oracle, and (2) execution plans do not take advantage of the fact that the index partition is equipartitioned with the table. Oracle only supports prefixed global index partitions (the indexes must be left prefixed with partitioning columns). For a global prefixed index partition, the last range value must be (`maxvalue, maxvalue, max`...). The global prefixed index can be unique or nonunique (see the example in

Appendix 46.5). In the example, the index is partitioned on `deptno` (the fact that the table is also partitioned on `deptno` is irrelevant) and the partitions are explicitly created. The index is created with global keyword and is on (`deptno`, `empno`), which is left prefixed on `deptno` (the column list of the partition). For the sake of example, the following would also give a global index partition:

```
CREATE UNIQUE INDEX U_GINDX ON EMP5 (DEPTNO,
   EMPNO, HIREDATE) GLOBAL PARTITION BY
   RANGE(DEPTNO, EMPNO) (PARTITION JX1 VALUES
   LESS THAN(10,3000), PARTITION JX2 VALUES
   LESS THAN (40, 9999), PARTITION JX3 VALUES
   LESS THAN(MAXVALUE,MAXVALUE));
```

Global indexes are more difficult to manage than local indexes: any maintenance of one table partition affects all index partitions because the global index partitions are not equipartitioned with the table.

Index Unusable (IU)

This is an attribute of nonpartitioned indexes or of an index partition. Once the partition is marked IU, then it must be either rebuilt or dropped and recreated. With an IU partition, no DML can be done against the index or the partition; however, that partition can still be split, dropped, renamed, or rebuilt. This is similar to direct load state of indexes using direct path of `sql*loader`.

When an index or a partition of an indexed partition is made IU, then the partition or the index needs to be rebuilt. There is no command to rebuild all partitions of a partitioned index: either repeat the rebuild for each partition, or drop the index and issue the `create index` command. The latter is more efficient because it only scans the table once to build all partitions of the index.

If an IU partition is split, then the new partition is also IU.

Unique/PK Constraints.

In Oracle8, it is not necessary to have a unique index to enforce a unique key constraint. Create a nonunique key and then use that to enforce the unique/pk constraint. However, if the existing index is partitioned, then the partitioning key columns for the index partition must also be a subset of the unique key columns list. Otherwise, Oracle will create an additional unique index to enforce the constraint.

Example: Create the table EMP5 as in Appendix 46.5, and create the global unique index `U_GINDX` as shown in the global index partitions. Now:

```
alter table emp5 add constraint pk_emp5 primary key (deptno,empno);
```

Although the index `U_GINDX` is unique, the statement above will create a new index `PK_EMP5` to enforce the primary key constraint because the partitioning key for the index partition (DEPTNO, EMPNO, HIREDATE) is not a subset of the indexing keys (DEPTNO, EMPNO). However, if we created the global index as follows:

```
CREATE INDEX NU_GINDX ON EMP5 (DEPTNO, EMPNO)
  GLOBAL PARTITION BY RANGE(DEPTNO, EMPNO)
  (PARTITION JX1 VALUES LESS THAN(10,3000),
  PARTITION JX2 VALUES LESS THAN (40, 9999),
  PARTITION JX3 VALUES LESS THAN(MAXVALUE,MAXVALUE));
```

and then create the primary key as above, we will get only one index because the partition key is a subset of the unique key, although the index NU_GINDX is nonunique.

Partition Maintenance

Index Partitions. Can only be RENAMED, SPLIT, REBUILD, DROPPED, or made UNUSABLE.

Table Partitions. Can be involved in MOVE, ADD, DROP, TRUNCATE, SPLIT, or EXCHANGE.

Move Partition

Example:

```
ALTER TABLE parts MOVE PARTITION depot2
  TABLESPACE ts094 NOLOGGING;
```

Typically, use ALTER TABLE MOVE PARTITION to move a table partition from an existing tablespace to a new tablespace, or to reorganize the segments of a partition. ALTER TABLE MODIFY PARTITION can be used to modify attributes other than the tablespace attributes. Moving a partition always creates a new segment and drops the old segment even if the tablespace is the same.

Index Partitions. Move is not valid for index partitions. However, when the table partition that is being moved is a local partition and contains data, MOVE PARTITION marks the matching partition in each local index unusable. For a table with global index partitions, all global index partitions and all non-partitioned indexes are always marked as unusable. These index partitions must be rebuilt after issuing MOVE PARTITION for a table partition.

Add Partition

Example:

```
alter table emp5 add partition jf values less than (80) tablespace indx
  storage(initial 100K next 100k pctincrease 1);
```

Table Partitions. Use ALTER TABLE ADD PARTITION to add a new partition as the last partition when the range bounds of the existing last partition are other than maxvalue. For this reason, ADD PARTITION does not make sense for an index because local partitions are equipartitioned and maintained by Oracle; thus, an add for table partition results in add for the matching index partition. For a global index the upper range bound is always maxvalue, so no more partitions can ever be added.

Index Partitions. Not valid for index partitions. For local index partitions, Oracle attempts to name the index partition the same as the table partition being added.

Drop Partition

Example: Create table EMP5 as follows:

```
CREATE TABLE EMP5 partition by range (deptno) (partition j1 values less
   than (10), partition j2 values less than (20), partition j_last values
   less than (70)) as select * from emp;
create unique index j4 on EMP5 (deptno, empno) GLOBAL partition by
   range(deptno) (partition jx1 values less than(10), partition jx2 values
   less than (40),partition jx3 values less than(maxvalue));
alter table emp5 add partition jf values less than (80) tablespace indx
   storage(initial 100K next 100k pctincrease 1);
create index j1 on EMP5 (empno, deptno) local (partition ji1, partition
   ji2, partition ji3, partition ji4); insert into emp5 (empno, deptno)
   values (1234, 79);
ALTER TABLE EMP5 DROP PARTITION JF;
```

Table Partitions. When a partition of a table with local index partitions is dropped, then the corresponding index partitions are also dropped.

For tables with global index partitions, the dropping of a table partition marks the global index partitions (and all nonpartitioned indexes) unusable *if* the partition being dropped contains any data. There are two options to drop a partition for a table containing global indexed partitions or unpartitioned indexes:

1. Drop the partition. Then rebuild all indexes (including nonpartitioned indexes). The rebuild can be done at the partition level, or drop the index and rebuild the entire index. The latter is more efficient because it scans the table for index build only once.
2. Delete all data from partition with DELETE. (Do not use TRUNCATE, as that also marks indexes as IU. See next section.) Then drop the partition.

The second method is useful if the amount of data is small, or if one needs to fire triggers for deleted data and generate redo and undo. Note that if this delete is only from one partition, then parallel DML (DELETE) cannot be used; hence, NOLOGGING will have no effect. But if more than one partition were to be dropped, then parallel DML can be used to do the delete and use the NOLOGGING option to speed up the delete.

Index Partitions. Drop can only be used for global index partitions (local index partitions can only be dropped if the corresponding table partition is dropped). The upper partition bounded by maxvalue can never be dropped. ALTER INDEX DROP PARTITION can be safely done when the index partition being dropped does not contain any index data. However, when a global index partition containing index data is dropped, it always marks the next higher partition unusable and that partition must be rebuilt. For example, if we dropped the global index partition jx2 of j4 for EMP5, then the partition jx3 will be marked IU.

Example: Alter index j4 drop partition jx2:

```
select i.index_name, i.partition_name, i.status
  from user_ind_partitions i, user_indexes t
  where t.table_name = 'EMP5' and i.index_name
  = t.index_name;
```

will show the index partitions that have been marked as unusable.

Truncate

Example: Alter table emp5 truncate partition jf.

Table Partitions. Truncate is only valid for TABLE PARTITIONS and is identical to drop in behavior. Truncating a local partition of a table automatically truncates the corresponding local index partition. Truncating a table partition with global index partition when there is no data in the partition being truncated poses no problem. Truncating a table partition that has data in the partition being truncated, and has global index partitions, will mark all global index partitions and nonpartitioned indexes as UNUSABLE and they should be rebuilt. Note that to execute a TRUNCATE, in addition to the steps laid out in DROP, you also will need to take care of foreign key constraints, if any, on the table. Drop them before the truncate and create them after the truncate.

Index Partitions. Not valid for index partitions.

Split

Table Partitions. An existing table partition can be split for reasons of size or performance. When a table containing local index partitions is split, then only the table partitions being created can be explicitly named. The split operation for the table automatically creates corresponding local index partitions, which Oracle attempts to name the same as the table partition names; when this fails, the index partitions get system-generated names. These would have to be renamed if needed. When a table partition containing data is split, it marks the local index partitions that have data in the associated table partition and all global index partitions as unusable. All of these must be rebuilt.

Example:

```
alter table emp5 split partition jf at (75)
   into (partition j75, partition j80 );
```

Here, the existing partition with a range of values less than 80 is split into two partitions j75, with values less than 75, and partition j80 with values less than 80.

Index Partitions. Local indexed partitions are maintained automatically, along with the splitting of table partitions. Global index partitions can be split as the table partitions.

Example: Create the emp5 table in the same way as drop. Drop the index J1. Then split the global partition J4 as follows:

```
alter index j4 split partition jx2 at (15) into
   (partition p15, partition p40);
```

The query on indexes shows the following:

```
INDEX_NAME    PARTITION_NAME    STATUS
----------    --------------    -------
J4            JX3               USABLE
J4            P15               USABLE
J4            JX1               USABLE
J4            P40               USABLE
```

The documentation claims that the two partitions P15 and p40 should be marked IU. I did not see that behavior.

Merging Partitions

There is no explicit merge partition command. It can be achieved by:

- Using EXPORT/IMPORT
- Doing a combination of DROP and EXCHANGE

Using `Export/Import` for Table Partitions

Assume a table TAB with partitions TAB_P1, TAB_P2, TAB_P3. The objective is to merge partitions TAB_P2 with TAB_P3.

If the table has no global indexes and no referential integrity constraints, then:

1. Export partition TAB_P2.
2. Drop partition TAB_P2.
3. Import partition TAB_P2 into TAB_P3.

Step 3 merges the corresponding local indexes. See more details later on using `Import/Export` with partitions.

Using `Drop` to Merge Global Index Partitions

The only way the local partitioned indexes can be merged is by merging the underlying table partitions. For global partitions, if `IPART_GA` and `IPART_GB` are two partitions, and `IPART_GA` does not contain any index data, then simply drop partition `IPART_GA`. If, however, `IPART_GA` contains index data, then it has to be a two-step operation:

1. `ALTER INDEX IPART` drop partition `IPART_GA`;—This marks `IPART_GB` IU.
2. Alter INDEX IPART rebuild partition `IPART_GB`;—Makes `IPART_GB` usable again.

Using `Exchange` to Merge Table Partitions

Example: Note that all empno in the demo table EMP are greater than 7000 and should all go into the partition j_last in the example below; there will be no records in any other partition.

```
CREATE TABLE EMP7 partition by range (empno) (partition j1 values less
   than (1000), partition j2 values less than (2000), partition j_last
   values less than (maxvalue)) as select * from emp where 0 = 1;
create table EMP8 as select * from emp;
ALTER TABLE EMP7 EXCHANGE PARTITION j1 with TABLE EMP8 WITHOUT VALIDATION;
select empno from EMP7 partition (j_last);
```

This will not select any rows; all rows that should have been in partition j_last were forced into partition J1 because of using `exchange` without validation.

```
select empno from EMP7 partition (j1);
```

This will show all rows from the table EMP8.

To identify all such rows that are in a partition to which they do not belong, create table INVALID_ROWS defined in file `UTLVALID.SQL` in the `rdbms/admin dir`. This table is similar to the table that provides details of chained rows. Then analyze the table:

```
ANALYZE TABLE <TABLE_NAME> VALIDATE STRUCTURE.
```

For the analyzed table, `INVALID_ROWS` will then have details of the rows in the partition that do not rightly belong to that partition.

Note: When using the exchange partition with table option (EMP8 in our example), the table has to be nonpartitioned. The exchange command actually does an update of the dictionary tables to change the data segments from one object to another. The physical attributes that are defined for the partitions are sort of dummy attributes. These are substituted with the physical attributes of the actual table.

For example, create table OLD_TAB (fld1...) tablespace USR storage (initial 1M, next 1M);

```
CREATE TABLE PART_TAB (.....) partition by
   range (fld1) (partition p1 values less
   than(100) tablespace INDX storage(initial
   1k, next 1K)),.........).
```

Also assume that table OLD_TAB contains data only for partition p1. Then `alter table part_tab exchange partition p1`, with table old_tab with validation, will exchange the partition segments with the table segments and vice versa. After the exchange, the table OLD_TAB will have 0 records, will be in tablespace INDX, and have storage (initial 1K, next 1K), and the partition P1 will have all records from `OLD_TAB`, be in tablespace USR, and have storage (initial 1M, next 1M).

Miscellaneous Items

Partition Extension to SQLPLUS

Use extension to `sqlplus` to specify a partition in DML as follows:

```
Select empno from emp partition (P1);
Following can use extensions to sqlplus;
INSERT, UPDATE, DELETE, LOCK TABLE and SELECT.
```

This is more efficient, as Oracle then does not have to compute the partition.

`Extension` currently has these limitations:

- It cannot be used in pl/sql.
- The table referenced cannot be in remote schema.
- The table referenced must be a base table (no views, synonyms, etc.).

Parallel DML with Partitions

An important point to consider with respect to using parallel DML with partitions is that a DML can only be parallelized across partitions. Within a partition, the degree of parallelism is always one. A table could have a DML using a degree of parallelism of *N* if the database is so configured. However, if the same table has 10 partitions, then everything else remains the same and depends on the partitioning; the maximum degree of parallelism that the DML can use is less than or equal to 10.

Using Export/Import for Partitions

For exporting or importing of only a specific partition, specify the partition name using the convention `SCHEMA.TABLE:PARTITION`. The behavior of import for a table that existed as a partitioned table at the time of export depends on the existence of the table in the current schema. We can effectively use this fact with export/import to merge partitions, or to convert a partitioned table into a nonpartitioned table or vice versa.

If the table now exists as a nonpartitioned table (and `IGNORE=Y` is specified), then import will put all rows from all of the partitions into the table, creating a nonpartitioned table. However, if the indexes were also exported and they were local partitioned indexes (and `INDEXES=N` was not specified for import), then the index creation will fail because the table is no longer a partitioned table.

If the table at export time was a partitioned table but is now partitioned differently from the original, then import will insert records into the table partitions where they belong as per the current schema. This might result in some rows being rejected because of the partition definition. The index creation may also fail, depending on the existence of local partitioned indexes, if any.

If the table does not exist in the current schema at the time of import, and only import of a partition is specified, then the import will first create the table as it existed at the time of export, then import the partition that was specified and, finally, create the necessary indexes.

If the table exists with the same definition as in the export file and data is imported into the table — and if indexes are not imported (`INDEXES=N`) — then any IU partitioned indexes that exist in the current schema are not maintained by import. We can use this side effect to our advantage if a lot of data is being imported in a specific partition. Instead of dropping the index to speed up the import, it may be advisable to make the local index partitions associated with the table partition IU, then rebuild them after import rather than letting import maintain the index partition. Issue `ALTER TABLE <TABLE> MODIFY PARTITION <PARTITION> UNUSABLE LOCAL INDEXES` before import.

Use `SKIP_UNUSABLE_INDEXES=Y` during import and, finally, after import issue:

```
ALTER TABLE <TABLE> MODIFY PARTITION <PARTITION>
  REBUILD UNUSABLE LOCAL INDEXES;
```

Appendix 46.1 A Unique Constraint Being Enforced by a Nonunique Index

```
drop table EMP1;
create table EMP1 as select * from emp;
REM CREATE A NON UNIQUE INDEX;
create index j1 on EMP1 (empno, deptno);
select index_name, uniqueness from user_indexes where table_name = 'EMP1';
alter table EMP1 add constraint pk_emp1 primary key (empno);
select index_name, uniqueness from user_indexes where table_name = 'EMP1';
```

This will show only one index J1 because the unique key constraint is enforced by the existing nonunique index.

Appendix 46.2 Creating Local Prefixed Index Partitions

```
DROP TABLE EMP2;
REM Table EMP2 partitioned on empno, deptno
CREATE TABLE EMP2 partition by range (empno,deptno) (partition j1 values
   less than
(1000,10), partition j2 values less than (2000,20), partition j_last
   values less than (maxvalue,
maxvalue)) as select * from emp;
REM NOW CREATE A LOCAL PREFIXED INDEX
create index j1 on EMP2 (empno, deptno) local (partition ji1, partition ji2,
   partition ji3);
alter table EMP2 add constraint pk_emp2 primary key (empno);
select index_name, uniqueness from user_indexes where table_name = 'EMP2';
```

This will shows two index J1 and pk_emp2. The uniqueness cannot be enforced by the existing index because to enforce uniqueness, the PARTITION COLUMN LIST of the index (`empno`, `deptno` which is the same as the table partition, owing to the fact that it is local partition) *must be a subset of the Unique/Primary Key Column List* (`empno`) and it is not.

Appendix 46.3 Local Prefixed Index Partitions

```
DROP TABLE EMP3;
CREATE TABLE EMP3 partition by range (empno) (partition j1 values
   less than (1000),
partition j2 values less than (2000),partition j_last values less than
   (maxvalue)) as select * from
emp;
REM CREATE A LOCAL PREFIXED INDEX PARTITIONS
create index j1 on EMP3 (empno, deptno) local (partition ji1, partition ji2,
   partition ji3);
alter table EMP3 add constraint pk_emp3 primary key (empno);
select index_name, uniqueness from user_indexes where table_name = 'EMP3';
```

This will give you only one index. The partitions column list, for the table and the index (`empno`) is a subset of the UNIQUE INDEX column list (`empno`, `deptno`).

Appendix 46.4 Local Prefixed Index

```
DROP TABLE EMP4;
REM Table EMP4 partitioned on empno, deptno
CREATE TABLE EMP4 partition by range (empno,deptno) (partition j1 values
   less than
(1000,10), partition j2 values less than (2000,20), partition j_last values
   less than (maxvalue,
maxvalue)) as select * from emp;
create index j1 on EMP4 (empno) local (partition ji1, partition ji2,
   partition ji3);
alter table EMP4 add constraint pk_emp4 primary key (empno);
select index_name, uniqueness from user_indexes where table_name = 'EMP4';
```

In this case, we first create a local prefixed index partition. Then we try to create and enforce a unique key constraint. Oracle cannot use the existing index to enforce the unique key constraint because the partitioning column list (`empno, deptno`) is not a subset of the index columns (`empno`). Oracle then attempts to create a new unique index on `empno`, which fails because there is already an existing (nonunique) index on `empno`.

Appendix 46.5 Drop Table Emp5

```
CREATE TABLE EMP5 partition by range (deptno) (partition j1 values
   less than (10), partition
j2 values less than (20), partition j_last values less than (maxvalue))
   as select * from emp;
REM CREATE NON PREFIXED INDEX. INDEX is on empno,
REM deptno and is not left prefix of
REM partition COLUMN LIST (deptno)
create index j1 on EMP5 (empno, deptno) local (partition ji1, partition ji2,
   partition ji3);
select index_name, locality, alignment from user_part_indexes;
REM CREATE A GLOBAL UNIQUE INDEX WITH PARTITIONS.
create unique index j4 on EMP5 (deptno, empno) GLOBAL partition by range(deptno)
   (partition
jx1 values less than(10), partition jx2 values less than (40), partition jx3
   values less than(maxvalue));
select a.index_name, a.locality, a.alignment, b.uniqueness from
   user_part_indexes a, user_indexes
b where b.index_name = a.index_name;
```

Appendix 46.6 Drop Table Emp6

```
CREATE TABLE EMP6 partition by range (empno) (partition j1 values less
   than (1000),
partition j2 values less than (2000), partition j_last values less
   than (maxvalue)) as select * from
emp;
REM Create local prefixed index. The index on empno,
REM deptno is left prefixed with the partition
REM column list (empno).
create index j3 on EMP6 (empno, deptno) local (partition ji1, partition ji2,
   partition ji3);
select index_name, locality, alignment from user_part_indexes;

   INDEX_NAME    LOCALITY   ALIGNMENT
   ----------    --------   ------------
   J1            LOCAL      NON_PREFIXED
   J3            LOCAL      PREFIXED
   PK_DEPT       LOCAL      PREFIXED
```

Chapter 47

Eliminating Space Reorganizations in Oracle8i

*Robin Schumacher**

Oracle has historically been a database that has forced reorganization tasks upon its database administrators. Reorganizations in Oracle are rarely pleasant tasks, due either to its complex nature or its feature-rich offerings of the RDBMS. Administrators have normally constructed elaborate SQL and server-side scripts to perform database and tablespace reorganizations, or have spent tens of thousands of dollars on expensive third-party software reorganization products. In addition, database downtime and many man-hours have been spent to rebuild an Oracle tablespace or database that has been injured by heavy fragmentation problems.

The fact is that reorganizations are not a permanent solution for the problems that necessitate their action. Instead, they act only as a band-aid solution at best and are certainly no substitute for proper up-front and continuous planning on the part of the DBA. However, the good news is that recently, in a very quiet manner, Oracle Corporation has introduced advancements into the database that are quickly making the need for reorganizations a thing of the past. This chapter discusses these new Oracle features and demonstrates easy and permanent methods that obsolete the need for reorganization for almost every Oracle database.

Why Reorganize?

The reason for performing a reorganization inside Oracle is primarily due to one problem that affects the database in two ways. Fragmentation is the problem, and the affected areas are particular Oracle objects (tables and

* ©2000 by Robin Schumacher. Printed with permission.

indexes mainly) and tablespaces. There are other minor issues beyond the scope of this work that cause reorganization to become necessary (e.g., index tree depth), but space fragmentation is the major culprit.

For objects, fragmentation takes on the form of an object growing into multiple space extents. For example, an administrator may have estimated that a particular table was going to need 20 MB of space and created the object with a single space extent of that amount. Over time, however, the amount of data flowing into that table has pushed it far from its original calculation, and now the table stands at over 300 MB. The way Oracle handles unexpected object growth is that it takes an object's NEXT space extent assignment (plus it may use the PCTINCREASE setting as well if set to a non-zero amount) and allocates another extent for the object to accommodate the necessary space enlargement request.

Object fragmentation has historically affected database performance and availability in three ways. First, the actual expansion of the object into multiple extents can take some time for Oracle to perform because extra extents are allocated and recursive calls occur to the Oracle data dictionary. Second, objects that have grown into hundreds of extents may take a longer amount of time to access, especially if the extents are scattered over different parts of the physical server disk. And third, availability of the database is threatened when an object attempts to grow into another space extent, but yet is prohibited because it has reached its maximum extent limit imposed by the DBA.

What can you do if you have objects that are nearing their imposed maximum extent limit? You could alter the objects to have UNLIMITED extents, although some database gurus frown upon such a setting. The alternative is to perform an object reorganization, accomplished using Oracle's export/import utilities. You can, depending on the version of Oracle being used, also reorganize indexes using the `ALTER INDEX ... REBUILD` command and tables by utilizing the `ALTER TABLE ... MOVE` command, both of which are very welcome additions to Oracle's command arsenal that have nearly obsoleted the need for third-party software object reorganization tools.

Tablespaces experience fragmentation as well, but the problem affects the database differently than does object fragmentation. Administrators have traditionally fought two types of tablespace fragmentation presentations: honeycombs and bubbles. Honeycomb fragmentation works like this: consider tablespace TEST whose object and free space extent map is presented in Exhibit 47.1. If we drop tables 2 and 3, the TEST tablespace map will then look like the one in Exhibit 47.2.

The extents occupied by tables 2 and 3 are now vacant and two adjacent free space chunks exist. This is known as honeycomb fragmentation. When another object is inserted into the tablespace, if it cannot fit into the free chunk formerly held by table 2, but could fit if the free chunk previously held by table 3 was included, then Oracle will coalesce the free chunks together and place the object inside the tablespace. As a DBA, you could help Oracle by manually performing the coalesce yourself by issuing the `ALTER TABLESPACE ... COALESCE` command. Oracle's SMON process is also supposed to coalesce tablespace honeycombs, but trusting SMON to coalesce free space is not very reliable or recommended.

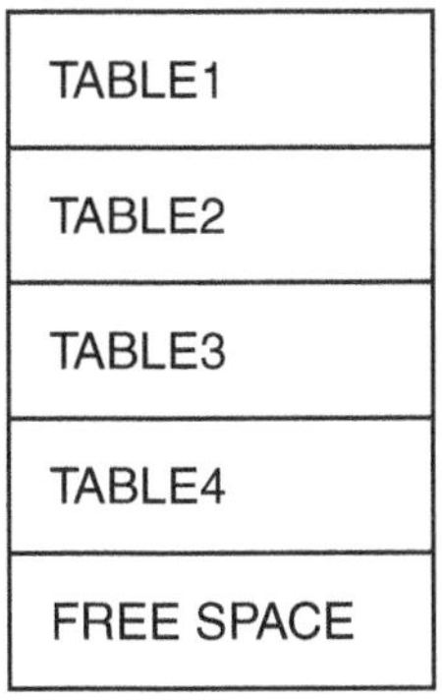

TABLE1
TABLE2
TABLE3
TABLE4
FREE SPACE

Exhibit 47.1 Tablespace for TEST Tablespace

Even after coalescing the free chunks in our example, we are still left with the second type of tablespace fragmentation, which is bubble fragmentation. Our tablespace now looks like the one in Exhibit 47.3.

A free space bubble is still trapped between tables 1 and 4. Why do we care? Because if an object is inserted into the tablespace whose INITIAL extent size is larger than the free space bubble, Oracle will ignore the bubble of free space and insert the object at the end of the tablespace (provided room exists). From a space utilization standpoint, it would be much better to have all free space exist in one chunk to avoid this type of free space wastage. Sadly, coalescing the free space in a tablespace does not remove bubbles, only honeycombs. The only solution for tablespaces that are experiencing high episodes of bubble fragmentation is a complete tablespace reorganization where everything is moved out of the tablespace, all the available space is coalesced, and then everything is brought back in.

But are tablespace and object reorganizations really the answer for database fragmentation problems? Or are they really only a temporary solution that must be repeated down the road? Is there another proactive, long-term

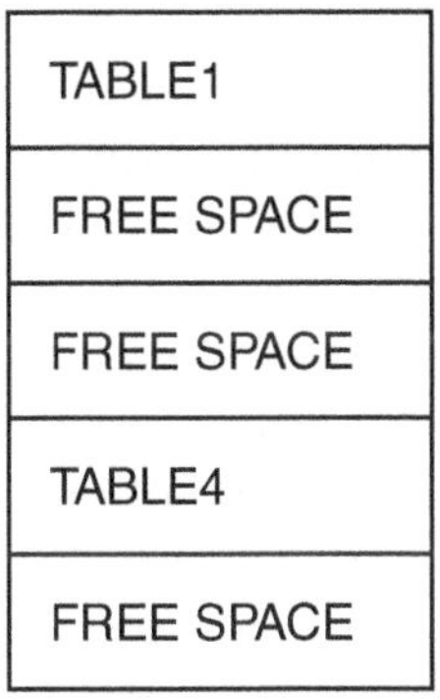

TABLE1
FREE SPACE
FREE SPACE
TABLE4
FREE SPACE

Exhibit 47.2 Tablespace Map after DROP Operation

TABLE1
FREE SPACE
TABLE4
FREE SPACE

Exhibit 47.3 Tablespace Map after Coalesce Operation

solution that DBAs can use up-front to protect themselves against fragmentation issues? Fortunately, now there is.

Using Locally Managed Tablespaces to Avoid Fragmentation

Beginning in Oracle8i, Release 8.1, the mechanism of *locally managed* tablespaces became available. The other form of tablespace extent management, *dictionary-managed* tablespaces, has been the norm for Oracle until now. In a dictionary-managed tablespace, Oracle manages extents in the tablespace by updating the appropriate tables in the data dictionary whenever an extent is allocated or released for reuse. Corresponding rollback data is stored by Oracle on each update of the dictionary tables that results from extent management operations. Updates to the data dictionary due to these types of space management tasks can cause problems for certain types of read-only databases (like a standby database) because write operations are sometimes required, such as those involved in a disk sort. This necessitates that the database be in write mode should such activity be allowed.

In Oracle8i, Release 8.1, locally managed tablespaces were introduced to alleviate such headaches and to deliver a better way of managing space. In a locally managed tablespace, space management tasks are handled by bitmaps stored within the tablespace itself. A bitmap is used to keep track of the status of blocks in each datafile — whether they are free or used. Each bit in the bitmap maps to a block or a group of blocks in the datafile. When extents are allocated or released (marked free), Oracle modifies the bitmap values to show the new status of each block. Part of the good news is that these changes do not generate rollback information because they do not update the system tables in the data dictionary, with the rare exception being cases such as tablespace quota updates.

Locally managed tablespaces offer many benefits to the database professional, including:

- OLTP systems profit from less dictionary concurrency problems due to Oracle managing space in the tablespace itself rather than the data dictionary. Recursive space management calls become a thing of the past. Those who endure parallel server installations will appreciate this success indicator, as "pinging" between nodes can be substantially reduced.
- Objects can have nearly unlimited numbers of space extents with seemingly no performance degradation being experienced. Such a feature eliminates the problem of object fragmentation outright.
- Free space found in datafiles does not have to be coalesced due to the fact that bitmaps track free space and allocate it much more effectively than dictionary-managed tablespaces. This benefit completely eliminates the problem of honeycomb fragmentation.
- Uniform or system managed extent sizes are automatically controlled for the database administrator, resulting in a much more efficient space management process. The result is an end to the problem of tablespace bubble fragmentation.

The last three points above speak directly to the problems identified previously regarding fragmentation. For the first time ever in an Oracle software release, the real potential exists for a database administrator to throw out (or just not purchase) expensive and time-consuming/error-prone tablespace reorganization tools and procedures. DBAs can convert any tablespace (except SYSTEM) to a locally managed tablespace, which means that an administrator can bear the burden of one last tablespace or database reorganization and then be done. DBAs can also choose to implement locally managed tablespaces for new databases up-front in their physical design so tablespace fragmentation and accompanying reorganizations can be eliminated right from the start.

Are there any drawbacks to using locally managed tablespaces? Only a few. The first thing to keep in mind from a planning perspective is that Oracle will use 64K in each datafile to contain the bitmap used for extent management. The second thing to understand is that because Oracle uses a bitmap to track extent information in each datafile, the information is never cached in Oracle's data dictionary. Instead, it must be obtained from the datafile bitmap blocks every time that space information is requested. Naturally, if the needed blocks are not in the buffer cache, quite a bit of physical I/O could be required, especially for databases with many datafiles.

Visual Examples of How Locally Managed Tablespaces Work

Walking through an example of how locally managed tablespaces work will demonstrate how they avoid the problematic reorganizations that are forced upon tablespaces. First, let us create a locally managed tablespace to work with. There are two ways to specify a locally managed tablespace: using the AUTOALLOCATE or UNIFORM SIZE specifications. With AUTOALLOCATE, the INITIAL value is used from an object's STORAGE creation clause; but from there on out, Oracle automatically sizes all other extents. If UNIFORM SIZE is used, then every extent will contain the same defined size, regardless of the overall size of the object.

For our example, we will create a locally managed tablespace with the following UNIFORM SIZE specification:

```
CREATE TABLESPACE HSER_DATA
DATAFILE 'D:\ORACLE\ORADATA\HSER\HSERIDX02.DBF' SIZE 100M
AUTOEXTEND ON NEXT 10M MAXSIZE UNLIMITED
EXTENT MANAGEMENT LOCAL UNIFORM SIZE 128K;
```

The tablespace HSER_DATA is 100 MB in size, has the AUTOEXTEND feature turned on to allow for unexpected growth, and has been created as locally managed with a uniform extent size of 128K.

Next, let's create a couple of test tables in the new tablespace to get things started:

```
CREATE TABLE TAB1 (COL1 NUMBER)
TABLESPACE HSER_DATA;
CREATE TABLE TAB2 (COL1 NUMBER)
TABLESPACE HSER_DATA;
CREATE TABLE TAB3 (COL1 NUMBER)
TABLESPACE HSER_DATA;
CREATE TABLE TAB4 (COL1 NUMBER)
TABLESPACE HSER_DATA;
```

In a locally managed tablespace, Oracle looks to allocate free space for each new extent by first locating a datafile in the tablespace and then searching that datafile's bitmap for the necessary number of adjacent free blocks. If that datafile does not have enough adjacent free space, Oracle looks in another datafile (if one exists) or extends the datafile if AUTOEXTEND is used.

Note that because of how Oracle manages space in locally managed tablespaces, certain storage options (such as PCTINCREASE, NEXT, MINEXTENTS and MAXEXTENTS) cannot be specified in the table's DDL.

Now let's peer inside the tablespace using the following SQL that will "map" out the tablespace's contents, in block id order:

```
SELECT 'free space',
   '     ' OBJECT_TYPE,
   '     ' OBJECT_NAME,
   block_id,
   bytes
FROM    SYS.DBA_FREE_SPACE
WHERE   TABLESPACE_NAME = 'HSER_DATA'
UNION
SELECT  SUBSTR(OWNER,1,15),
   SEGMENT_TYPE,
   SUBSTR(SEGMENT_NAME,1,30),
   BLOCK_ID,
   BYTES
FROM    SYS.DBA_EXTENTS
WHERE   TABLESPACE_NAME = 'HSER_DATA'
ORDER   BY 4,1,3
```

Using the above SQL gives us the following information regarding our locally managed tablespace:

```
                  OBJECT       OBJECT      BLOCK
OWNER              TYPE         NAME        ID          BYTES
-----             ------       ------      -----      ---------
SYS               TABLE         TAB1         9          131072
SYS               TABLE         TAB2        25          131072
SYS               TABLE         TAB3        41          131072
SYS               TABLE         TAB4        57          131072
FREE SPACE                                  73       104202240
```

As you can see, all the tables are nicely packed together while one large free chunk of space remains at the end of the tablespace — just like you would want it. In fairness to dictionary-managed tablespaces, the same would have occurred in any fresh tablespace. But now, let's drop tables 2 and 3 and see what the tablespace looks like:

```
DROP TABLE TAB2;
DROP TABLE TAB3;
```

```
                  OBJECT       OBJECT      BLOCK
OWNER              TYPE         NAME        ID          BYTES
-----------       -------      -------     ------     ---------
SYS               TABLE        TAB1          9          131072
free space                                  25          262144
SYS               TABLE        TAB4         57          131072
free space                                  73       104202240
```

What is interesting to notice in the above tablespace map is the complete absence of honeycomb fragmentation. In a dictionary-managed tablespace, we would have been left with two 128-K chunks of free space that were adjacent to one another and would have needed to perform a coalesce operation to combine the two chunks into one 256-K free space chunk. However, because locally managed tablespaces automatically track adjacent free space, the need to coalesce free extents (either manually or by Oracle itself during space allocation operations) is eliminated.

However, you may observe that we now have an episode of bubble fragmentation, and you would be correct. But with locally managed tablespaces, it's not a situation that creates a true fragmentation problem like those found in dictionary-managed tablespaces, as we will soon find out.

You also may have noticed that our first four tables were created with the default tablespace extent size of 128K. What happens when an object is created with a larger INITIAL extent size than the uniform extent amount imposed on the tablespace? Let's find out. We'll now create a new table that is 1 MB in size and then refresh our tablespace map to see what has happened:

```
CREATE TABLE TAB5 (COL1 NUMBER)
STORAGE(INITIAL 1M)
TABLESPACE HSER_DATA;
```

```
              TABLE        TAB1            9
SYS           OBJECT       OBJECT          BLOCK          131072
OWNER         -TYPE        -NAME           -ID            BYTES
-----         ------       ------          ------         ---------
SYS           TABLE        TAB1            9              131072
SYS           TABLE        TAB5            25             131072
SYS           TABLE        TAB5            41             131072
SYS           TABLE        TAB4            57             131072
SYS           TABLE        TAB5            73             131072
SYS           TABLE        TAB5            89             131072
SYS           TABLE        TAB5            105            131072
SYS           TABLE        TAB5            121            131072
SYS           TABLE        TAB5            137            131072
SYS           TABLE        TAB5            153            131072
free space                                 169            103415808
```

In a dictionary-managed tablespace, Oracle would have ignored the free space bubble that started at block 25 and would have inserted the entire 1-MB table at the end of the tablespace, leaving it still fragmented. Not so with our locally managed tablespace. Oracle neatly packed table 5 into two 128-K chunks at blocks 25 and 41 and then allocated the rest of table 5 at the end of the tablespace. Our bubble fragmentation problem has been rectified and the tablespace looks good again.

How about one last test? Let's drop table 1 and then allocate a new 1-MB extent for table 5 and see what happens:

```
DROP TABLE TAB1;
ALTER TABLE TAB5 ALLOCATE EXTENT (SIZE 1M);
```

```
              OBJECT       OBJECT          BLOCK
OWNER         -TYPE        -NAME           -ID            BYTES
-----         ------       ------          -----          ---------
SYS           TABLE        TAB5            9              131072
SYS           TABLE        TAB5            25             131072
SYS           TABLE        TAB5            41             131072
SYS           TABLE        TAB4            57             131072
SYS           TABLE        TAB5            73             131072
SYS           TABLE        TAB5            89             131072
SYS           TABLE        TAB5            105            131072
SYS           TABLE        TAB5            121            131072
SYS           TABLE        TAB5            137            131072
SYS           TABLE        TAB5            153            131072
SYS           TABLE        TAB5            169            131072
SYS           TABLE        TAB5            185            131072
SYS           TABLE        TAB5            201            131072
SYS           TABLE        TAB5            217            131072
SYS           TABLE        TAB5            233            131072
SYS           TABLE        TAB5            249            131072
SYS           TABLE        TAB5            265            131072
free space                                 281            102498304
```

Not surprisingly, Oracle plugs the 128-K free space hole at block 9 with the first 128K of table 5 and then fills in the rest at the bottom. All squeaky clean.

The key points to pull away from the above demonstration are that locally managed tablespaces conquer honeycomb fragmentation outright by automatically combining free space chunks when objects are removed from the tablespace; and that while bubble fragmentation may temporarily exist in a locally managed tablespace, it is not akin to the type of bubble fragmentation that can remain indefinitely in a dictionary-managed tablespace. The end result is tablespaces that free a DBA from having to perform time-consuming and error-prone reorganization procedures.

Locally Managed Tablespace Benchmarks

At this point, you may be wondering what the performance implications are on a locally managed tablespace that has objects whose extent totals may number into the thousands. Putting the fragmentation issue aside, how does this concept affect the bottom line as it relates to performance in a database? Oracle DBAs have always been taught that an object nestled perfectly into a single extent will always out-perform a like object whose extent counts are much higher and are scattered throughout the tablespace. But is this still the case? Let's find out.

We will perform a very informal benchmark of like objects in dictionary-managed tablespaces as well as locally managed tablespaces. Our tablespaces will be placed on non-RAID drives and will have these characteristics:

```
CREATE TABLESPACE HSER_LM_DATA
DATAFILE 'E:\ORACLE\ORADATA\HSER\HSERDATA_LM.DBF' SIZE 100M
AUTOEXTEND ON NEXT 10M MAXSIZE UNLIMITED
EXTENT MANAGEMENT LOCAL UNIFORM SIZE 128K;
CREATE TABLESPACE HSER_LM_INDEXES
DATAFILE 'D:\ORACLE\ORADATA\HSER\HSERIDX_LM.DBF' SIZE 50M
AUTOEXTEND ON NEXT 10M MAXSIZE UNLIMITED
EXTENT MANAGEMENT LOCAL UNIFORM SIZE 128K;
CREATE TABLESPACE HSER_DM_DATA
DATAFILE 'E:\ORACLE\ORADATA\HSER\HSERDATA_DM.DBF' SIZE 100M
AUTOEXTEND ON NEXT 10M MAXSIZE UNLIMITED;
CREATE TABLESPACE HSER_DM_INDEXES
DATAFILE 'D:\ORACLE\ORADATA\HSER\HSERIDX_DM.DBF' SIZE 50M
AUTOEXTEND ON NEXT 10M MAXSIZE UNLIMITED;
```

We have separated our data and index tablespaces on different drives just as good DBAs ought to and have identical drive placements for both locally and dictionary-managed tablespaces. Next, let us create a set of identical tables and indexes in both the locally and dictionary-managed tablespaces. The outcome is displayed in Exhibit 47.4.

Nothing will differ between any of the table and index definitions except their tablespace placement. Next, we will fill our two tables in both tablespaces with data: 500,000 rows will exist in the PATIENT table and 1,000,000 rows will be moved into the ADMISSION table. All tables and indexes will be updated with the COMPUTE STATISTICS function of the ANALYZE command and the Oracle database will be run in an optimizer mode of COST. Afterward, the demographics of both sets of objects looks like that shown in Exhibit 47.5.

Exhibit 47.4 Tables and Indexes in Locally and Dictionary Managed Tablespaces

```
-- TABLE: ADMISSION
CREATE TABLE ADMISSION(
          ADMISSION_ID            NUMBER(38, 0)       NOT NULL,
          PATIENT_ID              NUMBER(38, 0)       NOT NULL,
          ADMISSION_TIMESTAMP     DATE                NOT NULL,
          ADMISSION_DISCHARGE     DATE,
          INSURED                 CHAR(1)             NOT NULL,
          RELEASE_OK              CHAR(1)             NOT NULL,
          PATIENT_INSURANCE_ID    NUMBER(38, 0)       NOT NULL,
          CONSTRAINT ADMISSION_PK
          PRIMARY KEY
          (ADMISSION_ID,PATIENT_ID)
);

COMMENT ON TABLE ADMISSION IS 'admission represents an instance of a
  patient being admitted to the hospital for medical treatment/attention';
-- TABLE: PATIENT
CREATE TABLE PATIENT(
          PATIENT_ID              NUMBER(38, 0)       NOT NULL,
          PATIENT_FIRST_NAME      VARCHAR2(20)        NOT NULL,
          PATIENT_MIDDLE_NAME     VARCHAR2(20),
          PATIENT_LAST_NAME       VARCHAR2(30)        NOT NULL,
          PATIENT_SSN             NUMBER(38, 0)       NOT NULL,
          PATIENT_ADDRESS         VARCHAR2(50)        NOT NULL,
          PATIENT_CITY            VARCHAR2(30)        NOT NULL,
          PATIENT_STATE           VARCHAR2(2)         NOT NULL,
          PATIENT_ZIP             VARCHAR2(10)        NOT NULL,
          CONSTRAINT PATIENT_PK
          PRIMARY KEY (PATIENT_ID)
);


COMMENT ON TABLE PATIENT IS 'patient represents an individual seeking
  medical treatment/attention';
-- INDEX: admission_patient_id
CREATE INDEX admission_patient_id
  ON ADMISSION(PATIENT_ID);
-- INDEX: admission_insured
CREATE BITMAP INDEX admission_insured
  ON ADMISSION(INSURED);
-- INDEX: patient_ssn
CREATE UNIQUE INDEX patient_ssn
  ON PATIENT(PATIENT_SSN);
--
-- INDEX: patient_last_name
--

CREATE INDEX patient_last_name
  ON PATIENT(PATIENT_LAST_NAME);
```

Notice the large numbers of extents that the objects in the locally managed tablespace consume, whereas each object in the dictionary-managed tablespaces consists of only one extent each.

Next, let us put each set of objects through identical tests. Exhibit 47.6 lists informal benchmark results from a variety of SQL-related and Oracle utility

Exhibit 47.5 Object Demographic Information for Identical Objects in Locally and Dictionary-Managed Tablespaces

Object	*Object Type*	*Tablespace*	*Rows*	*Size*	*Extents*
ADMISSION_DM	TABLE	Dictionary	1,000,000	39MB	1
ADMISSION_LM	TABLE	Locally	1,000,000	39MB	301
ADMISSION_PK_DM	PK INDEX	Dictionary		23MB	1
ADMISSION_PK_LM	PK INDEX	Locally		23MB	175
ADMISSION_INSURED_DM	BITMAP INDEX	Dictionary		400K	1
ADMISSION_INSURED_LM	BITMAP INDEX	Locally		400K	3
ADMISSION_PATIENT_ID_DM	B-TREE INDEX	Dictionary		19MB	1
ADMISSION_PATIENT_ID_LM	B-TREE INDEX	Locally		19MB	140
PATIENT_DM	TABLE	Dictionary	500,000	40MB	1
PATIENT_LM	TABLE	Locally	500,000	40MB	304
PATIENT_LAST_NAME_DM	B-TREE INDEX	Dictionary		11MB	1
PATIENT_LAST_NAME_LM	B-TREE INDEX	Locally		11MB	79
PATIENT_PK_DM	B-TREE INDEX	Dictionary		9MB	1
PATIENT_PK_LM	B-TREE INDEX	Locally		9MB	66
PATIENT_SSN_DM	UNIQUE INDEX	Dictionary		10MB	1
PATIENT_SSN_LM	UNIQUE INDEX	Locally		10MB	75

operations on both the dictionary and locally managed tablespaces. SQL access paths have been verified as identical through EXPLAIN analysis.

The above tests show the locally managed tablespaces squeezing out a 34-second victory over the dictionary-managed tablespaces, primarily due to the margins obtained in the full DELETE and IMPORT operations. The really amazing story is found in the identical and near-identical response times recorded in many of the tests. Clearly, at least for this informal testing procedure, overall performance does not suffer one bit for objects that comprise hundreds of extents in a locally managed tablespace versus objects contained in a single extent in a dictionary-managed tablespace.

Conclusion

Oracle database administrators have enough on their plates these days without having to undergo the stressful, time-consuming, and error-prone operations of object and tablespace reorganizations that result from improper space management. With the introduction of locally managed tablespaces beginning in Oracle8i, Release 8.1, Oracle Corporation has quietly given the database professional a powerful, proactive weapon in the war of object and tablespace fragmentation. Properly implemented, locally managed tablespaces can obsolete nearly every Oracle reorganization software product on the market and eliminate a major administrative headache for today's database professional.

Exhibit 47.6 Benchmark Results of SQL and Utility Operations (Response Time in Seconds)

Operation	*Access Path/Explanation*	*Rows Affected/Returned*	*Dictionary Managed*	*Locally Managed*
SELECT	Full table scan count on PATIENT	500,000	4	5
SELECT	Full table scan count on ADMISSION	1,000,000	5	5
SELECT	Merge join between PATIENT and ADMISSION (full table scan on PATIENT, non-unique index scan on ADMISSION)	1	111	111
SELECT	Unique index access on PATIENT (PATIENT_SSN)	1	.25	.25
SELECT	Non-unique index access on PATIENT (PATIENT_LAST_NAME)	2	1	1
SELECT	Unique index access on ADMISSION	1	.25	.25
SELECT	Non-unique index access on ADMISSION (PATIENT_ID)	2	.30	.30
SELECT	Bitmap index access on ADMISSION	1	.5	.5
SELECT CURSOR	Loop through every record in PATIENT with cursor reading PATIENT_ID into declared variable. Sort (ASC) performed on PATIENT_ID	500,000	38	39
UPDATE	Full UPDATE on RELEASE_OK column of ADMISSION	1,000,000	350	355
DELETE	Full DELETE from PATIENT (no COMMITs)	500,000	872	841
EXPORT	FULL PATIENT TABLE (conventional)	500,000	36	35
IMPORT	FULL PATIENT TABLE (conventional) structure and indexes already in place)	500,000	349	340
ANALYZE	COMPUTE STATISTICS on ADMISSION TABLE	1,000,000	326	326
TOTALS			2,093.3	2,059.3

References

1. *Oracle8i Concepts Manual 8.1.5,* 1999.
2. *Oracle8i SQL Reference 8.1.5,* 1999.

Note

Benchmarks were conducted on an Oracle 8.1.5 database residing on a COMPAQ Intel P6 450 MHz Proliant 1700 Server with 320 MB RAM running Windows 2000 Server. Oracle SGA included a 17 MB data buffer cache and an 18 MB shared pool size.

Chapter 48

Determining the Table Rebuild Ratio for Oracle Tables

Roman Kab

Today's Oracle DBA is armed with sophisticated monitoring and analysis tools to alleviate the complexity of managing state-of-the-art Oracle systems. Many third-party tools offer automated table–index defragmentation based on prebuild thresholds, while some simply identify potential objects. But many experienced Oracle DBAs still prefer their own scripts and programs.

This chapter presents a technique to identify tables that will cause an Oracle database to consume unnecessary system resources during full-table scans. This is because Oracle will read all segment blocks below the high-water mark, regardless of the presence of data in these blocks. Appendix 48.1 provides a script that reports a rebuild ratio.

A *rebuild ratio* is a measure of the total number of blocks that are populated beneath the high-water mark (HWM) of a table. A table gets a high rebuild ratio when a large volume of deletes leads to empty blocks below the HWM. When there are a large number of empty blocks beneath the HWM, a full-table scan may take a large amount of time and consume exorbitant resources. Hence, the rebuild ratio is useful in determining which tables should be reorganized. We want to rebuild these tables to improve the performance of full-table scans against these tables.

How a Script Calculates the Table Rebuild Ratio

To compute the rebuild ratio, the following information is identified for the table:

0-8493-1139-X/02/$0.00+$1.50
©2002 by CRC Press LLC

- The total number of blocks that have been allocated for the table are identified.
- The total blocks and empty blocks are identified. Empty blocks are blocks above HWM.
- High-water mark is used to mark end of user data within a segment.

Note that empty block values will be populated by Oracle after the table has been analyzed.

To illustrate this technique, here is an example.

1. Let's create an Employee table with 50 blocks.

```
From DBA_SEGMENTS
EMPLOYEE(T)(50 Blocks)
|-----------------------------------|
```

2. Populate the table with some sample data and reanalyze it with compute statistics option.

```
From DBA_TABLES
EMPLOYEE(T)(2 Blocks) (47 Empty Blocks)
|==---------------------------------|
```

3. At this point, a full-table scan will only read two blocks, because Oracle knows the block that corresponds to the HWM. After additional rows are added to the employee table and the table is analyzed, here are the statistics.

```
From DBA_TABLES
EMPLOYEE(T)(49 Blocks) (0 Empty Blocks)
|=====================|
```

All 49 blocks are now populated with data and a full-table scan will read all blocks from this segment.

To perform a full-table scan, Oracle's optimizer may determine that to improve overall performance, reading of blocks will be done utilizing the `DB_MULTI_BLOCK_READ_COUNT` value that will yield fewer I/O calls. In this example, the value for `DB_MULTI_BLOCK_READ_COUNT` is 8. Simple math reveals 49/8 (`blocks/DB_ MULTI_BLOCK_READ_COUNT`): Oracle will perform seven I/O calls, of which six will return eight data blocks each and only one block for the seventh. That last call was expensive relative to the first six. During table creation, make all of the extents multiples of `DB_MULTI_BLOCK_READ_COUNT`. This also highlights problems with `PCTINCREASE` of values greater than zero.

Locating the Problem

To see the problem, let us delete a couple of hundred employees from the employee table. We then build statistics again — and Surprise!

```
From DBA_TABLES
EMPLOYEE(T)(49 Blocks) (0 Empty Blocks)
|======================|
```

Note that the HWM remains in place, although the table now has totally empty blocks that Oracle must read during full-table scans. This is normal behavior because these blocks are now on the freelist(s) and will be reused.

This is a good point to introduce and change some terminology. I will refer to EMPTY_BLOCKS column in the DBA_TABLE view as VIRGIN_BLOCKS. Blocks that are below the HWM and do not have any rows, I am going to call EMPTY BLOCKS. Blocks with row data will be called DIRTY_BLOCKS. All blocks below the HWM will be called TABLE BLOCKS.

Note: Do not confuse this definition with the dirty blocks that are read into the dirty buffer write cache in the Oracle SGA. These dirty blocks refer to actual blocks on disk.

The segment now has TOTAL BLOCKS, EMPTY BLOCKS, VIRGIN BLOCKS, DIRTY BLOCKS, and TABLE BLOCKS. The only unknowns at this point are EMPTY BLOCKS and DIRTY BLOCKS. The way to identify EMPTY BLOCKS is to subtract DIRTY BLOCKS from TABLE BLOCKS. Note that this SQL counts the first 8 bytes of each rowid in the table, thereby giving the number of dirty blocks in the table.

Oracle7

```
    select
       count(distinct(substr(rowid,1,8)))
       dirty_blocks
from EMPLOYEE ;
```

Oracle8

```
Select
count(distinct(dbms_rowid.rowid_block_number
   (rowid))) dirty_blocks
from EMPLOYEE;
```

We can now calculate EMPTY BLOCKS. In our example, the employee table has 49 TABLE BLOCKS, of which 37 are DIRTY BLOCKS.

Now that we have determined how many EMPTY BLOCKS are present below the HWM, calculate how much of the system resources are being consumed when this table is fully scanned by Oracle.

The complete SQ to report rebuild ratio is available in the Appendices to this chapter and at the *Oracle Internals* Web site (www.auerbach-publications.com/scripts).

Conclusion

An experienced Oracle DBA must reorganize tables wisely and not be intimidated by a high number of extents, which does not impede performance if the table is accessed by rowid. Tables that have lots of empty blocks, or blocks that are not fully packed with rows, will cause higher I/O calls during a full-table scan and are good candidates for rebuilding. With this technique, tables that will yield the highest returns if they are reorganized can be precisely identified.

How to enhance this script? It would be nice to see not only how many blocks have row data, but also the row distribution within blocks. If the blocks contain only a few rows and lots of free space, the rebuild ratio should be adjusted higher.

Also, a driver stored procedure that will populate a repository table with all tables and corresponding rebuild ratio from multiple instances will enable a DBA to quickly spot tables for rebuild:

```
create table rebuild_table
(
owner varchar2(30) not null,
table_name varchar2(30) not null,
add_dt date not null,
total_blocks number,
virgin_blocks number,
dirty_blocks number,
unused_blocks number,
blocks_by_rowid number,
rebuild_ratio number(6,2))
```

Appendix 48.1 To Report Rebuild Ratio

```
ttitle off

define owner=&&1
define table_name=&&2

set verify off
set feedback off
set termout off
set echo off

clear breaks
clear computes
clear columns

column totblk new_value _totblk noprint
column virgin_blks new_value _virgin_blks noprint
column table_blks new_value _table_blks noprint

select blocks totblk
from dba_segments
where segment_name = upper('&table_name')
and   owner = upper('&owner');

select blocks table_blks,
   empty_blocks virgin_blks
from dba_tables
where table_name = upper('&table_name')
and    owner = upper('&owner');


start comm_header.sql blocksus.sql "Blocks Utilization &owner..&table_name "

col dirty format 999999 heading 'Blocks/w|Rows' jus center
col virgin format 999990 heading 'Virgin|Blocks' jus center
col tableblk format 999990 heading 'All|Blocks|HWM' jus center
col totblk1 format 9999990 heading 'Allocated | Blocks' jus center
col unused format 999990 heading 'Unused|Blocks' jus center
col badness format 990.90 heading 'Rebuild|Ratio' jus center
set termout on

rem ttitle 'Blocks Utilization in &&1..&&2' skip 2

prompt ************************************************
prompt * Table must be rebuild if rebuild ratio > 25
prompt * Unless you are going to fill the table up with
prompt * data right away. Lots of empty blocks that Oracle
prompt * must scan.
prompt *
prompt ************************************************

select
   &&_totblk totblk1,
   &&_table_blks tableblk,
   count(distinct(substr(rowid,1,8))) dirty,
   (1-( count(distinct(substr(rowid,1,8))) / &&_table_blks )) * 100 badness,
   &&_virgin_blks virgin,
```

(continues)

Appendix 48.1 To Report Rebuild Ratio (continued)

```
   to_number('&&_totblk')-count(distinct(substr(rowid,1,8))) unused
     from &owner..&table_name ;

clear breaks
clear computes
undef 1
undef 2
undef owner
undef table_name
set termout on
set feedback on
set echo off

Output:

*********************************************
* Table must be rebuilt if rebuild ratio > 25
* Unless you are going to fill the table up with
* data right away. Lots of empty blocks that Oracle
* must scan.
*
*********************************************

       All
 Allocated     Blocks   Blocks/w     Rebuild     Virgin     Unused
    Blocks        HWM       Rows       Ratio     Blocks     Blocks
----------    -------   --------     -------    -------    -------
        50         49         37       24.49          0         13
```

Appendix 48.2 Populating a Table

Procedure that populates a table with owner and table_name and uses blocks in a table by counting distinct blockids. Then reports additional info from dba_tables and dba_segments.

Note: Script derives a rebuild ratio that serves as an indicator when table has lots of dirty blocks that Oracle must read during full tbs.

```
rem # RDBMS: Oracle 7.3.x.x
rem #
rem # NOTE: Must have execute on
rem # DBMS_SQL

create or replace procedure blkhwm (owner_in IN VARCHAR2 )
is

totblks number;          /* total blocks allocated */
virgin_blks number;      /* blocks above high water mark */
dirty_blks number;       /* blocks that have been touched */
badness number;          /* ratio on how badly table needs rebuild */
unused_blks number;
block_cnt number;

cursor_handle integer;
exec_feedback integer;

cursor tab1_cur is
   select
      table_name,
      blocks ,
      empty_blocks
   from
      dba_tables
   where
      owner = upper(OWNER_IN)
      and blocks > 0;

cursor seg1_cur(SEGMENT_NAME_CUR VARCHAR2,
      OWNER_CUR VARCHAR2) is
   select
      blocks
   from
      dba_segments
   where
      segment_name  = upper(SEGMENT_NAME_CUR)
   and       owner = upper(OWNER_CUR);

BEGIN
   FOR tab1_rec IN tab1_cur
   LOOP
      OPEN seg1_cur(tab1_rec.table_name,OWNER_IN);
      FETCH seg1_cur INTO totblks;
      CLOSE seg1_cur;

      /* Create Dynamic Cursor */
      cursor_handle := DBMS_SQL.OPEN_CURSOR;
      dbms_output.put_line('Table: '||tab1_rec.table_name);
```

(continues)

Appendix 48.2 Populating a Table (continued)

```
      DBMS_SQL.PARSE
           (cursor_handle,
         'SELECT count(distinct(substr(rowid,1,8)))
              FROM '|| OWNER_IN ||'.'||tab1_rec.table_name,
         DBMS_SQL.V7 );

      DBMS_SQL.DEFINE_COLUMN (cursor_handle, 1, block_cnt);
      -- DBMS_SQL.BIND_VARIABLE(cursor_handle, ':owner_in',owner_in);
      -- DBMS_SQL.BIND_VARIABLE(cursor_handle,
         ':table_name',tab1_rec.table_name);

      exec_feedback := DBMS_SQL.EXECUTE(cursor_handle);

      LOOP
           IF DBMS_SQL.FETCH_ROWS (cursor_handle) = 0
         THEN
           EXIT;
         ELSE
           DBMS_SQL.COLUMN_VALUE(cursor_handle, 1, block_cnt);
           dbms_output.put_line('Results: ' || to_char(block_cnt));
         END IF;
      END LOOP;
      DBMS_SQL.CLOSE_CURSOR(cursor_handle);
      INSERT INTO REBUILD_TABLE
         (owner,table_name,add_dt,total_blocks,virgin_blocks,
           dirty_blocks,unused_blocks,blocks_by_rowid,rebuild_ratio)
      VALUES
         (OWNER_IN,tab1_rec.table_name,sysdate,totblks,
         tab1_rec.empty_blocks,tab1_rec.blocks,totblks-block_cnt,block_cnt,
         (1 - (block_cnt / tab1_rec.blocks)) * 100
         );
   END LOOP;
commit;
END blkhwm;
/
```

Chapter 49

Oracle Parallel Query

Donald K. Burleson

One of the most exciting performance features of Oracle Version 7.3 and above is the ability to partition an SQL query into subqueries and dedicate separate processors to concurrently service each subquery. At this time, parallel query is useful only for queries that perform full-table scans on long tables, but the performance improvements can be dramatic. Here is how it works.

Parallel queries are most useful in distributed databases where a single logical table has been partitioned into smaller tables at each remote node. For example, a customer table that is ordered by customer name may be partitioned into a customer table at each remote database such that we have a phoenix_customer, a los_angeles_customer, and so on. This approach is very common with distributed databases where local autonomy of processing is important. But what about the needs of those in corporate headquarters? How can they query all of these remote tables as a single unit and treat the logical customer table as a single entity?

Although this "splitting" of a table according to a key value violates normalization theory, it can dramatically improve performance for individual queries. For large queries that may span many logical tables, the isolated tables can be easily reassembled using Oracle's parallel query facility:

```
Create view all_customer as
   select * from phoenix_customer@phoenix
   UNION ALL
   select * from los_angeles_customer@los_
   angeles
   UNION ALL
   select * from rochester_customer@rochester;
```

Note: The "@" references refer to SQL*Net service names for the remote hosts.

We can now query the all_customer view as if it were a single database table, and Oracle parallel query will automatically recognize the UNION ALL param-

0-8493-1139-X/02/$0.00+$1.50
©2002 by CRC Press LLC

eter, firing off simultaneous queries against each of the three base tables. It is important to note that the distributed database manager will direct each query to be processed at the remote location, while the query manager waits until each remote node has returned its result set. For example, the following query will assemble the requested data from the three tables in parallel, with each query optimized separately. The result set from each subquery is then merged by the query manager:

```
SELECT customer_name
FROM all_customer
WHERE
total_purchases > 5000;
```

Instead of having a single query server to manage the I/O against the table, parallel query allows the Oracle query server to dedicate many processors to simultaneously access the data.

To be most effective, the table should be partitioned onto separate disk devices such that each process can do I/O against its segment of the table without interfering with the other simultaneous query processes. However, the client/server environment of the 1990s relies on RAID or a logical volume manager (LVM), which scrambles data files across disk packs to balance the I/O load. Consequently, full utilization of parallel query involves "striping" a table across numerous data files, each on a separate device.

Parallel Create Table as Select

Parallel Create Table as Select (PCTAS) can be very useful in an Oracle data warehouse environment where tables are replicated across numerous servers or when pre-aggregating roll-up summary tables. PCTAS is also very useful when performing roll-up activities against an Oracle warehouse. For example, we could specify the number of parallel processes to compute the monthly summary values from our fact table. In the example below, we dedicate five processes to simultaneously read the blocks from the customer table:

```
create table region_salesperson_summary_03_97
parallel (degree 5)
as
select region, salesperson, sum(sale_amount)
from fact
where
  month = 3
and
  year = 1997;
```

Here we dedicate five query servers to extract the data from the fact table and five query servers to populate the new summary table. (See Exhibit 49.1.)

Again, we must remember that it is not necessary to have symmetric multiprocessing (SMP) or massively parallel processing (MPP) hardware to benefit from parallel query techniques. Even a single-processor UNIX system will experience some improvement from using parallel processes although all of the process run on the same CPU.

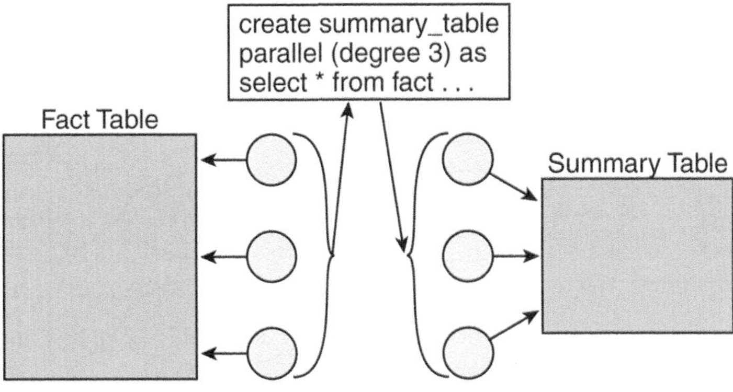

Exhibit 49.1 Parallel Create Table as Select

Parallel Index Building

Parallel index builds are often useful to the Oracle database administrator who needs to rebuild indexes that have either spawned too many levels or contain too many deleted leaf rows. Parallel index creation is also useful when importing Oracle data warehouse tables. Because data warehouses are so large, Oracle exports never capture the indexes and export only the row values. If a recovery of the table becomes necessary, the Oracle DBA can use parallel create to speed up the index recreation. Parallel index creation takes place by allowing the degree of parallelism to be specified in the create index statement.

```
alter index customer_pk
rebuild parallel 10;
```

Because this type of index creation always involves reading the old index structure and a large sort operation, Oracle is able to dedicate numerous, independent processes to simultaneously read the base index and collect the keys for the new index structure. Just like parallel query, each subquery task returns ROW-ID and key values to the concurrency manager. The concurrency manager collects this information for input to the key sorting phase of the index rebuild. For very large data warehouse tables, parallel index creation can greatly reduce the amount of time required to initially create or rebuild indexes.

Some Oracle professionals mistakenly believe it is necessary to have parallel processors (SMP or MPP) to use and benefit from parallel processing. Even on the same processor, multiple processes can be used to speed up queries. Oracle parallel query option can be used with any SQL SELECT statement — the only restriction being that the query performs a full-table scan on the target table.

Even if your system uses RAID or LVM, some performance gains are still available with parallel query. In addition to using multiple processes to retrieve the table, the query manager will also dedicate numerous processes to simultaneously sort the result sets from a large query (see Exhibit 49.2).

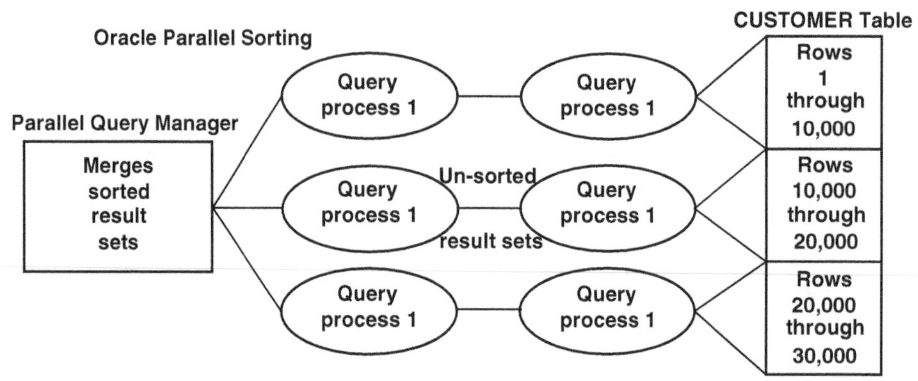

Exhibit 49.2 A Sample Parallel Sort

However, parallel query works best with SMP boxes, which have more than one internal CPU. It is also important to configure the system to maximize the I/O bandwidth, either through disk striping or high-speed channels. Because of the parallel-sorting feature, it is a good idea to beef up the memory on the processor.

Although sorting is no substitute for using a presorted index, the parallel query manager will service requests far faster than a single process. The data retrieval will not be significantly faster because all of the retrieval processes are competing for a channel on the same disk, but each sort process has its own sort area (as determined by the sort_area_size init.ora parameter), which speeds along the sorting of the result set. In addition to full-table scans and sorting, the parallel query option also allows for parallel processes for merge joins and nested loops.

Invoking the parallel query option requires all indexing be bypassed. The most important is that the execution plan for the query specifies a full-table scan. If the output of the explain plan does not indicate a full-table scan, the query can be forced to ignore the index by using query hints.

The number of processors dedicated to service an SQL request is ultimately determined by Oracle query manager, but the programmer can specify the upper limit on the number of simultaneous processes. When using the cost-based optimizer, the PARALLEL hint can be embedded into the SQL to specify the number of processes. For example:

```
SELECT /*+ FULL(employee_table) PARALLEL
   (employee_table, 4) */
   employee_name
   FROM
   employee_table
   WHERE
   emp_type = 'SALARIED';
```

If you use SMP with many CPUs, you can issue a parallel request and leave it up to each Oracle instance to use their default degree of parallelism:

```
SELECT /*+ FULL(employee_table) PARALLEL
   (employee_table, DEFAULT, DEFAULT) */
   employee_name
   FROM
   employee_table
   WHERE
   emp_type = 'SALARIED';
```

Several important init.ora parameters have a direct impact on parallel query:

- sort_area_size — The higher the value, the more memory available for individual sorts on each parallel process. Note that the sort_area_size parameter allocates memory for every query on the system that invokes a sort. For example, if a single query needs more memory and you increase the sort_area_size, all Oracle tasks will allocate the new amount of sort area, regardless of whether or not they will use all of the space.
- parallel_min_servers — The minimum number of query servers that will be active on the instance. System resources are involved in starting a query server, so having the query server started and waiting for requests will speed processing. Note that if the number of required servers is less than the value of parallel_min_servers, the idle query servers will consume unnecessary overhead and the value should be decreased.
- parallel_max_servers — The maximum number of query servers allowed on the instance. This parameter prevents Oracle from starting so many query servers that the instance is unable to service all of them properly.

To see how many parallel query servers are busy at any given time, the following query can be issued against the v$pq_sysstat table:

```
SELECT * FROM v$pq_sysstat
   WHERE STATISTIC = 'Servers Busy';

    STATISTIC          VALUE
   ------------    ------------
   Servers Busy         30
```

In this case, we see that 30 parallel servers are busy at this time. Do not be misled by this number. Parallel query servers are constantly accepting work or returning to idle status, so it is a good idea to issue the query many times during a one-hour period. Only then will you have a realistic measure of how many parallel query servers are used.

Hopefully, this chapter has shed some light on the process of how parallel query functions.

Chapter 50

Managing Oracle Table Freelists

Donald K. Burleson

One of the benefits of having a sophisticated database management system (DBMS) is that we are not concerned about the internals of how database objects are managed. However, the experienced Oracle professional must understand how Oracle manages table extents and free data blocks.

To become successful in managing high-volume simultaneous update activity, the Oracle database administrator (DBA) must intimately understand Oracle's table management strategy. This includes the behavior of freelists, freelist groups, and their relationship to PCTFREE and PCTUSED.

Oracle professionals must understand freelist management because there are many occasions when poor table performance directly relates to improper table settings. There have been cases where changing the table values has more than doubled the throughput of transactions against a table.

The most common mistake is not considering the average row length and block size when setting PCTFREE and PCTUSED for a table. When these settings are wrong, Oracle may populate freelists with "dead" blocks that do not have enough room to store a row, causing significant processing delays.

This chapter outlines all of the possible table scenarios and shows how to use an automated script to determine the optimal settings for a table.

Freelist Management

Freelists are critical to the effective reuse of space within the Oracle engine, and there is a direct trade-off between high performance and efficient reuse of table blocks. Hence, we need to decide if we desire high performance or efficient space reuse and set the table parameters accordingly.

0-8493-1139-X/02/$0.00+$1.50
©2002 by CRC Press LLC

Although freelists are most commonly associated with Oracle tables, all Oracle segments contain this information. To Oracle, a segment may be a table, an index (b-tree or bitmap), a rollback segment, or a temporary segment (used for sorting or index rebuilds).

Within the first block of every segment, Oracle stores internal information about the table. This information includes the following:

1. Extents table, an internal list of all segment extents
2. Freelists' descriptors
   a. Master freelist
   b. Transaction freelists
3. Segment high-water mark

Subsequent blocks in the Oracle segment may also have internal management information if multiple freelists have been defined.

Freelist Groups

With Oracle Parallel Server (OPS), internal table structures become even more complex. Oracle provides an additional OPS table parameter to define multiple freelist groups. With multiple freelist groups, extra segment header blocks are defined, and blocks immediately following block 1 will be used for the freelist groups. For example, assume the following table definition:

```
CREATE TABLE CUSTOMER( . . . )
STORAGE ( . . . FREELISTS 2 FREELIST GROUPS 2);
```

As a general rule, each Oracle instance in an OPS configuration should have a freelist group defined. Hence, if we see an OPS database with ten instances that access the CUSTOMER table, the CUSTOMER table must be defined with ten freelist groups.

In the syntax above, we see a table with two freelist groups and two freelists within each freelist group. As the table is allocated, Oracle will reserve three blocks at the front of the table for management chores. Oracle allocates block 1 for the segment header, block 2 for freelist group 1, and block 3 for freelist group 2. On blocks 2 and 3, we would see three freelists, two for the freelists and one master freelist. On block 1, we still have a freelist, which Oracle calls the "super master freelist." Oracle never uses the super master freelist directly for free blocks. Instead, the super master freelist is used to transfer free blocks to the lower-level freelists when the high-water mark is increased. (See Exhibit 50.1.)

It is imperative to understand how Oracle moves blocks onto the freelists. At table creation time, all blocks in the initial extent are eligible to receive rows, but Oracle will not become aware of these blocks until the high-water mark includes the blocks on the freelist. When the high-water mark is increased, Oracle will move the high-water mark up in increments of five

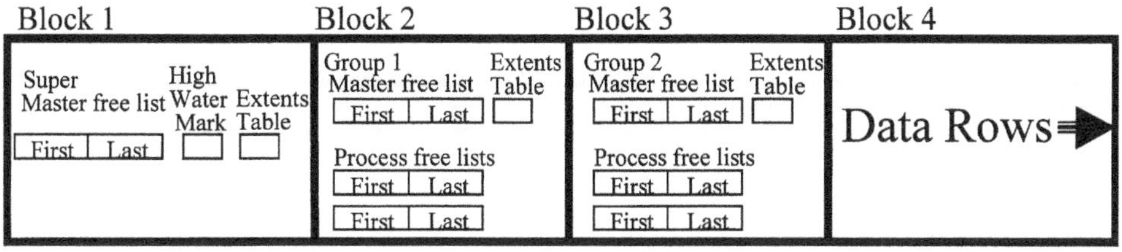

Block 1	Block 2	Block 3	Block 4
Super Master free list (First, Last); High Water Mark; Extents Table	Group 1 Master free list (First, Last); Extents Table; Process free lists (First, Last; First, Last)	Group 2 Master free list (First, Last); Extents Table; Process free lists (First, Last; First, Last)	Data Rows

Exhibit 50.1 A Segment Block Header

blocks and will add these blocks to the super master freelist. From the super master freelist, the free block DBAs are, in turn, fed to the individual freelist groups. Hence, it is possible to have a table in its initial extent where there are very few free blocks on the freelists, but there are several free blocks above the high-water mark.

Understanding the Relationship Between Freelists, PCTFREE, and PCTUSED

Whenever a request is made to insert a row into a table, Oracle goes to a freelist to find a block with enough space to accept a row. The sole purpose of the PCT_FREE and PCT_USED table allocation parameters is to control the movement of blocks to and from the freelists.

Although this is a very ordinary operation within Oracle, the settings for freelists' link (PCTUSED) and unlink (PCTFREE) operations can dramatically impact performance.

A row becomes available when a block's free space drops below the value of PCT_USED for the table. This freelist is kept in the block header of the table (i.e., the first several blocks of the table).

As a table has rows inserted into it, it will grow until the space on the block exceeds the threshold PCT_FREE, at which time the block is removed from the freelist. For example, with PCTFREE=10, blocks remain on the freelist while they are less than 90 percent full. Once an insert makes a block grow beyond 90 percent, it is removed from the freelist. Furthermore, it remains off the freelist *even if the space drops below 90 percent.* Only after subsequent deletes cause the space to fall below the PCT_USED threshold will Oracle put the block back on the freelist.

As rows are deleted from a table, the database blocks become eligible to accept new rows. This happens when the amount of space in a database block falls below PCT_USED and a freelist relink operation is triggered. For example, with PCTUSED=60, all database blocks that have less than 60 percent will be on the freelist, as well as other blocks that dropped below PCT_USED and have not yet grown to PCT_FREE. Once a block deletes a row and becomes less than 60 percent full, the block goes back on the freelist.

Many neophytes misunderstand what happens when a block is returned to the freelist. Once a block is relinked onto the freelist after a delete, it will

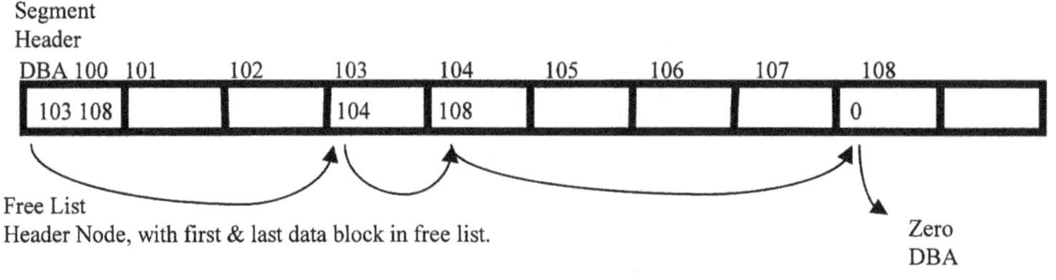

Exhibit 50.2 Basic Linkages of a Segment Freelist

remain on the freelist *even when the space exceeds 60 percent.* Only reaching PCT_FREE will take the database block off the freelist.

Adjusting Segment Pointers During Unlink and Relink Operations

Internally to Oracle, a freelist is a one-way linked list, with NEXT pointers indicating the data block addresses of the next free block. In addition, when a block is added to the freelist, a flag in the header of the free block is set to indicate that it is on the freelist chain, and another bucket in the block header will contain the data block address of the next free block in the segment.

The first node on the freelist (in the segment header) contains the data block address of the first block in the freelist and the data block address of the last block in the chain. The last data block in the freelist will have a zero value, indicating that it is the last free block in the freelist chain. (See Exhibit 50.2.) As new blocks are moved onto the master freelist, Oracle will use a "first in, first out" queue. That is, Oracle will place the new block at the front of the linked list, changing the pointers for the head and the newly freed block. Exhibit 50.3 illustrates the addition of block 106 onto the master freelist. This allows for very fast unlinking and relinking of data blocks from the freelist. (See Exhibit 50.3.)

To understand the operation of Oracle in a high-update environment, it is important to understand how Oracle gets free blocks to accept new rows. When an insert request is made, the following searches occur:

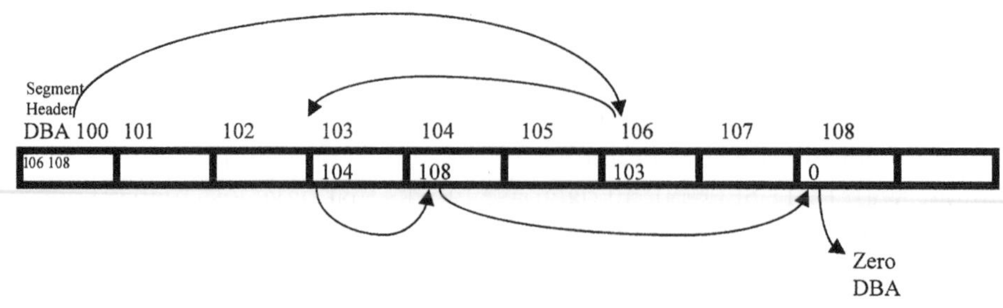

Exhibit 50.3 Adjusting Freelist Pointers for a New Free Block

1. Oracle first looks for the task's transaction freelist, looking for free blocks.
2. Oracle looks next into the process freelist group for a free block.
3. Oracle then attempts to move blocks from the master freelist to the process freelist. This operation is called a freelist merge and is normally done in chunks of five blocks. Note that Oracle will *not* look in other process freelists for free blocks.
4. Oracle then tries to get blocks from other task's transaction freelists, which have committed their rows. Oracle scans the transaction freelists, moving the committed blocks onto the master freelist.
5. Oracle then bumps up the high-water mark for the table by:
   a. Using n blocks and linking the blocks onto the master freelist
   b. Creating a new extent and linking n new blocks onto the master freelist

Note: When using RAW and LONG RAW columns in a row insert, Oracle will not attempt to insert the row below the high-water mark for the table and will immediately bump the high-water mark to get new blocks.

Multiple Freelist Groups and Oracle Parallel Server

When using OPS, it is necessary to have tables defined with a "freelist group" for each instance that accesses the database. The idea behind freelist groups is that each instance will get its own group, each with its own set of free blocks. This ensures that parallel instances do not compete from the same blocks within a table. Without freelist groups, both instances would contend for the master freelist in the segment header, causing slowdown. When using freelist groups, the freelist structure is disconnected from the segment header and resides on separate data blocks following the segment header. Of course, it follows that one freelist group may have free blocks that are unknown to the other instance.

In an OPS environment with multiple freelist groups, there are three types of freelists in each segment header:

1. *Master freelist (the common pool).* The master freelist exists for all Oracle segments. The master freelist resides in the segment header in the first block of the table. With OPS, you have a super master freelist on block 1 of the segment in addition to the master freelists that are dedicated to each freelist group.
2. *Process freelist (multiple freelists).* The process freelist is enabled using the FREELIST parameter when creating the table or index. A process freelist will acquire blocks in two ways. A process freelist can get blocks when a row is deleted, or when a "freelist merge" occurs. A freelist merge is a process whereby Oracle moves blocks from the master freelist to the process freelist, usually in chunks of five blocks (formula is presented later). If FREELIST GROUPS are not used, the process freelist will exist in the segment block header for the table, next to the master freelist. As we know, multiple process freelists can be defined whenever concurrent updates are expected against the table. Process

freelists greatly reduce contention for freelist in a non-OPS environment because each update process may read its own freelist. The downside is that each freelist exists independently of the other freelists, and blocks that appear on one freelist are not shared with the other freelists.

3. *Transaction freelist.* The transaction freelist is used by an in-flight program, which performs delete or insert operations. Unlike the master and process freelists, transaction freelists are allocated in the segment header on an as-needed basis. If there is no room in the segment header for the transaction freelist, the task will wait and incur a "wait on segment header." After the task has ended or committed, the entries are transferred from the transaction freelist to the process freelist in a first-in, first-out manner, with the most recently freed blocks being added to the head of the freelist chain.

Although process freelists minimize contention in non-OPS environments, a freelist group is used to minimize contention for space within a shared table that is being updated by multiple instances. In general, one freelist group is defined for each instance that uses a table concurrently, such that a system with two database nodes would define two freelist groups for all tables that would have concurrent inserts and deletes from the nodes.

After Oracle OPS release 7.3, it is possible to allocate table extents that are "dedicated" to a specific instance. Oracle says you can have more control over free space if you specifically allocate extents to instances. This has the side-benefit of reducing contention for resources.

```
alter table xxx allocate extents
   (size 100m datafile '/oracle/filename' instance 1);
```

Above we see an example where the customer table has increased by 100 megabytes, and these are exclusively dedicated to instance number one. Automatic table extension will never dedicate rows to an instance, and the space will go onto the master freelist.

Linking and Unlinking from the Freelists

As we know, the PCTFREE and PCTUSED table parameters are used to govern the movement of database blocks to and from the table freelists. In general, there is a direct trade-off between performance and efficient table utilization because efficient block reuse requires some overhead when linking and unlinking blocks with the freelist. As we may know, linking and unlinking a block requires two writes: one to the segment header for the freelist head node, and an update to the new block to make it participate in the freelist chain. The following general rules apply to freelists:

- An INSERT is effected by PCTFREE and may trigger a freelist unlink. Because INSERTs always use the free block at the head of the freelist chain, there will be minimal overhead in unlinking this block.

- An UPDATE that expands row length is effected by PCTFREE and may trigger a freelist unlink. An UPDATE may trigger an unlink of a block at any point in the freelist chain, causing significant processing overhead because the freelist chain must be walked from the beginning to locate the block.
- Deletes are affected by PCTUSED and may trigger a freelist link.

It is also important to understand how new free blocks are added to the freelist chain. At table extension time, the high-water mark for the table is increased and new blocks are moved onto the master freelist, where they are moved to process freelists. For tables that do not contain multiple freelists, the transfer is done five blocks at a time. For tables with multiple freelists, the transfer is done in sizes (5*(number of free lists + 1)). For example, in a table with 20 freelists, 105 blocks will be moved onto the master freelist each time a table increases its high-water mark.

Let us review the overhead associated with freelist links and unlinks. For the purposes of the following examples, use Exhibit 50.3.

1. **At INSERT time.** As new rows are inserted, the block may be removed from the freelist if the free space becomes less than PCTFREE. Because the block being inserted is always at the head of the freelist chain, only two blocks will be affected. In our example, assume the INSERT has caused block 106 to be removed from the freelist chain.

   Unlinking a block from the freelist (at INSERT time):

   a. Oracle detects that free space is less than PCTFREE and invokes the unlink.
   b. Oracle takes the data block address inside the segment freelist header (pointing to block 106).
   c. Oracle reads this block and captures the data block address from its freelist header. In this example, block 106 contains the address of block 103.
   d. Oracle moves this address (pointing to block 103) to the head of the freelist in the segment header. Block 106 no longer participates in the freelist chain, and the first entry in the freelist is now block 103. (See Exhibit 50.4.)

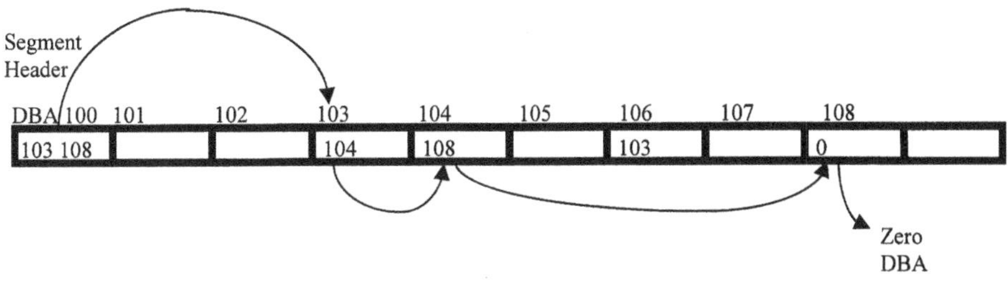

Exhibit 50.4 A Freelist Pointer after an Unlink

2. **At UPDATE time:** As updates to existing rows cause the row to expand, the block may be unlinked from the freelist if the free space in the block becomes less than PCTFREE. This will happen only if the row contains VARCHAR, RAW, or LONG RAW column data types because these are the only data types that could expand upon update. Because the updated block is not at the head of the freelist chain, the prior block's freelist pointer cannot be adjusted to omit the block, and hence the block is marked as "logically" deleted by setting the freelist indicator in the segment header.

Note: The "dead" block remains on the freelist although it does not have room to accept a row. This will cause additional overhead, especially if there are several "unavailable" blocks on the freelist. At runtime, Oracle will incur additional I/Os when reading these freelists and will try the freelist five times to find a block with enough room to store the new row. After five attempts, Oracle will raise the high-water mark for the table.

Note: Although it is most common for an UPDATE to trigger a freelist unlink, it is possible for an update to trigger a freelist link. This happens if an update to a VARCHAR or a RAW column results in a smaller row size.

Setting PCTFREE, PCTUSED Based on Average Row Length

It should now be clear that the average row length has a huge impact upon the settings for PCTFREE and PCTUSED. We want to set PCTFREE such that room is left on each block for row expansion, and we want to set PCTUSED so that newly linked blocks have enough room to accept rows.

Herein lies the trade-off between effective space usage and performance. If we set PCTUSED to a high value, say 80, then a block will quickly become available to accept new rows, but it will not have room for many rows before it becomes logically full again. The script below allows you to adjust the setting for PCTFREE and PCTUSED as a function of the number of rows that your want to store between I/Os.

Remember the rule: the lower the value for PCTUSED, the less I/O your system will have at insert time and the faster you will run. The downside, of course, is that a block will be nearly empty before it becomes eligible to accept new rows.

Here is the script to generate the syntax:

```
set heading off;
set pages 9999;
set feedback off;

spool pctused.lst;

define spare_rows = 2;

define blksz = 4096;
```

```
select
   ' alter table '||owner||'.'||table_name||
   ' pctused '||least(round(100-((&spare_rows
   *avg_row_len)/(&blksz/10))),95)||
   ' '||
   ' pctfree '||greatest(round((&spare_rows*avg_
   row_len)/(&blksz/10)),5)||
';'
from
   dba_tables
where
avg_row_len > 1
and
avg_row_len < 2000
and
table_name not in
   (select table_name from dba_tab_columns b
      where
data_type in ('RAW','LONG RAW')
)
and
owner in ('SSSS')
order by owner, table_name
;

spool off;
```

The Sparse Table Phenomenon

When using multiple freelists, there is a common problem relating to freelist imbalance. This freelist imbalance results in an Oracle table extending, although the table is largely empty and has thousands of free blocks. Fortunately, this imbalance is easy to remedy.

When the application fails to balance inserts and deletes across the freelists, as is the case with the sample CUSTOMER table, when rows are inserted with 20 simultaneous processes, but only one process deletes rows from the table, a "false" extension occurs. This example table is defined with two freelist groups, each having 20 freelists. This example illustrates some basic points about multiple freelists, especially that process freelists get blocks directly only when delete operations occur and that, within a freelist group, freelist entries are not shared.

Exhibits 50.5 through 50.7 demonstrate what happens to the CUSTOMER table when a system performs parallel inserts, but deletes rows from only one instance. The result is that the table has lots of free space but still extends.

Step 1

The table is created, and the initial extent blocks are linked to each group's master freelist, 105 blocks at a time, when the high-water mark is raised. The table is then populated via inserts and the blocks above the high-water mark are used, with all activity against each group's master freelist. At this time, only two of the 40 process freelists contain any blocks, and then, only those left over from the freelists merge.

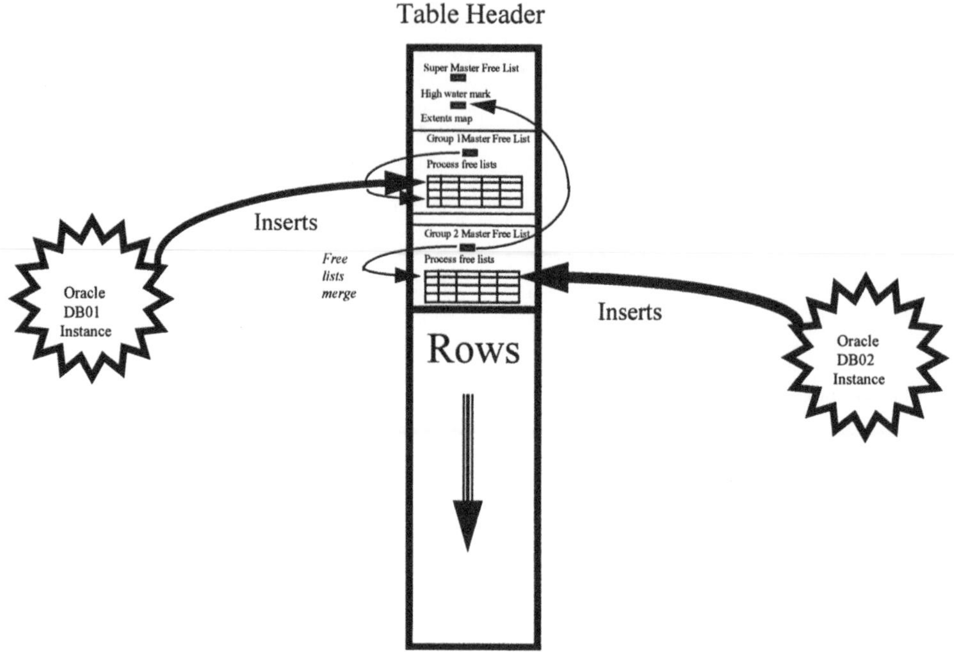

Exhibit 50.5 Simultaneous Inserts from Multiple Instances

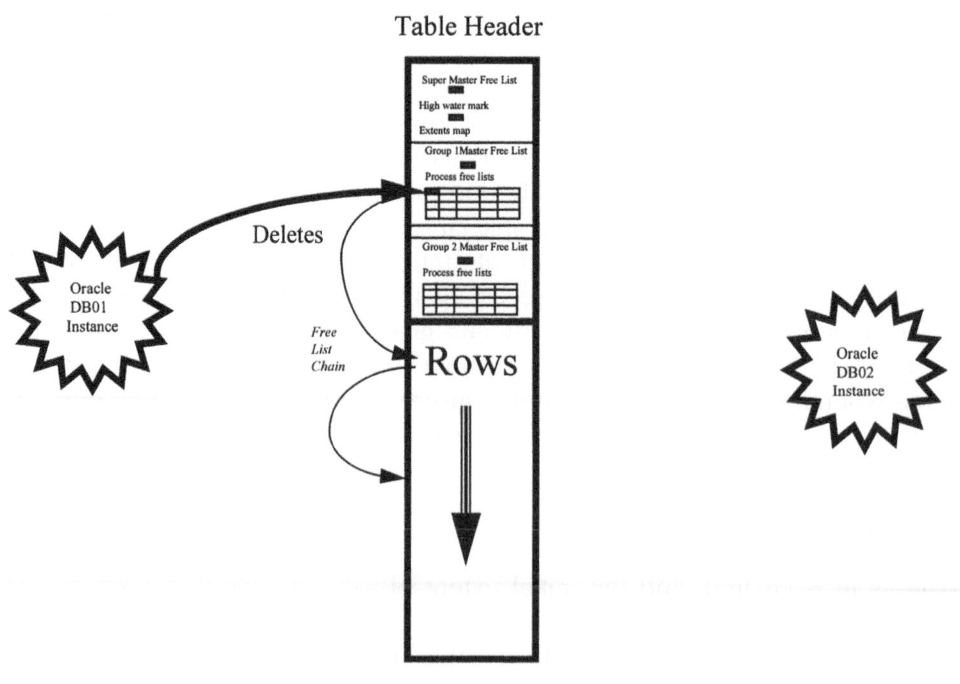

Exhibit 50.6 Deleting Rows from Only One Instance

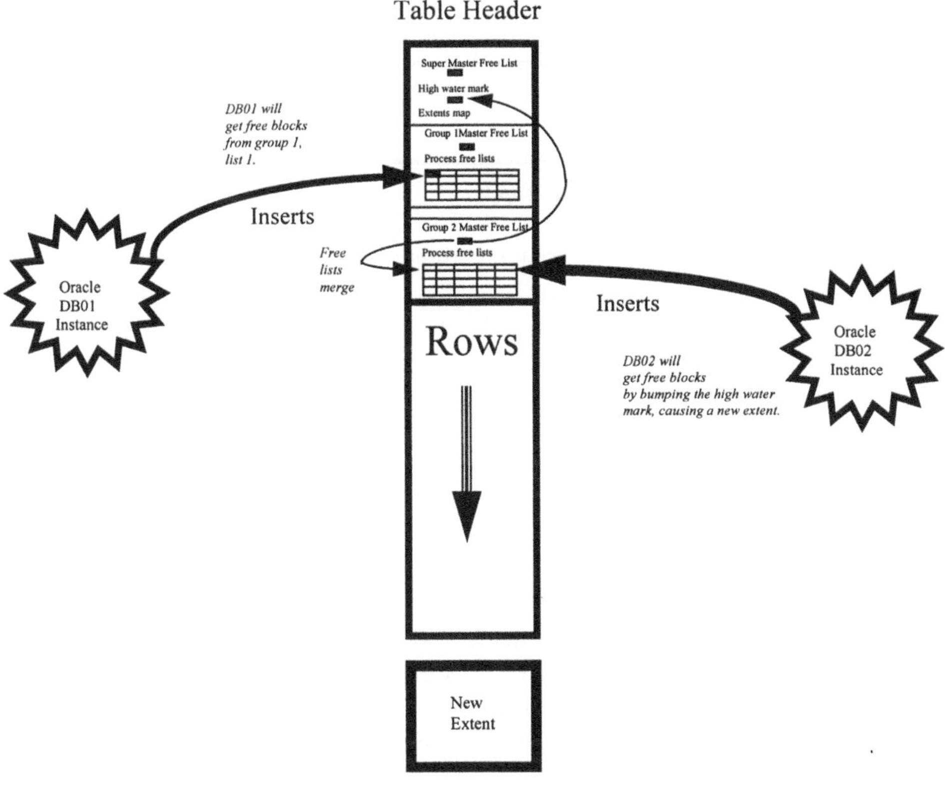

Exhibit 50.7 A Table with Unbalanced Freelists Extending

Step 2

Rows are deleted from the table using instance db01. Now we see the process freelist group 1, list 1, acquires all of the free blocks from the delete. The freelist group for db02 remains empty (Exhibit 50.6).

Step 3

Both instances now continue to add rows, with db01 using its process freelist, group 1, list 1. The db02 node does not know about free blocks in the other freelist group, so db02 requests a bump of the high-water mark, causing a new table extent.

Freelists and Long Rows

There are cases where large row lengths and an improper setting of PCTFREE can cause performance degradation. The problem occurs when a block becomes too full to accept another row, while the block remains on the freelist.

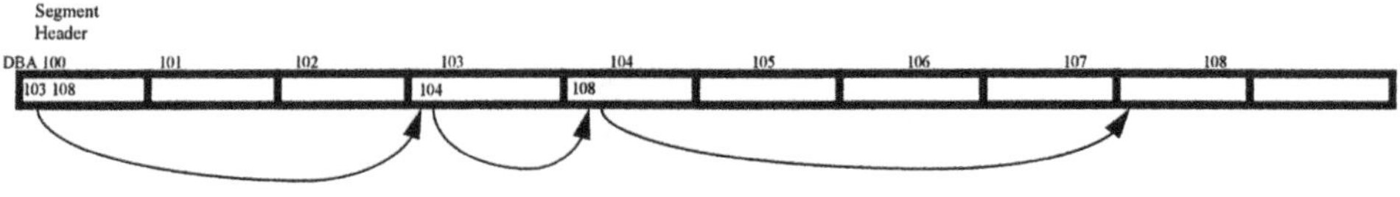

Exhibit 50.8 Searching for a Free Block

As rows are inserted, Oracle must fetch these blocks from the freelist, only to find that there is not enough room for a row. Fortunately, Oracle will not continue fetching freelist blocks forever. After retrieving a limited number of too-small blocks (probably five) from the freelist, Oracle assumes that there will be no blocks on the freelist that have enough space for the row, and Oracle will grab an empty block from the master freelist. This causes five extra I/O operations upon insert, and significant performance decline (see Exhibit 50.8).

This problem occurs when the row length for the table exceeds the space reserved on the block. For example, with 4K blocks and PCT-FREE= 10, the reserved space will equal 400 bytes (not counting block header space). Therefore, we may see this problem for any rows that are more than 400 bytes in length.

For example, consider a table with 1700 byte rows. After two rows are added to the block, 3400 bytes are consumed, and 600 bytes remain in the block. If PCTFREE=10, the block must reach 3600 bytes to be removed from the freelist, so the block will remain on the freelist although it cannot hold another entire row. The fourth row will not chain and Oracle will grab another free block from the freelist (Exhibit 50.9).

Freelist Behavior when SQL Updates Decrease Row Size

Because freelists are one-way linked lists, it follows that updates that trigger a link/unlink (where the target block is not at the head of the freelist chain) will not be able to dynamically perform the operation without some "trick." The trick is the unlink counter. Each time the block cannot be used because there is not enough space, the unlink counter is decremented. When this falls below a threshold, then the block is unlinked from the freelist. This way, Oracle tries not to keep the blocks that do not have enough space at the head of the freelist.

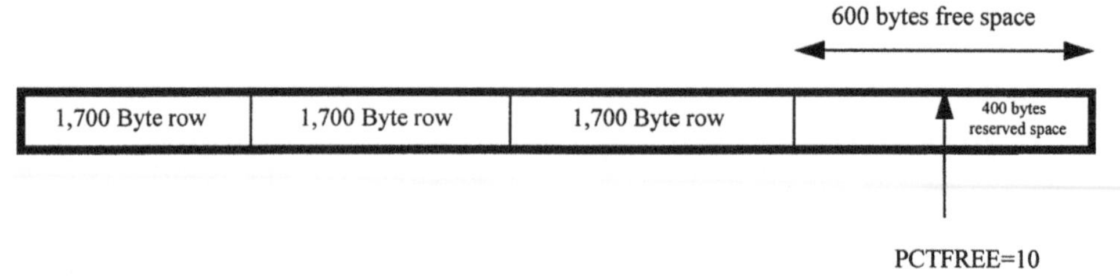

Exhibit 50.9 Block Layout for 4000-Byte Blocks with 1700-Byte Rows

Long Data Columns and Freelists

To avoid fragmentation of a row, Oracle will always want to insert table rows containing RAW or LONG RAW column types onto a completely empty block. Therefore, on insert, Oracle will not attempt to insert below the high-water mark (using freelists) and will always bump the high-water mark, pulling the free blocks from the master freelist.

So, if Oracle does not reference the freelists on insert, does this mean that multiple freelists are of no benefit for tables that contain RAW columns? No, it simply means that Oracle will not reuse blocks once they have been placed on the freelist chain. Multiple freelists are still useful in cases where there is heavy insert activity because free blocks are pulled from the master freelist onto each separate process freelist.

Therefore, if we make the assumption that freelists are only used to unlink freelist blocks after inserts or updates, then it follows that the PCTFREE parameter is far more important than the PCTUSED parameter for tables that contain RAW columns. But what should be the setting for PCTFREE? If the table does not experience any updates, then having a high PCTFREE only wastes space on the block.

We could carry this argument even further and state that we do not want blocks linked onto the freelist. Hence, we would want to make the value of PCTUSED very low, so that deletes will not invoke a freelist link operation. Therefore, for tables with RAW columns that are not updated, we will want to set both PCTFREE and PCTUSED to a low value.

Actually, free blocks below HWM (that is, blocks on the freelists) may be used for inserting LONGs, but only if the block is completely empty. If the block is partially used but still below the PCTUSED mark, it will not be used to insert the LONG data.

A Summary of Table Management Rules

The following rules govern the settings for freelists, freelist groups, PCTFREE, and PCTUSED. As we know, these values can easily be changed at any time with the ALTER TABLE command: the observant DBA should be able to develop a methodology for deciding the optimal settings for these parameters.

1. There is a direct trade-off between effective space utilization and high performance.
   a. *For high space reuse:* a high value for PCTUSED will effectively reuse space on data blocks, but at the expense of additional I/O. A high PCTUSED means that relatively full blocks are placed on the freelist. Hence, these blocks will be able to accept only a few rows before becoming full again, leading to more I/O.
   b. *For high performance:* a low value for PCTUSED means that Oracle will not place a data block onto the freelist until it is nearly empty.

The block will be able to accept many rows until it becomes full, thereby reducing I/O at insert time.

c. *For fast space acquisition:* turn off freelist links/unlinks. It takes fewer resources for Oracle to extend a table than to manage freelists. Freelists can be turned off by setting PCTUSED to 1. This will cause the freelists to be populated exclusively from new extents. Of course, this approach requires lots of extra disk space, and the table must be reorganized periodically to reclaim the wasted storage.

2. Always set PCTUSED to greater than the row length. We never want to have free blocks that do not have enough room to accept a row.
3. The presence of chained rows in a table means that PCTFREE is too low or DB_BLOCKSIZE is too small. In rare cases, LONG RAW row size may exceed the maximum block size for Oracle, making chained rows unavoidable.
4. If a table receives simultaneous inserts, it needs to have simultaneous deletes. Running a single purge job will place free blocks on only one freelist; all other freelists will not contain any free blocks from the purge.
5. Multiple freelists can waste disk — these tables will exhibit the "sparse table" phenomenon as the table grows and each freelist contains free blocks that are not known to the other freelists. For these tables, it is important to maximize table usage; we want the table to be placed onto a freelist as soon as it is capable of receiving more than two new rows. Hence, a fairly high value for PCTUSED is desired.

ORACLE SECURITY

With the advent of the new authentication server technologies and incorporation of Kerberos in Oracle8, Oracle security mechanisms are more complex than ever before. Oracle now offers sophisticated security mechanisms at both the database and network levels. In addition to the Oracle role-based security, we also find sophisticated PL/SQL encryption algorithms and a host of other tools, all designed to ensure that all Oracle information remains secure and manageable.

Chapters 51 through 53 are drawn from some of the foremost Oracle security experts in the industry. Especially interesting is Chapter 52 on row-level security, which shows how to protect access to Oracle database at the smallest level of granularity.

Chapter 51

Using Roles in Oracle Security

Mark B. Wallace

The purpose of this chapter is to help readers better understand an important aspect of Oracle7 and Oracle8 Server security. This will help readers plan a basic security implementation for their organizations, or evaluate one already in place. The approach presented works best for Oracle-based (i.e., two-tier client/server) security. If you choose (or your application software vendor chooses for you) application-based security, what is presented here will cover only part of your needs. Application-based security does not require users to connect directly to the database (instance). Instead, they log in to an application, or application server (as one might expect on the Web), and that application or server uses a master login to Oracle.

Brief Review of Security Basics

The Basic Principle

As readers will see, I construe security rather narrowly. For me, it is *the means of preventing man-made threats to your database from being carried out by the use of Oracle's client software (e.g., SQL*Plus).* Therefore, topics such as backup and recovery (the threat is computer failure — hardware, network, or software) or disaster recovery (the threat is an act of nature) will not be discussed at all. Nor will the more "exotic" man-made threats, such as hacking the operating system of your server hardware, or the physical destruction of a data center be addressed. Other non-Oracle-specific references are available on those topics.

The threat that will be investigated is *improper access to data.*

0-8493-1139-X/02/$0.00+$1.50
©2002 by CRC Press LLC

Improper access to data is for either read or write purposes. Improper read access is the reading (select) of data by someone who does not have permission to see it. Improper write access is the changing (insert, update, delete) of data by someone who does not have permission to change it.

Privilege Overview

Most of the Oracle security mechanism rests on Oracle "privileges" that are either held or not held by each UserID. (The UserID is also commonly referred to as the "user," "username," or "user name." Examples of UserIDs include "SYS," "SYSTEM," and "SCOTT.") There are two kinds of privileges, object and system. (In this context, "object" refers to an Oracle object that would appear in DBA_OBJECTS, such as a table, and not an object in the sense of object-oriented, such as Smalltalk, C++, or Java.) Object privileges give UserIDs, other than the owner of the object, the power to access it for specific purposes. System privileges give UserIDs the power to execute specific SQL commands. Certain system privileges (containing "ANY" in their names) can override the lack of object privileges.

The Security Matrix (Object Privileges)

Readers may find it helpful to use what I call the "security matrix" to decide which object privileges to grant to users (see Exhibit 51.1). The first part of that matrix shows UserIDs going down the left column and Oracle objects going across the top row. Each intersection of a UserID and an object needs to be analyzed in terms of access possibilities. Should access be permitted and, if so, which kinds?

The Security Matrix (System Privileges)

The second part of the security matrix shows the same UserIDs down the left column (see Exhibit 51.2), but now the top row includes the system privileges. For each UserID, one must consider which system privileges that user needs to make appropriate use of this database. Because the UserIDs are the same,

Exhibit 51.1 The Security Matrix (Object Privileges)

User/Object	*Obj1*	*Obj2*	*Obj3*	*Obj4*	*Obj5*	...
User1	?	?	?	?	?	
User2	?	?	?	?	?	
User3	?	?	?	?	?	
User4	?	?	?	?	?	
User5	?	?	?	?	?	
...						

Exhibit 51.2 The Security Matrix (System Privileges)

User/SP	*SysP1*	*SysP2*	*SysP3*	*SysP4*	*SysP5*	...
User1	?	?	?	?	?	
User2	?	?	?	?	?	
User3	?	?	?	?	?	
User4	?	?	?	?	?	
User5	?	?	?	?	?	
...						

this part of the matrix may be considered merely to represent additional columns that need to be analyzed. The analysis is the same: does the UserID need to hold the system privilege or not?

The "User Group" PUBLIC

It is possible to grant a privilege to the Oracle reserved word "PUBLIC." Privileges granted to PUBLIC are available to all users of the database, *as though those privileges had been granted to each UserID directly* (i.e., not through a role; see below). Sometimes, PUBLIC acts like a UserID, sometimes it acts like a role, and sometimes it acts like neither. Oracle calls it a "user group." It is the only such entity in the database, so there is no way to create another one. It seems that Oracle internals contain hard-coded logic that give special treatment to PUBLIC.

Roles

Basic Principles

Oracle7 introduced the "role" facility. The intent is to shrink the security matrix for analysis purposes. It can do this by allowing related (because they are all needed to run one application) privileges to be grouped together into one "bundle." It also allows related (because they all need to run one application) UserIDs to be grouped together into one "bundle." If it is the same bundle (role), then each of those UserIDs will, in effect, have been granted all of those privileges (each of which can be either a system or an object privilege). This has then been accomplished without having to grant each privilege to each UserID separately.

Role Administration

There are three steps to implementing a role-based security scheme. First, create a role; second, grant privileges to it; and third, grant it to UserIDs. In a more powerful (and difficult to administer) scheme, roles may be granted to more comprehensive roles. The initial roles might represent individual tasks, while the later roles might represent entire job descriptions. Some of this (granting roles to roles) can be very useful; but if it is overdone, the cure (roles) can become worse than the disease (difficulty of managing a large security matrix).

Role Consequences

In effect, each new role causes another row (because, like a UserID, it can receive privileges) and another column (because, like a system privilege, it can be granted) to be added to the overall security matrix. The savings come from the fact that the analysis effort is now proportional to the sum, instead of the product, of the rows and columns involved *for each role*. If too many roles are created, it can add up to more effort than managing the original matrix.

Typically, the number of roles in a well-run security scheme should range from a handful to (in the very largest shops) several dozen, at most. If you draw up your plans for security and find that they include hundreds of roles, most likely you are doing something wrong or you are not the target market for the role mechanism and probably should abandon it.

Role Management

Once a role has been granted to a UserID, there are two pairs of states that describe its relationship to that UserID. In the data dictionary, it is either default or non-default; and at runtime, it is either enabled or disabled. All roles start in the default state immediately after being granted. To set up a non-default role, use a two-step process. First, GRANT the role to the UserID. Second, issue an ALTER USER <x> DEFAULT ROLE <...> command to switch its state to non-default. Oracle automatically enables all default roles at connect time. Clients enable non-default roles during a session with the SET ROLE command. If a role is password-protected, the correct password must be supplied as part of that SET ROLE command.

Because the password can come from an executable program on the client side rather than be input by a human user directly, you can configure a limited version of application security with this mechanism. Simply set up a non-default, password-protected role for a UserID and enable that role with a SET ROLE command that is embedded in an executable client file. You do not need to disclose to the human users of that application even that there is a role, let alone that it is password-protected, and the password is stored internally in the executable. If those users access the database directly (e.g., through SQL*Plus), they will not have the additional privileges that come from the non-default role.

This is not industrial-strength security, however, as any human user who suspects what is going on can scan the executable with a disk editor, looking for the SET ROLE command, and find both the role name and its associated password. If you do not have any "power" users who would be that resourceful, this scheme can supply a modest amount of additional protection.

Tips and Techniques

As of Oracle7 and later releases, never GRANT a privilege WITH [GRANT | ADMIN] OPTION. One of the main benefits of roles is the elimination of most justifications for that "pass it on" syntax, which was always extremely dangerous. And do not ever grant a *role* WITH ADMIN OPTION. That defeats the entire purpose of the role mechanism.

Installing Roles in Your Shop

What is a reasonable process for implementing roles in your shop? I suggest starting with your production users (not developers or database administrators). Try to collect them into groups based on the particular applications they run or, if necessary, the particular data they access. Then, for each separate group, identify the Oracle privileges needed by its member UserIDs to do their work. (I would start with the group with the largest number of UserIDs because that is where the benefits will be the greatest. Alternatively, one could start with the group that is easiest to analyze in terms of the privileges its members require.) Now you are ready to implement role-based security for that group.

First, create a role to hold the privileges. Second, grant those privileges to that role. Third, set up a new UserID and grant the role to it. Fourth, test your analysis by attempting to run each transaction needed by members of that group from your new UserID (it should not hold any privileges except those from the new role). If you are successful, you are ready to grant the role to all UserIDs in the group. The final step is to revoke all direct grants of privileges to UserIDs that are redundant with the privileges they are holding through the role. You might want to do this a few UserIDs at a time, at least in the beginning, and have a restore script ready to regrant the revoked privileges if it turns out you missed something in your analysis.

If this goes well, continue onto the next group of users, repeating the steps as appropriate. You will end up with a security system that is far easier to administer.

Security Anomalies

An anomaly is a state of affairs that is both unexpected and undesired. A colloquial definition is "nasty side effect." The Oracle security system unfortunately has several areas where it behaves in ways that may be both surprising and dangerous (of course, what is surprising to you depends on what you already know). Look at some involving roles:

- Privileges that you hold through a role are useless for creating a stored procedure or view. You need direct grants to create stored software.
- The INDEX and REFERENCES object privileges cannot be granted through a role.
- Most disturbingly, none of the following commands has any effect on the target UserID's current session:

```
[GRANT | REVOKE] <role> [TO | FROM] <user>;
DROP <role>;
```

This means that if you revoke a role from a UserID, or even drop the role entirely, the user can continue to make use of all privileges received through that role until disconnect (which could be hours, or even days, later). This is in sharp contrast to normal REVOKEs, which take effect immediately (i.e., with the next SQL command issued by the UserID).

It should be noted that a role GRANT can be taken advantage of without reconnecting if the user knows enough to enable it with the SET ROLE command.

Data Dictionary Views

How can you find out what security provisions are in effect? This can be ascertained from the *Oracle Data Dictionary*. Several views are useful in this regard. Some of them are as follows:

- DBA_SYS_PRIVS (system privileges granted to users)
- DBA_TAB_PRIVS (object privileges granted to users, except for those in the next view)
- DBA_COL_PRIVS (column-level object privileges granted to users)
- DBA_ROLES (master list of all roles in the database)
- DBA_ROLE_PRIVS (roles granted to users)
- DBA_USERS (master list of all users in the database)
- ROLE_ROLE_PRIVS (roles granted to other roles)
- ROLE_SYS_PRIVS (system privileges granted to roles)
- ROLE_TAB_PRIVS (object privileges granted to roles, including column-level ones)

This last view is defective under Oracle8.0.3, 8.0.4, and 8.0.5 (at least). The defect did not exist in Oracle7, and it has been repaired in Oracle8.1.5, but I have not been able to check any earlier 8i releases. The defect causes the view to report *only* the column-level privileges and not the non-column-level ones.

Future Topics

Candidate topics for the future include (1) general security tips and techniques and dealing with Oracle anomalies, (2) new Oracle8 security features, and

(3) new Oracle8i security features. Suggestions as to what you would find valuable are eagerly solicited.

Acknowledgments

Thanks to reviewers John ("John B.") Beresniewicz, Kelly McDonald Cox, and Lynda Whitley for valuable suggestions. If any errors remain, responsibility for them is mine alone.

Chapter 52

Managing Row-Level Security in Oracle8i

Michael R. Ault

New to Oracle8i is the concept of row-level access restriction. For years DBAs have requested some form of conditional grant where access to specific rows can be easily restricted or granted, based on user or group membership. Oracle has finally given DBAs the functionality of conditional grants in the form of row-level security.

Row-level security is managed using a combination of Oracle8i contexts, stored procedures, database level triggers, and the `DBMS_RLS` package. The entire row-level security concept is tightly bound to the concept of a database policy. Generally speaking, a policy will require a:

1. Context
2. Procedure to implement the context
3. Database (Oracle8i) level trigger that monitors login activity
4. Security procedure to implement the policy
5. Policy declaration

Row-level security control requires certain environment variables, known as contexts, to be set. The `DBMS_CONTEXT` package is used to set the various context variables used by the RLS policy. Exhibit 52.1 is a flowchart showing how to implement a simple security policy.

The process is not complex. Let us examine each step and see what is really involved.

In the first step, a context package or procedure is developed which will then be used by a login trigger to set each user's context variables. This step is vital: if the context variables are not set, it is many times more difficult to implement row-level security using the `DBMS_RLS` package. The package or

0-8493-1139-X/02/$0.00+$1.50
©2002 by CRC Press LLC

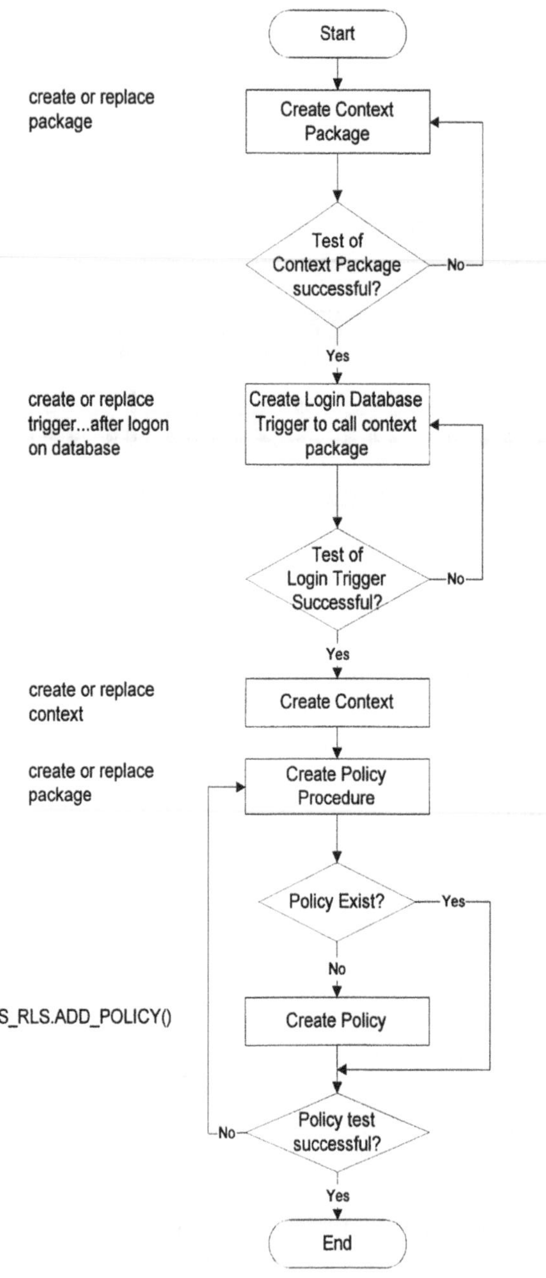

Exhibit 52.1 Steps to Implement a Security Policy

procedure used to set the context variables should resemble the one shown in Exhibit 52.2.

In the package in Exhibit 52.2 are two procedures, one that retrieves a user graphics function from a prebuilt and populated table (`GET_GRAPHICS_FUNCTION`); the other is used to set the user's context variables, based on

Exhibit 52.2 Example of Context Setting Procedure

```
CREATE OR REPLACE PACKAGE graphics_app AUTHID DEFINER AS
PROCEDURE get_graphics_function(usern IN VARCHAR2, graphics_function OUT
   VARCHAR2);
PROCEDURE set_graphics_context(usern IN VARCHAR2);
END;
/
SET ARRAYSIZE 1
SHO ERR
CREATE OR REPLACE PACKAGE BODY graphics_app AS
graphics_user VARCHAR2(32);
graphics_function VARCHAR2(32);
PROCEDURE get_graphics_function(usern IN VARCHAR2, graphics_function OUT
   VARCHAR2) IS
BEGIN
SELECT user_function INTO graphics_function FROM
   graphics_dba.graphics_users
WHERE username=usern;
END get_graphics_function;
PROCEDURE set_graphics_context(usern IN VARCHAR2) IS
BEGIN
graphics_app.get_graphics_function(usern,graphics_function);
DBMS_SESSION.SET_CONTEXT('GRAPHICS_SEC','GRAPHICS_FUNCTION',
   graphics_function);
DBMS_SESSION.SET_CONTEXT('GRAPHICS_SEC','GRAPHICS_USER',usern);
END set_graphics_context;
END graphics_app;
/
SHOW ERR
```

using the DBMS_SESSION.SET_CONTEXT procedure provided by Oracle (SET_GRAPHICS_CONTEXT).

Of course, the procedures in Exhibit 52.2 would not be much use without a trigger that could run the procedure whenever a user logged onto the system. Until Oracle8i, this would have involved setting auditing on for login, moving the aud$ table from SYS ownership, and setting the ownership to another user, resetting all of the synonyms pointing to aud$, and then building an on-insert trigger to perform the actual work. In Oracle8i, all we have to do is build a database level trigger similar to the one shown in Exhibit 52.3.

Exhibit 52.3 Example Database Login Trigger

```
CREATE OR REPLACE TRIGGER set_graphics_context AFTER LOGON ON DATABASE
DECLARE
username VARCHAR2(30);
BEGIN
username:=SYS_CONTEXT('USERENV','SESSION_USER');
graphics_app.set_graphics_context(username);
EXCEPTION
WHEN OTHERS THEN
NULL;
END;
/
```

Exhibit 52.4 Sample Context Package

```
CREATE OR REPLACE PACKAGE graphics_sec AUTHID DEFINER AS
FUNCTION graphics_check(obj_schema VARCHAR2, obj_name VARCHAR2)
RETURN VARCHAR2;
PRAGMA RESTRICT_REFERENCES(GRAPHICS_CHECK,WNDS);
END;
/
SET ARRAYSIZE 1
SHOW ERR
CREATE OR REPLACE PACKAGE BODY graphics_sec AS
FUNCTION graphics_check(obj_schema VARCHAR2, obj_name VARCHAR2)
RETURN VARCHAR2 AS
d_predicate VARCHAR2(2000);
user_context VARCHAR2(32);
BEGIN
   user_context:=SYS_CONTEXT('graphics_sec','graphics_function');
   IF user_context = 'ADMIN' THEN
     d_predicate:=' 1=1'; dbms_output.put_line(d_predicate);
   ELSIF user_context = 'GENERAL USER' THEN
     d_predicate:=' graphics_usage='||chr(39)||'UNRESTRICTED'||chr(39);
       dbms_output.put_line(d_predicate);
   ELSIF user_context='DEVELOPER' THEN
     d_predicate:=' 1=1'; dbms_output.put_line(d_predicate);
   ELSIF user_context IS NULL THEN
     d_predicate:='1=2';
   END IF;
   RETURN d_predicate;
END graphics_check;
END;
/
SHOW ERR
```

Once we have an operating context setting package and a database login trigger, we can proceed to create the required context checking package and the context it checks. Exhibit 52.4 shows a sample context checking package.

The entire purpose of the package in Exhibit 52.4 is to return a `d_predicate` value based on a user's `graphics_function` context value. The `d_predicate` value is appended to whatever WHERE clause is included with the command, or is appended as a WHERE clause whenever there is no preexisting clause.

The creation of our graphics security context is rather simple. Once we have finished the preliminary work, it boils down to one command:

```
CREATE OR REPLACE CONTEXT graphics_sec USING
  sys.graphics_app;
```

The final step is to set the policy into the database. This is done with the DBMS_RLS package, using the procedure ADD_POLICY:

```
BEGIN

dbms_rls.add_policy('GRAPHICS_DBA','INTERNAL_GRAPHICS','GRAPHICS_POLICY',
  'GRAPHICS_DBA', 'GRAPHICS_SEC.GRAPHICS_CHECK','SELECT,
  INSERT,UPDATE,DELETE');
END;
```

The above policy simply ties the components we previously defined into a coherent entity called `GRAPHICS_POLICY` and implements this policy against the table `INTERNAL_GRAPHICS`, which is in the schema `GRAPHICS_DBA`. The policy `GRAPHICS_POLICY` is owned by `GRAPHICS_DBA` and uses the procedure `GRAPHICS_SEC.GRAPHICS_ CHECK` to verify that users can perform select, insert, update, and delete operations.

The table `graphics_users` is required in the example above. The table contains the username and graphics function.

Policy Usage

Policy usage is controlled internally by the Oracle system and adheres to the following usage guidelines:

1. SYS user is not restricted by any security policy.
2. The policy functions that generate dynamic predicates are called by the server. The following is the required structure for the function:

```
FUNCTION policy_function (object_schema IN VARCHAR2, object_name
  VARCHAR2)
RETURN VARCHAR2
```

Where:

`object_schema` = the schema owning the table of view
`object_name` = the name of table of view that the policy will apply

3. The maximum length of the predicate that the policy function can return is 2000 bytes.
4. The policy functions must have the purity level of WNDS (write no database state).
5. Dynamic predicates generated out of different policies for the same object have the combined effect of a conjunction (ANDed) of all the predicates.
6. The security check and object look-up are performed against the owner of the policy function for objects in the subqueries of the dynamic predicates.
7. If the function returns a zero-length predicate, then it is interpreted as no restriction being applied to the current user for the policy.
8. When a table alias is required (for example, the parent object is a type table) in the predicate, the name of the table or view itself must be used as the name of the alias. The server constructs the transient view as something like "select c1, c2, … from tab where <predicate>."
9. Checking of the validity of the function is done at runtime for ease of installation and other dependency issues of import/export.

`DBMS_RLS` Package

The entire concept of row-level security is based on the use of policies stored in the database. The only way to store policies in the database is to use the `DBMS_RLS` package.

Exhibit 52.5 Procedure in DBMS_RLS Package

Procedure	Purpose
ADD_POLICY	Creates a fine-grained access control policy to a table or view.
DROP_POLICY	Drops a fine-grained access control policy from a table or view.
REFRESH_POLICY	Causes all the cached statements associated with the policy to be reparsed.
ENABLE_POLICY	Enables or disables a fine-grained access control policy.

The DBMS_RLS procedures cause current DML transactions, if any, to commit before the operation. However, the procedures do not cause a commit first if they are inside a DDL event trigger. With DDL transactions, the DBMS_RLS procedures are part of the DDL transaction.

For example, a trigger may be created for CREATE TABLE. Inside the trigger, a column can be added through ALTER TABLE and a policy added through DBMS_RLS. All these operations are in the same transaction as CREATE TABLE, even though each one is a DDL statement. The CREATE TABLE succeeds only if the trigger is completed successfully.

The DBMS_RLS package has the procedures shown in Exhibit 52.5.

The syntax for calling these procedures is shown in the next sections.

Syntax for the ADD_POLICY Procedure

```
DBMS_RLS.ADD_POLICY (
   object_schema       IN VARCHAR2   := NULL,
   object_name         IN VARCHAR2,
   policy_name         IN VARCHAR2,
   function_schema     IN VARCHAR2   := NULL,
   policy_function     IN VARCHAR2,
   statement_types     IN VARCHAR2   := NULL,
   update_check        IN BOOLEAN    := FALSE,
   enable              IN BOOLEAN    := TRUE);
```

Where:

```
object_schema   = schema owning the table/view, current user if null
object_name     = name of table or view
policy_name     = name of policy to be added
function_schema = schema of the policy function, current user if null
policy_function = function to generate predicates for this policy
statement_types = statement type that the policy apply, default if any
update_check    = policy checked against updated or inserted value?
enable          = policy is enabled?
```

Syntax for the `DROP_POLICY` Procedure

```
DBMS_RLS.DROP_POLICY (
   object_schema      IN VARCHAR2   := NULL,
   object_name        IN VARCHAR2,
   policy_name        IN VARCHAR2);
```

Where:

`object_schema`	= schema containing the table or view (logon user if null)
`object_name`	= name of table or view
`policy_name`	= name of policy to be dropped from the table or view

Syntax for the `REFRESH_POLICY` Procedure

```
DBMS_RLS.REFRESH_POLICY (
   object_schema IN VARCHAR2  := NULL,
   object_name IN VARCHAR2  := NULL,
   policy_name IN VARCHAR2  := NULL);
```

Where:

`object_schema`	= schema containing the table or view
`object_name`	= name of table or view with which the policy is associated
`policy_name`	= name of policy to be refreshed

Syntax for the `ENABLE_POLICY` Procedure

```
DBMS_RLS.ENABLE_POLICY (
   object_schema IN VARCHAR2  := NULL,
   object_name IN VARCHAR2,
   policy_name IN VARCHAR2,
   enable IN BOOLEAN);
```

Where:

`object_schema`	= schema containing the table or view (logon user if null)
`object_name`	= name of table or view with which the policy is associated
`policy_name`	= name of policy to be enabled or disabled
`Enable`	= true to enable the policy, false to disable the policy

Through the use of the above procedures, DBAs and developers can easily manage policies.

Summary

Oracle has given DBAs and developers a powerful new tool to manage row-level security. This new tool is a combination of contexts, triggers, and packages, plus a new package named `DBMS_RLS` through which security policies are implemeneted.

Through the proper use of policies, contexts, packages, and database level triggers, row-level security can be easily integrated in Oracle8i applications.

Chapter 53

Auditing Oracle

Frederick Gallegos
Joseph C. Yin

This chapter provides a basic explanation of the auditing facility provided in the Oracle database system and how to audit by using the auditing scripts included in this guide. The chapter is divided into three sections. The first describes the auditing script for creating audit trails for any user-specific administrative application's access grants table. The second describes the security features in Oracle and the necessary auditing scripts to be run by the auditors or security professionals in the daily relational database management system (RDBMS) operations. The final chapter section deals with the client/server administrator security while using Oracle7.

Creating Audit Trails of Access Grants Tables

A common element of any administrative application is a placeholder (database table) that contains information on accesses and grant privileges on each application user (see Exhibit 53.1). This type of validation table will be checked each time a user attempts to call an application, accessing data from the database, a process, or an executable routine during the active application session. If the user's privilege fails during the validation checking process, an error message is usually displayed on the application window that stops the user from continuing with the request and process.

This type of table provides auditors with a great bundle of auditing trails in keeping track of each authorized application user's privileges and therefore ensuring the security-level check within the internal operation of administrative application. The following scripts will generate the needed auditing trails on users' privileges. Auditors should run this report initially for every single application user and determine to see if hard copy of the output is necessary, depending upon needs. Then this script should be run every time a new user

0-8493-1139-X/02/$0.00+$1.50
©2002 by CRC Press LLC

Exhibit 53.1 A Typical Table Format

Name	*Null Condition*	*Type*
USER_NAME (Authorized username)	NOT NULL	VARCHAR2 (30)
PROCESS_NAME (Authorized user form, process, report, or executable)	NOT NULL	VARCHAR2 (30)
TYPE_IND (Type of BANNER activities)	NOT NULL	VARCHAR2 (1)
CAPACITY_IND (User's Privileges: query, maintenance (all access), or execute)	NOT NULL	VARCHAR2 (1)
ACTIVITY_DATE (Date of activity performed on the records of this table)	NOT NULL	DATE

is created or any old account changes are performed. By doing so, the audit file can always be updated in a continuous manner:

```
Shell Script (which calls the "secure" SQL script)
clear
echo "*****************************************************"
echo "* APPLICATION Security Listing *"
echo "*****************************************************"
echo "set verify off">secure_program_cmds.sql
echo "set pagesize 100" >> secure_program_cmds.sql
echo "set echo off" >> secure_program_cmds.sql
echo "spool Security_Listing_Report" >> secure_program_cmds.sql
echo. "@secure.sql" >> secure_program_cmds.sql
echo "spool off" >> secure_program_cmds.sql
echo "exit" >> secure_program_cmds.sql
chmod 700 secure_program_cmds.sql

#
#Enter Database Username
#
while:
do
   echo "Enter your database username->\c "
   read username
   case $username in
" ")echo "\nA database username must be entered\n";;
     *) break ;;
   esac

done
#
#Enter Database Password
#
while:
```

```
do
   echo "Enter your database username->\c "
   stty -echo
   read pass
   stty echo
   case $pass in
" ")echo "\nA database username must be entered\n";;
      *) break ;;
   esac
done

echo " "

sqlplus -silent $username/$pass @ secure_program_cmds
sed 's/$*/ /' Security_Listing_Report.1st>Security_Audit_Log
#---------------------------------------------------------
# Generate Output Report
#---------------------------------------------------------
echo " "
read OUT?"Print Log? (Y=Yes, N=No) "
[[ $OUT = "N"]] && exit;
read PRINTER?"Enter Printer Name: "
[[ $PRINTER = " " ]] && PRINTER=(your printer name)
```

This shell script will only be available to auditors or security professionals by setting up file permission control within the UNIX operating system. Furthermore, this also requires that a unique database account be created to access the aforementioned database table by the DBA. The actual secure SQL script is listed below:

```
rem
rem   APPLICATION Security Audit Log Creation
rem
prompt
prompt Enter the User Name for Auditing.
accept name char prompt 'Enter Name:'
column user_name heading 'Name' format a30
column process_name heading 'Process' format a15
column type_ind heading 'Type' format a15
column capacity_ind heading 'Priv' format a15
column activity_date heading 'Date' format DATE
break on capacity_ind skip page
compute RECORD of process_name on
     capacity_ind
select user_name, process_name,
decode(type_ind, 'E', 'Executable', 'F', 'Form',
   'P', 'Process', 'R', 'Report'),
decode(capacity_ind, 'Q', 'Query', 'M', 'Maintenance',
   'E', 'Execute'), activity_date
from table (your table name)
where user_name=&name
order by capacity-ind;
```

The result of this report is displayed in Exhibit 53.2. (The authors have performed the audit procedures and scripts against my work's administrative

Exhibit 53.2 Results of the Report

NAME	PROCESS	TYPE	PRIV	DATE
YIN	GJAJOBS	FORM	QUERY	22-JAN-93
YIN	GJAPCTL	FORM		22-JAN-93
YIN	SWGEOPS	FORM		22-FEB-95
	**********	FORM	***************	
	3			
YIN	SGASTDN	FORM	MAINTENANCE	22-JAN-93
YIN	SCARRES	FORM	MAINTENANCE	22-JAN-93
	**********		***************	
	2		RECORD	
5 ROWS SELECTED				

application (BANNER), and the report in Exhibit 53.2 is from BANNER's GURSECR database table.)

The output gives a clear accounting of all application's (in this case, it is the BANNER application) internal accesses granted to an individual. Auditors or security professionals can therefore perform a periodic review of the audit log to see if any exceptions have occurred on selected individual account application's access makeup. Also, auditors can run the script as desired to maintain the security level of application access and allow the audit log to serve as an alternate checking mechanism other than the online application security ad hoc query.

Oracle Security Features

Because the makeup of the other applications' security processes within the client/server architecture includes the Oracle security layer beside itself, it is important to gain the basic understanding of what Oracle, as an application, can offer to the auditors in regard to auditing the desired application usage. Under the Oracle database environment, security is broken down into three layers: operating system, user security, and object security. This chapter focuses on only the latter two layers due to the complex nature of the operating system configuration and the authors' actual work experiences in Oracle application developments. For detailed information related to the first layer, please consult with the individual operating system group and user manuals. (All actual Oracle SQL language commands listed from this point on have been cross-verified against Oracle SQL Language Manual for accuracy.)

User Security

Each database user must have the necessary access to connect to the database in order to obtain authorized information while using any database application.

Therefore, the DBA has to set up the user by issuing the following SQL command:

```
GRANT {CONNECT|RESOURCE|DBA} TO username IDENTIFIED by password
```

This command will grant the privileges to the user for connecting to the appropriate database. The password is set to default during the initial granting process; the user will then be able to change the password to his or her own password. The actual password for each user is stored in the data dictionary under an encrypted format, which cannot be decrypted by any users or the DBA. The password is internally decrypted through Oracle's software algorithm when a user connects to the database. Oracle also provides automatic logins for the user on an as-needed basis; the DBA can create an Oracle account that begins with the letters 'OPS$', followed by the operating system username of the user. The user will not need to provide a username or password during an active session when connecting to the database because this type of account relies on the operating system to validate user identification; if it is validated, Oracle will not revalidate again.

Audit Recommendation

From an auditing point of view, it is recommended that an audit log file be created to record every time the GRANT command is used by the DBA. In addition, all automatic logins should be eliminated to ensure the security of the database. If automatic logins are needed by the users, then it is recommended that all automatic login accounts have different passwords assigned, which are randomly changed on a periodic basis by the DBA.

Object Security

This layer of security deals with granting each database application user the privileges to access objects within a database, such as tables, views, and sequences. All information is stored within different objects of a database. Thus, each user needs the necessary access privileges to be granted by the owners of those objects to continue an operation while using the needed database application. All grantable object privileges are listed in Exhibit 53.3. (Yes indicates the privilege's availability under each object type.)

As one can see, granting the proper privilege is a critical task; it can directly affect the data integrity stored within the object and database as a whole.

Audit Recommendation

From an auditing point of view, it is recommended that log files be created on only the critical objects within the database during the object privileges granting process. It is neither efficient nor effective to track all object granting processes due to the immense amount of audit record logging processes. The

Exhibit 53.3 All Grantable Object Privileges

Object Privileges/ Object Type	*Table*	*View*	*Sequence*	*Procedure (Database Stored Procedures/Functions/Packages)*
ALTER	Yes		Yes	
DELETE	Yes	Yes		
EXECUTE				Yes
INDEX	Yes			
INSERT	Yes	Yes		
REFERENCES	Yes			
SELECT	Yes	Yes	Yes	
UPDATE	Yes	Yes		

database administrators and auditors need to identify those critical objects and then implement the audit log creation process to log every instance of granting privileges against those objects. In addition to the creation of those audit logs, Oracle provides an auditing facility to assist systems staff in obtaining and maintaining proper audit trails at the system level. This facility needs to be turned on by modifying the INIT.ORA file, which contains the database start-up parameters. The DBA needs to set the AUDIT_TRAIL parameter value to "TRUE," thus enabling the creation of an audit trail. After restarting the database with this parameter value change, the audit trail process can begin. No audit trail will be written to the audit trail tables until the authorized user issues the following SQL command.[1]

- For System Auditing (logging event on user connection to the database)

```
AUDIT {[CONNECT] [RESOURCE] [DBA] [NOT EXISTS]|ALL}
   [WHENEVER [NOT] SUCCESSFUL]
```

- For Object Auditing (login event on user action to the object of the database)

```
AUDIT action ON object [BY {SESSION|ACCESS]} {WHENEVER [NOT] SUCCESSFUL]
```

Once the AUDIT command is issued, the audit trail table in the data dictionary may grow to a considerable size if it is not periodically purged or achieved by the authorized system personnel. The audit trail table is the only tape of data dictionary tables that can be modified by the authorized personnel without affecting the data integrity of the database. However, a word of caution — it will affect the auditing integrity if undocumented or unauthorized changes are made.

Each audit action that can be audited is assigned a numeric code within the database. These codes are accessible to systems analysts using the following SQL command script, `audit_action.sql`, against the AUDIT_ACTION view:

```
rem
rem SQL script to list all available audit actions and codes
rem
spool audit_action
set pagesize 500
set verify off
select action,    /*Action Code*/
name              /*Name of the action*/
from audit_action
order by name
spool off
!enscript-G -b' Audit Action Listing"
        -rfCouier8 audit_action.1st
!rm audit_action.1st
```

Knowing these action codes, one can then perform the desired audit trail recreation against the database, both on the system level and the object level. It is also critical to understand that each audit trail creation requires the authorized user to issue the AUDIT command to start the logging process of desired database event. Without the issuance of this command, there will be no audit trails written to the audit trail tables. Once the audit concern is no longer needed by the authorized user, one can issue the NOAUDIT command to stop the logging process immediately.

There are two special audit scripts described below to handle login audit and action audit. One is auditing login (logging all attempts to connect to the database):

```
rem
rem   SQL script to generated a format file on tracking
rem   all login events to the database. A hard copy of the audit trail
rem   will be directed to the appropriate printer
rem

set pagesize 500
set verify off

spool Login_Audit_Trail

select username,             /*ORACLE user account name*/
terminal,                    /*Terminal ID used*/
decode(returncode, '0', 'Connected',
   '1005', 'Failed due to NULL value',
   '1017', 'Failed', returncode),/*Failure check*/
to_char(timestamp, 'DDD-MON-YY HH24:MI:SS), /*Login time*/
to_char(logoff_time, 'DD-MON-YY HH24:MI:SS') /*Logoff time*/
from dba_audit_connect

order by timestamp
spool off

   !enscript -G -b'Login Audit Listing'
   -rfCouier8 Login_Audit_Trail
```

This script will allow authorized users to generate an audit trail report that displays all login failure attempts and all successful login attempts, along with their logon and logoff times.

The other is an action audit (logging user-specified audit action to objects within the database):

```
rem
rem   SQL script to generated a format file on tracking
rem   specified action the database object. A hard copy of the audit
        trail
rem   will be directed to the appropriate printer
rem

set pagesize 500
set verify off

spool Action_Audit_Trail

select username,          /*ORACLE user account name*/
terminal,                 /*Terminal ID used*/
owner,                    /*Object owner*/
obj_name,                 /*Object name*/
action_name,              /*Action Code*/
to_char(timestamp, 'DD-MON-YY HH24:MI:SS'), /*Login time*/
to_char(logoff_time, 'DD-MON-YY HH24:MI:SS') /*Logoff time*/
from dba_audit_trail

order by timestamp
spool off
   !enscript -G -b' Action Audit Listing'
       -rfCouier8 Action_Audit_Trail
```

This script will allow authorized users to generate an audit trail report that displays the specified action performed against the database object and their logon and logoff times.

There are no outputs available for those audit scripts because limited system resources were provided during the write-up of this guide from the auditee. The systems analyst team should take those scripts and enhance them according to their needs. Moreover, those scripts provide a basic understanding of the Oracle auditing facility tool. Again, it is important for the team to obtain further understanding of referencing to the Oracle manual and customizing their audit trail programs to make them suitable for the operating environment. In addition, here are some data dictionary views the authors have used that can be utilized by the team in performing the audit trail review. These views are supported by *Security & Control in an Oracle Environment,* a publication by The EDP Auditors Foundation, Inc. (now Information Systems Audit and Control Foundation). The following data dictionary views contain relevant information to the systems analyst team regarding security auditing:

- DBA_OBJECTS: a listing of every object contained in the database
- DBA_TAB_COMMENTS: a description of every table contained in the database
- DBA_COL_COMMENTS: a description of every column of every table in the database
- DBA_USERS: the user profile of every user defined in the database

- DBA_TAB_GRANTS: the object privileges granted on every column of every table
- DBA_TAB_AUDIT_OPTS: the auditing options enabled for every table in the database
- DBA_AUDIT_TRAIL: the audit trail of every database event that has been logged
- DBA_SYS_AUDIT_OPTS: the systemwide auditing options enabled for the database

These views can greatly assist the authorized system staff in maintaining proper control over the database access while using any database application.

Client/Server Administrator Security with Oracle7

In a typical client/server environment, the database administrator is often required to manage multiple databases across the network. Although the responsibility of the database administrator may be too much for any one person to fulfill, it is, however, cost-effective under management's view within this new client/server environment. In the earlier releases of Oracle, all privileged administrator connections were accomplished using INTERNAL to connect to the database server. This type of connection, using a centralized administration account, disables any accountability tracing as to who actually performs those powerful administrative operations. Thus, it can be a serious matter, especially when there is more than one user who knows the centralized administrative account and concurrently logging onto the server to perform their authorized or unauthorized tasks. With the new version of Oracle, one can ensure that accountability and proper control of all privileged administrator account connections are in place by performing the following steps:

1. **Create a password file by using the ORAPWD utility.**

```
orapwd FILE=filename PASSWORD=password ENTRIES=integer
```

This syntax will create an encrypted file that the host computer's operating system manages. It is important to ensure that the operating system assigns the access file privileges against this file only to authorized users. As a part of the syntax, the option ENTRIES is essential. This option allows one to assign the number of entries that are allowed in the password file and in turn creates a limit on how many database users can become administrators.

2. **Grant SYSOPER and SYSDBA roles to your administrative users.** In granting those roles to individuals, the Oracle7 server includes the user's privilege as an entry in the external password file. Moreover, by using the role-granting process, accountability can be now directly associated with the individual database user because the grantee no longer uses one centralized administrative account to logon to the database server.

3. **Set the REMOTE_LOGIN_PASSWORDFILE server parameter.** The parameter should be set to EXCLUSIVE because Oracle7 allows individual grantees of the SYSOPER or SYSDBA privileges to establish secure, privileged administration connections using their own accounts. By doing so, there is an audit trail available when needed for the DBA or auditors. The risk of not having accountability for all administrative connections is reduced to the minimum level.
4. **Use special view to audit password file members.** An auditor can utilize V$PWFILE_USERS view to generate a listing of all user accounts possessing the SYSDBA and SYSOPER system privileges. It is an essential tool in ensuring that security is not being compromised when the above steps are implemented by a business entity, especially the implementation of the REMOTE_LOGIN_PASSWORDFILE server parameter.

Most importantly, the latest Oracle implementation in regard to object and access security control is applying the concept of "role"-based security. Simply stated, the direct objects or access grants no longer need to be issued to each user account. Instead, one or more database roles will be created, with the necessary objects or accesses grants first. After the roles are created, management then dedicates which user will be granted to the specified role/roles to perform his or her jobs. The advantages of using role-based security are: (1) There is a central way to maintain all object/access privileges, any changes can be applied and these affect every user with the affected database role without any delays. In addition, there are fewer items for the DBA to maintain in regard to user privileges because one specific database role can contain numerous objects grants, and the role can be assigned to multiple users. (2) Roles can be separately defined with certain privileges against the same database objects (e.g., Role_1 can update and delete the data, but Role_2 can only select (view) the data); thus, segregation of duties can be controlled among all database users. (3) The database role can also be used to validate a user's application access privileges. One can set up the application to utilize the database roles to determine which part of the application a user can access. (4) The database role itself can be set up with password protection; thus, the user must also know the role password to access the privileges against the objects grants within the role. The role password essentially provides secondary protection when database objects are being accessed or changed.

Moreover, database role security can also be enhanced using an application to enable the database roles to the users. To accomplish this enhancement, the database roles must be assigned to the users' accounts as a non-default role, and this method will enable the assigned database roles to the user only when the user utilizes the application. Once the user exits the application, the database roles become inactive. Instead of letting the user know the password for the database roles, the application will handle the necessary password needed to enable the database role and its associated objects grants. By doing so, user access to the database objects is further controlled because the user cannot access the objects granted within a database role any other way except using the specified application. Auditor and security staff can therefore focus their attention on the application usage and security when auditing a database environment.

Conclusion

With a basic understanding obtained from this guide, auditors and security professionals can carefully plan the necessary auditing steps under their own client/server application environment. Only through a solid understanding of the aforementioned recommendations and scripts can management obtain the highest level of security access through any client/server application and Oracle RDBMS.

Note

1. *Security and Control in an Oracle Environment,* The EDP Auditor Foundation, Inc., pp. 33–36.

ORACLE DATA WAREHOUSING

The foremost advantage of Oracle8 was its claim to be able to support very large databases structures. In fact, Oracle offers a wealth of tools such as Oracle partitioning and Oracle parallel features that are directly aimed at the very large database.

Oracle also offers a wealth of internal tools for data warehousing, including star query joins, hash joins, bitmapped indexes, and other tools and techniques that are primarily designed for the management of very large-scale data warehouse applications.

Chapters 54 through 58 are drawn from some of the foremost experts in the Oracle data warehousing industry. Foremost, we see tips and techniques for undocumented features of Oracle's Express product, which is the OLAP front-end for Oracle. We also present excellent chapters relating directly to issues of volume of scale, including tips and techniques for Oracle stress testing and how to manage the overall load upon the very large Oracle database.

It is no longer sufficient for Oracle administrators to confine themselves within the domains of the standard Oracle engine. Multi-terabyte databases are becoming commonplace today and it is imperative that the Oracle administrator understand the issues relating to large volumes of data and the data warehouse tools within Oracle.

Chapter 54

What's Wrong with My Data?

Jeffery Feldman

You've probably heard the expression, "Garbage in, garbage out." A computer system utilizing the most technologically sophisticated architecture, elegant user interfaces, and intuitive report generation capabilities can still become nearly useless if the data it relies upon is fundamentally flawed. While investigating and correcting "bad" data may be among the least glamorous tasks to perform, it is absolutely critical if organizations are to realize the full potential of the systems they've developed (often at a considerable cost in time, resources, and dollars).

Why Should I Care?

Perhaps you are not quite convinced that data integrity should be a major concern or, at any rate, not for the applications you are dealing with. After all, the existing systems are running just fine with the current data, aren't they? And any required data cleansing can be done at some point in the future when time and resources become more available.

Well, maybe. Much depends on just how the data is being used, and on the organization's tolerance for risk. Let's say, for example, that the only use of the data is to support a company-internal management information system, and that about 5 percent of the data is known to be in error. A cost-benefit analysis that compares the effort required to correct the data versus the increased value of the system to its users might well conclude that the 5 percent error rate is acceptable.

On the other hand, what if that error rate was actually 30 percent? Or what if the application in question was sending bills to your customers? It is unlikely that faulty data could be tolerated for long in either situation.

0-8493-1139-X/02/$0.00+$1.50
©2002 by CRC Press LLC

Just because existing systems can use a particular set of data, that does not necessarily imply ease-of-use for a new system — among other things, there may be a great deal of hard-coded logic in the old systems that allows them to bypass problems in the raw data. And there are a host of potential new problems once you start merging data from several different existing systems in order to feed your new system.

And postponing the cleansing effort is generally inadvisable. The initial data propagation/transformation efforts can require significant revision and reexecution. Considerable additional effort and cost may be needed to repair data, to make it accessible, and to prevent continued corruption. However, once the users have started to access the system, its credibility (and your own) are on the line. There may not be any funds available for continued work if the system's users are not satisfied with the initial release. And does time and additional resources ever really become easier to get onto a project at a "later date"?

Potential Impacts

Some potential impacts of unreliable data include the following:

- *Increased cost of database marketing.* Poor quality data affects direct mail, telemarketing, and marketing collateral costs. A large automobile manufacturer purged its customer files and cut direct-mail costs by U.S.$500,000 the first year, and lowered the costs of managing this data long term.[1]
- *Increased operational costs.* The time that resources must spend to detect and correct errors can be very significant. One estimate for the cost of poor data quality is 8 to 12 percent of revenue; for service organizations, a "good working estimate" might be 40 to 60 percent of expenses.[2] There is also a related negative impact on employee morale.
- *Lowered customer satisfaction.* Multiple mailings sent to the same customer can be annoying; they can cause the customer to question your enterprise's competence and can harm the customer relationship. This is especially true if the information within a given mailing or statement pertaining to a customer is incorrect.
- *Reduced use of system.* If the believability or the objectivity of the data comes into question, then the resulting poor reputation will cause reduced use of the system and underlying databases.[3] Considering the effort and cost of developing these systems, anything impairing their value or use is clearly counterproductive.
- *Risk to health/safety.* The quality of data in (for example) medical records is clearly of major importance, as the diagnosis and procedure must be recorded correctly. Other examples of critical systems include those controlling aircraft movement and traffic signals, chemical plants and nuclear reactors, jail security, and many others.

What Problems Might There Be?

Let us take the following as our working scenario: a new data warehouse is being constructed, and the data from several operational legacy systems/databases will be used to populate it. These legacy feeder systems will remain in production for some time. We are therefore concerned with the quality of the available data not only for the purpose of the initial load of our data warehouse, but also because any problems that currently exist will continue to contaminate our data until they are fixed. This is a hypothetical but common situation, and provides the context for further discussion.

Potential Problems

1. Missing Data

In Exhibit 54.1:

- Lee does not have a *Smoker* status code/flag, while Frank does not have a value in the *Sex* field. The degree to which either is an issue will depend on whether or not they are mandatory fields. If one or the other is mandatory, how will you go about getting that information?
- Record 525 is not present. Does this indicate a deletion, or a problem with missing records in this particular file?
- Smith and Yu have a zero *Age*. Either they are less than a year old, or 00 is the default or dummy value given to the *Age* field. Do the business rules help you to determine which is which? If 00 is the dummy value, then this data is missing.
- There is another kind of missing data — data that is needed by the new application, but was not captured by any of the older feeding systems. If you are fortunate, it will be possible to derive the new value by manipulating the old data. Otherwise, the effort to capture and record new information can be considerable.

Exhibit 54.1 Example of Missing Data

Identifier	*Last Name*	*Sex*	*Age*	*Smoker*
523	Smith	M	00	N
524	Jones	F	23	Y
526	Lee	M	42	
527	Frank		17	Y
528	Yu	M	00	N

Exhibit 54.2 Example of Redundant Data

Identifier	*Last Name*	*Sex*	*Age*	*Smoker*
Data File "A"				
523	Smith	M	00	N
524	Jones	F	23	Y
526	Lee	M	42	
527	Frank		17	Y
528	Yu	M	00	N
Data File "B"				
523	Smith	M	00	N
524	Jones	F	22	N
525	Samuelson	M	54	Y
526	Lee	F	42	
527	Frank		17	Y

2. Redundant Data, with Inconsistencies

In Exhibit 54.2:

- Our hypothetical data warehouse draws information from both Files "A" and "B" (assume each has unique fields of interest not displayed in the above example). Because each file was developed and used separately by different divisions of the company, redundant information is stored. Which will you use as your primary source for those fields available from both?
- Note that the information for Jones is not consistent. Is it safe to assume that File "A" has more recent information, and therefore that Jones took up smoking at age 23? Regardless of the answer, how do we account for the difference in *Sex* for Lee?
- Data File "B" has a record 525 not present in File "A." Should we then merge the records from the two files to get a complete set? Or perhaps File "B" is out of date, and the record should have been deleted from File "B" as well? This is another illustration of inconsistency.

3. Different/Changing Business Rules or Logic

In Exhibit 54.3, our hypothetical data warehouse draws information from both Files "A" and "C":

- Notice that Lee's *Smoker* status is "Y" in File "C." This is a result of a business rule in the application logic which says "Unless the individual specifically indicates that they are a nonsmoker, give them the smoker code." That rule is not present in the application producing File "A," causing the discrepancy.

Exhibit 54.3 Example of Different Logic

Identifier	*Last Name*	*Sex*	*Age*	*Smoker*
Data File "A"				
523	Smith	M	00	N
524	Jones	F	23	Y
526	Lee	M	42	
527	Frank		17	Y
528	Yu	M	00	N
Data File "C"				
523	Smith	M	99	N
524	Jones	F	22	N
525	Samuelson	M	54	Y
526	Lee	F	42	Y
527	Frank			

- Is there disagreement on Smith's age between the two files? No, it's just that the dummy value for File "C" happens to be "99" rather than "00."
- Is File "C" missing more data for Frank than File "A"? Yes, but it's intentional — the logic for File "C" refuses to store values for *Age* and *Smoker* unless all mandatory fields (including *Sex*) are completed.
- Note that these types of inconsistency can appear within a single file just as easily as between files, if the business rules/application logic changes over time.

4. Missing/Nonunique Primary Key

In Exhibit 54.4, our hypothetical data warehouse draws information from both Files "A" and "D":

- Data File "D" does not have the *Identifier* field, and in fact does not have a unique primary key. If we assume File "A" does not have the *First Name* field, then will you match record 523 with Fred Smith or with Sid Smith? Which File "D" record will you match record 528 with?
- At first glance, record 526 might seem an easy match. But can we really assume the 536 Lee is the same person as the File "D" Tom Lee?
- The bottom line here is that the lack of a primary key can be a major obstacle to accessing the data you need, even when the data is present in the files themselves.

5. Nonstandardized or Multi-element Fields

In Exhibit 54.5:

Exhibit 54.4 Example of Primary Key Problems

Identifier	*Last Name*	*Sex*	*Age*	*Smoker*
Data File "A"				
523	Smith	M	00	N
524	Jones	F	23	Y
526	Lee	M	42	
527	Frank		17	Y
528	Yu	M	00	N

Last Name	*First Name*	*Department*	*Yrs Employed*	*Salary*
Data File "D"				
Smith	Fred	40	2	50,000
Smith	Sid	40	3	75,000
Lee	Tom	30	3	60,000
Yu	Robert	50	1	45,000
Yu	Ted	30	6	80,000

- Do all these people work for the same company? If there were 5000 records to look at instead of just five, would you be able to identify the variations? Company names have not been standardized, and this is just a flavor of the possible result.
- In the *Name and Title* field, there is an even worse lack of standards. Some titles are spelled out in full ("Vice President"), others are abbreviated ("Sr V.P.") Some names are accompanied by designations ("Mr."), others aren't. And do we include the department or division ("I.S."), or don't we?
- The positioning of the information in the *Name and Title* field is also inconsistent, with some last names first, some first names first, one title (marketing representative) preceding the name while the others follow the name, and so on.
- In fact, there are several individual elements contained within the *Name and Title* field, which is a large part of the problem. These elements include the First Name, Last Name, Initial (if any), Designation (e.g., Mr., Dr.), Title, the Department (e.g., I.S., Operations), and even in one case, degrees (B.Comm.)
- The individual elements within *Name and Title* are almost impossible to work with as they are now. Even a simple alphabetical report sorted by last name could be impractical. Clearly, separate fields for separate elements makes life much easier.

Exhibit 54.5 Example of Nonstandardized and Multi-element Fields

Name and Title	*Company*
George Taylor, B.Comm.,Vice President	DEC
Levi, Dr. Harold P. Sr V.P.	Digital Equipment
Marketing Representative Tim Hanlon	Digital
O'Leary Don, Operations	Digital Corporation
Mr. E.Rourke, Mgr I.S.	Dec Corp

6. Invalid Values

The constraints defining what constitutes a "valid" value for any given field should be clearly defined within each database or file, as it will be different in every case, and can even change for the same field over time.

In Exhibit 54.6:

- If the only valid values for Sex are "M" or "F," then records 524 and 527 have invalid values. In the case of Jones, we know what was meant. In the case of Frank, however, the "N" might be a keystroke error, or it might mean "Not Known," or anything. Thus, without the proper edits, coded values can easily become corrupted.
- Age should always be numeric, which makes Lee's age invalid as entered (what if we tried to add or subtract from it?). Also, it is clear that Yu's age cannot be correct. The first problem illustrates that it is possible to get character data where numeric data is desired (and vice versa); the second illustrates that without edits, values can be entered outside the acceptable range or domain for that field.
- Which Social Insurance Numbers are valid? Certainly, Lee's and Yu's are not valid and, depending on our formatting rules, Jones' may or may not be OK as is. Text fields are often the most difficult to validate, which is why when there is a choice (such as with SIN) it is generally better to look for alternatives.

Exhibit 54.6 Example of Invalid Values

Identifier	*Last Name*	*Sex*	*Age*	*SIN*
523	Smith	M	00	143-476-987
524	Jones	Female	23	547198234
526	Lee	M	Forty-two	657-432-89
527	Frank	N	17	654-975-298
528	Yu	M	222	674-A27-897

Exhibit 54.7 Example of Incorrect Values

Last Name	*First Name*	*Department*	*Yrs Employed*	*Salary*
Data File "D"				
Smith	Fred	40	2	50,000
Smith	Sid	40	3	75,000
Lee	Tom	30	3	60,000
Yu	Robert	50	1	45,000
Yu	Ted	30	6	80,000

Department	*Total Years*	*Total Salary*	*Total Staff*	*Avg Salary*
Data File "E"				
30	8	140,000	2	70,000
40	5	125,000	2	65,000
50	1	45,000	1	45,000

7. Incorrect Values

In Exhibit 54.7, our hypothetical data warehouse draws information from both Files "D" and "E":

- Although the *Avg Salary* should have been the result of dividing the *Total Salary* by the *Total Staff,* somehow a mistake was made for Department 40, as 125,000/2 = 62,500, not 65,000. Derived or calculated data can be in error within the same record or file.
- Although the *Total* columns in File "E" were intended to sum the data of File "D," a calculation mistake was made in the *Total Years* (of experience) for Department 30 (should be 9, not 8). Thus, derived or summary data in one file can also be incorrect based upon the data in a completely different file.
- These types of erroneous values can easily corrupt other results. For example, there may be a field in a third file containing the difference in average wages between men and women. Depending on whether File "E" is used for source data (*Avg Salary*), the resulting calculation may be accurate, or not.

8. Referential Integrity Violations

Referential integrity is a constraint to ensure that relationships between rows of data exist, and in particular that one row of data will exist if another does (generally in different tables).

In Exhibit 54.8, our hypothetical data warehouse draws information from both Files "A" and "F":

Exhibit 54.8 Example of Referential Integrity Problems

Identifier	*Last Name*	*Sex*	*Age*	*Smoker*
Data File "A"				
523	Smith	M	00	N
524	Jones	F	23	Y
526	Lee	M	42	
527	Frank		17	Y
528	Yu	M	00	N

Identifier	*Current Salary*	*Yr-1 Salary*	*Yr-2 Salary*	*Yr-3 Salary*
Data File "F"				
523	0	0	55,000	45,000
523	75,000	65,000	0	0
524	63,000	58,000	53,000	50,000
525	53,500	48,800	45,000	42,300
527	51,800	47,700	43,500	40,200
528	45,000	45,000	38,500	37,500

- Although Data File "F" has *Identifier* as a key, unfortunately it is not unique, as can be seen from the two 523 rows. While under some circumstances this would boil down to a primary key issue (possibly combined with a missing, invalid, or redundant data issue), in this particular case it appears we should be consolidating the data in the two rows.
- There is no entry in File "F" corresponding to record 526 from File "A." This is a clear violation of referential integrity, as Lee must (at the very least) have a current-year salary recorded.
- Record 525 in File "F" has no corresponding entry in File "A," so just who is this a salary record for? This is an example of an "orphaned" record (does not have a "parent" record).

9. Special Case: Dates

Dates can be tricky to work with for a number of reasons:

- Many possible representations, including:
  - Multiple date formats (e.g., YYDDD, CCYYMMDD, DDMMYY)
  - Multiple internal storage options, depending on language, OS, etc.
  - Dates are often stored in pure numeric fields, or within text fields
- There are a large number of ways default or dummy dates have been established, some of which can be quite confusing:
  - Is 99365 (Dec 31, 1999) a dummy value, or a legitimate date?
  - How about 010101 (Jan 1, 2001)? 999999?
  - If your programs run across 000000 in the Year 2000, what action will they take? What action should they take?

- The year 2000 itself will cause many of the existing dates and formats to become unacceptable, whereas up to now they may have worked just fine.
  - Two-digit years will need to be accompanied by two-digit century values, **or**
  - Some interim solution based (for example) on sliding date windows will need to be adopted, **or**
  - A business decision to accept the risks and potential consequences of inaccurate processing will need to be made by the enterprise

10. Special Case: Addresses

Addresses can be complicated to work with because they routinely combine many of the issues we have described into just a few fields, with the resulting combination being particularly challenging to unravel or to correct. These problems can include[4]:

- No common customer key across records and files
- Multiple names within one field
- One name across two fields
- Name and address in same field
- Personal and commercial names mixed
- Different addresses for the same customer
- Different names and spellings for same customer
- "Noisy" name and address domains
- Inconsistent use of special characters
- Multiple formats within disparate data files
- Legacy data buried and floating within free-form fields
- Multiple account numbers blocking a consolidated view
- Complex matching and consolidation
- Data values that stray from their descriptions and business rules

Conclusion

Knowing your enemy is the first step toward defeating him. In this case, the enemy is "bad" data, and this chapter has illustrated several ways in which poor-quality data can be present in your files. The task for you, the reader, is to use the examples provided and apply them to your own specific systems and databases. Assess the severity of the situation, evaluate the cost-effectiveness or desirability of taking corrective action, and proceed accordingly.

Notes

1. Brethenoux, E., "Data Quality — The Missing Link in Data Mining." *Gartner Group* (October 29, 1996).
2. Redman, T.C., "The Impact of Poor Data Quality on the Typical Enterprise." *Communications of the ACM* (February, 1998).
3. Strong, D.M., Lee Y.W., and Wang R.Y., "Data Quality in Context." *Communications of the ACM* (May, 1997).
4. "The Five Legacy Data Contaminants You Will Encounter in Your Warehouse Migration." White paper provided by Vality Technology Incorporated. Obtained from http://www.datawarehouse.com.

Further Reading

1. Zimmer, M., "Data Conversion: Doing it Right the First Time." *Handbook of Data Management 1999.* S. Purba, Ed. 1999. Auerbach Publications, Boca Raton, FL.
2. "Customer Data Quality." White paper provided by *i.d.Centric.* Obtained from http://www.idcentric.com.

Chapter 55

Oracle Express Development in the Enterprise

Paul Mundell

The road from business data to business information is often tortuous, requiring countless hours of authentication and transformation. It seems that those who most need access to the business information are destined to articulate their needs in terms of what they already "don't have." A first pass at an Online Analytic Processing (OLAP) application is often little more than a proof of concept. Conventional OLAP applications anticipate the general need for authentication and transformation and provide easy-to-use tools to accommodate these aspects of the OLAP process. Generally, they sow the seeds of their own limitations with modifiers such as Desktop OLAP (DOLAP), Multidimensional OLAP (MOLAP), Relational OLAP (ROLAP), and Hierarchical OLAP (HOLAP). In fact, Oracle's Express satisfies all of these flavors of OLAP. These tools typically represent a finished application with a functionality that has been wholly specified "out-of-the-box." Deviation from the script quickly results in less-than-supportable workarounds. Thus, OLAP applications fail when they are required to adapt to a constantly changing business process with the accompanying sets of new business rules. It is here that Oracle Express comes in. More than a language, Express is a complete OLAP development environment that can support development of extensible OLAP applications. This chapter examines those features of Oracle Express that make it a world-class platform for the staging of OLAP development.

Data Analysis and Data Collection

Data collection and data analysis are sister processes, neither of which should be subordinate to the other. Computer-aided analysis has been part of the

0-8493-1139-X/02/$0.00+$1.50
©2002 by CRC Press LLC

enterprise for as long as computers have been used to capture business activity. Any time there is a large body of data, there is an analysis requirement. These requirements include the following:

- Exception reporting
- Auditing
- Summarization

Historically, because of its excessive demands on computing resources, analysis was performed in batches overnight when the computer resources were generally more available. System requirements focused on the maximum number of simultaneous users making simple requests. Analysis requirements that were more difficult to estimate would be addressed later or not at all.

Today, business information is expected to be delivered in a timely manner. Analysis cannot be allowed to interfere with the support of direct revenue-generating processes, nor will today's user community tolerate it being banished to the discretionary realm of batch reporting. Separate and scalable resources for analysis are a requirement of any large-scale enterprise. Analysis of business information at all levels is critical to the successful operation of the enterprise.

In data collection, the underlying data and application models are slowly changing. Generous accommodation is made for simultaneous access, but the resources allocated to an individual request is presumed small and manageable. An institutional framework exists for modifying the underlying data and application models, which has the effect of slowing future system evolution to an administratively manageable pace. On the other hand, the nature of analysis requirements, by its essential definition, defies scoping and "pigeon-holing."

In analysis, a single query may consume all available resources. In data collection, there is a presumption of the smallness and locality of the data addressed or changed. In analysis, there can be no such assumptions; by its very nature, analysis requirements imply simultaneous non-local access to all of the business data. Data collection will typically take small incremental changes from many sources at the same time, creating a large operational data store, which in aggregate will be too voluminous to review on a line-by-line basis. Data analysis will take this voluminous source and condense it into a reviewable form suitable for use in basic activities, such as the aforementioned audit, exception reporting, and summarization.

The OLAP Problem

Scalability in the OLAP world is far less predictable and needs a different and more flexible scalability strategy. In particular, commonly interpretable business aggregates (dimensions) need to be identified and common OLAP queries need to be stratified based on the "depth" and complexity. For example, an FAQs (frequently asked queries) dictionary needs to be compiled. Finally, to support these aggregates with elemental data, dynamics links back to the supporting data must be maintainable.

The business goal of OLAP is the effective selection and mapping of flexible business dimensions and processes. These entities are contained in various operational data stores throughout the enterprise. Thus, both the initial choice of mapping and the ability of the environment to adapt to significant changes in the business environment in great measure determines the success of OLAP. Information is collected from diverse areas of the enterprise that may not have incentives to cooperate. (Often, it is not until an exchange of information is agreed upon that provides benefit to all parties involved that the reliability of the effort can be assured.) This often suggests an iterative "slow-roasting" approach, allowing all of the disparate data stores to "uncoil" gently and mesh with each other (much like the proteins in a roast). Attempts to hurry the process can result in the disparate data stores springing open chaotically, leading to confusion and lack of data integrity.

Oracle Development and the OLAP Problem

Oracle's approach to the OLAP problem is two-phased. First, introduce the user community to the basic data store through Oracle's Discoverer product and use the information gathered to identify the needs for more sophisticated analyses. Then use Express as a platform to build a flexible OLAP application that will be able to adapt to changing business analysis requirements. Discoverer is an easy-to-use and easy-to-administer ROLAP tool that will often satisfy an enterprise's initial analysis requirements. From the administrative perspective, Discoverer provides a graphical user interface (GUI) tool for creating and managing virtual dimensions, measures, and hierarchies. From the user perspective, dimensions, measures, and hierarchies are transformed into configurable views with the ubiquitous rotates and drills. These views can be stored either in the database for shared/published use or locally as files. Through the creation and management of these views, the user community can become familiar with the basic configurable access to the underlying data.

Discoverer serves the all-important frontline role of creating the demand for OLAP information. Discoverer does not represent a complete OLAP solution. It fails to satisfy several scalability requirements. These include sharing the computing resources with the data collection process (because it is ROLAP-based) and providing only limited support for sequential investigation. What follows are some features of Express that address the OLAP scalability problem:

1. *The Express platform for a clean separation of the analysis platform from the data collection platform.* Express is an autonomous OLAP platform that can (and should) be installed on separate hardware. An Express database can exist independently of any underlying relational database.
2. *The Express instance is separate from the Express data.* An Express database is a simple file or, when it goes to extraordinary size, a group of files. By making these files accessible to multiple instances of Express running on different hardware platforms, it is possible to isolate the

impact of one platform's query on the other. For example, one could allocate certain deep, resource-intensive queries to an instance of Express that would be allowed to devote 100 percent of its resources to executing that query, while another instance of Express remains dedicated to handling the more routine queries. This presents unique options for scalability just by adding platforms. In this case, there is a *de facto* clustering solution where the queries or data requests get assigned to the most appropriate hardware based on query depth and often along with hardware availability. Note that from the relational database perspective, all of this management happens on the application level.

3. *The Express database is dimensionally aware.* Express acts on its multidimensional variables as a relational database table would if it supported automatic indexing for each of its dimensional elements.
4. *Support for a fine level of control about where and when the elements of the business aggregates are calculated and stored as well as access to intermediate results.* Using Express, it is possible to decide where aggregation and transformation take place. With Express, one can force the relational database to do certain aggregations on the relational side and then bring the data into Express database. Alternatively, the detailed tables can be brought into Express and aggregated and transformed by the Express platform. The detail or aggregate data can then be stored in Express either temporarily or permanently. Express provides for dynamic and simultaneous access to multiple data sources while allowing for the final assembly and display to take place on the desktop. The final assembly is defined as the result that can reasonably be reviewed by an analyst (certainly thousands of rows are plausible, but tens of thousands probably pushes the envelope). Part of the process that needs to precede final assembly would likely include compressing the delivered result using the aforementioned principles of audit, summarization, and exception.
5. *Support for intra-server communication.* Express instances can communicate directly with one another, allowing for the coordinated distribution of tasks among themselves. These tasks executed on the remote instance of Express (the server side) can incorporate information from the calling instance of Express (the client side) in the same call. This information can include any aspect of the calling instance's operating environment or elements of calling instance's attached Express databases.
6. *Support for a powerful, dimensionally aware fourth-generation language (4GL).* Express maintains support for a comprehensive programming language. Most OLAP products support a scripting language. A scripting language maintains a first level of lexical consistency that allows for the interpretation and execution of simple commands concatenated into a script. Express's 4GL maintains a robust level of support for programming, including a full-featured debugging and program

trace facility. Beyond the basics, it is possible to develop a palette of Express tools in support of the particular OLAP application.

7. *Support for dynamic and mutable scenario creation (what-if analysis).* By default, Express users attach to an Express database in read-only mode. This allows them to view a snapshot of the database based on when they attached. Express then allows the user to make changes to their snapshot of the underlying database, run Express 4GL programs against their changes, and analyze the results. As it does this, the underlying database remains unchanged and available to other users for viewing.
8. *Support for persistent user-aware Web sessions across a Common Gateway Interface.*

More on the Express Development

Express is at once a combination of database, application development environment, and application in its own right. Perhaps surprisingly, among the more important things stored in a typical Express application is data about the application itself (not to exclude the programs). The integration of a database with a development environment is especially appealing when you consider the possibilities of using database query tools on the application support data (particularly the programs). Express maintains a global and programmatically accessible dictionary of all global elements and their properties. This access and these properties prove extraordinarily useful when developing general application tools. One of the little-considered aspects of Express development is what happens when your integrated development environment includes a full-featured database. This is what causes Express development to fit awkwardly between three programming paradigms. With its liberal use of and reliance on "global" information, Express applications may appear to be "data driven." On the other hand, given the structure and procedural nature of its 4GL, Express can appear to fall into the structure programming camp of development. Finally, exploitating its dimensionally aware expressions (objects) and its use of runtime resolutions of executable expressions (late binding) will make Express seem object-oriented.

By way of illustration, what follows is a short example of some Express 4GL code that loops through a list of Express instances that in turn establish connections to relational databases and update these remote Express databases with data from the relational databases. Note that many simplifying assumptions have been made for the sake of brevity. If we have a dimension called `_datamart` and variables of the form `_dmart.*` dimensioned by `_datamart`, then our little code snippet could look like this:

```
PROGRAM _DATAMANAGER
comset type socket
For _datamart
   Do
   connect server _dmart.server id _dmart.user password _dmart.psswrd
```

```
    _dmart.sess = comunit
    xopen on _dmart.sess
    execute joinchars('database attach ' _dmart.db ' rw') on _dmart.sess
    export &_dmart.load to eif pipeline dfns on _dmart.sess
    execstart joinchars('call ' _dmart.load '(' _dmart.con ')') on
      _dmart.sess
    execute 'update'
    doend

  while true
    do
    limit _datamart to _dmart.status eq 0 ifnone alldone
    for _datamart
      do
      _dmart.status = execstatus( on _dmart.sess )
      if _dmart.status eq 1
        then show joinchars(_dmart.name ' - Successfully Loaded')
      if _dmart.status eq -1
        then show joinchars(_dmart.name ' - An Error Occurred')
      doend
    doend
  alldone:
  show 'Loading Completed'
  END
```

And it has an actual loading program that looks like this:

```
PROGRAM _DATALOADER
argument connectstring text

SQL.DBMS = 'ORACLE'
SQL connect &connectstring
SQL declare c1 cursor for -
select branch,sum(sales) from datatable group by branch
SQL open c1
while SQLCODE eq 0
  SQL fetch c1 into :append branch,:sales
SQL close c1
SQL rollback
END
```

Even without knowledge of the Express 4GL, the preceding can be reviewed as an indication of the unique way Express does things. This code snippet highlights several of the aforementioned features that make Express extensible and scalable. The *connect thru xopen* commands establish what are called XCA (Express Communications Architecture) dialogs with other Express instances for each dimension value of `_datamart`. Then the following execute command executes the Express command built up by the joinchars function on the remote Express instance and waits for completion before returning control back to the calling instance (synchronously). This will attach the Express database of the remote instance with a name that is contained in the Express variable `_dmart.db` of the calling instance. Here, as throughout this Express program, you can see the transparent simultaneous mixing of both client and server data in a "single" Express command. The name of the database comes from the calling instance, while the action applies to the remote instance. Next, the data-loading program, which is defined and stored in the calling instance is "injected" into the remote instance, with the export command. This data-loading program is then executed on the remote instance asynchronously with the *execstart* command. Control is immediately returned to the calling instance, and the calling instance moves on the next `_datamart` to initiate then next data-loading program. The `while` loop following the initial loop cycles through the Express instances, checking the completion status and terminating when all of the instances have completed their data loads. The `_DATALOADER` program would be called by each remote Express instance in which `_dmart.load` contained the text value `_DATALOADER`. In other words,

```
->Show _dmart.load
_DATALOADER
```

Notice that even in the data-loading program, the freedom aggregate is either on the relational database side, as is done here, or it reads the elemental data on the Express side and Express does the aggregation. The actual path chosen depends on the relative needs of each platform (the relational database or the Express Platform). In managing the scalability, having the flexibility to easily shift the computer resources around is key to being able to adapt to ever-changing user requirements.

Very few OLAP products can provide a framework for developing of applications that efficiently adapt to the ever-changing business process. Unlike many other OLAP development efforts in the enterprise, Express development — once it takes root — tends to grow in usefulness and scope. That is because the initial OLAP specification generally represents only a first draft and merest shadow of the final user requirement. The road to business information is heavily mined with partially conceived user requirements and political intrigue. Bringing OLAP to the enterprise is fraught with the risk of satisfying those requirements while losing the hearts and minds of the intended user community. Express represents the opportunity to accommodate the current requirements while maintaining a framework for future expansions and adaptation.

Chapter 56

An Approach to Load Analysis and Stress Testing

J.B. Sastry

The issues discussed in this chapter are relevant to data-server load analysis and stress testing of custom or packaged applications on Oracle RDBMS. A comprehensive, enterprise-level test suite should also include components for network and middle-tier software/process server evaluation. The concepts described here may form the strategic back plane for application and site-specific solutions for performance and scalability testing needs on Oracle platform.

Changing Business Needs

Businesses are increasingly being driven in their IT strategies through rapid application development, enhancement, and deployment made possible by innovative technologies and solution suites. While some of these changes are ornamental in value, some others have deep impact and are voluminous. Furthermore, the effects of changes are not readily known until actual deployment into production systems, leading to experimentation at high risk. Often, the cost of such high risks forces organizations to be "laggards" in implementing technological advancements, a clearly disconcerting situation with high opportunity costs of nonadoption for the IT houses and a dearth in market for the software developer.

Means and *modus operandi* to enhance the ability of IT managers in developing rational and effective models to successfully tackle the predictive problems form the core intent of this chapter. Ability to simulate targets and stress testing are perennially challenging tasks. These attempts strive to develop

0-8493-1139-X/02/$0.00+$1.50
©2002 by CRC Press LLC

capabilities for quantification of verifiable load definitions, and recognition and extrapolation of system load patterns, among other aspects.

Before delving into the mechanics of quantitative load modeling, let us take a look at some compulsive scenarios that demand a proactive stance from IT managers:

Rapidly Growing Environments

High growth in the number of users or, as is more often the case, addition of user communities to existing applications, results in increased data volumes and connections. Changing IT paradigms such as Web enabling existing client/server operations, object orientation, extensible framework for multimedia and other nonconventional database applications drastically alter the variables and bring in hitherto-unknown system load patterns.

Morphing Application Logic

The need is to predict the effects of a change to a software module or a version change in existing software. The software change needs to be tested in a reliable environment that closely resembles the production environment. This is the only way to reliably account for interdependencies between user processes and inevitable resource contention. Also, at a more subtle level, consider a change in user populations and the mix of their application roles. A change of 30–70 mix of `READ-ONLY` to `INSERT-UPDATE` users has different aggregate load characteristics when compared to a 50–50 system.

Hardware- or Architectural-Related Changes

Rearchitecture options demand the most economic solutions: the biggest bang for the buck. They are also very expensive and long-thought-out processes. Developing the ability to simulate current loads, and playing with "what-if" alternative and migratory situations adds tremendous value to such strategic planning. Integration of multiple applications systems into central data warehouses is another trend facilitated by dynamic and extensible architectures such as NUMA, and robust software solutions such as Web servers, Universal DBs, and so on. The older, nicer practice of dividing and managing smaller applications may not work well with changing needs to integrate the whole breadth and spectrum of data for CRM and other emerging data-hungry analytical pursuits.

Performance Tuning

For a cost-effective solution, a data center needs to correctly identify and tune resources in an efficient and proactive manner. Experimentation on a test server running closely comparable loads to production provides an excellent opportunity to hypothesize, experiment, and evaluate the effects of tuning critical parameters.

Service Level Agreements (SLAs)

Many large organizations have contractual responsibilities to their customers to provide a certain level of service. Often this is expressed in terms of response times for some number of concurrent users on given transactions. To live up to these commitments, an organization needs an extremely accurate testing model to ensure that the technical environment that is ultimately used can support the required number of users and data volumes. I would be remiss in not mentioning the latest marketing concept of business-online offering. Business houses, Oracle included, are offering IT services to businesses at large with captive control over application and data administration. It is probable that under such offloaded IT businesses, the customer contracts would mostly hinge around SLAs on selected business transactions.

Problems and Issues

While there are excellent scaling and capacity planning tools available, their capability to closely simulate realistic client environments is limited.[1] Test results from these tools may point to laboratory rather than actual conditions, depending upon the assumptions made in planning the test. Several test designs have been observed to be limited by a theoretical vacuum when faced with reality checks such as, What loads are we simulating? What period of future growth are they corresponding to? How do we validate the exercise?

Duplicating an entire production environment in a test center is also a very expensive solution, due to the difficulty of imitating actual transaction volumes and the randomness of the transaction mix. If played back through middle-tier application and method servers, providing for large numbers of such servers can be an expensive proposition.

There are many SQL and Window-action replay software packaged solutions that can efficiently copy the end-user-generated SQL or mouse-clicks to play back on the data servers. However, the issue appears to be the rationalization of the test dynamics, rather than the ability to replay load. Consider, for example, the constraints of randomization of Data Manipulation Language (DML), which otherwise tend to skew results owing to prevailing data-access mechanisms, such as data caching, delayed writing, and shared or exclusive locking asides of I/O subsystem spread. The test loads should not create inadvertent contention, which does not otherwise exist in production.

The inability to accurately define and measure the "load" thus is a difficult problem to resolve. Capacity planning tools, on the other hand, rely on extrapolating prevailing numbers on production servers to predict problem thresholds under limitations of backbone of validity and empirical evidence. Today's high-cost environments demand complete authentication of the results and assumptions prior to investments on migrations or rearchitectures.

Problems with Application Scaling and Some Possible Remedies

Traditional stress testing approaches generally involve capture and replay of some user SQL and on-the-screen behavior. Depending on the objectives of such testing efforts, one might find a few issues cropping up at analysis time. See Appendix 56.1 for a table presenting such issues.

A General, Methodological Solution

The ideas presented above are for a conceptually variant methodology that splits and redefines the server loads into multiple dimensions of the Oracle server's internal processes. This is a minor paradigm shift from the normal and conventional load and capacity measurements such as CPU utilization. The ability to split the loads into database-related activities automatically facilitates "fashioning" of loads into scenarios, making it possible to simulate skewed loads on the test servers specific to peak load situations in the multi-user production system. Principally aimed at resolving scaling issues at the data-server level, this methodology provides opportunities to create a test lab environment that can easily change loads to suit different data server stress situations. Mathematical modeling enables load optimization through integer programming and other techniques. Loads can be "concocted" to variant situations, such as "before noon peak OLTP" scenario versus "5 P.M. batch job runs," as long as we measure what the loads are in production. Even in a multi-tier interactive environment, reliability of scalability testing can be enhanced through modeling background loads on the data servers while checking response times from the client stations.

The main components of this tool-technique are:

- Load profiling:
  - Profile existing production
  - Load profile extensions for future
- Load generation/modeling:
  - Generate generic load
  - Generate application load
  - Generate "what-if ..." load
  - Generate loads for tuning
  - Select combinations of SQL
  - Project loads based on business proxies
- Analyzing results

Exhibit 56.1 illustrates the workflow in this methodology. The rest of this chapter concentrates on introducing the principal idea of load definition and its applicability to business intense situations.

Immediate Gain

Background Loads

An obvious advantage is the ability to routinely create desired load-effects as background loads to check performance of software releases or upgrades, leveraging their performance testing.

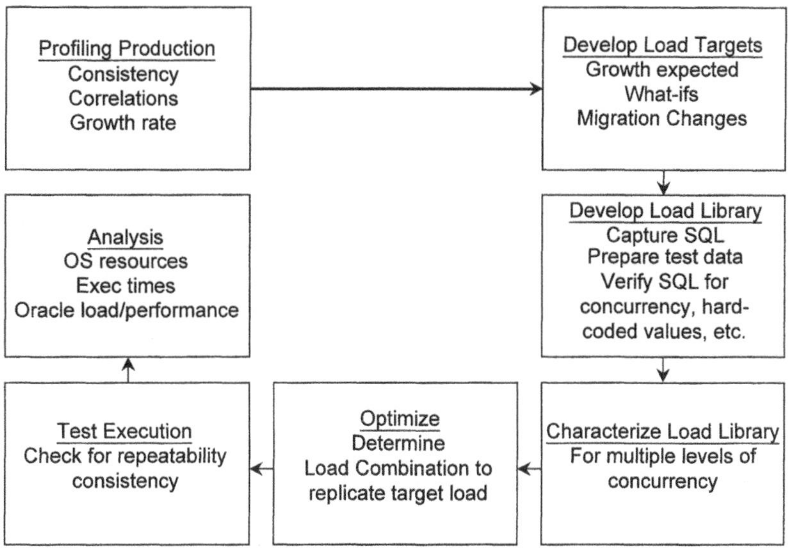

Exhibit 56.1 Process Flow in Stress Testing Methodology

What-if Testing

Configuration options of Oracle database installations can be evaluated in a realistic environment. Tuning options can be projected, evaluated, and tested beforehand for one-shot implementation in production units. On busy 24 × 7 systems, this can be a great advantage because trials and failures are prohibitively expensive.

Service Level Agreements

SLAs on user-specified transactions can be checked against simulated background loads for mutual acceptance.

Scaling for the Future

The methodology can be extended through mathematical simulation models for projecting into the future. This can serve vital capacity planning and other strategic needs of mid- to long-term planners in IS departments.

Technical Concepts

Load Factors (Oracle-Reported System Statistics)

Oracle server reports statistics on the whole set of activities taking place in the system on a continuous basis. These are reported at both a user session level and at the aggregate system level. Further, some of these are reported on a

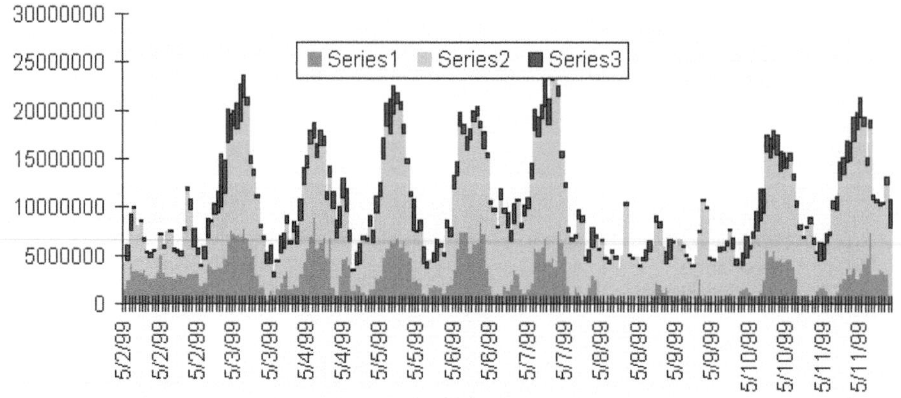

Exhibit 56.2 Intensity of Physical Reads in the Oracle Database Across Weekdays/Hours

cumulative basis (since the start-up of the instance) and some as of that instance of time. By organizing a periodic collection of these statistics and computing their periodic differences (deltas), we can derive the amount of the activity over that period of time. Some generic scripts can easily be developed to LOG these extractions from the `V$SYSSTAT` view. The deltas (hourly increments) against specific clock hours (for example, 8 A.M. through 9 A.M.) can then be used to trend over a period of time and chart the load characteristics, differentiating peak OLTP loads from batch loads, or other situations, such as `READ-INTENSIVE-HIGH-USER_LOGIN` situations versus `WRITE-INTENSIVE-BATCH-UPDATE` processes. A quick look at the following set of charts illustrates the point.

Exhibit 56.2 shows the load patterns (in this case, `PHYSICAL READS` performed) of a system of overlapping Oracle databases.

The `SORTING` activity in the system at the corresponding times is shown in Exhibit 56.3.

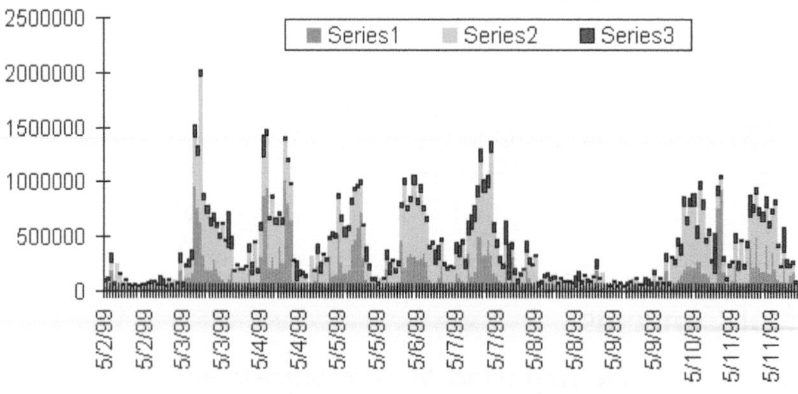

Exhibit 56.3 Intensity of Sorts (Rows) in the Oracle Database Across Weekdays/Hours

The shapes on weekdays of 05/03/99 through 05/07, and 05/10 and 05/11 are distinctly different from those on the weekends. The consistent shapes are also suggestive of steady-state loads. Finding patterns among these leads took some useful assumptions and deductive work.

Some deductions follow:

- Repetitive patterns are pointing to the steady-state aggregate behavior in the applications. A further look into hourly or half-hourly numbers would indicate load intensities across specific time frames. Such time series data is very advantageous in load balancing activities through activity scheduling. For example, the deferred surges between peaks of London to New York stock markets can nicely allow proactive planning of computing resources scheduling!
- The shapes of different load factors (statistics) tends to be different based on the activity and the load dimension they are reflecting. Additional discussion is provided later on these factors and what they represent in load dimensions. To illustrate the point, consider a combination of `PHY READS`, `WRITES`, and `SORTS` to be representative of an intensive batch operation as against a `RECURSION` and `PARSE` of an intensive OLTP activity.
- Steady-state patterns automatically mean statistical trending and reproducibility. However complex they may be, repetitive patterns may be related to correlation analysis. Multiple regression modeling comes to the rescue by also predicting the R-squared values, as a measure of reliability and confidence on such predictive equations.
- The patterns emerge out of the aggregate application behavior, as dictated by the user community and business needs. This is the most essential part needing reproduction during test simulations!

Load Factors

Among the 180+ statistics reported by Oracle through the view `V$SYSSTAT`, the following few are chosen to represent various dimensions of the system load. This selection is purely experiential, and may shrink or expand depending on the load situation being studied, accuracy desired, and the operational logic of the business application.

Some of the important factors that are considered representative of load intensity are[2]:

- User logins, calls, commits, rollbacks
- Write requests, physical reads and writes
- Redo entries, size, DB block changes
- Table fetches by rowid, full-table scans
- Parse counts, parse-time CPU, opened cursors cumulative
- Sorts — rows, in memory and on disk

Exhibit 56.4 Critical Oracle Statistics

BYTES RECEIVED VIA SQL*NET FROM CLIENT
BYTES RECEIVED VIA SQL*NET FROM DBLINK
BYTES SENT VIA SQL*NET TO CLIENT
BYTES SENT VIA SQL*NET TO DBLINK
CLUSTER KEY SCANS
CONSISTENT CHANGES
CONSISTENT GETS
CR BLOCKS CREATED
CURSOR AUTHENTICATIONS
DB BLOCK CHANGES
DB BLOCK GETS
DBWR BUFFERS CANNED
DBWR FREE BUFFERS FOUND
DBWR LRU SCANS
DBWER MAKE FREE REQUE
DBWR SUMMED SCAN DEP
DIRTY BUFFERS INSPECTED
ENQUEUE CONVERSIONS
ENQUEUE RELEASES
ENQUEUE REQUESTS
EXECUTE COUNT
FREE BUFFER INSPECTED
LOGONS CUMULATIVE
MESSAGES RECEIVED
OPENED CURSORS CUMULATIVE
PARSE COUNT
PARSE TIME CPU
PHYSICAL READS
PHYSICAL WRITES
RECURSIVE CALLS
RECURSIVE CPU USAGE
REDO BLOCKS WRITTEN
REDO ENTRIES
REDO SIZE
REDO SMALL COPIES
REDO WASTAGE
REDO WRITES
ROLLBACK CHANGES – UNDO RECORDS APPLIED
ROLLBACKS ONLY – CONSISTENT READ GETS
SESSION LOGICAL READS
SORTS (MEMORY)
SORTS (ROWS)
TABLE FETCH BY ROWID
TABLE SCAN BLOCKS GOTTEN
TABLE SCAN ROWS GOTTEN
TABLE SCANS (LONG TABLES)
TABLE SCANS (SHORT TABLES)
USER CALLS
USER COMMITS
USER ROLLBACKS
WRITE REQUESTS

As generally known, these factors combine with the Wait events (resources), I/O subsystem, and Data volumes to complete the picture.

It is best to track all the critical statistics over a period of time, and then choose the ones meaning the most to us. The typical start-up list is shown in Exhibit 56.4.[3] Relative rankings are dependent upon the target load scenario being studied. Parsing activity may have a higher priority in an OLTP load and against a write intensity under a batch situation. In choosing our representative load factors, we are effectively defining the dimensions in which our load manifests.

Interfactor Prioritization and Ranking

It is recommended to identify and group the factors into "strata" of importance. The first layer may comprise up to 15 factors that are directly driven by the application. For example, these might include user connections, cursors, parsing, execute calls, tablescans, rows/blocks loaded into cache, consistent blocks, and so forth. These primary factors can thus be examined for covariance with application-related logical factors (business proxies).[4]

Interfactor ranking would enable formulating the load factor matrix that is representative of a given load scenario. This matrix is then our quantified measure of the system load.

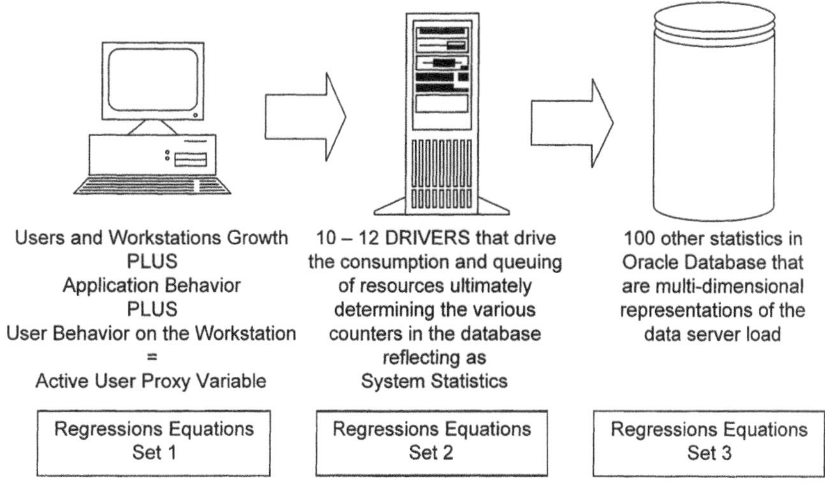

Exhibit 56.5 Multi-stage, Multi-variate Regressions

Regression Models

The next capability is the development of regression equations which would enable projections of these load factors into the future. Exhibit 56.5 explains this idea with different stages of regression.

- The first set is the identification and quantification of business proxies. These are variables that denote changes in the application usage. Some sample variables are the number of manufactured units or population of users.
- The second set in Exhibit 56.5 represents primary factors that are influenced by business proxies.
- The third set is the rest of the load factors that are driven by the primary factors. These are largely configuration driven.

Thus, in the multi-stage regression[5] scheme we are attempting to account for multiple forces:

- Business growth scenarios
- Primary load vectors from business growth variables, reflective of translation of business logic into primitive work operations
- Their cumulative effect on the entire system, accounting for the application configuration and system architecture

Applications of Quantitative Load Definitions[6]

Having cracked the enigma of metricating loads, prioritization and their projection into the future enriches our stress testing and performance management

Exhibit 56.6 Individual Characterized Loads Pool Together to Simulate a Desired Load Dimension

		4	5	6	7	8	9	10	11
		c1roll	c2cpux01	s1idle01	s1idle02dd	s1idle03	s1read01	s1read02	s1read03
Load Factor	Rank	217	100	116	326	656	1108	1128	1380
		0	0	30	8	5	2	1	1
		1	0	31	11	5	3	1	2
BYTES RECEIVED VIA SQL*NET F		722827	197249	1608211	5143927	10111122	3134279	9942604	22665876
BYTES RECEIVED VIA SQL*NET F		0	22249	1562	37210	27266	0	0	0
BYTES SENT VIA SQL*NET TO CL		327085	128034	2389109	6267149	13332050	2003695	5808684	12948268
BYTES SENT VIA SQL*NET TO DE		0	73639	1355	34219	21162	0	0	0
CLUSTER KEY SCANS	3	5074	307	556	1935	3682	2876	7367	19024
CONSISTENT CHANGE	1	2648	230	867	2337	17263	84	1229	5100
CONSISTENT GETS	2	341387	50119	161993	679793	1891211	153222	893117	2645501

abilities in many ways. These techniques can be deployed for many applications, some of which are discussed below.

Load Mixing in Test Scenarios

Having extrapolated the target load as a set of numbers, it is possible to put together a mix of load generating SQL/application replays. We can even measure the proximity of such load mixes to the target set of numbers for evaluating confidence levels. A fictitious miniature scenario is presented in Exhibit 56.6 for illustration. Column numbers 4 through 11 represent the "effect" of each test script run on the system. The shaded rows are the number of executions of the script within the load mix for accomplishing a given target load.[7]

Test Evaluation

Because we are working in measurable load definitions, it is possible to compare and evaluate the execution of a load test. The variations of the select few load factors from target to accomplishments would give us the acceptability of test results and validate the observations. As a corollary, any major deviations from target loads would portray load deviations. Unpredictable test behaviors can then be diagnosed and the tests invalidated. Without such a measurable basis, we cannot infer operational skews merely by looking at aggregate resource consumption statistics.

Target Simulations

Because any load target is a matrix of load factor-intensity values, we will be able to develop complex load simulations through resolving them into number games. This adds versatility to an otherwise dry topic of load simulations. In more complex systems involving multi-application interactions, it is now possible to individually load interactive systems to desired target proximity. This would authenticate the test processes and philosophy.

Test Scenarios and Failure Thresholds

Multifarious test scenarios can be developed through various load combinations and possibilities. On the failure threshold determination, it is possible

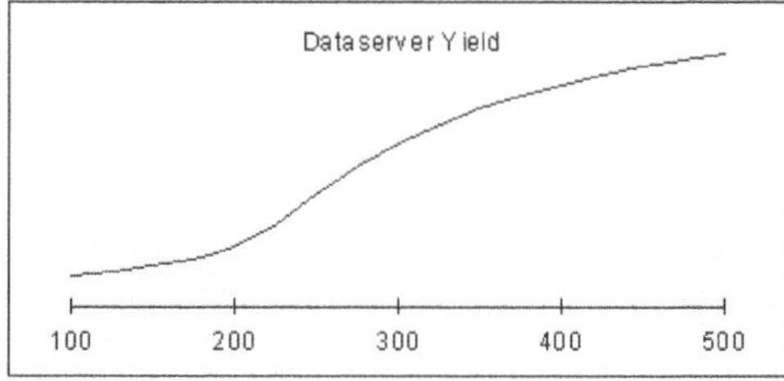

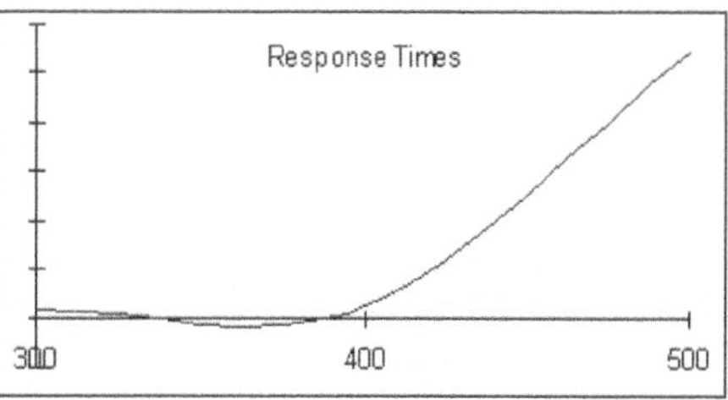

Exhibit 56.7 Dataserver Yield Restrictions Flattening the Curve at Threshold Load Levels; Response Times to User/Batch Operations Rise Accordingly

to establish the resources that will crunch as growing levels of loads are simulated. Taking a look at Exhibit 56.7, we see that the yield from the data server maximizes as the test loads are scaled from 100 to 500 percent of current production system. The response times, however, steeply go up — showing a decay in system performance. Observations during the tests would reveal that accomplished load factors fall short of targets. Due to the chokes in the system, operations will not progress at desired rates. The same decay in the system (noted by the response time surge) can also be measured and represented as a ratio of the load shortfall.

Tuning Considerations

By freezing a load mix and running under different tuned configurations, the response time changes would relatively evaluate the choices. The way to organize this facility is through the following steps:

1. Determine the target load scenario under which tuning would become necessary; for example, when some OLTP jobs are running with heavy CPU utilization. Tuning for parsing activity may reduce CPU bottlenecks. Brute-force solutions of adding resources do not always work and are often too expensive.
2. Once the tuning premise is established, determine the test that would reflect the tuning issues accurately. The load mix that will generate the test load simulation can be computed and frozen for the test duration.
3. Execute the test load the first time before tuning; note the response times and statistics. Tune and make changes and rerun the test loads. Comparisons will reveal the effects of tuning.

Tracking and Monitoring Growth

As part of the stress testing, businesses will identify the threshold points before which rearchitecture or resource augmentation is needed. Proactive management steps would then monitor the present growth rates and track load factors as the system progresses toward the breakpoints established by the stress tests. By virtue of quantifiable load factors, we can evolve certain critical performance ratios applicable to specific business environments and keep tabs on them. Performance ratios can be tracked on a peruser or per-unit-of-time basis, on a time series for progressive, qualitative evaluation.

Conclusion

This chapter attempted to present a newer approach to stress testing of Oracle-based application systems, with components that add value to the system-load testing efforts. Interested readers can contact the author for more information. As with any other innovation, this method may contain some debatable arguments and assumptions. Constructive discussions are welcome. All opinions expressed are the author's own and are not endorsed by Oracle Corporation.

Notes

1. Consider the issue of test data, for an example. All `SELECT`s in the test SQL should select valid rows. All `UPDATE`s should address valid existing rows and `INSERT`s should abide by the integrity and other business constraints. Then there are configuration issues, such as data volume spreads. If all the test data is "loaded" into the system for use during test, how much are we spreading the I/O, as it occurs in production? Ability to extract these anomalies is fairly limited without a more intricate approach.
2. Descriptions and definitions of these statistics can be found in any standard Oracle book or Oracle-supplied manuals.
3. Ranking among items facilitates grouping and classification, in addition to prioritization.
4. For a brief description, suffice it to say that business proxies are the variable influencing the primary load factors. In almost all cases, user population, concurrency, mix of their roles on the system, and data volumes relate to primary load factors very closely.
5. One small but important note is that the regressions in each stage are multivariate and nonlinear in nature. This is easy to foresee in such a complex environment involving shared resources and optimization thresholds. They are similar to econometrics used in policy formulations.
6. Readers should note that each of these applications deserve high attention and detail for actual implementation and are not covered in such detail. The main purpose here is to introduce an idea offering new solutions to a vexing old problem.
7. The solution is a typical OR problem involving integer (optionally linear) programming technique. We determine the load mix that maximizes the number of load factors within acceptable tolerance range. Please see http://www.Math.net/workload-modeling.html for a mathematical model and a detailed discussion on this aspect in a co-authored paper.

Appendix 56.1 Sample Problems and Solutions

Problem Area 1

Scaling is generally through a few selected transactions by increasing the number of concurrent users. This process may be less effective due to resource limitations of application and method servers.

Potential Remedy

Ability to operate at the back end through measuring and scaling the actual work done at the data server may help demystify the load generating process.

Problem Area 2

Inability to replicate the bundle (mix) of transactions that typically exist in the production server can be a constraint. The right mix of transactions and their multiplicity at any point of time is impossible to reproduce accurately in a test lab. Even if it could be reproduced, we do not have a way of confirming whether the resulting load is identical to that in production.

Potential Remedy

Determining the effects of such load causing user activities at the lowest, atomic levels opens up a broad new range of opportunities. The "load" in its final manifestation results in a set or a bundle of activities. Metrication and attributing these sets of resultant operations to a given business process or a transaction modifies our view of the "load" considerably. Such a paradigm shift also enables usage of quantitative and modeling techniques, for example, use of regression analysis to find an optimum mix of transactions that produce the desired load. The efficiency of such loads is measurable because we are now dealing with a set of atomic operations and their quantified intensities over a period of time under observation.

Problem Area 3

When multiple simulated users are fired up against specific transactions, a "data query skew" can occur if the concerned data is not realistically spread out across disk drives. In a normal production system tuned for performance, the data distribution and volumes are generally more balanced than in a data "copy" used for a typical test.

Potential Remedy

Dealing at an atomic level generally overcomes such skews. Also, the metrics of low-level operations readily indicate such behaviors and are useful in validating the quality of a test.

Problem Area 4

The transactions chosen for scaling may not be representative of a large spectrum of operations in the production system. It is very difficult to include all transactions in such a mix.

Potential Remedy

Our new-found ability to translate all loads into a set of atomic operations isolates the "causes" from "effects." Inherent advantages of this approach are obvious. We are intent on matching the metrics of a set of universal activities without worrying about the details of the jobs that caused them.

Problem Area 5

It is often assumed that the growth in number of users is representative of the application implementation growth. In fact, there are other hidden dimensions, such as data volumes and their spread, configuration of OS and DB, SQL logic changes in software version upgrades, etc.

Potential Remedy

Our ability to link and relate the low-level operations to the variations (covariance) to the business parameters opens an exciting possibility to define complex mathematical relationships for translating business variables into system loads. The dependencies among the variables and growth factors and the load defining low-level operations can help us develop regression models.

Problem Area 6

If two applications are interactive, it is very difficult to reproduce the resultant stresses at the time of testing due to mutual loading. Say, for example, system A1 stresses A2. Then to test A1, we also have to stress A2 because the ultimate performance of A1 is dependent upon response times from A2.

Potential Remedy

By focusing on the final load placed on the data server(s), we already take into account load factors such as interfaces and interdependencies of connected systems. These intricate details are typically not addressed by more traditional approaches.

Problem Area 7

It is impossible to simulate the behavioral habits (ergonomic, social) of end users on the system. They depend on perceived response times, human needs, and activity rates. Traditional stress testing methods string transactions together at increased user levels — resulting in an artificially high intensity of stress. The load is artificially high because breaks in user activity are not included or distributed in the test. A cyclical break (sleep) pattern is a poor substitute for natural randomness.

Potential Remedy

In our new approach, we are aiming to reproduce a whole scenario in a given period of time. The cyclic nature and quantum of activities are embedded within our target models, thus we are catering to these vagaries without explicitly working for them.

Problem Area 8

Load is generally measured as CPU. This leaves out many important, fine-grained factors, especially considering the numerous technological advancements in operating systems and database operations. Issues such as buffer contention and block contention, arising out of user competition for the same data, are very practical problems and therefore important to address.

Potential Remedy

Load factors include the full range of reported statistics from the Oracle server. In addition to considering the individual stresses of these many factors, we can analyze interdependencies of resources. In many cases, high stress on one resource may affect other resources and cause a cascading loss of performance. We can locate the resources that are most taxed as well the critical points at which they may fail. Needless to say, this is the essence of proactive stress testing and performance management.

Note: The methodology suggested in these remedies has been successfully adopted in some of the author's engagements at client sites. The methodology is formally known as Oracle Data-Server Stress Simulation (ODSS) and is available as an Oracle consulting service.

Chapter 57

Undocumented Express

William G. Brown

In 1995, Oracle Corp. realized that its product offerings lacked the functionality of a multidimensional database. Moving quickly to fill this critical need, the company examined writing a new multidimensional database while evaluating the major multidimensional vendors' offerings. The purchase of the Express multidimensional database and applications from Information Resources, Inc. made it a market leader in the growing business intelligence market.

Express has greatly expanded Oracle's ability to deliver business intelligence to the user community. Coupled with Oracle's strong relational database and query tools, Express and its related applications (Oracle Sales Analyzer and Oracle Financial Analyzer) fill a critical gap in Oracle's solution for online analytical processing (OLAP).

Express' strength lies in its flexibility of design and rich Stored Procedure Language (SPL). What follows is a description of a series of undocumented Express tips and functions that are useful because they take advantage of Express' flexibility.

Undocumented Express Tips and Functions

The tips and functions can be classified into these nine categories:

1. MCALC
2. Worksheets
3. Time dimensions
4. TCONVERT
5. Capstones
6. XCA
7. Faster SQL-based loaders
8. Custom functions
9. Conjoints

0-8493-1139-X/02/$0.00+$1.50
©2002 by CRC Press LLC

MCALC

MCALC is an undocumented function in Express written for Oracle Sales Analyzer (OSA). Although officially MCALC is supported only with OSA, developers have used it for years in custom Express applications. MCALC is used to calculate custom aggregates, such as user-defined dimension members that have not been precalculated.

The MCALC function is attached to a formula that users will access for reporting. There are five components to MCALC: variable, screenby, method, members, and weight.

The basic syntax for MCALC has the following format:

```
MCALC(variable, SCREENBY boolean method OF members, WEIGHTBY weight)
```

An example that uses the MCALC syntax follows:

```
define F.SALES formula decimal <GEOG PROD TIME>
Eq MCALC(v.sales, SCREENBY if V.SALES eq NA
  THEN NO else YES, TOTAL of MEMBERS.G, TOTAL of MEMBERS.P,
  TOTAL of MEMBERS.T)
```

Now look at each MCALC component, its definition, and a specific example for each component.

Variable

The data variable (or formula) users are reporting on. For example:

```
define V.SALES variable decimal <PRODGEOG <PROD GEOG> TIME>
```

Screenby

This is an optional variable or formula that controls the handling of NAs and calculations. Information Resources, Inc. added SCREENBY to OSA before OSA was acquired by Oracle. SCREENBY supports the type of census data Information Resources sells and is normally used to distinguish a product that is unavailable in a market from a product that is not sold in a market. Generally, in custom applications this option is set to return a NO if the variable is NA and YES if the variable is not NA. For example:

```
SCREENBY if V.SALES eq NA then NO else YES
```

This setting will allow custom aggregates to be calculated, but NAs will be reported as NAs and will not be converted to ZERO on reports. However, if any cell of a custom aggregate is NA, the custom aggregate will be NA.

Method

Six methods are available to calculate a custom aggregate. The possible values for METHOD are: AVERAGE, FIRST, LAST, LARGEST, TOTAL, and NONADD.

- AVERAGE: A simple or weighted average (see option WEIGHTBY).
- FIRST: The first value in the member list. This is typically used with time dimensions.
- LAST: The last value in the member list. This is typically used with time dimensions.
- LARGEST: The largest value from the member's list. If all values are negative, MCALC returns a zero.
- TOTAL: Sums the values from the member's list.
- NONADD: Returns NA in all cases.

Member List

This is a text variable dimensioned by one of the formula's base dimensions. For precalculated dimension members, this variable contains an NA value. For custom aggregates, this variable contains a list of dimension members that will be used to calculate the aggregate value. For example:

```
define MEMBERS.P variable text <PROD>
limit PROD to 'MYCUSTAGG'
rpr down PROD MEMBERS.P
PROD         MEMBERS.P
MYCUSTAGG    PROD_BIKE
             PROD_CAR
             PROD_WAGON
```

If the Express option MCALCINT is set to YES (default), Express expects integer values representing dimension member positions. Setting MCALCINT to NO and using dimension members in the member list is recommended. In the above example, the custom aggregate MYCUSTAGG is made up of dimension members PROD_BIKE, PROD_CAR, and PROD_WAGON instead of the integer values 1, 2, and 3 that would have been the default values had MCALCINT been set to YES. This way, as new members are added, the member list does not have to be updated to reflect possible changes in the order of the dimension members.

Weightby

This is an optional variable or formula that allows for weighted averages. Omitting this argument assigns all dimension members a weight of one. If a weight is NA, it is omitted from the custom aggregate. If WEIGHTBY is used, the following formula is used to calculate the average:

```
Sum of(weight*value*sign of the number)/sum of (weight * sign)
```

MCALC is a complex function. If you wish to use MCALC, please experiment with it until you fully understand its abilities and limitations. In the meantime, to help you get started, below are several MCALC limitations and some methods to mitigate them.

Dynamic Member Lists

Once built, a member list is static and remains unchanged until someone manually updates it. To generate a dynamic member list, you can use a formula. This is useful in situations where there are two sources for the member list, such as a system where some members on the member list were generated by the system and other members were generated by an end user.

We can fool MCALC using Express' versatile text manipulation tools. For example,

```
Define MEMBERS.P formula text <PROD>
Eq uniquelines(joinlines(USERMEM.P, SYSMEM.P))
```

Display of NAs and ZEROS

As discussed briefly in the SCREENBY section, the display of NAs and ZEROS is often confusing with MCALC. Using the SCREENBY option, MCALC can either

- Translate all NAs to ZERO, which translates all NAs on a report to ZEROS. NA and ZERO have considerably different meanings, so this behavior is not desirable.
- Not translate NA to ZERO; however, if any member in the custom aggregate is NA, the custom aggregate will result in an NA.
- Treat NA as ZERO for only custom aggregates, which provides a solution that combines the best of both options by allowing you to report NAs as NAs and to correctly calculate custom aggregates using ZEROS when appropriate.

Using the example from the members list section above, one can illustrate each of the above behaviors:

- Translate all NAs to ZERO:

```
dfn F.SALES_ZERO formula dec <PROD GEOG TIME>
eq Eq MCALC(v.sales, TOTAL of MEMBERS.G, TOTAL of MEMBERS.P,
  TOTAL of MEMBERS.T)
Rpr down PROD F.SALES_ZERO
PROD          F.SALES_ZERO
PROD_BIKE          10
PROD_CAR           20
PROD_WAGON          0
MYCUSTAGG          30
```

- Do not translate NA to ZERO, to show that there is no data for PROD_WAGON in the SALES cube:

```
dfn F.SALES_NOZERO formula dec <PROD GEOG TIME>
eq Eq MCALC(v.sales, SCREENBY if V.SALES eq NA THEN NO else YES,
  TOTAL of MEMBERS.G, TOTAL of MEMBERS.P, TOTAL of MEMBERS.T)
rpr down PROD F.SALES_NOZERO
PROD            F.SALES_NOZERO
PROD_BIKE             10
PROD_CAR              20
PROD_WAGON            NA
MYCUSTAGG             NA
```

- Treat NA as ZERO for only custom aggregates by changing the formula so that the MCALC function is not required until a custom aggregate is calculated:

```
Dfn f.sales formula dec <PROD GEOG TIME>
eq if MEMBERS.P ne na or MEMBERS.G ne na or MEMBERS.T ne na -
then F.SALES_ZERO else V.SALES
```

If a custom aggregate is not being calculated, the formula returns the data from the variable; otherwise, MCALC calculates the custom aggregate, treating NA as ZERO.

Worksheets

Worksheets are an old Express feature originally used to import and export data to Lotus spreadsheets. Although they have not been enhanced to handle Excel or other spreadsheets, they have some interesting and useful properties.

A worksheet is a two-dimensional object. Unlike other Express objects, each worksheet cell can contain different data types. The WKSDATA function is used to determine which data type is in each cell. Worksheets are useful to buffer or store data when one is uncertain of the data type.

Time Dimensions

Usually, time dimensions are just standard text dimensions that use application code to enforce special rules. When the administrator defines a time dimension, a series of objects are created that allow Express to properly calculate time series data (LAG, YTD). However, Express has the ability to define "true" time dimensions that have an implicit knowledge of time. These time dimensions are broken into homogeneous pieces, with a dimension for each level in a hierarchy (such as MONTH, QUARTER, and YEAR).

Time dimensions have many properties that an application designer might wish to use. Time dimensions are often used to control and populate traditional text dimensions for reporting time periods. Time dimensions have implicit relations: A developer can limit months to year without a defined relation. For example,

```
Limit YEAR to 'YR99'
Limit MONTH to YEAR
```

will result in the 12 months of 1999.

Because true time dimensions are homogenous — they store only one level of data — and proper order is maintained, you can easily find equivalent periods using positional logic. For example, to find a time period one year ago,

```
Limit month to 'DEC99'
Limit month to month-12
```

Using this method, the code returns DEC98. Compare this with using a text time dimension, which is heterogeneous. Unless you are careful with your code, 12 members back could be any time period.

Sometimes, time hierarchies are not easily derived from the source system or time information such as Day of Week is not available. It can be faster to simply maintain the time dimensions in Express. For maintaining a text time dimension, Express has many useful functions with implicit relations describing time dimensions, including the following:

DAYOF: Day of week for a date
DDOF: Day of month for a date
MMOF: Month of a date

Using time dimensions, one can also design smaller and more efficient databases using TCONVERT.

TCONVERT

The TCONVERT function allows data to be aggregated or allocated from one time dimension to another, thereby reducing the size of the database considerably. For example, a sales system with two years of monthly level data normally requires eight quarters and two years of precalculated data, making a time dimension of 34 members. Using TCONVERT, one can reduce the size of the dimension to 24-month members, with a corresponding reduction in size of the cubes. In addition, TCONVERT supports average and last value as aggregation methods.

Although allocations are rarely used, TCONVERT also supports spreading data down to lower levels from higher levels. This can be useful if quota is set at the quarter level but users want to compare their current sales against their quarterly quotas.

Using TCONVERT adds some complexity to the database, but the complexity can be completely hidden from end users. Continuing with the above sales example, we can define the following:

```
Define MONTH dimension month
Define QUARTER dimension quarter
Define YEAR dimension year
Define V.SALES variable decimal <PRODGEOG <PROD GEOG> MONTH>
Ld Where the data is stored

Define Q.SALES formula decimal <PRODGEOG <PROD GEOG> QUARTER>
Eq TCONVERT(V.SALES, QUARTER, SUM)

Define Y.SALES formula decimal <PRODGEOG <PROD GEOG> YEAR>
Eq TCONVERT(V.SALES, YEAR, SUM)
```

None of these objects will be visible to end users. Define the following formula for end users:

```
Define F.SALES formula decimal <PROD GEOG TIME>
eq if isvalue(TIME YEAR) then Y.SALES(YEAR TIME ) else
If isvalue(TIME QUARTER) then Q.SALES(QUARTER TIME)
else if ISVALUE(TIME MONTH) then V.SALES(MONTH TIME) else na
```

Now, users have a text time dimension with embedded totals, but the aggregate numbers are calculated dynamically. Performance of TCONVERT is directly related to the amount of data being calculated. For example, a year value calculated from months is considerably faster than one calculated from days.

The formula that presents the data to end users has little or no overhead. Both F.SALES and V.SALES demonstrate identical performance characteristics for stored data.

Capstones

Currently, Express is not a multi-processor database. Capstones are a way to physically partition the databases to allow parallel processing. Although capstones add to the database complexity, there can be vast performance improvements.

There are two issues in using capstones as a design technique: how to physically separate the data and how to logically integrate it for transparent reporting.

Physically separating the data is the most challenging. However, there are some simple guidelines to follow:

- Split the data to avoid duplication of derived or input data.
- Split measures among databases only when the databases have different dimensionality or different densities.
- Split by time periods only when forced to by tight load windows.

Integrating the data requires a fairly simple set of formulas. The formulas are similar to those given in the TCONVERT example above for creating a user-accessible formula. Use the ISVALUE function on each dimension to determine the data's location. If we assume the SALES data is split into two pieces, we can use the following formula:

```
Dfn F.SALES FORMULA DECIMAL <PROD GEOG TIME>
Eq if isvalue(DB1_PROD PROD) and isvalue(DB1_GEOG GEOG and
   isvalue(DB1_TIME TIME)
then DB1_SALES(DB1_PROD PROD DB1_GEOG GEOG DB1_TIME TIME)
else if isvalue(DB2_PROD PROD) and isvalue(DB2_GEOG GEOG) and
   isvalue(DB2_TIME TIME)
then DB2_SALES(DB2_PROD PROD DB2_GEOG GEOG DB2_TIME TIME)

else na

define DB1_SALES VARIABLE DECIMAL <DB1_PROD DB1_GEOG DB1_TIME>
define DB2_SALES VARIABLE DECIMAL <DB2_PROD DB2_GEOG DB2_TIME>
```

No matter how the databases are split, there appears to be no performance penalty using this approach.

In larger applications using both TCONVERT and capstone functions, placing the TCONVERT formulas in the data databases and not in the capstone database will provide the best performance.

Express Communication Architecture

Express Communication Architecture (XCA) is Express' original method of communicating between a client and a server. With the release of Express Server 5.0, this communication method was replaced with Structured N-Dimensional Programming Interface (SNAPI). However, XCA has the following useful features:

- Using the pipeline option, you can move database objects directly from database to database without resorting to EIF files.
- Server-to-server connections can be established, allowing data, programs, and files to be moved from server to server.
- Using Personal Express, data can be sliced down to fit on a client machine and run in disconnect mode.

In Express Server 6.2, a new set of XCA functions was released to support Oracle Financial Analyzer.

EXECSTART allows you to issue a command to another Express database while continuing to process the first database. Using XCA, you can attach another database and move a cube of data. EXECSTART will allow you to roll-up the data and then bring the calculated data back to the primary database.

A code fragment using this technique follows:

```
cd /databasedir
dtb attach data.db rw
" Initiate the secondary session
comset type local   "Connect to the same machine you are on
connect
xopen   "Open XCA port
" In the secondary session, attach database read-only

execute 'cd /databasedir
execute 'dtb ro data.db'
" In the secondary session, rollup sales dollar variable
execstart 'call ROLLUP_PRG(\'SALES_DOL\')'
" At the same time rollup the sales unit variable
call rollup_prg('SALES_UNT')
upd
" In the primary session, attach and detach the
"   database in order to clear Express memory
dtb detach acme
dtb attach acme rw
" Wait for the secondary rollup. Test for errors.
trap on errwait
xca_err = execwait
trap off
```

```
" In the secondary session, export the sales dollar cube back to the
  primary session
execute 'export SALES_DOL to eif pipeline'
upd
dtb detach acme
xclose
disconnect
return
errwait:
"Handle the execwait error
return
END
```

The advantage of XCA over capstones is that the database design and code stream is simpler. However, moving the data from the secondary session to the primary session can be slow. This process works best with several smaller cubes.

You can create more than one secondary session by specifying a session number. You should create only as many sessions as you have available CPUs and adequate memory to support the process.

Faster SQL-Based Data Loaders

Express can read data from a relational database. However, it can be slower than reading from flat files because Express requires two passes through the data. The first pass maintains the dimensions, and the second pass loads the data. Skipping the two-pass approach will save some processing time but will cause the database to become disorganized.

If performance is an issue, you can write a SQL-based data load program that makes one pass through the data. The program performs all the dimension maintenance and buffers the data. As a post process in the program, the data is copied into the cubes, avoiding a second pass. Benchmarking indicates that this is as fast as creating a data file and writing a traditional flat file loader. A code example is shown in Appendix 57.1.

Custom Functions

Functions are Express routines that take an argument and return a result. There are hundreds of functions built into Express and you can expand on that list by writing your own functions. Writing custom functions is quite easy in Express.

Formulas allow complex calculations that act on two or more cubes, or act along a dimension. For example, we can compute variance as ACTUALS-BUDGET and a three-month moving average as movingaverage(f.sales, –3, 1, 1).

We can also combine the flexibility of formulas with the power of functions. We can write a function that performs a more complex calculation than a formula and can assign the function to the formula definition. For example:

```
Define F.SALES formula decimal <PROD GEOG TIME>
Eq f.sales.prg

Dfn F.SALES.PRG
Prg
Vrb result dec
"Simple program to calculate data on the fly
"Data is stored in a different cube DATA_SALES, with a relation
"linking PROD to D_PROD, GEOG to D_GEOG, etc.
limit D_PROD to PROD_DATA
limit D_GEOG to GEOG_DATA
limit D_TIME to TIME_DATA
result = total(DATA_SALES, -
DATA_PROD PROD DATA_GEOG GEOG DATA_TIME TIME)
return result
end
```

Assigning a newly created function to a formula definition is a useful and powerful technique. It is critical to note that performance directly relates to the complexity and amount of data the function is calculating.

Conjoints

Conjoints were originally developed to control data sparsity. In the 6.x releases of Express, composites were developed to replace conjoints. Although conjoints have slipped away from the developer's toolkit, they still have numerous uses.

Many-to-Many Relations

OLAP applications often require establishing a relationship between two dimensions. Perhaps the most common is the relationship between a company and its currency for performing exchange rate calculations. The object to support this might be defined as follows:

```
define COMPANY_CURRENCY relation CURRENCY <COMPANY>
```

This will work as long as each company has one and only one currency (which is usually the case).

However, if the need for a many-to-many relationship arises, you can create one using a conjoint. For example, each department could have employees with many titles, and the same titles could be used throughout the company. Although this is impossible to create with the standard relation object, with a conjoint, a many-to-many relationship can be defined like this:

```
define DEPT_TITLE dimension <DEPT TITLE>
```

If you also need to know that titles are valid in a department, the commands are:

```
limit DEPT to 'XXX'
limit DEPT_TITLE to DEPT
limit TITLE to DEPT_TITLE
```

The status of the title dimension contains the valid members for department XXX.

Performance

Although composites are the simplest method of controlling data sparsity, conjoints offer greater control and, in some cases, better performance. Loading data into a conjoint is fairly well documented, but Oracle does not document the method to aggregate data along a conjoint. After loading the input level data, the embedded totals (also known as aggregate levels) and relations for the ROLLUP command still need to be created and maintained.

Here is a code fragment that will maintain one dimension of a conjoint. To maintain each subsequent dimension, just repeat the code.

```
"Define the relationship to rollup the geography dimension over the list
  of geography "hierarchies
"GEOGPROD is the conjoint, GH is the list of geography hierarchies.

if not exists('GEOG_GHIER')
  then define GEOG_GHIER relation GEOGPROD <GEOGPROD GH>

for GH               "For each GEOG hierarchy
do
limit GEOG to all    "Select all geographies

while statlen(GEOG) ne 0
do
"Each loop will step up the hierarchy until reaching the top (statlen is
  equal to 0)
  limit GEOG remove ancestors using PRNTREL.G
  limit GEOGPROD to GEOG    "Only loop over the required geographies
"Add parent level (stored in PRNTREL.G) while filling in relationship
  mnt GEOGPROD merge <PRNTREL.G(GEOG key(GEOGPROD GEOG)) KEY(GEOGPROD
  PROD)> relate GEOG_GHIER
"Set status to next level, if statlen equal 0 then stop, else continue
  limit GEOG to PRNTREL.G
doend"statlen ne 0 loop

doend"Loop over GH
```

You can aggregate data over the conjoint using the conjoint parent-child relationship illustrated below (use one ROLLUP command for each dimension in the conjoint).

```
rollup V.SALES over GEOGPROD using GEOG_GHIER
```

If your application requires the additional functionality of composites but you want to speed up the aggregation process using conjoints, you can switch back and forth between them simply.

Use the CHGDFN command as follows to change from composite to conjoint and back again:

```
chgdfn GEOGPROD composite    "Turns GEOGPROD to a composite
chgdfn GEOGPROD dimension    "Returns GEOGPROD to a dimension
```

One important difference between composites and conjoints is that composites can be used only with variables. In the example below, any other object dimensioned by GEOGPROD must first be deleted before issuing the

CHGDFN command. For example, after running the conjoint maintenance code above, the following commands must be issued before changing the conjoint back to a composite:

```
if exists('GEOG_GHIER')
  then delete GEOG_GHIER database &obj(database 'GEOG')
chgdfn GEOGPROD composite
```

Leveraging Express

As you can see, Express' rich stored procedure language can help you develop creative solutions to a wide range of business problems. By following the tips and techniques summarized in this chapter, you will be on your way to taking advantage of Express' power and flexibility.

Appendix 57.1 Buffer SQL Data Loader

```
"|-----------------------------------------------------------------------"|
"| Name: READ_SALES                                                      "|
"| Description: Simple example of buffered SQL data loader               "|
"| Author: WGBROWN (Symmetry)                                            "|
"| Date: 05/07/98                                                        "|
"| Date   Who  Change                                                    "|
"| ------ ---- ----------------------------------------------------------"|
"| ----------------------------------------------------------------------"|
arg  _month date
vrb  _time  text
vrb  _geog  text
vrb  _prod  text
vrb  _cnt   int
vrb  _sec   int
vrb  _sales dec

trap on error
call prg_init('READ_SALES')
pushlevel 'READ_SALES'

trap on error
"------------------------------------------------------------------------
" Define all the buffer objects required for the database if not exists('REC')
   then define REC DIMENSION INT database BASE

if not exists('REC_MONTH')
   then define REC_MONTH relation MONTH <REC> DATABASE BASE temp

if not exists('REC_STORE')
   then define REC_STORE RELATION STORE <REC> DATABASE BASE temp

if not exists('REC_PROD')
   then define REC_PROD RELATION STORE <REC> DATABASE BASE temp

if not exists('REC_SALES')
   then define REC_SALES DEC <REC> DATABASE BASE temp

"add a 5000 dimension members to store the data.
mnt rec dlt all
mnt rec add 5000
"------------------------------------------------------------------------
call prg_msgs(joinchars('Starting SALES for '_day))

_cnt=0
_sec=seconds

sql declare c1 cursor for -
   select MONTH, GEOG, PROD, SALES -
     from SALES where MONTH = :_month
   order by MONTH, GEOG, PROD

if sqlcode ne 0
   then signal sqlerr 'Cursor declare failed'

sql open c1
call prg_msgs(joinchars('Reading Sales, Cursor opened'))
```

(continues)

Appendix 57.1 Buffer SQL Data Loader (continued)

```
while sqlcode eq 0
do

   sql fetch c1 into :_time, :_geog, :_prod, :_sales

   if _geog eq na
     then goto skip

   _cnt = _cnt+1                          "record counter

   if not isvalue(MONTH _time)
     then signal 'BADTIME' 'Invalid time period in READ_SALES'

   mnt GEOG merge _geog
   mnt PROD merge _prod

   REC_DAY   (REC _CNT) = _time
   REC_GEOG  (REC _cnt) = _geog
   REC_PROD  (REC _CNT) = _prod
   REC_SALES (REC _CNT) = _sales

   if rem(_cnt 5000) eq 0
     then do
       update
       call prg_msgs(joinchars('Read in '_cnt ' records in 'seconds-_sec))
       mnt rec add 5000
       doend
skip:
doend

call prg_msgs(joinchars('Read in '_cnt ' records in'seconds-_sec))

sql close c1
sql rollback work

"-----------------------------------------------------------------------------
"Move data from buffers to the real cubes

limit.sortrel=n
oknullstatus=y
limit TIME to rec_month ifnone done

for TIME "For each time member that has been read into the buffedo
   limit rec to TIME "Select the months records

   call prg_msgs(joinchars('Starting assign of data for ' TIME)
     "Sum the data from the buffer into the cube.
   SALES = total(REC_SALES, REC_GEOG REC_PROD)

   update
   DATA_LOADED(MEASURE 'SALES')=YES "set data loaded flag for reference

   call prg_msgs(joinchars('Finished assign of data for ' MONTH)

   update
doend
```

Appendix 57.1 Buffer SQL Data Loader (continued)

```
done:

call prg_done
return

error:

sql close c1
sql rollback work
signal errorname errortext
return
```

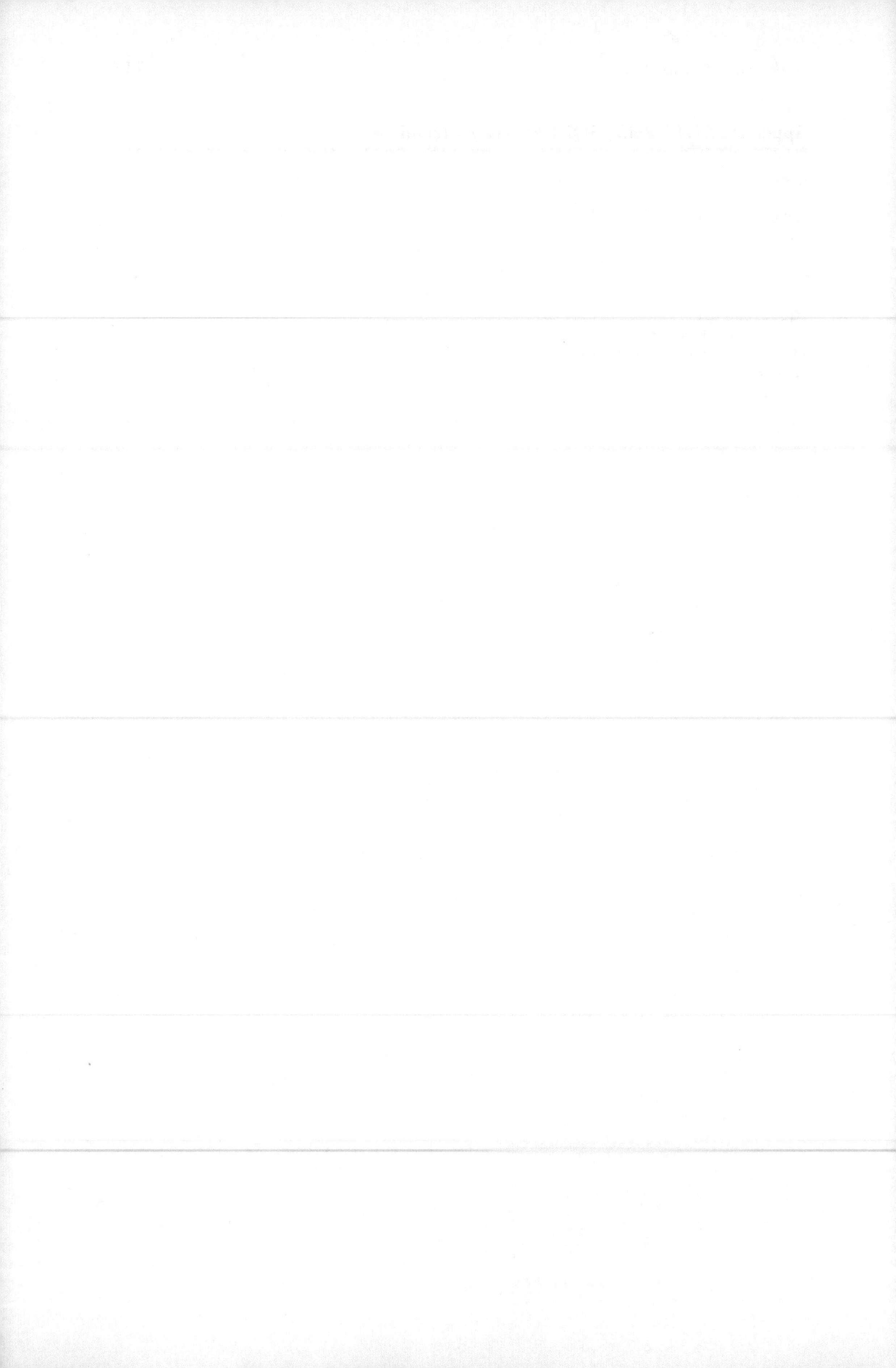

Chapter 58

Enterprise Transformation and Data Management

Richard Lee

Globalization and rapid technological change have forever changed the competitive landscape. There has been a great advance in information technology and telecommunications that accelerate productivity and supply-chain integration. This rising sophistication, and expectations of customers around the world, has given rise to implications in the way companies manage processes and data.

Whether it is through the Internet, information kiosks, or some other means, there now exists the "virtual customer" who decides what, when, where, and how they will purchase goods and/or services. Customers have virtual access through "cyberspace" to products and services to which they previously could not gain access. Not only do customers now have access, they will demand products and services "online" and almost in "zero-time." Consequently, this will have dramatic effects on the way companies manage, process, and organize data. Organizations that traditionally retrieve and use "old data" to plan, forecast, and execute will have a difficult time in meeting customers' needs in the future.

Leading organizations have shifted their focus from cost to growth strategies. These companies are building flexibility and rapid-response capabilities into their products and services. They are redesigning business processes and leveraging technology to develop innovative, integrated solutions. Studies (conducted by Deloitte Consulting) conclude that the speed of adaptability to customers — not incumbency, size, or technological elegance — has become the chief determinant of success in the industry. In all regions and sizes of organizations, the ability to innovate and respond quickly to changing market

0-8493-1139-X/02/$0.00+$1.50
©2002 by CRC Press LLC

conditions was cited as the most critical advantage. The most profitable companies recognize the power of twenty-first century customers and are adapting to a new customer value paradigm and proactively changing the basis of competition.

Organizations that collect, leverage, and utilize data effectively will have a distinct advantage over their competitors. Organizations that excel at data management will be more efficient at rolling out their key capabilities into new markets. Success depends on linking the organization's strategic objectives with data management. There must be clear strategic decision-making for data sharing, and the appropriate infrastructure — both technical and non-technical. As well, organizations must address a number of issues, including the mindset to share data, the resources to capture and analyze the data, and the ability to find the right people and data.

Improvement on Processes

Almost all enterprise transformations have involved some degree of reengineering, whether it has been minor incremental improvements or major dramatic change. Regardless of the degree of change, any transformation of an enterprise necessitates a reevaluation of the management of data.

Many enterprise transformations have improved processes through information technology integration and centralized data management. The advantage of integration allows a worldwide organization to run as a small business. Standardizing business processes all over the world with one system allows an organization to manage data in multiple languages and multiple currencies more effectively. Most IT managers cite that standardizing business processes is the primary advantage for integrating computer systems. Organizations also benefit by generation of better data through more effective utilization of resources. As well, the data that can be monitored through integrated systems allows an organization to know how it is actually producing, instead of knowing the forecasted or theoretical capacity of an operation. Once an integrated system is in place, it can also be less expensive to operate.

Finding Profits in Data

Companies must recognize the potential for utilizing data for profit. Improved processes and integrated systems do not necessarily make enterprises more successful. To sustain growth and take advantage of the enterprise transformation improvements, companies are consolidating internal databases, purchasing market-research data, and retaining data longer in efforts to better focus their marketing efforts. To serve their customers better, organizations are analyzing behavioral characteristics of customers. If organizations can start tracking a customer's purchasing behavior, the kinds of things he or she likes and doesn't like, the organization can use the organization's data mining tools and data warehouses developed to target-market the customer. There would be a lot less "junk mail" and better deals that the customer really cares about.

However, building and managing data through centralized or decentralized databases is not an easy task. Many organizations have had difficulty in finding adequate tools to manage such an ordeal. Many IT departments have found that the tools required to manage these databases are inadequate, immature, and possibly nonexistent.

The business process should dictate the tools and data required for users to perform the responsibilities that enhance the enterprise. Business processes should be developed to maximize the value of the enterprise to customers, employees, and shareholders. Identifying the correct tools and data translate into specific business goals that match the organization's unique objectives.

Critical Success Factors

Enterprise transformation not only impacts technical and organizational structures, but data structures as well. Companies must recognize the importance of managing information as an asset. Successful companies recognize the need to carefully manage their data as well as they manage other valued assets. Critical success factors include managing data from an enterprisewide basis, managing data quality, assigning data ownership and empowerment, and developing long-term data strategies to support the enterprise.

Managing Data from an Enterprisewide Basis

An effective approach to managing data on an enterprise scale is to transform data from a "functional silo" view to a business-unitwide and enterprisewide view. The data should address not only functional areas, such as sales, financial, and products, but also how their relationships with enterprise processes, such as marketing, finance, and distribution, are mapped.

The culture of an organization usually dictates how data is distributed across its business units. A large multinational organization that has business units operating autonomously may have disparate technology architectures and distributed local databases. This environment provides more of a challenge than companies that have a strategy of centralizing data for current and detailed historical data, while allowing each business unit to retain corresponding summary data.

The purpose of an enterprisewide view of data is to:

- Share data between multiple organizations or among business units that are critical to the enterprise
- Identify and control data that has dependencies with other systems or subsystems
- Improve the quality of data resources

- Establish effective data change management processes that maximize the value of information while ensuring data quality
- Minimize data duplication due to collecting and processing information
- Facilitate external partner data access and sharing

Many companies can benefit from managing data on an enterprisewide basis. Data just sitting in a local database is just data. However, when data is shared on an enterprisewide scale, then other business units may be able to take advantage of that data. From a customer relationship perspective, when demographics and psychographics are added to customer data, the company can gain extensive knowledge about that customer. Business intelligence is gained when the results of a competitive analysis are added to base customer data. When this intelligence is utilized within the enterprise's planning process, it will result in value-added ways to manage and expand the customer base.

Managing Data Quality

One of the many benefits for improved data management through enterprise transformation is improved data quality through elimination of data duplication. Most companies have many individuals throughout different parts of the organization that enter data relating to a certain process or business function. Consequently, it is very difficult to identify the integrity of the various types of data that is entered.

Data error can be attributed to a number of factors, including:

- Multiple data entries from multiple users
- Lack of corporate standards
- Data distributed across disparate sources and legacy systems
- Data redundancy between different applications
- Data entry errors

An example of this was cited in an article in *Automotive Manufacturing & Production,* a first-tier automotive supplier having seven divisions that shared some of the same vendors, but not the same vendor codes. Each division not only assigned a unique identification number to each of those vendors, but each division also had its own descriptions for the components supplied by those vendors. Also, the seven divisions had a mix of legacy hardware platforms, software applications, and financial systems. To say the least, monthly roll-ups for divisional product sales, as well as component and supplier costs, were difficult for the parent company to obtain.

To improve the quality of data, there have been a number of approaches utilized throughout industry. Companies have achieved improved labor time and cost by achieving gains in speed and accuracy of data entry. Directly related to this is the higher degree of work satisfaction from staff because the users will not have to re-key the information. As a result, companies that invest an amount up-front in improving labor and data entry processes will save an organization a substantial amount of effort and cost providing batch work solutions later.

Assigning Data Ownership and Empowerment

Enterprise transformation typically leads to a change of responsibility for users. As a result, it is very important for organizations to manage data effectively. A number of roles involved in creating and distributing data are important for effective data management. Roles have been identified as:

- *Business process owners.* The business process owner defines and maintains the processes and sub-processes across multiple business functions. Operational business processes may include market products/services, perform order management, procure materials/services, manage logistics and distribution, and provide customer support. Infrastructure business processes may include the following: perform financial management, manage human resources, manage information systems, and provide support services. Business process owners have the responsibility of evaluating and managing the proposed changes to data if it has an impact on their business process.
- *Data owner.* The data owner is usually a business-function manager who is responsible for the data resource. For example, a person in the finance department should own the tax-rate data. A data owner should be able to assess the validity of the data from a business point of view, and not necessarily a computer programmer. The data owners should drive and review proposed changes to the data and assess the impact on their own data.
- *Data user.* The data user is anyone that completes a simple, fill-in-the-field change to a data item. A data user tends to be a task-based role rather than a position, and can be anyone from a customer-support representative to the head of a plant temporarily changing the inventory capacity for a given item. Data entry should be performed under careful access, security, and data-validation controls.
- *Data custodian.* The data custodian is a person who often resides in an information technology department or MIS, providing services to several data owners. The data custodian is a person who actually manipulates the data structure for the data owner. Data custodians manage data dictionaries under change-control processes, implement proposed functional changes at the data level, and assess the broader impacts of proposed data changes. This role typically involves a combination of a database administrator, a data analyst, and an application-knowledgeable analyst.

Transforming enterprises usually occurs through technology-enabled business processes. This transformation must include an in-depth knowledge of the enterprise's application, data, and technical infrastructures. Just as important as the technical infrastructure is the organizational infrastructure that must be in place. This includes a strong management committee that is involved in program management, selection committees, implementation teams, and ongoing support teams.

To achieve a successful enterprise transformation, extensive training, education, and overall project leadership are required. Resources must be both technically and business knowledgeable. Achieving an effective data management process during enterprise transformation is not easy, but it is essential to achieve the business improvements required in today's competitive economy.

Developing Long-Term Data Strategies to Support the Enterprise

Enterprises that undergo transformation look to improved data planning and access through the use of appropriate methods, tools, and technologies. Companies must learn to promote, internally and externally, the importance of data as a valuable resource and properly manage its creation, use, storage documentation, and disposition.

In a survey of 500 organizations, conducted by and published in *LAN Times,* it was found that a vast majority of the businesses had already implemented technology to provide intranet or browser-based access to corporate data. The major driving forces toward this Internet- or intranet-based technology is the demand for mobile knowledge workers and the opportunities for revenue and efficiency by E-commerce. As a result, enterprises are now reformulating their data strategy to take advantage of the benefits of the Internet. Most companies have a long way to go, but are now looking at the most efficient ways to build database infrastructures and user-friendly, standardized access paths. The benefits are tremendous for enterprises looking to get useful information directly to the people, inside or outside the company, who need them most.

The Internet

The Internet provides companies with the ability to distribute data to end users. Through consolidation and simplifying data on one universal client, companies can contact their customers and work with their business partners much more easily. The Internet makes it easier for companies to manage geographically distributed databases and organizations. Companies are now identifying ways to consolidate data onto a central server to allow access from users anywhere, with the proper data security and integrity features in place.

Allowing customers to gain access to a company's database via the Internet provides many benefits to organizations. Customers can obtain information regarding billing, invoices, and their accounts via the Internet. Cost savings is just one of the reasons for companies managing their distributed databases via the Internet. According to the *LAN Times*, "A lot of organizations are interested in decentralizing the IT management operations because database administrators are so expensive. Rather than have a database administrator for each regional office, you can have one DBA team in the central office that can manage all the regional databases. The Internet will move that paradigm along because in the world of the Internet, physical location is more or less irrelevant."

The leading application for companies tends to be customer support, followed by decision support, financial transactions, E-commerce, and EDI. Other internal uses are support for mobile employees, interactive intranet-based databases, and sales-force automation.

Conclusion

Enterprise transformation requires a robust strategy for enterprisewide data management. Managing data on an enterprisewide basis is increasingly crucial to running almost every aspect of today's business. Effective data management requires a combination of efficient processes, robust and flexible technology infrastructures, and skilled people. There is a growing need for enterprises to manage data on an enterprisewide basis, through data ownership and empowerment while maintaining data quality. Companies are also developing long-term data structures to meet the business needs. The Internet is just one of the tools that enterprises are utilizing to manage their data.

References

Anonymous, "Data Cleanliness is Next to Enterprise Efficiency." *Automotive Manufacturing & Production*, Vol. 10, Issue 6, June 1998, p.66.

Bartlett, Jeffrey, "Business Needs Driving Data Dependency," *LAN Times*, May 11, 1998, Vol. 15, No. 10, p15(1).

Caron, Jeremiah, "Access methods change it all.," *LAN Times*, May 11, 1998, Vol. 15, No. 10, p7(1).

Deloitte Consulting, Deloitte & Touche, "1998 Vision in Manufacturing" study, 1998.

Gibbs, Jeff, "The Power of Enterprise Computing." *Internal Auditor*, February 1997.

Greenfeld, Norton, "Enterprise Data Management." *Unix Review*, February 1998.

Miller, Ed, "A Solution Approach to PDM." *Computer-Aided Engineering*, April 1998.

Moriarty, Terry, Swenson, Jim, "The Data Requirements Framework." *Database Programming & Design*, April 1998 Vol. 11, No. 4, p.13(3).

Mullin, Rick, "IT Integration Programmed for Global Operation." *Chemical Week*, Vol. 159, Issue 6, Feb. 12, 1997, p.21–27.

Perez, Ernest, "Savings from Data Entry Engineering." *Database*, Vol. 21, Issue 3, June/July 1998, p.76–78.

Schwartz, Karen, D., "Distributed Databases, Distributed Headaches." *Datamation*, June 1998.

Singh, Colin and Hart, Max, "Changing Business Culture: Information is the Key." *Australian CPA*, Vol. 68, Issue 8, September 1998, p.50–52.

Trussler, Simon, "The Rules of the Game." *Journal of Business Strategy*, Vol. 19, Issue 1, January/February 1998, p.16–19.

ORACLE DATABASE INTERNALS MANAGEMENT

Chapters 59 through 69 derive from numerous and sundry articles submitted by *Oracle Internals* experts to provide an in-depth treatment of the internal workings of various Oracle components. These techniques can dramatically improve the performance and manageability of your Oracle systems.

These include discussions by Brad Brown, chief architect at The Ultimate Software Consultants (TUSC), who reveals some internal hardware operations and shows how you can tune your hardware for optimal Oracle performance. We also see some great chapters that discuss Oracle concurrency management, metadata schema usage, the use of triggers in high-volume applications, as well as discussions on the new features of Oracle8i using the DBMS_LOCK package to improve the performance of the Oracle8i database.

Chapter 59

Getting a Quick Start with Oracle8i

Roman Kab

This chapter focuses on a few very powerful Oracle8i features. Oracle8i is packed with new features and enhancements to the existing, but not fully developed, features introduced in Oracle8. If you are a veteran database administrator who transitioned from Oracle version 6 to Oracle 7.0 and then to 7.1, you will quickly see a trend in feature and functionality introductions. Oracle 7.0 was dramatically different from version 6, but 7.1 really brought Oracle into a new level of relational database management systems (RDBMS). This chapter does not attempt to address new Java Virtual Machine (JVM) support in Oracle8i.

Transportable Tablespaces

The first feature is TRANSPORTABLE TABLESPACES. This option enables tablespace(s) to be copied and plugged into another database. This eliminates long-running, error-prone exports/imports to move operational data to the data warehouse. It is possible to archive large tablespaces faster and with much easier restore. The restore process could be applied to any database, providing more flexibility.

Here are some steps to follow to unplug/transport/plug tablespace(s):

1. Identify tablespaces that will not introduce orphans when moved (i.e., indexes without tables). Run:

```
execute dbms_tts.transport_set_check('ts1,ts2', TRUE);
select * from transport_set_violations;
```

0-8493-1139-X/02/$0.00+$1.50
©2002 by CRC Press LLC

2. Make the target tablespace READ ONLY.
3. EXP sys/change_on_install TRANSPORT_TABLESPACE=y TABLESPACES=t1,t2 TRIGGERS=y CONSTRAINTS=y GRANTS=y FILE=tt.dmp
4. Copy corresponding data files.
5. Import entries for the transported tablespaces — a very quick import.

```
IMP TRANSPORT_TABLESPACE=y DATAFILES='/db/t1_jan','/db/t2_feb'
TABLESPACES=t1,t2,... TTS_OWNERS=scott
FROMUSER=scott TOUSER=scott FILE=tt.dmp
```

Transportable tablespaces can be used to distribute data to other databases as well as to consolidate data (see Exhibit 59.1).

Optimizer Plan Stability

If you work at a vendor that builds applications on Oracle databases or an information technology (IT) development shop that needs the application to perform as well at the client site as during system testing, you need to use stored outlines.

Oracle8i offers stored outlines to ensure that the optimizer generates the same execution plan regardless of changes to the system configuration, init parameters, or object statistics.

This feature also benefits high-end Online Transaction Processing (OLTP) sites by having Structured Query Language (SQL) execute without having to invoke the cost-based optimizer at each SQL invocation.

Using CREATE OUTLINE, the command user will create a stored outline that contains an execution plan for each SQL statement. The execution plan remains the same for all SQL statements associated with this outline name. There may be a need to create multiple outlines for the same SQL statements, depending on the time of day they execute (i.e., batch versus daily OLTP reports). This dynamic switching between outlines provides great flexibility and ensures proper application executions. See Appendix 59.1 for an example.

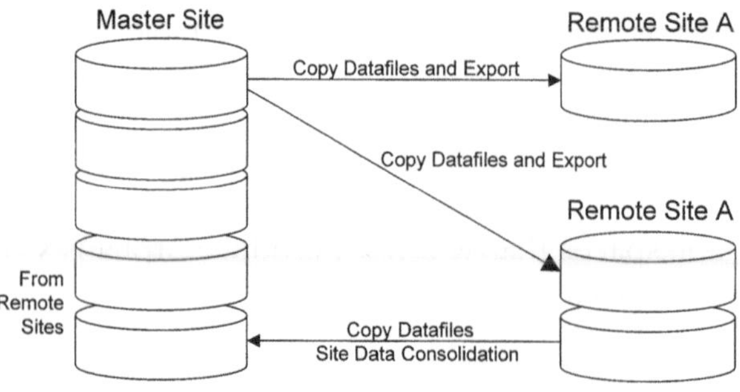

Exhibit 59.1 Data Distribution with Portable Tablespaces

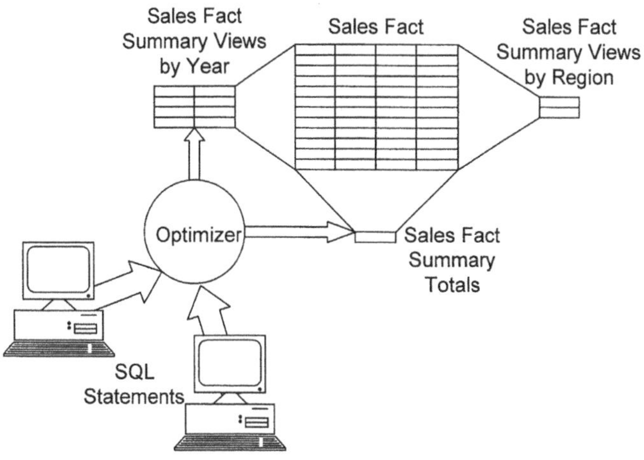

Exhibit 59.2 Oracle Transparently Rewrites SQL Statements to Utilize Materialized Views

Materialized View

Oracle8i introduces many powerful features designed especially for large data warehouses. One of them is summary management using materialized views.

A materialized view is implemented by existing Oracle8 replication technologies. If you have worked with replication, the concept of materialized views will seem familiar. It features a snapshot-like setup with tables storing precomputed summary results. The power of the materialized views comes from transparent access to the views. The Oracle8i database server automatically rewrites queries to use the summary data, rather than retrieving data from detail tables by doing expensive joins and aggregate operations. As shown in Exhibit 59.2, this query rewrite facility is totally transparent to the application, which is not aware of the materialized view. The rewrite capability will appear in other features of the Oracle8i engine.

The CREATE MATERIALIZED VIEW statement is used to create a materialized view. This statement includes a subquery, typically a join or a data aggregation (GROUP BY), the results of which comprise the materialized view. Once created, the view is maintained much like snapshots. The refresh process either completely or incrementally refreshes the data.

Like the replication set of Application Program Interface (API), Oracle provides a collection of materialized view analysis and advisory functions that are callable from any PL/SQL program. These are packaged in the DBMS_OLAP package. See Appendix 59.2 for an example.

Logminer

The ability to analyze data in an online redo or archived redo log file may not appear at the top of a DBA's list. But when logical data corruption occurs, UNDO SQL statements can be constructed to remedy the problem.

Logminer can enhance application auditing by tracking specific changes to the tables based on username, table name, time, or transaction. Logminer can analyze log files from other databases, as long as they were created on the same operating system and use the same version. See Appendix 59.3 for an example.

Virtual Private Database

Today's applications and databases require server-enforced and granular access control because clients are connecting from local desktops and external Internet sessions. This new, powerful feature provides the means to access application data from many sources. The virtual private database feature has two components: fine-grained access control and application context. Here is how they work together to implement a safe and consistent security policy across applications.

Fine-Grained Access Control

Access control is implemented by attaching security policies to individual tables. These policies are created using PL/SQL stored packages or functions. The Oracle-supplied DBMS_RLS package is used to associate the security policy functions with the table or view. Oracle8i dynamically rewrites SQL statements by appending a WHERE condition derived from the execution of security policy functions. The logic in these functions determines appropriate WHERE condition values based on the **application context.** The security policy can be enabled or disabled via the DBMS_RLS package.

Application Context

The application context provides a way to set the context for a namespace. This context is used by fine-grained security policies to determine WHERE conditions. To set or establish the context value, you need to develop the PL/SQL packages or functions that the applications will call during the initialization process. Once the packages have been created, use the CREATE CONTEXT command to associate context name with the package name. The context value is set by calling the DBMS_SESSION.SET_CONTEXT( ) function.

Here is how it works. During initial application login, a stored procedure needs to be executed to set application context. Application context is simply a value stored in a named memory location within an Oracle 8i instance. This location is referenced by the context name created with the CREATE CONTEXT command. Each session has its own private context(s). Do not confuse application context with the database security roles. Application context provides row-level application security. Context value can be set and reset based on the application's needs. Once the context value is set, it is accessed by

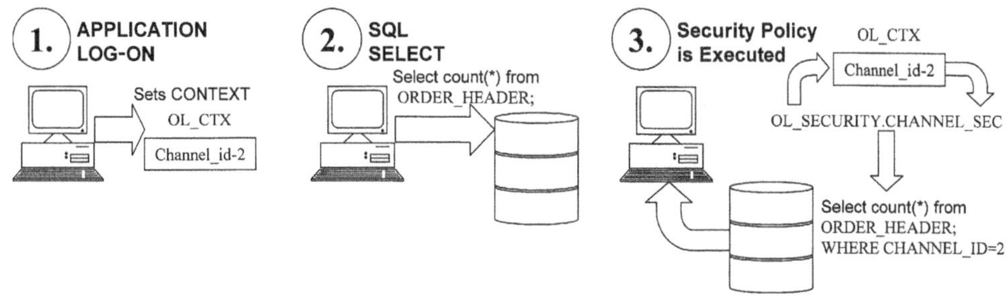

Exhibit 59.3 Fine-Grained Application Security — Steps

the SYS_CONTEXT function from any SQL statement or stored procedure. In this example, context value is referenced by security policies attached to the application tables without any user awareness. The RDBMS engine during table access events executes security policies. Table security policies use system function calls to access context value. Through evaluation of its value user's SQL statements, they are rewritten to enforce row-level security. Row-level security is accomplished by appending additional WHERE predicates. In addition, application context value provides an easy method for establishing a session's responsibilities and functions within an application.

Fine-Grained Application Security

In the example in Appendix 59.4, the requirement is to secure an ORDER_HEADER table and provide access to the records based on the distribution channel. This is a Web-based system that multiple distributors can access. The first step is to build a stored procedure that executes the application during the initial log-in process and set the context value. Using DBMS_SESSION.SET_CONTEXT, the context is set. The context name will be OL_CTX, with CHANNEL_ID as the variable that will hold the context value (see Exhibit 59.3).

Locally Managed Tablespaces

Prior to Oracle8i, the management of free and used extents within a tablespace relied heavily on the data dictionary tables. Oracle has introduced a mechanism to track extent information in the tablespace, using bitmaps.

Bitmaps manage space allocation efficiently and require no dictionary access to allocate or update extents for the tablespace. The result is better space management, reduced fragmentation, and increased reliability. Locally managed tablespaces are ideal candidates to hold temporary tables and their indexes, eliminating unnecessary transactions against system catalogs.

Locally managed tablespaces require UNIFORM or AUTOALLOCATE space allocation methods. UNIFORM allocations mean that all extents in the tablespace will be the same size. You can establish a default size or let the system pick one for you. With AUTOALLOCATE, you need to establish initial extent; the system determines the next extent size. Temporary tablespaces that are created as locally managed can only use UNIFORM.

Parameters such as NEXT, PCTINCREASE, MINEXTENTS, and MAXEXTENTS are not valid with locally managed tablespaces.

Temporary Tables

These tables store intermediate results and are created in the user's temporary tablespace. The data in these tables is visible to the session that inserted it. You can specify how Oracle8i retains records in the temporary table with an ON COMMIT PRESERVE ROWS or ON COMMIT DELETE ROWS clause.

Example

```
CREATE GLOBAL TEMPORARY TABLE pulled_orders (
  Item_id NUMBER,
  Location VARCHAR2(10),
  Qty NUMBER)
  ON COMMIT PRESERVE ROWS
TABLESPACE LOCAL_TEMP ;
```

Nonpartitioned Table Reorganization

Oracle8i has the ALTER TABLE MOVE command for simple table reorganization. All grants, views, procedures, and dependent objects remain in place and valid with the exception of indexes. Indexes on reorganized tables become UNUSABLE and must be rebuilt or dropped and recreated. The power behind this feature is that it enables quick table reorganization, table relocation to a different tablespace, or new storage settings implementation.

Today's VLDBs require fast reorganization of tables and indexes within a small time frame. ALTER TABLE MOVE can be executed against many tables at the same time and can be aborted if need be. Remember, with Oracle7 and Oracle8, most of the reorganizations were accomplished via drop or truncate and reload, but the new MOVE command does not require data to be truncated; it simply builds a new table as a temporary segment until the operation succeeds and then renames a temporary segment to the designated table name.

Export and Import Utilities

Query

With Oracle8i, a query can be specified for the select statement. The query feature with the EXP utility enables you to selectively extract data or create dmp files based on the range of keys. You are not limited to the WHERE predicate; ORDER BY is another option to reorder records or to unload data for an operational data mart in predefined order.

Be careful with query statements because Oracle will try to apply it to every table.

Example

Export ORDER_HEADER into multiple files based on channel_id:

```
exp scott/tiger file=order_header_ch2.dmp tables=order_header
  query=\"where channel_id = 2\"
direct=n

exp scott/tiger file=order_header_ch1.dmp tables=order_header
  query=\"where channel_id = 1\"
direct=n
```

Multiple Output Files

The export utility now supports multiple output files. This feature enables large exports to be divided into files whose sizes will not exceed the operating system's limit.

Provide filenames and fullpaths in the FILE parameter and the export utility will write the database information into each file according to the FILESIZE parameter. The FILESIZE parameter establishes the byte count of the output export file(s).

When importing from multi-file export, you must provide the same file names, in the same sequence as in the FILE parameter.

Example

Multi-file Export:

```
EXP SCOTT/TIGER FILE=D:\output\scott1.dmp,E:\output\scott2.dmp FILE-
  SIZE=5m LOG=scott.log direct=n

Log File Sample:

  exporting table    PRODUCTS      36 rows
                                   exported
  exporting table    SALES
continuing export into file e:\output\
  scott2.dmp
110166 rows exported
  exporting table    SALESPERSON   0 rows
                                   exported
```

Invoker Rights

Stored procedures can now be built to execute with the rights of the user who invoked the procedure. The invoker-rights model is another step toward the creation of reusable code. A stored procedure can be used by multiple users to manage data stored in their schemas.

```
CREATE [OR REPLACE] FUNCTION [schema_name.]function_name
[(parameter_list)] RETURN datatype
[AUTHID {CURRENT_USER | DEFINER}] {IS | AS}
```

This feature also enables greater application security because the user executing the stored procedure will adhere to his or her current privileges.

Appendix 59.1 Use of Stored Outlines

Let us take ORDER_LINE table. During the night operation, I want to make sure that the report is executed using the full-table scan. There is no index on the ITEM_ID column that will be used for report selection.

```
SYS>Grant priv create any outline to scott;
SCOTT>create an outline for BATCH processing;

create outline cust002 for category BATCH
on
select order_id,item_id,sales,cost,sales-cost
from order_line
where item_id = 'P243467-28' and sales - cost > 15000

Select Statement Cost=162 Card=573 Bytes=18336
   Table Access (Full) on SCOTT.ORDER_LINE Cost=162 Card=573 Bytes=18336

SQL> alter session set use_stored_outlines=BATCH;
SQL>create index item_id_i1 on order_line ( item_id)
SQL>analyze index item_id_i1 compute statistics;
Run the same SQL.
Explain - Execution remained the same!
Select Statement Cost=162 Card=573 Bytes=18336
   Table Access (Full) on SCOTT.ORDER_LINE Cost=162 Card=573 Bytes=18336

SQL> alter session set use_stored_outlines=false;

Session altered.
Run the same SQL.
Execution - Without outline Oracle uses new INDEX.
-----------------------------------------------------------------
Select Statement Cost=51 Card=573 Bytes=18336
   Table Access (By Index Rowid) on SCOTT.ORDER_LINE Cost=51 Card=573
        Bytes=18336
      Index (Range Scan) on SCOTT.OL_ITEM_ID_I1 - Non-Unique Cost=21 Card=573
```

Oracle8i provides a set of OUTLN_PKG API PL/SQL packages to manage outlines.

Appendix 59.2 Materialized Views

Summary SQL without materialized views:

```
select ac.ac_name,sum(ol.sales) AS sum_of_sales from
order_header oh,account ac, order_line ol
where oh.account_id = ac.account_id
and oh.order_id = ol.order_id
group by ac.ac_name;

Explain:
Select Statement Cost=16619 Card=24 Bytes=2376
   Sort (Group By) Cost=16619 Card=24 Bytes=2376
      Hash Join Cost=2127 Card=110166 Bytes=10906434
         Table Access (Full) on SCOTT.ACCOUNT Cost=1 Card=24 Bytes=1176
         Hash Join Cost=2032 Card=110166 Bytes=5508300
            Table Access (Full) on SCOTT.ORDER_HEADER Cost=7 Card=6023
               Bytes=144552
            Table Access (Full) on SCOTT.ORDER_LINE Cost=162 Card=110166
               Bytes=28643
```

Build materialized view:

```
create materialized view account_sales_mv
pctfree 0 tablespace orc2_userdata
storage ( initial 16k next 16k )
parallel build immediate
refresh complete
enable query rewrite
as
select ac.ac_name,sum(ol.sales) AS sum_of_sales from
order_header oh,account ac, order_line ol
where oh.account_id = ac.account_id
and oh.order_id = ol.order_id
group by ac.ac_name;
```

Enable the QUERY REWRITE:

```
alter session set query_rewrite_enabled=TRUE;
analyze table account compute statistics;
analyze table order_header compute statistics;
analyze table order_line compute statistics;
```

Run the same SQL:

```
Explain:
Select Statement Cost=1 Card=204 Bytes=6528
   Table Access (Full) on SCOTT.ACCOUNT_SALES_MV Cost=1 Card=204
      Bytes=6528
```

Appendix 59.3 Logminer

Build dictionary file to translate object numbers to object names:

```
execute dbms_logmnr_d.build(dictionary_filename =>
   'orc2_logminer.ora',dictionary_location =>
   'd:\orant_851\oradata\orc2_utldir');
```

Add log files to be analyzed:

```
execute dbms_logmnr.add_logfile(Options => dbms_logmnr.NEW,LogFileName =>
   'D:\ORANT_851\ORADATA\ORC2\REDO01.LOG');
execute dbms_logmnr.add_logfile(Options => dbms_logmnr.ADDFILE,
LogFileName => 'D:\ORANT_851\ORADATA\ORC2\REDO02.LOG');
```

Start the logminer:

```
execute dbms_logmnr.start_logmnr(DictFileName
   =>'d:\orant_851\oradata\orc2_utldir\orc2_logminer.ora');
```

Test SQL:

```
update system.emp
set sal=800 where empno=7369;
```

Build UNDO SQL for changes made by ROMAN:

```
SELECT sql_redo, sql_undo FROM v$logmnr_contents
WHERE username = 'ROMAN'
```

Output:

```
REDO: update SYSTEM.EMP set SAL = 100 where ROWID = 'AAAAv7AAHAAAAnqAAA';
UNDO: update SYSTEM.EMP set SAL = 800 where ROWID =
   'AAAAv7AAHAAAAnqAAA';

execute dbms_logmnr.end_logmnr
```

Appendix 59.4 Fine-Grained Application Security

Procedure for setting context:

```
CREATE OR REPLACE PACKAGE scott.ol_sec_ctx IS
PROCEDURE set_channel_id;
END ol_sec_ctx;
/
CREATE OR REPLACE PACKAGE BODY scott.ol_sec_ctx IS
PROCEDURE set_channel_id IS
d_channel_id NUMBER;
BEGIN
d_channel_id := 2; -- This could be dynamic
/* set channel_id attribute under namespace 'ol_ctx'*/
DBMS_SESSION.SET_CONTEXT('ol_ctx', 'channel_id', d_channel_id);
END set_channel_id;
END ol_sec_ctx;
```

Create the context and associate it with the package:

```
(as SYS)>CREATE CONTEXT ol_ctx USING scott.ol_sec_ctx;
```

The security procedure that will enforce access to the ORDER_HEADER table is based on the context value. The context value is obtained by calling the SYS_CONTEXT function and the predicate is then constructed. This procedure is called every time there is a SELECT issued against the ORDER_HEADER table.

```
(as SCOTT)
CREATE or replace PACKAGE Ol_security AS
FUNCTION channel_sec (D1 VARCHAR2, D2 VARCHAR2)
RETURN VARCHAR2;
END;
/
CREATE OR REPLACE PACKAGE BODY Ol_security AS
FUNCTION channel_sec (D1 VARCHAR2, D2 VARCHAR2) RETURN VARCHAR2
IS
   D_predicate VARCHAR2 (2000);
   BEGIN
   D_predicate := 'channel_id = SYS_CONTEXT(''ol_ctx'',''channel_id'')';
   RETURN D_predicate;
   END channel_sec;
END Ol_security;

(as SYS)
grant execute on dbms_rls to scott;
```

Once the security procedure is created, it needs to be attached to the ORDER_HEADER table `(as SCOTT) attach ol_policy to order_header`. Enforce the policy using the `ol_security.channel_sec` package.

```
exec sys.DBMS_RLS.ADD_POLICY ('scott', 'order_header', 'ol_policy',
   'scott','ol_security.channel_sec', 'select');
```

Now that everything is in place, let us test it. The application context-channel id will be set to 2. Without application context, count would return 0.

Appendix 59.4 Fine-Grained Application Security (continued)

```
SQL> exec ol_sec_ctx.set_channel_id();
```

Now execute an SQL against ORDER_HEADER. Because a security policy was enabled and the context value for CHANNEL_ID was 2, this query returned a count of 2261 orders:

```
SQL> select count(*) from order_header;
   COUNT(*)
   --------
       2261
```

Disable policy enforcement. Every distributor has access to the whole table.

```
SQL> exec dbms_rls.enable_policy('scott','order_header','ol_policy',FALSE);
SQL> select count(*) from order_header;
   COUNT(*)
   --------
       6023
```

Results with security policy disabled return count for the whole table.

Chapter 60

Oracle Sessions Monitoring

Serg Shestakov
Dmitry Petrov

One of the most challenging tasks for an Oracle DBA is to keep an eye on sessions. Standard Oracle tools aimed at solving this problem are rather heavy-weighted, and it is not that easy to deploy and customize these tools for particular DBA needs. It is good practice for a DBA to write scripts for sessions monitoring. Sometimes there can be a situation when graphical tools like Top Sessions Monitor cannot be used; all that is left for a DBA may be just a UNIX command console. More importantly, when writing these scripts, the DBA gets a clear understanding of how to work with the Oracle dictionary structures responsible for storing vital sessions information — what resources are allocated for a session, what types of locks are being used, etc. Also, the DBA will become aware of major problems with user sessions and possible workarounds for these problems.

Let us indicate the most critical things we want the tool to monitor. First, we consider how to monitor active user sessions and their resources, and how to reveal heavy problematic queries. Second, we discuss how to extract SQL code for problematic queries running against our database. Third, we show how to deal with locks: monitor resource locks, track locking, and waiting transactions. The next thing to discuss is how to monitor rollback segments usage. Finally, we'll see what the options are to terminate a problematic session and write a handy utility for terminating a session from the operating system side.

Assume the following environment: SPARC Solaris 2.6 and Oracle Enterprise 8.0.5. Write the monitoring tool using Korn shell and Oracle SQL. Simple and reliable Korn shell scripts can be started from Telnet or run as a batch job using cron; and Oracle SQL can be executed from Korn shell using sqlplus.

0-8493-1139-X/02/$0.00+$1.50
©2002 by CRC Press LLC

Monitoring Resources Allocation

To simplify SQL execution from the UNIX command line, we write a wrapper for this sqlplus utility — Korn shell called sp.sh. First, assign Korn shell to execute this script and put some comments. In the first section, check the number of parameters passed to the script. If there are no parameters passed, print the usage note and exit. In the second section, analyze the first parameter; if it equals "-h," we print the help message and exit. The first and second sections of code are listed below.

```
#/bin/ksh
# sp.sh - Executes Oracle SQL

# Section 1. Print a usage note and exit:
if [ -z "$1" ] ; then
   echo "Try 'sp.sh -h' for help!"
   exit
fi

# Section 2. Print a help message and exit:
if [ "_$1" = _-h ] ; then

cat 1>&2 <<EOF

Script to execute Oracle SQL.
Parameters:
1    - SQL Script to execute (required)
2..5 - SQL script parameters (optional)

EOF
exit
fi
```

The third section is more complex and needs a detailed explanation. Prepare two environment variables — USERNAME and USERPASSWORD — storing Oracle username and its password. Read these values from the oralogin file where this information is stored with field separator #. Each line is stored in the form: <Oracle SID>#<User name>#<Password>. This is done for increased security and for DBA convenience when managing multiple database instances. The script scans the oralogin file for a string starting with the current SID and reads the second and third fields. To read the fields, use the "cat" command with -d option to point the field separator (#) and the -f option to tell what field number we want to read. An exemplary line in oralogin for a database instance called *ORCL*, user *scott,* and password *tiger* should look like this: ORCL#scott#tiger.

Once the environment has been prepared, we run sqlplus. Note that we run "sqlplus" commands using standard input. Data is passed to sqlplus until the EOF keyword is encountered for a second time. For security reasons, avoid running sqlplus with command-line arguments (username/password); on UNIX systems, any user can issue a "ps -ef|grep sqlplus" command and see a string revealing the password, something like "sqlplus scott/tiger." Script takes up to five parameters; the first parameter is a must and can be either

"-h" for help or SQL script name to execute. All additional parameters are passed directly to SQL script when running it with sqlplus. One can see the third section code below.

```
# Section 3. Prepare parameters and run sqlplus:
USERNAME=`grep "^${ORACLE_SID}" oralogin | cut -d# -f2`
USERPASSWORD=`grep "^${ORACLE_SID}" oralogin | grep $USERNAME |
   cut -d# -f3`

sqlplus <<EOF
$USERNAME/$USERPASSWORD
SET SERVEROUTPUT ON;
@$1 $2 $3 $4 $5
exit
EOF
```

The Oracle environment variables ($ORACLE_HOME, $TNS_ADMIN, etc.) are not defined because we want to run this utility in interactive mode, and shell will inherit the appropriate environment from its parent. To run script as a cron job, we need to add a code in the beginning of Section 3 to define all the necessary variables.

Having defined a script to run SQL commands, let's get closer to Oracle processes. Sessions data is gathered by Oracle and can be extracted from certain dictionary views. Information is scattered among many dictionary views. The question is: what views will be enough to collect vital session data? For resources allocation monitoring, this tool will take into account six views:

v_$session
v_$process
v_$sesstat
v_$statname
v_$sqltext
v_$sess_io

Note that we address the v_$ views directly to avoid addressing its public synonyms, the v$ views.

The sys.v_$session view is a basic view that holds data for all current identification information: operating system and Oracle user names, session identifier, and session serial number.

We want to monitor user sessions. Let us see what the options are for the end user to open an Oracle session. Sessions are created by operating system users, represented in this monitoring tool output by the OSUSER column. Note that the OSUSER field corresponds to OS username for the client machine. It is also very important to know the OS process identifier (OSPID column); this may help the DBA to monitor system resources allocation (CPU time, memory usage) for resource-consuming sessions on the OS level. For this purpose, utilities like top and ps (on UNIX systems) can be used. For example, once the OS process identifier 13158 is known, we can issue the ps -efo 'pid vsz pcpu' | grep "^13158" command to see memory and CPU utilization. This is important because, in Oracle versions prior to 8.1.6, CPU utilization statistics gathering was incorrect. We can prepare and spool operating-system commands like the one described above to temporary shell file and execute it. This kind of Oracle–UNIX integration will be described in the Terminating a Session section.

Each OS user can open one or more concurrent connections to the database instance under one or more Oracle users represented by the USERNAME column. Each opened Oracle connection is uniquely identified by session identifier (SID column) and session serial number (SERIAL# column).

Also from the v_$session we read session status (STATUS column), command being executed (COMMAND column), session log-on time (LOGON TIME column), server type (SERVER column), and program name (PROGRAM column). Session may have one the following statuses: ACTIVE, INACTIVE, KILLED, CACHED, or SNIPED. Sessions monitoring the KILLED and SNIPED statuses are of particular interest, and we discuss them in detail in the Terminating a Session section. As for the commands being executed, Oracle stores command type as a number. For better presentation, use the DECODE function to convert most of the codes. If command type name cannot be found in DECODE list, its code will be printed instead.

From other views, vital session data can be read. Reference the sys.v_$process view using the process address field (PADDR) to get the OS process identifier (OSPID column) already mentioned above. Information on resources allocated for the current session is obtained from the sys.v_$sesstat view, referencing it with session identifier. We read UGA and PGA sizes from the sys.v_$sesstat, and print it in Mbytes (UGA and PGA columns, respectively). We read the number of open cursors (CURSORS column) from the sys.v_$sesstat. For each session, there can be several rows holding the statistics. To collect those data, use the sys.v_$statname view, referencing it with the STATISTIC# field.

Calculate the I/O statistics hit ratio using the sys.v_$sess_io view, referencing it with the session identifier. To get the hit ratio, use the following formula:

$$100*[(\text{Consistent gets} + \text{Block gets}) - \text{Physical reads}] \\ /(\text{Consistent gets} + \text{Block gets})$$

The corresponding SELECT statement fetching information for active sessions monitoring is given in Appendix 60.1.

How can we customize this script? First of all, to avoid printing excessive information, we can filter sessions using resource limit thresholds. Threshold values depend on the specific application. For example, print only those sessions exceeding the UGA limit or print the top five cursor-intensive transactions. To calculate the thresholds, run additional queries. Sometimes, the DBA may be interested in top time time-consuming sessions. Sessions with the lowest hit ratio may also be important for application code tuning.

All sessions are ordered by OS username, Oracle username, session identifier, and serial number. Note that we filter sessions removing information concerning Oracle background processes like PMON, SMON, etc. These processes do not require session-level administering. Thus, focus only on user sessions and avoid information overload for the DBA. To turn on monitoring for background processes, the DBA should modify the WHERE clause, removing the AND ses.username IS NOT NULL clause.

From the above statement's output, the DBA can detect long-running and resource-intensive sessions. Once suspicious sessions have been detected, we may want to look at the lines of SQL code to detect the root cause. This task is discussed in the next chapter section.

Extracting an SQL Code

To see an SQL statement being executed in the session, we must address two dictionary views: the v_$session and v_$sqltext. Reference the v_$sqltext from v_$session using the SQL address and SQL hash value. These fields uniquely identify the SQL statement being executed. SQL text is broken into blocks of 64 characters; each block has a number stored in the PIECE field. We restrict our monitoring tool output to 100 SQL text blocks (see Appendix). Note that the v_$sqlarea view also contains SQL text corresponding to the current session, but truncated to the first 1000 characters. That's why the v_$sqlarea view is not used. As before, filter sessions using the WHERE clause.

And, of course, we can filter sessions in the WHERE clause using threshold criteria based on application-specific or session identification information. The best way to optimize a sophisticated query is to use specialized software. For example, problematic queries can be analyzed using Oracle's EXPLAIN PLAN, SQL Trace, TKPROF, or AUTOTRACE. Oracle also supplies a very handy utility with graphical interface — SQL Analyzer included in Tuning Pack.

Dealing with Locks

When many users access database objects concurrently, there can be situations when a transaction not committed by one user session locks the resource requested by another session. For example, one user may issue an UPDATE statement and leave for a coffee break. Some table rows become locked. Another user, attempting to update one of these rows, will have to wait until the first user returns and either commits or rolls back. There may be many similar situations causing resource locks. The client machine may hang or crash, leaving the Oracle server process waiting for a reply. A user may issue a DDL operation on an object locked by another user for DML operation; this causes Oracle to produce an error like "ORA-00054: resource busy...." There may be more sophisticated scenarios; for example, when two users cross-block each other's resources. This causes another Oracle error — "ORA-00060: deadlock detected while waiting for resource."

We are primarily concerned with two lock types: DML locks (TM and TX) and DDL locks. The TM type corresponds to row-level locks and is applied when a row is being updated, deleted, or inserted. The TX type corresponds to table-level or partition-level locks and serves to protect the object from being modified with some DDL operations. Note that each DML operation automatically causes shared TM lock for the object and exclusive TX lock for the rows being accessed. DDL locks are applied to protect the object from conflicting DDL operations.

Locks can be analyzed in two dimensions: (1) resource (object name) and (2) user/session (waiting or holding a lock). But for resource-oriented analysis as well as for user-oriented analysis, we need a function to detect if the given session is waiting or not. The v_$lock view is holding information on requested lock mode (REQUEST field). Given the session identifier, count the number of rows in the v_$lock table, indicating requested mode different from None. The script for the function (IS_WAITING) should be run under the same Oracle user you want to monitor sessions. The function creation script is listed below; it can be saved to the func.sql file and compiled running sp.sh func from the UNIX command console.

```
rem############################################
rem  Function IS_WAITING.
rem  Parameters: Session Identifier.
rem  Returns 0 if transaction is not waiting.
rem  Otherwise transaction is waiting.
rem############################################

CREATE OR REPLACE FUNCTION IS_WAITING (sess_id NUMBER)
RETURN NUMBER IS
is_waiting NUMBER;
BEGIN
SELECT count(*) INTO is_waiting FROM sys.v_$lock d
WHERE d.sid= sess_id and d.request!=0;
RETURN is_waiting;
END;
/
```

How can sessions that cause resource locks be detected? Oracle stores information on current locks in the v_$lock and v_$locked_object dictionary views. For Oracle Parallel Server, there are two more dictionary views holding information on locks. Our monitoring tool uses information stored in the v_$lock. Reference the v_$lock view from v_$session using the session identifier. From v_$lock, take the lock type, actually applied lock mode, and the lock mode requested by the session. Convert all these codes to string values using the DECODE function (LOCK TYPE, MODE HELD, and MODE REQUESTED columns, respectively). We also use the dba_objects view to get the locked object name (OBJECT column), referencing it with the object identifier. The statement to extract information on locks for resource-oriented analysis is listed in Appendix 60.3.

The output is sorted according to the object name. Looking at the output, the DBA can see an overall picture: who is causing resource locks; what resource is being locked most of all; and what sessions are waiting because of it.

To detect exactly which session is causing another session to wait, write another SELECT statement (see Appendix 60.4). It is based on v_$lock b and sys.v_$session views joined by a session identifier. What is most important is its WHERE clause. Fetch data only for sessions requesting a lock and its corresponding waiting sessions, which are detected using the ID2 and ID2 fields of the v_$lock view. Fetch sessions that were assigned an equal pair of ID2 and ID2 fields and have conflicting lock modes.

Now see how to use both scripts for locks analysis. For example, suppose users JOHN and MIKE try to update a row in the scott.emp table using the following statement:

```
UPDATE emp SET deptno=30 WHERE empno=7369;
```

User JOHN issued an update first and does not commit. Thus, MIKE's transaction is waiting for a resource (table EMP) to be unlocked. If we run the first lock-monitoring script, we see what objects are locked and what transactions are waiting. From the exemplary output, table EMP has some rows locked by JOHN, and user MIKE is waiting and ready to lock a row.

```
###############################################
Object Locks:
###############################################
                       USER
OBJECT    OSUSER     NAME     SID    SERIAL#    WAIT
EMP       JOHN       JOHN       8          9
EMP       MIKE       MIKE      10         62    WAIT

LOCK      MODE                MODE
TYPE      HELD                REQUESTED
-------   ------------------  ----------------
DML       Row-X (SX)          None
DML       Row-X (SX)          None
```

To establish exactly which transaction is holding the lock requested by the waiting transaction, run the second lock-monitoring script. From its output we see that JOHN's transaction holds the exclusive lock and, because of it, MIKE's transaction (requesting exclusive lock) is waiting; these transactions have an equal pair of ID1 and ID2 fields and conflicting lock modes. So we see the root cause: it's a session with identifier 8 and serial number 9 opened by JOHN.

```
############################################
Locking and Waiting Transactions:
############################################
          USER                              MODE
OSUSER    NAME     SID   SERIAL#    WAIT    HELD
JOHN      JOHN       8         9            Exclusive
MIKE      MIKE      10        62    WAIT    None

MODE
REQUESTED             ID1         ID2
None               131077           6
Exclusive          131077           6
```

To detect exactly which data block/row is causing the lock, address the v$session view and get the ROW_WAIT_BLOCK# and ROW_WAIT_ROW# fields, respectively. Once the root cause is known, the next thing to do is to call the person whose transaction is holding a lock and ask them to commit or roll back. Another option is to kill a session, which causes delays in mission-critical operations. For this operation, we need a session identifier and serial number from the script's output. Later, we discuss how a session can be killed manually. A session can be terminated using Oracle Lock Manager: run a Lock Manager, select a session, and choose from the menu "Locks > Kill Session."

Tracking Rollback Segments Usage

It is also important to monitor how active transactions use rollback segments. To get this information, we need the following dictionary views: the v_$session, v_$process, v_$rollname, v_$rollstat, v_$transaction, and v_$sqlarea. The v_$transaction is a basic view where we read active transactions start time and status. To detect if the transaction is a space transaction, recursive transaction, or nonundo transaction, analyze three fields using the DECODE function and print results in a single column called STATUS. Reference the v_$rollstat using the transaction rollback segment id (XIDUSN field). From v_$rollstat, revoke segment statistics — the number of allocated extents and size in Mbytes (EXTENTS and MB columns, respectively). Also reference v_$rollname using the USN field to detect the rollback name. For DBA convenience, get and print the first 100 characters of the current SQL statement from the v_$sqlarea view referenced by the session address. This also ensures that only active transactions are analyzed. The SQL statement addressing dictionary views for information on rollback segment usage is listed in Appendix 60.5.

The SQL script in Appendix 60.5 can be very useful to track rollback segment growth and to reveal transactions that intensively use rollback segments. The DBA can create tables to gather the statistics. For detected rollback segment-intensive transactions, the DBA may want to manually assign large rollback segments using SET TRANSACTION USE ROLLBACK SEGMENT <Segment Name>. Moreover, before running a large report, it is sometimes reasonable to manually lock all the rollback segments using simple UPDATE statements from different sessions and issue a commit for these waiting transactions only upon report completion.

Finally, we may want to format the output of our monitoring tool. Because sqlplus is used, it is relatively straightforward. Put all the SQL statements into a script file called ses.sql. Before running queries, limit the line and page sizes for the report using the "set" command, issue the "break" command to avoid repetitive printing of equal session identification information like OSUSER name, and limit the output width using the "column" command. The corresponding section of code is listed in Appendix 60.6.

Terminating a Session

In general, there are two ways to terminate a problematic session: from within Oracle and from the operating system. When a session is killed from within Oracle, it is marked as KILLED in v_$session and the PMON process takes control of rolling back the transaction if required. The ALTER SYSTEM KILL SESSION command should be used to kill a session. It requires two arguments uniquely identifying the session: session identifier and serial number. For example, to kill a session with session id 8 and serial number 9, log on to Oracle as a user with ALTER SYSTEM privilege (e.g., sys or system) and run:

```
ALTER SYSTEM KILL SESSION '8,9';
```

Upon completing this command, the user may get an error message like "ORA-00028: your session has been killed." Note that if the user attempts to kill the current session, the command will fail. Another important thing is that when terminating an inactive session, the user will get an error when attempting to use the killed session.

The DBA may encounter various difficulties when killing a session from within Oracle. Sometimes, the session will hang in KILLED mode or enter the SNIPED mode. The latter situation is very typical of Oracle7 servers. It happens when the process exceeds the limits defined in a user profile (IDLE_TIME setting). What's most unpleasant with SNIPED sessions is that when the user reconnects, coordinates for communicating with the old session may get lost and the SNIPED session will just consume memory resources. In both cases, it is rather problematic to kill a session from within Oracle. Only shutdown and start-up may help, and this is an unacceptable option for nonstop systems. The DBA can try another way: kill a process from the operating system side. Note that after attempting to kill a session from the operating system, the user may get a TNS error message like "ORA-12571: TNS:packet writer failure."

The DBA can analyze the monitoring tool output, and detect and write down the session identifier and serial number for a problematic session. After this, the DBA can try to kill a session from within Oracle using the ALTER SYSTEM KILL SESSION command. If this attempt fails, hangs, or the session becomes marked as KILLED or SNIPED and does not disappear from the v_$session for a long period of time (and the DBA sees it should not take so long a time for a PMON to roll it back), the DBA can try to kill a session from the operating system side. To simplify this operation, we have written a Korn shell utility, ses_kill.sh. Its code is listed in Appendix 60.7. The utility logic is rather straightforward. Note that this is an interactive utility; it is not designed to be run as a cron job, so there is no need to define Oracle environment variables. In Section 1, read the script parameters — session identifier and serial number. The next section runs the SQL script called ses_kill.sql using the sp.sh shell described earlier. This SQL script creates a shell file containing the "kill -9 <OSPID>" command. Then change mode for a newly spooled file (kill_process.sh) to make it executable. The code in the third section actually does the killing; it runs the kill_process.sh and then removes this temporary file from disk.

As mentioned before, ses_kill.sql spools to a shell file, kill_process.sh, containing the kill -9 <OSPID> command for the session to be killed. The script addresses the v_$process and v_$session views. Note that "kill" commands are also added for all SNIPED sessions indicated in the v_$session view. The ses_kill.sql code is listed in Appendix 60.7.

We have considered a sessions monitoring tool and utility for session killing. The monitoring tool consists of sp.sh (Korn shell script) and two SQL scripts (ses.sql and func.sql). Before first usage, you compile a function running the sp.sh func in the UNIX command prompt. To run the monitoring tool, simply type sp.sh ses. The utility for session killing consists of ses_kill.sh (Korn shell script) and ses_kill.sql (Oracle SQL). Here, we also use the sp.sh script. To run the utility, type ses_kill.sh in the UNIX command prompt. You will be asked for parameters. Before running the Korn shell scripts, make sure the proper rights for this have been set, issuing a chmod u+x *.sh command.

The sessions monitoring tool and utility for session killing are very reliable and useful tools. The basic advantage is that these scripts can be easily modified to fit particular DBA needs. Sessions can be filtered and analyzed according to the specific applications. An interesting way to enhance functionality and improve interface is to deploy these scripts to the Web.

Appendix 60.1 Active Sessions Monitoring

```
prompt ##################################################
prompt Resources Allocation:
prompt ##################################################
SELECT status,
NVL(decode(ses.command,1,'CRT TABL', 2,'INSERT', 3,'SELECT',
4,'CRT CLST', 5,'ALT CLST', 6,'UPDATE', 7,'DELETE', 8,'DROP',
9,'CRT INDX', 10, 'DRP INDX', 11,'ALT INDX', 12,'DRP TABL',
15,'ALT TABL', 17,'GRANT', 18,'REVOKE', 19,'CRT SYNM',
20,'DRP SYNM', 21,'CRT VIEW', 22,'DRP VIEW', 26,'LOC TBLE',
27,'NOTHING', 28,'RENAME', 29,'COMMENT', 30,'AUDIT', 31,'NOAUDIT',
32,'CRT XTDB', 33,'DRP XTDB', 34,'CRT DBSE', 35,'ALT DBSE',
36,'CRT RSEG', 37,'ALT RSEG', 38,'DRP RSEG', 39,'CRT TBSP',
40,'ALT TBSP', 41,'DRP TBSP', 42,'ALT SESS', 43,'ALT USER',
44,'COMMIT', 45,'ROLLBACK', 46,'SVEPOINT','IDLE'),'?') "Command",
   ses.osuser "OSUSER",
   DECODE(ses.USERNAME,null,ses.osuser,ses.USERNAME) "USERNAME",
   ses.sid "SID",
   ses.SERIAL# "SERIAL#",
   p.spid "OSPID",
   TO_CHAR(opencur.value,'999') "Cursors",
   TO_CHAR(ses.LOGON_TIME,'MM-DD HH24:MI') "Logon Time",
   ROUND(statuga.value/(1024*1024),2) "UGA",
   ROUND(statpga.value/(1024*1024),2) "PGA",
   SUBSTR(DECODE((io.consistent_gets+io.block_gets),0,'None',
      (100*(io.consistent_gets+io.block_gets-io.physical_reads)/
      (io.consistent_gets+io.block_gets))
      ),1,4)||'%' "HITRATIO",
   ses.server,
   ses.program "PROGRAM"
FROM  sys.v_$session ses,
      sys.v_$sesstat statuga, sys.v_$sesstat statpga,
      sys.v_$statname nuga, sys.v_$statname npga,
      sys.v_$process p, sys.v_$sess_io io, sys.v_$sesstat opencur
WHERE nuga.name = 'session uga memory'
      AND statuga.statistic# = nuga.statistic#
      AND statuga.sid=ses.sid
      AND npga.name = 'session pga memory'
      AND statpga.statistic# = npga.statistic#
      AND statpga.sid=ses.sid AND p.addr = ses.paddr
      AND io.sid=ses.sid
      AND opencur.sid=ses.sid AND opencur.statistic#=3
      AND ses.username IS NOT NULL
ORDER BY 3 asc, 4 asc, 5 asc, 6 asc;
```

Appendix 60.2 Extracting an SQL Statement

```
prompt  ##################################################
prompt  SQL Code:
prompt  ##################################################

SELECT  s.osuser  "OSUSER",
        DECODE(s.USERNAME,null,s.osuser,s.USERNAME) "USERNAME",
        s.sid     "SID",
        s.serial# "SERIAL#",
        b.piece,
        b.sql_text
FROM  sys.v_$session s,
      sys.v_$sqltext b
WHERE s.sql_address = b.address
      AND s.sql_hash_value = b.hash_value
      AND b.piece < 100
      AND s.username IS NOT NULL
ORDER BY 1 asc, 2 asc, 3 asc, 4 asc, 5 asc;
```

Appendix 60.3 Extracting Information on Locks for Resource-Oriented Analysis

```
prompt ####################################################
prompt Object Locks:
prompt ####################################################
SELECT a.object_name "OBJECT",
    c.osuser "OSUSER",
    DECODE(c.USERNAME,null,c.osuser,c.USERNAME) "USERNAME",
    c.sid "SID",
    c.serial# "SERIAL#",
    DECODE(IS_WAITING(c.sid),
       0,'',
       'WAIT') AS "WAIT",
    DECODE(b.type,
       'MR', 'Media Recovery',
       'RT', 'Redo Thread',
       'UN', 'User Name',
       'TX', 'Transaction',
       'TM', 'DML',
       'UL', 'PL/SQL User Lock',
       'DX', 'Distributed Xaction',
       'CF', 'Control File',
       'IS', 'Instance State',
       'FS', 'File Set',
       'IR', 'Instance Recovery',
       'ST', 'Disk Space Transaction',
       'TS', 'Temp Segment',
       'IV', 'Library Cache Invalidation',
       'LS', 'Log Start or Switch',
       'RW', 'Row Wait',
       'SQ', 'Sequence Number',
       'TE', 'Extend Table',
       'TT', 'Temp Table',
       b.type) "LOCK TYPE",
    DECODE(b.lmode,
       0, 'None',
       1, 'Null',
       2, 'Row-SELECT (SS)',
       3, 'Row-X (SX)',
       4, 'Share',
       5, 'SELECT/Row-X (SSX)',
       6, 'Exclusive',
       to_char(b.lmode)) "MODE HELD",
    DECODE(b.request,
       0, 'None',
       1, 'Null',
       2, 'Row-SELECT (SS)',
       3, 'Row-X (SX)',
       4, 'Share',
       5, 'SELECT/Row-X (SSX)',
       6, 'Exclusive',
       to_char(b.request)) "MODE REQUESTED"
FROM sys.dba_objects a, sys.v_$lock b, sys.v_$session c
WHERE
    a.object_id = b.id1 AND b.sid = c.sid
    AND c.username IS NOT NULL
ORDER BY 1 asc, 2 asc, 3 asc, 4 asc, 5 asc;
```

Appendix 60.4 Detecting What Session Is Causing Another Session to Wait

```
prompt ################################################
prompt Locking and Waiting Transactions:
prompt ################################################

SELECT c.osuser "OSUSER",
   DECODE(c.USERNAME,null,c.osuser,c.USERNAME) "USERNAME",
   c.sid "SID",
   c.serial# "SERIAL#",
   DECODE(IS_WAITING(c.sid),
      0,'',
      'WAIT') AS "WAIT",
   DECODE(b.lmode,
      0, 'None',
      1, 'Null',
      2, 'Row-SELECT (SS)',
      3, 'Row-X (SX)',
      4, 'Share',
      5, 'SELECT/Row-X (SSX)',
      6, 'Exclusive',
      to_char(b.lmode))     "MODE HELD",
   DECODE(b.request,
      0, 'None',
      1, 'Null',
      2, 'Row-SELECT (SS)',
      3, 'Row-X (SX)',
      4, 'Share',
      5, 'SELECT/Row-X (SSX)',
      6, 'Exclusive',
      to_char(b.request))  "MODE REQUESTED",
      b.id1 "ID1",
      b.id2 "ID2"
FROM sys.v_$lock b, sys.v_$session c
WHERE
   b.sid = c.sid
   AND c.username IS NOT NULL
   AND (b.request<>0 OR (b.request=0 AND b.lmode!=4
      AND (b.id1,b.id2) IN
         (SELECT d.id1, d.id2 FROM v_$lock d
           WHERE d.request<>0
              AND d.id1=b.id1
              AND d.id2=b.id2)))
ORDER BY 5 asc, 6 asc, 4 asc;
```

Appendix 60.5 Tracking Rollback Segments Usage

```
prompt ##################################################
prompt Rollback Segments Usage:
prompt ##################################################
SELECT
   s.osuser "OSUSER",
   DECODE(s.USERNAME,null,s.osuser,s.USERNAME) "USERNAME",
   s.sid "SID",
   s.SERIAL# "SERIAL",
   p.spid "OSPID",
   t.start_time "Start Time",
   r.name "ROLLBACK", rs.EXTENTS,
     ROUND(rs.RSSIZE/(1024*1024),3) "MB",
   DECODE(t.space, 'YES', 'SPACE TX',
     DECODE(t.recursive, 'YES', 'RECURSIVE TX',
       DECODE(t.noundo, 'YES', 'NO UNDO TX', t.status))) status,
   s.program,
   RPAD(a.SQL_TEXT,100) "SQL TEXT"
FROM  sys.v_$transaction t,
      sys.v_$rollname r,
      sys.v_$session s,
      sys.v_$process p,
      sys.v_$rollstat rs,
      sys.v_$sqlarea a
WHERE t.xidusn = r.usn and rs.usn = r.usn
      AND p.addr = s.paddr
      AND a.ADDRESS=s.SQL_ADDRESS
      AND t.ses_addr = s.saddr;
```

Appendix 60.6 Formatting Output of Monitoring Tool

```
prompt ***********************************************
prompt ****** Sessions Monitoring Tool *******
prompt ***********************************************

set linesize 132
set pagesize 60

break on "OSUSER" on "USERNAME" on "SID" on "SERIAL";

column "Command"          format a10;
column "Logon Time"       format a11;
column "Start Time"       format a11;
column "Cursors"          format a7;
column "USERNAME"         format a10;
column "OSUSER"           format a10;
column "SID"              format 99999;
column "SERIAL"           format 999999;
column "OSPID"            format 99999;
column "UGA"              format 99.99;
column "PGA"              format 99.99;
column "PROGRAM"          format a10;
column "SQL TEXT"         format a10;
column "OBJECT"           format a15;
column "PROGRAM"          format a15;
column "LOCK TYPE"        format a15;
column "MODE REQUESTED"   format a15;
column "ROLLBACK"         format a10;
column "MODE HELD"        format a15;
```

Appendix 60.7 Terminating a Session

```
#!/bin/ksh
# ses_kill.sh - Terminates Oracle session from
operating system

# Section 1. Reading the session coordinates:
echo "\nSession ID: \c"
read SessionID
echo "\nSerial Number: \c"
read SerialNumber

# Section 2. Making a command file:
sp.sh ses_kill ${SessionID} ${SerialNumber}
chmod 755 kill_process.sh

# Section 3. Killing a session:
kill_process.sh
rm kill_process.sh
exit 0

rem ##################################################
rem Creates a shell script to terminate Oracle session:
rem ##################################################

set feedback off
set pagesize 0
set termout off
set heading off
set echo off
set verify off

spool kill_process.sh ;

SELECT 'kill -9 '||spid FROM sys.v_$process
   WHERE addr IN (SELECT paddr FROM sys.v_$session
      WHERE (sid=&1 AND serial#=&2) OR status ='SNIPED');

spool off;
```

Chapter 61

The Object/Relational Features of Oracle8

Donald K. Burleson

There has been a huge debate about the benefits of adding objects into mainstream database management. For years, a small but highly vocal group of object-oriented bigots preached the object revolution with an almost religious fervor. However, the object-oriented databases languished in the backwaters until the major relational database vendors made a commitment to incorporate objects into their relational engines. Now that object-orientation is becoming a reality, Oracle developers are struggling to understand how the new object extensions are going to change their lives.

Oracle's commitment to objects was not just acknowledgment of a fad; the benefits of being able to support objects are very real, and the exciting new extensions of Oracle8 are going to create the new foundation for database systems of the twenty-first century.

When glancing at the Oracle8 documentation, these extensions seem mundane. These new features essentially consist of user-defined data types, pointers to rows, and the ability to couple data with behavior using methods. However, these new additions are anything but mundane. They are going to change the way that databases are designed, implemented, and used in ways that Oracle developers have not been able to imagine.

Oracle database designers will no longer need to model their applications at the most atomic levels. The new "pointer" construct of Oracle8 will allow for the creation of aggregate objects, and it will no longer be necessary to create Oracle "views" to see composite objects. Relational databases need to be directly able to represent the real world. Object-oriented advocates argue that it does not make sense to dismantle the car when one arrives home each night, only to reassemble it every time one wants to drive it. In Oracle7, we must assemble aggregates using SQL joins every time that we want to see

0-8493-1139-X/02/$0.00+$1.50
©2002 by CRC Press LLC

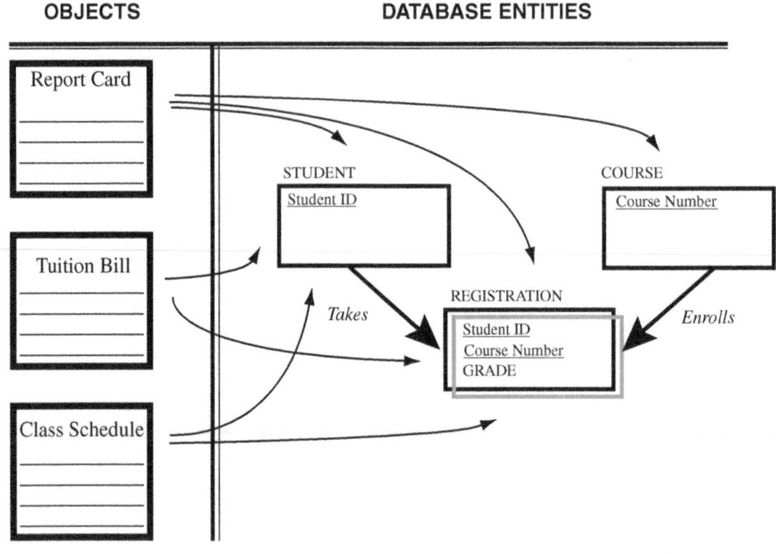

Exhibit 61.1 Objects Made Up of Atomic Relational Entities

them. Finally, relational designers will be able to model the real world at all levels of aggregation, not just at the third normal form level.

This ability to prebuild real-world objects will allow the Oracle designer to model the world as it exists, without having to recreate objects from their pieces each time that they are needed. These real-world objects also have ramifications for Oracle's SQL. Rather than having to join numerous tables together to create an aggregate object, the object will have an independent existence, even if it is composed entirely of pieces from atomic tables (Exhibit 61.1).

This modeling ability also implies a whole new type of database access. Rather than having to use SQL, Oracle8 databases may be "navigated," going from row to row, chasing the pointer references without ever having to join tables together. Navigational data access will allow Oracle designers to create faster links between tables, avoiding some of the time-consuming SQL join operations that plague some systems.

Finally, the ability of Oracle8 to tightly couple data and behavior will change everything. Rather than having all process logic in external programs, the process code will move into the Oracle database and the Oracle engine will manage both the data and the processes that operate on the data. These "methods" were first introduced into the object-oriented model to provide encapsulation and reusability. *Encapsulation* refers to the requirement that all data inside an object can be modified only by invoking one of its methods. By having these pretested and reliable methods associated with the object, an Oracle object "knows" how to behave and the methods will always function in the same manner, regardless of the target objects. *Reusability* is achieved by eliminating the "code hunt." Before methods were introduced, an Oracle programmer had to scan through Pro*C programs or stored procedures to search for the necessary code. With methods, the developer only needs to know the name of the class associated with the object, and the list of methods can easily be displayed. The availability of these reusable methods will change the role of Oracle programmers from being code craftsmen. Just as the introduction of reusable parts changed the way American manufacturing functioned, the introduction of reusable code will change the way Oracle systems are constructed and maintained.

However, this reusability does not come without a price. The structure of the aggregate objects must be carefully defined, and the Oracle developer must give careful thought to the methods associated with objects at each level of aggregation. Libraries of reusable code will develop to be used within new Oracle systems.

Now that we have seen the compelling benefits of object/relational databases, let us take a closer look at how Oracle8 has implemented these features. Oracle has implemented the object/relational model in stages, introducing objects in Oracle 8.0 and inheritance in Oracle 8.2.

User-Defined Data Types

The ability of Oracle to support user-defined data types (sometimes called abstract data types, or ADTs) has profound implications for Oracle design and implementation. User-defined data types will allow the database designer to:

- Create aggregate data types. These are data types that contain other data types; for example, a type called `full_address` could contain all subfields necessary for a complete mailing address.
- Nest user-defined data types. Data types can be placed within other user-defined data types to create data structures that can be easily reused within Oracle tables and PL/SQL; for example, a data type called `customer` could be defined that contains a data type called `customer_demographics`, which in turn contains a data type called `job_history`, and so on.

Pointers and Oracle

One of the new user-defined data types in the object/relational model is a "pointer" data type. Essentially, a pointer is a unique reference to a row in a relational table. The ability to store these row IDs inside a relational table extends the traditional relational model and enhances the ability of an object/relational database to establish relationships between tables. The new abilities of pointer data types include the following.

Referencing "Sets" of Related Rows in Other Tables

It is now possible to violate first normal form and have a cell in a table that contains a pointer to repeating table values. For example, an employee table could contain a pointer called job_history_set, which in turn contains pointers to all relevant rows in a job_history table. This technique also allows for aggregate objects to be prebuilt in such a way that all specific rows that comprise the aggregate table can be preassembled.

Allowing "Pointers" to Nondatabase Objects in a Flat File

A table cell, for example, could contain a pointer to a flat file that contains a nondatabase object, such as a picture in GIF or JPEG format.

Establishing Data Relationships

The third feature is the ability to establish one-to-many and many-to-many data relationships without relational foreign keys. This alleviates the need for relational JOIN operations, since table columns can contain references to rows in other tables. By dereferencing these pointers, rows from other tables may be retrieved without ever using the time-consuming SQL JOIN operator.

Now that we have a high-level understanding of these Oracle8 features, let us take a closer look at how they are implemented.

Implementing Data Types

One of the shortcomings of the relational model was the requirement to model all data at their smallest level. For example, if we want to select all address information for a customer, we are required to manipulate street_address, city_address, and zip_code as three separate statements. With abstract data typing, we can create a new data type called full_address, and manipulate it as if it were an atomic data type. While this may seem like a huge improvement, it is interesting to note that prerelational databases supported this construct, and the COBOL language had ways to create data "types" that were composed of subtypes. For example, in COBOL, we could define a full address as follows:

```
05 CUSTOMER-ADDRESS.
   07 STREET-ADDRESS     PIC X(80).
   07 CITY-ADDRESS       PIC X(80).
   07 ZIP-CODE           PIC X(5).
```

We can then move the customer address as if it were an individual entity:

```
MOVE CUSTOMER-ADDRESS TO PRINT-REC.
MOVE SPACES TO CUSTOMER-ADDRESS.
```

By the same token, Oracle8 will allow the definition of a customer_address data type:

```
CREATE TYPE customer_address (
   street_address   char(20),
   city_address     char(20),
   zip_code         char(5));
```

We can then treat customer_address as a valid data type, using it to create tables and select data:

```
CREATE TABLE customer (
   full_name        cust_name,
   full_address     customer_address,
   . . .
   );
```

Now that the Oracle table is defined, we can reference full_address in our SQL, just as if it were a primitive data type:

```
SELECT DISTINCT full_address FROM CUSTOMER;

INSERT INTO customer VALUES (
   full_name ('ANDREW','S.','BURLESON'),
   full_address('123 1st st.','Minot,
   ND','74635');

UPDATE CUSTOMER (full_address) VALUES ' ';
```

Note that the SQL changes with user-defined data types. Here is the syntax to select a component of full_address:

```
SELECT full_address.zip_code
WHERE
full_address.zip_code LIKE '144%';
```

Nesting Data Types

Now, take this concept one step further and consider how user-defined data types can be nested within other data types. A basic example would be to create a data type that encapsulates all of the data in a table:

```
CREATE TYPE          customer_stuff (
   full_name         customer_name,
   home_address      customer_address
   business_address  customer_address);
```

With the customer_stuff type defined, table definition becomes simple:

```
CREATE TABLE CUSTOMER (customer_data customer_stuff);
```

Using this type of user-defined data type, we are essentially duplicating the object-oriented concept of encapsulation. That is, we are placing groups of related data types into a container that is completely self-contained and has the full authority of the innate relational data types, such as int and char.

```
Select customer_stuff.customer_name.zip_code
   from customer
where customer_stuff.customer_name.zip_code like '144%';
```

Using Pointer References

The ability to define data types that contain pointers to rows in other database tables will profoundly change the way that databases are created and maintained.

These extensions to the relational model will allow a cell in a table to reference a list of values, or another entire table. This ability will allow the designer to define and implement "aggregate objects" containing pointer references to the components, rather than having to define a relational view on the data. This will also allow the database designer to more effectively model the real world, reduce overhead, and also provide a way to attach "methods" or behaviors to aggregate objects.

Repeating Groups and Abstract Data Types

Let's take a look at how repeating values appear in Oracle8. Oracle PL/SQL uses the VARRAY construct to indicate repeating groups, so we can use the VARRAY mechanism to declare our job history item. Here we create a type called job_history with a maximum of three values:

```
CREATE TYPE customer_address (
   street_address       char(20),
   city_address         char(20),
   zip_code             char(5));

CREATE TYPE job_details (
   job_dates            char(80),
   job_employer_name    char(80),
   job_title            char(80)
   job_address          customer_address);

CREATE TYPE job_history (
   VARRAY(3) OF REF job_details);
```

Now that we have defined the data types, here is how we can create the Oracle table using the data types:

```
CREATE TABLE CUSTOMER (
   customer_name            full_name,
   cust_address             customer_address,
   prior_jobs               job_history);
CREATE TABLE JOB_HISTORY (
   job_stuff                job_details);
```

Now that we have created a repeating list within our Oracle definition, in addition to dereferencing the data type, we also need to subscript the prior_jobs to tell Oracle which one we want:

```
SELECT customer.prior_jobs.job_title(3)
FROM CUSTOMER
WHERE customer.customer_name.last_name LIKE 'JONES%';
```

Establishing Data Relationships to Other Tables

Now that we have violated first normal form and upset Chris Date, let's carry this argument one step further. If it is possible to allow for repeating values within a table cell, why not a reference to an entirely new table? Imagine a database that allows nesting of tables within tables, such that a single cell of one table could be a pointer to another whole table. While this concept may seem foreign on the surface, it is not too hard to understand if we consider that many real-world things, or objects, are made up of subparts.

It has always been a shortcoming of the relational database that only atomic things could be directly represented, and relational "views" were required to assemble aggregate objects. The object technology professors always made fun of the relational model's inability to represent aggregate objects, comparing it to the "dismantled car" analogy mentioned earlier. At last, nested abstract data types allow Oracle users to represent real-world things without resorting to views.

Now, let's take a look at how this type of recursive data relationship might be represented within Oracle8. The following definition creates a type definition for a list of orders. This list of pointers to orders might become a column within an Oracle table.

```
CREATE TYPE order_set
  AS TABLE OF order;

CREATE TYPE CUSTOMER_STUFF (
  customer_id             integer,
  customer_full_name      full_name,
  customer_full_address   customer_address,
  . . .
  order_list              order_set);
CREATE TABLE customer OF customer_stuff;
```

Here we see the new style of table creation syntax. Both of the following table declarations are identical, except that the `CREATE TABLE OF` syntax will establish Object IDs (OIDs), so that other tables may contain references to rows in the customer table.

Without OIDs:

```
CREATE TABLE customer (cust_data customer_stuff);
```

With OIDs:

```
CREATE TABLE customer OF customer_stuff;
```

In either case, we have now defined a pointer column called `order_list` in the customer table. This will point to a list of pointers. Each cell of this list will contain pointers to rows in the order table (Exhibit 61.2).

Here we have nested the order table within the customer table! And here comes the cool part. We can now "prejoin" with the order table to add the three order for this customer:

```
UPDATE customer
  SET order_list (
    select REF(order)/* this returns the OIDs from all order rows */
    from order
    WHERE
```

```
      order_date = SYSDATE
      and
      order.customer_ID = (123)
   )
```

Now let us take a look at how we can navigate between tables without having to join tables together.

```
SELECT DEREF(order_list)
from CUSTOMER
where
customer_id = 123; /* this will return 3 rows in the order table */
```

The important point is that we have navigated between tables without ever performing an SQL join. Consider the possibilities. We would *never* need to embed the foreign key for the customer table in the order record, since we could store the pointers in each customer row. Of course, we would never be able to perform a relational join between the customer and order tables, but this does not really make any difference as long as we have maintained the ability to navigate between customers and orders with pointers.

Of course, these are one-way pointers from customer to orders, and we do not have a method to get from the order table to the customer unless we embed a pointer to point to the row that contains the customer for each order. We could do this by creating an "owner" reference inside each order row that contains the OID of the customer who placed the order.

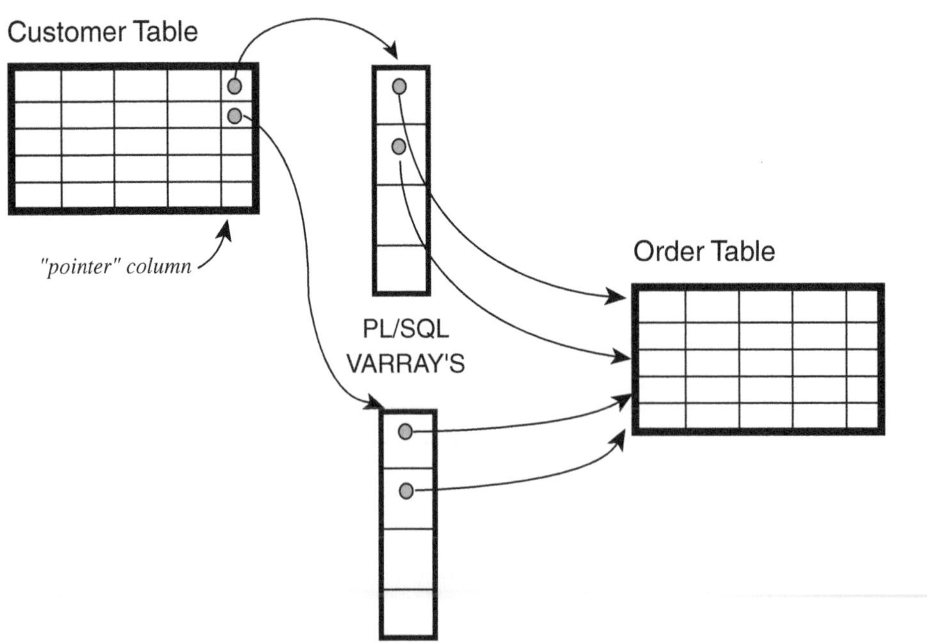

Exhibit 61.2 Pointers to VARRAYs of Row Pointers

Summary

While the syntax extensions for Oracle8 seem minor, the ramifications for Oracle database design and administration are gigantic. We are now able to design systems that support all major object-oriented features, including pointer-based data navigation, coupling data and behaviors, polymorphism, and, in Oracle8.2, support for inheritance. The new object features are going to revolutionize the nature of Oracle systems, and herald a new age of database design where the promises of object-orientation will become reality.

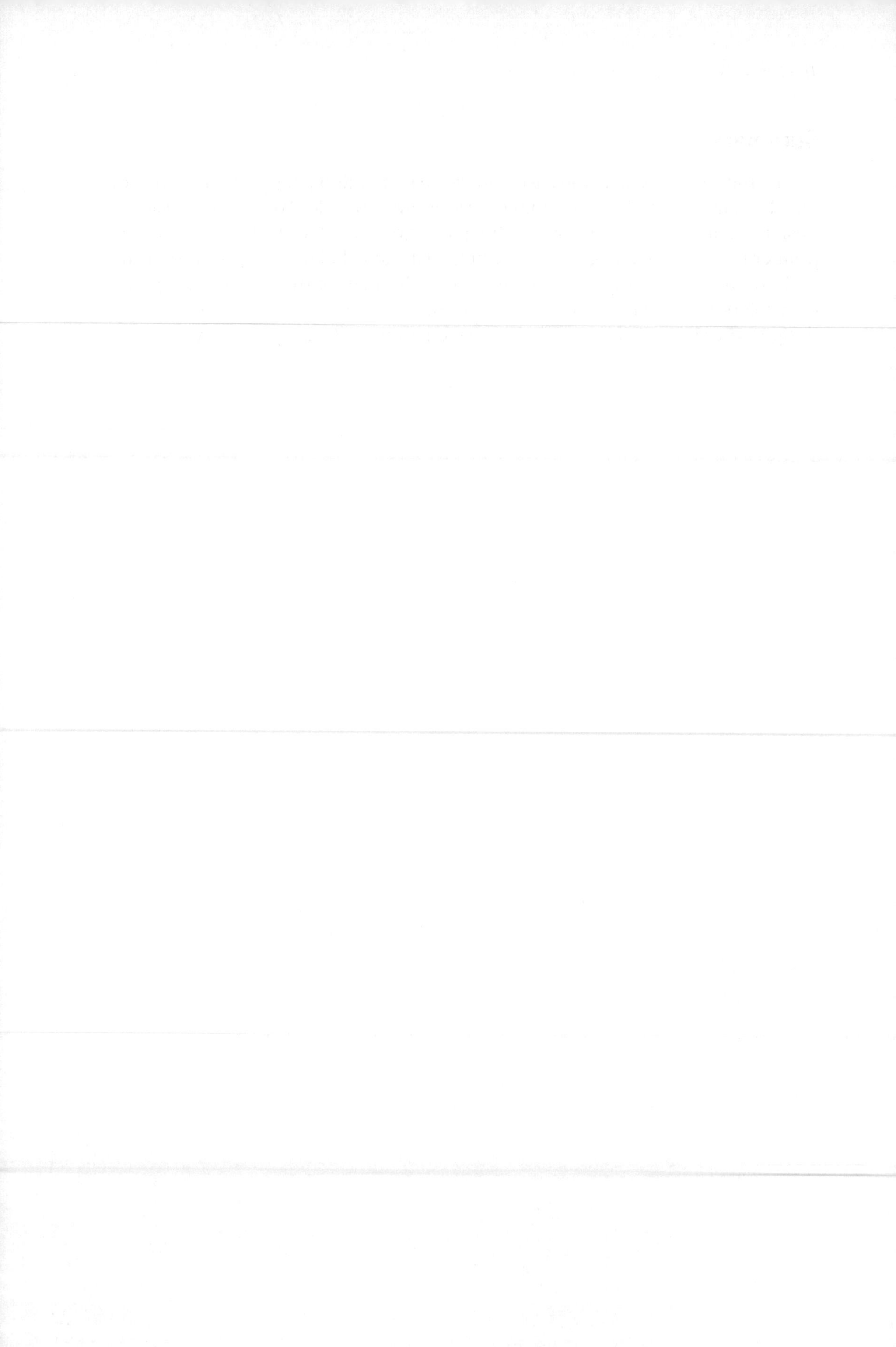

Chapter 62

Hardware Considerations

Bradley D. Brown

With the exploding growth of the Internet, choosing the right hardware for a Web-based application is critical to successful deployment. The hardware you choose will need to balance cost, reliability, service support, uptime, and performance requirements with the capability to scale with your user base.

Selecting A Vendor

The first step in selecting hardware is choosing your vendor. Many factors should be considered as part of this decision. Your choice should be based on the combination of these factors and the production environment in which your system will operate.

Support Priority

One often-overlooked consideration when selecting hardware is how widely the platform is supported. Groups of products tend to ship earlier on certain platforms, and some products are not available on all platforms.

Service

The quality of vendor service should play a key role in selecting a hardware platform. Especially with an external Web site, you must ensure that hardware installations, upgrades, and replacements will go smoothly to avoid costly downtime.

Several publications periodically rate hardware vendors' service. While these surveys are a useful guide, no substitute exists for talking with people who are actually using the hardware. Speak with as many people as you can.

0-8493-1139-X/02/$0.00+$1.50
©2002 by CRC Press LLC

Compatibility

Ensure that your choice of hardware vendor is in line with the information systems strategy of your company. Each vendor will offer different levels of compatibility and pricing. Having a single vendor can also minimize the variety of platform-related issues. Every platform will have issues unique to the vendor.

Upgradability

You always want to guarantee that a path exists to upsize your application — you need to leave yourself room to grow. Make sure an easy upgrade path is available if you need to grow rapidly due to heavy system usage, and try to plan ahead for large promotions to avoid an issue.

Be skeptical of scalability solutions that require more exotic hardware configurations. For fast-growing companies, the skill set to administer more complex configurations may not be available. Solutions that can scale in a single server, or a more manageable number of servers, may save you downtime due to administrator error.

Performance

Performance is more important than many people might like to think. It is one of the attributes that shapes your customers' view of your company. Bandwidth is key to a successful Web site.

Choosing and properly configuring the right hardware can make or break a Web site's performance. While performance might be improved with faster hardware, application tuning should be the first step to improving performance.

Minimizing network roundtrips through the use of JavaScript and other browser-side code can drastically improve performance. The ultimate test of Web site congestion immunity is to check the Web site's performance the next time a new version of Netscape Navigator or Internet Explorer is released.

Another important and often-overlooked performance factor is the speed of your internal network. A common recommendation is the use of a switched network. Building your network with switch technology offers several benefits, including increased speed by enabling servers to communicate at dedicated speeds of 100MB to 1GB. Network switches provide additional management features and fault tolerance.

Availability

External users will expect your Web site to be available 24 × 7, and they want to access the site at their convenience. Users will quickly become frustrated and find another site to frequent.

Several factors affect availability; the choice of hardware platform, redundancy/fault tolerance, and choice of backup method are only some of the decisions that dictate Web site availability. When selecting a provider to host your Web site, confirm that they have redundant Internet connections to disparate providers; otherwise, you are a candidate for an unexpected outage.

Sizing the Web Server and Related Hardware

Sizing a system is more of an art than a science. Every configuration will have a bottleneck; the trick is to have the system reach all of its bottlenecks at the same time.

Benchmarks can be a good guideline for relative system performance. If a benchmark shows that a particular configuration can process 100,000 transactions per hour, do not assume that your application will perform the same. Typically, benchmark transactions are less complex than real-world transactions.

Two sites to visit for benchmarks are http://www.tpc.org and http://www.spec.org. The biggest problem with benchmarks is they are rarely current enough to have results for hardware you are ready to purchase. The other caveat related to benchmarks is to choose the benchmark carefully. SPECfp is not an appropriate benchmark to judge database or Web server performance, because these applications rarely perform floating-point operations.

Getting Enough Processors

Megahertz is not everything. Do not fall into the common trap of comparing processors from different vendors based on megahertz alone. The architecture of each processor is different. Some are 32-bit and some are 64-bit; some can execute two instructions at a time and some can execute four instructions at a time.

The best way to determine the number of processors of a given type you need for your system is to take your application for a test drive. Measure the CPU time required by your workload mix and scale the result to the number of users you will have.

Unfortunately, this is rarely practical. In the absence of a test box of your own, you can use information from several sources to size the number of processors. Find a standardized benchmark that best fits your application. Use the benchmarks as a general comparison of processors from different manufacturers. Do not forget that benchmarks are not perfect, but they are good in the absence of a test machine.

Because technology changes so rapidly, you will be able to get the most for your dollar by deferring hardware purchases as long as possible. If you plan on a project lasting six months, buy your development boxes today and defer the purchase of your production box until closer to the go-live date. In Exhibit 62.1, you will see the processor's logical performance increase over time. In Exhibit 62.2, we look at processor trace size over time.

In general, a fewer number of fast processors perform better than a large number of slower processors. This is largely because of the inability to

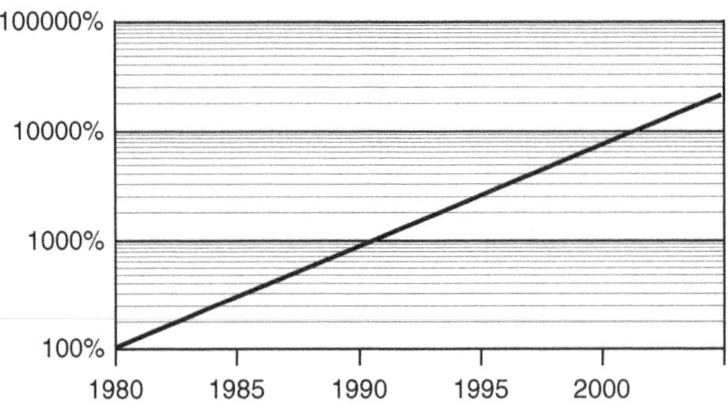

Exhibit 62.1 Processor Logical Performance Increase

parallelize certain operations; if an operation cannot be parallelized, a risk of having idle CPUs is encountered. If you are compelled to run on one processor, the speed of the CPU will limit your application. The potential to have idle CPUs is mitigated by having a large number of users.

Try to find someone else running a similar application. Ask what hardware they are using. You can always estimate what you will need, but a reasonability check is nice to have.

Another technique is to estimate the CPU seconds needed per user; then determine the number of users you need to handle during peak processing times and estimate the number of processors necessary. For example, if a user requires 10 seconds of CPU time to complete processing, and you need to process 2000 users during the peak hour, you will need 20,000 CPU seconds per hour. With the preceding specs, you should have at least six processors:

$$20{,}000/3600 = 5.6$$

This calculation is not always easy to do because response time does not necessarily equate to CPU time, but it is a good technique.

Do not be afraid to order some equipment now and some tomorrow. It is more important to have a machine that is in the right ballpark than to get

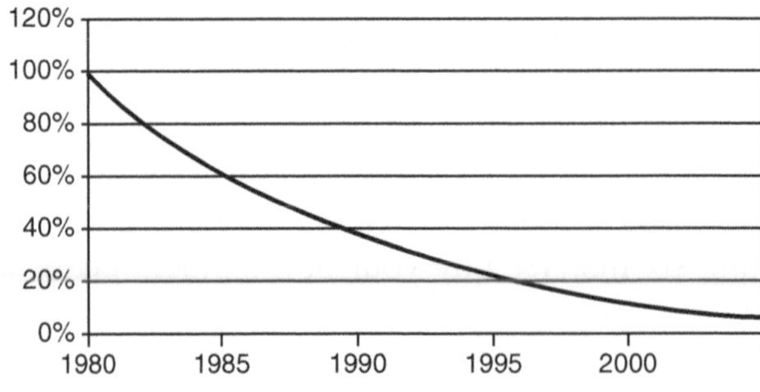

Exhibit 62.2 Processor Trace Size

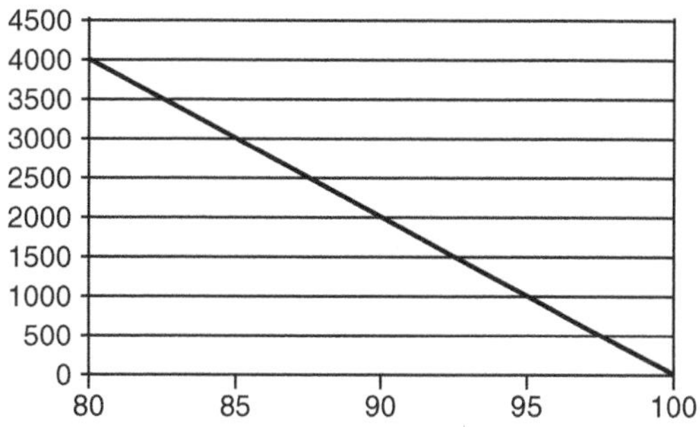

Exhibit 62.3 Response Time versus Cache Hit Ratio

the right number of processors on the first try. It is far more expensive to buy a machine already at capacity and then find out that you need to replace it.

Getting Enough RAM

RAM makes the machine. Because hard disk access can be thousands of times slower than memory access, purchasing and installing enough memory to effectively cache frequently accessed data and prevent O/S paging can improve system performance by an order of magnitude.

Memory is needed by the database to cache data, by the Application Server to cache code, by the Web server to cache HTML pages, and by the O/S to cache the file system. It is rare that someone has too much memory.

As you can see from Exhibit 62.3, response time is directly correlated to cache hit ratios. A 99 percent cache hit ratio is five times faster than a 95 percent cache hit ratio and 20 times faster than an 80 percent cache hit ratio. While not all applications can achieve a 99 percent cache hit ratio, less than a 90 percent cache hit ratio is almost certainly due to not allocating enough memory to the cache.

Cache is not the only use for memory. Applications and user processes also require memory.

As a general rule, the data cache for database should be 1 to 5 percent of the database size. This breaks down for very large databases, where the percentage is usually less; and for small databases, where the percentage is usually more.

DRAM capacities have been quadrupled every three years. Unfortunately, DRAM speeds have not improved as rapidly. This mismatch in technology advances may lead to applications being increasingly memory bandwidth bound. It is evident from Exhibit 62.4 how much DRAM technology advances have improved over time.

Getting Enough Storage

It is important to consider your storage needs — from drive size to cache to host adapters.

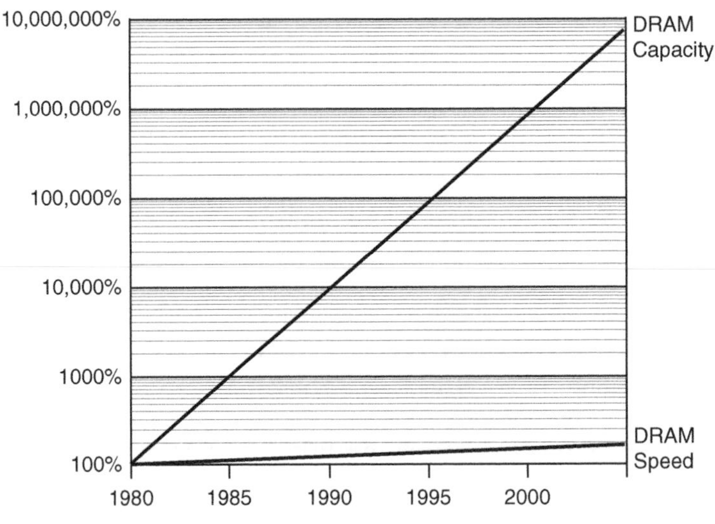

Exhibit 62.4 DRAM Technology Advances as a Function of Time

Drive Size

With ever-increasing drive sizes, tuning application I/O becomes increasingly more challenging. The following are three typical modes of operation for an application:

- *Random I/O:* in which the drive access time is the bottleneck
- *Sequential I/O:* in which, given enough I/O buses, drive throughput is the bottleneck
- *CPU intensive:* in which the system's CPUs are the bottleneck

Of the preceding three most common performance bottlenecks listed, two are related to storage.

Determine if your application will be bottlenecked on random I/O. If your application might be bottlenecked on random I/O, do not be tempted by the cost savings of larger hard drives. The way to process additional I/Os per second is to have additional hard drives.

Drive capacities have quadrupled every three years, similar to DRAM capacities. Unfortunately, drive speeds have not improved as rapidly.

Cache

A large amount of disk cache can be a double-edged sword. Disk cache can dramatically improve write performance by registering a successful write as soon as the write reaches the cache. Because memory is thousands of times faster than disk, writes can be completed 10 to 1000s of times faster than writing to disk.

Regardless of the amount of cache, read and write performances are ultimately limited by the underlying drives. For example, if you have one drive that can write at 10 Mbps, you may be able to achieve better throughput for short periods.

Host Adapters

The choice of host adapters and number of host adapters affect performance. There are many types of I/O buses in use today. The more popular interfaces for open systems are Fast-Wide SCSI, Ultra SCSI, Ultra2 SCSI, and Fibre Channel.

Fiber Channel, renamed to Fibre Channel, does not require fiber optics. Fibre Channel interface cards are available using either fiber-optic or copper cables.

Having enough host adapters can greatly improve performance. Even with the fastest interfaces available today, as few as seven drives performing sequential reads can saturate a single I/O controller. While it is usually impractical to have enough host adapters to handle the maximum possible sequential I/O bandwidth, having as many host adapters will improve bandwidth to the disks.

Multiple host adapters are a must if a system uses software-based RAID 1. With drive mirroring, performance is noticeably degraded when both copies of a volume are on the same I/O bus.

RAID

The choice of RAID (redundant array of independent disks, formerly redundant array of inexpensive disks) level can greatly impact performance. The following is a brief discussion of some common RAID levels. For a further detailed discussion of RAID, refer to "An Introduction to RAID Technology," a booklet available at http://www.mti.com.

RAID 5

RAID 5 provides the most economical protection for your data. With RAID 5, any single disk can fail without interrupting access to your data. RAID 5 provides significant read performance benefits over those of a single disk. Because reads are spread over n disks, read performance can be as much as n times faster than a single disk. When a RAID 5 write occurs, the original image of a block must be read, the parity information for the stripe must be read, the new data must be written, the new parity must be computed, and the new parity information must be written to disk.

RAID 1

RAID 1 is based on mirroring. At least two copies of each data file exist. Read performance can range from 2 to $2N$ times the performance of a single disk.

Write performance is not significantly different from a single disk. Performance is dictated by the application's capability to spread out I/O activity across several disks. If there are read hotspots, performance will be close to two times the performance of a single disk. If read activity can be spread out over several devices, read performance will be close to 2*N* times that of a single disk. RAID 1 should be used when I/O activity can be evenly spread across several file systems.

RAID 1+0

RAID 1+0 is based on mirroring combined with striping across several disks. As with RAID 1, at least two copies of each data file exist. Read performance is typically 2*N* times the performance of a single disk. Write performance ranges from 1 to *N* times that of a single disk. The advantage that RAID 1+0 has over RAID 1 is the transparent striping of I/O activity. RAID 1+0 offers enhanced data protection over that of RAID 5 because multiple disks in a RAID 1+0 can fail before there is data loss. RAID 1+0 is usually the best choice for your storage subsystem.

Hardware versus Software RAID

Little performance difference exists between hardware and software RAID. The main difference is where the processing occurs. With software RAID, the processing occurs in the host system's CPUs. With hardware RAID, the processing occurs either in the host interface or in a RAID array. If your environment requires a storage area network (SAN), hardware RAID array is the best choice.

Choosing an Operating System

While the choice of hardware usually dictates the operating system, several situations exist for which this is not the case.

Compaq Tru64 UNIX versus Windows NT on Alpha Processors

Traditionally, this has been an easy decision. Tru64 UNIX, formerly Digital UNIX, was usually a better choice than Windows NT. With Compaq acquiring Digital, the choice may not be as clear. Although Compaq has stated publicly that it intends to continue to actively support Tru64 UNIX, the empirical evidence is clouded. With Oracle, all evidence points to Tru64 UNIX being the preferred operating system. Oracle has consistently shipped products for Tru64 UNIX prior to shipping for Windows NT on Alpha.

While the future direction may not be clear, unless you have a compelling reason to run Windows NT on Alpha, Tru64 UNIX is more stable and is better supported by Oracle.

Windows NT versus Linux on Intel Processors

Windows NT and Windows 2000, on Intel hardware, are very widely supported operating systems. The downsides to Windows NT have traditionally been stability, scalability, and overhead. While Linux was thrust into the limelight by many factors, including a government antitrust investigation of Microsoft, it is a viable alternative to Windows NT.

Who has the performance edge? It is difficult to say because it changes all the time.

Refer to Exhibit 62.5 for a result summary. The main trend one notices when digging deeper into the benchmarks is that NT takes better advantage of multiple processors than Linux. This is probably because multiprocessor support is relatively new to Linux.

As Linux continues to mature, expect the multiprocessor performance gap to close. Linux is less resource-intensive an operating system than NT (Linux runs respectably on a 486 with 32 MB of RAM); therefore, performance will likely be better on Linux.

Based on recent product release dates, Windows NT is better supported by Oracle. However, Oracle has stated that it intends to fully support Linux. At the time of writing, Oracle8i, Oracle Application Server 4, and WebDB were all available for Linux. In addition, Developer Server 6.0 was available in beta release. Oracle has plans to release Oracle Applications for Linux.

With major hardware vendors including Dell, Compaq, and IBM supporting Linux, it will be around for the long haul. Silicon Graphics has even talked about dropping Irix in favor of Linux.

For people who are cost conscious, already have UNIX expertise in-house, or do not have a compelling reason to run Windows NT, Linux is a good option. If you only have Windows NT expertise in-house, Windows NT is probably the better choice.

Linux on Non-Intel Processors

While Linux is available on many non-Intel platforms, the other platforms are not as well supported at this time. At the time of writing, running Linux on anything other than Intel-based hardware is not recommended. Currently, Oracle only supports Linux on Intel.

Researching Available Patches

Staying current with operating system and firmware patches can improve system security, stability, and performance. The best place to look for patches is usually the vendor's Web site.

Some vendors, such as Sun, provide a patch analysis tool. The patchdiag tool can be downloaded from http://sunsolve.sun.com. Microsoft has a security patch e-mail list. To subscribe to the list, visit http://www.microsoft.com/security.

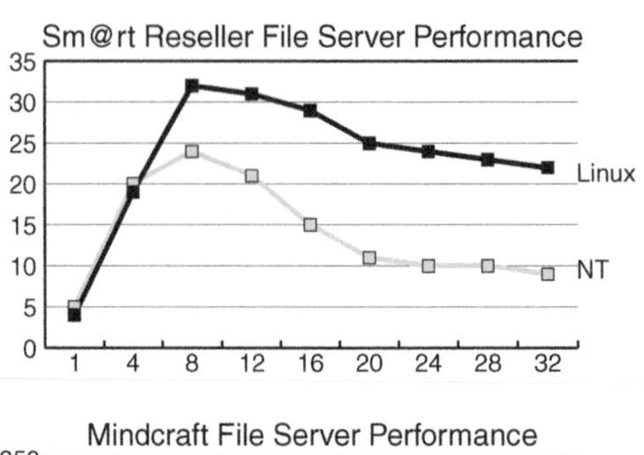

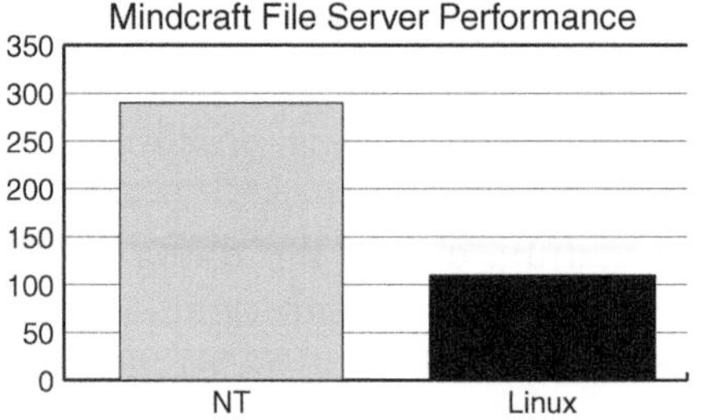

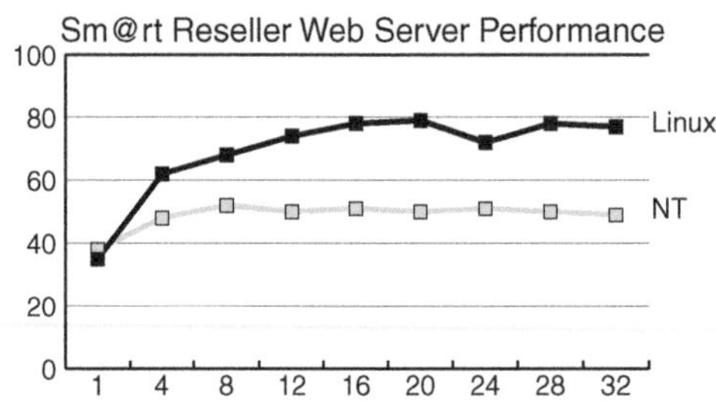

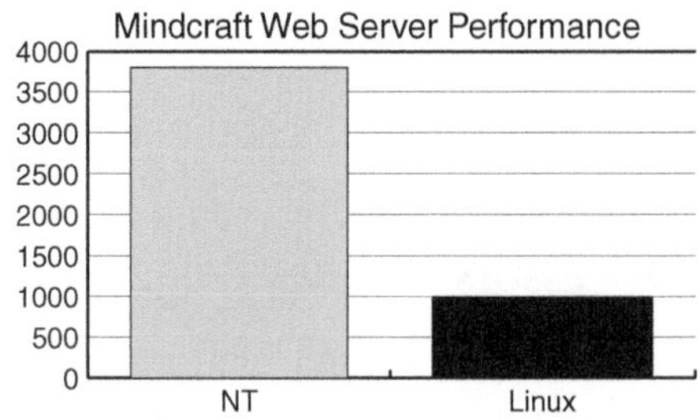

Exhibit 62.5 Result Summary

Another useful mailing list to be on is the CERT advisory e-mail list. Visit http://www.cert.org. Available patches for Oracle can be found on Oracle's MetaLink Web site, http://metalink.oracle.com.

Summary

Hardware is one of the more important components of your Web applications. It is also the place to begin your Web journey. Take time to build a powerful infrastructure for the future. Think through your decisions; ask others for their opinions; and make choices that last.

References

1. "Technology Trends, Cost/Performance, and Instruction Sets" Prof. Saul Levy – Rutgers University, 1997.
2. Sm@rt Reseller, January 28, 1999.
3. Mindcraft, June 15, 1999.

Chapter 63

Oracle Extras

Bradley D. Brown

As developers, we are on a constant search for tools and utilities to make our lives easier in the Web development world. A number of tools, toolkits, other miscellaneous Oracle products, applications, and freebies are discussed in this chapter. Today, Oracle offers most of their freebies on its TechNet site (technet.oracle.com).

Establishing a Web Development Toolkit

Do you always have access to necessary programs or codes to complete the task at hand? Maybe they are on your laptop, your machine at home, or at the office. Wherever you are working, you are bound to run into the situation where you need your tools and do not have them, unless you have a library of specific code or programs right at your fingertips. Having the necessary tools, and being prepared and knowledgeable, are the bases of Rapid Application Development (RAD). This can be accomplished with little effort.

Jump-Starting Your Applications

I am never without my trusty CD of programs and code examples. Everyone has code examples and programs, but are they in one location or are they strewn about on a multitude of floppies and zip disks? The solution is to create your own CD of cool tools and code that you need constantly. The price to produce your own CDs has come down significantly over the past couple of years. In fact, you can buy the media for about one dollar. If you do not have a writeable CD drive, I am sure that you know somebody who has a CD burner; there might even be one at your local library.

0-8493-1139-X/02/$0.00+$1.50
©2002 by CRC Press LLC

If you are certain that you will always have access to the Web, store this information on a Web server for quick access at any time. Web-deploying your toolkit can make it easier to publish it to your group. However, the CD has proven to be the best all-around media, primarily because it is available anywhere, anytime, and you do not need to dial up to the network or to the Internet to access the information.

Finding Cool Tools

Where do you find these cool tools? Finding the tools is easier than you might think. First, you can download many of the tools from the TUSC Web site (www.tusc.com). You can also find useful tools at www.jumbo.com, www.download.com, and www.shareware.com.

Finding and Using Oracle Freebies

You will find that Oracle offers utilities and scripts at no charge. Usually, these are unsupported or beta versions. Some utilities, such as WebAlchemy, are available for download and widely used, but are unsupported and seemingly lost in the OAS shuffle. You will usually find the Oracle freebies on the Oracle TechNet site (technet.oracle.com).

Using WebAlchemy

WebAlchemy is a GUI tool written in MS Visual C++ for translating HTML pages into PL/SQL procedures to be used with the OAS PL/SQL cartridge. You can obtain WebAlchemy from your local Oracle representative. At the time this chapter was written, WebAlchemy was not available on the TechNet site; however, watch the TUSC site for further information on this tool.

Converting from HTML to PL/SQL

Start the WebAlchemy application and then click the Open File icon, choose Open on the File menu, or hit `CTRL-O` to open the desired HTML file to convert into PL/SQL Toolkit code. Once you have the HTML file open, convert the file to PL/SQL by clicking the Generate icon, choosing Generate PL/SQL on the Generate menu, or pressing `CTRL-G`.

Using Positional Versus Named Notation

You can configure WebAlchemy to convert the HTML into PL/SQL with positional notation, as opposed to named notation for input parameters. This is a matter of personal preference and standards within your organization, but WebAlchemy can support the generation of either notation.

Generating Graphs Using OWA_CHART

OWA_CHART is available from your Oracle representative, but also keep an eye on the TUSC site for further information about OWA_CHART. This package enables you to draw horizontal and vertical bar charts from data extracted using a Select statement. In the words of an OWA_CHART developer, it is a "package to display the results of a query in a bar chart."

Using Oracle's Java Plug-In — JInitiator

Oracle JInitiator is Oracle's version of JavaSoft's Java Plug-In. Oracle JInitiator is implemented as a plug-in for Netscape Navigator or an ActiveX component for Microsoft Internet Explorer. JInitiator provides the capability to specify the use of a specific Java Virtual Machine (JVM) on Web clients instead of relying on a browser's default JVM. Oracle JInitiator enables customers to execute Oracle Developer Server applications in any Netscape Navigator 4.0 browser or subsequent releases and in Microsoft Internet Explorer 4.0 browser or subsequent releases. Oracle JInitiator is currently available for Windows95, Windows NT 4.0, and Windows 98. Certification for Windows98 will follow shortly. You can download JInitiator from technet.oracle.com.

Using the Web Publishing Assistant

The Web Publishing Assistant aids in the publishing of data from queries against your Oracle database in an HTML format. Queries can be executed and published once or scheduled to execute on a regular basis. The Web Publishing Assistant uses a Create Web Page Wizard to help you publish your data quickly and easily. Web Publishing Assistant is a great way to publish data on a daily, weekly, or monthly basis — such as a weekly management report. Although the Web Publishing Assistant cannot generate dynamic reports, the advantage of the tool is that queries are executed and published as static HTML data. This way, if 100 managers need the weekly management report, all 100 of them are viewing a single static HTML file rather than taking valuable processing power to dynamically execute the same report 100 times.

Exhibit 63.1 illustrates the initial Web Publishing Assistant page. After clicking on the Create Web Page button, the wizard will prompt you through four steps to publish the data.

Understanding the Web Publishing Assistant Template Language

Three sample templates are included with the Web Publishing Assistant. By opening the sample templates and reading them, you will quickly discover the intricacies of templates. However, these are simple examples compared to the power and capability of the complete template language.

```
Keyword <%begindetail%>, <%enddetail%>
```

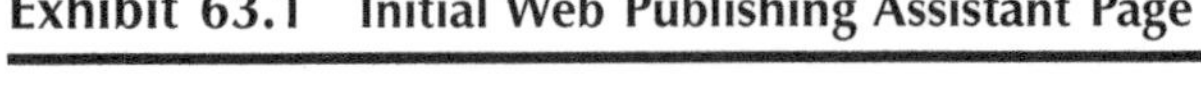

Exhibit 63.1 Initial Web Publishing Assistant Page

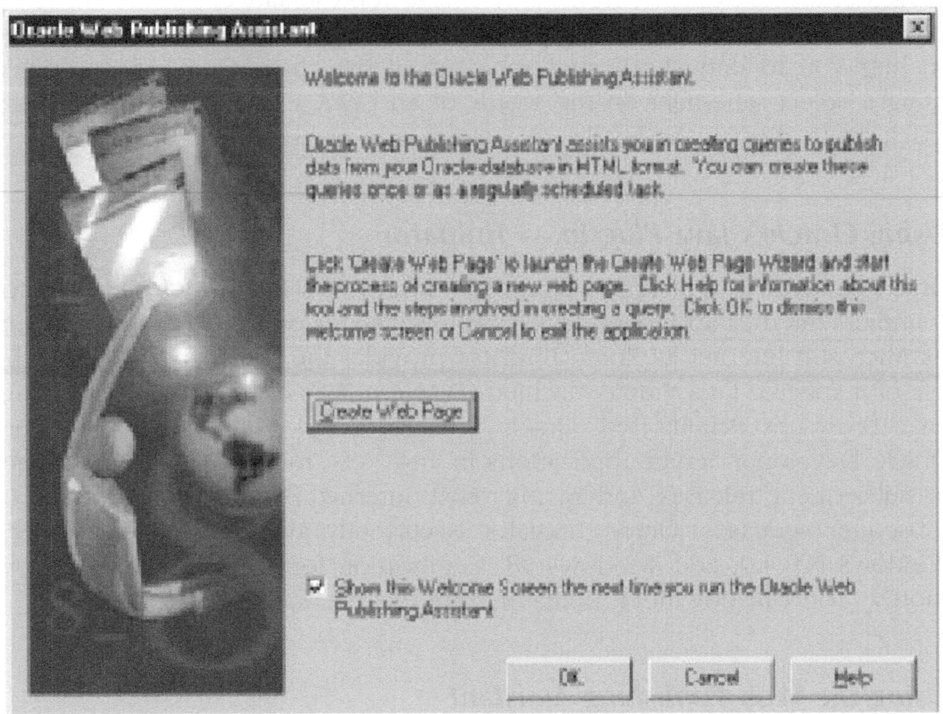

These keywords, `begindetail` and `enddetail`, surround a section of the HTML template with which the data output from the Oracle database will be merged. Within this section, the column names are denoted with <% and %>, used to mark the position of the data returned from the query.

Your template can contain conditional logic with an if-then-else statement to control how the Web page is constructed. One common use of an if-then-else statement is to insert a condition to display the results from the query on the first row with a `<%begindetail%>` section. If no records are returned by the query, you typically want a message similar to the following to appear in the resulting HTML file.

Using the `<%if%>` statement and a built-in variable named CurrentRecord, you can tailor the output so that a message is displayed when no records are returned by the query. Conditional logic statements must exist entirely before, inside, or after the `<%begindetail%>` and `<%enddetail%>` block; they cannot span the begin and end detail commands. Nested `<%if%>` statements are not allowed; you cannot place an `<%if%>` statement within a `<%if%>` statement.

CurrentDate

The CurrentDate variable shows the date and time of the Web page generation. This variable cannot be used inside `<%if%>` statements. If you do not specify a date format, the default format used is DD/MMM/YYYY (for example, 05/OCT/1997). The default time format is HH:MM:SS A.M./P.M. (for example, 10:01:15 A.M.). You can change the date and time format using the codes shown in Exhibit 63.2.

Configuring SQL*Net

SQL*Net is a fundamental component of the Oracle product line. This chapter section discusses SQL*Net as it relates to OAS. If you install the Oracle database on one machine and OAS on another, you will need SQL*Net to connect OAS to the database.

Understanding SQL*Net Parameters

To connect to a database, you will need to edit the following two files that will be created during the SQL*Net installation:

- sqlnet.ora
- tnsnames.ora

Reviewing the sqlnet.ora File

The sqlnet.ora file is used on the database server to establish parameters every time you connect to the database from OAS, TOAD, Procedure Builder, or SQL*Plus. The sqlnet.ora file is a server-side SQL*Net file.

Reviewing the tnsnames.ora File

The tnsnames.ora file is used by the client to connect to a database. The tnsnames.ora file is used by clients and distributed database servers to identify potential destinations and contains local naming parameters.

Establishing Your SQL*Net Parameters

You can edit the tnsnames.ora file manually with any text editor. The file is located in the following directory:

- *On Windows95:* Orawin95/Network/Admin
- *On Windows NT:* Orant/Network/Admin
- *On UNIX:* \$ORACLE_HOME\network\admin

Configuring and Using SQL*Plus

Another fundamental component of the Oracle RDBMS is SQL*Plus. SQL*Plus enables you to access the database to perform queries, database modifications,

Exhibit 63.2 Date and Time Format Codes

Format Code	*Description*
`%a`	Abbreviated weekday name
`%A`	Full weekday name
`%b`	Abbreviated month name
`%B`	Full month name
`%c`	Date and time representation appropriate for locale
`%#c`	Long date and time representation, appropriate for current locale; for example, Tuesday, March 14, 1995, 12:41:29
`%d`	Day of month as decimal number (01–31)
`%#d`	Day of month as decimal number without leading zero (1–31)
`%H`	Hour in 24-hour format (00–23)
`%#H`	Hour in 24-hour format without leading zero (0–23)
`%I`	Hour in 12-hour format (01–12)
`%#I`	Hour in 12-hour format without leading zero (1–12)
`%j`	Day of year as decimal number (001–366)
`%#j`	Day of year as decimal number without leading zero (1–366)
`%m`	Month as decimal number (01–12)
`%#m`	Month as decimal number without leading zero (1–12)
`%M`	Minute as decimal number (00–59)
`%#M`	Minute as decimal number without leading zero (0–59)
`%p`	A.M./P.M. indicator for 12-hour clock in current locale
`%S`	Second as decimal number (00–59)
`%#S`	Second as decimal number without the leading zero (0–59)
`%U`	Week of year as decimal number, with Sunday as first day of week (00–51)
`%#U`	Week of year as decimal number, with Sunday as first day of week without the leading zero (0–51)
`%w`	Weekday as decimal number (0–6; Sunday is 0)
`%W`	Week of year as decimal number, with Monday as first day of week (00–51)
`%#W`	Week of year as decimal number, with Monday as first day of week without the leading zero (0–51)
`%x`	Date representation for current locale
`%#x`	Long date representation, appropriate to current locale; for example, Tuesday, March 14, 1995
`%X`	Time representation for current locale
`%y`	Year without century, as decimal number (00–99)
`%#y`	Year without century, as decimal number without the leading zero (0–99)
`%Y`	Year with century, as decimal number (for example, 1998)
`%#Y`	Year with century, as decimal number without the leading zeros (for example, 1998)
`%z`	Time zone abbreviation; no characters if time zone is unknown
`%Z`	Time zone name; no characters if time zone is unknown

and other maintenance operations. At one point, SQL*Plus was used by end users to perform ad hoc queries, by database administrators, and as the primary reporting tool. A variety of tools are used for reporting and maintenance today, although SQL*Plus remains a useful tool.

*Modifying SQL*Plus Configure Files*

The glogin.sql and login.sql files can be configured to make your life easier when using SQL*Plus. These files enable you to set SQL*Plus parameters at the time of login, instead of manually setting them each time. The glogin.sql file is used globally on the machine where SQL*Plus is installed. When someone starts SQL*Plus, these parameters will be used. The login.sql can be customized for each individual user. Each person could create his or her own login.sql file.

*Setting Your Working Directory in SQL*Plus*

To create a shortcut of the SQL*Plus executable in Windows, right-click the executable and choose Create Shortcut from the menu. Once you have a shortcut created, right-click on it and select Properties from the menu. When the dialog box appears, click the Shortcut tab. Change the "Start in" directory to the directory in which you will be working.

Creating Your glogin.sql and login.sql Files

The glogin.sql is located in the following directory: D:\ORAWIN95\PLUS33 for Oracle 7.x and D:\ORAWIN95\PLUS80 for Oracle 8.x. The login.sql file is located in the directory you set as your working directory.

Making the Most of Oracle File Packager

The Oracle File Packager enables you to create an installation script to be executed using the standard Oracle Installer utility. Oracle File Packager creates the files and the necessary install script all in the directory you specify. Once the files are in the directory, you can copy them to a CD or the media of your choice.

Using Oracle's Enterprise Manager

This chapter section addresses Enterprise Manager only from a Web development perspective. Oracle Enterprise Manager is primarily meant to be used by DBAs; therefore, many of the functions will not be discussed, including Backup Manager, Data Manager, and Storage Manager.

Instance Manager

The Instance Manager is useful when developing Web applications because from time to time you may need to abort or kill sessions that are taking an unusually long time to execute, or perhaps if an infinite loop has occurred. The Instance Manager enables you to click on the Sessions menu and then click Disconnect to kill the specific session.

Schema Manager

The Schema Manager is useful to view, create, and edit database objects, including clusters, database links, functions, indexes, package bodies, package specifications, procedures, refresh groups, sequences, snapshot logs, snapshots, synonyms, tables, triggers, and views. Privileges can also be granted on objects through the Schema Manager. The Schema Manager uses an Explorer-like interface to enable you to drill into an object type (for example, functions), and then shows the schemas containing the object type that can be drilled into to view the specific object. The object can be edited directly in the window.

Security Manager

If your application uses database authentication, the Security Manager is useful for granting and revoking privileges to your packages and procedures. The Security Manager enables you to grant and revoke (system and object) privileges and roles to users. Profiles can also be managed through the Security Manager. Profiles enable you to control a session's resources, including CPU time per session, CPU time per call, overall connect time, and session maximum idle time. Database services can also be limited through the use of profiles. Database services include the maximum number of concurrent sessions per user, maximum reads per session/call, and maximum private SGA Kbytes.

SQL Worksheet

The SQL Worksheet is more effective than using SQL*Plus for your ad hoc queries during Web development. The SQL Worksheet is a GUI and contains a command history so you can retrieve, edit, and execute your previously typed SQL queries.

Software Manager

Oracle Software Manager (OSM) enables you to automate many of the administrative tasks common in a distributed environment. Fortunately, in a Web environment, the browser is often the only piece of software that resides on the client. However, if you are using Oracle JInitiator, that is another client component — and there may be more, depending on your implementation.

OSM could be used to manage the distribution of your client software. In a large development environment, OSM could be used to manage the distribution of all development software. In conjunction with Oracle Enterprise Manager, OSM registers, distributes, installs, and tracks all software on network machines with Oracle Intelligent Agents.

Using Oracle's GUI PL/SQL Editor — Procedure Builder

Procedure Builder is a great product when it comes to Web development because it enables you to create, edit, and debug your Web packages, procedures, and functions through a GUI tool. For Web development, use only the server-side editing capabilities of Procedure Builder.

Building Program Units

By selecting the Program Units node in the Object Navigator and clicking the Create button, you can create a new program unit. Upon clicking the Create button, Procedure Builder will open the Program Unit editor. To open the Program Unit editor for an existing program unit, you can double-click on the icon next to the unit. When you select a program unit in the Object Navigator, it also becomes the active program unit in Procedure Builder's debugging window, called the PL/SQL Interpreter.

The Object Navigator enables you to drag and drop objects to change the relationships between objects. For example, if you drag a program unit into an open library, the program unit will be added to the library. For Web development, it is important to execute your code on the server. Program units in the Stored Program Units node are executed directly from the server.

Debugging Program Units

The PL/SQL Interpreter is the central debugging workspace where you can set debug actions and test the program unit in runtime simulation. Click a Program Unit icon in the Object Navigator to display its source in the Source pane of the Interpreter window, including line numbers. Breakpoints suspend execution of a compiled program unit, enabling you to step through code and troubleshoot runtime errors. You can also set conditional breakpoints, called debug triggers. When the procedure is running, execution will halt at these breakpoints so that you can debug your PL/SQL code.

Building a Library

Libraries (packages) are collections of program units stored on the client side or server side for easy reuse by multiple applications. For Web development, remember that you only want server-side development.

Summary

When you review the extensive list of Oracle products and tools, it is amazing. At one point in time, if you knew SQL*Plus, SQL*Forms, and RPT, you were king of the Oracle development world — no more. From WebAlchemy to OWA_CHART to JInitiator to the Web Publishing Assistant, Oracle's depth of Web tools is extensive. SQL*Net has provided Oracle with a competitive scalability and distributability advantage for years. SQL*Loader provides powerful capabilities for mass loading and converting data from other systems. Oracle's Enterprise Manager and Procedure Builder get you into the GUI world of database management and development. No matter what, when it comes to developing a Web solution, Oracle certainly will exceed your expectations with its breadth of tools to help you do the job.

Reference

Brown, Bradley, *Oracle8i Web Development,* 1999.

Chapter 64

Oracle's Triggers

Richard Earp
Sikha Bagui

A trigger is a PL/SQL procedure that executes when a table-modifying event (insert, delete, or update) occurs. Triggers may be fired for each row affected (FOR ANY ROW [WHEN] ...), or may be fired at the statement level for an insert, update, or delete operation. Triggers may be fired before or after an event (a triggering action) takes place. There are therefore 12 categories of triggers (before/after, row/statement, update/insert/delete):

- Before update row-level
- Before update statement-level
- After update row-level
- After update statement-level
- ...plus four for insert and four for delete

A trigger's category is defined by the type of triggering transaction (before update, after update, before insert, etc.), and by the level at which the trigger is executed (statement or row). The execution of a trigger may often be transparent to the user.

There are four general uses for triggers:

1. To enforce new or complex business rules for table-modifying operations — rules that are more complex than may be ordinarily available with an SQL constraint or command. By being able to enforce these complex data integrity rules using triggers, developers can centralize the enforcement of complex business rules and also keep the amount of network traffic to a minimum.
2. To compute a value that is based on other values or circumstances.
3. To audit an insert, delete, or update action
4. To implement security measures.

0-8493-1139-X/02/$0.00+$1.50
©2002 by CRC Press LLC

A few well-placed database triggers, written in the correct way, can reduce application coding and testing times. On the other hand, poorly written database triggers can destroy an application. Triggers may cascade; and hence, when one trigger fires another trigger, which may fire yet another trigger, trigger control can get out of hand in a hurry. One way of dealing with this "infinite loop" problem in triggers is to include a database trigger *"warning"* in every trigger. In this way, programmers and DBAs will be aware of all database triggers that are being fired in an application.

What a trigger cannot do:

1. A trigger cannot be attached to a `SELECT` SQL statement.
2. Database triggers can be accidentally disabled or dropped by a person with sufficient privileges, thus compromising the integrity of the database.
3. When a database update fails, the offending statement and all previous trigger updates are rolled back in that transaction. The only way to get an output from such a failed database update is to report the error via a non-update activity such as a database pipe (Gurry and Corrigan, 1996).
4. Oracle's triggers cannot be associated with any table owned by user SYS (i.e., the data dictionary).

A Simple Trigger Example

Suppose that you want to update the student table (see Exhibit 64.1) such that if there is a change in the major attribute from anything to a Master's in computer science (MACS), then you want to set the value of the class attribute to 6.

Exhibit 64.1 Student Table

Stno	Sname	Maj	Class	Bdat
2	Lineas	ENGL	1	15-APR-80
3	Mary	COSC	4	16-JUL-78
8	Brenda	COSC	2	13-AUG-77
10	Richard	ENGL	1	13-MAY-80
13	Kelly	MATH	4	12-AUG-80

The `update` command that changes a major to `MACS` could look like this:

```
UPDATE student
SET maj = 'MACS'
WHERE stno = 2;
```

This update should change student number 2's (`stno=2`) major to `MACS`. A trigger, which would fire every time there is an update of the Student table, could be created with a CREATE TRIGGER command containing a PL/SQL block (BEGIN .. END) like this:

```
CREATE OR REPLACE TRIGGER upd_student_trig
BEFORE update
OF maj
ON student
FOR EACH ROW
BEGIN
   if :new.maj = 'MACS' then :new.class := 6;
   end if;
END upd_student_trig;
```

The PL/SQL syntax of the command is that the trigger name is "upd_student_trig." This is a "BEFORE update" trigger on table Student for updates involving the "maj" attribute. BEFORE is necessary because we want to "compute" the `class` value *before* the row is updated. The `FOR EACH ROW` part of the trigger is necessary when each row in the table might change. In this case, although we are updating only one row, the `FOR EACH ROW` is necessary to use `new` and `old` references, which are not allowed in statement-level triggers.

Row-Level Triggers versus Statement-Level Triggers

Row triggers are useful if the trigger action relies on the data-related activities. Row-level triggers execute once for each row affected by a command. Statement triggers, however, are not often used for data-related activities. Statement-level triggers can be used to enforce undeclared security measures on transactions performed on a table. Statement-level triggers execute once for each table-modifying command. For example, if a `DELETE` command deletes 100 rows into a table, a statement-level trigger will only execute once.

Execution of Triggers

Triggers only affect commands of specific types (table modifying commands), and only while the triggers are enabled. Any transaction created prior to a trigger's creation will not be affected by the trigger. Triggers do not retroactively check the database. A trigger is enabled when it is created. To enable or disable a trigger, the `alter trigger` command is used:

```
alter trigger trigger_name enable;
```

or

```
alter trigger trigger_name disable;
```

To enable all triggers for a particular table:

```
alter table table_name enable all triggers;
```

Triggers may be dropped by the drop trigger command:

```
drop trigger trigger_name;
```

Trigger Syntax and Values in the Trigger

When referring to values in the table being modified in row-level triggers, the general format is:

```
:new.attribute or :old.attribute
```

(with the colons and periods). In the PL/SQL body, attributes in the tables are indicated with (colon)(new/old)(.)(attribute-name); for example, `:old.stno` or `:new.class`, which would stand for the old value of `stno` or the new value of `class`, respectively.

Our first example illustrated a trigger that affected the value of `class` when a new value for major was placed into the `Student` table. The trigger would be fired with any update statement involving the `maj` attribute in the `Student` table, and action would ensue when the new value of the major attribute (`maj`) was set to `MACS`. The action in the example was that you would set the new value of `maj` to `MACS`, but you would also set the new value of class to 6 (essentially, automatically).

Using `WHEN`

Another way to handle the syntax of the PL/SQL body is to use the `WHEN` clause. The trigger creation of our first example with a `WHEN` clause would look like this:

```
CREATE OR REPLACE TRIGGER upd_student_trig
BEFORE update
OF maj
ON student
FOR EACH ROW
WHEN (new.maj = 'MACS')
BEGIN
   :new.class := 6;
END upd_student_trig;
```

Syntactically, the `FOR EACH ROW` is necessary if the `WHEN` clause is used. Also, there is a slight change in the syntax of the "new/old" modifier in the `WHEN` clause in that it does not use a colon before `new` or `old`.

There are some performance issues regarding triggers in general and the `WHEN` clause in particular. Triggers were not compiled before version 7.3 of Oracle. Some users tended to use this non-compilation as a reason not to use triggers. Also, if triggers are used, there may be multiple triggers on the same table ... one for delete — before and after, one for update with each a trigger for each different attribute, more before and afters, statement- and row-level triggers, etc. Generally, the more triggers one puts into play, the poorer the performance (but possibly, the better the integrity). At any rate, the `WHEN` clause of a trigger, if present, is executed first. If the trigger is meant to fire only under a restricted set of circumstances, and particularly if the trigger contains a lot of PL/SQL code, it is prudent to use a `WHEN` to bypass the

PL/SQL if it is not necessary to execute it. In this sense, the WHEN is not strictly an alternative to using IF logic inside of the PL/SQL block — it is generally better to use WHEN.

A Trigger Where One Table Affects Another Trigger

We will now consider several examples of triggers to illustrate their utility. What follows is an example that illustrates a trigger that checks one table and updates another based on what happens in the first table. Suppose you have a table called atrig(stno, name, class) that looks like this:

```
SQL>          select *      from atrig;
Stno          Name            Class
100           Adam              1
200           Bob               2
300           Chuck             3
400           Dave              1
500           Ed                2
600           Frank             4
700           George            2
777           Extra             3
```

Now, suppose further that you create another mirror table called btrig (st, nam, cl) [different attribute names with the same attribute types]:

```
SQL> insert into btrig select * from atrig;
8 rows created.
```

Now, suppose you want a signal if class is changed to 5. If putting a value of 5 in class is out-and-out wrong, you would, of course, create the atrig table in the first place with a check constraint on class to prevent anyone from changing class to 5. However, let's suppose that changing class to a value of 5 is allowable, but you just want to get an indication if that change was made.

For your signal, you may add an *after*-the-fact "check" on class using a trigger which "fires" when the update to the class attribute changes its value to 5. A before trigger is used to fix a value for a table *before* an insert or update takes place. You may also compute a value for inserting into (or updating) the table with a before trigger. An after trigger is used to audit what happened when a row or rows are inserted, updated, or deleted. In this case, the action of notification of a change in the value of the class attribute to 5 is more of an auditing action, so we choose to use an after trigger.

To illustrate this trigger, we create a script called "create_trig1" which contains the CREATE TRIGGER command. This trigger is "row-level, update triggered, after." It looks like this:

```
CREATE OR REPLACE TRIGGER trig1
AFTER update
OF class
```

```
ON atrig
FOR EACH ROW
WHEN (new.class=5)
BEGIN
   update btrig set btrig.nam = upper(btrig.nam)
   where btrig.st = :old.stno;
END;

SQL> @create_trig1;
Trigger created.
```

When this script is run, it creates a trigger whose name is "trig1." Now, **after** an update on table `atrig` is performed, the trigger fires if an **update** occurs on the `class` attribute. As the trigger body indicates, the trigger fires *after* the updating takes place and each row in the table is checked. If the value of `class` in `atrig` is set to 5, the `btrig` table gets updated. The result:

```
SQL> update atrig set class = 5 where stno = 200;

1 row updated.

SQL> select * from btrig;
St   Nam       Cl
100  Adam      1
200  BOB       2
300  Chuck     3
400  Dave      1
500  Ed        2
600  Frank     4
700  George    2
777  Extra     3
```

Here, `btrig` mirrors the `atrig` table with the old values for the student number, the old values for the class, and a slightly modified value for name (now shown in capital letters).

A Trigger that Acts as an Automatic Backup

In our next example, we consider a different role for the `btrig` table — an automatic backup. Suppose that `btrig` is originally empty. Then, as rows are deleted from `atrig`, we back up our delete by putting the old `atrig` values into `btrig`. The trigger script might look like this:

```
CREATE OR REPLACE TRIGGER trig2
AFTER delete on atrig
FOR EACH ROW
BEGIN
   Insert into btrig values (:old.stno, :old.name, :old.class);
END;
```

Here, a row-level trigger fires after a row is deleted from `atrig`. The trigger then inserts values that were in `atrig` into `btrig`.

```
SQL> delete from atrig where rownum<5;

4 rows deleted.

SQL> select * from btrig;
St   Nam        Cl
100  Adam        1
200  BOB         2
300  Chuck       3
400  Dave        1
```

Statement-Level Trigger that Performs Different Operations if an Update, Delete, and/or Insert is Done — An Audit Example

In the next example, we illustrate a trigger to audit an action. Suppose that a table, `resultx`, has been created like this:

```
create table resultx (out varchar(100));
```

Then, consider this trigger creation script:

```
CREATE OR REPLACE TRIGGER trig3
BEFORE delete or insert or update of name
On atrig
BEGIN
  if inserting then insert into resultx values
   ('atrig had an insertion'||SYSDATE);
  end if;
  if deleting then insert into resultx values
   ('atrig had a deletion'||SYSDATE);
  end if;
  if deleting then insert into resultx values
   ('atrig was updated'||SYSDATE);
  end if;
END;
```

If we execute this statement:

```
SQL> insert into atrig values (333,'Me',8); 1 row created.
```

we get this result in table `atrig`:

```
SQL> select * from atrig;

Stno   Name    Class
100    Adam     1
200    Bob      2
300    Chuck    3
400    Dave     1
500    Ed       2
600    Frank    4
700    George   2
777    Extra    3
333    Me       8
```

This insert triggers trig3 and causes a record (an audit) of the insert to be made in resultx.

```
SQL> select * from resultx;
OUT
--------------------------------
atrig had an insertion 23-SEP-00
```

Of course, other information could be added to resultx as well; for example, who performed the action (user), what the terminal was (terminal-id), the old value in atrig, etc.

Mutating Tables: A Problem

A mutating trigger is a trigger that attempts to modify the same table that initiated the trigger in the first place. You cannot issue an insert, delete, or update command from a trigger on the table that is causing the trigger to fire. In our first example, we used "old" and "new" to modify an attribute in a table; we could not have used an **update** command in the trigger itself. In the second example, we modified btrig when the event that caused the trigger was in atrig. When modifying atrig, it could be said to be "mutating." Regard this sequence of syntactically correct commands:

```
CREATE OR REPLACE trigger trig
AFTER update
OF class
ON atrig
FOR EACH ROW
WHEN (new.class=5)
BEGIN
   INSERT INTO atrig VALUES (555,'XXX',1);
END;

SQL> save create_trig_v1
Created file create_trig_v1
SQL> /

Trigger created.
```

The CREATE trigger compiles and everything looks okay. But look at what happens when we execute the following command:

```
UPDATE atrig
SET class = 5
WHERE stno = 700;
*
ERROR at line 1:
table ATRIG is mutating, trigger/function may not see it
at "TRIG", line 2
error during execution of trigger 'TRIG'
```

This error occurs because you cannot issue an **insert** on atrig command when you are already doing another table-modifying command on the same table.

One way to work around a mutating update is to replicate all required data into a second mirror table and deal with the update later.

Required System Privileges

To create a trigger on a table, the user must have `CREATE TRIGGER` system privileges, `ALTER` privileges for the table, or `ALTER ANY TABLE` privileges. To alter a trigger, the user must have `ALTER ANY TRIGGER` system privileges.

Performance Tuning Issues with Triggers

Programmers and DBAs need to be aware of the overhead associated with database triggers. Also, row-level database triggers can be very expensive, particularly if there are many rows. A few suggestions to reduce trigger overhead include:

1. Exploit the `WHEN` clause. The `WHEN` clause is stored in compiled form as part of a database trigger header and is executed before the trigger body (Gurry and Corrigan, 1996). Therefore, properly constructed `WHEN` clauses can dramatically reduce the runtime overheads.
2. The size of the trigger text should be kept as small as possible. Database triggers prior to Oracle 7.3 were not stored in parsed form and needed to be reparsed on every reference (Gurry and Corrigan, 1996). In versions after Oracle 7.3, triggers are not held in compiled (PL/SQL pcode) form. Every time a trigger is fired, the code must be recompiled. Overhead will be reduced if the trigger is already in the shared buffer pool. Another alternative is for each trigger to call a stored procedure to perform the work. The procedure is precompiled, and hence the trigger code is reduced to a handful of lines.
3. Because trigger code is repeatedly parsed and re-parsed when it is executed multiple times, retaining the "parse tree" in memory helps performance. This can be done by monitoring the shared buffer pool and increasing the size of the pool if it is not retaining cursor information long enough (Gurry and Corrigan, 1996).
4. If the SQL code contained within the PL/SQL segment is tuned based on an EXPLAIN PLAN, triggers should work better.
5. A final suggestion would be to try to avoid triggers altogether. In many cases, a trigger can be replaced by a table-level check constraint or column-level default values. When used, triggers should be well-planned. They should be identified during the initial database design phase, rather than being used as "a quick bug fix" or a post-implementation audit control feature.

Summary

A trigger is a PL/SQL entity that executes when a table-modifying event occurs. The purpose of this chapter was to introduce the concept of triggers and suggest several uses for triggers. We have illustrated different types of triggers for computing values, auditing, and creating backups. We have also discussed the mutating trigger problem that can arise if triggers are improperly written.

References

Gurry, M. and Corrigan, P. (1996). *Oracle Performance Tuning (2nd ed.),* Sebastopol, CA: O'Reilly & Associates, Inc.

Chapter 65

Concurrency

Rick Greenwald

The issue of concurrency lies at the very heart of the power and complexity of the modern relational database. After all, the basic database functions of storing and retrieving data are relatively easy to solve. It is somewhat more complex to guarantee transactional integrity, but even this functionality is relatively easy to implement — for one user. The challenge of providing concurrent access to reliable data is the inevitable result of more than one person using a database.

The Goal of Concurrency

The goal of concurrency may be to allow many users to share access to data, but the effect of concurrency controls is more solitary. A concurrency scheme is designed so that each user feels that they, and they alone, have access to data. If the data is being shared with other users, they should remain blissfully unaware of the repercussions of that sharing.

All is well and good on the sharing front when it comes to sharing data that is only read. But as soon as one user writes to the database, the issue of data integrity rears its nasty head.

Data integrity dictates that users can depend on the validity of their data. There are a number of data integrity problems that can occur in a multi-user database:

- *Dirty reads:* where one user is reading data which has been changed by another user, but the transaction which has made the change has not yet been committed. The end result of this problem is an inconsistent view of data because the uncommitted transaction can always be rolled back and the changes removed.

0-8493-1139-X/02/$0.00+$1.50
©2002 by CRC Press LLC

- *Orphans:* where a row is selected by a query, but deleted by another user during the duration of the query. The end result of this problem is data in the query results that no longer exists in the database.
- *Phantoms:* where a row that would have been selected for a query is added by another user while the query is executing. The end result of this problem is an incomplete set of data.

Implementing Concurrency

To avoid these problems, databases implement some type of concurrency scheme. The purpose of the concurrency scheme is to allow a user to be isolated from the changes that other users make.

Concurrency schemes use a system of locks to implement user isolation. The good news about a lock is that it protects data integrity by protecting one user's view of the data from other users' changes. The bad news about locks is that they introduce a phenomenon known as *contention*. As multiple users contend for the same data, locks on the data prevent them from actions that could result in conflicting values for data. When a piece of data is locked, its availability is limited, which in turn can have a dramatic effect on the overall throughput of the database.

Because of this rather dire consequence of locking, most databases have two types of locks. When a user writes data to the database, an exclusive lock is placed on the data. An exclusive lock means that no one else can access the data because it is in the process of being changed.

When a user reads data, a shared lock can be placed on the data. A shared lock allows others to read the data, but does not allow anyone to place an exclusive lock on the data. If someone were allowed to change the data while others were reading it, the integrity of the data read would be violated. Shared locks have no impact on other readers, but can contribute to contention by making writers wait.

Most databases simply use shared or exclusive locks to implement concurrency schemes. And, because of the inevitability of contention, especially in databases with large user populations, some of these databases offer concurrency schemes that allow integrity violations like dirty reads in the service of database performance. For example, a database may allow a user to read uncommitted, dirty data to avoid contention imposed by exclusive locks.

The Oracle Solution

But Oracle is different. The Oracle database, since Version 6, has used a fairly unique solution to the problems posed by concurrency with a technology called *multi-version consistency* (see Exhibit 65.1).

Rather than guarding data integrity with a restrictive locking approach, the Oracle database avoids the problem entirely by maintaining multiple versions

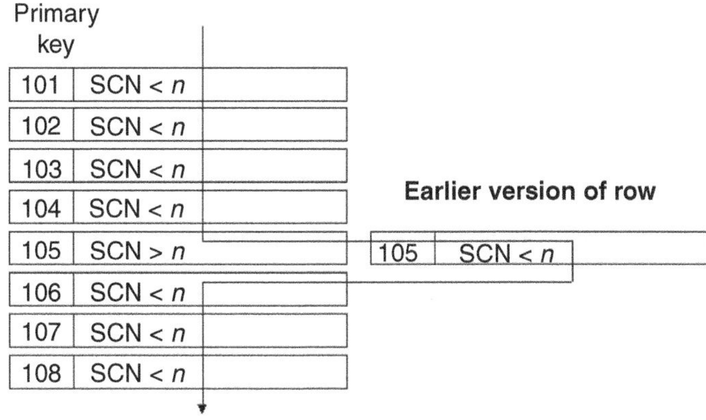

Exhibit 65.1 Data Retrieval for Query with System Change Number (SCN) of *n*

of the same data. When a user changes a piece of data, the Oracle database will create a new version of the data. In Exhibit 65.1, the value of the piece of data with the primary key of 105 has been changed, so Oracle has created another version of that row.

When a query accesses the database, Oracle returns the data as it existed at the start of the query. In the illustration, the query began before the above change was committed, so Oracle automatically reads the older version of the data.

This solution frees the Oracle database from the need to have any shared locks to protect the integrity of data which has been read. Because a query is always returning a consistent view of the data, there is no need to isolate data accessed by a query from changes made by other users.

How Oracle Implements Multi-Version Consistency

For the Oracle database to properly implement its scheme of multi-version consistency, there must be a way to determine when a database operation takes places, at least with regard to other operations. Oracle uses an internal value called a *system change number* to determine the order of database requests. A system change number is assigned to each database request. Subsequent requests get higher system change numbers. In Exhibit 65.1, the Oracle database knew that the system change number for the database query was lower for the query than for the write operation that changed the data, so it returned an earlier version of the data.

The Oracle database tracks the system change number of the oldest active transaction. If the system change number associated with a new version of a row is lower than the oldest active transaction number, that version of the row is no longer necessary, so it can be dropped from the database.

Oracle has designed the internal operations of the database so that it can still deliver optimal performance, even while maintaining multiple versions. Oracle developers get the benefits delivered by significantly lower contention without paying the price in database performance or having to adjust the design of their applications to compensate for a potential loss of data integrity.

The end result of using multi-version concurrency is that a user will get a snapshot view of the data as it existed at the time a query began.

Virtues of the Multi-Version Consistency

Multi-version consistency delivers a number of benefits for Oracle users. First and foremost is *reduced contention in the database*, which contributes to improved throughput. Because there are no shared locks on the database, there is no contention caused by read activities. Although there still may be contention caused by conflicting attempts to write to the same row in the database, this type of contention is essentially inevitable to protect data integrity.

Second, multi-version consistency gives a reader a *consistent view of a database at a point in time*. The process of collecting data requested by a query inevitably takes time. A row requested by a query could be changed after the query began, but before the database reached the row to retrieve it. With multi-user consistency, the Oracle database knows exactly what version of a row to use.

Finally, the reduced number of locks means *less overhead for lock management*. In fact, Oracle stores all locks as part of a database page, so there is no need for a lock manager at all. There is a distributed lock manager process but this process is used to coordinate locks between multiple server instances.

Flavors of Isolation

Multi-version consistency is used to implement Oracle's concurrency scheme. Oracle does, however, support two different *isolation levels*. An isolation level describes the amount of isolation that a single user has from the actions of other users.

The most commonly used isolation levels available with your Oracle database are:

- *READ COMMITED*. The READ COMMITTED isolation level is the default isolation level for an Oracle database. This isolation level only holds write (exclusive) locks for the duration of the SQL statement. Changes made by a statement in a transaction with this isolation level can be seen by other transactions before the transaction is complete.
- *SERIALIZABLE*. The SERIALIZABLE isolation level ensures that each transaction will appear as a discrete operation; as if potentially conflicting transactions actually occurred in serial form. With this isolation level, all write locks are held for the duration of the transaction. Changes made by a transaction with this isolation level cannot be seen by others until the transaction is complete.

There is another isolation level, READ ONLY, which does not allow any write activity.

How to Set Isolation Levels

As mentioned above, the default isolation level for the Oracle database is READ COMMITTED. If you wish to use another isolation level, you can change the level in one of two ways.

To change the isolation level for the duration of a session, you use the ALTER SESSION ISOLATION_LEVEL command, with either the SERIALIZABLE or the READ COMMITTED keywords. Once you modify an isolation level with the ALTER SESSION command, the isolation level remains in effect until the session ends or another ALTER SESSION ISOLATION_LEVEL command is issued.

If you only want to change the isolation level for the duration of a transaction, you can use the SET TRANSACTION ISOLATION LEVEL command, followed by the appropriate keywords. Once the current transaction is complete, the isolation level reverts back to the isolation level in place before the current transaction was begun. The SET TRANSACTION LEVEL must be the first SQL statement issued in a transaction.

If you want to allow the use of the SERIALIZABLE isolation level, you must set the INITRANS parameter of a table to at least 3. This parameter allocates enough space in each block in the table to allow for the storage of control information necessary to implement this isolation level.

Repercussions of Isolation Levels

The isolation level you select can have a number of different repercussions, in terms of data integrity as well as database operations. First of all, the READ COMMITTED isolation level allows for the existence of phantom rows. Because the changes made by one transaction can be seen by other transactions, a row inserted by another transaction could be seen by a transaction that uses READ COMMITTED isolation. If the row were inserted after the reading transaction began, it would result in the existence of a phantom.

This scenario results in a condition called a *non-repeatable read*. A non-repeatable read occurs when the same query, executed at two different times in a transaction, can return different results. Because a phantom row would show up in a later query, an application that assumes a consistent state for the database throughout the duration of the transaction could be undermined.

The different isolation levels also differ in how an application reacts to a lock. When a query issued in a READ COMMITTED isolation level encounters an exclusive lock, the query can simply wait until the SQL statement responsible for the lock is completed. The completion will release the lock, which will allow the transaction to read the data. This sequence is permissible with the READ COMMITTED isolation level because changes made by other transactions are visible.

However, the same scenario would have a different result with a SERIALIZABLE isolation level. If a query is issued with this isolation level, the game is over. Even if the writing transaction completes, it would still imply that the data has been changed since the reading transaction was issued. There is no sense in waiting for the lock to be released, so the query receives an ORA-08177 error, "cannot serialize access." At this point, the issuing transaction has to either commit or rollback the work done up to this point, ending the transaction, or attempt to use some other SQL query that will not encounter the same problem. The most typical solution for this scenario is to rollback the current transaction and begin the work again.

The Oracle database uses the information kept in its rollback buffers to enforce multi-version consistency. If there is not enough room in the rollback buffers to keep all the information needed to reconstruct an earlier value, the Oracle database will return an ORA-01555 error, "snapshot too old (rollback segment too small)." This error usually occurs when a long-running query is executed against a database with a lot of update activity. You can correct this error by increasing the size of the rollback buffers.

The ORA-01555 error can also occur if you are using discrete transactions, which are special transactions that circumvent the normal process of creating undo files in order to optimize performance. Because a discrete transaction must be explicitly started, you should be aware of this possible occurrence.

There are ways that you can explicitly override the locking scheme implemented by your chosen isolation level. For example, you could use the SELECT… FOR UPDATE statement, which places a non-exclusive lock on the rows selected to prevent other transactions from modifying the rows until the issuing transaction is completed. Oracle also allows you to explicitly lock a table with the LOCK TABLE syntax.

Choosing an Isolation Level

All of the isolation levels available in Oracle provide a high level of data consistency. But which isolation level should you use?

If your transactions do not write to the database, you can use the READ ONLY isolation level. The READ ONLY isolation level provides transaction-level read consistency, but of course does not allow you to write to the database.

If you need an absolute level of consistency across a transaction, such as the ability to use repeatable reads, you will have to use the SERIALIZABLE isolation level.

Of course, the SERIALIZABLE isolation level can have an impact on both database performance, through the introduction of more contention, and application performance, because application developers will have to include code to handle a situation where a transaction cannot be serialized.

Typically, the level of data integrity is not a gray area — an application system, or a specific transaction in an application, needs to be able to depend on repeating a query with the same results, or not. Your Oracle database can provide this level of data integrity on a session or transaction basis, while allowing other transactions to use the READ COMMITTED isolation level.

Chapter 66

The Supporting GROUPS

Anunaya Shrivastava

Group actions are required in data processing development environments. Usually, we apply group functions on the dataset and make groups by using the GROUP BY clause. The Group functions such as AVG, SUM, COUNT, etc. do not provide all the actions that are required in the business programming environment. The Group functions also have severe restrictions in SQL because they can be used only with GROUP BY clause. However, in the data manipulations requirements/data massaging operations, we sometimes want to apply actions to groups that are not provided by the actions provided by the standard Group functions. This is especially true when a logical group records spans over many physical records.

A typical case of the aforementioned scenario is any table that stores transactional information. In such a scenario, one would like to accumulate all the physical records that make up a logical record and then apply the action to the entire logical record. I try to explain this concept with the help of a simple invoice table in this chapter. This chapter discusses my implementation of the Grouping algorithm using PL/SQL. You can easily modify the code to suit your needs.

How to Group

To overcome the challenges of applying actions to a group of records, we need to first group them, then hold the group, and finally apply an action. I have tried to define a GROUPS package. The logic for this package is simple. This approach relies on ordering the records in a superset of records. It then scans the records; if the previous data in the record is the same as, or belongs to the group, then it groups it and performs an action. In our case, we apply the operator "+" for each member in the group. We can also try any other action that is deemed feasible by the business requirements. Hence, we can

0-8493-1139-X/02/$0.00+$1.50
©2002 by CRC Press LLC

process a subset group as a single logical record that is actually spanning several physical records.

In this approach, we group records on the basis of the value of the column to be grouped. This approach is explained by a simple illustration. Consider a small table with two columns. Let us call this table "alphabet with two columns letter, position" having data as:

Letter	*Position*
a	1
b	2
c	3
a	1
d	4

Now that we have this record group, we want to accumulate the records into distinct groups. The approach here is to sort the records in a cursor such as select c1as "select letter, position from alphabet order by letter." The cursor internal picture after sorting looks like this:

Letter	*Position*
a	1
a	1
b	2
c	3
d	4

When we manipulate this cursor, we can form groups by following logic in plain English.

In an ordered data set

IF previous record = current record then

form a group and perform group action

This approach slices the data in required subsets of groups. The action in this case is addition for the group; so the desired output is:

Letter	*Position*
a	2
b	2
c	3
d	4

Implementing the Grouping Logic in PL/SQL

In coding for the GROUPING logic in PL/SQL, I have used the DBMS_SQL package to dynamically load a PL/SQL table of two columns. One of the columns carries the value to group and the other column carries the value of the groups. These groups are formed by concatenation of data values. Also, in the dynamic **sql** package, the dataset is also ordered before loading it into the PL/SQL table. I then loop the PL/SQL table to check whether the grouping columns data value is similar to that in the previous record. If it is similar, then I perform the Group action. The first time the previous record variable is null and last group record stays there with the loop execution finishing. To process the last record, we have to repeat the action outside the loop to be executed once in the end.

Using the Groups Package

The GROUPS package shown in Appendix 66.1 is easy to use in any code development effort. For example, you are developing a huge package and one of the requirements is that you want the group's line to be multiplied by a factor that you are picking up from the database associated with that group. Thus, you can add a function convert_factor to the main GROUPS function and call it in your PL/SQL construct. The SUMS procedure here displays the output of the Group action of summation. The SUMS program unit can also be made into a function returning PL/SQL table and the PL/SQL table can be used further into the program.

You can also use the GROUPS package in an anonymous PL/SQL block as shown below:

```
Begin
GROUPS.SUMS('emp','Sal','deptno');
End;
```

The above block will display the output of groups of `deptno` with sum of salary for the `deptno`.

An implementation of this approach is developed in the code package called GROUPS. The action performed in our case is addition/concatenation, depending upon the datatype. An example of the usage of this can be seen in a scenario where we have an INVOICE table such as:

Invoice Number	*Invoice Description*	*Invoice Amount*
A1234	This is invoice for cust#1 05/01/00	100
A1234	This another charge 05/05/00	200
A1234	Another charge on 05/07/00	300
B4000	There is invoice for cust# 2 -05/07/00	400
B4000	This is another charge -05/08/00	500

The return from the Groups function is a pl/sql table holding groups with the action performed on the group. This table output is displayed via standard package — the DBMS_OUTPUT.PUT_LINE. This pl/sql table can be used in any programming effort where we need to group records and perform a group action and return the records after the action is performed.

The output of the calls to GROUPS.SUMS is displayed in Exhibits 66.1 and 66.2.

Exhibit 66.1 Summing the Invoice Amount for Invoice Numbers

```
Begin
GROUPS.SUMS('INVOICE','Invoice_Amount','Invoice_Number');
End;

OUTPUT
-------------
A1234 600
B4000 900
```

Exhibit 66.2 Concatenating the Invoice Description for Invoice Numbers

```
Begin
GROUPS.SUMS('Invoice','Invoice_description', 'Invoice_number');
End;

OUTPUT

A1234 This is invoice for cust#1 05/01/00 This is another charge
 05/05/00 Another charge on 05/07/00
B4000 There is invoice for cust# 2 -05/07/00 This is another charge
 05/08/006
```

Conclusions

The Groups function described in this chapter gives you an easy way to group data within a PL/SQL program rather than resorting to the GROUP BY clause or using Group functions. The GROUPS package can be used as is in your PL/SQL development effort or you can use any new actions (functions/procedure) in the package just like the SUMS procedure.

Any way you use it, you will find it to be a handy method to apply group actions without resorting to the GROUP BY clause and Group functions that cannot handle your business requirements.

Appendix 66.1 The GROUPS Package

```
--AUTHOR : Anunaya Shrivastava
--DATE :18-APR-2000
--USAGE:
--PURPOSE:
--DEPENDENCIES     : DBMS_SQL package
--
--Acknowledgement : Suganthi Natrajan
--
-- GENERAL NOTES  : This package processes the records from a table.
-- 1. Groups the records
-- 2. Applies the group sum function
-- 3. Returns the data in a pl/sql table
-----------------------------------------------------------------------
-- record to define the structure of the table.
TYPE GROUPER IS RECORD
(col1 Varchar2(32000),
col2 Varchar2(32000));

-- table of records to hold the values from the dynamic cursor
TYPE GROUPER_TAB IS TABLE OF GROUPER
INDEX BY BINARY_INTEGER;

---Procedure performing group action
PROCEDURE SUMS (table_name in Varchar2,group_column in Varchar2,
grouping_columns in Varchar2,p_delimiter in Varchar2 default NULL);
g_datatype Varchar2(200);

END GROUPS;

CREATE OR REPLACE PACKAGE BODY GROUPS IS
---Private function to build the query string based on parameters.
FUNCTION query_build (table_name in Varchar2,group_column in Varchar2,
grouping_columns in Varchar2)
RETURN Varchar2 IS

Begin
RETURN 'SELECT
'||group_column||','||replace(grouping_columns,',',','||')||' From
'||table_name||
' Order by '||grouping_columns;
End query_build;

---Private function to return a dynamic PL/SQL table after accepting query
string as an input
--- This function uses DBMS_SQL to excute the cursor that is formed at runtime.

FUNCTION Load_temp_tab (query_string in Varchar2)
RETURN GROUPER_TAB
IS
c INTEGER;
grouping_columns   Varchar2(32000);
col_to_group       Varchar2(32000);
exec_cur           INTEGER;
v_query_string     Varchar2(32000);
group_tab          GROUPS.GROUPER_TAB;
next_row           NUMBER;
```

(continued)

Appendix 66.1 The GROUPS Package (continued)

```
BEGIN
C:=DBMS_SQL.OPEN_CURSOR;
DBMS_SQL.PARSE(c,query_string,DBMS_SQL.V7);
DBMS_SQL.DEFINE_COLUMN(c,1,col_to_group,2000);
DBMS_SQL.DEFINE_COLUMN(c,2,grouping_columns,2000);
exec_cur :=DBMS_SQL.EXECUTE(c);
   LOOP
      IF DBMS_SQL.FETCH_ROWS(c)=0
      THEN
      EXIT;
      ELSE
      next_row:=nvl(next_row,0) +1;
      DBMS_SQL.COLUMN_VALUE(c,1,group_tab(next_row).col1);
      DBMS_SQL.COLUMN_VALUE(c,2,group_tab(next_row).col2);
      END IF;
   END LOOP;
   DBMS_SQL.CLOSE_CURSOR(c);
RETURN GROUP_TAB;
END Load_temp_tab;

--This private procedure processes the pl/sql table and makes groups and
performs
-- group actions

Procedure process_temp_tab (temp_tab Grouper_tab, l_delimiter in
Varchar2 default NULL) IS
v_current_rec      Varchar2(32000);
v_prev_rec         Varchar2(32000);
next_row           NUMBER:=0;
v_total            NUMBER :=0;
v_totaled_group    Varchar2(32000);
tot_tab            Grouper_tab;
V_concat_total     Varchar2(32000);
BEGIN
For i in temp_tab.First.. temp_tab.LAST
LOOP
   v_current_rec := temp_tab(i).col2;
   IF (v_prev_rec is null) or (v_prev_rec=v_current_rec) Then
      If g_datatype='NUMBER' Then v_total:=v_total+temp_tab(i).col1;
      ELSE
      v_concat_total:=v_concat_total||l_delimiter||temp_tab(i).col1;
      End if;
   v_totaled_group:= v_current_rec;
   ELSE
      next_row:=NVL(tot_tab.LAST,0)+1;
   IF g_datatype='NUMBER' THEN
         tot_tab(next_row).col1:=v_total;
      tot_tab(next_row).col2:=v_totaled_group;
   ELSE
      tot_tab(next_row).col1:=v_concat_total;
      tot_tab(next_row).col2:=v_totaled_group;
   END IF;
      If g_datatype='NUMBER' Then v_total:=0;
         v_total:=v_total+temp_tab(i).col1;
      ELSE
         v_concat_total :=NULL;
         v_concat_total:=v_concat_total||l_delimiter||temp_tab(i).col1;
```

Appendix 66.1 The GROUPS Package (continued)

```
      End if;
      v_totaled_group:= v_current_rec;
   End if;
   v_prev_rec:=v_current_rec;
END LOOP;
   next_row:=NVL(tot_tab.LAST,0)+1;
   IF g_datatype='NUMBER' THEN
      tot_tab(next_row).col1:=v_total;
      tot_tab(next_row).col2:=v_totaled_group;
   ELSE
      tot_tab(next_row).col1:=v_concat_total;
      tot_tab(next_row).col2:=v_totaled_group;
   END IF;
For i in tot_tab.FIRST..tot_tab.LAST
LOOP
dbms_output.put_line(tot_tab(i).col2||'-----'||tot_tab(i).col1);
End loop;
End process_temp_tab;

---Public function to validate the table and find the datatype
---Also display by various calls to the private functions
---the grouped output with the group actions of Summation performed.

PROCEDURE SUMS (table_name in Varchar2,group_column in Varchar2,
grouping_columns in Varchar2, p_delimiter Varchar2 default NULL) IS
v_query_string    Varchar2(32000);
v_tab             grouper_tab;
v_table_name      Varchar2(60);
v_column_name     Varchar2(60);
BEGIN
v_table_name:=Upper(table_name);
v_column_name :=Upper(group_column);
   Begin
   SELECT data_type
   INTO
   g_datatype
   from
   All_tab_columns
   WHERE Table_name =v_table_name
   AND column_name = v_column_name;
   Exception
   When no_data_found then
   RAISE_APPLICATION_ERROR(-25000,'Did not find anything');
   When too_many_rows then
   RAISE_APPLICATION_ERROR(-25001,'Too many rows');
   When others then
   RAISE_APPLICATION_ERROR(-25002,'Others Errors');
   End;

-------Process the grouping logic-----------------------
v_query_string:=query_build(table_name,group_column,grouping_columns);
v_tab:=LOAD_TEMP_TAB(v_query_string);
PROCESS_TEMP_TAB(v_Tab,p_delimiter);
END SUMS;

END GROUPS;
/
```

Chapter 67

Registering a Metadata Schema

Alex Watts

Many applications use metadata and many also hold their metadata in relational databases. Typically, this metadata is updated regularly. A change to the metadata for one application may cause another application using the same metadata to stop working. This is a familiar configuration management problem that its similar to the problem of changing common program code when working in a team. The solution requires a configuration management tool that operates at the level of rows in a database.

Oracle Designer 6i provides such a tool. It includes a set of configuration management tools and the ability to "register" a metadata schema within the Designer 6i Repository. With these features, it is possible to checkout and checkin metadata rows. Each checkout creates a private editable copy of the metadata row that cannot be seen by other users until it is checked in. Each checkin makes the metadata row non-editable and allocates a unique version number to that row. Designer enables users to work with metadata rows on branches and add them into configurations that are equivalent to code labels. These configuration management features apply to all objects held in the Designer 6i Repository — not just metadata.

The Designer 6i configuration management features are a large topic in their own right. Key concepts are Workareas, Containers, and Configurations. Workareas are the working environment of Designer 6i and are based on workarea rules that determine what is visible within the workarea. Containers work in the same way as folders in a file system. There are two types of containers: Folders and Application Systems. Every object that exists in the Repository must exist in a container within a workarea. Configurations are the equivalent of a "label" or "stripe." They allow a user to group related Repository objects and include this group of objects in a workarea using the workarea rules.

0-8493-1139-X/02/$0.00+$1.50
©2002 by CRC Press LLC

How Registration Works

Registration requires your original metadata schema to exist as an Oracle database user outside the Designer 6i Repository. Registration creates a new set of database objects in the Repository that look and behave like the original set of objects, but the rows can be versioned and used in configurations and workareas. The objects are implemented differently from the originals in order to support versioning and configuration management. For example, a constraint is implemented as a trigger and a table as a view. The metadata can be created, updated, and deleted in the Repository using ordinary SQL. The data can be configuration managed using the new Designer 6i PL/SQL and Java APIs, as well as the Repository Object Navigator (RON) and the Repository Command line (CMT) tools. Alternatively, the data can be manipulated with the Designer 6i CDAPI.

How to Register a Schema

To register a schema, you need to execute a number of functions in the jr_registration PL/SQL package.

Step 1

Execute jr_registration.register ('<SCHEMA NAME->',-true,true,true,'<OUTPUT DIRECTORY>'), where the schema name contains the metadata schema and the output directory has been configured as a utl_file_dir in the init.ora. This step populates the Designer metadata that describes the registered schema in the Repository.

Step 2

Execute jr_registration.generate ('<SCHEMA NAME->' ,'<OUTPUT DIRECTORY>' ,'<OUTPUT DIRECTORY>'). This step creates the Repository database objects that implement the schema in the Repository.

Step 3

Execute jr_registration.migrate ('<SCHEMA NAME->' , '<WORKAREA>' , '<CONTAINER>' , '<OUTPUT DIRECTORY>' ,'<OUTPUT DIRECTORY>'). This step is optional. If run, it will copy all data from the original schema into the Repository implementation of that schema.

The output directories will contain the logs from these three steps as well as the SQL and PL/SQL created by registration. The latter can be modified and rerun to add extra functionality or fix bugs in the generated code.

How to Use the Registered Metadata Using SQL

Existing SQL that refers to a table in the original schema should just work against the view in the registered schema because tables are registered as views in the Repository. However, there are a few extra things that you will need to do. In every SQL connection, you will need to execute two PL/SQL commands before using the schema. These are:

```
jr_context.set_workarea ('<WORKAREA NAME>')
jr_context.set_working_folder ('<CONTAINERNAME>')
```

Also, your SQL needs to allow for the fact that there are additional columns in the registered views to support versioning and configuration management. Insert statements should specify the columns to be inserted (e.g., insert into tableA (col1,col2) values('abc',123);). You do not need to populate the additional columns created by registration because these columns will be automatically populated by the Repository. You should not use `select *` unless your code can cope with retrieving these additional columns.

You can checkin and checkout your metadata rows using the Repository tools. Alternatively, you can use the published Designer PL/SQL and Java APIs to perform versioning and configuration management in your own tools, or an SQL/PLUS session using, for example, the PL/SQL functions

```
jr_version.check_out(…), jr_version.check_in(…)
```

or

```
jr_version.check_in_changes_on_branch(…)
```

You may find it useful for different users or teams to work in different workareas using the workarea rules to control what versions of objects are visible in each workarea. In this way, each user can work on his or her own version of a metadata row and fully test it before making it available to other users.

The Designer CDAPI

The Designer CDAPI is the PL/SQL API used by all Designer tools to perform operations on Designer objects and to maintain transaction control. For a long time, Designer has provided the User Extensibility (UE) feature, which is similar to Registration. UE is the capability to add your own element types to the Repository and to add properties to existing element types. This can only be done using the CDAPI. A key difference between Registration and UE is that the former creates Repository objects that can be manipulated using ordinary SQL as well as the CDAPI.

General Restrictions

Oracle ran out of time on 6i and was not able to invest as much development time in Registration as it would have liked. This has resulted in a large number of restrictions. Most of the restrictions apply to using the Designer CDAPI with registered objects.

This chapter section describes two general restrictions that apply to all registered objects, while the next chapter section shows you how to work around the restrictions relevant to the CDAPI. Note that there are other restrictions in addition to the ones described in this chapter. You should carefully read the Designer 6i documentation and release notes before registering your schema in the Repository.

1. You can add new tables to your original schema and run the `jr_registration` functions again. Registration will register these new tables correctly and add them into the Repository. However, if you change a table that has already been registered, then registration ignores the changes. The only way to change or remove registered tables is to remove the entire registered schema from the Repository using the PL/SQL function `jr_registration.drop_schema ('<SCHEMA NAME>' ,'<OUTPUT DIRECTORY>')`. This is a big restriction in the current release of the Repository because it removes all the version history as well as the registered objects and their data. However, it is easy to write SQL to extract the data from the Repository and insert into the new format schema to save the data. The new format schema can then be registered and the data migrated as described above. However, all version history and configuration membership will be lost.
2. It is not possible to reference existing Designer objects from registered tables. For example, if you want to create a foreign key from your own table to the Designer Domain object, registration will not allow you to do this.

Registering a Schema to Use the CDAPI Successfully

When registering a schema that works with the CDAPI, you need to work around a number of restrictions. It is difficult to separate the list of restrictions from the description of what you need to do to get it to work. Therefore, I will combine the two topics.

Designer 6i objects can be primary or secondary. Only primary objects are versioned, and primary objects own secondary objects. For example, the RON shows that Table Definitions own Columns and Modules own Module Components. Registration assumes that this relationship is defined declaratively by a CASCADE DELETE foreign key. The restrictions are:

1. The foreign key must reference a primary key and not a unique key.
2. The keys must be numeric.
3. The key must be single column.

If you do not have a natural numeric foreign key, then you can create an artificial one and populate it with a sequence and a trigger, as in the following example. Registration will copy the trigger into the Repository for you and use it to populate the numeric value when you create an instance of the object. The example below creates a primary object, called DATA STRUCTURE, owning a secondary object, called DATA_ITEM. The relationship must be defined by specifying the 'Owning object via Foreign key' (OFK) pragma. The column used when a name is displayed is defined using the NAME_COLUMN pragma or defaults to any column called NAME.

```
create table DATA_STRUCTURE (
id number(38) not null
,name varchar2(100) not null
);

ALTER TABLE DATA_STRUCTURE
   ADD (CONSTRAINT DATA_STRUCTURE_PK PRIMARY KEY (ID)
);

create sequence DATA_STRUCTURE_ID_SEQ;
CREATE OR REPLACE TRIGGER DATA_STRUCTURE_ID_TRG BEFORE INSERT
   ON DATA_STRUCTURE for each row
DECLARE
itemp number;
BEGIN
      if :new.id is null then
         select DATA_STRUCTURE_ID_SEQ.nextval into itemp from dual;
      :new.id := itemp ;
   end if;
END;
/

PROMPT *** Creating Table >DATA_ITEM< ***
create table DATA_ITEM (
data_structure_id number(38) not null
,item varchar2(100) not null
,datatype varchar2(100)
,length number(4)
);

COMMENT ON TABLE DATA_ITEM IS '#repos_pragma-{OFK=DI_DS_FK}';
COMMENT ON COLUMN DATA_ITEM.NAME is '#repos_pragma{name_column=item}';

ALTER TABLE DATA_ITEM
   ADD (CONSTRAINT DATA_ITEM_PK PRIMARY KEY (ID)
);

ALTER TABLE DATA_ITEM
   ADD (CONSTRAINT DI_DS_FK FOREIGN KEY (data_structure_id)
   REFERENCES DATA_STRUCTURE (id) ON DELETE CASCADE
);
```

Please note that there is a bug in Designer 6i caused by the generation of error handling code. This code is not required when a trigger exists and results in the trigger being created but never executed. This can be fixed by editing the generated PL/SQL package Jro<TABLE NAME> to remove the following code in the procedure pre_con-straint_check.

```
-- Check mandatory properties are not null
   if pl.v."ID" is null then
      rmmes.post( property_not_null_fac, property_not_null_code

                 , 'DATA_STRUCTURE', 'ID');
      raise property_not_null;
   end if;
```

Designer supports a foreign key reference to another table in your schema that is not the owning foreign key. This will allow you to select an object of that type using the RON. This reference must also use a single numeric column.

To create a dropdown list in the property palette of the RON, you must update the Designer metadata for the registered types to set the OF_DOMAIN column of the RM_PROPERTIES table to refer to the relevant column on the RM_DATA_VALUES table. The following SQL can be used to do this, where tablename and columnname are the table and column in the original schema and datatypename is the name of the Designer data type in the RM_DATA_TYPES table whose values you wish to appear in the dropdown list.

```
update rm_properties
set of_domain =
(select dt.IRID
from rm_data_types dt
where dt.name = '&datatypename')
where irid = (select p.IRID
from rm_element_types et ,rm_properties p
where p.defined_against = et.id
and et.name = '&tablename'
and p.name = '& columnname ') ;
undefine columnname;
undefine tablename;
undefine datatypename;
```

There are two further restrictions worth noting here.

Registration will allow you to create more than two levels of objects; for example, DATA_STRUCTURE owns DATA_ITEM owns DATA_VALIDATION. This will work until you try to change the instance of DATA_STRUCTURE that owns DATA_ITEM. For example, you might move the DATA_ITEM account-_number from DATA_STRUCTURE account_rec1 to account_rec2. At this point, the reference from the DATA_VALIDATION tertiary object will not be changed and will still point to account_rec1. It is therefore best to limit any object structure to two levels.

Copying registered objects using the Designer copy functions only works if the primary key of the secondary object happens to be called IRID. The workaround is to include a column called IRID in the table definition of secondary objects and create a primary key on this column.

Conclusions

If you just want to register your metadata schema in the Designer 6i Repository so that you can use your existing applications for maintaining the metadata as well as the Designer 6i versioning and configuration management tools, then you should encounter few problems. Your biggest restriction is that you will lose your version history when you make changes to the structure of the schema.

If you want to register your metadata to be able to use the Repository tools and the CDAPI to manage your metadata, then you will need to work around a number of restrictions. You will need to evaluate whether the advantages of accessing the registered schema using existing applications justify the workarounds. If not, then I would recommend that you use the Designer User Extensibility feature instead. This allows you to model your metadata and integrate it with Designer objects using the CDAPI alone. You will still be able to use the full versioning and configuration management features of the Repository.

Chapter 68

ORADEBUG: A Useful (Undocumented?) Utility

Biju Thomas

> **Warning:** This is a powerful internal tool used by Oracle to debug and trace Oracle sessions. If not used properly or if you are not sure what you're doing, the results could be destructive. The author or the publisher does not take any responsibility for any damages caused to your database by using this utility. This document is for information purposes only.

ORADEBUG is a debugging tool that sends its commands through the server manager. This is a very powerful tool that can manipulate and dump internal structures. You must have administrator privileges to use this tool (CONNECT INTERNAL). Prior to version 7.3.2.3, this utility was called oradbx. This tool is primarily used by Oracle worldwide customer support.

There is very little documentation available on ORADEBUG in Oracle manuals. Minimal online help is available in Server Manager. The following is the help information available when you execute the command "oradebug help" from server manager line mode (svrmgrl) on an Oracle8 database in UNIX.

```
SVRMGR> oradebug help
HELP          [command]                   Describe one or all commands
SETMYPID                                  Debug current process
SETOSPID      <ospid>                     Set OS pid of process to debug
SETORAPID     <orapid> ['force']          Set Oracle pid of process to debug
DUMP          <dump_name> <level>         Invoke named dump
DUMPSGA       [bytes]                     Dump fixed SGA
DUMPLIST                                  Print a list of available dumps
EVENT         <text>                      Set trace event in process
SESSION_EVENT <text>                      Set trace event in session
DUMPVAR       <p|s|uga> <name> [level]    Print/dump a fixed PGA/SGA/UGA variable
SETVAR        <p|s|uga> <name> <value>    Modify a fixed PGA/SGA/UGA variable
```

0-8493-1139-X/02/$0.00+$1.50
©2002 by CRC Press LLC

```
PEEK           <addr> <len> [level]      Print/Dump memory
POKE           <addr> <len> <value>      Modify memory
WAKEUP         <orapid>                  Wake up Oracle process
SUSPEND                                  Suspend execution
RESUME                                   Resume execution
FLUSH                                    Flush pending writes to trace file
TRACEFILE_NAME                           Get name of trace file
LKDEBUG                                  Invoke lock manager debugger
CORE                                     Dump core without crashing process
IPC                                      Dump ipc information
UNLIMIT                                  Unlimit the size of the trace file
PROCSTAT                                 Dump process statistics
CALL           <func> [arg1] ... [argn] Invoke function with arguments
SVRMGR>
```

If used carefully, ORADEBUG can be used to troubleshoot many problems and to find process and shared memory information. Basically, you set the session to the process you want to debug and execute the appropriate ORADEBUG command. Each time an ORADEBUG command is to be executed, it has to be prefixed by the utility name "oradebug." Take a look at a few of the commands in ORADEBUG in detail.

To Find Which Shared Memory Segment Is Associated with the SGA of Database

From UNIX level, to find the shared memory and semaphore allocation, use the "ipcs" command.

```
$ ipcs -smb
IPC status from <running system> as of Mon Dec 20 10:29:10 1999
T     ID          KEY           MODE          OWNER      GROUP    SEGSZ
Shared Memory:
m     0           0x000057de    --rw-rw-r--   root       FS       139264
m     1           0x000081aa    --rw-rw-r--   root       FS       147456
m     602         0x0000af5e    --rw-rw-r--   root       FS       3352
m     759903      0x0e46a413    --rw-r-----   oracle     dba      37019648
m     755107      00000000      --rw-------   oracle     dba      110592
m     483308      0x03847c10    --rw-rw----   oracle     dba      17448960
m     151509      00000000      --rw-------   oracle     dba      1212
m     351610      0x1aaa67f4    --rw-rw----   oracle     dba      57229312

T     ID          KEY           MODE          OWNER      GROUP    NSEMS
Semaphores:
s     133890048   00000000      --ra-r-----   oracle     dba      100
s     78512130    00000000      --ra-------   oracle     dba      2
s     70713347    00000000      --ra-ra----   oracle     dba      50
s     21037060    00000000      --ra-------   oracle     dba      2
s     9961478     00000000      --ra-ra----   oracle     dba      100
$
```

The flags given with the "ipcs" command are **s** for shared memory, **m** for semaphores, and **b** for the size in bytes. We see here that Oracle owns many shared memory segments; there are three database instances running on this server. To find out which shared memory segment is associated with the instance, we can make use of the ORADEBUG utility.

Connect to the database using svrmgrl and issue the command "oradebug ipc," which gives the following information:

```
SVRMGR> ORADEBUG ipc
Shared memory information written to trace file.
-------------------- Semaphores --------------------
Total number of semaphores = 50
Number of semaphores per set = 50
Number of semaphore sets = 1
Semaphore identifiers:
70713347
SVRMGR>
SVRMGR>
```

Now, it is known that the semaphore id 70713347 from the "ipcs -smb" is associated with this instance. Note from the above listing that the shared memory information is written to a trace file. Look at the trace file written to your USER_DUMP_DEST directory; it will have the shared memory id and more information about how the shared memory is used. ("show parameters dump" from svrmgrl will show the value for USER_DUMP_DEST set to the instance.) The "shmid" in the trace file generated by the above command had 483308, whose shared memory segment size from the "ipcs" command is 17MB. In Oracle7, the shared memory information is shown on the Server Manager screen. Normally, if the output from "oradebug" command produces only a few lines of output, the output is relayed to the Server Manager. Here is an output from an Oracle7 database.

```
SVRMGR> oradebug ipc
-------------- Shared memory --------------
Seg Id       Address     Size
521          c6295000    657272832
Total: # of segments = 1, size = 657272832
-------------- Semaphores ----------------
Total number of semaphores = 500
Number of semaphores per set = 500
Number of semaphore sets = 1
Semaphore identifiers:
6141
SVRMGR>
```

Here, Seg Id 521 is the shared memory segment id and 6141 is the semaphore identifier.

Sometimes, the Oracle database does not shut down properly and the shared memory and semaphores are left hanging (mostly when you do a shutdown abort); then the UNIX admin may need to remove them manually by using the "ipcrm" command. (You might get an ORA-600 [SKGMBUSY] error when starting the instance. Rebooting the server will clear all segments, but this is not always practical.) The ORADEBUG utility is useful to find the id of the instance to remove the proper shared memory and semaphore segment.

```
Current sessions in Oracle
O/S                                    Oracle     Oracle     UNIX
Login       Oracle      Session        Session    Serial     Process     Oracle
ID          User ID     Status         ID         No         ID          PID
--------    --------    --------       -------    -------    -------     ------
b2t           B2T       INACTIVE          10        8972       14743        12
b2t           SYS       INACTIVE          11        7673       14588        11
oracle        B2T       ACTIVE             9          31       14475        10
```

To Suspend and Resume an Oracle Session

ORADEBUG can be used to suspend an active Oracle session. You need to know the pid value from the v$process view of the session you want to suspend. Use the following query to get the session information. You may add the appropriate 'where' condition to filter the query.

```
set pages 999 lines 80 trims on echo off verify off pau off
ttitle 'Current sessions in Oracle'
column pu format a8 heading 'O/S|Login|ID' justify left
column su format a8 heading 'Oracle|User ID' justify left
column stat format a8 heading 'Session|Status' justify left
column ssid format 999999 heading 'Oracle|Session|ID' justify right
column sser format 999999 heading 'Oracle|Serial|No' justify right
column spid format 999999 heading 'UNIX|Process|ID' justify right
column ppid format 999 heading 'Oracle|PID' justify right

select s.osuser pu,
  s.username su,
  s.status stat,
  s.sid ssid,
  s.serial# sser,
  lpad(p.spid,7) spid,
  p.pid ppid
from v$process p,
    v$session s
where  p.addr=s.paddr
and    s.username is not null
order by 1,2,7
/
```

Let's now suspend the SID 9. Log in to server manager and connect as internal. Set the Oracle PID of the process to debug using the "setorapid" command in ORADEBUG. It displays the UNIX process id and the database instance name so you can be sure of what session you are playing with.

```
SVRMGR> oradebug setorapid 10
Unix process pid: 14475, image: oracleDBTEST
SVRMGR> oradebug suspend
Statement processed.
SVRMGR>
```

To resume the session, do the same as above to set the PID and do "oradebug resume":

```
SVRMGR> oradebug setorapid 10
Unix process pid: 14475, image: oracleDBTEST
SVRMGR> oradebug resume
Statement processed.
SVRMGR>
```

Alternatively, you can also set the session using the UNIX process id (here, it is 14475). When you set the session using UNIX process id, the Oracle PID value is displayed.

```
SVRMGR> oradebug setospid 14475
Oracle pid: 10, Unix process pid: 14475, image: oracleDBTEST
SVRMGR>
```

To debug the current session (normally used to trace current session), use the "oradebug setmypid" command.

To Wake Up an Oracle Process

Have you ever wondered when the SMON and PMON processes wake up? Have you ever thought of getting the SMON process to clean up the temporary segments that are no longer used? Well, ORADEBUG can be used to wake up a process. Find the PID from v$process for the process you want to wake up. For example, to find the PID of SMON process, do the following query:

```
SQL> select pid, program
   from v$process
   where program like '%SMON%';

         PID PROGRAM
----     ------------------------------------
           6 oracle@myserver (SMON)

1 row selected.

SQL>
```

To wake up the SMON process, connect as internal in server manager and issue command "oradebug wakeup 6," where 6 is the PID of the SMON process from the above query.

As a side note, from Oracle8, you can clean up the temporary segments by setting an event:

```
alter session set events 'immediate trace name DROP_SEGMENTS level
   TS#+1';
```

The parameter to pass in is ts# + 1 for the level. Basically, it is the tablespace number found in ts$ plus 1. If the value is 2147483647, then temp segments in ALL tablespaces are dropped; otherwise, only the segments in a tablespace whose number is equal to the LEVEL specification are dropped. To find the tablespace number, run the following query:

```
select name, ts#
from ts$;
```

This will return the tablespace number that you must pass in the query.

To Dump Internal Database Structures

ORADEBUG can be used to obtain information about internal database structures. Use the command "oradebug dump" to get a named dump. For example, to invoke an errorstack dump, do "oradebug dump errorstack 10." To see all the available list of dumps, use the "oradebug dumplist" command. It is very useful to know the dump list, because it is not documented with "alter session set events." You can also use the "alter session set events" command to take a dump.

Appendx 68.1 provides the output from the dumplist command for the following example: "alter session set events 'immediate trace name CONTROLF level 10'" to take a control file dump.

The dump file size of the trace files are limited to the MAX_DUMP_FILE_SIZE parameter in the init.ora file. To remove the file size limit, use the "oradebug unlimit" command.

To obtain the process status information of a session, use the "oradebug procstat" command. Appendix 68.2 provides a sample of process status information. All the output is written to the USER_DUMP_DIRECTORY. To dump the core without crashing the process, do "oradebug core" after setting the appropriate PID.

What's New?

In 8i, ORADEBUG is OPS-aware. Many commands can be executed on a group of instances or on all instances of a database. This makes diagnosing hangs and other problems somewhat easier. The new -GOPS-command prefix and the new SETINST option are used to set the instance list. The syntax is as follows, where DEF stands for default.

```
ORADEBUG [-g [DEF | INSTLIST]] subcommand subcommand-parameters
```

The lock debugger (lkdebug) utility within the ORADEBUG utility is new from version 8.0; "oradebug lkdebug help" will give the options that can be used with lkdebug.

Summary

ORADEBUG is a very useful utility for DBAs to troubleshoot. Use the commands only if you know what you're doing. The DBA can use the ORADEBUG utility to clear shared memory or semaphore segments, to take process or system state dump, or to suspend an oracle session. This chapter has reviewed usage of the following ORADEBUG commands:

Help:	setmypid	setorapid	setospid
Dump:	dumplist	event	wakeup
Suspend:	resume	unlimit	procstat

Create a test database on a nonproduction server and try these and other ORADEBUG commands before you start using them on a production database.

Appendix 68.1 Example Output

```
SVRMGR> oradebug dumplist
TRACE_BUFFER_ON
TRACE_BUFFER_OFF
LATCHES
PROCESSSTATE
SYSTEMSTATE
INSTANTIATIONSTATE
REFRESH_OS_STATS
CROSSIC
CONTEXTAREA
HEAPDUMP
HEAPDUMP_ADDR
POKE_ADDRESS
POKE_LENGTH
POKE_VALUE
POKE_VALUE0
GLOBAL_AREA
MEMORY_LOG
ERRORSTACK
TEST_STACK_DUMP
BG_MESSAGES
ENQUEUES
SIMULATE_EOV
ADJUST_SCN
NEXT_SCN_WRAP
CONTROLF
BUFFERS
SET_TSN_P1
BUFFER
PIN_BLOCKS
RECOVERY
LOGHIST
ARCHIVE_ERROR
REDOHDR
LOGERROR
OPEN_FILES
DATA_ERR_ON
DATA_ERR_OFF
TR_SET_BLOCK
TR_SET_ALL_BLOCKS
TR_SET_SIDE
TR_CRASH_AFTER_WRITE
TR_READ_ONE_SIDE
TR_CORRUPT_ONE_SIDE
TR_RESET_NORMAL
LOCKS
CLASSES
FILE_HDRS
KRB_CORRUPT_INTERVAL
KRB_CORRUPT_SIZE
KRB_PIECE_FAIL
KRB_OPTIONS
KRB_TRACE
DROP_SEGMENTS
TREEDUMP
LONGF_CREATE
```

Appendix 68.1 Example Output (continued)

```
ROW_CACHE
LIBRARY_CACHE
MTSSTATE
SAVEPOINTS
KXFPCLEARSTATS
KXFPDUMPTRACE
KXFPBLATCHTEST
KXFXSLAVESTATE
KXFXCURSORSTATE
OBJECT_CACHE
```

Appendix 68.2 Process Status Information

```
Dump file /dump/DBTEST/udump/dbtest_ora_14475.trc
Oracle8 Enterprise Edition Release 8.0.5.0.0 - Production
With the Partitioning and Objects options
PL/SQL Release 8.0.5.0.0 - Production
ORACLE_HOME = /home/app/oracle/product/8.0.5
System name:   SunOS
Node name:     myserver
Release:       5.5.1
Version:       Generic_103640-29
Machine:       sun4u
Instance name: DBTEST
Redo thread mounted by this instance: 1
Oracle process number: 10
Unix process pid: 14475, image: oracleDBTEST

*** 1999.12.20.11.32.35.000
*** SESSION ID:(9.31) 1999.12.20.11.32.35.000
----- Dump of Process Statistics -----
User level CPU time = 2393
System call CPU time = 552
Other system trap CPU time = 0
Text page fault sleep time = 0
Data page fault sleep time = 0
Kernel page fault sleep time = 0
User lock wait sleep time = 0
All other sleep time = 156878
Wait-cpu (latency) time = 0
Minor page faults = 0
Major page faults = 6858
Swaps = 0
Input blocks = 7
Output blocks = 1
Messages sent = 0
Messages received = 0
Signals received = 4
Voluntary context switches = 7247
Involuntary context switches = 961
System calls = 42372
Chars read and written = 830982753
Process heap size = 385028
Process stack size = 49152
```

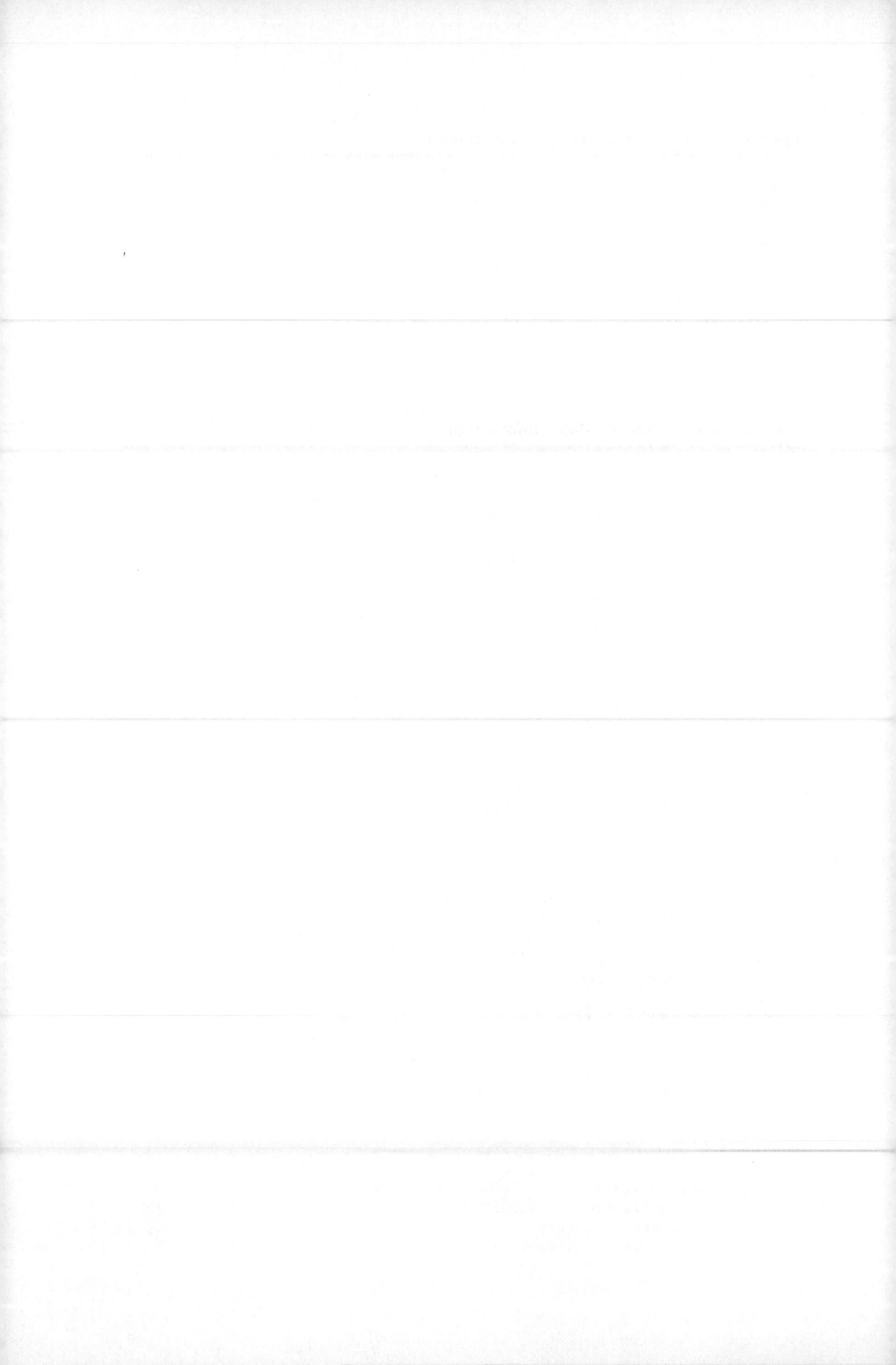

Chapter 69

Using the DBMS_LOCK Built-In Package

John Beresniewicz

What Is DBMS_LOCK?

The Oracle RDBMS uses locks internally to provide serialized access to shared resources. DBAs and developers are most familiar with Oracle's use of locking to control and manage concurrent access to data at the table and row levels. The DBMS_LOCK package makes the Oracle Kernel's lock management services available to user-written applications.

Application locking implemented using DBMS_LOCK is functionally identical to native RDBMS locking at the levels of lock modes and compatibility, deadlock detection, and visibility through V$ views.

Some possible uses of DBMS_LOCK are to:

- Provide for exclusive access to an external device or service (e.g., a printer)
- Coordinate or synchronize application processing in parallel
- Signal the availability of services
- Disable or enable program execution
- Coordinate access to a shared database pipe

DBMS_LOCK Programs

The DBMS_LOCK package presents a relatively straightforward interface containing two procedures and three functions. These are summarized in Exhibit 69.1.

Exhibit 69.2 presents a formatted version of the calling signatures of all DBMS_LOCK programs. Note that the REQUEST, CONVERT, and RELEASE

0-8493-1139-X/02/$0.00+$1.50
©2002 by CRC Press LLC

Exhibit 69.1 The `DBMS_LOCK` Programs

ALLOCATE_UNIQUE	Procedure	Generate lock handle for a given lock name
REQUEST	Function	Request lock in a specific mode
CONVERT	Function	Convert lock from one mode to another
RELEASE	Function	Release previously acquired lock
SLEEP	Procedure	Suspend session for a specified time

programs are overloaded on the parameter that identifies the lock. The VARCHAR2 lockhandle parameter is used for named locks. The INTEGER id parameter is used for numbered locks. The first basic decision to make when programming using `DBMS_LOCK` is which of the two lock identification methods to use.

Named or Numbered Locks?

Named locks are generally preferable to numbered locks for the simple reason that naming conventions can be used to ensure that applications do not mistakenly use the same locks for different purposes. With numbered locks, it is much more difficult to separate applications with disjoint sets of lock ids.

Named locks also allow better tracking of lock usage as the `V$LOCK` virtual table can be joined to `SYS.DBMS_LOCK_ALLOCATED` to map user sessions to the lock names they are holding or waiting for.

One apparent advantage of using integer lock identifiers is that they are somewhat faster because they avoid the catalog lookup involved in associating a named lock's handle with its internal identifier. Investigation of this performance

Exhibit 69.2 Calling Signatures of `DBMS_LOCK` Programs

```
PROCEDURE DBMS_LOCK.ALLOCATE_UNIQUE
   (lockname IN VARCHAR2
   ,lockhandle OUT VARCHAR2
   ,expiration_secs IN INTEGER DEFAULT 864000);

FUNCTION DBMS_LOCK.REQUEST
   (id IN INTEGER || lockhandle IN VARCHAR2
   ,lockmode IN INTEGER DEFAULT X_MODE
   ,timeout IN INTEGER DEFAULT MAXWAIT
   ,release_on_commit IN BOOLEAN DEFAULT FALSE)
RETURN INTEGER;

FUNCTION DBMS_LOCK.CONVERT
   (id IN INTEGER || lockhandle IN VARCHAR2
   ,lockmode IN INTEGER
   , timeout IN NUMBER DEFAULT MAXWAIT)
RETURN INTEGER;

FUNCTION DBMS_LOCK.RELEASE
   (id IN INTEGER || lockhandle IN VARCHAR2)
RETURN INTEGER;

PROCEDURE DBMS_LOCK.SLEEP
   (seconds IN NUMBER);
```

difference revealed that, although the relative difference was significant over thousands of calls to DBMS_LOCK functions, the additional per-call overhead of named locks on a Personal Oracle7 database was less than 0.001 second. Very few applications will require these additional microseconds. For these reasons, I strongly recommend using named locks and lockhandles, rather than integer identifiers.

The ALLOCATE_UNIQUE *Procedure*

The ALLOCATE_UNIQUE procedure returns a unique "handle" to the lock specified by the parameter lock name. This handle is used to identify the named lock in calls to other DBMS_LOCK programs. Multiple calls to ALLOCATE_UNIQUE for the same value of lock name will always return the same handle. Lock names can be up to 128 characters in length. Note also that lock names prefixed with "ORA$" are reserved for use by Oracle Corporation and should not be used in applications.

When ALLOCATE_UNIQUE is first called, a row is inserted for the named lock into the catalog table SYS.DBMS_LOCK_ALLOCATED. Subsequent calls for the same lock name will find the row and use it to build the unique lockhandle. The expiration_secs parameter of ALLOCATE_UNIQUE determines how long this row will persist before it is removed from the table. This aging mechanism keeps the table from accumulating rows for named locks that are no longer used (which could negatively impact performance).

One disadvantage of the ALLOCATE_UNIQUE procedure is that it always performs a COMMIT. This is problematic in that it forces a transaction boundary, and transaction control should normally be maintained at the highest possible level. Another implication of the COMMIT is that ALLOCATE_UNIQUE cannot be called from database triggers.

We can mitigate the impact of ALLOCATE_UNIQUE by calling it at most once per named lock in any session. Because ALLOCATE_UNIQUE will always return the same lockhandle for a given lock name, we can save the handle in a persistent package variable and reuse it later. Exhibit 69.3 demonstrates how this technique might be used in an application where access to a printer is serialized using DBMS_LOCK. The function get_printer_lockhandle always returns the correct lockhandle but calls ALLOCATE_UNIQUE only once for the printer lock.

One subtle danger with the technique in Exhibit 69.3 is that, if the session persists longer than the value of expiration_secs for the lock specified in the call to ALLOCATE_UNIQUE, the lock's entry in SYS.DBMS_LOCK_ALLOCATED could age out and invalidate the stashed lockhandle. The default lock expiration time is 10 days, making this an unlikely possibility under most circumstances. We could enhance the get_printer_lockhandle function in Exhibit 69.3 to avoid this danger by adding an expiration time variable and calling ALLOCATE_UNIQUE if the lockhandle is NULL or the expiration time has been reached since the last call.

Exhibit 69.3 Minimizing Calls to ALLOCATE_UNIQUE Using a Persistent Package Variable

```
PACKAGE BODY printer_access
IS
printer_lockname VARCHAR2(128) := 'printer_lock';
printer_lockhandle VARCHAR2(128);

FUNCTION get_printer_lockhandle
RETURN VARCHAR2
IS
BEGIN
   IF printer_lockhandle IS NULL
   THEN
   DBMS_LOCK.ALLOCATE_UNIQUE
   (lockname => printer_lockname
   ,lockhandle => printer_lockhandle);
   END IF;

   RETURN printer_lockhandle;
END get_printer_lockhandle;

END printer_access;
```

The REQUEST *Function*

The REQUEST function requests the specified lock in the mode identified by lockmode. The function is overloaded on the lock identifier, which can be either an integer or the lockhandle of a named lock returned by ALLOCATE_UNIQUE. If the lock cannot be acquired immediately, the requesting session will block and wait up to the value of the timeout parameter (in seconds) to get the lock. The default value for timeout is 32767 seconds, which is probably longer than most application users are willing to block and wait. Thus, be sure to specify timeout values that are realistic whenever calling this function.

The REQUEST function also takes a Boolean parameter called release_on_commit. Passing TRUE for release_on_commit causes the lock to be released automatically when the current transaction ends with a COMMIT or ROLLBACK. A value of FALSE allows the session to hold the lock across transaction boundaries. This can be an important feature when serializing access to non-data resources while simultaneously executing database transactions, as the locks need not be reacquired after each COMMIT.

The DBMS_LOCK.REQUEST return values and their meanings are as follows:

- 0 = Success
- 1 = Timed out
- 2 = Deadlock
- 3 = Parameter error
- 4 = Lock already owned
- 5 = Illegal lockhandle

Exhibit 69.4 Encapsulating REQUEST in a Function Returning a Boolean

```
PACKAGE BODY printer_access
IS

FUNCTION printer_locked
RETURN BOOLEAN
IS
   temp_return INTEGER;
BEGIN
   temp_return := DBMS_LOCK.REQUEST
   (lockhandle => get_printer_lockhandle
   ,lockmode => DBMS_LOCK.x_mode
   ,timeout => 1
   ,release_on_commit => FALSE);

   RETURN (temp_return IN (0,4));
END printer_locked;

END printer_access;
```

One usability issue with using the REQUEST function arises from having to check these return codes and proceed conditionally, based on whether the lock was acquired or not. Basically, if the return value is 0 or 4, then the lock has been acquired; otherwise, not. One simple yet powerful technique to enhance the REQUEST function is to encapsulate it in another function that returns the Boolean TRUE if the lock has been acquired and FALSE otherwise. This is illustrated in Exhibit 69.4, which extends the printer_access package example of Exhibit 69.3.

In Exhibit 69.4, the printer_locked function will return TRUE if the printer lock can be acquired in exclusive mode within one second, otherwise it returns FALSE. Note that the function calls the get_printer_lockhandle function defined earlier to efficiently obtain the proper lockhandle.

Using the printer_access package makes our main line code far cleaner and easier to understand, as illustrated below:

```
IF printer_access.printer_locked
THEN
/* OK, use the printer here */
ELSE
/* cannot lock printer, send message to user */
END IF;
```

The printer_access package functions effectively shield our code from the details of using either REQUEST or ALLOCATE_UNIQUE, allowing us to write a simple IF … THEN block testing for exclusive control of the resource.

The CONVERT *Function*

The CONVERT function changes the mode of an already acquired lock to the mode specified by the lockmode parameter. CONVERT is overloaded on the first parameter, accepting either an integer lock identifier or lock handle.

Return values for CONVERT function are the same as for REQUEST above, with one exception: the value 4 means that the lock is not owned and thus cannot be converted.

Most applications do not require sophisticated multimode locking schemes and thus will not need to convert between lock modes. One usage note is that CONVERT can only succeed where the lock has already been acquired using REQUEST. Thus, applications need to ensure the proper calling order of these functions.

As with REQUEST, CONVERT function calls will block and wait up to timeout seconds until the lock mode conversion can be completed. Again, the default value for timeout is very long, so be sure to provide a suitable value for the application.

The RELEASE *Function*

The RELEASE function releases the lock. Return values and their meanings are:

- 0 = Success
- 3 = Parameter error
- 4 = Do not own lock
- 5 = Illegal lockhandle

Checking the return code for RELEASE is a bit tedious. After all, regardless of the return code, the session should not own the lock once the function completes.

The SLEEP *Procedure*

The SLEEP procedure suspends the calling session for the duration specified by the seconds parameter. It can be used to implement low overhead wait times in applications requiring delay and retry logic. Note that passing a NULL value for seconds may generate ORA-600 errors on some platforms.

Lock Modes and Compatibility Rules

There are six locking modes available to applications using DBMS_LOCK. The following public package constants are declared in DBMS_LOCK to identify these modes:

```
nl_mode    CONSTANT    INTEGER    := 1;    -- NULL mode
ss_mode    CONSTANT    INTEGER    := 2;    -- Sub-share
sx_mode    CONSTANT    INTEGER    := 3;    -- Sub-Exclusive
s_mode     CONSTANT    INTEGER    := 4;    -- Share
ssx_mode   CONSTANT    INTEGER    := 5;    -- Sub-share exclusive
x_mode     CONSTANT    INTEGER    := 6;    -- Exclusive
```

Exhibit 69.5 Compatibility of Null, Share, and Exclusive Locking Modes

Request=>Held	nl_mode	s_mode	x_mode
nl_mode	Succeed	Succeed	Succeed
s_mode	Succeed	Succeed	Fail
x_mode	Succeed	Fail	Fail

Lock modes should be specified using these named constants when calling DBMS_LOCK, REQUEST, or CONVERT. This provides better code readability, as well as insulation from DBMS_LOCK implementation details (i.e., the specific integers corresponding to given lock modes).

```
BEGIN
/* rather than this */
DBMS_LOCK.REQUEST(id=>1000, lockmode=>6);

/* better to do this */
DBMS_LOCK.REQUEST(id=>1000, lockmode=>DBMS LOCK.x_mode);
END;
```

Null, share, and exclusive mode locks should be sufficient for almost all applications. The other modes can be used to support complex locking schemes for compound objects beyond the scope of this chapter.

As discussed, all locks have an identifier and are held in one of the available modes. When a user session holds a lock in a specific mode, another session may request that lock in the same or another mode. The lock compatibility rules specify whether the requesting session can obtain the lock, based on both the requested mode and held mode. When a lock cannot be obtained in the desired mode, the requesting session will block and wait for up to the specified timeout for the lock to become available. The compatibility rules for null, share, and exclusive locks are summarized in Exhibit 69.5.

From Exhibit 69.5 we see that null mode locks can always be acquired and do not block other modes. Share mode locks allow share mode requests but block exclusive mode requests. Finally, exclusive mode locks block both share and exclusive mode requests.

Best Practices for DBMS_LOCK

The discussion thus far has pointed out several recommendations for best practices when using DBMS_LOCK:

- Use named locks instead of integer lock ids.
- Use naming conventions to separate locks by application.
- Minimize calls to ALLOCATE_UNIQUE using persistent package variables.
- Specify reasonable (nondefault) timeout values.
- Encapsulate calls to REQUEST or CONVERT with functions that return Boolean values.
- Release locks quickly to minimize the potential for contention.

I have encapsulated several of these practices into a package called DBLOCK that simplifies and standardizes the usage of named locks.

The DBLOCK Package

Appendix 69.1 shows the package specification for DBLOCK. The package includes the following features:

- Automatic association of any lock name to its lockhandle, using a persistent PL/SQL table
- Function to return lockhandles by lock name
- Minimizes calls to ALLOCATE_UNIQUE
- Defaults to reasonable timeouts and allows a global timeout setting
- Function returning Boolean indicating successful lock acquisition
- Combined encapsulation of REQUEST and CONVERT functions
- Release locks without checking return codes

The examples that follow illustrate using the DBLOCK package to implement applications of DBMS_LOCK locking. The source code for the package body of DBLOCK appears as in Appendix 69.2.

Previous listings have suggested how DBMS_LOCK might be used to serialize exclusive access to a printer. There are many potential uses for non-data related locking. Two examples I have had occasion to use in the past are:

1. Controlling access to a shared database pipe
2. Signaling the availability of a service process

Accessing a Shared Database Pipe

Database pipes created using the DBMS_PIPE built-in package are an example of a sharable Oracle resource not automatically controlled by RDBMS locks. Database pipes usually do not require rigidly serialized access by concurrent users because multiple sessions can write separate messages to a pipe simultaneously. However, suppose we have a pipe onto which we want to load a single message that will be accessed and shared by multiple users, perhaps a status message. In this case, users need to read the message and replace it on the pipe for the next user. For a brief time the pipe is empty, and an application user reading the pipe at that moment may timeout and not get the message. The application cannot distinguish between this situation and the pipe being truly empty. Serializing access to the pipe using DBMS_LOCK prevents reading from the empty pipe when another session is using the shared message.

Assuming the shared message is read from and written to the pipe by a procedure called read_write_app_pipe, the code might look like this:

```
IF dblock.get_lock_TF('APP_PIPE')
THEN
read_write_app_pipe;
dblock.release_lock('APP_PIPE');
ELSE
RAISE cannot_lock_pipe;
END IF;
```

Because `get_lock_TF` defaults to exclusive mode, only one user can access the pipe at a time. The lock is released immediately after using the pipe to minimize the time that it is locked. The application can trap the exception, in case some special processing is required when the pipe cannot be locked.

Signaling Service Availability

A slightly more complex example involves using `DBMS_LOCK` to indicate that a service process is available for access by user sessions. The service process acquires and holds a lock in exclusive mode when it is available for use by clients. Clients of the service attempt to obtain the lock and failure to do so indicates that the service is running. Appendix 69.3 illustrates how this functionality might be implemented in a package called `app_service`.

Client programs use the `service_active_TF` function to test for availability of the server. Note that this function attempts to acquire the lock in shared mode, while the server acquires it in exclusive mode. Shared mode ensures that two clients testing for service availability simultaneously do not result in one of them "fooling" the other into thinking the service is available by preventing lock acquisition. Again, the lock is released immediately to avoid having a client hold the lock long enough to prevent a server process from starting. A consequence of the server acquiring the lock in exclusive mode is that there can be at most one server active at any time. If we want to allow multiple concurrent servers, then shared exclusive mode should be used.

Conclusion

The Oracle RDBMS is evolving many new features and capabilities beyond the original "tables of rows" relational. Database pipes, objects, and abstract data types, external program calls, Internet file services, and Java all portend much greater application variety and sophistication. Applications will increasingly be faced with managing concurrent access to non-data services and facilities. `DBMS_LOCK` provides the necessary tools to implement these requirements and, with a little help from an encapsulation package like `DBLOCK`, it can become a relatively simple matter.

Appendix 69.1 Package Specification for DBLOCK

```
CREATE OR REPLACE PACKAGE dblock
   /*
   || Adds value to DBMS_LOCK by allowing easier manipulation
   || of named locks. Calling programs use lock names only,
   || corresponding lockhandles are automatically identified,
   || used and saved for subsequent use.
   ||
   || Author: John Beresniewicz, Savant Corporation
   ||
   || 12/30/98: added set_timeout and curr_timeout
   || 10/26/97: added expiration_secs_IN to lockhandle
   || 10/21/97: added release
   || 10/21/97: added dump_lockhandle_tbl
   || 10/17/97: created
   ||
   || Compilation Requirements:
   ||
   || PL/SQL 2.3 or higher
   || EXECUTE on DBMS_LOCK
   || EXECUTE on DBMS_SESSION
   ||
   || Execution Requirements:
   ||
   */
AS
   /* variables to anchor other variables */
   lockname_var VARCHAR2(128);
   lockhandle_var VARCHAR2(128);

   /* sets the default timeout */
   PROCEDURE set_timeout(timeout_IN IN INTEGER);

   /* returns the current timeout setting */
   FUNCTION curr_timeout RETURN INTEGER;

   /*
   || returns TRUE if a COMMIT has taken place between
   || subsequent calls to the function
   || NOTE: returns TRUE on first call in session
   */
   FUNCTION committed_TF RETURN BOOLEAN;

   /*
   || returns lockhandle for given lockname, only calls
   || DBMS_LOCK.ALLOCATE_UNIQUE if lockhandle has not been
   || previously determined
   */
   FUNCTION lockhandle
      (lockname_IN IN lockname_var%TYPE
      ,expiration_secs_IN IN INTEGER := 864000)
   RETURN lockhandle_var%TYPE;

   /*
   || returns TRUE if named lock is acquired in mode
   || specified
   */
```

Appendix 69.1 Package Specification for DBLOCK (continued)

```
   FUNCTION get_lock_TF
      (lockname_IN IN lockname_var%TYPE
      ,mode_IN IN INTEGER := DBMS_LOCK.x_mode
      ,timeout_IN IN INTEGER := curr_timeout
      ,release_on_commit_TF IN BOOLEAN := FALSE)
   RETURN BOOLEAN;

   /* releases named lock */
   PROCEDURE release (lockname_IN IN lockname_var%TYPE);

   /* print contents of lockhandle_tbl for debugging */
   PROCEDURE dump_lockhandle_tbl;

END dblock;
/
```

Appendix 69.2 The DBLOCK Package Body

```
CREATE OR REPLACE PACKAGE BODY dblock
AS

   /* used by committed_TF, unique to each session */
   commit_lockname lockname_var%TYPE :=
                      DBMS_SESSION.UNIQUE_SESSION_ID;

   /* default timeout value */
   timeout_var INTEGER := 1;

   /* rectype to pair handles with names */
   TYPE handle_rectype IS RECORD
      (name lockname_var%TYPE
      ,handle lockhandle_var%TYPE
      );

   /* table to store lockhandles by name */
   TYPE handle_tbltype IS TABLE OF handle_rectype
      INDEX BY BINARY_INTEGER;

   lockhandle_tbl handle_tbltype;

   FUNCTION committed_TF RETURN BOOLEAN
   IS
      call_status INTEGER;
   BEGIN
      /* get unique lock, expire in one day */
      call_status := DBMS_LOCK.REQUEST
                        (lockhandle => lockhandle(commit_lockname,86400)
                        ,lockmode => DBMS_LOCK.x_mode
                        ,timeout => 0
                        ,release_on_commit => TRUE);

      RETURN (call_status = 0);
   END committed_TF;

   FUNCTION get_lock_TF
      (lockname_IN IN lockname_var%TYPE
      ,mode_IN IN INTEGER := DBMS_LOCK.x_mode
      ,timeout_IN IN INTEGER := curr_timeout
      ,release_on_commit_TF IN BOOLEAN := FALSE)
   RETURN BOOLEAN
   IS
      call_status INTEGER;

      /* handle for the named lock */
      temp_lockhandle lockhandle_var%TYPE := lockhandle(lockname_IN);

   BEGIN
      call_status := DBMS_LOCK.REQUEST
                        (lockhandle => temp_lockhandle
                        ,lockmode => mode_IN
                        ,timeout => timeout_IN
                        ,release_on_commit => release_on_commit_TF
                        );
      /*
      || if lock already owned, convert to requested mode
      */
```

Appendix 69.2 The DBLOCK Package Body (continued)

```
   IF call_status = 4
   THEN
      call_status := DBMS_LOCK.CONVERT
                     (lockhandle => temp_lockhandle
                     ,lockmode => mode_IN
                     ,timeout => timeout_IN
                     );
   END IF;

   RETURN (call_status = 0);
END get_lock_TF;

FUNCTION lockhandle
   (lockname_IN IN lockname_var%TYPE
   ,expiration_secs_IN IN INTEGER := 864000)
RETURN lockhandle_var%TYPE
IS
   call_status INTEGER;
   temp_lockhandle lockhandle_var%TYPE;

   temp_index BINARY_INTEGER;

BEGIN
   /*
   || if lockhandle_tbl empty must call ALLOCATE_UNIQUE
   */
   IF lockhandle_tbl.COUNT = 0
   THEN

      DBMS_LOCK.ALLOCATE_UNIQUE
         (lockname => lockname_IN
         ,lockhandle => temp_lockhandle
         ,expiration_secs => expiration_secs_IN);

      lockhandle_tbl(1).handle := temp_lockhandle;
      lockhandle_tbl(1).name := lockname_IN;

   /*
   || check lockhandle_tbl for matching lockname
   */
   ELSE
      FOR i IN lockhandle_tbl.FIRST..lockhandle_tbl.LAST
      LOOP
         IF lockhandle_tbl(i).name = lockname_IN
         THEN
            temp_lockhandle := lockhandle_tbl(i).handle;
         END IF;
      END LOOP;
   END IF;

   /*
   || if temp_lockhandle still null, call ALLOCATE_UNIQUE
   || and load entry into lockhandle_tbl
   */
   IF temp_lockhandle IS NULL
   THEN
      DBMS_LOCK.ALLOCATE_UNIQUE
         (lockname => lockname_IN
         ,lockhandle => temp_lockhandle);

      /*
```

(continued)

Appendix 69.2 The DBLOCK Package Body (continued)

```
        || add to end of lockhandle_tbl
        */
        temp_index := lockhandle_tbl.LAST+1;
        lockhandle_tbl(temp_index).handle := temp_lockhandle;
        lockhandle_tbl(temp_index).name := lockname_IN;

      END IF;

      RETURN temp_lockhandle;
   END lockhandle;

   PROCEDURE release (lockname_IN IN lockname_var%TYPE)
   IS
      call_status INTEGER;
   BEGIN
      call_status := DBMS_LOCK.RELEASE
                       (lockhandle => lockhandle(lockname_IN));
   END release;

   PROCEDURE dump_lockhandle_tbl
   IS
   BEGIN
      DBMS_OUTPUT.PUT_LINE('LOCKNAME.HANDLE');

      FOR i IN lockhandle_tbl.FIRST..lockhandle_tbl.LAST
      LOOP
         DBMS_OUTPUT.PUT_LINE
            (lockhandle_tbl(i).name||'.'||lockhandle_tbl(i).handle);
      END LOOP;
   END dump_lockhandle_tbl;

   PROCEDURE set_timeout(timeout_IN IN INTEGER)
   IS
   BEGIN
      IF timeout_IN >= 0
      THEN
         timeout_var := timeout_IN;
      END IF;
   END set_timeout;

   FUNCTION curr_timeout RETURN INTEGER
   IS
   BEGIN
      RETURN timeout_var;
   END curr_timeout;

END dblock;
/
```

Appendix 69.3 Signaling Service Availability Using DBMS_LOCK

```
PACKAGE app_service
IS
   service_lockname CONSTANT VARCHAR2(20):= 'service_lock';

   PROCEDURE server
   IS
   BEGIN
      IF dblock.get_lock_TF
         (lockname_IN => service_lockname
         ,mode_IN => DBMS_LOCK.x_mode
         ,timeout_IN => 1
         ,release_on_commit_TF => FALSE);
      THEN
         /* perform the service code here */
      ELSE
         /* another server active, exit */
         RETURN;
      END IF;
      dblock.release_lock(service_lockname);
   END server;

   FUNCTION service_active_TF
   RETURN BOOLEAN
   IS
   BEGIN
      IF dblock.get_lock_TF
         (lockname_IN => service_lockname
         ,mode_IN => DBMS_LOCK.s_mode
         ,timeout_IN => 0
         ,release_on_commit_TF => TRUE);
      THEN
         /* lock acquisition means service not active */
         dblock.release_lock(service_lockname);
         RETURN FALSE;
      ELSE
         RETURN TRUE;
      END IF;
   END service_active_TF;

END app_service;
```

Index

A

B

C

D

E

F

G

H

I

J

K

L

M

N

O

P

Q

R

S

T

U

V

U

V

W

X

W

X

Y

The only insider's guide to mastering Oracle

Oracle Internals

Edited by **Donald K. Burleson**, *Oracle DBA*

The Auerbach Publications monthly newsletter that lets DBAs get inside Oracle

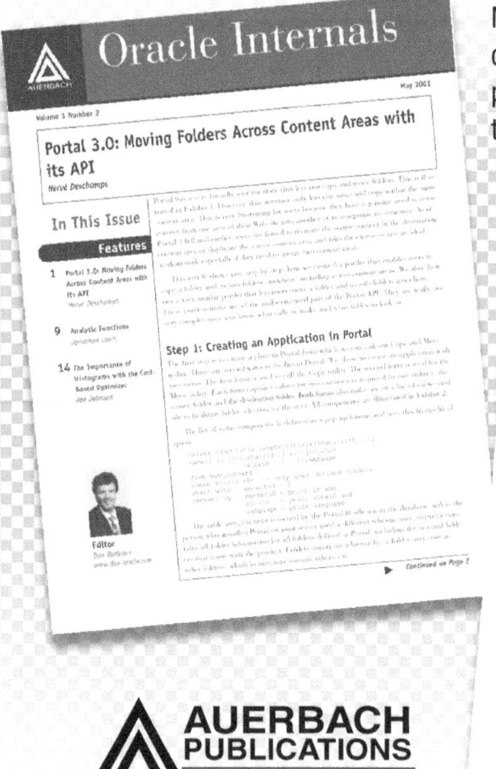

Make no mistake, **Oracle Internals** is not for dilettantes or beginners. Written and edited by professionals for professionals, it is the most technical Oracle periodical on the market.

AUERBACH PUBLICATIONS

Catalog no. A6, 12 issues annually, $145.00

Call 1-800-272-7737 or visit http://www.auerbach-publications.com/oi

In North & South America, Asia, and Australasia:

CRC PRESS
2000 N.W. Corporate Blvd., Boca Raton, FL 33431-9868, USA
Tel: 1-800-272-7737 or Fax: 1-800-374-3401
From Outside the Continental U.S.
Tel: 1-561-994-0555 or Fax: 1-561-989-8732
e-mail: orders@crcpress.com

www.crcpress.com

In Europe, Middle East, and Africa:

CRC PRESS UK
Pocock House, 235 Southwark Bridge Road, London SE1 6LY, UK
Tel: 44 (0) 20 7450 5083 or Fax: 44 (0) 20 7407 7336
e-mail: enquiries@crcpress.com
Post, fax, phone, or e-mail your order to:
CRC PRESS, ITPS
Cheriton House, North Way, Andover, Hants, SP10 5BE, UK
Tel: 44 (0) 1264 342932 or Fax: 44 (0) 1264 342788
e-mail: crcpress@itps.co.uk

Mention code **511FA** *when ordering online to receive your 10% discount.*

AU1139AD
5.3001BB

OTHER AUERBACH PUBLICATIONS

ABCs of IP Addressing
Gilbert Held
ISBN: 0-8493-1144-6

Application Servers for E-Business
Lisa M. Lindgren
ISBN: 0-8493-0827-5

Architectures for e-Business
Sanjiv Purba, Editor
ISBN: 0-8493-1161-6

A Technical Guide to IPSec Virtual Private Networks
James S. Tiller
ISBN: 0-8493-0876-3

Building an Information Security Awareness Program
Mark B. Desman
ISBN: 0-8493-0116-5

Computer Telephony Integration
William Yarberry, Jr.
ISBN: 0-8493-9995-5

Cyber Crime Field Handbook
Bruce Middleton
ISBN: 0-8493-1192-6

Enterprise Systems Architectures
Mark Goodyear, Editor
ISBN: 0-8493-9836-3

Enterprise Systems Integration, 2nd Edition
Judith Myerson
ISBN: 0-8493-1149-7

Information Security Architecture
Jan Killmeyer Tudor
ISBN: 0-8493-9988-2

Information Security Management Handbook, 4th Edition, Volume 2
Harold F. Tipton and Micki Krause, Editors
ISBN: 0-8493-0800-3

Information Security Management Handbook, 4th Edition, Volume 3
Harold F. Tipton and Micki Krause, Editors
ISBN: 0-8493-1127-6

Information Security Policies, Procedures, and Standards: Guidelines for Effective Information Security
Thomas Peltier
ISBN: 0-8493-1137-3

Information Security Risk Analysis
Thomas Peltier
ISBN: 0-8493-0880-1

Information Technology Control and Audit
Frederick Gallegos, Sandra Allen-Senft, and Daniel P. Manson
ISBN: 0-8493-9994-7

Integrating ERP, CRM, Supply Chain Management, and Smart Materials
Dimitris N. Chorafas
ISBN: 0-8493-1076-8

New Directions in Internet Management
Sanjiv Purba, Editor
ISBN: 0-8493-1160-8

New Directions in Project Management
Paul C. Tinnirello, Editor
ISBN: 0-8493-1190-X

Oracle Internals: Tips, Tricks, and Techniques for DBAs
Donald K. Burleson, Editor
ISBN: 0-8493-1139-X

Practical Guide to Security Engineering and Information Assurance
Debra Herrmann
ISBN: 0-8493-1163-2

TCP/IP Professional Reference Guide
Gilbert Held
ISBN: 0-8493-0824-0

Roadmap to the e-Factory
Alex N. Beavers, Jr.
ISBN: 0-8493-0099-1

Securing E-Business Applications and Communications
Jonathan S. Held
John R. Bowers
ISBN: 0-8493-0963-8

AUERBACH PUBLICATIONS

www.auerbach-publications.com
TO Order: Call: 1-800-272-7737 • Fax: 1-800-374-3401
E-mail: orders@crcpress.com

The only insider's guide to mastering Oracle

Oracle Internals

Edited by **Donald K. Burleson**, *Oracle DBA*

The Auerbach Publications monthly newsletter that lets DBAs get inside Oracle

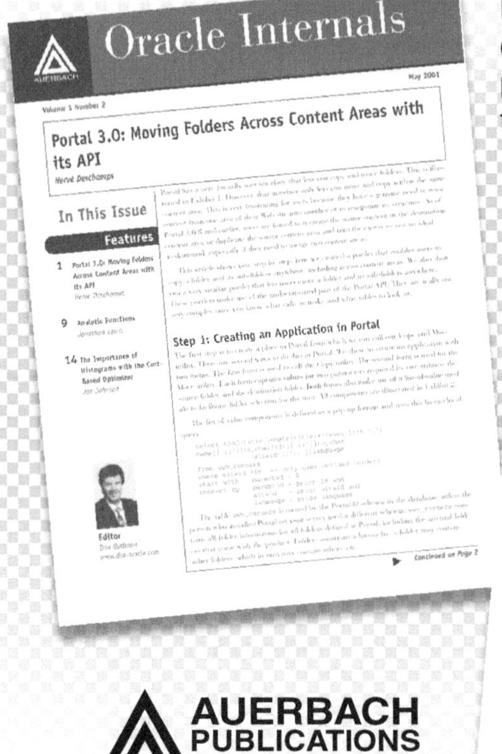

Make no mistake, **Oracle Internals** is not for dilettantes or beginners. Written and edited by professionals for professionals, it is the most technical Oracle periodical on the market.

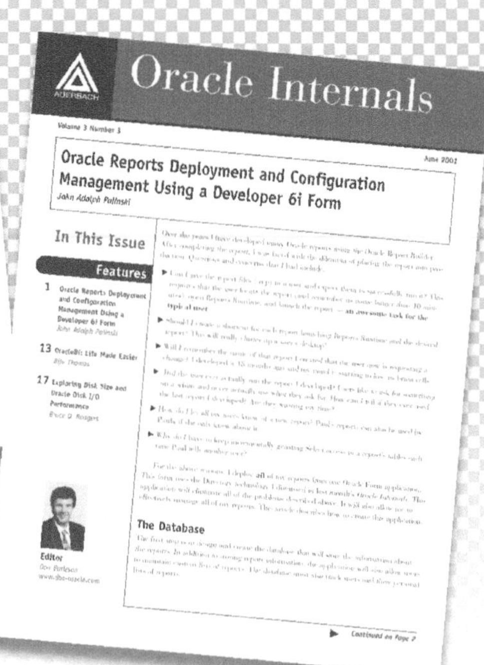

AUERBACH PUBLICATIONS

A CRC Company

Catalog no. A6, 12 issues annually, $145.00

Call 1-800-272-7737 or visit http://www.auerbach-publications.com/oi

In North & South America, Asia, and Australasia:

CRC PRESS

2000 N.W. Corporate Blvd., Boca Raton, FL 33431-9868, USA
Tel: 1-800-272-7737 or Fax: 1-800-374-3401
From Outside the Continental U.S.
Tel: 1-561-994-0555 or Fax: 1-561-989-8732
e-mail: orders@crcpress.com

www.crcpress.com

In Europe, Middle East, and Africa:

CRC PRESS UK

Pocock House, 235 Southwark Bridge Road, London SE1 6LY, UK
Tel: 44 (0) 20 7450 5083 or Fax: 44 (0) 20 7407 7336
e-mail: enquiries@crcpress.com
Post, fax, phone, or e-mail your order to:
CRC PRESS, ITPS
Cheriton House, North Way, Andover, Hants, SP10 5BE, UK
Tel: 44 (0) 1264 342932 or Fax: 44 (0) 1264 342788
e-mail: crcpress@itps.co.uk

Mention code **511FA** *when ordering online to receive your 10% discount.*

AU1139AD
5.3001BB

OTHER AUERBACH PUBLICATIONS

ABCs of IP Addressing
Gilbert Held
ISBN: 0-8493-1144-6

Application Servers for E-Business
Lisa M. Lindgren
ISBN: 0-8493-0827-5

Architectures for e-Business
Sanjiv Purba, Editor
ISBN: 0-8493-1161-6

A Technical Guide to IPSec Virtual Private Networks
James S. Tiller
ISBN: 0-8493-0876-3

Building an Information Security Awareness Program
Mark B. Desman
ISBN: 0-8493-0116-5

Computer Telephony Integration
William Yarberry, Jr.
ISBN: 0-8493-9995-5

Cyber Crime Field Handbook
Bruce Middleton
ISBN: 0-8493-1192-6

Enterprise Systems Architectures
Mark Goodyear, Editor
ISBN: 0-8493-9836-3

Enterprise Systems Integration, 2nd Edition
Judith Myerson
ISBN: 0-8493-1149-7

Information Security Architecture
Jan Killmeyer Tudor
ISBN: 0-8493-9988-2

Information Security Management Handbook, 4th Edition, Volume 2
Harold F. Tipton and Micki Krause, Editors
ISBN: 0-8493-0800-3

Information Security Management Handbook, 4th Edition, Volume 3
Harold F. Tipton and Micki Krause, Editors
ISBN: 0-8493-1127-6

Information Security Policies, Procedures, and Standards: Guidelines for Effective Information Security
Thomas Peltier
ISBN: 0-8493-1137-3

Information Security Risk Analysis
Thomas Peltier
ISBN: 0-8493-0880-1

Information Technology Control and Audit
Frederick Gallegos, Sandra Allen-Senft, and Daniel P. Manson
ISBN: 0-8493-9994-7

Integrating ERP, CRM, Supply Chain Management, and Smart Materials
Dimitris N. Chorafas
ISBN: 0-8493-1076-8

New Directions in Internet Management
Sanjiv Purba, Editor
ISBN: 0-8493-1160-8

New Directions in Project Management
Paul C. Tinnirello, Editor
ISBN: 0-8493-1190-X

Oracle Internals: Tips, Tricks, and Techniques for DBAs
Donald K. Burleson, Editor
ISBN: 0-8493-1139-X

Practical Guide to Security Engineering and Information Assurance
Debra Herrmann
ISBN: 0-8493-1163-2

TCP/IP Professional Reference Guide
Gilbert Held
ISBN: 0-8493-0824-0

Roadmap to the e-Factory
Alex N. Beavers, Jr.
ISBN: 0-8493-0099-1

Securing E-Business Applications and Communications
Jonathan S. Held
John R. Bowers
ISBN: 0-8493-0963-8

AUERBACH PUBLICATIONS

www.auerbach-publications.com
TO Order: Call: 1-800-272-7737 • Fax: 1-800-374-3401
E-mail: orders@crcpress.com

The only insider's guide to mastering Oracle

Oracle Internals

Edited by **Donald K. Burleson,** *Oracle DBA*

The Auerbach Publications monthly newsletter that lets DBAs get inside Oracle

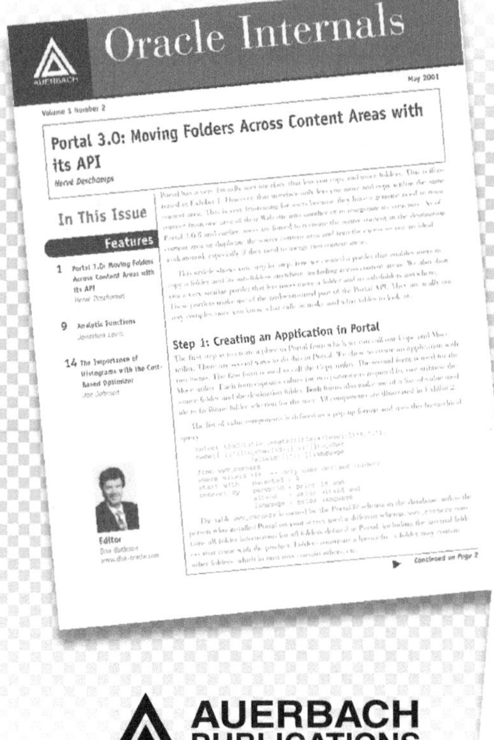

Oracle Internals

AUERBACH

May 2001

Volume 1 Number 2

Portal 3.0: Moving Folders Across Content Areas with its API

Hervé Deschamps

In This Issue

Features

1 Portal 3.0: Moving Folders Across Content Areas with its API

9 Analytic Functions

14 The Importance of Histograms with the Cost-Based Optimizer

Step 1: Creating an Application in Portal

Editor

Don Burleson

Continued on Page 2

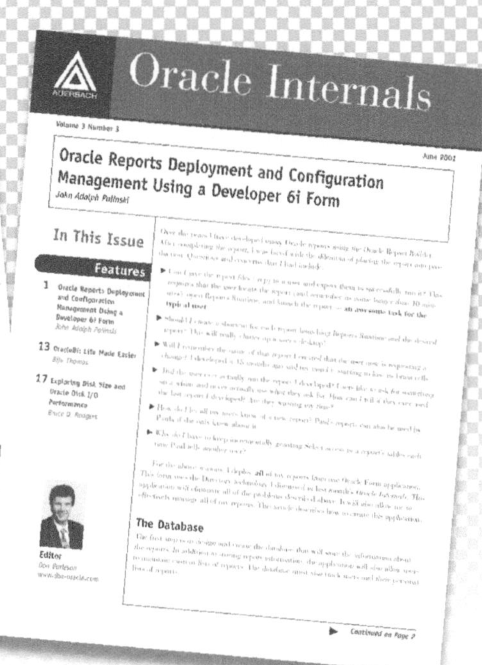

Oracle Internals

AUERBACH

Volume 3 Number 3

June 2001

Oracle Reports Deployment and Configuration Management Using a Developer 6i Form

John Adolph Palinski

In This Issue

Features

1 Oracle Reports Deployment and Configuration Management Using a Developer 6i Form

13 OracleBit Life Made Easier

17 Exploring Disk Size and Oracle Disk I/O Performance

The Database

Editor

Don Burleson

Continued on Page 2

Make no mistake, **Oracle Internals** is not for dilettantes or beginners. Written and edited by professionals for professionals, it is the most technical Oracle periodical on the market.

AUERBACH PUBLICATIONS
A CRC Company

Catalog no. A6, 12 issues annually, $145.00

Call 1-800-272-7737 or visit http://www.auerbach-publications.com/oi

In North & South America, Asia, and Australasia:

CRC PRESS
2000 N.W. Corporate Blvd., Boca Raton, FL 33431-9868, USA
Tel: 1-800-272-7737 or Fax: 1-800-374-3401
From Outside the Continental U.S.
Tel: 1-561-994-0555 or Fax: 1-561-989-8732
e-mail: orders@crcpress.com

www.crcpress.com

In Europe, Middle East, and Africa:

CRC PRESS UK
Pocock House, 235 Southwark Bridge Road, London SE1 6LY, UK
Tel: 44 (0) 20 7450 5083 or Fax: 44 (0) 20 7407 7336
e-mail: enquiries@crcpress.com
Post, fax, phone, or e-mail your order to:
CRC PRESS, ITPS
Cheriton House, North Way, Andover, Hants, SP10 5BE, UK
Tel: 44 (0) 1264 342932 or Fax: 44 (0) 1264 342788
e-mail: crcpress@itps.co.uk

Mention code **511FA** *when ordering online to receive your 10% discount.*

AU1139AD
5.3001BB